LIGHTS OF CREATION & TRANSCENDENCE

David Birnbaum / Mesorah Matrix Series

expanded edition May 2019

www.MesorahMatrix.com

MESORAH MATRIX
V·O·L·U·M·E·2

TIKKUN OLAM
JUDAISM, HUMANISM & TRANSCENDENCE

LIGHTS OF CREATION & TRANSCENDENCE | Mesorah Matrix Series
David Birnbaum

Editors

David
Birnbaum & Martin S. **Cohen**

Associate Editor: **Saul J. Berman**

New Paradigm Matrix®

EXPLORING HIGHER DIMENSIONS

Published by NEW PARADIGM MATRIX

Library of Congress Cataloging-in-Publication Data

Birnbaum, David.

Tikkun Olam / David Birnbaum and Martin S. Cohen.

ISBN 978-0-9961995-0-6

1. Tikkun Olam.   2. Jewish Spiritual.   I. Title.

21st CENTURY PUBLISHING

New Paradigm Matrix
att: David Birnbaum
Tower 49
Twelve E. 49th St.,
11th Floor,
New York, NY 10017

www.NewParadigmMatrix.com

Direct contact to Editor-in-Chief

David.Birnbaum.NY@gmail.com

Schwarz
Treiger-Bar-Am
Berkovits
Claussen
Hammer-Kossoy
Broyde
Kurtz
Chipman
Cardin
Zion
Bulka
Jacobson-Maisels
Labovitz
Cohen
Gordon
Greyber
Wittenberg
Kwall
Glazer
Krygier
Jacobs
Dorff
Berkowitz
Blech
Kosman
Landau
Artson
Bedzow

Tikkun Olam

Repair/Perfect the World

David Birnbaum and Martin S. Cohen

Editors

NEW PARADIGM MATRIX

www.NewParadigmMatrix.com

David Birnbaum & Martin S. Cohen

Tikkun Olam

Repair/Perfect the World

with essays by

Bradley Shavit Artson, Raḥel Berkovits, Adena K. Berkowitz, Benjamin Blech,
Michael J. Broyde & Ira Bedzow, Reuven P. Bulka, Nina Beth Cardin,
Yehonatan Chipman, Geoffrey Claussen, Martin S. Cohen, Elliot N. Dorff,
Aubrey L. Glazer, Jeremy Gordon, Daniel Greyber, Meesh Hammer-Kossoy,
Jill Jacobs, James Jacobson-Maisels, Admiel Kosman, Rivon Krygier,
Vernon H. Kurtz, Roberta Rosenthal Kwall, Gail Labovitz, Melanie Landau,
Sid Schwarz, Kim Treiger-Bar-Am, Jonathan Wittenberg, and Noam Zion

Saul J. Berman
Associate Editor

New Paradigm Matrix Publishing
New York
2015

21st CENTURY PUBLISHING

ב״ה

From the Editor-in-Chief

May 10, 2015

It is a privilege to be serving as Editor-in-Chief of this unique 10-theme series. I am honored to be working with world-class editors Benjamin Blech, Martin S. Cohen, Saul J. Berman, and Shalom Carmy.

It is our hope and prayer that the series be a catalyst for intellectual and spiritual expansion – as well as a unifying force both for our people as well as for individuals of good will globally.

Sincerely,

David Birnbaum

דוד אריה בן אברהם יעקב הלוי   5775 אייר 21

Mesorah Matrix series

jewish thought & spirituality

10-theme

10-volume

200+ original essays

150+ global thought leaders

a decade-long unified endeavor

genre: *applied scholarship*

www.MesorahMatrix.com

21st CENTURY PUBLISHING

Mesorah Matrix series

A POTENTIALLY ICONIC LEGACY SERIES
FOR THE 21ST CENTURY

10-VOLUME SERIES......200+ ESSAYS......A GLOBAL EFFORT

150+ ESSAYISTS....SPANNING THE WORLD'S TOP JEWISH THOUGHT LEADERS

A DYNAMIC CONTEMPORARY GLOBE-SPANING ENDEAVOR AND COLLEC-TION

ESSAYISTS COVER A VERY WIDE SPECTRUM OF JUDAISM:

THE COMPLETE SERIES TO DATE IS AVAILABLE ON-LINE GRATIS
IN FLIP-BOOK FORM......AND DOWNLOAD-ABLE GRATIS
+
AVAILABLE IN SOFTCOVER VIA AMAZON
+
AVAILABLE IN E-BOOK FORM VIA VARIOUS MODALITIES

A UNIQUE STUDY AND REFERENCE TOOL FOR CLERGY, ACADEMICS,
STUDENTS & LAY INTELLIGENSIA

A STELLAR CORE COURSE OF STUDY – WHETHER FOR ONE SEMESTER OR
MULTI-YEAR

AND... AS AN UNINTENDED CONSEQUENCE, THE SERIES HAS
BROKEN DOWN BARRIERS - AND SERVED AS A FORCE-MULTIPLIER –
IN UNIFYING THE JEWISH PEOPLE

IN DEPTH & BREADTH......SCOPE & SPECTRUM
A LANDMARK SERIES
UNIQUE ACROSS THE 3,500+ YEAR SPAN OF JEWISH HISTORY

This New Paradigm Matrix work
is available via multiple modalities:

amazon: www.AmazonX1000.com

eBooks: www.eReader1000.com

online: www.MesorahMatrix.com

contact: NPM1000@yahoo.com

The ten volumes of the Mesorah Matrix series amount to a contemporary encyclopedia of the best of traditional and new creative thinking on the central issues of Jewish Spirituality for the 21st century. People grappling with the place of truth, personal virtues and social values in their lives, will find multiple essays which challenge them to grow intellectually and spiritually in their Jewish identity. The ideas are all deeply rooted in Jewish texts in ways that enlighten the early texts and brighten the path into the future of the Jewish People.

- Rabbi Saul Berman
  Yeshiva University
  Chanukah, 2018

About the Editors

Martin S. Cohen has been a Senior Editor of the inter-denominational Mesorah Matrix series since 2012.

From 2000-2014, he served as Chairman of the Editorial Board of the quarterly journal *Conservative Judaism*, which was published under the joint auspices of the Jewish Theological Seminary and the Rabbinical Assembly.

Rabbi Cohen also served as the senior editor of *The Observant Life*, a landmark compendium of Jewish law and custom published by the Rabbinical Assembly in 2012.

His weekly blog can be viewed at www.TheRuminativeRabbi.blogspot.com. He has served as rabbi of the Shelter Rock Jewish Center in Roslyn, New York, since 2002.

Rabbi Cohen was educated at the City University of New York and at the Jewish Theological Seminary, where he was ordained a rabbi and received his Ph.D. in Ancient Judaism. He is the recipient of fellowships at the Hebrew University in Jerusalem in 1983 and Harvard University in 1993.

Martin Cohen has taught at Hunter College, the Jewish Theological Seminary, the Institute for Jewish Studies of the University of Heidelberg, as well as at the University of British Columbia and the Vancouver School of Theology.

His published works include *The Boy on the Door on the Ox* (2008) and *Our Haven and Our Strength: A Translation and Commentary on the Book of Psalms* (2004), as well as four novels and four books of essays.

Rabbi Cohen is currently writing a translation and commentary on the Torah and the Five Megillot.

MARTIN S. COHEN MAJOR WORKS

As Senior Editor

Mesorah Matrix series 2012 - present

Conservative Judaism 2000 - 2014

The Observant Life 2012

As Author (Non-Fiction)

Travels on the Private Zodiac: Reflections on Jewish Life, Ritual and Spirituality (1995)

In Pursuit of Wholeness: The Search for Spiritual Integrity in a Delusional World (1996)

Travels on the Road Not Taken: Towards a Bible-Based Theology of Jewish Spirituality (1997)

Sefer Ha-ikarim Li-z'maneinu (2000)

Our Haven and Our Strength: The Book of Psalms (2004)

Siddur Tzur Yisrael (2005)

Zot Nechamati for the House of Mourning (2006)

Riding the River of Peace (2007)

The Boy on the Door on the Ox (2008)

As Author (Fiction)

The Truth About Marvin Kalish (1992)

Light from Dead Stars (1996)

The Sword of Goliath (1998)

Heads You Lose (2002)

About the Editors

David Birnbaum is a philosophical writer, historical chronicler and *conceptual theorist*. His first work *God and Evil* (KTAV, 1988) is considered by many to be a breakthrough *modern day classic* in the field of theodicy. See God-And-Evil.com.

Editor-in-Chief Birnbaum is known globally as "the architect of Potentialism Theory" – a unified philosophy/cosmology/metaphysics. The paradigm-challenging theory (see ParadigmChallenge.com) is delineated in Birnbaum's 3-volume *Summa Metaphysica* series (1988, 2005, 2014). See Philosophy1000. com.

A riposte to *Summa Theologica* of (St.) Thomas Aquinas, the Birnbaum treatise challenges both the mainstream Western philosophy of Aristotelianism and the well propped-up British/atheistic cosmology of Randomness. See Potentialism Theory.com.

The focus of 150+ reviews/articles, Summa Metaphysica has been an assigned Course Text at over 15 institutions of higher learning globally. See SummaCover-age.com.

Summa Metaphysica was the focus of an international academic conference on Science & Religion in April 16-19 2012 (see Conference1000.com). The work has been very widely covered globally. See RewindSumma.com.

David Birnbaum is the Editor-in-Chief of the *Mesorah Matrix* series on Jewish thought and spirituality. The *sui generis* series spans 10-volumes and 10 themes. The entire series is comprised of 200+ specially commissioned original pieces from 150-180 global Jewish thought leader essayists. See Mesorah1000.com.

In the history realm, David Birnbaum is the author/chronicler of the 2-volume *The Crucifixion – of the Jews*, and of the 7-volume *Jews, Church & Civilization*. His Crucifixion series, in particular, traces a direct trajectory from the Canonical Gospels in the First Century to Auschwitz in the Twentieth. See History1000.com.

David Birnbaum has served on the faculty of the New School for Social Research in Manhattan. He is a graduate of Yeshiva University High School (Manhattan), CCNY (City College of New York) and Harvard. His commentary blog is www.ManhattanObserver.com.

DAVID BIRNBAUM MAJOR WORKS

As Author

4-volume *Summa Metaphysica** (www.philosophy1000.com)

2-volume *The Crucifixion* (www.crucifixion1000.com)

7-volume *Jews, Church & Civilization* (www.civilization1000.com)

As Editor-in-Chief

10-volume *Mesorah Matrix* (www.mesorah1000.com)

As Conceptualizer

3-volume *Summa Spinoffs* (www.Spinoffs1000.com)

8-volume *Potentialism Theory* via Graphic-Narrative
(www.TheoryGraphics1000.com)

As Commentator

www.ManhattanObserver.com

YouTube channels

Summa Metaphysica

Mesorah Matrix

*

Summa I: Religious Man / God and Evil
 Summa II: Spiritual Man / God and Good
 Summa III: Secular Man / The Transcendent Dynamic
 Summa IV: Quantum Man / Morphed Cosmic Order

DAVID BIRNBAUM MAJOR WORKS

FOCUS ON 4-VOLUME -

Summa Metaphysica series

presenting new paradigm
Potentialism Theory
a universal, unified, seamless & fully-integrated
overarching philosophy

www.SummaMetaphysica.com

Summa I:
Religious Man: God and Evil: focus: *theodicy & eternal origins* [1988]**

Summa II:
Spiritual Man: God and Good: focus: *metaphysics & teleology* [2005]

Summa III:
Secular Man: The Transcendent Dynamic: focus: *cosmology & evolution* [2014]

Summa IV:
Quantum Man: Morphed Cosmic Order: focus: *quantum-potential* [2020]

see also secondary site PotentialismTheory.com

see also: Rewindsumma.com 222+ panel Scroll-Down tour

YouTube Channel: Summa Metaphysica

see also Supplement: Articles on Summa
(only online - on www.SummaMetaphysica.com)

** see also: www.GodOfPotential.com
** see special YouTube channel: www.UnifyingScienceSpirituality.com

www.BirnbaumAcademic.com

www.David1000.com

www.Major1000.com

Tikkun Olam

Tikkun Olam

TABLE OF CONTENTS

The term *tikkun olam* has had various meanings during the last two thousand years, acquiring its current meaning of social action in its broadest terms only within the last fifty years or so. It denotes, however, deep Jewish values and duties—described in part by such terms as *ḥesed*, *tzedek*, and *mishpat*: in biblical and rabbinic literature—and it includes obligations to the environment, society, and family.

Tikkun olam has its biblical source in one of the names of God, key to the covenant of circumcision made with Abraham.

Tikkun ha-olam is often understood as the rationale by which the rabbis intervened in the Jewish legal system in order to ameliorate a problematic or even unjust situation that could arise from strict adherence to the letter of the law. This essay, through a close reading of the sources and parallel materials, suggests a more complicated understanding of how *tikkun ha-olam* functioned in the tannaitic context, which allows for a more complex and interesting understanding of the challenges of making and interpreting law, advancing social welfare through law, and creating a system of justice and social benefit.

A thorough literary analysis of the two *mishnayot* from tractate Gittin that discuss the concept of *darkhei shalom* ("the interest of peace") paints a visual picture of the physical structure of a Jew's community and the people with it. The Mishnah includes those not only those with whom one identifies with because of similar beliefs and practices, but also those usually on the periphery of normative communities: the poor, the disabled, Jews with other religious practices, and non-Jews. The text emphasizes that they too must be treated with respect and dignity, for all human beings are God's creations.

The *mitzvah* of pilgrimage to Jerusalem is not just about visiting God in the exclusive ancient cultic center. When examined in its larger spiritual context, if can be understood to suggest a moral and spiritual *aliyah* ("ascent"), which by its nature symbolizes moral *tikkun*. Translated into modern geopolitical terms, this can be taken as a call to Jews and Arabs in today's Middle East to undergo the kind of interior moral mutation that could lead to the renouncing the concept national hegemony to sacred space. This building of a true "city of God" reflects the universalistic ideal of Judaism.

The article's main point is that tikkun olam is more than a generic slogan, and is instead a precise concept addressing a fundamental responsibility central to Judaism.

Unless otherwise indicated, all translations here are the authors' own work. Biblical citations foot-
noted to the "NJPS" derive from the complete translation of Scripture published under the title
Tanakh: The Holy Scriptures by the Jewish Publication Society in Philadelphia in 1985.

Preface

Martin S. Cohen

One of the signs that any civilization or society has retained its vitality and its vibrancy will rest in its ability—and also in its willingness—to allow even its most foundational ideas to morph forward and develop along lines that their original formulators may well have found unexpected, even perhaps foreign.

Tikkun olam is an example of just such a concept. The phrase is in wide use today to denote the struggle for social justice and ecological responsibility, but meant something quite different when it was first used in early rabbinic times. Is that kind of linguistic development a bad thing because it obfuscates the term's original meaning? Or is it essentially a good thing because it is exactly the ability of old words and phrases to come to mean new things that points to the dynamic vibrancy of a spiritual or cultural tradition? The essays gathered together in this volume present cogently argued, strongly put, and very emotionally satisfying responses to those very questions. Some argue that the process that has led modern-day Jews to see the struggle for social justice as part and parcel of Judaism should be viewed as positive and healthy. Others find the way the phrase *tikkun olam* is used today to be wan and uninspiring…and dare to suggest ways to understand the concept that will be more stirring than bland. And still others focus primarily on those ancient sources themselves in an attempt to find meaning there that appears to have escaped even moderns who know these texts well.

Taken together, the essays in this volume evince a profound, inspiring willingness to engage with the literary heritage of ancient Judaism in an effort creatively to fashion a Jewish world for contemporary Jews that is somehow both faithful to history without being slavishly dependent on its vagaries. All are rooted in ancient texts. And all are the work of rabbis and scholars who feel called upon to translate the Judaism of antiquity into something moderns can embrace enthusiastically and wholeheartedly— without bowdlerizing the texts they are analyzing or intentionally misreading the lessons bequeathed by their ancient forebears.

The work in this book is meant to inspire. Each essay is rooted in the supposition that the mission of every generation of Jewish people is to focus the past through the present in order to create a kind of naturally evolved Judaism that all can embrace, without feeling any concomitant need to abandon their own intellectual, moral, or spiritual integrity. And this is precisely how Jewish people from every corner of the Jewish world can set off on the great redemptive journey that leads to Jerusalem, to the city of God that itself symbolizes the highest and finest aspirations of all humankind. Each of our authors, myself surely included, is somewhere along the way on that journey. We thus write as individuals to set forth our own ideas, but also as a group that has come together between the covers of this book to invite readers to come along on this specific journey, on this lifelong effort to create the spiritual context in which it becomes possible to live authentically Jewish lives suffused with faith, with meaning, and with confidence in the future of the House of Israel...and also endowed with a clear sense that the obligation endlessly to interpret and re-interpret our Jewish heritage should be considered ennobling rather than burdensome, and as a sacred challenge.

Our authors represent Jewish spiritual learning at its finest and more variegated. They are men and women who hail from Great Britain and from France, from Israel and Canada, as well as from the United States. They are at many different stages of their professional careers. Many are formally affiliated with different inner-Jewish denominations, but others live and work outside the denominational framework. Some are seasoned writers who have published widely, while others are relatively new authors. Some are academics, some work as active clergy people, and still others are independent authors. They are, therefore, all very different people... and yet at the same time, they are very similar in the one specific way that counts the most profoundly: all believe in the power of the written word to inspire fresh thinking and to inform passionate commitment...and thus also to change the world.

For the sake of creating a unified volume that readers will find appealing and easy to read, our authors were asked to adhere to certain stylistic guidelines, particularly as pertains to transliteration of ancient texts. Any volume such as this one is necessarily built around consensus and compromise; my hope is that readers will find our efforts to produce a book that "feels" unified to outweigh the irritation of not having granted our authors an entirely free hand to write as they might otherwise have seen fit. The four-letter name of God, *yod-hei-vav-hei*—whose original pronunciation is unknown, and is generally enunciated as either "Adonai" or "Hashem" by contemporary Jews—is rendered as "the Eternal" or "the Eternal One" in this volume, as it will be in subsequent books in the series.

I must acknowledge the world class contributors to this volume who willingly agreed to be part of this innovative venture and who were collectively such a pleasure for me personally to work with, through a painstaking editorial process. And, of course, I would like also to salute Sanctification's Rabbi Benjamin Blech and my other fellow editors in the Mesorah Matrix series, Rabbi Saul J. Berman and Professor Shalom Carmy.

In his own category, however, is the Editor-in-Chief, architect and 'guiding light' of the Mesorah Matrix series, David Birnbaum. It was David who first conceived of this immense landmark project – and who personally brought me into the project in the summer of 2012. Readers interested in learning more about the larger project can visit the Mesorah Matrix website at www.mesorahmatrix.com. David is to be commended for having the vision, the assiduity, the intellect, and the passion to engineer and guide this formidable and potentially historic endeavor.

Finally, I would like to acknowledge the men and women of the Shelter Rock Jewish Center in Roslyn, New York, who have embraced my literary pursuits as part and parcel of what it means for me personally to be a rabbi. Rather than seeing my writing and editing as a hobby that takes me away from my "real" job, my thoughtful, good-hearted congregants understand that it is precisely my effort to create Jewish books—to write, to edit, to publish, and to draw others into books like this one—that allows me personally to feel worthy of occupying the pulpit of their synagogue. I am more fortunate than I could ever say to serve a congregation like Shelter Rock as its spiritual leader, and this book and its sister volumes are merely the tangible proof of that fact. To all, then, I say thank you…and may we all together move forward to create many more books that inspire, inform, challenge, and enthuse.

Martin S. Cohen
Roslyn, New York
November 23, 2014
הוא יום השנה הל״ה לפטירת אמי מורתי ע״ה וז״ל

A Note from the Editors

Every effort has been made to retain a good level of consistency between the essays that appear here in terms of the translation and transliteration of Hebrew. Many of our decisions have, needs be, been arbitrary, but we have done our best to create a book that will be as accessible to newcomers to the study of Judaism as it is inspiring to cognoscenti. The four-letter name of God, left unpronounced by pious Jews as a sign of reverence, is mostly rendered in this volume as "the Eternal" or "the Eternal One." Other divine names are either transliterated or translated to create in English something akin to the way the text reads in Hebrew. All translations are their authors' unless otherwise indicated.

Essays

What Is *Tikkun Olam* and Why Does It Matter? An Overview from Antiquity to Modern Times

Elliot N. Dorff

Jews today speak of *tikkun olam* as a central Jewish precept; concern for literally "fixing the world" by making it a better place, through activities we often call "social action," is certainly at the heart of a contemporary Jewish perspective on life. That meaning of the term *tikkun olam*, however, is itself very new in Jewish history.

The first occurrences of the phrase *tikkun olam* in the Jewish tradition appear in the Mishnah and Tosefta (both edited c. 200 C.E.), which state that the rabbis instituted a number of changes in Jewish law *mi-p'nei tikkun ha-olam*, "for the sake of *tikkun olam*."[1] In these earliest usages, the term probably means—as the Alcalay and Even-Shoshan dictionaries suggest as their first definition—guarding the established order in the physical or social world (with derivative nouns *t'kinah*, meaning "standardization," and *t'kinut*, meaning "normalcy, regularity, orderliness, propriety").[2] In the twelfth century, Maimonides expands on this considerably, claiming that the rabbis created *all* of their rulings, customs, and decrees—that is, the entire rabbinic legal tradition—in order "to strengthen the religion and order [i.e., fix] the world."[3] In this earliest meaning of the term, then, the rabbis sought to repair the legal and social worlds by making Jewish law apply fairly and effectively in their contemporary circumstances, thus giving the world proper proportion and balance.

The next time the phrase is used, now with a different meaning, occurs in the second paragraph of the Aleinu prayer, which was first used in Jewish liturgy in the fourteenth century. That paragraph is much less often sung than the first and therefore it is much less well known, even though it is the core of the prayer's meaning. The first paragraph says that we Jews have a duty to praise God for making us a distinct nation and for creating and ruling the world. The second paragraph then states:

> Therefore we hope in You, Adonai our God, soon to see the glory of Your might, sweeping idolatry away so that false gods will be utterly destroyed, *to fix [perfect] the world by [to be] the Kingdom of the Almighty (l'takkein olam b'malkhut shaddai)* so that all human beings will pray [call out] in Your name, bringing all the wicked of the earth back to You, repentant. Then all who dwell on earth will acknowledge and know that to You every knee must bend and every tongue pledge loyalty. Before You, Adonai, our God, they will bow and prostrate themselves, and they will give honor to Your name. All of them will accept the yoke of Your sovereignty, and You will rule over them soon and forever; for sovereignty is Yours, and You will rule with honor always and forever, as it is written in Your Torah, "The Eternal will rule forever and ever" (Exodus 15:18). Furthermore, it is said [in the Prophets], "And the Eternal will be acknowledged sovereign over the whole earth, on that day the Eternal will be one and God's name one" (Zechariah 14:9]).[4]

Notice several things about the concept as it appears in this prayer (where it is expressed as a verbal form: *l'takkein olam*, "to fix [or perfect] the world"). First, because God chose us, created the whole world, and rules it alone (that is, without the aid of any other god), as the first paragraph asserts, we hope and pray that *God* will fix the world. This is definitely not the modern notion that we *human beings* are called to do that.

Second, the "fixing" about which the prayer speaks is *not* what moderns reference as social action. It is rather theological in nature: that Adonai—the God of Israel—will be recognized by all human beings (literally, "all creatures of flesh"), and not solely by Jews, as the one and only God. This will make God's rule, and therefore God's moral standards, absolute and universal, forcing "all the wicked [people] of the earth" to turn to God—and, presumably, to change their ways. A "fixed" world will thus involve universal recognition and acceptance of a clear and exclusive standard of behavior, with all people adjusting their expectations, attitudes, and behavior to conform to that standard. But while this prayer envisions a moral renaissance as a corollary to universal recognition of the one and only God, it does not speak of a world rid of war, poverty, dissension, and disrespect—except, perhaps, implicitly. That is, if everyone is following God's rules and aspiring to God's ideals for human beings, that may well produce a world in which those limitations no longer exist—but that kind of moral ideal is not the explicit message of this prayer. It is rather an expression of a hope for a theological ideal, that of monotheism.

The third time the phrase appears in Jewish history, in Lurianic Kabbalah, it has yet another meaning. Isaac Luria (1534–1572) created his own distinctive form of Kabbalah. From the time the Zohar was written in the thirteenth century until Luria's own time, Kabbalists had depicted a God consisting of ten spheres (*s'firot*), with multiple interactions among the spheres. Human beings were to try to become one with God through study of the esoteric meanings of the Torah and through obeying God's commandments, which were also given new, mystical meanings.

Luria, however, claimed that in creating the world, God had used too much of the divine energy and benevolence, thus shattering the finite vessels that God had created. (Those "vessels" include all finite beings, both inanimate and animate: mineral, vegetable, animal, and, especially, human.) When Jews study the Torah, especially its esoteric meanings, and when Jews fulfill their obligations under God's commandments, Luria maintained, they literally help to fix the shattered world. Jews thus potentially have immense power—a comforting message to Jews battered by the pogroms and massacres of Luria's time—for even if they are often helpless victims in their lives on earth, in the celestial realm they can do nothing less than fix God's vessels and the world God created.

For Luria and his followers, obeying the commandments certainly included what we would call the social and moral imperatives of our tradition, but those social ideals were not their primary emphasis. They focused instead, as did all Kabbalists, on fixing one's own life by making one's will and one's very being one with God. For Luria, Jews observing the commandments would also, quite audaciously, fix the *s'firot* that collectively are the God that humankind may know. In a world physically, economically, culturally, politically, socially, and religiously hostile to Jews, one can readily understand how Jews needed to find meaning and hope by turning away from that world and focusing instead on their own inner lives—and, for Luria, that included the world of divine being as well.

The Maharal of Prague (Rabbi Judah Loew ben Bezalel, 1525–1609) uses the phrase *tikkun olam* in yet two other senses. First, he maintains that the whole purpose of the Torah is to teach us how to fix the world, ridding it especially of our penchant to do evil. Thus we—that is, all Jews—fix the world when we obey the dictates of the Torah, because we thereby purge evil from the world.[5] This is not the modern conception of social action, because the Maharal means both more and less than what moderns have in mind: more, because he clearly thinks that Jews must obey not only the moral dictates of Judaism but also its ritual commandments in order to free the world from evil (while moderns usually do not have rituals in mind as part of what they mean by *tikkun olam*); and less, because freeing the world from the desire to do evil is not the equivalent of the much broader social agenda that most moderns intend by the phrase (since they mean to include also the need to feed the hungry, house the homeless, and so on).

In another place, the Maharal uses the phrase in yet another sense—namely, to assert that sometimes societal conventions, based on our desire to fix the world (i.e., make the world work efficiently), contradict the Torah's laws. He maintains that such customs violate Jewish law unjustly, whether they produce a stringency or leniency:

In chapter 2 of [the talmudic tractate] Bava Metzia, the rabbis said that a person does not have to return a lost object to its owner once the latter has given up looking for it. But this seems far-fetched to people: that a person should take something that is not one's own and for which one did not work or toil, and covet the property of another. This is not according to societal conventions (*dat ha-nimusit*), for such conventions requires that one return an object even after the owner has given up on finding it. The reason that is so is because societal conventions require us to do that which is suited to fix the world, even if reason does not require such an act [as a matter of justice]; but rather, that is simply the way of *tikkun ha-olam* [i.e., of fixing the world]. Thus: sometimes societal conventions are stringent with regard to a given issue, even if reason and the plain law do not require something. But sometimes conventions are more lenient in a given matter, even though reason does not approve—namely, when the act is not necessary to fix the world. Thus according to societal conventions, one must return a lost object after the owner has given up on finding it, and that is a stringency [i.e., it goes beyond the legal requirement of the halakhah]. On the other hand, if one found a silver or gold vessel and announced once or twice that one had found it, and nobody sought after it for a year or two, one may then take possession of it and use it, for there is no fixing of the world [in not doing so] after announcing it several times and waiting for a year or two or more, for the owner will no longer come for it [after that]. But that is not according to the Torah, for if one found a silver or gold vessel and announced it many times [and still nobody claimed it], one may never use it. It must just sit there forever until [the prophet] Elijah comes [to announce the messianic era], which is a great stringency.[6]

The Maharal then claims that in both instances the Torah, which is fully rational and wise, is actually right and societal conventions are wrong.[7] Property merely belongs to a person; it is not his or her flesh and blood. Therefore, if a person gives up hope of ever finding something, the despair (*yei·ush*) of ever retrieving it is enough to sever the item from its owner. As a result, it becomes ownerless (*hefker*), and any finder may keep it. On the other hand, if it is clear (from the value of the property, for example) that the owner would never give up hope of finding it, then the connection between the item and owner is not severed, and so the finder must forever simply keep it without using it. (The Maharal uses the traditional turn of phrase "until Elijah comes" to say as much.) Thus, the Maharal is using the term *tikkun olam* to indicate common sense—or accepted, utilitarian norms, intended to make the world work efficiently—and he is claiming that sometimes Jews must *not* seek to "fix" the world in that way, but rather must obey Jewish law.

It is only in the mid-twentieth century that the term *tikkun olam* came to mean that we human beings (and not just rabbis) may fix the world of concrete objects, animals, and persons by engaging in both environmental and social care and repair. Possibly a creation of the Civil Rights Movement of the 1960s, the term with that meaning gained its most widespread use first in the Reform Movement, which was heavily invested in civil rights work. In the 1960s the phrase was not well defined, but *tikkun olam* was intended to be a Jewish term denoting any humanitarian action. Conservative and even some Orthodox Jews who gradually began to use the term with that meaning were interested in identifying *tikkun olam* with specific, traditional commandments to work toward social ends, as well as in exploring the legal discussion of those commandments. Now it is used by Jews of all sorts to denote the broad Jewish mandate to care for others.[8]

Related Terms and Concepts in Older Texts

I once was on a panel with a very learned Jew who claimed that *tikkun olam* as it is used now is not a Jewish concept, and that its current usage is by those who want to abandon traditional Judaism and to remake Judaism into a religion solely concerned with social action. He was clearly right about the historical roots of the term; as I explained in the previous section of this essay, the term gains its present meaning only late in Jewish history, and its earliest meanings were significantly different from what we mean by the phrase today. The meaning of *tikkun olam* as environmental and social actions to repair the world is very new, spanning only five or six decades—like yesterday in Jewish time—and the types of action called for by the current sense of *tikkun olam* certainly cannot (and should not) replace all other forms of Jewish practice. At the same time, as I pointed out to my co-panelist, there are other terms in classical Jewish sources that denote some of the same things that we now mean by the phrase *tikkun olam*. Because these other terms have an ancient pedigree, one that continues throughout Jewish literature to our own day, one certainly cannot maintain, as he did, that social concern is a new form of Judaism, unrelated to the Jewish past. He was right, of course, in asserting that social concern is not the whole of Judaism; but it *is* a central feature of it, as moderns claim—even though this concern is expressed in different words than it was in earlier eras. The closest of those classical words for what we mean today by *tikkun olam* are *ḥesed*, on the personal level, and *tzedek* and *mishpat*, on the communal level.

Ḥesed originally meant loyalty—to God and to one's neighbor. It therefore comes to mean what one does in faithfulness to God and to one's neighbor—namely, acts of love, kindness, and care. So, for example, Abraham's servant uses the language of *ḥesed* when he asks God to be loyal to his master, Abraham, in identifying the right woman to marry Isaac (Genesis 24:12, 14); God shows loyalty (*ḥesed*) to Joseph by making the chief of the jail into which he has been thrown like him (Genesis 39:21), and then Joseph uses the same language to ask the cup-bearer to show loyalty to him for interpreting his dream favorably by mentioning him to Pharaoh so that he can get out of jail (Genesis 40:14); and Jacob uses that same word when he asks Joseph to show loyalty to him by burying him in Canaan rather than Egypt (Genesis 47:29). With regard to the last case, the rabbis speak of burying the dead as *ḥesed shel emet*, a true act of loyalty, because the dead person cannot pay us back.[9] A later term is *g'milut ḥasadim*, extending acts of *ḥesed*.

Tzedek means justice, as in the famous verse "Justice, justice shall you pursue" (Deuteronomy 16:20). The Torah's vision of justice includes both procedural and substantive elements. That is, the Torah demands that in court we ensure fairness by following specific procedures in judging people ("procedural justice"), and in society generally we must guarantee that there is a substantial safety net so that the most vulnerable members of our society—traditionally identified as orphans, widows, and the poor—get what they need to live, get an education, and find a mate ("substantive justice").[10]

Mishpat comes from the root *shin-pei-tet*, from which the word for "judge," *shofeit*, is derived; thus mishpat originally meant the decision of a judge, or a precedent. It has that meaning, for example, in the very first verse of Exodus 21, the opening of the weekly portion called Mishpatim—for as biblical scholars have pointed out, the norms contained in that section of the Torah probably originated as judicial precedents. From this origin, the word *mishpat* expands to mean "law" more generally, especially in the plural form. For example: "See, I [Moses] have imparted to you laws (*hukkim*) and rules (*mishpatim*), as the Eternal my God has commanded me" (Deuteronomy 4:5);[12] "God issued divine commands (*d'varav*) to Jacob, divine statutes (*hukkav*) and rules (*u-mishpatav*) to Israel; God did not do so for any other nation, and of such rules (mishpatim) they know nothing" (Psalm 147:19–20); "You came down on Mount Sinai and spoke to them from heaven; You gave them right rules (*mishpatim y'sharim*) and true teachings (*v'torot emet*), good laws and commandments (*hukkim u-mitzvot tovim*)" (Nehemiah 9:13).

Finally, already in the Bible the word *mishpat* expands yet further to mean "justice." For example: "The Rock!—God's deeds are perfect, Yea, all of God's ways are just (*mishpat*)" (Deuteronomy 32:4); as well as the famous verse from Micah: "God has told you…what is good, and what the Eternal requires of you: only to do justice (*mishpat*), to love goodness (*hesed*), and to walk modestly with your God" (6:8).[13]

As this last verse exemplifies, the values of justice and kindness are often spoken of together in both the Bible and rabbinic literature, to indicate that they balance and reinforce each other. So, for example, in a verse Jews recite three times each day, the psalmist asserts: "The Eternal is righteous (*tzaddik*) in all ways and kind (*hasid*) in all actions" (Psalm 145:17).[14] More expansively, using many of the Hebrew words that have been historically used to express aspects of our contemporary notion of *tikkun olam*, the psalmist (36:6–8) declares:

O Eternal, Your kindness (*hasdekha*) reaches to heaven;
Your steadfastness (*emunat'kha*) to the sky;
Your righteousness (*tzidkat'kha*) is like the high mountains;
Your justice (*mishpat'kha*) like the great deep;
humans and beast You deliver, O Eternal.
How precious is Your loving care (*hasd'kha*), O God!
Humanity shelters in the shadow of Your wings.

This intermixing of terms continues in rabbinic literature—as, for example, in this passage:

> Rabbi Eleazar quoted this verse, "God has told you, O mortal, what is good, and what the Eternal requires of you: only to do justice (*mishpat*), to love goodness (*ḥesed*), and to walk modestly with your God" (Micah 6:8). What does this verse imply? "To do justice" means to act in accordance with the principles of justice. "To love goodness" means to let your actions be guided by principles of lovingkindness. "To walk modestly with your God" means to assist needy families at their funerals and weddings [by giving humbly, in private]. Rabbi Eleazar said: Whoever does deeds of charity (tzedakah) and justice (mishpat) is considered as having filled the entire world, all of it, with lovingkindness (*ḥesed*), as it is written, "God loves what is right (*tzedakah*) and just (mishpat); the earth is filled with the lovingkindness of the Eternal" (Psalm 33:5). Should you suppose that one may achieve this easily, Scripture says, "How precious is Your loving care, O God" (Psalm 36:8).[15] Should you suppose that difficulty in executing charity and justice also affects those who fear heaven, Scripture says, "But the Eternal's steadfast love (*ḥesed*) is for all eternity toward those who fear God, and divine beneficence (*tzidkato*) is for children's children for those who keep God's covenant" (Psalm 103:17).[16]

Clearly, then, from the Jewish perspective doing justice is *not* restricted to abiding by or judging according to the rules; it certainly does demand that,[17] but it also requires that one balance justice with kindness.

The rabbinic tradition goes further than that. It values acts of kindness for the objective good they accomplish, regardless of the motive that may have prompted a person to do them. Thus, it prefers acts of kindness to charity (even though it values that as well), for kindness can fix the world in more ways than charity can:

> Our rabbis taught that deeds of lovingkindness (*g'milut ḥasadim*) are superior to charity (*tzedakah*) in three respects. Charity can be accomplished only with money, while deeds of lovingkindness can be accomplished through personal involvement as well as with money. Charity can be given only to the poor, while deeds of lovingkindness can be done for both rich and poor. And charity applies only to the living, while deeds of lovingkindness apply to both the living and the dead....[18]

At the same time, the rabbis were not blind to the importance of motive. Thus while they valued all acts of kindness for the good they achieve, regardless of the reasons for which people perform those acts, the rabbis judged the moral worth of such acts according to the degree to which they are done with selfless, benign motives:

> Rabbi Eleazar said: The reward for acts of justice (*tzedakah*, usually translated as "charity") depends upon the degree of lovingkindness (*ḥesed*) in them, as it is written, "Sow justice (tzedakah) for yourselves; reap according to [your] goodness (*ḥesed*)" (Hosea 10:12).[19]

Thus, if possible, our acts of kindness should affect our inner being as well as the world at large. Here, though, one must remember the fundamental rabbinic educational psychology—namely, that although it is best to do good things for the right motives, one should do the right thing even for the wrong reason if one must, for "from doing the right thing not for its own sake, one will come to do it for its own sake."[20] That is, we should to do the right thing now, rather than wait to be inspired by the proper motive. I would suggest that the rabbis maintained this for three reasons: first, the right motive may never come; second, even if one does the right thing for an improper motive (e.g., to get a good reputation or a favor from someone else), the good act hopefully accomplishes an objective good in society; and third, the way we learn good motives is by doing good acts (as the rabbis themselves said, in the text just cited).

The Importance of *Tikkun Olam* and Its Related Values

The values we are discussing are among the most important of the Torah's values. As the Talmud asserts, *hesed* runs through the Torah from beginning to end:

> Rabbi Simlai taught: The Torah begins with deeds of lovingkindness and ends with deeds of lovingkindness. It begins with deeds of lovingkindness, as it is written, "And the Eternal, God, made garments of skins for Adam and for his wife and clothed them" (Genesis 3:21). It ends with deeds of lovingkindness, as it is written, "And God buried him [Moses] in the valley in the land of Moab" (Deuteronomy 34:6).[21]

> Once, as Rabbi Yoḥanan was walking out of Jerusalem, Rabbi Joshua followed him, and upon seeing the Temple in ruins, he said: "Woe unto us that this place is in ruins, the place where atonement was made for Israel's iniquities!" Rabbi Yoḥanan responded: "My son, do not grieve, for we have another means of atonement that is as effective. What is it? It is deeds of lovingkindness (*g'milut ḥasadim*), concerning which Scripture says, 'I [God] desire goodness (*hesed*), not sacrifice'" (Hosea 6:6)."[22]

Furthermore, to refuse to care for others is to deny the reality of God: "Rabbi Judah said: When a person denies the duty of lovingkindness, it is as though he or she had denied the Root [i.e., God]."[23] Conversely, engaging in acts of *hesed* is nothing less than modeling oneself after God:

> "To walk in all God's ways" (Deuteronomy 11:22). These are the ways of the Holy One: "compassionate and gracious, slow to anger, abounding in kindness (*hesed*) and faithfulness, extending kindness (*hesed*) to the thousandth generation, forgiving iniquity, transgression, and sin..." (Exodus 34:6). This means that just as God is compassionate and gracious, you too must be compassionate and gracious....Just as God is righteous, you too must be righteous...as it is said, "The Eternal is righteous in all ways and kind in all actions" (Psalm 145:17). Just as the Holy One is righteous, so you too must be righteous. Just as the Holy One is kind (or: loving, *hasid*), so too you must be kind (loving).[24]

> "Follow the Eternal your God" (Deuteronomy 13:5). What does this mean? Is it possible for a mortal to follow God's Presence? The verse means to teach us that we should follow the *attributes* of the blessed Holy One. As God clothes the naked...you should clothe the naked. As the Holy One visited the sick...so you should visit the sick. As the Holy One comforted those who mourned...so you should comfort those who mourn. As the Holy One buried the dead...so you should bury the dead.[25]

Finally, *hesed* is one of the three values on which the very existence of the world depends, as we learn in this famous passage from the mishnaic tractate Pirkei Avot ("Ethics of the Fathers")—famous both because it comes at the very beginning of the tractate, and also because it has been set to music and has become a popular song in modern times: "Simeon the Just...used to say: The world depends on three things—on Torah, on worship, and on acts of lovingkindness (*g'milut hasadim*)."[26]

The other Hebrew terms found in ancient texts that describe aspects of what we now mean by *tikkun olam* are *tzedek* (justice) and *mishpat*, especially in the latter term's broadest sense of justice. As indicated earlier, in many ways *hesed* denotes the personal, individual aspects of *tikkun olam*, while *tzedek* and mishpat denote its communal elements. Furthermore, similar to *hesed*, *tzedek* and *mishpat* are indeed core values of the Jewish tradition. Thus, at the end of the first chapter of Pirkei Avot, we read an alternative list of values on which the world depends: "Rabbi Simeon ben Gamliel used to say: The world depends on three things—on judgment (*din*), truth, and peace, as the Bible says, 'Judge in your gates truth and justice (*u-mishpat*) and peace' (Zechariah 8:16)."[27]

Like *hesed*, the justice aspects of *tikkun olam* are also part of God's very essence. As the psalmist declares, "Righteousness and justice (*tzedek u-mishpat*) are the base of Your throne; steadfast love and faithfulness (*hesed ve-emet*) stand before You" (Psalm 89:15; see also 97:2).

The Book of Proverbs similarly asserts that if a person pays attention to wisdom, "then you will understand the fear of the Eternal and attain knowledge of God....God reserves ability for the upright and is a shield for those who live blamelessly, guarding the paths of justice (*mishpat*), protecting the way of those loyal to God. You will then understand what is right, just and equitable (*tzedek u-mishpat u-meisharim*)—every good course" (2:5, 7–9). Consequently, to seek God is to seek justice: "Listen to Me, you who pursue justice (*tzedek*), You who seek the Eternal....For teaching (torah) will go forth from Me, My way (*mishpati*, literally "my justice") for the light of peoples.... Listen to Me, you who care for justice (*tzedek*), O people who lay My teaching to heart!" (Isaiah 51:1, 4, 7). From the Bible's point of view, then, the tasks of discerning the just and the good and then acting on that knowledge are not just central to Jewish identity; they are what God demands of us: "Do what is right and good in the sight of the Eternal..." (Deuteronomy 6:18).

Many philosophical questions immediately arise from this last verse and the other passages we have been considering: What do we mean by the terms "kind," "just," "right," and "good" in the first place, and how are they different from each other? How shall we determine the courses of action that are right or good in morally ambiguous situations? What, for example, should we do when the kind act is not the just act? And how is God related to our moral discernment and action? I have delved into these deeper philosophical questions in several of my other writings.[28] For now, though, suffice it to say that *tikkun olam* and its component values have deep roots in the Jewish tradition, identifying core values in the identity of both Jews and God.

American vs. Jewish Views of Individuals and Community[29]

Most American Jews immediately warm to the idea of *tikkun olam*. In fact, for many, this tenet actually defines the most important part of their Jewish identity, the duty they see embedded in Judaism that makes them proud to be Jews. Many American Jews believe that commitment to repairing the world is widely shared by non-Jews as an imperative of their American identity. The truth, however, is that although non-Jewish Americans may feel a duty to repair the world on the basis of their religious convictions, the American identity of both Jews and other American citizens does not strongly support this duty. The same can be said for people living in other countries influenced by Enlightenment ideology.

American law is strongly rooted in Enlightenment assumptions, as articulated in the United States' Declaration of Independence: "We hold these truths to be self-evident, that all men are created equal, that they are endowed by their Creator with certain unalienable rights, that among these are life, liberty, and the pursuit of happiness." The ideological foundation on which American law is based, then, is that all people are individuals with rights. Whether we get these rights from our Creator, as Jefferson asserts, or from being recognized by legislators and courts, as the long history of "the rights of the Englishman" and the common law would suggest, much of American law—and, indeed, the American psyche—is based on claims of rights.

Like American law, Jewish law demands that each person be treated with respect, but for a different reason. In American law, this is because "all men are endowed by their Creator with certain unalienable rights." For Judaism, the reason is instead that all human beings have been created in the image of God.[30] In neither system, though, does this respect for persons mean that everything that a person does is to be applauded or even condoned. Hence there are laws defining what people must and must not do, and penalties are prescribed for violating the laws. Still, even those condemned to death for committing a capital offense must, according to the Torah, be removed before nightfall from the post on which they were hanged, for, as the Torah says, "an impaled body is an affront to [literally, 'a curse of'] God" (Deuteronomy 21:23). That is, the image of God in each of us must be respected, even with regard to someone who has committed the most egregious of crimes—even if that person is in the process of being punished for that crime.

In American legal theory, and as Americans generally see it, every community is voluntary. I may join or leave any group at any time, including my religious community. This applies even to the United States itself. Gaining American citizenship is hard, but if I am already an American citizen and have not committed a felony, I may leave the country and renounce my citizenship at any time.[31]

This voluntary nature of American notions of community should not be overstated. For all of their individualism—a more pronounced individualism than exists even in other Western democracies—Americans nevertheless put great stock in their multiple forms of association with others. President Barack Obama has stated this well:

If we Americans are individualistic at heart, if we instinctively chafe against a past of tribal allegiances, traditions, customs, and cases, it would be a mistake to assume that this is all we are. Our individualism has always been bound by a set of communal values, the glue upon which every healthy society depends. We value the imperatives of family and the cross-generational obligations that family implies. We value community, the neighborliness that expresses itself through raising the barn or coaching the soccer team. We value patriotism and the obligations of citizenship, a sense of duty and sacrifice on behalf of our nation. We value a faith in something bigger than ourselves, whether that something expresses itself in formal religion or ethical precepts. And we value the constellation of behaviors that express our mutual regard for another: honesty, fairness, humility, kindness, courtesy, and compassion. In every society (and in every individual), these twin strands—the individualistic and the communal, autonomy and solidarity—are in tension, and it has been one of the blessings of America that the circumstances of our nation's birth allowed us to negotiate these tensions better than most.[32]

Even with this proper notice of communal ties in American society, the individualism at the heart of American culture and law makes communities in America, and American citizenship itself, voluntary.

In contrast, the Jewish tradition conceives of the Jewish community as organic. Classical Jewish law defines a Jew as someone who is born to a Jewish woman or reborn, as it were, into the Jewish community through the rites of conversion. Once a Jew, a person cannot relinquish that status. A Jew who converts to another religion becomes an apostate, a *m'shummad* (one whose faith has been spiritually destroyed) or a *poshei·a yisrael* (a rebellious Jew).[33] Apostate Jews are subject to some penalties in Jewish law: their testimony is inadmissible in court[34] (except to free a woman legally chained to her first husband[35]); they cannot marry even retroactively through sexual intercourse, because they are assumed to be licentious (like other non-Jews);[36] the court may exclude them from their father's inheritance and pass it on to other members of the family who have not apostatized;[37] the Jewish community has no duty to redeem them from captivity and is actually forbidden to do so;[38] and Jews should not observe mourning rites for such people.[39] In modern Israel, the Supreme Court has ruled that an apostate cannot claim Jewish status under the Law of Return (the Brother Daniel case).[40] Still, the Talmud asserts that "a Jew, even though he has sinned, remains a Jew,"[41] and so if an apostate marries a Jew or even another apostate, the marriage is valid in Jewish law, and a male apostate would need to give his wife a formal writ of Jewish divorce (a *get*) if they wanted to dissolve their marriage.[42] That is also true for a convert to Judaism who subsequently returned to his or her original faith or became part of yet another faith community: once the person has become Jewish, even for an ulterior motive, the conversion makes the person part of the Jewish people, and a convert's betrothal of a Jew or another apostate is valid, requiring a Jewish writ of divorce to dissolve.[43] Furthermore, as a Jew, a female apostate passes Jewish identity on to her offspring.[44] Jewish identity, then, is construed as being part of the Jewish body politic; and just as a part of a body cannot on its own decide to leave the rest of it, so too no Jew can sever himself or herself from the Jewish community.

This thick, organic sense of community has widespread legal implications not only with regard to membership and apostasy, but also in a host of other areas. Most importantly for purposes of this essay, this organic Jewish view of community makes all Jews liable for each other's welfare: as the Talmud says, "All Israelites are responsible for one another" (*kol yisrael areivin zeh ba-zeh*).[45] So, for example, if I see someone drowning or accosted by robbers, I must, according to Jewish law, take steps to save the person (while still protecting my own life).[46] In contrast, in American law until recently, when most states passed "Good Samaritan laws," if I tried to help someone in need and unintentionally hurt the person in the process, I could actually be sued for any harm done. Conversely, only three states— Vermont, Rhode Island, and Minnesota—have enacted statutory duties that require individuals to perform non-risky rescues, and Wisconsin has a statute that requires persons present at the scene of a crime either to report the crime to the police or personally to assist the crime victim. All other American states accept the Common Law, which imposes no duty to rescue.[47]

Thus the Jewish concept of *tikkun olam* and its parallels in other religions are important complements to the American focus on individual rights. Frankly, the reverse is true as well: American commitment to individual liberty is an important balancing factor to the strong sense of community and duty embedded in such Jewish concepts as *tikkun olam*. To see this complementary balancing, however, one must first see that the American and Jewish traditions in fact differ in their approach to the duty to repair the world along the lines described above, one example of the larger distinction between them in their differing emphases on rights vs. duties.

The Arenas of *Tikkun Olam*

In what aspects of our lives should the values articulated by the Jewish value of *tikkun olam* find expression? Although there are many, the ones where Jewish writers have most often applied the term are these:

A. The Environment

"Repairing the world" can literally mean fixing the damage that we have done to our physical environment—and taking steps to preserve what we have now. Often called "Jewish environmental ethics," the roots for this concern begin in the Torah, are developed further in the rest of the Bible and in rabbinic and medieval literature, and find significant expansion in contemporary Jewish thought. This is not surprising, given that it is only in our time that the human population of the planet has exceeded seven billion, with the associated strains that that puts on the air, water, and food supply; and it is only since the Industrial Revolution and the development of modern modes of transportation that we have polluted the air as much as we have.

The theological root of Jewish concern for the environment goes back to the opening chapters of Genesis, where God creates the world. Although the Industrial Revolution has in many aspects of our lives severed the connection between creation and ownership—the person who puts the cog on the wheel does not own the car—it still is the case in some areas of our lives that one who creates something owns it. So, for example, one who writes something and copyrights it, or one who invents something and patents it, owns it and can determine the conditions under which others may use it. In the Torah, the fact that God created the world means immediately that God is *koneih shamayim va-aretz*, "creator of heaven and earth" (Genesis 14:19, 22)—where *koneih* means not only the creator but in fact the owner, and "heaven and earth" is a merism, meaning the heavens, the earth, and everything in between. Thus the Torah says explicitly: "Mark!

The heavens belong to the Eternal, our God; the earth and all that is on it!" (Deuteronomy 10:14). We humans, then, may use the earth only subject to the conditions that God sets in the Torah, generally stated already in chapter 2 of Genesis. We read there that Adam and Eve are placed in the Garden of Eden to "work it and preserve it" (2:15).

This theological basis for our duties to preserve the world (and repair it when we have damaged it) is probably best articulated in the following rabbinic passage:

> "See the work of God. Who can fix that which he has ruined?" (Kohelet 7:13). At the time that the blessed Holy One created the first human being, God took him on a tour of all the trees of the Garden of Eden, and God said to him, "See My works, how beautiful and praiseworthy they are! Everything I created, I created for you. Pay attention that you do not ruin or destroy My world, for if you ruin it, there is nobody to fix it after you.[48]

This theological tenet explains a number of laws in the Torah itself and in later Jewish law. Thus the Torah requires that the land lie fallow one year out of seven (Leviticus 25:1–7), even on land that a person owns. When the Israelites go to war, they may only use those trees that do not bear fruit to build their siege works (Deuteronomy 20:19–20)—and the rabbis later extend this commandment to become a general commandment prohibiting wastefulness, that is, destroying anything that is not needed (*bal tash·ḥit*).[49] They also took steps to avoid bad odors, so tanning yards had to be located to the east (or, according to Rabbi Akiva, north or south) of town so that the prevailing westerly winds would not bring the foul odors produced by tanning leather into the town.[50] The rabbis also took steps to limit noise and air pollution (as, for example, in the forms of dust or smoke), as well as other environmental factors that can harm someone's person or property.[51]

Modern authors have expanded on these themes significantly, taking into account the modern realities of overpopulation, pollution, global warming, and limited resources.[52] Given their general desire to preserve the tradition as it has been handed down, Orthodox writers have been less willing to extend the tradition in these ways than Conservative and, especially Reform, Reconstructionist, and secular Jewish writers have been, but even some Orthodox writers have sought to apply these traditional moorings to modern environmental realities.[53]

B. The Society

This is probably the other main area where many contemporary Jews think of the duties of *tikkun olam*. Efforts to prevent or alleviate poverty; to provide housing, clothing, education, jobs, and health care; and to guarantee that workers are treated fairly, are all part of what contemporary Jews commonly understand to be their duties under the Jewish value of *tikkun olam*.

Exactly how a person or group should work toward these ends is sometimes a matter of dispute. For example, if one wants to provide jobs for people out of work, does that, or does that not, entail working with unions? Which of these goals takes precedence over which? Or, given that one cannot possibly repair the entire world and that all of these are important needs, should a person or group just pick one of these needs and work on that? To what extent should these efforts be directed toward getting new laws or regulations passed by people in government? To what extent, if any, should a Jewish group support particular political candidates because of their positions on these issues? How should Internal Revenue Service regulations and, more generally, our interest in the separation of religion and state in the United States, affect the way we interact with the government?

On some of these issues Jewish sources abound, but others require more of a stretch to apply the Jewish tradition to modern circumstances. So, for example, in my own writings, I have fairly easily summarized what a Jewish approach to relieving poverty should look like in our time because the Jewish tradition has dealt with this question extensively.[54] On the other hand, until very recently in human history, health care was largely ineffective and therefore cheap, and so applying the Jewish tradition to the distribution of health care—who should get what, and who should pay for it—is much harder, requiring analogizing from other areas of Jewish law to this one.[55]

In my book on *tikkun olam*, I included several areas of social action that have strong roots in Jewish sources but are often omitted when contemporary Jews think about *tikkun olam*. Among these is the duty to be present for people in their times of need or joy. This includes, for example, visiting the sick and attending weddings and funerals, but it also includes responding to the needs of family and friends on an ongoing basis for comfort, advice, or just listening, for that is what members of a community should do for each other. In that book I also discuss Jewish duties to ransom captives and Jewish norms about how we talk to and about each other, all as communal forms of *tikkun olam* that are rarely discussed as part of that general concept.[56]

C. The Family

In the same vein, my book on *tikkun olam* include discussion of another arena of everyone's life that is not usually thought of when contemporary Jews speak about *tikkun olam*, namely, spousal and parent–child relations. In some ways, it is easier to participate in fixing everyone else's problems than it is to deal with one's own personal issues, and so people would rather focus on what they can do in general society. The Jewish tradition, however, pays considerable attention to how spouses, parents, and children should and should not interact with each other. It even establishes legal duties that each member of the family has to the others, and it also deals with the ugly side of some families, where violence takes place.[57] Fixing our family lives may be the hardest type of *tikkun olam* to accomplish, but it also may be the most important.

Repairing the World as a Divine Call to Action

We have seen that the phrase *tikkun olam* has meant a variety of things, from its very first usage in the Mishnah to its contemporary meaning of fixing the world in its environmental, social, and familial aspects. We have also seen that although the tradition has used other terms for what contemporary Jews mean when they speak of *tikkun olam*—words like *ḥesed*, *tzedek*, and mishpat—the Jewish tradition from its very beginning has demanded such action of us, however it is described linguistically. So the tradition is clear about the essence and imperative nature of *tikkun olam*: God calls Jews to act to make this a better world, in all the ways described above.

At the same time, *tikkun olam* is not the whole of Judaism. In the Shema (Deuteronomy 6:5), we are commanded to love God "with all your heart, with all your soul, and with all your might," and that can happen only, as the rabbis remind us, if we commit ourselves to acting in all three of the realms upon which the world rests: "Torah, worship, and acts of *ḥesed*."[58] In addition, we Jews inherit a rich cultural tradition and strong links to Jews in the present, past, and future. May we all find the richness and fulfillment embedded in Jewish life as a whole, including its important imperative of *tikkun olam*.

NOTES

[1] M. Gittin 4:2–7, 9; 5:3; 9:4; M. Eiduyot 1:13; T. Ketubot 12:1; T. Gittin 3:12, 13; 6:10; T. Bava Batra 6:6. See also B. Ketubot 52b and Y. Pesaḥim 14b.

[2] Reuben Alcalay, *The Complete Hebrew-English Dictionary* (Bridgeport, CT: The Prayer Book Press, 1965), p. 2835; Abraham Even-Shoshan, *Milon Ḥadash* (Jerusalem: Kiryath Sepher, 1970), vol. 7, p. 2898. I want to thank my good friend Rabbi William Cutter, Professor of Hebrew Literature at Hebrew Union College in Los Angeles, for calling my attention to this original meaning.

[3] M.T. Hilkhot Mamrim 1:2.

[4] The translations of biblical passages throughout this essay are generally based on the "new JPS" translation of the Tanakh (Philadelphia: Jewish Publication Society, 1985), hereafter referred to as NJPS.

[5] Maharal of Prague, *Tiferet Yisrael* (ed. Yehoshua David Hartman; Jerusalem: Makhon Yerushalayim, 5760 [1999-2000]), vol. 2, pp. 906–908.

[6] Maharal of Prague, *Be'eir Ha-golah* 2:6 (ed. Yehoshua David Hartman; Jerusalem: Makhon Yerushalayim, 5763 [2002–2003]), vol. 1, pp. 182–183. The passage from the Talmud cited is located at B. Bava Metzia 21b.

[7] The Maharal is using the word "Torah" here to refer to Jewish law in all its amplified complexity, not just the laws that actually appear in Scripture.

[8] For more on the evolution of the term *tikkun olam* over the last half-century, see the first chapter of my book The Way Into *Tikkun Olam*: Repairing the World (Woodstock, VT: Jewish Lights Publishing, 2005), and also Earl Schwartz, "*Tzedakah, Tikkun Olam*, and the Pitfalls of Loose Talk," in *Conservative Judaism* 63:1 (Fall 2011), pp. 3–24.

[9] Bereishit Rabbah 96:5.

[10] I explore some of the more important aspects of both the procedural and substantive meanings of the term in my book *To Do the Right and the Good: A Jewish Approach to Modern Social Ethics* (Philadelphia: Jewish Publication Society, 2002), chapters 5 and 6.

[11] See, for example, Umberto Cassuto, *A Commentary on the Book of Exodus*, trans. Israel Abrahams (Jerusalem: Magnes Press [Hebrew University], 1967), pp. 260–264, who points out that if Exodus 21–24 were really a law code, it should have clear rules about normal activities in life, such as contracting business deals and getting married. The fact that these chapters do not address such common things indicates that what we have in this section is simply a collection of judicial precedents on a variety of topics, rather than an attempt to give a full and systematic exposition of the law.

[12] The term is also used this way and appears in the NJPS translation as "rules" in Deuteronomy 4:8 and 14; Ezekiel 20:25; and Malachi 3:22.

[13] The term possibly also has the meaning of justice—as well as judgment—in Psalm 103:6: "The Eternal executes righteous acts and judgments [or, more generally, justice; *u-mishpatim*] for all who are wronged."

[14] It is possible that the original meaning of this verse is different—namely, that

both *tzaddik* and *ḥasid* are synonyms for "faithful" or "trustworthy." That would preserve the parallelism common to biblical poetry. The rabbis of ancient times, however, understood these words as they are translated here, and so at least in rabbinic theology, if not in biblical thought, righteousness and kindness are put in balance.

[15] Note that the word *yakar* can mean "rare," as Rabbi Eleazar is choosing to interpret it here in order to make his homiletical point. Its original meaning in its biblical context, however, is probably "precious" (as was translated above), because it is juxtaposed with verses that glory in God's care for those who keep the divine covenant. The rabbis frequently cite verses out of context and "misunderstand" them for homiletical purposes; this is fine, according to their procedures, as long as a given interpretation does not countermand Jewish law or values but rather reinforces them, for "there are seventy faces to the Torah" (Bemidbar Rabbah 13:15–16).

[16] B. Sukkah 49b.

[17] See note 10 above.

[18] B. Sukkah 49b.

[19] Ibid.

[20] B. Pesaḥim 50a.

[21] B. Sotah 14a.

[22] *Avot d'Rabbi Natan* 4:5.

[23] Kohelet Rabbah 7:1, §4.

[24] Sifrei D'varim, *Eikev*, on Deuteronomy 11:22.

[25] B. Sotah 14a.

[26] Pirkei Avot 1:2.

[27] Pirkei Avot 1:18.

[28] See, in particular, *Love Your Neighbor and Yourself: A Jewish Approach to Modern Personal Ethics* (Philadelphia: Jewish Publication Society, 2003), chap. 1 and Appendix; *The Way Into Tikkun Olam* (cited in note 10, above), chap. 3; and For the Love of God and People: A Philosophy of Jewish Law (Philadelphia: Jewish Publication Society, 2007), chap. 6.

[29] For a more thorough treatment of the first part of this section, see chapter 1 of my book *To Do the Right and the Good* (cited in note 10, above).

[30] Genesis 1:26–27; 5:1; 9:6.

[31] See http://travel.state.gov/content/travel/english/legal-considerations/us-citizenship-laws-policies/renunciation-of-citizenship.html, which is the State Department website that describes the right to renounce one's American citizenship, as provided for in Section 349(a)(5) of the Immigration and Naturalization Act, and the ways in which it must be done—namely, by (1) appearing in person before a U.S. consular or diplomatic officer, (2) in a foreign country (normally at a U.S. Embassy or Consulate); and (3) signing an oath of renunciation.

[32] Barack Obama, *The Audacity of Hope: Thoughts on Reclaiming the American Dream* (New York: Crown, 2006), p. 55.

[33] Other terms that are used are a *mumar* (one who changes [faiths]), *apikoros*

(heretic), and *kofeir ba-ikkar* (one who denies a fundamental principle of Jewish faith).

[34] M.T. Hilkhot Eidut 10:1–3; S.A. Hoshen Mishpat 34:1–3.

[35] S.A. Even Ha-eizer 17:3.

[36] Israel B. Pethahiah Isserlein, *T'rumat Ha-deshen* (New York: Keren Menashe v'Sarah Lehman, 1991), vol. 1, pp. 64–65 and 83–84. Isaac b. Sheshet, *Responsa* (Jerusalem, 1967), no. 11; *Piskei Din shel Batei Din Ha-rabbanim B'yisrael* (Jerusalem: Weiss, 1980), 7:35, 39–44; but cf. 54–55.

[37] A son is heir to his father by the mere fact of kinship (Numbers 27:8; B. Bava Batra 108a, 111a; M.T. Hilkhot Nahalot 1:1; and S.A. Hoshen Mishpat 271:1). Nevertheless, the Mordecai (Kiddushin, chap. 1) ruled that an apostate does not inherit from his father. Most authorities maintain that by strict law he does still have the right of inheritance, but in order to discourage apostasy, the court is authorized to pass his inheritance to family members who have not apostatized, on the strength of the rule *hefker bet din hefker*, i.e., the court has the right of expropriation. For that principle, see B. Yevamot 89b and B. Gittin 36b. For its use to deny apostates their inheritance, see Asher ben Yehiel, *Kitzur Piskei Ha-Rosh* to B. Kiddushin, chap. 1, #23; Responsa of Rabbi Solomon Cohen 3:37; M.T. Hilkhot Nahalot 6:12; S.A. Hoshen Mishpat 283:2.

[38] M.T. Hilkhot Matnot Aniyim 8:14.

[39] M. Sanhedrin 6:6; S.A. Yoreh Dei·ah 345:5 (unless the apostate met a sudden death, in which case it is assumed that he or she repented just before death; see S.A. Yoreh Dei·ah 340:5, gloss; and cf. 157 and Hoshen Mishpat 266:2).

[40] Israel's High Court Case of *Rufeisen* (Brother Daniel) 72/62, *Piskei Din* 16:2428–2455.

[41] B. Sanhedrin 44a; see Nahmanides on Deuteronomy 29:14.

[42] B. Yevamot 30b; M.T. Hilkhot Ishut 4:15; S.A. Even Ha-Eizer 44:9.

[43] M.T. Hilkhot Issurei Biah13:17.

[44] M. T. Hilkhot Ishut 4:15.

[45] B. Shevuot 39a.

[46] B. Sanhedrin 73a. For an extended treatment of this duty in Jewish law, see Aaron Kirschenbaum, "The 'Good Samaritan' in Jewish Law," *Dine Israel* 7 (1976), pp. 7–85 (Hebrew); reprinted in summary form in English as "The Bystander's Duty to Rescue in Jewish Law," in the *Journal of Religion and Ethics* 8 (1980), pp. 204–226.

[47] David A. Hyman, "Rescue Without Law: An Empirical Perspective on the Duty to Rescue," in *Texas Law Review* 84:3 (February, 2006), pp. 653–738, at p. 683. As Hyman demonstrates, four states have enacted laws requiring people who witness a person in distress, whether a medical emergency or a victim of a crime, at least to notify rescue personnel or police, depending on the nature of the emergency, and, if possible, to aid the person oneself if that can be done without significant danger to the rescuer—specifically, Vermont, Rhode Island, Minnesota, and Wisconsin. Several other states have imposed limited duties to report crimes: Florida, with regard to reporting sexual batteries; Hawaii, applying

to all crimes in which the victim suffers "serious physical harm"; Massachusetts, requiring the reporting of aggravated rape, rape, murder, manslaughter, or armed robbery to the extent that one can do so without danger to oneself or others, and requiring the reporting of hazing; Ohio, requiring the reporting of a felony; and Washington, applying to certain crimes against children and violent offenses.

[48] Kohelet Rabbah 7:19.

[49] B. Shabbat 67b, 129a, 140b; B. Bava Kamma 91b; B. Hullin 7b.

[50] M. Bava Batra 2:9; M.T. Hilkhot Shekheinim 11:4.

[51] For example, M. Bava Batra 2:3, 5, 8; B. Bava Batra 22b–23a.

[52] See, for example, Ellen Bernstein, ed., *Ecology and the Jewish Spirit: Where Nature and the Jewish Spirit Meet* (Woodstock, VT: Jewish Lights Publishing, 1998); Arthur Waskow, ed., *The Torah of the Earth: Exploring 4,000 Years of Ecology in Jewish Thought* (Woodstock, VT: Jewish Lights Publishing, 2000), 2 vols.; Jeremy Benstein, *The Way Into Judaism and the Environment* (Woodstock, VT: Jewish Lights Publishing, 2006).

[53] See, for example, Barry Freundel, "Judaism's Environmental Laws," in Bernstein, *Ecology and the Jewish Spirit*, pp. 214–225, and Norman Lamm, "Ecology in Jewish Law and Theology," in Waskow, *Torah of the Earth*, vol. 1, pp. 103–126.

[54] See my *To Do the Right and the Good*, chap. 6; and my *The Way Into Tikkun Olam*, chap. 5.

[55] Elliot N. Dorff, *Matters of Life and Death: A Jewish Approach to Modern Medical Ethics* (Philadelphia: Jewish Publication Society, 1998), chap. 12.

[56] *The Way Into Tikkun Olam*, chaps. 4–7. For an example of a book that neglects these topics under this title, see David Shatz, Chaim I. Waxman, and Nathan J. Diament, eds., *Tikkun Olam: Social Responsibility in Jewish Thought and Law* (Northvale, NJ: Jason Aronson Press [The Orthodox Forum Series of Rabbi Isaac Elchanan Theological Seminary of Yeshiva University], 1997).

[57] See my *Love Your Neighbor and Yourself*, chaps. 3–5, and my *The Way Into Tikkun Olam*, chaps. 8–10. These topics are also omitted in the volume on *tikkun olam* edited by Shatz, Waxman, and Diament referenced in the previous note.

[58] Pirkei Avot 1:2, in a remark attributed to Simeon the Just.

The Biblical Source for *Tikkun Olam*

Benjamin Blech

*"When I use a word," Humpty Dumpty said in rather a scornful
tone, "it means just what I choose it to mean—neither more nor less."
"The question is," said Alice, "whether you can make words mean
so many different things."
"The question is," said Humpty Dumpty, "which is to be master—
that's all."*

—Lewis Carroll

The problem with the contemporary usage of the phrase tikkun olam
is that it has come to mean so many different things that we can
hardly be sure it truly means anything at all.

In the past half-century the term has come to be identified
primarily with a call for social justice. It serves as the guiding slogan
for the many organizations catering to communal needs and defining
Judaism by the performance of good works for the larger world. Jill
Jacobs perceptively points out: "In its current incarnation, *tikkun olam*
can refer to anything from a direct service project such as working in
a soup kitchen or shelter, to political action, to philanthropy. While
once regarded as the property of the left, the term is now widely
used by mainstream groups such as synagogues, camps, schools, and
federations, as well as by more right-wing groups wishing to cast
their own political agendas within the framework of *tikkun olam*."[1]
She concludes by noting: "Some have suggested imposing a ban or
hiatus on the term *tikkun olam,* given the general confusion about the
meaning of this phrase."

Shortened to one word, simply *tikkun*, and chosen as the name for the left-leaning liberal publication founded in 1986 by Michael Lerner, it was meant to suggest the very essence of Judaism.

Going back to the Middle Ages, it was in the sixteenth-century mystical school of Lurianic Kabbalah that the word *tikkun* first came to be invested with deep spiritual meaning, but in a far different context.[2] For Isaac Luria (1534–1572), the foremost leader of the community of mystics in Safed in the Galilee and considered the father of contemporary Kabbalah, the idea of *tikkun olam* was based on the notion that the ten vessels that contained the perceptible world of divinity had shattered, bringing evil into the world. The broken vessels required repair, and this would become the greatest mission of humanity. The way to restore the divine light to its proper place was through prayer, study of Torah, and the performance of *mitzvot*. It seems clear that for Luria, tikkun was not seen as synonymous with a call for social justice; rather, it was a challenge to strive toward perfecting oneself. Human life on its own, without reference to any communal context, was perceived as having meaning, since every person's actions have the capacity to affect the cosmos—and, with daring audacity, even God's perceptible reality.

Whereas the modern understanding of *tikkun olam* has to do with the idea of changing the world at large, the earlier medieval mystics had understood it as charging humankind with the primary mission of spiritually changing itself. The difference of emphasis may well hinge on an ancient philosophic question that remains to be resolved: is our quest for universal improvement better served by concentrating on the individual, or on humanity as a whole?

Both the early and later understandings, however, share an acknowledgment of *tikkun olam* as a fundamental and all-important principle of our faith. But what is remarkable is that there seems to be very little source material to justify the kind of prominence that this concept has taken on in the Jewish tradition. It may come as a surprise to learn that the phrase *tikkun olam* is not found anywhere in the entire Torah; neither is it counted by any of the commentators as one of the 613 *mitzvot*. Indeed, in the whole of the Mishnah it appears as the rationale for rabbinic decrees in a mere ten instances—hardly indicative of a primary place in the pantheon of Jewish values.[3]

In this essay, I will argue that *tikkun olam* has a biblical source from a concept implicit in the word "Shaddai," which is one of the seven major names of God found in the Torah that are identified by Maimonides as so sacred that they may never be erased.[4] In so doing, I believe we will also gain a far better understanding of the authentic parameters that ought to define the meaning of the phrase *tikkun olam*.

The link between the name Shaddai and the ideal of *tikkun olam* has an early precedent. This conjoining is familiar to us from a phrase in the Aleinu prayer, with which we close every synagogue service and which is second only to the Kaddish (in all of its forms) as the most frequently recited prayer in current synagogue liturgy.[5] In its concluding paragraph, we express the hope that we may soon see the Almighty's mighty splendor, the removal of detestable idolatry from the earth, and be enabled *l'takkein olam b'malkhut Shaddai*—that is, "to perfect the world beneath the sovereignty of Shaddai."

The words of this prayer have an ancient source. Although there is a tradition that its authorship goes back to Joshua, the disciple of Moses,[6] almost all contemporary scholars find this improbable.[7] Yet another suggestion attributes the prayer to the Men of the Great Assembly during the period of the Second Temple.[8] What is indisputable, though, is that Aleinu was incorporated into the Musaf service on Rosh Hashanah as a prologue to the Malkhuyot portion of the Amidah[9] by the talmudic sage Rav, who lived in Babylonia in the third century.[10] At the very least, then, its text dates back to early talmudic times. And it is in this prayer that the concept of *tikkun olam* finds expression (in the verbal formulation *l'takkein olam*) as a key element of the ultimate vision of messianic fulfillment. Achieving *tikkun olam* is what will lead to the realization of the prophetic promise with which the Aleinu prayer closes: "The Eternal shall be sovereign over all the earth; in that day the Eternal will be one and His name will be one" (Zechariah 14:9).

To my mind, this makes the Aleinu prayer the most significant indicator of the importance that the talmudic sages attached to the concept of *tikkun olam*. Here, the idea has moved beyond its most frequent valence in the Talmud, as the rabbinic motive for curbing possible corruptions of the halakhic system,[11] and it has come to signify an all-embracing goal of Jewish life and law, one whose acceptance would make possible the fulfillment of prophetic visions of a glorious universal future.

From the perspective of the Aleinu, it is clear why the obligation "to perfect the world beneath the sovereignty of Shaddai" is not one of the 613 commandments: it cannot be *one* of them because it is the *summary of all of them*. This fact readily explains why *tikkun olam* is not found as a *mitzvah* in the Torah. Including it would have diminished its importance, because each individual *mitzvah* is part of a larger panoply of commandments, each with its own specific claim on our attention and performance. *Tikkun olam*, however, is not really a specific commandment; rather, it is an overarching category under which is subsumed all of divine law, by way of purpose and goal.

The task of humanity is clearly defined: to perfect the world. But what is most intriguing is the particular name of God that is used in conjunction with this mission. The expression of our duty is linked to the phrase "the sovereignty (*malkhut*) of Shaddai." The name of God that occurs most frequently in Scripture (6828 times) is, of course, the Tetragrammaton, the name liturgically pronounced as Adonai and more casually referenced simply as "*the* Name," *Ha-sheim*, which functions as the distinctive personal name of the God of Israel.[12] Yehudah Halevi[13] (along with Maimonides[14] and others) emphasizes that this name, *the* Name, is the only proper name of God; all other names are simply attributive descriptions. It is remarkable that the summary of human responsibility for *tikkun olam* is connected to a name of God that is descriptive rather than distinctive—one of the six names that reflects attributes of the Almighty but that is not the one that confirms God's primary essence.

I believe that it is precisely the unique significance of God's name as Shaddai that makes it possible for us to fulfill our historic mission of perfecting the world—for the very same reason that it was the name used by God when establishing the covenant of *b'rit milah* with Abraham, who was to become the spiritual founder of the Jewish people.

The Theological Problem of Circumcision

Rabbi Elijah ben Shelomo Zalman Kremer, commonly known as the Gaon of Vilna (1720–1797), often stressed the importance of examining the very first appearance of a word in the Torah in order to best understand its most correct and primary meaning.[15] With this in mind, it is crucial to recognize the context in which God initially self-identifies as Shaddai: "Abram was ninety-nine years old when the Eternal appeared to him and said, 'I am El-Shaddai; walk before Me and be perfect'" (Genesis 17:1).[16] This introductory statement serves as a preface both to the name change of Abram to Abraham, as well as to the commandment of circumcision to mark the covenant between God and the spiritual "father of a multitude of nations" (Genesis 17:5).

Circumcision was the sign of Abraham's selection. It was a *mitzvah* to be carried out by all future generations of his descendants as well: "This is My covenant, which you shall observe between Me and between you and between your seed after you, that every male among you be circumcised" (Genesis 17:10). Yet circumcision is an act that seems profoundly paradoxical to the idea of a divine Creator. Rabbi Moses Alshikh (1508–1600), called the Maharam, states the problem clearly in his classic commentary to the Torah:

Before we discuss those verses, we will address questions raised about *b'rit milah*, namely: how is it possible that the Creator of everything, the One whose deeds have no faults— but rather, who only does works that shall be praised, as it is stated in Midrash Rabbah: "Look and see how good is the work of the Eternal"—how it could be possible that the supreme sovereign of sovereigns…created man with a fault so grievous that he is forced to remove part of the flesh with which God created him?[17]

In somewhat different form, an ancient rabbinic midrash had already posed the same question, from the mouth of an unidentified "philosopher":

A philosopher asked Rabbi Hoshaya: "If circumcision is so precious, why was it not given to Adam?"

"If [that is a valid question]," he replied, "[let me ask you] why you shave the corners of your head and leave your beard?"

He answered, "Because it grew with me in folly [in childhood and youth, before I reached the use of discretion; hence it is of lesser value and I cut it]."

"If so, you should blind your eye and cut off your hands [since you have these too from birth]."

"To such an argument have we come!" he [the philosopher] observed [i.e., your arguments are mere sophistries].

"I cannot send you away empty-handed," the rabbi responded. "[The real reason is this:] Whatever was created during the first six days requires further preparation. For example, mustard needs sweetening, vetches [any of a genus of herbaceous twining leguminous plants] need sweetening, wheat needs grinding, and man too needs to be completed [i.e., by circumcision]."[18]

Clearly the midrash intended this debate, between a devotee of Greek philosophy and a spokesman for Jewish belief, to leave us with appreciation for the rabbi's victorious response. Yet the reader is left unsatisfied. The final words of the story don't seem to fully address the philosopher's problem. We are informed that God's created works are incomplete, that they still require additional effort to bring them to their ultimate state of perfection. But that still does not offer any *reason* to explain this state of affairs. The midrash begs the question of why the Creator—who is obviously capable of producing masterpieces—permits the divine handiwork to be diminished by seeming flaws that bespeak imperfection and require further correction and improvement.

Perhaps the midrash expected us to intuit its meaning. Its point, though, becomes clear in light of yet another midrash on the same theme. This text describes a somewhat similar discussion between Rabbi Akiva and Turnusrufus:[19]

> The evil Turnusrufus asked Rabbi Akiva, "Which are better, things made by the Almighty or things made by flesh and blood?"
>
> He [Akiva] replied, "Things made by flesh and blood are better!"
>
> Turnusrufus said to him, "But heaven and earth—can a human being make anything like these?"
>
> Rabbi Akiva said, "Don't talk to me about things that are above created beings, that can't be controlled; rather, talk to me about things that are to be found among humanity."
>
> He [Turnusrufus] said, "Why do you circumcise?"
>
> He [Akiva] replied, "I knew you would ask me about that, which is why I pre-empted and told you that things made by humans are better than things made by the Almighty."
>
> Rabbi Akiva brought him wheat and cakes and said to him, "These are made by the Almighty and these are made by humans. Aren't these [cakes] better than the wheat?"

Turnusrufus retorted, "If God wanted circumcision, then why doesn't the baby come out circumcised from his mother's womb?" Rabbi Akiva responded, "Because the Almighty didn't give *mitzvot* to Israel for any reason other than to refine humanity through them."[20]

This conversation reflects a deep theological chasm between Rabbi Akiva and the Roman leader. For the Roman, creation belongs exclusively to God. Rabbi Akiva, however, sees divine purpose in the world's incompleteness—a purpose that is central to the reason for the observance of all the commandments. God intentionally created humanity imperfect, in order to leave room for us to become God's partners in creation. Indeed, God placed us into an imperfect world and charged us with the responsibility of perfecting it. "Things made by humans are better than things made by the Almighty," insists Rabbi Akiva. God will not do it all; human dignity requires that we be left with a role to play as well. The pagan couldn't understand how Jews could take a gift of God, a newborn baby boy, and immediately alter a portion of his anatomy. Rabbi Akiva saw in this the very meaning of circumcision as *b'rit* (literally "covenant"), implying a partnership of mutual responsibility between God and humanity.

The commandments are meant to refine humanity. Just as metal needs to be purified, so too is the case with people: though we were created by an all-perfect God, we are in need of additional refinement. A child comes forth from the womb with an imperfection, and we are commanded to complete the task of creation.

The *Sefer Ha-ḥinnukh*, a classic work that systematically discusses the 613 commandments of the Torah,[21] explains the rationale for the *mitzvah* of circumcision by way of this concept:

God desired that the completion be through the hand of a human [partner], and so did not create the male complete from the womb [specifically] in order to hint that, just as the completion of the form of his body is to be by his [own] hand, so too is it in his hand to complete the formation of his soul by way of the improvements of his actions."[22]

This is what Rabbi Akiva says is the ultimate purpose of all *mitzvot*, when he observes that the commandments "were given for no other reason than to refine humanity through them."[23] As the Meiri[24] explains it, the commandments were given "to refine humankind through them—that is to say, to acquire for those who perform them the perfection that is required of them."[25]

The question posed by Turnusrufus has been asked in many other contexts, concerning the permissibility of change in humanity's relationship to the world. Do we have a right to interfere in a world created by God? Dare we heal the sick? May we feed the hungry? Is it allowed to clothe the naked? If God had wanted any of these things, shouldn't the religious response be that God would have done them personally? And doesn't the fact that God chose not to do so then imply that things are to remain exactly as they are?

If the world as it currently is expresses God's ideal, then all change would be impermissible. Progress would be a sin. Human intervention of any kind would be nothing less than tampering with the divine will. All human efforts to improve life would be a disrespectful affront to the Almighty.

But the fact that circumcision appears as the very first *mitzvah* given to Abraham is highly symbolic: it is meant to teach us the error of this approach. *A Jew dare not simply accept the world as it is, rationalizing its inadequacies as the will of God.* Humanity was given a mission to imitate God—to be, in the words of the Talmud, "partners with God in the act of creation."[26] That means that we too must share in the task of creating a better world. For that reason, God did not complete creation—for only an imperfect world affords humankind the opportunity to play a part in its ultimate perfection.

Rabbi Akiva's response to Turnusrufus with regard to circumcision has a fascinating sequel in the Babylonian Talmud. In another discussion between these two very same disputants, it becomes clear that the debate between them had far greater ramifications:

> It has been taught: Rabbi Meir used to say, "The critic [of Judaism] may bring the following argument: 'If your God loves the poor, why does God not support them?' If that happens, answer as follows: 'So that through them we may be saved from the punishment of Gehinnom.'" This question was actually put by Turnusrufus to Rabbi Akiva: "If your God loves the poor, why does God not support them?" He [Akiva] replied: "So that we may be saved through them from the punishment of Gehinnom."[27]

God did not eradicate poverty, so that those who support the poor may gain the great merit of charitable giving. In this way, the wealthy are granted the opportunity to share in the divine task of sustaining the needy.

The world is not perfect, so that we can work toward perfecting it.

The story of creation concludes with the words *asher bara Elohim la·asot* (Genesis 2:3). This is often awkwardly translated as "which God created in the making," or something along those lines. Literally, the text means "which God created to make," and so the real question is: what exactly does that mean? For example, to whom is the last word, la·asot (rendered into English as "to make"), addressed? Rabbi Ḥayim Paltiel (born c. 1240) suggests that this text teaches that at a certain point in creation, God transferred the responsibility for its completion to humankind—whose specific obligation it is to assist God in "making" the world. This is what the word *la·asot* suggests.[28]

This reading suggests that there is an early biblical hint about the concept of *tikkun olam*, which underlies the very first *mitzvah* that would later come to define the male Jew. Circumcision continues creation, by improving on what God had purposely left imperfect. It grants us not only permission but also the obligation to change the world for the better. And its focus is the male sexual organ, the very source of our ability to procreate—and hence become partners with God in the act of ongoing human creation.[29]

I heard from my revered teacher, Rabbi Joseph Soleveitchik (1903–1993), that this may well account for the fact that a *b'rit* is to be performed on the eighth day. Seven days represent the week of creation on the part of God; the eighth day begins the time when this task is transferred to us. We are thus meant to continue God's work, and through our own efforts help bring it to perfection.[30]

Shaddai

This helps us to understand why, in the passage discussing the mitzvah of circumcision, the Torah refers to God as "Shaddai."

What is the meaning of this name, which refers not to God's essence but rather to an attribute? Many suggestions have been offered by scholars, but the traditional rabbinic explanation offers us the greatest insight into the appropriateness of using the name "Shaddai" in the context of the mitzvah of *b'rit milah.* The Talmud preserves a midrash that explains the name Shaddai as a kind of contraction of two other words: *she-amar* ("who said") and *dai* ("enough").[31] The idea is that the name Shaddai is meant to evoke the image of God seeing creation unfolding and then saying "Enough!"—even before all was perfectly in order. And in that thought rests our conviction that we have the right, and perhaps even the obligation, to alter the world.

Had God simply declared that the work of creation was done, there would have then been no greater sacrilege than for us to suggest that the world would still benefit from any human improvements— which effort would then reasonably taken be taken as something akin to touching up Michelangelo's frescoes or Leonardo da Vinci's paintings, attempting to make them brighter or better. But instead, we are allowed to know that God—acting specifically in the divine guise of El-Shaddai—intentionally left room for us to contribute our own efforts to the work of creation. It is as if God has said, "Remove the defect of the foreskin that I left on your son, so that you do not fear to continue to do away with all the other imperfections you will find on earth—imperfections that are meant to allow you to join your creative labors with those of the divine Creator." The verse from Genesis may thus be understood: "I am El-Shaddai, [therefore] walk before Me"—and do not fear sharing the same path upon which I Myself walk—"and become perfect"—for I did not make you perfect, in the hope that you would come to achieve it on your own.

In the Torah, the divine name Shaddai is used in introducing the first *mitzvah* given to Abraham. In our prayers, the use of the name Shaddai reveals to us the theological justification for *tikkun olam*. The Aleinu prayer reminds us that our mission is *l'takkein olam b'malkhut Shaddai*—that is, literally, "to perfect the world beneath the sovereignty of Shaddai." If the world were already perfect, then *tikkun olam* would be a meaningless slogan: not only unnecessary, but also indefensible, as an effort to "fix" what God had already made, according to the divine will. But if the faults and the flaws of the world are divinely ordained by a God who chooses to give humankind the honor of rectifying them, then *tikkun olam* is nothing less than our reason for being, and it speaks to our opportunity to live up to God's aspirations for us.

What Does *Tikkun Olam* Demand?

To complete what God left unfinished. To become God's "partners in the work of creation." To use our God-given gifts to enhance the lives of others. To fight evil and injustice. To utilize our talents and abilities in the service of humanity. To employ our freedom responsibly. To be creators and not destroyers. To live meaningfully, so that we may make a difference in the grand story of history. To live in such a way that we reflect nobly upon our presence on earth, as those designated as having been created "in God's image." To ensure that the world is a little bit better when we leave it than it was when we first arrived.

That is why, as Jonathan Sacks put it so beautifully in his closing message to his United Kingdom community upon his retirement as chief Rabbi,

> Judaism was the world's first religion of protest. The exodus in the days of Moses was an unprecedented event: the supreme Power intervening to liberate the supremely powerless. Elsewhere, religion in ancient times was a conservative force. The gods were on the side of the established power. They legitimated hierarchy. They reconciled the masses to a life of ignorance and servitude. How could you challenge the status quo? It was the will of the gods, the structure of the cosmos, on earth as it was in heaven. That is what Karl Marx meant when he called religion the opium of the people.
>
> Judaism opposed this entire constellation of values. It laid the foundations for an egalitarian society based not on equality of wealth or power but on equal access to education, welfare, and human dignity. The prophets never argued that there is injustice, poverty, disease, and violence in the world because that is how God wants it to be. Judaism is God's call to human responsibility, to bring *the world that is closer to the world that ought to be.*
>
> That is why Jews are to be found disproportionately as doctors fighting disease, lawyers fighting injustice, educators fighting ignorance, economists fighting poverty, and scientists extending the frontiers of human knowledge. The Greeks believed in fate and gave the world masterpieces of tragedy. Jews believed there is no fate that cannot be averted

by penitence, prayer, and charity. Judaism is the principled rejection of tragedy in the name of hope.[32]

The concept of *tikkun olam* is revolutionary in the history of religion. It defines faith in dual terms: just as people are to have faith in God, God has faith in people. We are to offer God devotion; God in turn provides us with dignity. Progress is the purpose of the covenant between the Creator and those entrusted with the task of emulating the Divine. History is the story of humanity's struggle to fulfill the obligations imposed upon us, as part of the divine partnership.

Tikkun olam demands that we not accept the world as it is, but rather that we view it as it might become. That remains still an unfinished task. Yet our glory is the extent to which we help to narrow the gap between the world as it is, in its actuality, and the world as it might become, its potential.

NOTES

[1] Jill Jacobs, "The History of Tikkun Olam," in *Zeek: A Jewish Journal of Thought and Culture* (June 2007), at www.zeek.net/706tohu.

[2] Gershom Scholem, *Major Trends in Jewish Mysticism* (1941; rpt. London: Thames & Hudson, 1955), pp. 244–286.

[3] See for example M. Gittin 4:2, regarding divorce law, or M. Gittin 4:3, about the collection of the *k'tubbah* money for a widow, and cf. also the laws regarding the limit on payments to redeem captives (M. Gittin 4:6), the purchase of religious articles from non-Jews (M. Gittin 4:6), the way in which previously spoken vows might undermine the legitimacy of a divorce (M. Gittin 4:7), and the question regarding the status of first fruits grown on land purchased from non-Jews (M. Gittin 4:9). Several additional uses of the phrase are found in M. Gittin 5:3. During the talmudic period, the principle of *mi-p'nei tikkun ha-olam* is applied to a very limited number of additional cases; see, for example, B. Pesaḥim 88b. Many of these passages are discussed at length in other essays in this volume.

[4] Maimonides, M.T. Hilkhot Yesodei Hatorah 6:2. The names are: the Tetragrammaton (i.e., *yod-hei-vav-hei*), Adonai, El, Elo·ah, Elohim, Shaddai, and Tz'va·ot. Some editions of Maimonides' code include the name Ehyeh, found in Scripture at Exodus 3:14. Cf. also B. Shevuot 35a.

[5] Barry Freundel, *Why We Pray What We Pray: The Remarkable History of Jewish Prayer* (New York: Urim, 2010), p. 204; Macy Nulman, *The Encyclopedia of Jewish Prayer* (Lanham, MD: Rowman and Littlefield, 1993), p. 24.

[6] Nulman, *Encyclopedia*, p. 24; Freundel, *Why We Pray*, pp. 205–206. Among the authorities who support the attribution to Joshua are Rav Hai Gaon (d. 1038), Eleazar of Worms (d. 1230), Rabbi Natan ben Rabbi Judah (13th century), and the *Kol Bo*, a sixteenth-century halakhic compendium of uncertain authorship.

[7] There is much evidence that Aleinu could not have been composed by Joshua. For one thing, the prayer cites verses from the prophet Isaiah, who lived centuries later. Additionally, the term "blessed Holy One" (*ha-kadosh barukh hu*) appears in Aleinu, but this was not used as an appellation for God in biblical times. Finally, the Hebrew word *olam* had a temporal sense only in biblical times; it took on a spatial sense ("world") only in the post-biblical period (see, e.g., the *Daat Mikra* commentary to Psalms by Amos Hakham [Jerusalem: Mosad Harav Kook, 1983] to Psalm 89:3, p. 138, nn. 4 and 5). Moreover, terms found in Aleinu are characteristic of the so-called *heikhalot* literature that came into being in the rabbinic period, at least a millennium after Joshua's day. (See in this regard Elliot R. Wolfson's essay, "Hai Gaon's Letter and Commentary on Aleynu: Further Evidence of Moses De León's Pseudepigraphic Activity," in *Jewish Quarterly Review* 81:3–4 (1991), pp. 365–410, particularly pp. 379–380.

[8] Nulman, *Encyclopedia*, p. 24; Freundel, *Why We Pray*, p. 207. This attribution was also supported by the seventeenth-century Kabbalist Manasseh ben Israel.

[9] Malkhuyot, "kingship" or "sovereignty," is one of three special sections that

are added to the central portion of the Musaf Amidah on Rosh Hashanah; it focuses on the idea of God's rule over the whole world. The other two sections are Zikhronot, "remembrances," which focuses on those ideas and events that God has promised to recall forever; and Shofarot, which focuses on the ways in which the shofar plays a role in Jewish history.

[10] Bernhard Salomon Jacobson, *The Weekday Siddur: An Exposition and Analysis of Its Structure, Contents, Language and Ideas*, trans. Leonard Oschry (Tel Aviv: Sinai, 1973), p. 307; Nulman, *Encyclopedia*, p. 24.

[11] For examples of this usage, see the examples provided in note 3 above.

[12] In this volume, the Tetragrammaton is usually rendered in English as "the Eternal" or "the Eternal One."

[13] This is Halevi's argument in his most famous work, the *Kuzari* II 2, trans. Hartwig Hirschfeld (1905; rpt. New York: Schocken, 1964), p.83.

[14] M.T. Hilkhot Yesodei Hatorah 6:2.

[15] Cf. the comment of Rabbi Tzadok Hakohen of Lublin in his *Sefer P'ri Tzaddik* (Lublin: Shteinmesser and Hershenhorn, 1901), vol. 1, p. 38a; cf. idem, *Sefer Yisrael K'doshim* (1928; rpt. B'nei B'rak: Yahadut, 1973), pp. 33b–34a.

[16] The name El-Shaddai (literally, "God-Shaddai") appears six times in the Torah, five of them in Genesis and one in Exodus, and one sole time in the Bible elsewhere, at Ezekiel 10:5. Of special interest is Exodus 6:3, which specifically notes that El-Shaddai was the name by which the patriarchs (and presumably the matriarchs) of Israel knew God.

[17] *Sefer Torat Mosheh* (ed. Warsaw 1879), p. 45a. The midrash cited is found at Bereishit Rabbah 12:1.

[18] Bereishit Rabbah 11:6.

[19] In all probability, he was the governor of Judea in the first century C.E. Rufus was governor at the time of the outbreak of the Bar Kokhba war, and may well have had frequent interactions with Rabbi Akiva.

[20] *Midrash Tanhuma*, *Tazria* §5, ed. Solomon Buber (1885; rpt. New York: Hotzaat Sefer, 1946), p. 18a.

[21] The sixteenth-century author Gedaliah ibn Yahyah credited the *Sefer Ha-hinnukh* to Rabbi Aaron Halevi of Barcelona (1235–c. 1290) but others disagree, as the views of the book contradict opinions set forth by Halevi in other works. This has led to the conclusion that the true author of *Sefer Ha-hinnukh* was a different Aaron Halevi, this one a student of Rabbi Shelomo ben Aderet (called the Rashba 1235–1310). The work circulated anonymously in thirteenth-century Spain.

[22] *Sefer Ha-hinnukh*, *mitzvah* 2, ed. Hayyim David Chavel (Jerusalem: Mosad Harav Kook, 1960), p. 56.

[23] Rabbi Akiva's explanation for *mitzvot* has another source in Bereishit Rabbah 44:1: "What does it matter to God if an animal is slaughtered by cutting its neck through the spine or the throat? [The answer is:] The commandments were given only in order to refine humanity."

[24] Rabbi Menahem ben Shelomo Meiri (1249–1315), one of the leading

talmudists of the medieval period.

[25] *Beit Ha-b'hirah* to B. Berakhot 34b, ed. Shemuel Dickman (Jerusalem: Makhon Ha-talmud Ha-yisraeli Ha-shaleim, 1965), p. 120, s.v. *ha-mishnah ha-sh'lishit.*

[26] B. Shabbat 10a and 119b, and cf. B. Sanhedrin 38a.

[27] B. Bava Batra 10a. In rabbinic parlance, Gehinnom is roughly equivalent to the Western notion of Hell.

[28] Commentary of Rabbi Ḥayyim Paltiel to Genesis 3:2. Rabbi Isaac Samson Lange personally published the commentary, properly called *Sefer Peirushei Ha-torah L'rav Ḥayyim Paltiel*, in 1981; it has now been entered into the Bar Ilan Responsa Project.

[29] Cf. B. Kiddushin 30b: "There are three partners in the creation of a human being: the father, the mother, and the blessed Holy One."

[30] In this vein, I believe that the sign of the covenant was exclusively reserved for males and has no corresponding sign for women because the underlying concept—that all Jews are called to serve as God's partners in creation through the covenant—does not need to be "added" to women's bodies, because they are already God's partners in creation through their ability to conceive and give birth. For other interesting approaches to this question, see Shaye J. D. Cohen, *Why Aren't Jewish Women Circumcised: Gender and Covenant in Judaism* (Berkeley, CA: University of California Press, 2005).

[31] B. Ḥagigah 12a.

[32] Jonathan Sacks, "A Judaism Engaged with the World" (delivered on June 24, 2013, and available on-line at http://www.rabbisacks.org/a-judaism-engaged-with-the-world; the passage quoted here appears on p.16 of the pdf).

Mi-p'nei Tikkun Ha-olam in Tannaitic Literature:
The Challenges of Law, Justice, and the Social Welfare

Gail Labovitz

Introduction

Rabbinic, and more particularly tannaitic texts—that is, the Mishnah
and other roughly contemporaneous texts—are widely recognized as
the earliest sources to reference the concept of tikkun olam.[1] Many
other writers who have previously addressed this topic, however, have
already observed that the language and concept as found in these
sources is not identical to tikkun olam as we tend to understand and
use the phrase today. In fact, they note that the actual phrase *tikkun
olam* never appears as such in these earliest rabbinic documents;
rather, the phrasing is *tikkun ha-olam*, with the definite article (the
prefix *ha-* means "the"; this is, in fact, a more grammatically correct
wording). Yet despite using the term multiple times and in multiple
contexts, the texts are not especially forthcoming on its actual meaning
and import.[2] The verbal root *taf-kof-nun*, from which the noun form
tikkun is derived, has multiple valences, as the definitions provided by
Marcus Jastrow[3] demonstrate: "(1) to straighten, mend, repair, set in
order, prepare... (2) to establish, institute, introduce a legal measure,
ordain." The word *olam* means "the world" in its broadest sense, but
might in this phrase have the more limited meaning of "the world
of the rabbis"—i.e., something more like "the entire community," or
"the (rabbinic) system/way of life."

Moreover, tannaitic texts never mention only *tikkun ha-olam*, but rather always use the phrase *mi-p'nei tikkun ha-olam*, "because of *tikkun ha-olam*."[4] That is, *tikkun ha-olam* is not, apparently, a concept or goal in and of itself but is rather seen as grounds for explaining and/or justifying certain types of rabbinic legislative action. Many if not most of those who have written about the tannaitic (and related talmudic) examples of the phrase argue that the intent of the enactments described and justified by the phrase (as well as, for that matter, enactments merely included by implication in the category) has to do with corrective measures in the legal system, typically to respond to and ameliorate a problematic or even unjust situation that could arise from strict adherence to the letter of the law. A few examples of this type of analysis by contemporary writers will suffice to demonstrate the point:

> These rabbinic amendments modify existing laws because in particular circumstances the laws produce unjust or undesirable results.[5]

> In the Talmud, *tikkun ha-olam* is a response...to a perception of overarching injustice, a sense that existing law must be modified to create a more balanced society.[6]

> Within the Mishnah, this phrase is invoked in response to situations in which a particular legal detail threatens to cause the breakdown of an entire system...By invoking the concept of *tikkun ha-olam*, the Rabbis repair the flaw that endangers the stability of the system as a whole, and in doing so, they improve the system.[7]

Possible ways of translating *tikkun ha-olam* into English thus might be something like "for the sake of good order" or "the improvement of society."[8]

My aim here is not to dispute this sort of definition or description. What I will attempt to demonstrate, however, is that there are a number of difficulties revealed when we read the mishnaic sources more closely, and especially when we read them in conjunction with parallel materials elsewhere in the Mishnah and other tannaitic texts—difficulties that have not always been sufficiently acknowledged, and that complicate any understanding of how the concept of *tikkun ha-olam* functions in the tannaitic context. I hope that through my analyses here, a more complex and interesting picture will emerge about the challenges of making and interpreting law, advancing social welfare through law, and creating a system of justice and social benefit.

Mishnah Gittin, Chapters 4–5

Before turning to the substance of my analysis, I must begin by introducing the primary source for the concept of *tikkun ha-olam* in tannaitic literature. It is noteworthy that the bulk of the occurrences of the phrase "because of *tikkun ha-olam*" appear together in a single passage in the Mishnah, in tractate Gittin. On the surface, the Mishnah appears to be organized topically.[9] In practice, however, as any student of the text quickly becomes aware, there are a number of different organizational principles that may guide the flow of subject matter and information in the Mishnah. It is thus not uncommon to encounter sections of Mishnah that depart from the apparent topic at hand, to instead collect diverse rulings and statements linked by some other factor—such as the name of the sage making the ruling, linguistic similarity, or a common underlying conceptual theme. Chapters 4 and 5 of Mishnah Gittin—the tractate dedicated to the laws and procedures of divorce and the document by which it is effected—is an example of the latter instance: a collection of disparate materials connected by a common underlying conceptual theme, in this case *tikkun ha-olam*.

As is often the case, the collection begins with a ruling that is relevant to the topic of the tractate, and to the chapter of the tractate in which it is found. In order to understand the text, however, a few preliminary words about the rabbinic understanding of marriage and divorce are in order.[10] Marriage in rabbinic law is a unilateral process in which a man "sets aside" a woman as his wife, typically by giving her an item of value (in current practice a ring) and declaring "Behold, you are betrothed to me," with the result (among others, of course) that he has exclusive sexual access to her during the course of the marriage.[11] So too, then, divorce is a similar one-sided process in which the husband relinquishes his prior claim on the wife. This is done by the writing of a document (known as a get) in which the (about to be ex-) husband states, "Behold, you are permitted to any man." The document becomes effective at the moment it is delivered to the wife, or to her appointed representative.[12] Failure to execute any part of this process properly has potentially significant ramifications in Jewish law, both for the woman and her ability to remarry, and also for the legitimacy of her children from a new man—should she remarry, only to have the validity of her original divorce later thrown into question.[13]

The phrase mi-p'nei tikkun ha-olam is first introduced in the second mishnah of the fourth chapter of Gittin. The immediately preceding mishnah (4:1) explains that since a get is not valid until it has actually reached the wife, it is possible for the husband to change his mind and annul it while it is still in transit. He may do this by overtaking the messenger carrying the get (either himself or by sending a second messenger after the first) to cancel the delivery process, or by informing his wife (again, either in person or through another messenger), any time before the arrival of the get to her, that it is null. The next mishnah, 4:2, presents two cases relevant to divorce (the first of which follows directly from the rule of 4:1), and the phrase tikkun ha-olam is included in both cases:

(a) At first, he [i.e., the husband] would convene a court
    in another place and nullify it [i.e., the divorce document].
    Rabban Gamliel the Elder enacted that they should not
    do thus, because of *tikkun ha-olam*.
(b) At first, he [i.e., the husband] would use an alternate
    version[14] of his name and her name [in the text of the
    get] at will, or of the name of his city and the name of
    her city. Rabban Gamliel the Elder enacted that he
    should write "the man so-and-so and all names that he
    has," "the woman so-and-so and all names that she has,"
    because of *tikkun ha-olam*.[15]

What follows in the rest of this chapter of Mishnah and into the first
part of chapter 5 is a series of rulings on a variety of topics of all sorts,
including laws pertinent to personal relations and status, financial
transactions, land ownership, slavery, and communal obligations.
For example, we find statements that communities are forbidden to
pay excessive ransoms to redeem captives (4:6), that under certain
circumstances slaves may be freed, although required to repay their
value to their former owner (4:4, 5), and that someone returning a
lost object does not need to take an oath (5:3).[16] Some, but far from
all, cases in these *mishnayot* are formally justified "because of *tikkun
ha-olam*"; though the phrase appears thirteen times between 4:2 and
5:3, there are several *mishnayot* in which it does not appear at all, or in
which it is applied to one case but not another. The grouping of these
cases together suggests, to many scholars who have examined this
unit, that the principle has a broader application to the collection as
a whole, including to those cases in which it is not explicitly cited.[17]
It is also possible, however, that any given case that is included with
the rationale of *tikkun ha-olam* might also bring in its wake similar
or related cases, in a secondary chain of associative connections.
Below, I will offer a suggestion (which should be recognized as just
a suggestion at this stage of my research) as to why certain rulings
might not carry this justification of *tikkun ha-olam* with them.

Reading Mishnah Gittin 4–5 in Light of Tannaitic Parallels

When read on its own, M. Gittin 4:2 presents a pattern in its two cases. First, the original state of the law is described. Moreover, the *mishnah* implies that the original state of affairs has some significant potential negative consequence for one or more of the parties involved, although that consequence is not stated explicitly.[18] That is: in each example, an original practice or legal situation is described, but the reader is to recognize that each also has the capacity to create significant confusion as to the validity of a divorce and whether a woman has been released from the marriage or not. In the first case (labeled "a" above), a man has sent a divorce document with an emissary to be delivered to his wife. In this instance, unlike the case described in 4:1, the husband nullifies the document in such a way that neither the emissary nor the woman necessarily know that he has done so; the obvious risk is the wife's subsequent confusion as to whether she is in fact divorced or not. Moreover, it is an established principle that a divorce document must be written specifically for the divorcing couple. In the second case (labeled "b"), confusion of names could easily result in confusion as to whether the divorce document was in fact written by *this* husband, for *this* wife. At stake is her ability to document that she is in fact legally severed from her original husband, on which hinges the legitimacy of any subsequent relationship she might enter. Following the presentation of these problematic possible outcomes of the original law, then, is a statement describing subsequent rabbinic intervention. Rabban Gamliel the Elder, who lived in the mid-first century C.E., issues an enactment regarding each situation:[19] in one case forbidding the act in question, even though according to the rabbinic understanding of the law of the Torah it is technically legal and effective; in the other, putting additional safeguards into the written form of the divorce document, which resolves any possible problem. The stated motive in each case is "because of *tikkun ha-olam*."

This seems, then, an ideal source on which to base an argument that *tikkun ha-olam* represents the reason for and justification of rabbinic legal activism. Cases like these suggest that in order to create more just outcomes and to forestall serious societal problems, the rabbis of the tannaitic period felt empowered (or perhaps even obligated) to intervene in Jewish law, as they understood its demands, so as to alter its direction. Yet when we turn to the parallel toseftan passage to M. Gittin 4:2, we already see the first break into this narrative of intervention and repair.

We find this corresponding discussion in T. Gittin 3:3. It cites the case of the Mishnah, and then comments on it:

> "At first he would convene a court in another place and nullify it..."
> If he nullified it, it is nullified; [these are] the words of Rebbe [Rabbi Judah the Patriarch].
> Rabban Shimon ben Gamliel says: He cannot nullify it, nor add to its conditions.[20]

This rabbinic debate is predicated on Rabban Gamliel the Elder's enactment, as described in the *mishnah*.[21] Prior to the enactment, it was certainly the case that if a husband cancelled a get in this manner, it was legally cancelled. What Rebbe and Rabban Shimon ben Gamliel[22] are disputing, then, must be: what happens if a man tries to cancel a get in this manner after—*and in spite of*—Rabban Gamliel the Elder's ruling? As noted above, according the rabbinic understanding of the law of the Torah, it is always within the husband's discretion to nullify the get prior to the moment it reaches the wife and takes effect. The method by which he does so is less relevant than the fact that the choice to preserve or undo the marriage must be his. Rabban Gamliel the Elder has attempted to close off one possible means of cancelling a *get*, because of the confusion that is likely to result if it is cancelled in that manner. But what if a man ignores and violates Rabban Gamliel's ruling? Although Rabban Gamliel attempts to impose a solution on a genuine problem, the Tosefta introduces the possibility that the rabbinic intervention might not be observed. Moreover, it records that the later *tanna·im* were not unified in their response to this challenge.

As hinted at above, the following *mishnah* (M. Gittin 4:3) is the first indication that this chapter of the Mishnah (and the next) will deviate from a topical structure, into an associative pattern based on the phrase *mi-p'nei tikkun ha-olam*. It includes three cases, only one of which addresses divorce:

(a) A widow does not collect payment [of her marriage contract] from the property of the orphans, except through an oath. They refrained from imposing an oath on her. Rabban Gamliel the Elder enacted that she should vow[23] to the orphans whatever they desire, and collect her marriage contract.

(b) The witnesses sign on the divorce document because of *tikkun ha-olam*.

(c) Hillel enacted *prozbul*[24] because of *tikkun ha-olam*.

For my purposes here, I will concentrate on the first two cases of this *mishnah* (marked as "a" and "b"). The first (the widow attempting to collect her marriage settlement; case "a") has a nearly identical structure to the two cases of enactments by Rabban Gamliel the Elder in the previous *mishnah*: a legal situation that becomes problematic, and an enactment instituted by Rabban Gamliel the Elder that attempts to resolve the problem. Although the topic has shifted from divorce to a different area of marital law, both the name of the sage and his legal step of making an enactment link this case to the preceding *mishnah*, and likely explain the presence of this material here. Yet the rationale of *tikkun ha-olam* is not explicitly cited to justify this enactment.

Is it implied? Many scholars have in fact read this entire mishnaic passage as a coherent unit.[25] In considering a response to that question, it is intriguing to note that this case does not appear where it might seem most likely to have been included: in chapter 9 of Mishnah Ketubot (the tractate dedicated to, among other topics, financial arrangements between spouses, including the details of marriage contracts and their collection)—where a number of *mishnayot* discuss when a widow might be required or exempted from the obligation to take an oath to collect her marriage settlement. Its placement here instead, then, may be suggestive: one might argue that while Mishnah Ketubot describes the system as it ideally functions, when the system falters in some way and must be corrected (via *tikkun ha-olam*), then, since that given specific case would no longer "fit" there, it was therefore placed in the collection in Mishnah Gittin instead.

However, it should also be noted that there are also some significant questions to be raised about the problem itself, notably: who refrained from making widows take oaths, and why? As Aryeh Cohen has observed, "The Mishnah's declaration 'they refrained from imposing an oath on her'...can actually be interpreted in two ways. Either passively as 'they were restrained from administering...[by some unidentified outside force],' or actively as 'they stopped (or no longer) administered....'"[26] He further notes that "[a] reading of the Mishnah in the context of M. Gittin 4 might just as easily support the passive reading. The first *mishnahs* are all dealing with responses to 'historical' events in the form: (1) ruling; (2) occurrence which no longer allowed for ruling to occur; (3) *takanah*."[27] Understood either way, the source of the problem may be a significant factor distinguishing this case from those of the previous *mishnah*: here, it is not sticking to the letter of the law that triggers a potential problem and evokes Rabban Gamliel the Elder's enactment in response, but rather some outside circumstance that prevents the law from being properly observed. Were the law to function as originally intended, it would seem, there would be no need for intervention; widows would take the appropriate oath (thereby reassuring the orphans of the validity of their claims), and collect what had been duly promised to them as a marriage settlement. Moreover, if it was in fact the rabbis themselves (or the rabbinic courts) who had stopped administering oaths for some unstated reason, then the difference is especially acute. Read this way, the *mishnah* itself acknowledges that Rabban Gamliel the Elder must intervene—not to amend the law, but precisely because of a rabbinic failure (or unwillingness) to observe the letter of the law! Perhaps when a rabbi attempts to resolve a problem of outside origins, or even of (other) rabbis' own making, then *tikkun ha-olam* is not the most immediate rationale to be invoked.

In the second case of M. Gittin 4:3, we return to a ruling (case "b") that both addresses the topic of divorce documents and also that is said to be motivated by *tikkun ha-olam*: "The witnesses sign the divorce document because of *tikkun ha-olam*." As noted above, according to rabbinic law a divorce does not take place until the moment that the divorce document (*get*) reaches the wife's hands; strictly speaking, witnesses to the delivery would be sufficient to establish the validity of the divorce. Under this new enactment, witnesses signed on the document itself, once it was written, thereby attesting to the husband's intent and that they had seen proper procedures followed. Although there is no description of what might have been the problem arising from the prior practice that this ruling is meant to correct,[28] some possible advantages of having the witnesses' names written on the divorce document can be readily imagined. Doing so ensures, for example, that the woman does not need to produce actual witnesses (who might not be available)—either to the writing of the document or its delivery—in order to validate her status as divorced, should questions ever arise in that regard in the future; the signature of the witnesses on the document, together with the fact that the document is now in her possession, is sufficient to prove that she is indeed divorced.

Whereas the previous case (regarding widows' oaths) did not have parallels in its more "natural" location (in M. Ketubot), this ruling is in fact cited in several other tannaitic sources, including a parallel *mishnah* and toseftan *halakhah* elsewhere in tractate Gittin.[29] These two passages further complicate matters by questioning whether this ruling is in fact a requirement—or, put another way, whether the motive of *tikkun ha-olam* is sufficient to make this change mandatory. The mishnaic parallel, M. Gittin 9:4, reads:

> Three divorce documents are invalid, but if she [re]marries [on the strength of them] the offspring [from the second marriage] is valid: he wrote it in his handwriting but there are no witnesses on it; there are witnesses on it but no date; there is a date on it but there is only one witness on it—these three divorce documents are invalid, but if she [re]married the offspring is valid.
>
> Rabbi Eliezer says: Even if there are no witnesses on it, but rather he gave it to her in the presence of witnesses, it is valid...because the witnesses only sign on the divorce document because of *tikkun ha-olam*.

In this text, we observe that the move to require witnesses to sign a divorce document was in fact a contested matter among tannaitic authorities—or, at least, there was one prominent authority (Rabbi Eliezer) who dissented, and who deemed witnesses' names within the document itself altogether unnecessary, so long as there were witnesses to the delivery of the document (in keeping with the original law, as noted above). This may further mean (much as emerges when M. Gittin 4:2 is compared with T. Gittin 3:3) that the rabbinic enactment described in M. Gittin 4:3 requiring the signature of witnesses may not have been universally accepted, despite the seemingly categorical language of M. Gittin 4:3. It is true that in his statement Rabbi Eliezer does not entirely dismiss the new enactment, but he does reinterpret the rationale of *tikkun ha-olam* so that it becomes not a motive for requiring absolutely that witnesses sign on a divorce document, but at best a reason why doing so is good practice.

What is more, there may be significant ramifications to imposing a legal requirement that insists on having witnesses' signatures on a divorce document, as emerges from T. Gittin 6:9:

> A basic divorce document on which one witness is written [or] a folded divorce document[30] on which two witnesses are written [or][31] its witnesses are within it, she must leave [her subsequent marriage] and the "thirteen things" [are applied] to her; the words of Rabbi Meir (that he said in the name of Rabbi Akiva).[32]
>
> But the sages say: the witnesses only sign on the divorce document because of *tikkun ha-olam*.

Several things are noteworthy in this passage. First, if one insists on having witnesses sign a divorce document as a legal requirement, then it follows that failure to meet this requirement could call the validity of the divorce document into question, with considerable negative results. The "thirteen things" are a series of consequences suffered by a woman who remarries under a misapprehension either that her first husband was dead or that her divorce was valid; these include: she may not remain married to either man, her children by the latter husband are *mamzeirim*,[33] and she loses her entitlement to her marriage settlement or any other financial support from either man.[34] Rabbi Meir in fact holds that this is precisely how the law must be applied. In contradiction to the rule of M. Gittin 9:4, he rules that if only one witnesses signed on the document, not only the document but also the woman's subsequent remarriage is entirely invalid, and the woman (and her children from the latter marriage) may suffer these very legal repercussions. In other words, an enactment that was meant to effect some sort of needed repair and adjustment—that is, to effect *tikkun ha-olam*—might instead (or in addition) lead to other, equally problematic results.

The opinion attributed to an individual in M. Gittin 9:4 (Rabbi Eliezer), on the other hand, becomes here in the Tosefta the collective (and hence, in rabbinic thinking, more authoritative) view. *Tikkun ha-olam* does not mandate a new practice or irrevocably overturn the old, but rather simply recommends a certain procedure. By deeming the ruling that witnesses sign the document to be merely good advice, in this case the rabbis can effect a different "repair"—namely, protecting the remarried woman and the status of her children. By changing the meaning and valence of *mi-p'nei tikkun ha-olam*, it seems that another potential *tikkun ha-olam* has been effected. Understood yet another way, what these two sources also suggest is that there are circumstances in which the *tikkun ha-olam* of the legal change, if made into an absolute requirement, could become the opposite of *tikkun ha-olam*—and function quite to the detriment of the woman in divorce.

Finally, while the underlying issues are somewhat more complex than I want to discuss here in detail, I would like to conclude this section by making brief note of M. Gittin 5:6, particularly as analyzed by Jeffrey L. Rubenstein,[35] as another case that pulls together several of themes discussed here. The case is one that responds to conditions that come from outside of the rabbinic legal system—namely, land seizures by non-Jewish authorities as a result of the Jewish rebellion(s) against Roman rule. In short, the *mishnah* addresses questions arising when another Jew, other than the original owner, seeks to purchase confiscated land from the non-Jew now in possession of it: what are the rights, if any, of the original Jewish owner to first rights of purchase, or to reclaim the land or some part of its value from the latter Jewish purchaser? The rabbinic response passes through several stages, with the ultimate ruling that the purchaser does take title and owes only minimal recompense to the original owner. This conclusion is (therefore?) not explicitly justified as a measure "because of *tikkun ha-olam*," though Rubenstein suggests this motive may be implied. It may be notable that the toseftan parallel, T. Gittin 3:10 cites an alternate concern: "because of settlement of the country" (*mi-p'nei yishuv ha-m'dinah*)—that is, bringing real estate in the Land of Israel back into Jewish hands, rather than *tikkun ha-olam*. Moreover, as Rubenstein further observes (quite forcefully), the rabbinic ruling to address this situation does not result in a just solution as regards the original owner of land, who does not recover the property or even receive back its full value when it is repurchased by someone else from the person now occupying it: "Jewish law essentially recognizes Roman appropriation of the land and 'collaborates' in the injustice by legitimating the sale..."[36]

Conclusion

Law—making it, interpreting it, applying it—is a complex process. A legal system can be challenged at multiple points, and in multiple ways. The rabbinic legal enterprise entails not just rabbinic oversight and intervention but communal compliance as well—which may not be forthcoming. What is just, or even what will produce a just outcome, is not always (or often) clear. Rabbis themselves can create, and not just recognize, unjust or unworkable situations. Moreover, they can even create a new unjust situation in the very attempt to resolve a prior difficulty.

Modern analyses of the phrase *tikkun ha-olam* as it is used in early rabbinic sources, it seems to me, have often carried with them a subtle, even hidden, but nonetheless detectable subtext: not only an argument that the rabbis, during at least one time in Jewish history, felt empowered enough to make explicit emendations to the law when it led to unjust or damaging results, but also a further implication that perhaps rabbis and Jewish leaders of our own day should exercise similar courage in our approach to Jewish tradition and practice. Certainly, there is much to be said for encouraging this sort of proactive approach to Jewish law and practice at this time. My argument here, however, has been that the rabbinic texts themselves, from the very outset (that is, both from introduction of the concept in the earliest rabbinic texts, and in the first *mishnayot* of the series in Gittin chapter 4) carry their own subtle, and at times even hidden—but nonetheless detectable—subtext. This is a complicated subtext, one that challenges our reliance on law as a medium that should move inexorably in the direction of justice, or of repairing the community—and perhaps even the world. This reading I have offered here challenges us to think more deeply about what it is that we are doing—or could be doing—as we interpret and modify and apply the laws of our tradition, and particularly when we invoke that process as a pathway to a more just and equitable society. And may we do so *mi-p'nei tikkun ha-olam.*

NOTES

[1] The Mishnah is the first and foundational redacted work of rabbinic Judaism, produced in the land of Israel and dated to approximately the beginning of the third century C.E. It is divided into six "orders" (*s'darim*), each covering a broad area Jewish law and practices: Zera·im ("Seeds," dealing with agricultural laws); Mo·eid ("Appointed Times," dealing with holidays and calendrical laws); Nashim ("Women," dealing with marital law); Nezikin ("Damages," dealing with torts, as well criminal and civil judicial procedures); Kodashim ("Holy Things," dealing with sacrificial law and ritual slaughter); and Tohorot ("Purities," dealing with matters of ritual purity and impurity). Each *seder* is further subdivided into tractates (*massekhtot*) whose titles, on the whole, indicate the specific topics that they cover; for example, Nashim includes tractates such as Ketubot (marriage contracts), Kiddushin (betrothals), and Gittin (divorce documents). Tractates are divided into chapters, and chapters into individual units, each of which is also referred to as a *mishnah* (using the lower case, to distinguish from the work as a whole, i.e., Mishnah, capitalized), or *mishnayot* in the plural. An individual *mishnah* typically covers one or two cases, including possible rabbinic disagreements on a ruling. The Tosefta roughly follows the format and structure of the Mishnah and typically parallels its content, often adding additional material (hence its name, which is derived from the Hebrew/Aramaic root meaning "to add or increase") that does not appear in the Mishnah or that elucidates mishnaic materials. Although likely redacted after the Mishnah, there is ongoing scholarly debate as to the provenance of the materials it contains, some of which may predate mishnaic materials. An individual unit in the Tosefta is refererd to as a *halakhah* (plural, *halakhot*). This essay will refer primarily to these two works, and indeed to comparisons and contrasts between them. There are also several exegetical (midrashic) collections attributed to rabbinic circles of this time period, but references to the subject at hand are very few in this corpus. Rabbis cited in these works are known as *tanna·im* (singular, *tanna*).

[2] David S. Widzer, for example, writes: "Nowhere in the Talmud is the phrase *mi-p'nei tikkun ha-olam* explicitly defined, nor is a set of parameters given to determine whether or not the concept applies in a given instance"; see his "The Use of Mi-p'nei Tikkun Ha-Olam in the Babylonian Talmud," in *CCAR Journal* 55:2 (2008), p. 35.

[3] Compiler of the most widely used English dictionary for rabbinic terminology; see Marcus Jastrow, *A Dictionary of the Targumim, the Talmud Babli and Yerushalmi, and the Midrashic Literature* (1886; rpt. New York: The Judaica Press, Inc., 1996), pp. 1691–1692.

[4] With one exception, in T. Ketubot 12:2—which is perhaps the exception that proves the rule: after a ruling is described and justified with the phrase *mi-p'nei tikkun ha-olam*, Rabbi Yose asks/challenges: "But what tikkun ha-olam is there in this [ruling]?" See Saul Lieberman, *Tosefta Ki-feshutah: Be'ur Arokh La-*

Tosefta, 2nd ed., vol. 3 (1962; rpt. New York: Jewish Theological Seminary of America, 1995), p. 370.

[5] Jeffrey L. Rubenstein, *Talmudic Stories: Narrative Art, Composition, and Culture* (Baltimore and London: The John Hopkins University Press, 1999), p. 160. To be fair, Rubenstein also notes that the example that is of most relevance to his topic (M. Gittin 5:6) itself may result in a different unjust outcome. I will return to this case below.

[6] Jane Kanarek, "What Does *Tikkun Olam* Actually Mean?" in *Righteous Indignation: A Jewish Call for Justice* (Woodstock, VT: Jewish Lights Publishing, 2009), p. 21.

[7] Jill Jacobs, *There Shall Be No Needy: Pursuing Social Justice Through Jewish Law & Tradition* (Woodstock, VT: Jewish Lights Publishing, 2009), p. 54.

[8] Rubenstein, Talmudic Stories, p. 160 and Gilbert S. Rosenthal, "Tikkun HaOlam: The Metamorphosis of a Concept," in The Journal of Religion 85:2 (2005), p. 219, respectively. Similarly, Kanarek offers "a recalibration of the world" (p. 19) and Jacobs suggests "for the sake of the preservation of the system as a whole" (p. 33). In this vein, see also Eugene J. Lipman, who lists several more ways the term has been rendered in English by scholars and translators in his "*Mipne Tikkun Ha'Olam* in the Talmud: A Preliminary Exploration," in *The Life of the Covenant: The Challenges of Contemporary Judaism*, ed. Joseph A. Edelheit (Chicago: Spertus College of Judaica Press, 1986), pp. 107–108.

[9] As suggested above in note 1.

[10] It may be noted that the following general principles continue to guide the practice and rituals of marriage and divorce in Jewish law to this day.

[11] See Gail Labovitz, "'The Language of the Bible and the Language of the Rabbis': A Linguistic Look at *Kiddushin*, Part 1," in *Conservative Judaism* 63:1 (2011), pp. 25–42, and idem, "'He Forbids Her to All': A Linguistic Look at Kiddushin, Part 2," in Conservative Judaism 63:2 (2011), pp. 27–48.

[12] Although there are grounds on which a woman may petition for a divorce and a rabbinic court may rule that a divorce is indeed in order, the power to grant the divorce remains with the husband.

[13] If she is not properly divorced from the prior husband, then the subsequent relationship is legally adulterous. Children born of an adulterous relationship are deemed *mamzeirim* in Jewish law, and are severely restricted in their ability to marry within the Jewish community: they may only marry others of their own status, and in any case they pass their status on to their descendants.

[14] Literally: "he would alter." Nearly all commentators understand that what is at issue here is a person (or place) known by more than one name—that, is, his/her name has been altered at some point. Think, for example, of someone who is known to some by an English name and to others by a Hebrew name, or who is known to some (but not all) by a nickname that is not immediately obvious as a diminutive of one's given name. See also the end of M. Gittin 8:5 and T. Gittin 6:5, which also address situations in which someone may be known by more than one name (and/or may be considered a resident of more than one

location), and the implications of these situations for the proper drafting of a divorce document.

[15] All translations of primary sources in this essay are my own.

[16] That is, an oath that the individual is returning in full the article that he or she found—as, for example, in a case where the finder found less than the entirety of the item(s) that was originally lost.

[17] See, for example, J. N. Epstein, *M'vo·ot L'sifrut Ha-tana·im: Mishnah, Tosefta, U-midr'shei-Halakhah* (Jerusalem: Magnes and Tel Aviv: D'vir, 1957), p. 995, Rubenstein, *Talmudic Stories*, p. 162, or Widzer, "The Use of *Mi-p'nei Tikkun Ha'Olam*," pp. 44–45, n. 27.

[18] This issue is thus a topic frequently addressed in the talmudic commentaries.

[19] An important question some scholars have explored is that of the relationship of measures adopted "because of *tikkun olam*" to the *takkanah*, a form of rabbinic ordinance or decree. After M. Gittin 4:3, the use of the verb *tav-kof-nun* to describe the process of instituting the change is absent from the rest of the mishnaic passage. Are these changes nonetheless to be understood as *takkanot*? Note, for example, that while the title of Lipman's article suggests that its topic is "*Mi-p'nei Tikkun Ha'Olam* in the Talmud," he dedicates several pages to cataloguing and discussing rabbinic uses of the verb *tav-kof-nun* in the sense of a legal enactment, before he turns to the phrase *mi-p'nei tikkun ha-olam* itself. Similarly Rosenthal, "*Tikkun HaOlam*: The Metamorphosis of a Concept," pp. 215–217.

[20] A get may be given with conditions included, so that the divorce is valid only if the conditions are met. An example of such a condition might be, "if you give me 200 *zuz*"—from the time that she gives the money, she is divorced, whereas of she does not give the money, she is not divorced.

[21] Indeed, this is the understanding of the Babylonian Talmud, which cites and discusses the implications of this tradition in B. Gittin 33a. See also Lieberman, *Tosefta Ki-feshutah* (*Nashim*), p. 829.

[22] Both are descendants of Rabban Gamliel the Elder, and son (Rebbe) and father (Rabban Shimon ben Gamliel) to each other, though I do not know exactly what to make of this fact.

[23] While both vows (*n'darim*) and oaths (*sh'vu·ot*) are binding and taken quite seriously in rabbinic law, a vow is of lesser severity than a court-imposed oath.

[24] The *prozbul* is a "rabbinic enactment allowing for loans to be collected after the Sabbatical Year...The Torah requires all loans to be cancelled at the end of the seventh year of the seven-year cycle (see Deuteronomy 15:1–11). If, however, the loan contract has been given to the court for collection, the loan is not cancelled...Hillel's innovation lay in making this arrangement...public by means of...a document formalizing the transfer of authority to the court." Quoted from Adin Steinsaltz, *The Talmud: A Reference Guide* (New York: Random House, 1989), p. 247.

[25] See, for example, those cited in note 17 above.

[26] Aryeh Cohen, *Rereading Talmud: Gender, Law and the Poetics of Sugyot*

(Atlanta, GA Scholars Press, 1998), p. 156; brackets in original.

[27] Ibid., n. 3.

[28] In a similar vein, the last of the three cases of the *mishnah* (case "c")—the *prozbul*—includes the language of "Hillel instituted" and the rationale of *mi-p'nei tikkun ha-olam*, but no explanation of the problematic situation that Hillel's enactment was meant to correct. This information appears in M. Sheviit 10:3, but without the rationale of mi-p'nei tikkun ha-olam. See also Sifrei Devarim §113 (ed. Finkelstein, 1940; rpt. New York: Jewish Theological Seminary, 5753 [1992–1993], pp. 173–174), which in some manuscripts includes a citation/conflation of these two *mishnayot*.

[29] And see also T. Gittin 7:13, which I will not discuss here.

[30] As explained by Steinsaltz, *Reference Guide*, p. 175: "In contrast to a regular document, a [folded document] was folded a number of times and sewn at the folds. At least three witnesses were required for such a [document] and one witness had to sign on the outer side of each fold. The original purpose of this elaborate procedure was to delay a hasty decision by a priest to divorce his wife..."

[31] See Lieberman, *Tosefta Ki-f'shutah* (*Nashim*), p. 899 regarding the proper reading here.

[32] But see Lieberman, ibid.

[33] For an explanation of this term, see note 13 above.

[34] See M. Yevamot 10:1 and M. Gittin 8:5 for a complete listing.

[35] See Rubenstein, *Talmudic Stories*, p. 162.

[36] Rubenstein, *Talmudic Stories*, pp. 160–163; citation from p. 162.

The "Stuttering" *Halakhot* and *Tikkun Olam*

Martin S. Cohen

Introduction

The notion that the path to knowing, worshiping, and serving God lies in strict observance of the laws of the Torah is one of the truly foundational ideas of rabbinic Judaism. Indeed, when Rabbi Oshaya famously imagined Creator God peering into an already-existent Torah while creating the world (somewhat in the manner of an builder consulting already drawn-up blueprints), he was merely suggesting that we human beings, the created, may see in the commandments of the Torah a path to follow back to our Creator...and thus to an ongoing sense of divine presence in our lives, in our communities, and in our personal ambits.[1] In the rabbis' conception, the Torah's narrative was a useful literary frame—for the deeds of Israel's ancestors were, they intuited, intended to serve as the basis for countless moral lessons for their descendants—but it was the laws of the Torah and all of their derivative details that were imagined as the paving stones that constitute the specific spiritual path forward toward God that an individual seeking "to seek God and thus truly to live" might follow.[2] Indeed, it was to make that specific point that Rabbi Akiva stressed that both the legal principles of the Torah and their endless applications—the *k'lalot* and the *p'ratot*, to use his own terms—were not only revealed to the Israelites at Sinai, but were repeated (presumably, all of them) first to Moses in the Tent of Meeting, and then again to all of Israel on the Plains of Moab.[3] By following the laws and remaining faithful not merely to the theoretical *concept* of a covenant that binds the nation and its God but actually to the minutiae of observance that characterize the behavior of the fully faithful member of the House of Israel, each individual Jewish soul becomes capable of living a life in and of God.[4]

In that God was taken as the ground of all morality, the question of whether any of God's laws could reasonably be considered by their nature "immoral" could not be asked by the ancient rabbis. And, indeed, the question of whether strict observance of the law could possibly lead an individual to behave unethically does not seem to have occurred to the ancients in anything like those terms.[5] Nevertheless, our ancient sources are filled with instances in which circumstance required that an adjustment—and often one wholly unwarranted by the original law as presented in Scripture—be made in the *halakhah*, lest the observance of some specific law lead not to a finer, better world of individuals more fully reminiscent of the Creator in whose image they were created, but instead to a world made both less just and less decent because the law was followed slavishly and counterproductively to an essentially negative outcome.

Adjustments to the Halakhah:
Mi-p'nei Tikkun Ha-olam, Mi-p'nei Darkhei Shalom, Mi-p'nei Eivah

A large number of these "adjustments" to what was then the existing *halakhah* are justified by noting that they were enacted *mi-p'nei tikkun ha-olam*, a phrase cited in many essays included in this volume and which, in its original rabbinic context, means something like "for the sake of the decent functioning of society." I would like to introduce some of those laws here, but also to note that there are also other groups of analogous adjustments to the law that were enacted for the specific sake of making the world more just, decent, fair, and equitable than would have been the case if the law had been observed in its original, unaltered form. And, indeed, in addition to the *mi-p'nei tikkun ha-olam* revisions of the law, also relatively well known are a second such group of laws, enacted "for the sake of the ways of peace [in the world]" (*mi-p'nei darkhei shalom*), and a third group, enacted "for the sake of [eliminating] animosity" (*mi-p'nei eivah*). But a fourth group of laws, labelled in the Yerushalmi[6] as "stuttering *halakhot*" (*halakhot shel im·um*), are relatively unknown even to halakhic cognoscenti. It is this group of laws that I would particularly like to present in this essay. Furthermore, I would like to suggest that the specific approach to "fixing" the law embodied by the "stuttering *halakhot*" could reasonably inspire the adoption of a larger, more general concept of "fixing" the law for the sake of bringing the Torah more into sync with the norms of behavior that a specific generation recognizes as inherently moral and ethically just—and that this should be the framework that we modern Jews bring to the concept of *tikkun olam* as part of our ongoing effort to perfect the world and, in so doing, to effect its ultimate redemption.

The formal *mi-p'nei tikkun ha-olam* passages are mostly straightforward. For example, the fourth chapter of tractate Gittin in the Mishnah, the oldest extant code of rabbinic law,[7] opens with a discussion of the possibility of a man annulling a bill of divorce that he has dispatched to his wife but that has not yet reached her hand. The basic law itself is clear: a man who sends off a bill of divorce to his wife by means of an agent retains the ability to void the document merely by telling as much to the agent either orally or in writing.[8] And he also retains the ability to cancel the divorce by telling the same thing to his wife, also either directly or in writing.[9] Nor is there any question about how the law works once the get (that is, the bill of divorce) has finally reached the wife's hand: *im mi-she-higia ha-get l'yadah shuv eino yakhol l'vatlo* ("once the *get* comes into her hands, he no longer has the right to void it"). And now we get to the point. Apparently, it was originally the case that a husband could void a get already dispatched to his wife merely by convening a *beit din* and voiding it in their presence even absent the knowledge of his wife—and it was that specific practice that the Mishnah sought to do away with. Thus Rabban Gamliel the Elder forbade the original practice *not* because he determined it to *actually* be illegal, but simply because the possible repercussions of allowing such a practice would have proven inimical to the smooth functioning of society. Specifically: absent the "adjustment" requiring that voiding of a get be communicated directly to the delivery agent or the woman herself, the original *halakhah* could have resulted in the creation of a class of women who thought themselves to be unmarried (because they had received a *get*), but who actually were still married (because their husbands, unbeknownst to them, had convened a court of three and voided the get without informing them either directly or indirectly).[10]

Similarly, the law theoretically permits a *get* to be written using whatever names are submitted to the scribe for a husband, a wife, and their place of residence. But in a world without birth certificates, passports, or other documents of the kind we moderns use legally to certify our names, this practice led to the problem of divorce documents being issued to people who only sometimes used the names that appeared in them. And so the same Rabban Gamliel the Elder decreed, *mi-p'nei tikkun ha-olam*, that henceforth bills of divorce should be issued in the husband's and wife's names (as provided in the original *halakhah*), but that those names appear in the get as "so-and-so, or by whatever names he [or she] may be otherwise known"—thereby clearing the way for the *get* to be deemed valid even if one of the parties to it is known in some other venue by a different name.[11]

Nor was it solely within the context of marriage and divorce law that such adjustments to the *halakhah* were applied. One must never redeem a captive for more than his or her fair market "price" *mi-p'nei tikkun ha-olam*—lest the community's generosity encourage further instances of kidnapping and hostage-taking.[12] A physician who errs in good faith and does harm rather than good is not to be prosecuted *mi-p'nei tikkun ha-olam*.[13] A priest serving in the Temple who inadvertently renders a sacrifice invalid by unintentionally resolving to consume some of the flesh of the animal, meat that will licitly come to him as a priestly emolument, past the scriptural deadline for such consumption, need not feel liable to make restitution to the sponsor of the sacrifice *mi-p'nei tikkun ha-olam*.[14] It is also worth noting that the concept of laws revised *mi-p'nei tikkun ha-olam* was specifically not restricted to situations of societal good unrelated to Torah law. Thus, the Mishnah also records that Hillel the Elder's innovation of the *prozbul*, a legally valid way to avoid the dissolution of debts that the Torah mandates in the Sabbatical year, was specifically motivated by the desire to act *mi-p'nei tikkun ha-olam*.[15] In all these examples, the phrase denotes the same basic principle: it is both licit and desirable to outlaw legal procedures that are formally permissible, let alone actually to close real loopholes in the law, when the alternative would be to tolerate a result that would impact upon society or its citizens negatively by creating situations characterized by injustice, mean-spiritedness, or cruelty. I could offer many other examples, but the ones mentioned above should give readers the general idea.[16]

The second set of laws I mentioned above are those enacted *mi-p'nei darkhei shalom*, "for the sake of the ways of peace." These appear through our ancient sources, but many of them are collected conveniently in the Mishnah in fifth chapter of tractate Gittin.[17] The administrators of Jewish charity funds may solicit funds from non-Jewish donors and distribute alms to the non-Jewish poor *mi-p'nei darkhei shalom*.[18] Similarly, Jews are to assist in burying the indigent non-Jewish dead and even in arranging that a proper eulogy be delivered over their biers, both *mi-p'nei darkhei shalom*.[19] If one notices among those gleaning in one's fields some "poor" whom one knows not truly to be in need, one can protest if one thinks one will get them to desist—or alternatively, if one judges that one will only stir up a huge brouhaha without accomplishing anything meaningful, one can let it go *mi-p'nei darkhei shalom*, and leave it at that.[20] Nor is one compelled to protest if non-Jewish indigents glean in one's field, or collect one's "forgotten sheaves," or come to take the produce in the corners of one's field that one has left for the poor: even though these gifts are specifically designated by Scripture for the Jewish poor, one may opt to say nothing when non-Jewish needy arrive to collect some of one's charity grain, again *mi-p'nei darkhei shalom*.[21] And even though ownership is understood by Jewish law to be a function of the will to possess, taking away a found object from a mentally challenged individual incapable of exerting that kind of formal will to own is considered theft, again *mi-p'nei darkhei shalom*.[22] There are many other examples I could offer, but all simmer down to the same thing: when observance of the law according to its strict letter may lead to strife, harshness, inner-societal contentiousness, or possibly even to violence, then we do not follow the law *sensu stricto*. Instead, we "fix" the law so that it leads not to strife at all but instead to feelings of peacefulness and harmony among all segments of society, including people outside the Jewish community.

The *mi-p'nei eivah* passages are yet another example of the rabbis' elastic approach to *halakhah* when the outcome struck them as potentially deleterious to the smooth functioning of society— particularly when it was feared that absent a "fixing" of the *halakhah*, feelings of ill will, and even animosity, would ensue. For example, the law is completely clear that among the activities forbidden on Yom Kippur is washing.[23] The same passage in the Mishnah that adumbrates the pleasures forbidden on the Day of Atonement, however, also notes *en passant* that both "kings and brides are permitted to wash their faces."[24] The Mishnah offers no explanation, but the Yerushalmi does: kings are permitted to wash their faces because a high standard of personal hygiene is part of the majestic bearing kings must bring to their office, and brides are permitted to wash their faces *mi-p'nei eivah*, i.e., lest they appear uncomely to their husbands and thus inadvertently trigger inner-marital strife.[25] In another interesting passage, Rabbi Yoḥanan suggests that the word of an unlettered peasant be accepted in the context of a wedding feast regarding whether food had been properly tithed even though such testimony would normally be considered suspect to the point of unacceptability, and that that should be our practice *mi-p'nei eivah*, lest the rejection of such testimony lead to inner-societal Jewish animosity.[26] Interestingly, a different rabbi says the same thing in an adjacent passage, but justifies his ruling as necessary *mi-shum darkhei shalom*.[27]

All of the above categories are relatively well known, but the same cannot be said of the *halakhot* of *im·um*, to which I would now like to turn my attention.

Halakhot of Im·um

What the word *im·um* itself means is a question in its own right. Marcus M. Jastrow, relating the term to words with similar roots denoting "dimness" or "obscurity," defines the verbal root of *im·um* as meaning "to disregard the law" or "to act irregularly in an emergency."[28] This was the opinion of earlier scholars as well, but others relate the word to the more familiar *gimgum*, meaning "stuttering" or, less clinically, "speaking indistinctly or unclearly."[29] In either event, the meaning of the phrase *halakhot shel im·um* becomes clear from the context and unmistakably denotes laws that the sages consciously chose to suppress under certain circumstances for the sake of making the world a more peaceful place. Given the rabbis' deep devotion to the law, their willingness to "stutter" in certain specific settings for the sake of making the world a better place is especially striking. After I explain some of these instances, I will set forth my reasons for considering this to be a potentially meaningful model for moderns seeking to embrace and deepen the concept of *tikkun olam*.

The concept of *halakhot shel im·um* comes to the fore in a passage that appears in full twice in the Yerushalmi: once in tractate Sheviit and once in Maaser Sheini. (Part of the passage also appear in tractates Shabbat and Avodah Zarah.) In each section of the passage, the underlying idea is that the duty of legal decisors is to guarantee that the observance of the law invariably leads to a finer world and never to the contrary…and not even when to do so requires a bit of self-induced stuttering.

The text in tractate Sheviit brings together several laws that all qualify as examples of halakhic *im·um*. The first involves a landowner saying to a worker during the Sabbatical year, "Here is an *issar* coin— go collect some greens for me." In such a case, none of the sanctity of the Sabbatical year inheres in the coin; because he received the money as wages for his labor rather than specifically to pay for the vegetables, the worker is free to use the money however he wishes. If, however, the landowner says, "Gather me up some greens for today against this *issar*," then the sanctity of the Sabbatical year does attach itself to the coin and the worker can only use it in the specific way that the law permits the use of "Sabbatical year funds."[30] That much is part of the Mishnah, but the Yerushalmi's discussion notes that the distinction between the two cases mentioned seems negligible, in that the same worker is doing the same thing for the same wage in both cases. Ah, Rabbi Avin (quoting Rabbi Yossi ben Ḥananiah) demurs, but this is one of the *halakhot shel im·um*, one of the places in which the sages consciously "stuttered," thus creating a straw distinction where none really exists. Doing so effectively benefits a poor laborer in need of funds to pay off a debt: by detecting enough of a difference between the two cases mentioned, the world becomes a better place…and that, apparently is a good enough reason to warrant enshrining an otherwise barely real distinction in law.[31]

The other examples are similar. There is a *mishnah* in tractate Maaser Sheini that likewise makes a distinction between two nearly identical situations. Second tithe produce must be taken to Jerusalem and consumed there. Interestingly, the Torah itself (at Deuteronomy 14:24–26) foresees the possibility of that being difficult to manage and specifically permits one to sell the produce at home and then bring the money to the Holy City in order to save the hassle of transporting what could for some be huge amounts of produce over long distances. The case discussed in the Mishnah, however, is a bit different and wonders about the case of a landowner who hires someone to bring his second-tithe produce to Jerusalem by saying, "Bring this produce to Jerusalem and we'll settle up there." In other words, the owner specifically stipulates that the worker's wages be paid out of the produce itself upon arrival, and that is forbidden! But if the owner were to say, "Bring the produce up there so that we can consume it together in Jerusalem," that would be licit—because the owner would in effect have invited the worker to eat there as his guest, and one has the right to do whatever one wants with one's produce as long as it is consumed in the Holy City. Again, the Yerushalmi notes that the two situations are almost identical: in both scenarios the same worker does the same thing for the same wage. And the answer is the same (albeit this time taught by Rabbi Zeira in the name of Rabbi Yonatan): this is one of the *halakhot* of *im·um* in which the sages consciously "stuttered" in pronouncing the law, so as to avoid creating a situation in which it would become difficult to find someone to hire to bring one's produce to Jerusalem.[32]

A third example has to do with the laws of Sabbath rest. There is a *mishnah* in the twenty-third chapter of tractate Shabbat that determines that one may borrow wine or oil from a neighbor on Shabbat, as long as one does not specifically ask using language that implies that the exact substance involved will be replaced but not specifically returned. In other words, when one borrows a cup of sugar from a neighbor and then returns the next day with a cup of sugar to that same neighbor's door, it is obviously not the same sugar in the cup as the day before! That, however, qualifies as a business transaction of the kind forbidden on Shabbat. However, borrowing from a neighbor is permitted if one merely asks to "borrow" some oil or wine, using vaguer language that does not suggest that something other than that which is taken will be returned. Taken seriously, that makes no sense: why in the world would someone borrow a cup of oil and then return the very same oil the next day? If one doesn't need to use the oil, then why is one "borrowing" it in the first place? And here too, Rabbi Zeira notes in the name of Rabbi Yonatan that we are dealing with a "stuttering" *halakhah*, one that the sages enacted by willing themselves to see a distinction where none really exists— in this case for the sake of helping out a householder who needs a neighbor's help dressing a salad for Shabbat lunch.[33]

Of more consequence is the final *halakhah* in the sequence. The passage begins with another statement of Rabbi Yonatan, this one transmitted by Rabbi Yaakov bar Aḥa, who notes that the law regarding bread baked by non-Jews is another of the "stuttering" laws. The Yerushalmi then goes on to note that when Rabbi Yaakov was asked to expatiate on Rabbi Yonatan's comment, he offered the following explanation: although it would make sense to forbid the bread of gentiles even in places where Jewish bread is not available, the *halakhah shel im·um* permits gentile bread in such a setting— so that nourishment may be provided for the hungry.[34] What is of particular interest is the comment of Rabbi Mana, made *en passant* in the part of the passage I glossed over, to the effect that these laws of *im·um* invariably permit that which might otherwise be forbidden, but never vice versa. In other words, the way to "adjust" the law in a halakhically permissible way, to ensure that society never suffers as a result of allegiance to Torah, is for the law to become more liberal, but never more severe or restrictive.

This, then, was the sages' concept of *tikkun olam* as I understand it: that ongoing fidelity to the law must always improve the world, and that it is vital to take whatever steps are necessary to prevent the opposite from taking place...even if the way to take those steps requires a bit of consciously undertaken "stuttering" about the specific legal detail under discussion. I have mentioned several categories of laws designed with this goal in mind, starting with those actually labeled by the sages as laws promulgated *mi-p'nei tikkun ha-olam* and moving on to other laws that under separate rubrics accomplish the same thing. My proposal is that we understand them all as variations on the same theme and, taking our sages intellectual and spiritual flexibility to heart, that we work to guarantee that faithfulness to the commandments only ever leads to a more just, more kind, and more peaceful world.[35]

Conclusion: Implications for Understanding *Tikkun Olam* in Modern Parlance

If one were merely to read modern books about Judaism that mention *tikkun ha-olam* (usually rephrased in English contexts somewhat ungrammatically as *tikkun olam*), one would gain a very different impression. The term is widely used, even in English-language book titles intended for readers who presumably do not speak Hebrew,[36] but it is no longer used simply to denote innovations in the law intended to make society function more smoothly or more justly. Instead, it most often seems to reference a concept left unnamed in earlier books about Jewish life: the obligation to struggle for the betterment of the world "out there" without reference to the *halakhah* at all. Take, for example, this passage from Brenda Shoshanna's 2008 book, *Jewish Dharma*: "[*Tikkun olam*] means to heal, balance, and correct the world...The Torah teaches that not only do we have to fix...ourselves, but ultimately it is our responsibility to fix and heal the entire world."[37] Or this glossary entry from a widely-read introduction to Judaism, Ted Falcon and David Blatner's *Judaism for Dummies*: "*Tikkun* literally means improvement, repair, or correction. However, the term is at the core of an important Jewish teaching: that the greater purpose of Jewish identity and observance has to do with the healing of both our planet and ourselves. The phrase *tikkun olam* is sometimes translated as the 'healing of the world,' and refers to world peace, global security, social justice, or—in the more mystical tradition—the completion of all of God's creation."[38] Or this quote from Richard G. Hirsch's 2000 book, *From the Hill to the Mount*: "*Tikkun olam* is a corporate enterprise, to be achieved through the striving of the entire Jewish people here and now, to shape the future of the world and to establish peace and brotherhood among all the families of humankind."[39] Clearly, the term is being used in these works to denote something at a considerable remove from the definition I am proposing in this essay. My suggestion is that instead of this wan use of the term to denote any kind of effort at all that has at its heart the desire to improve the world, forward-thinking Jews should seek to anchor their efforts to bring about the redemption of the world—the ultimate *tikkun*—by working to improve the law that binds Israel to its God, by guaranteeing—to the best of their ability—that fidelity to the codicils of the covenant never lead to anything even tangentially immoral or ethically untoward.

In other words, if we are eager to repair the world and to work personally for its final redemption, we need to embrace wholehearted, unambiguous fidelity to the Torah and its laws—the *k'lalot* and the *p'ratot*, as mentioned on the first page of this essay—and then, in the context of that level of unremitting allegiance to the law, to work to fix not the world, but the laws of the Torah—which, as noted above, the *midrash* imagines God consulting while creating the world in the manner of a builder or a contractor reading pre-prepared blueprints. To tamper with divine law sounds as though it should be, at best, an iffy enterprise. Yet the Jewish people has long embraced this concept and determined that an obligation, not merely a right, exists continually to fix, adjust, and repair the law—*precisely* so that its observance will lead always and invariably to treating the oppressed justly, to generous caring for the needy, to the mending of the tears in the fabric of society, and ultimately to the redemption of the world—

may it come speedily and within our day—because those praying daily for that redemption will already have done their part on the ground to make the world worthy of, and ready for, salvation in God. And therein lies our right to consider ourselves the harbingers of the world's redemption through the medium of unremitting fidelity to the covenant that binds us to God. The pursuit of that goal of perfecting the law is what *tikkun olam* means to me. And it is also, I believe, what it can and should mean to Jewish people everywhere.

NOTES

[1] Bereishit Rabbah 1:1, ed. Theodor-Albeck (1903–1929; rpt. Jerusalem: Wahrman, 1967), p. 2.

[2] Regarding the supposition that the Torah's narrative frame is meant to present moral lessons to future generations, cf. Ramban's comment to Genesis 12:6, s.v. *va-ya·avor avram ba·aretz ad m'kom sh'khem.*

[3] B. Zevaḥim 115b (=B. Ḥagigah 6b and Sotah 37b). The reference to the Plains of Moab presumably means that Moses spoke aloud but apparently failed to record (or rather, to re-record) in Deuteronomy those of the Torah's laws that appear elsewhere in the Torah.

[4] Cf. the statement of Rabbi Ḥananiah ben Akashya, who said that God gave Israel the Torah and its commandments for the express purpose of making them worthy, i.e., worthy of being linked in covenant to the Almighty (M. Makkot 3:16, cf. *Avot D'rabbi Natan,* text A, ch. 41, ed. Schechter [1887; rpt. New York: Feldheim, 1967], p. 134).

[5] Cf. David Weiss Halivni's essay, "Can a Religious Law Be Immoral?," published in *Perspectives on Jews and Judaism: Essays in Honor of Wolfe Kelman,* ed. Arthur Chiel (New York: Rabbinical Assembly, 1978), pp. 165–170.

[6] The Yerushalmi is the Talmud of the Land of Israel, sometimes called the Palestinian Talmud or the Jerusalem Talmud, and was edited in the fourth century C.E.

[7] Compiled by Rabbi Judah the Patriarch in the land of Israel c. 200 C.E.

[8] M. Gittin 4:1.

[9] Ibid.

[10] M. Gittin 4:2. Rabban Gamliel, the grandson of Hillel the Elder, lived in the first century C.E. A *beit din* is a court, consisting minimally of three members, convened to adjudicate matters of *halakhah.*

[11] Ibid.

[12] M. Gittin 4:6.

[13] T. Gittin 3:8, ed. Lieberman (New York: Jewish Theological Seminary, 1973), vol. 2, p. 257. (The text goes on at 3:9 specifically to mention a physician performing an abortion authorized by the *beit din* who inadvertently harms the mother, and notes that he too is not to face charges *mi-p'nei tikkun ha-olam.*) The idea there too is clear: prosecuting physicians who err in good faith will discourage anyone from wishing to practice medicine, and the smooth functioning of the world requires that there be medical doctors in it. The Tosefta is an ancient collection of rabbinic dicta dating to the age of the Mishnah but that were not included in the Mishnah itself.

[14] Ibid. The idea here is that priests will decline to serve at the altar if they face financial liability for even a momentary lapse of concentration, and the better functioning of the world requires that this not be the case. The inverse is also true, however, and the Mishnah also notes that priests who intentionally commit this specific sacrilege *are* considered liable to make restitution—and this

law too was enacted *mi-p'nei tikkun ha-olam*, presumably so as not to discourage people from sponsoring sacrifices in the Temple by making it possible for a priest maliciously to invalidate a sacrifice merely by saying, even falsely (since none could offer proof to the contrary), that he consciously planned to consume the meat coming to him at some time past the legal limit.

[15] M. Gittin 4:3. The idea, as developed in more detail in the Gemara ad locum (at B. Gittin 36a), was that people with the potential to lend funds to the poor were declining to do so as the Sabbatical year approached and they were threatened with the dissolution of the debts owed them, just as the Torah itself forecast could possibly one day be the case at Deuteronomy 15:9. The *prozbul*, then, was intended to speak directly to that phenomenon once it became clear that a mere admonishment, even one with scriptural *bona fides*, was not going to be enough to get people to lend much-needed funds to the poor as the likelihood of being repaid diminished with the approach of the Sabbatical year. The word *prozbul* itself derives from the Greek, probably from an expression meaning "before the counselors' assembly" or something to that effect.

[16] A comprehensive list of instances in which the phrase *mi-p'nei tikkun ha-olam* appears in the Bavli and the Yerushalmi may be found in Gilbert Rosenthal's essay, "*Tikkun ha-Olam*: The Metamorphosis of a Concept," The Journal of Religion 85:2 (April 2005), p. 217, n. 10. To these may be added the following tannaitic sources: Mekhilta D'rabbi Yishmael, *Parashat Mishpatim, Massekheta D'kaspa, parashah* 20 (ed. H. S. Horovitz and I. A. Rabin, 2nd ed. [1931; rpt. Jerusalem: Wahrman, 1970], p. 330); M Gittin 4:2 (two instances), 4:3 (two instances), 4:4, 4:5, 4:6 (three instances), 4:7, 4:9, 5:3 (two instances), 9:4; M. Eiduyot 1:13; T. Terumot 1:14 (two instances), 1:15; T. Ketubbot 12:1; T. Gittin 3:8, 3:12, 3:13 (four instances), 6:10; and T. Bava Batra 6:6 (two instances).

[17] M. Gittin 5:8.

[18] T. Gittin 3:13, ed. Lieberman (New York: Jewish Theological Seminary, 1973), p. 259. The idea is clearly that the fund was specifically set up to assist the needy within the Jewish community, and its administrators must now decide whether to reach beyond its charter.

[19] Ibid. Here too the idea is clearly that a charity fund to assist the Jewish indigent was set up and its administrators must now decide whether to reach beyond the scope of their original charter.

[20] T. Pei·ah 3:1, ed. Lieberman (New York: Jewish Theological Seminary, 1956), p. 50. The Torah specifically ordains that dropped produce be left on the ground for the poor (Leviticus 19:9–10), but does not establish any specific criteria regarding how poor precisely the individual seeking to glean in another's field must be. Cf. Maimonides' comments regarding the right of an individual to self-define as poor, and thus qualify to receive the gifts for the poor that the Torah commands the prosperous to offer (at M.T. Hilkhot Matnot Aniyim 7:2, 5, and particularly 6, where one's obligations to a stranger who simply says that he is hungry are discussed; but cf. also 10:19, where the author solemnly imprecates the scoundrel who accepts gifts of charity that he does not really

need—thus implying that one may receive such gifts merely by self-defining as needy).

²¹ M. Gittin 5:8. Scripture notes (at Leviticus 19:10) that these gifts are *le-ani v'la-geir*, for the "poor and the sojourner," but the "sojourner" was taken by the rabbis to denote converts to Judaism, not non-Jews in general. Cf. Maimonides' comment at M.T. Hilkhot Matnot Aniyim 1:9, where he writes unambiguously that the Hebrew word *geir*, translated here as "sojourner," refers solely to the righteous proselyte (that is, the *geir tzedek*) in the context of these gifts that Scripture offers to the poor.

²² M. Gittin 5:8.

²³ M. Yoma 8:1.

²⁴ Ibid.

²⁵ Y. Yoma 8:1, 44d. That brides need to worry about their attractiveness in a way that grooms apparently do not is a function of the androcentricism that is basic to the larger worldview of the Yerushalmi and rabbinic works in general.

²⁶ Y. Demai 4:2, 24a.

²⁷ Ibid. The Hebrew *mi-shum* means the same thing as *mi-p'nei* in the other passages cited.

²⁸ Marcus M. Jastrow, *A Dictionary of the Targumim, the Talmud Babli, and Yerushalmi, and the Midrashic Literature* (New York : G.P. Putnam, 1903), p. 1089.

²⁹ Cf. the comment of Rabbi Shlomo Sirilio (d. c. 1558) to Y. Shevi·it 8:4, s.v. *mei-hilkhot shel im·um*, in which he offers both possibilities as reasonable. But cf. the commentary *ad locum* of Rabbi Elijah of Fulda (1650-c.1720), who clearly favors the latter explanation.

³⁰ M. Sheviit 8:4. Sabbatical year funds can be used to purchase food, but not to pay off debts; cf. the explanation of Leviticus 25:6 at B. Avodah Zarah 62a.

³¹ Y. Sheviit 8:4, 38a and Maaser Sheini 3:1, 54a.

³² Ibid.

³³ Ibid.

³⁴ Ibid. This passage also appears in Y. Shabbat 1:7, 3c and Y. Avodah Zarah 2:9, 41d.

³⁵ Related to the "stuttering" *halakhot* but not quite identical are the laws the Yerushalmi declares were enacted *al y'dei ilah* "for a [relatively] paltry reason," i.e. one that was clearly a pretext intended formally to justify a legal decision deemed societally desirable, for example the passage in Y. D'mai 4:1, 23d, where the testimony of a witness who would otherwise be considered untrustworthy is deemed acceptable for the sake of enhancing the Shabbat observance of someone who might go hungry if that person's testimony is not accepted at least temporarily. The term is used in the Bavli as well, e.g. at B. Nazir 65b (=B. K'tubbot 20b) where Resh Lakish is quoted as saying that the rabbis of old seized on any reason at all, even the least substantial one, to declare the Land of Israel to be in a state of a priori purity. There are other examples in both the Yerushalmi and the Bavli as well.

[36] Cf., e.g., Elliot Dorff, *The Way Into Tikkun Olam: Repairing the World* (Woodstock, VT: Jewish Lights Publishing, 2005) or David Shatz, Chaim I. Waxman, and Nathan J. Diament, eds., *Tikkun Olam: Social Responsibility in Jewish Thought and Law* (Northvale, NJ: Jason Aronson, 1997). For that matter, cf. also Vivian Newman's *Tikkun Olam Ted* (Minneapolis: Kar-Ben Publishing, 2013), a children's board book.

[37] Brenda Shoshanna, *Jewish Dharma: A Guide to the Practice of Judaism and Zen* (Cambridge, MA: Da Capo Press, 2008), pp. 249-250.

[38] Ted Falcon and David Blatner, *Judaism for Dummies* (2001; rpt. Hoboken: John Wiley and Sons, 2013), glossary.

[39] Richard G. Hirsch, *From the Hill to the Mount: A Reform Zionist Quest* (Jerusalem and New York: Gefen Publications, 2000), pp. 114–115.

Back to the Cave! Rabbi Shimon Bar Yoḥai's Dilemma: Torah or *Tikkun Olam*?

Noam Zion

Introduction: The Rabbinic Turn Toward Social Activism

Rabbi Jonathan Sacks tells a hasidic tale about rebuking an overzealous scholar, which echoes God's critique of the great scholar-cum-mystic Shimon bar Yoḥai. That rebuke led to the latter's spiritual transformation into an activist reformer. The tale is as follows:

[Rabbi Dov Ber of Mezritch][1] was once so intent on his studies that he failed to hear the cries of his baby son. His father[2] heard, and went down and took the baby in his arms until he went to sleep again. Then he went approached his son, still intent on his books, and said, "My son, I do not know what you are studying, but it is not the study of Torah if it makes you deaf to the cry of a child."

Jonathan Sacks sums up the message as follows: "To live the life of faith is to hear the cry of the afflicted, the lonely and marginal, the poor, the sick and disempowered, and to respond. For the world is not yet mended, there is work still to do, and God has empowered us to do it—with him, for him, and for his faith in us."[3]

Like this overly studious rabbi, Rabbi Shimon bar Yoḥai (also known as Rashbi) was so absorbed in his own learning that he could not hear the needs of others or appreciate those who were engaged in taking care of the material needs of people. He was drawn to the *vita contemplativa* at the expense of *tikkun olam*—that is, his intellectual life was so absorbing that he could not hear the pressing needs for repairing the world. He was committed uncompromisingly to an unworldly, even anti-worldly, Torah. Yet, as we shall see in the literary masterpiece to be analyzed in this essay, the rabbis re-imagined his career as transformed into a life of moderate *tikkun olam*. While this tale may have little to recommend it as a historical document, it has much to teach us of the ancient rabbis' rationale of world-affirming reform and of the attractions and excesses of world-destroying spiritual and political revolution.

Conceptually, this essay contributes to a nuanced view of the now popular term *tikkun olam*. That term, popular in American Jewish parlance, can refer to anything that purports to improve something in the world—whether a large-scale redistribution of wealth and power, a pursuit of social justice in a particular sector of society, or even the smallest act of human kindness, such as the grandfather comforting the crying baby, in the story brought by Sacks. In rabbinic law, the concept of *tikkun ha-olam*,[4] as well as the linguistically related concept of takkanot (legislation or amendments of the law), often apply to legal predicaments that may have potentially untoward results for the functioning of society. In that sense, the ideal of *tikkun* is not about revolutionizing a corrupt system but rather about making piecemeal improvements to an imperfect world. Mystical meanings of *tikkun* in the Zohar and in its Lurianic interpretation need not be considered here. But it is interesting to note that the putative author of the Zohar, the second-century sage Rashbi, is the hero of a tale that often uses the root of the word *tikkun* in a wholly non-mystical, mundane context. *Tikkun* refers in this narrative to Roman institution-building (bridges, markets, public baths)—which Rashbi initially condemns in revolutionary terms, along with all earthly pursuits of greater material amenities. At the beginning of the tale, Rashbi is politically and spiritually committed to an uncompromising rejection of mundane civilization, whether Roman or Jewish. He seeks a radical *tikkun ha-olam* (although he himself does not use that term), in the sense of wanting to destroy what is and to create instead an alternative world free of bodily dependence. Yet by the end of the narrative, it is Rashbi himself who has been fixed or repaired—and I use the term *tikkun* here metaphorically, to describe Rashbi's self-corrective process of repentance. He becomes a judicial authority and municipal activist who fixes up the markets and enjoys the baths. Within this tale there is implicitly (and sometimes explicitly) a debate between various understandings of what it means to "fix the world." By analyzing this fascinating narrative in depth, perhaps we can contribute to a more nuanced understanding of *tikkun olam*, which understands the danger of extremists, whose revolutionary or even antinomian efforts may lead to destruction, and seeks to temper radical approaches to *tikkun olam* with a more moderate approach, which sees law as a positive force that can effect piecemeal reform and improvement in the world.

Shimon Bar Yoḥai's Cave (B. Shabbat 33b–34a)[5]

Prologue

    Rabbi Judah and Rabbi Yose and Rabbi Shimon [bar Yoḥai] were sitting, and Judah ben Gerim [literally, "Judah son of converts"] was sitting beside them.

Act I: Crime and Punishment

Scene 1: The Debate

    Rabbi Judah opened and said, "How pleasant are the acts of this nation: they established (*tikknu*) markets; they established bathhouses; they established bridges!"

    Rabbi Yose was silent.

    Rashbi answered and said, "Everything they established, they established only for their own needs: They established markets—to place prostitutes there; bathhouses—to pamper themselves; bridges—to take tolls."

Judah ben Gerim went and retold their words, and it became known to the government.

Scene 2: The Verdict

They [i.e., the Roman government] said: "Judah who extolled—let him be extolled. Yose who was silent—let him be exiled to Sepphoris. Shimon who disparaged—let him be killed."

Act II: The Great Escape
Scene 1: Beit Ha-Midrash

He [Rashbi] went with his son and hid in the academy (*beit midrash*). Each day his wife brought them bread and a jug of water and they ate. When the decree became more severe, he said to his son, "Women's minds are easily changed. They may torture her (*m'tza·arah*) and she will reveal [us]."

Scene 2: The Cave

He went and together they hid in a cave. A miracle happened for them and a carob tree and a spring were created for them. By day they sat and studied, removing their clothes and sitting up to their necks in sand. When the time came to pray, they went out and dressed and covered themselves and went out and prayed. Then again they took off their clothes, in order that they should not wear out. They dwelled in a cave for twelve years.

Act III: The Reprieve, Its Revocation, and Rehabilitation
Scene 1: Elijah

Elijah came to the opening of the cave. He said, "Who will inform Bar Yoḥai that the emperor has died and the decree is annulled?"

They [i.e., Rashbi and his son] went out and they saw men plowing and sowing. They said, "They forsake eternal life (*ḥayyei olam*) and busy themselves with temporal life (*ḥayyei sha·ah*)?!" Everywhere they turned their eyes [in disapproval] was immediately burned. A heavenly voice went out and said to them, "Did you go out to destroy My world?! Return to your cave!"

Scene 2: The Heavenly Voice
They dwelled [in the cave] for [an additional] twelve months. They[6] said, "The sentence of the wicked in Hell[7] is twelve months." A heavenly voice went out [and said], "Go out from your cave." They went out. Wherever Rabbi Eleazar [Rashbi's son] smote, Rashbi healed.
He said, "My son, you and I are sufficient for the world."

Scene 3: Shabbat Spices
They saw a certain old man who was holding two branches of myrtle running at twilight.
They said to him, "Why do you need these?"
He said to them, "To honor the Sabbath."
[They said:] "Would not one suffice for you?"
He said, "One for [the command] *Remember* [*the Sabbath*, Exodus 20:8] and one for *Observe* [*the Sabbath*, Deuteronomy 5:12]."
He [Rashbi] said to him [his son:] "See how dear is a commandment (*mitzvah*) to Israel!"
[Their minds were set at ease.]

Scene 4: The Bathhouse
Rabbi Pinḥas ben Yair, [Rashbi's] father-in-law, heard and went out to greet him. He took him to the bathhouse. He [Pinḥas ben Yair] was massaging his [Rashbi's] flesh. He saw that there were clefts in his flesh. He was weeping and the tears were falling from his eyes and hurting (*m'tza·ari*) him [i.e., Rashbi].

He said to him, "Alas that I see you so!"
He replied, "Happy that you see me so. For if you did not see me so, you would not find me so [learned]." For originally when Rashbi raised an objection, Rabbi Pinḥas ben Yair solved it with twelve solutions. Subsequently [i.e., after studying in the cave for thirteen years] when Rabbi Pinḥas ben Yair objected, Rashbi solved it with twenty-four solutions.[8]

Act IV: Restitution and Tikkun

Scene 1: Jacob's Model

He [Rashbi] said, "Since a miracle occurred, I will go and fix (*atkin*) something, since it says, 'And Jacob came whole (*shaleim*)' (Genesis 33:18)."

Rav [who explicated that same verse] said, "Whole in his body, whole in his money, whole in his Torah, as the verse says: 'and he [Jacob] showed grace to (*va-yiḥan*; literally, "camped before") the city, and Jacob fixed (*va-yiken*; literally "purchased") a field...' (Genesis 33:18)."

Rav said, "He established (*tikkein*) coinage for them."[9]

Samuel said, "He established (*tikkein*) markets for them."

Rabbi Yoḥanan said, "He established (*tikkein*) bathhouses for them."

Scene 2: Urban Renewal and its Detractors

He [Rashbi] said, "Is there something to fix (*l'takkonei*)?"

They said to him, "There is a place of doubtful impurity and it bothers (*tza·ara*, literally "causes pain"), since the priests need to go around it [i.e., to avoid walking on an area suspected of impurity]."

He said, "Does anyone know if there was a presumption of purity here?"

A certain old man said, "Here and there [Yoḥanan] ben Zakkai cut down lupine beans for *t'rumah*."[10]   He [Rashbi] did the same [i.e., treating at least part of the ground as pure]. Wherever it [the ground] was hard packed, he [Rashbi] ruled it pure. Wherever it was loose [where a potential grave might have been dug], he marked it [as potentially impure, so the priests could simply avoid that spot without going around the whole field].

A certain old man said [derisively], "The son of Yoḥai made a cemetery pure."[11]

He [Rashbi] replied, "If you had not been with us, or even if you had been with us but had not voted with us, you would have spoken well. But now that you were with us and voted among us, should they say: '[Even] prostitutes daub make-up on one another [to make them look better]'? How much the more so [should] scholars [protect one another's public face from shame]!"[12]

He [Rashbi] cast his eyes at him and his soul departed.

Epilogue: Payback Time for an Informer

He [Rashbi] went out to the market. He saw Judah ben Gerim. [He said,] "Is this one still in the world?" He set his eyes upon him and made him a heap of bones.

The Dilemma: *Vita Contemplativa or Vita Activa?*

The rabbis debated: what is more important—*talmud* or *ma·aseh*, study or action? Rabbi Tarfon argued for action and Rabbi Akiva for study. The assembled scholars responded in a way that recognized the validity of each view and softened the opposition between the *vita contemplativa* and the *vita activa*, as the Romans called the alternatives in this perennial debate. They concluded: "Greater is *talmud torah*." But why? "Because study leads to action."[13] Most rabbis sought to maintain a balance between intellectual pursuit and worldly activity, Oral Torah and *derekh eretz*, to sustain human civilization.[14]

Yet a few rabbis did live only for the life of the mind, without any intention that their study should be for the purpose of preparing themselves to better the world. *Torah li-sh'mah*, study for its own sake as an end in itself, was their calling—and they condemned those who used study simply as an means to get ahead on the ladder of social prestige, disdaining those who engaged in worldly work. Rabbi Shimon bar Yoḥai was one such militant eccentric, who not only retreated from the world to an ivory tower but who in fact devalued the whole material world, together with all earthly creativity and productivity. Bar Yoḥai dismissed the value of simple farmers, as well as pretentious political leaders—whether Roman or Jewish—who devoted their lives to public service by improving the facilities of municipal life, thus improving the quality of everyday life. His conception of a life of Torah is not justified by the rationale that resolved the debate between his own teacher, Rabbi Akiva, and Rabbi Tarfon: "*Talmud* (study) is greater because it brings about *ma·aseh* (action)." Bar Yoḥai would accept no compromises—at least, not until the rabbis constructed a different ending to the story of his life as a revolutionary.

Bar Yoḥai's Single-Minded Commitment to *Torah Li-sh'mah*, Torah Study for Its Own Sake

By reading the tale of the cave against the backdrop of other rabbinic textual material about Rashbi, we can see how radically the rabbis reconstructed both his personality and his ideology, in their surprise ending. Bar Yoḥai's repentance is uncharacteristic for an individual so exceptionally arrogant about his own knowledge of Torah. He is reported to have said:

I [by my value] could exempt the whole world from
punishment, from the day I was born until now. And if
Eleazar my son were with me, [we could exempt it] from the
time that the world was created until now...
I have seen those destined to ascend [i.e., the spiritual elite
who will gain access to divine knowledge] and they are few.
If they are one thousand, I and my son are among them. If
one hundred, I and my son are among them. If two, I and
my son are they.[15]

Rabbi Shimon bar Yoḥai devalues anything but Torah, and anyone
but brilliant male Jews. When discussing the cause of a plague called
askara, Bar Yoḥai explains: "It is caused by the sin of neglect of
Torah,"[16] and he maintains that theory againt all statistical evidence
to the contrary:

They said to Rashbi: "[The case of] women disproves [your
scientific claim that *askara* is a disease caused exclusively
by neglect of Torah, for women are exempt from Torah
study, yet they too contract that disease]."
[But Rashbi could respond:] "They cause their husbands to
neglect Torah!"
[They countered:] "Gentiles disprove [your claim, for
gentiles are exempt from Torah study, yet they too contract
that disease]."
[He responded:] "But they cause Israel to neglect Torah!"
[They countered:] "Children disprove [your claim, for they
are minors exempt from Torah study, yet they too
contract that disease]."
[He responded:] "But they cause their fathers to neglect Torah!"[17]

Even though Bar Yoḥai's wife had been his mainstay while he was
hiding in the beit *midrash*, he nevertheless denigrated her character
and gave her no credit. Life is dependent, he argued, solely on Torah

study. Therefore Rashbi burned to death those farmers who devoted their time to agriculture, while God intervened to feed him and his son by creating a carob tree and revealing a spring in the cave, so that he did not need to concern himself about physical needs while studying Torah. The following text illustrates this point:

> Our rabbis taught: "You shall gather in your new grain"
> (Deuteronomy 11:14). What does this teach? [It sets a
> limit on the interpretation of another verse,] which says,
> "Let not this Torah cease from your lips [but recite it day
> and night]" (Joshua 1:8). Should this [second] verse be
> taken literally?
> No, for the first verse teaches, "You shall gather in your new
> grain"—that is, perform worldly occupations (*derekh
> eretz*) together with them (*talmud torah*)." These are the
> words of Rabbi Ishmael.
> However, Rashbi says: "Is it possible that a man should plow
> in plowing season, sow in sowing season, harvest in
> harvest season, thresh in threshing season, and winnow
> when the wind blows? What, then, would become of
> Torah?! Rather: When Israel fulfills the will of God,
> their work is done by others, as it is said: "Strangers
> shall stand and pasture your flocks; [aliens shall be your
> plowmen and vine-trimmers]" (Isaiah 61:5). When they
> do not fulfill the will of God, they themselves must do
> their own work, as it is said: "You shall gather in your
> new grain" (Deuteronomy 11:14). And even more so,
> they have to do the work of others, as it is written: "You
> shall serve your enemy" (Deuteronomy 28:48).
> Abaye said, "Many acted in accordance with Rabbi Ishmael
> and they prospered; those who acted in accordance with
> Rashbi did not prosper."
> Rava said to the sages: "I ask you not to appear before me [to
> study] in the month of Nisan and in the month of Tishrei

[i.e., during the spring planting and fall harvesting seasons], in order that you not be distracted by concern for your sustenance during the rest of the year."[18]

Abaye's critique of Bar Yoḥai is wryly pragmatic and self-serving, while Rava demonstrates a moral concern for the welfare of his community of non-scholars whose Torah study is to be integrated with maintaining their economic basis for survival without relying on miracles. Rashbi, in this view, cares neither for his own prosperity nor for that of the community.

The Historical Context:
Sedition against and Secession from Society

Bar Yoḥai's critique of material culture applies with special vehemence to the Roman political and economic imperialism that destroyed Torah study in Judea. The story of the cave is dramatically set some seventy years after the Romans had destroyed all of Jerusalem; it takes place in the immediate aftermath of the Bar Kokhba Revolt (132–135 C.E.), which totally depopulated Judea and left only a tiny remnant in the Galilee.

Rashbi's own teacher, Rabbi Akiva—who, as we saw above, preferred study to action—had taken a religious–political position in supporting the revolt against Rome, declaring Bar Koziba to be the Messiah and renaming him Bar Kokhba.[19] Akiva was later imprisoned and tortured by the Romans; he died as a martyr while reciting the Shema and affirming his belief in God, even as he was scourged with iron combs raking off his skin in the arena of Caesarea.[20] The crime for which Akiva was punished was his refusal to stop teaching Torah publicly after the failure of the Bar Kokhba Revolt. The tradition reports that he ordained five rabbis; after the collapse of the revolt in 135 C.E. and the depopulation of all the Jews of the Land of Israel (except for the northern Galilee area), these five rabbis were the only hope to keep alive the long oral tradition that had been brought to its peak by Rabbi Akiva, who would soon be captured and executed by the Romans. One of these five young rabbis was Shimon bar Yoḥai; another was Rabbi Judah son of Ilai (who was probably the debating partner called simply "Judah" in our story).

Rabbi Shimon Bar Yoḥai's vilification of Roman culture—or its "anti-culture," as he understands it—is more readily understood in light of this cycle of political, national, and biographical traditions. The three rabbis were discussing Roman civilization, and they were most likely doing so in Roman-occupied Galilee. After the destruction of the last war, they may have been contemplating the reconstruction or urban renewal brought by the Romans to the war-ravaged Land of Israel. When the Roman Empire (especially under Hadrian) built buildings, roads, aqueducts, and bridges, however, they left their cultural mark on their world-renowned engineering feats, which were named for and probably decorated with their pagan statues and the reliefs of deified emperors. The spread of Roman material civilization was thus a conscious ideology of emperors. The rabbis responded in different ways to the Empire's physical transformation of the face of the Land of Israel.

Rabbi Judah praised the Romans for *tikkun*: "for building markets, for building bridges, and building public baths." He related to the national enemy objectively and ignored the Roman Empire's status as a national or imperial military oppressor and as a society promoting religious paganism, even emperor worship. From a neutral, pragmatic perspective, he saw the massive building program as good government that benefits its citizens. Rome's historic function was not to create a new civilization, but rather to take the Hellenistic civilization that it had conquered and establish it firmly on the whole of the Mediterranean world.[21] Politically, the Roman achievement was to turn the whole world into a single country—uniting conquerors and conquered in one community.[22]

Why did Rabbi Judah feel it important to open this conversation with such praise? Was he baiting Rabbi Shimon bar Yoḥai "to get a rise out of him"? Was he trying to put a positive face on a process of incremental imperial conquest that could not be stopped? When we first hear Rabbi Judah begin to praise a nation for pleasant acts, we would probably expect the nation to be Israel and the acts to be *mitzvot*.[23] But the object of Rabbi Judah's praise was Rome—whose pursuit of conspicuous consumption and populist entertainment, often sadistic and murderous, angered Rabbi Shimon bar Yoḥai.

Actually, Israel is commanded to engage in such acts of *tikkun ha-olam*—meaning, literally: construction of the world for human habitation. According to Moshe Halbertal the earliest use of the term *tikkun ha-olam* in rabbinic sources appears in the Mishnah, where a legal reform (*tikkun*) is instituted to permit marriage and procreation.[24] Halbertal has suggested that the term originally refers to the **civilizational mission** to settle the world—embraced not only by Rome, but also by the rabbinic understanding of God's partnership with human beings. In this *mishnah*, the value of procreation is buttressed with a verse from Isaiah 45:18 that speaks of God's concern that human beings help settle the earth and not leave it as an uninhabited chaos (*tohu va-vohu*), as it was before God's creation.

In the discussion among the three rabbis, Rabbi Yose was silent. Why? Did he have no opinion about this hot political topic? The text says that he "kept silent" (*shatak*)—suggesting that he did have an objection of some sort, but he chose to suppress it. This may have been due to fear of Roman retaliation, or fear of challenging the firebrand Bar Yoḥai, or perhaps even prudence in the face of a bystander— Judah ben Gerim, who might have then relayed the conversation to his parents, who were of pagan origin.[25] (Note that Judah ben Gerim is not the same person as Rabbi Judah.) Our story appears in a larger talmudic context dealing with the dangers of gossip. It is possible that Judah ben Gerim was irresponsible in gossiping about Rashbi, and Rabbi Yose thus maintained his silence in order not to risk the dissemination of even more *lashon ha-ra* (gossip).[26]

Rabbi Shimon bar Yoḥai condemned all of the Roman accomplishments out of hand, and he reinterpreted the "generosity" of Roman government toward its Jewish citizens as a self-serving cult of the body and of material benefit—existing only to exact tolls, promote prostitution, and pamper the body. Had our text given Rabbi Judah a voice in responding to Bar Yoḥai, perhaps he would have replied along the following lines:

- True, the imperial government is not interested altruistically in the well-being of its residents and citizens; but there may still be some benefit to be reaped, even if it originates from a place of self-interest.
- Thanks to its extensive roadworks, Rome is helping the world to become more closely connected, enhancing trade and communication; pax romana unifies much of the civilized world.
- The baths, the epitome of Roman culture, cultivate not only physical pleasures but also promote good hygiene; they also provide a public culture where citizens meet to exchange views.

In the end, Judah ben Gerim relays the conversation to others, who perhaps inform on Bar Yoḥai or perhaps simply pass on the gossip. Not surprisingly, Roman intelligence-gathering is adequate to catch the heretical and seditious arguments by suspected rabbinic revolutionaries.

Father and Son Hiding Out: Spiritual Retreat to the *Beit Midrash* and to the Cave

Rabbi Shimon bar Yoḥai and his son escape, first to the *beit midrash* and then to a miracle cave. Both of these venues represent not only temporary hiding places, but in fact alternative, competing worlds to the world of Roman civilization. Let us examine how this is so.

1. The *beit midrash*, the study hall, represents the values of the Jews' **civilizational mission**. According to the rabbis, "a person who has no knowledge of Bible, Mishnah, or the ways of the world (*derekh eretz*) is not one of the *yishuv*"[27] (i.e., one who belongs to the settled world, such as a citizen of the *polis*). Such a person ought to withdraw to the desert and their testimony is not acceptable in court. To maintain his standing as a civilized person Bar Yoḥai must continue to study, so he must take his son with him as a *ḥevruta*, a study partner, in order to continue to pursue Torah's oral, dialogic culture.

2. The *beit midrash* is a **retreat from the world of Roman conquest to a world of intellect**, not concerned with the earthly task of civilization that belongs to the temporal and social world (*ḥayyei sha·ah*).

3. The cave is not a human institution but is rather a **return to a natural haven, a Garden of Eden** where primordial waters flow and miraculous trees nourish and sustain both knowledge and life. It is **a retreat from all human civilization**, not merely a political protest against the latest empire. Perhaps that is why Rabbi Shimon bar Yoḥai and his son remove all their clothes: they are nude, as were Adam and Eve in their state of innocent bliss in the Garden.

4. Bar Yoḥai's solitude is not only a political necessity; in fact, it is a spiritual choice. In ways it is reminiscent of fourth-century Christian monks (whose name derives from the Greek word *monos*, meaning "solitary"), who withdrew from society in order to live in absolute solitude. Originally monks lived alone in caves (not in groups in monasteries), and they were called "hermits." The turn to the desert is often called a "conversion," quite literally a "turning away" from society to the desert as the ideal **place of spirituality**.

5. The removal of clothing may represent **transcendence of the body**. Prayer seems to require a higher form of modesty or mental concentration than does studying. For prayer, one must wear clothes; and so, ostensibly to save them from wearing out,[28] Bar Yoḥai and his son remove their clothes while studying and cover themselves up to their necks in sand, as an alternative form of covering their bodies. The narrator paints a picture of two talking heads buried up to their necks in the cave, and yet studying incessantly. Here, then, is **a retreat from one's own body**, one's own physical embodiment at birth, and it hearkens to the pre-birth world as a place where the child learns Torah before entering this world.[29] Rashbi and his son have buried themselves, their bodies, as if dying in body but being spiritually reborn as mono-functioning intellects, disembodied minds. In fact, this line of interpretation would be even clearer if they had stopped praying—for Rashbi elsewhere remarks that he would have wished for two mouths: one to pray for temporal needs and one to study Torah.[30] If prayer is about requesting divine aid for worldly needs (and rabbinically, *t'fillah* refers only to the Amidah), then in the cave where all needs are taken care of miraculously there is no reason to pray.

6. The cave may also be **a foretaste of the rabbinic world to come, where one studies all day**.[31] The cave is at once a foretaste of the world to come as well as a throwback to both the Garden of Eden and to the womb. Yet while the images of the womb and the Garden of Eden include women (as mother and as lover), the cave is not only womanless (as is the rabbinic *beit midrash*), but is in fact suspicious of women. We may well ask: Why does Rashbi so distrust his wife and all women? Why doesn't he appreciate her help in keeping him alive with food and water while he and his son hide, fugitives from his own impulsive mouthing-off against the Romans?

7. Rabbinic society, like the Greek philosophical culture, has a misogynist theme related to the privileging of the intellect over the body—hence, of men over women. It is for this same reason that Bar Yoḥai will later dismiss (and even kill) the *am ha-aretz*, the culturally ignorant farmer—just as he cursed the Romans, who were engaged in material culture. All of these value priorities and oppositions are congruent: male/intellect (i.e., the world of Torah) versus female/*am ha-aretz*/non-Jews (i.e., the world of secular civilization).

8. If all civilization is suspect, as Rabbi Shimon bar Yoḥai's condemnation of Roman material civilization implies, then procreation is also superfluous—because therein lies the main value of women and the purpose of marriage. The ideal couple of the Garden—man and woman—has been displaced by the ideal rabbinic couple: father and son studying Torah.

9. Bar Yoḥai is suspicious of women (including his devoted, supportive wife), because they are considered weak-minded, weak in character, or easily influenced (*da·atan kalah*). While this characterization may sometimes refers to women's vulnerability to sexual seduction, here it refers to their lack of fortitude to resist interrogation when subjected to Roman torture.

Our analysis of this text suggests that we see here a **three-way cultural battle**. Initially there are three realms, with the beit *midrash* supported by the low technology of simple village life in the Land of Israel: farmers plow, and wives serve the scholars.[32] The *beit midrash* is allied with simple Jews who are supportive of the *beit midrash* and who resent high culture's introduction of taxation and prostitution and elite bathhouses (that resemble today's country clubs). The beit midrash keeps to basics so as not to be tempted by material luxuries and so as not to overburden the poor people who support them. It represents national solidarity marshaled against the foreign invader. The following chart makes clear these relationships:

Beit Midrash	Wife / Farmer	Romans
Torah culture	low culture (bread, jug)	high culture (markets, etc.)
Torah society	elementary society (marriage)	complex society
Torah knowledge	easily changed mind	secular knowledge (technology)

Rabbi Shimon bar Yoḥai undergoes a significant shift, from his initial alliance with the people against the Roman Empire, to his later condemnation of the simple Jewish farmers—as if they were as bad as the Roman bridge-builders. Both fall together, for him, under the pejorative rubric of *ḥayyei sha·ah*—that is, focused only on temporal life. Ultimately, this stance will alienate Bar Yoḥai from God-the-Creator, who appears to be at odds with the God-of-Torah in the cave. The move to the cave pits Rashbi against two alternative worlds: that of the Romans, as well as that of the simple Jew—and, thus, God's creation.[33] Rashbi is, then, not merely a political freedom fighter against colonialism, but he is in fact an ascetic nihilist.

Abraham Joshua Heschel, in his book *The Sabbath*, portrays Rabbi Shimon bar Yoḥai as a radical critic of Roman materialism, viewing their building projects not in terms of their products—civilization or *tikkun olam*—but only in terms of their motives and their implicit theology—self-idolization:

Rome was at the height of her glory...Signs of immense progress in administration, engineering, and the art of construction were widely visible....Rabbi Shimon fled from the world where eternity was the attribute of a city and went to the cave where he found a way to endow life with a quality of eternity![34]

It was not the force of despair that bred Rabbi Shimon's contempt for the affairs of this world. Behind his blunt repudiation of worldliness, we may discern a thirst for the treasures of eternity and a sense of horror at seeing how people were wasting their lives in the pursuit of temporary life, thus neglecting the pursuit of eternal life.

The First Reprieve and Its Revocation

In the talmudic tale, Elijah appears to announce the end of the Rabbi Shimon bar Yoḥai's persecution: "Elijah came to the opening of the cave. He said, 'Who will inform Bar Yoḥai that the emperor has died and the decree is annulled?'" Here, Elijah's task as an angel of God is to bring good tidings: the persecution is over. Rome itself has not fallen, but the cruel emperor who sought to suppress Judaism (most probably Hadrian) is no longer.[35]

As Bar Yoḥai returns, leaving his "temporary" political asylum furnished with only a bare minimum of necessities for life, he should be happy to re-enter the real world. Jews living in the Land of Israel no longer need to fear the suppression of Torah study; there is freedom of thought, without fear of uttering remarks that might be seen as seditious or traitorous. We might now expect Rashbi to become the new redeemer, similar to Moses. After all, Rashbi's life-story recalls that of Moses: he too rebelled against tyranny (Pharaoh) and then fled (to Midian), and was later recalled (to Egypt) by God's announcement that it was safe to return (Exodus 4:19). Upon his return from exile, Moses became the prophet of liberation from Pharaoh; so too, perhaps upon his return from hiding Rashbi will likewise seek to aid his oppressed Jewish compatriots.

However, Rabbi Shimon bar Yoḥai is the ever-uncompromising idealist, and he seeks to destroy God's world and his own people's lives and livelihood. He sees as corrupt not only the world of foreign domination by Rome, but also the unspiritual activity of ignorant

Jewish farmers—even if they are simply seeking to produce food in order to sustain human life. These farmers are working the land, and they are doing so for their own sake—not for the sake of a higher purpose. They are men trying to support their families, while Bar Yoḥai has turned his back on his own wife, who had tried to support him. The point of Rashbi's derision against Roman *tikkun olam* can no longer be understood merely as a nationalist and xenophobic response to a cruel empire; it must be seen also as a defense of a spiritualized understanding of Torah—that is, single-handed pursuit of eternal life, opposed absolutely to temporal life. It is no surprise that Rashbi is later identified as the author of the Zohar, for his mystical tendencies are already manifest in the talmudic tale. He sees the world ruled by Rome as evil—but it is not only imperial civilization that he destroys, but also simple farmers earning a living. The Torah that Rashbi studied could not have been merely the exoteric Torah filled with laws about life, about agriculture, about how to build houses and maintain roads so that the public is not harmed. Rashbi's Torah was not "study that brings one to action."

While Rabbi Shimon bar Yoḥai's active condemnation of the world of sowing and planting is extreme among the rabbis, his disdain for a life of economic activity—as opposed to one of study—was an attitude shared by many of the rabbis. Consider this prayer, intended to be recited upon leaving the *beit midrash*, which was composed in the generation after the Bar Kokhba revolt by Rabbi Neḥunyah ben Hakaneh:

> Rabbi Neḥunyah ben Hakaneh used to say a short prayer as he entered the *beit midrash* and as he left it....On his leaving, what did he say? "I give thanks to You, O Eternal my God, that You have set my portion with those who sit in the *beit midrash* and You have not set my portion with those who sit in [street] corners: for I rise early and they rise early, but I rise early for words of Torah and they rise early for temporal things; I labor and they labor, but I labor and receive a reward

and they labor and do not receive a reward; I run and they run, but I run to the life of the world to come and they run to the pit of destruction."[36]

The cave of Shimon bar Yoḥai must have been, for him, more than just a temporary political refuge. The cave has become a sort of Garden of Eden, by virtue of Bar Yoḥai's uniquely intense Torah study. The biblical associations of the Garden include the miraculous growth of a tree and the flowing of a spring, prepared by God for humans. Leaving the cave, which is reminiscent of the original divinely planted Garden, thus represents not liberation but rather loss of purity and perfection. It is to re-enter a mundane world of material needs and economic activity—the men sowing and plowing, which so upset Bar Yoḥai. The Garden of Eden as an image of primordial existence and future otherworldliness is preferable to any world— with or without Roman rule.

The cave represents not a world of plenty and comfort, but in fact an ascetic and spare retreat center for meditation, study, and prayer. Torah is learned here at a level never to be reached in a world of distractions, even if the beauty of the body is marred by the harsh conditions. This has become the whole world, the eternal world— and for Rabbi Shimon bar Yoḥai and his son, that is all that is needed. Caves are also places for burying the dead in the Land of Israel, and many rabbinic tales report meetings with dead ancestors or divine beings in caves. It is in this liminal existence between life and death, between temporary existence and angelic eternal existence, that Rabbi Shimon bar Yoḥai had spent all those years. Here, the transcendent Torah was accessible. Here, the world of natural and supernatural were interwined. Bar Yoḥai has returned to the womb— to be nurtured by God, and then reborn as a superhuman hero. His heroism is intellectual and his learning is nourished in a womblike space—reminiscent of the popular midrashic myth about the fetus who learns the whole Torah effortlessly while in the womb.[37] But emerging from the womb and from the cave is traumatic, just as one might be resurrected from a tomb.[38] In the midrash, the all-knowing fetus loses its Torah knowledge when expelled into the mundane world. And as we have seen, upon exiting the cave Bar Yoḥai becomes utterly destructive to the mundane world.[39]

Therefore God—the God of Creation, the God who is the greatest constructor of worlds, literally, engaged in *tikkun olam*—exiles Rabbi Shimon bar Yoḥai back into the cave. The cave is no longer a Garden of Eden for study, nor a political refuge from an unjust foreign ruler. It is now a penal cell. Return to the cave is a punishment reminiscent of Gehenna, where the righteous suffer in purgatory until purified after twelve months—which is the same period of time that comprises the divine sentencing for Rashbi, the hero-turned-criminal not only in the eyes of Rome, but now also in the eyes of the God whose Torah he has been studying. The God who protected and sustained Bar Yoḥai and his son miraculously in the cave with water and fruit now repudiates this radical revolutionary, who has become too radical and destructive. The voice[40] from heaven is shockingly allied with the Roman government in its concern to contain Bar Yoḥai's destructive influence on its civilizing project.

Back to the Cave: The Turning Point for God

The turning point of our narrative is found in God's voice:

> They [i.e., Rashbi and his son] went out and they saw men plowing and sowing. They said, "They forsake eternal life (*ḥayyei olam*) and busy themselves with temporal life (*ḥayyei sha·ah*)?!" Everywhere they turned their eyes [in disapproval] was immediately burned. A heavenly voice went out and said to them, "Did you go out to destroy My world?! Return to your cave!"[41]

And we must ask ourselves: What is God's point of view on Bar Yoḥai's revolutionary actions?

Until this point in the narrative, there had been every reason to assume God is on the same side as Rabbi Shimon bar Yoḥai:

- The Romans destroyed God's Temple, invaded God's land, massacred God's people, and forbade the teaching of God's Torah.
- Bar Yoḥai is a persecuted political and religious refugee whose freedom of expression was undermined by an informer (or, at least, by criminally negligent gossip).
- Bar Yoḥai is a man of the *beit midrash*, the last refuge of God in the world after the destruction of God's other house, the *beit mikdash*, the Temple—and this remaining house, the *beit midrash*, is now being assaulted by Hadrian's prohibition of teaching Torah.
- The creation of the spring and the carob tree in order to feed the refugees could only have been effectuated by God.
- God must have sent Elijah to announce to Bar Yoḥai the fall of his enemy, the Emperor.
- Bar Yoḥai's ability to kill with his eyes must derive from his Torah study (not some magical formula), and must therefore be considered a divine gift.

But at this point in the story, it seems that God switches sides. God laments the destruction to "**My** world"—claiming divine ownership for the world disparaged and destroyed by Bar Yoḥai. It is no longer the eternal world of Torah that is valued as *ḥayyei olam*; rather the world that is valued is now the world of the Creator. God is thus aligned with both the Romans and the Jewish farmers, against the destructive religious anarchy of Bar Yoḥai. While God might be expected to side against Rome in support of the political or religious plight of the people Israel, God refuses to side against the material world and humanity—and thus cannot side with the mystic/ philosophic/scholar Bar Yoḥai. God does not seek to kill Bar Yoḥai as traitor or revolutionary (as Hadrian did), but simply to reeducate the arrogant rabbi, who thought he was equal to the whole world and could bear the punishment of the whole world because he was so righteous. God therefore sentences him to a further stay in the cave, as a sort of corrective punishment. The cave is no longer Paradise, but Gehenna; it is a purgatory, but not a life sentence. Bar Yoḥai's sentence is to last for twelve months. But will God's "reeducation project" succeed?

The Second Reprieve and the Shabbat Spices

They dwelled [in the cave] for [an additiona] twelve months. They said, "The sentence of the wicked in Hell is twelve months." A heavenly voice went out [and said], "Go out from your cave." They went out. Wherever Rabbi Eleazar smote (*maḥei*), Rashbi healed (*masei*). He said, "My son, you and I are sufficient for the world."

The inseparable father and son, the dynamic study duo, now see their paths in the world diverge: Eleazar continues the path of his uncompromising father, while Rabbi Shimon mellows and does an about-face. He heals not only the places where he has himself caused damage, but he must also clean up after the son whom he has mis-educated.[42] The crucial question to ask, is: How does the father respond to his son, who continues to destroy the world that God-the-Creator has told them not to destroy?

First, Rabbi Shimon bar Yoḥai takes responsibility for his son's destruction by healing whatever damage the latter effects. Perhaps the father also means to demonstrate to his son the alternative path of creation and rebuilding that he has discovered. And Rashbi is also modeling a path of repentance and compensation, after having pursued a path of destructive judgment for many years.

Yet why does Bar Yoḥai say to this destructive son: "My son, you and I are sufficient for the world"? Doesn't this statement underscore his arrogance, as if they see themselves as two mythic titans fighting off the whole world? Maybe what Rashbi means is: we are not equal to the world in value, but we **are** sufficient in spiritual power to redeem the world—but only if we join together in healing, just as previously we joined together in learning. Bar Yoḥai thus suggests a renewed alliance between father and son: not to destroy the corrupt world, but to repair it.

The father seeks to win his son over by pointing to the spiritual beauty of simple people celebrating Shabbat. Shabbat is a taste of the world to come, a spiritual withdrawal from the mundane—just as their period of isolation in the cave had been.

> They saw a certain old man who was holding two branches of myrtle running at twilight. They said to him, "Why do you need these?" He said to them, "To honor the Sabbath." [They said:] "Would not one suffice for you?" He said, "One for [the command] *Remember* [the Sabbath, Exodus 20:8] and one for *Observe* [the Sabbath, Deuteronomy 5:12]." He [Rashbi] said to him [his son:] "See how dear is a commandment (*mitzvah*) to Israel!" [Their minds were set at ease.]

Melila Hellner-Eshed believes that Rabbi Shimon bar Yoḥai is truly transformed by the vision of the old man and the spices, though his much-scarred son remains destructive (both of himself and toward others).[43] The world of the cave contrasts markedly with the world of the old man, which so captivates Bar Yoḥai. The cave represents the intellect, while the old man worships God with a delicate and sensuous fragrance. The cave is for eternal truths enlightened in timeless environment where there is no change of day and night and no cycle of six days of work, while the old man runs so as not to miss a fleeting moment between dusk and sundown, to honor God on Shabbat. A whiff of Shabbat is a taste of the eternal embedded in the everyday. The cave represents Bar Yoḥai's egocentric, megalomaniacal claims that he and his son are equal in value to the whole world. Yet the old man's concern to perform a single *mitzvah*—and, in fact, the practice of bringing two myrtle branches with their fine scent to honor of Shabbat is technically only a custom and not a commandment—evokes Rashbi's exuberant praise of the simple people of Israel, for their love of *mitzvot*. Thus Rashbi is on his way to becoming a healer and a supporter of civilized life. He honors a man who honors Shabbat, which is the sacred day that honors God's creation.

But Eleazar, the son of Rabbi Shimon, is permanently damaged. In the cave he was his father's only companion; there, Bar Yoḥai had the singular opportunity to create in his own image, to prove that he and his son were worth the whole world that they had denounced and left behind. Denied maternal love and even his mother's nurturing meals, Eleazar lived a life on the run from the Romans, ascetically living out his father's way of life and suffering the consequences of his father's demanding idealistic vision. Here is, perhaps, a child of a great public figure who is scarred not by neglect, but rather by the too great demands of his imposing parent. Is Eleazar another version of Isaac, bound and sacrificed by his father Abraham on the altar of his father's own religious quest? In rabbinic lore,[44] Eleazar first becomes a policeman and a brilliant detective, punishing criminals, and then an informer who hands over tax-evading Jews to the Roman authorities for execution—the same Romans who had once persecuted and pursued him and his father! His body, which once subsisted on the Spartan fare of water and carobs, becomes distended into an obesity beyond belief, and that deformity is likely to make sexual intimacy and reproduction impossible.

The Hasidic Inspiration from Bar Yoḥai's Revelation

Rabbi Shimon bar Yoḥai is rebuked by God for his misguided religious worldview that denigrates and devalues the mundane activities of the farmers, but then he learns his lesson. The lesson is not simply about the need to be pragmatic in tending to the bodily needs before attending to the spiritual. Rather, it is about the importance of being engaged with the material world, as its own embodiment of spirituality. Rabbi Jacob Joseph Hakohen of Polonne (1710–1784) discovers in the tale of Bar Yoḥai's spiritual about-face a spiritual revolution congruent with the hasidic innovation of his teacher, the Baal Shem Tov. He explains:

> They [Bar Yoḥai and his son] were first of the opinion that worship of God consists solely in a person engaging in Torah [study], prayer, fasting, weeping etc. Therefore, when they saw people who were not engaged thus [i.e., the two farmers plowing their fields], they were incensed [and killed them].[45]

But God displays divine wrath, rejecting that form of service by Bar Yoḥai and leading him to reevaluate the nature of religiosity:

> They sensed that this cannot be but to instruct them of a more equitable path, the path of mercy [*raḥamim*. Namely,] that paying one's attention to the fact that in all the details of a person's occupation, there too is the blessed divine name [present], and that is considered worship of God.

Menachem Lorberbaum explains the implications of this text as follows: "Awareness of God's all-encompassing presence in the most mundane of our activities is worship of God, not only partaking in the official norms of the *halakhah*. It is 'the path of mercy' because it concomitantly entails an acceptance of the world."[46]

Rabbi Jacob Joseph continues:

> It is not only one who engages solely with Torah and prayer that is considered a worshiper of God. For by thus behaving one arouses [divine] antagonism against the people of the world who do not behave likewise. Rather, a person is considered a ladder—even when it is poised on the earth, the lowest rung is in the earthly grossness of matter.[47]

Lorberbaum explains as follows:

> Jacob's ladder is here located within each person in his quality as a microcosm, and it reaches from the highest rung on which the deity hovers to the lowest, "the earthly grossness of matter." Piety that construes the sincere occupation with the here and now as religious laxity evokes divine wrath, while acceptance inspires divine grace. *Tikkun olam* is thus transformed to a salvific stature. To quote Gershom Scholem with regard to Lurianic Kabbalah: "Salvation means actually nothing but restitution, re-integration of the original whole, or *tikkun*, to use the Hebrew term."[48]

In conclusion, the student of the Baal Shem Tov learns, from Bar Yoḥai's illumination, the lesson of Proverbs: "In all your ways know God" (Proverbs 3:6).

A Visit to the Spa: Rest and Relaxation for the Revolutionary's Sores

> Rabbi Pinḥas ben Yair, [Rashbi's] father-in-law, heard and went out to greet him. He took him to the bathhouse. He [Pinḥas ben Yair] was massaging his [Rashbi's] flesh. He saw that there were clefts in his flesh. He was weeping and the tears were falling from his eyes and hurting (*m'tza·ari*) him [i.e., Rashbi].

Has Rabbi Shimon mellowed? Has he repented for the crime for which God exiled him back to the cave?

Rabbi Shimon bar Yoḥai has certainly suffered terribly in a physical sense. The Yerushalmi's version of our story states: "Rashbi hid in a cave for thirteen years, in a cave of…carobs, until his body became covered with sores."[49] Yet in his conversation with his empathetic father-in-law,[50] Bar Yoḥai shows no bitterness—as he had earlier evinced toward both Rome and the farmers. His own suffering and the lost years in the cave do not fuel his indignation; his idealism is not tainted with personal vengeance in this case. But his mellow response is not necessarily derived from a change of perspective concerning the material world. Rather, he continues to downgrade the physical and to justify suffering as a necessary means to greater Torah learning, demonstrated by his prowess in fending off intellectual challenges. Bar Yoḥai is as sharp as ever in mind, and so the loss of his skin's beauty and the pain when the salty tears drop into his cracked skin is not of real consequence.

Yet something must have changed. Rabbi Shimon Bar Yoḥai, who had condemned the bathhouses of Rome as places to pamper one's body, is himself now in a bathhouse—his own convalescent resort, as it were. Bar Yoḥai allows his father-in-law to pamper him, even if he denies his need for healing. Years earlier, he had shown no appreciation of his wife's concern for his physical well-being and, in fact, he had disdained any dependence on others; now, however, he accepts graciously that kind of loving physical care from his father-in-law.

Back to the Material World: The Turning Point for Bar Yoḥai

He [Rashbi] said, "Since a miracle occurred, I will go and fix (*atkin*) something, since it says, 'And Jacob came whole (*shaleim*)' (Genesis 33:18)."

Rabbi Shimon bar Yoḥai's healing process is also reinforced by his sense of gratitude for having been saved from Roman persecution. Life is important to him after all, even in the mundane sense. Bar Yoḥai now celebrates life and enjoys a good bath—even though the bathhouses were built by Rome. So as one who thanks God for the gift of divine grace in saving one's life, Bar Yoḥai goes beyond recognition in words and now wants to repay his community for their kindness to him. Recalling Jacob's near-death experience upon returning from twenty years of exile and meeting Esau—the father of Edom, the ancestor of Rome in rabbinic midrashic genealogy—Bar Yoḥai too wishes to thank God for maintaining his wholeness.[51]

What does Bar Yoḥai learn from Jacob, who also fought a life-long struggle and found rest only after twenty years? Let us begin with the literal meaning of the Torah, and then see how the rabbis read it—integrating into our cave story notions of *t'shuvah* and *tikkun*, repentance and reparation. The Torah relates:

> Jacob arrived whole in the city of Shechem, which is in the land of Canaan—having come thus from Paddan-aram—and he encamped (*va-yiḥan*) before the city. The parcel of land where he pitched his tent he purchased from the children of Ḥamor, Shechem's father, for a hundred *kesitahs* (coins). He set up an altar there, and called it *El Elohei Yisrael*. (Genesis 33:18–20)

Jacob arrived "complete" (*shaleim*), which means he did not lose his life, his wealth, his children; he was, however, limping, so his wholeness stands in tension with the injury sustained in his struggle with the angel (of Esau?). Finished running, he now settles down in Shechem, a city, and purchases a piece of land—his first permanent home. He then builds an altar to his God, named by his own new name, "Israel." The altar is built from a sense of gratitude, for Jacob is aware of how far he has come and how God has answered the prayer he made before meeting Esau.[52] Since the Hebrew verbs for "to camp" and "to placate" sound very similar, the word *va-yiḥan*, which literally means "camped," can also be reinterpreted midrashically to mean that Jacob "placated the face" of the city fathers, from whom he bought the land (Genesis 33:19). Similarly, Jacob placated Esau with material gifts (Genesis 33:8).[53] Perhaps he also requested a permit of domicile as a resident alien, as Abraham did in Hebron when he purchased a burial cave and a field (Genesis 23:4).

The rabbis' explanation of this verse transforms it from simply a financial transaction, conducted by a nomad settling on land outside a city, into an act of beneficence for the city that resonates with the notion of classic Hellenistic philanthropic contributions to public institutions. But they have also shaped the gift in the form of the fulfillment of a vow in gratitude for being rescued:

> He [Rashbi] said, "Since a miracle occurred, I will go and fix (*atkin*) something, since it says, 'And Jacob came whole (*shaleim*)' (Genesis 33:18)."
> Rav [who explicated that same verse] said, "Whole in his body, whole in his money, whole in his Torah, as the verse says: 'and he [Jacob] showed grace to (*va-yihan*; literally, "camped before") the city, and Jacob fixed (*va-yiken*; literally "purchased") a field...(Genesis 33:18).'"
> Rav said, "He established (*tikkein*) coinage for them."
> Samuel said, "He established (*tikkein*) markets for them."
> Rabbi Yohanan said, "He established (*tikkein*) bathhouses for them."

For Rav, "whole in his Torah" means that Jacob has not lost his Torah learning during his long exile. This is fitting as well for Bar Yohai, who has grown in his own Torah learning in the harsh conditions of his own long exile, in the cave. But Rav gives pride of place to physical blessings ("whole in his body, whole in his wealth") before even commenting on spiritual blessings ("whole in his Torah").

In corresponding measure to the physical and financial blessings he has received, Jacob shows his gratitude not to God nor to Esau, but to the non-Jewish population of this *polis*.[54] The nomadic shepherd turns out to be an activist for urban development with a fine sense for markets and coinage. In short, Jacob embodies the great world-civilizing impulses of Greece and Rome in his *tikkun*, his development and his repair of public space.

How can Rabbi Shimon bar Yoḥai follow this model? Only by making amends, by repairing all the damage he has done, and by reversing his whole revolutionary ideology. Torah itself will now become a means to bring about reconstructive action; it can no longer be an idealistic stance from which to disparage the world of civilization.

Literarily, the same words are invoked at both the beginning and ending of the story of Bar Yoḥai, so that we as readers can measure the changes in him, word for word. Repeated are key terms: baths, markets, and the money collected at toll-bridges. All of these are for our own good, for our own physical benefit, for society—and they are precisely the elements that Bar Yoḥai had originally condemned, by declaring: "Everything they established (*tiknu*), they established only for their own needs: They established markets—to place prostitutes there; bathhouses—to pamper themselves; bridges—to take tolls." The root of the most frequently repeated word in the narrative is *tav-kof-nun*, which means "repaired" or "constructed" or "instituted"; and the world to be improved is not the eternal one of Torah-study, *ḥayyei olam*, but rather the social–material one, *ḥayyei sha·ah*. Jacob's *va-yiken*—purchase of land—resonates with this root as well, and so perhaps his action is also being reinterpreted as *tikkun*.

The danger of *tikkun olam* is that may provide a temptation to destroy the established world before building a new one. In the lyrics of the socialist anthem "Internationale," translated into Russian by the Jewish poet Arkady Yakovlevich Kots in 1902 and later translated into Hebrew by members of the Labor Movement in Israel, the workers speak of destroying the foundations of the world in order to build on its ruins a new world:

Arise, you branded by a curse, you whole world of the

starving and enslaved! Our indignant intellect boils, ready to lead us into a fight to the death. **We will destroy this world of violence down to the foundations, and then we will build our new world.** He who was nothing will become everything!

This is close to the spirit of Rabbi Shimon bar Yoḥai at the beginning of the tale. Roman rule is described with the term *tiknu*, in terms of the civilization they have established. And that is precisely what Bar Yoḥai wishes to destroy: he wishes to do a *tikkun* of the divine kingdom. As used in the fourth-century Aleinu prayer, this language speaks to calling all the inhabitants of the world to bend their knee to God, destroying all idolatry and the earthly rule of all that is inimical to the sovereignty of God. However, at the end of the tale, Bar Yoḥai has changed: he not only abandons his earlier commitment to a completely destructive tikkun of the prevailing social order, but he even expresses a desire to join in an effort to do a piecemeal *tikkun* that accommodates human life in its wholly mundane search for the amenities of civilization. He no longer seeks thoroughgoing revolution requiring the dismantling of all of civilization—even though Roman urban civilization is also implicated in the suppression of Torah study and of his people's desire for freedom.

Tikkun Olam: Urban Renewal and Its Detractors

Let us return to the opening question in this essay: Is there necessarily an opposition between *talmud torah* and *ma·aseh*, between study and action? At the end of the tale, Rabbi Shimon bar Yoḥai asks, hoping to be helpful: "Is there something to fix (*l'takkonei*)?" In posing this question, is he following in Jacob's footsteps and going to work in the city engineering department; or does he mean to suggest that there may be some way in which Torah can bring about action to effect improvement of civil society? The answer is: he is doing both. Bar Yoḥai marks off a hard path for priests to walk though the graveyeard without becoming ritually contaminated. Death is the primary source of impurity in the Torah, and Bar Yoḥai is now committed to life—to everyday life, to making things more comfortable for our physical existence. To this end, he will seek to help the priests maintain their purity, as rabbinic law mandates, even though the Temple is long gone. He wants to save them the bother of a long walk around the field of suspected impurity, and he does so by identifying where precisely bodies were most likely buried (i.e., where the soil is still loose), thus permiting them to walk on the hard-packed earth.

Melila Hellner-Eshed notes quizzically that this *tikkun* of Rabbi Shimon bar Yoḥai's merely provided a shortcut for a minority of the residents, as it saved the priests the inconvenience walking around the suspected old cemetery area.[55] But surely Tiberias—the largest Jewish city left, after the destruction of all southern Judea in the Bar Kokhba revolt—had more pressing needs than a shortcut for priests! Even Jacob innovated much more practical projects for Shechem, as did the Roman builders for all of the Land of Israel. Why was Bar Yoḥai's effort at *tikkun* so circumscribed?

Perhaps we ought to see Bar Yoḥai's most important contribution as keeping alive the Oral Torah, which was almost lost after the revolt. His *tikkun* in the urban realm can be seen as a part of the self-corrective mechanisms of the rabbinic system. My teacher David Hartman often spoke of the "pathology" of the *halakhah*—that is, the ways that legalism and intellectual elitism can create unhealthy forms of service of God. The fear of suspected impurity, and the resulting interference of religious strictness in daily life, are pathologies that must be put in their place by greater and more flexible knowledge, and the ultra-conservative religious fanatics must be silenced. Bar Yoḥai's apparent leniency with the law of impurity for the sake of greater ease in daily life invited zealots to denounce him and tear down what he had tried to fix. For those opposed to Bar Yoḥai, the purity of death took precedence over the sanctity of life:

> A certain old man said, "The son of Yoḥai made a cemetery pure [i.e., he tried to what is conceptually impossible and hence hypocritical, since by definition no cemetery can be pure of the impurity of death]."

This detractor, who was spreading ugly innuendoes and gossip (the larger topic of this talmudic section), turns out to have been part of the very *beit din* (court) in which Bar Yoḥai ruled that priests were permitted free passage through the carefully marked field. The old man has thus betrayed the collegial loyalty among judges. In condemning the traitorous old judge, Rashbi compares him unfavorably to the professional ethos of prostitutes, who loyally help each other dress up and apply cosmetics, acting with more solidarity and cooperation among themselves than the judge himself does among his own colleagues. In effect Bar Yoḥai, has corrected his pejorative comments about prostitutes, whom he had associated initially with hedonist Roman urban culture that he condemned, and he has instead criticized the kind of supercritical rabbinic scholar that he himself may have been, at one time.

Epilogue: Payback Time

> He [Rashbi] went out to the market. He saw Judah ben Gerim. [He said,] "Is this one still in the world?" He set his eyes upon him and made him a heap of bones.

Note that Rabbi Shimon bar Yoḥai has now been domesticated almost completely—he is no longer a critic of civilization, but now one of its promoters; no longer an otherworldly Torah scholar, but now a world-repairing scholar who uses his legal wisdom to make life easier for priests going to market. He heals rather than damages; he feels gratitude rather than disdain for the material world and his own body.

However, he has *not* become a milquetoast, a *nebbishy* peacenik, and neither is he seen as the lover of peace always seeking compromise, celebrated by Hillel's understanding of Aaron the priest. Bar Yoḥai still uses his charismatic powers to punish extra-legally, in a vigilante way. He does kill the seditious fellow judge, who had undermined Rashbi's ruling by taking part in the court yet refuting its conclusions publicly. That is a very radical punishment, which is unjustifiable and disproportionate in legal terms; but psychologically and literarily, as revenge for betrayal, it is very satisfying. Bar Yoḥai may have seen in that super-pious judge an image of his own former self, as a zealot of uncompromising truth. In killing the judge, he perhaps kills an aspect of himself. The process of self-transformation requires expulsion of the old self.

Yet ironically, this shows that Bar Yoḥai's extremism has not been eradicated but simply redirected. He kills Judah ben Gerim for being a traitorous informer (or, at least, for being a loose-lipped gossip), whose revelation of Rashbi's private comments caused the latter years of persecution.[56]

Rabbi Shimon bar Yoḥai believes that forms of worldly corruption can be eradicated, and so he acts decisively to remove two traitors who threatened him personally—but he does not condemn the whole world. Bar Yoḥai is still militant, but now he maintains solidarity with simple people and with urban society. He has modified his attitude toward human civilization and changed into a piecemeal reformer. His changing conception of the good and how to achieve it contributes to a new way of imagining the human pursuit of social good: "The philanthropic tradition is the social history of the moral imagination—imagining a vision of the public good and inventing forms of voluntary action to advance that good."[57]

The starting point is imagining "the good" in the Platonic

tradition. Bar Yoḥai in the cave has an individual's good in mind—a contemplative one, also an idea central to Plato—which he believes is diametrically opposed to the world empire that rules the public sphere (namely: Rome). He imagines his own personal spiritual good as an ideal that exists in opposition to an existing reality and independent of any physical needs, which are met supernaturally while he is in hiding. He communes through God and Torah with this otherworldly, private good for twelve years in the cave. However, when he emerges—after an additional thirteenth year, meted out as a type of divine punishment—he is changed: now, Bar Yoḥai embraces a "public good" that is achieved not by study or asceticism but by legal activism on the municipal level. His goal is simple: to improve the material and social life in the polis, so that priests can more conveniently traverse public space. This concern for others makes his imagination "moral," while his legal activity is "a voluntary action to advance that good."[58] Biblical, rabbinic, and governmental legislation all show that the "vision of public good" can be achieved by judicial action. Moral imagination, nurtured by the prophets and the philosophers, helps us to imagine a world better than the one we have—and we can then invent ways to make repairs in a flawed world.

Rabbi Shimon bar Yoḥai, then, arrives—through his own path of self-transformation and *tikkun*—at a view expressed beautifully by Rabbi Joseph B. Soloveitchik:

> We have always considered ourselves to be an inseparable part of humanity and we were ever ready to accept the divine challenge, "Fill the earth and subdue it" (Genesis 1:28). We have never proclaimed the philosophy of *contemptus* or *odium seculi* [rejection of the secular world]. We have steadily maintained that involvement in the creative scheme of things is mandatory.[59]

Men of old who could not fight disease and succumbed in

multitudes to yellow fever or any other plague with degrading helplessness could not lay claim to dignity. Only the man who builds hospitals, discovers therapeutic techniques, and saves lives is blessed with dignity....The brute is helpless, and therefore not dignified. Civilized man has gained limited control of nature and has become in certain respects her master, and with his mastery he has attained dignity as well. His mastery has made it possible for him to act in accordance with his responsibility.[60]

When God created the world, God provided an opportunity for the work of God's hands—man—to participate in God's creation. The Creator, as it were, impaired reality in order that mortal man could repair its flaws and perfect it.[61]

Here we have completed our narrative, which is best described as a reluctant journey toward *t'shuvah*, repentance, or to *tikkun*, repair. It is Rashbi's attitude to the world, even more than the world itself, that is fixed. This is what Maimonides calls *tikkun ha-nefesh*, repairing the soul, the character, the mind, and beliefs—and which he says is even more important than repairing the body, *tikkun ha-guf*.[62] In it, Rabbi Shimon bar Yoḥai's legendary reputation as a mystic revolutionary undergoes a radical facelift. He is remolded from a militant, anti-worldly monk to an urban reformer concerned with micro-planning in order to improve accessibility, by permitting a path through the graveyards for the comfort of the priests. He is no longer an ivory-tower or cave-dwelling academic, but rather a legal activist seeking compromise in the real world.

Our task is now complete, as we sought to illuminate the idea of *tikkun olam* from an *aggadah* that probably has no historical claim to authenticity. It goes against everything the other rabbinic sources teach us about Rabbi Shimon bar Yoḥai. But that is the point: *tikkun olam* is an approach that differs from other attempts to make a better world (with which it should be not confused), by adopting an attitude of total transformation. It comes to replace revolution with reform. It lowers expectations and therefore allows for compromises. It is not apocalyptic, even when its enemy is no less globalized and all-powerful than the Roman Empire. The master of *tikkun olam* must cultivate particular virtues and dispositions. While young rebels may be moved to action in very extremist ways, they must mature in their labor for justice and learn to tame their self-righteous, arrogant, and destructive passions—such as the ones that Bar Yoḥai "fixed" in himself. Fixing the world must never lose its love and high valuation of God's creation. Otherwise, the would-be purists of universal justice must be sent back to the cave for another "time-out."

NOTES

[1] Also known as the Mitteler Rebbe (1773–1827), who became the second Lubavitcher Rebbe.

[2] Reb Shneuer Zalman of Lyadi (1745–1812), the first Lubavitcher Rebbe.

[3] Jonathan Sacks, *To Heal a Fractured World* (New York: Schocken, 2007), p. 82.

[4] The term as it appears in classical sources includes the definite article, *tikkun ha-olam*. In modern parlance, the article is elided and the concept is referred to simply as *tikkun olam*.

[5] Translation adapted from Jeffrey Rubenstein, *Talmudic Stories: Narrative Art, Composition, and Culture* (Baltimore: Johns Hopkins University Press, 2003), pp. 106–108, based on ms. Munich 95.

[6] The identity of the speakers is uncertain; perhaps this is an anonymous editorial insertion.

[7] I use "Hell" and "Gehenna" interchangeably in this essay.

[8] Apparently as a result of Rashbi's time in the cave, he now surpassed Pinḥas ben Yair, who had once been a more brilliant scholar than Rashbi.

[9] Rabbi Judah Loew ben Betzalel of Prague (c. 1520–1609, called the Maharal) suggests that Jacob's "fixing the face of the city" may refer to the face on the coins of the city.

[10] Lupine beans are a typical Mediterranean plant with a bitter taste, used mainly for animal fodder. Thus Ben Zakkai must have regarded at least part of this field as pure; otherwise he could not have harvested lupines to be given to the priest as a *t'rumah* offering. Some say Ben Zakkai was himself a priest; if so, he would not have entered the field if it was impure.

[11] Since a human corpse is the the greatest possible source of ritual impurity, a cemetery can never validly be declared pure. The old man implied that while Rashbi may have thought that he was only marking off a few suspected graves, he could not, in fact, turn that which is essentially impure into a wholly pure area.

[12] In other words, Rashbi accuses the old man of not even showing the minimal solidarity with his colleagues and fellow judges that would have been shown even by competitive prostitutes—rather, he publicly attacked the joint ruling of the other rabbis.

[13] B. Kiddushin 40b.

[14] Ibid.

[15] The passage is found in B. Sukkah 45b, following the translation of Jeffrey Rubenstein in *Talmudic Stories*, p. 117. Elsewhere, Rabbi Shimon bar Yoḥai is reported to have said, "Learn my principles, for my principles are loftier than [my teacher] Rabbi Akiva's highest principles" (B. Gittin 67a).

[16] B. Shabbat 33b.

[17] Ibid.

[18] B. Berakhot 35b.

[19] Y. Taanit 4:8 (68d). Akiva expounded the following verse, "A star (*kokhav*) has risen from Jacob" (Numbers 24:17) and so nicknamed the rebel as *Kokhba*, "the

star," rather than *Koziba*. Upon seeing Bar Kokhba, Akiva would say: "This is the King Messiah!".

[20] B. Berakhot 64b.

[21] Henri Irénée Marrou, *A History of Education in Antiquity*, trans. George Lamb (New York: Sheed and Ward, 1956), p. 413.

[22] Ibid., p. 392. Marrou observes that Rome's senatorial class of aristocrats saw their empire as "fulfilling its historic mission to preserve civilization and culture in the face of the barbarians; and their culture came more and more to mean the classical literary tradition." The Italians who conquered Greece in the second century B.C.E. had since absorbed its language and culture and the elite now spoke, read, and educated their children in Greek alongside Latin. By virtue of the *pax Romana*, Rome was able to turn the Mediterranean world into one cultural community. While some oppressed Judeans might see the Romans only through the eyes of their sword and their taxes, others—like Rabbi Judah, son of the converts—might concur with one Greek aristocrat Aelius Aristides in Ionia, who addressed the Roman emperor extolling the philosophic benefits of the Empire's law and order: "The whole world seems to be on holiday. It has laid aside garments of iron so that it shall be free to devote itself entirely to beauty and the joy of living. The cities have forgotten their old rivalries—or rather the same spirit of emulation animates them all, the desire to be considered first in beauty and charm. On all sides can be seen gymnasiums, fountains, *propylaea*, temples, workshops, schools." (Arstd. XXVI, K, 97).

[23] Rubenstein, *Talmudic Stories*, p. 110.

[24] This point was made in a lecture at the Hartman Institute in Jerusalem given to their annual rabbinic seminar; the source is M. Gittin 4:5.

[25] Martin Cohen points out that *geirim* may not mean "converts" here, but simply "resident aliens." He notes correctly that it is a violation of rabbinic ethics to remind descendants of converts of their ancestors (B. Baba Metzia 58b). Nevertheless, in this rabbinic narrative that profiles the generally xenophobic Bar Yoḥai, it is not inappropriate to identify Bar Yoḥai's rival in a way that may suggest a slur on his foreign lineage.

[26] The motif of the threesome who speak out on the imperial program of an evil emperor who is suppressing the Jewish people is echoed in a midrash about the three wise men who advise Pharaoh about his decree to kill the Jewish babies in Egypt (Shemot Rabbah 1:9). The advisors in that source are identified as Balaam, Job, and Jethro. Job is the silent one there, but his silence is not neutral or excusable—he was later punished with great suffering. The midrash sees God as parallel to the Romans, in issuing decrees against those who remain silent. In Egypt, maintaining silence enabled the Pharaoh to carry out his decrees against the Israelites. In light of this comparison, Rashbi is to be praised as a moral hero, not condemned as an arrogant intellectual who was secretly jealous of Roman achievements.

[27] M. Kiddushin 1:10.

[28] Rashbi's food in the cave is supplied miraculously, just as God provided

manna from heaven for the Israelites in the desert. However, the analogy does not extend to clothing: unlike the Israelites' clothing, which did not wear out (Deuteronomy 8:3–4), care is needed to be taken to preserve Rashbi's clothing.

[29] B. Niddah 30b.

[30] Y. Berakhot 1:3 (3b).

[31] The heavenly *beit midrash* is where the righteous join God in study of the Torah (*Tanna D'vei Eliyahu Rabbah* 1, 3, 4, 5, 8, 9): "One who accustoms oneself to go to the *beit ha-k'neset* and *beit ha-midrash* in this world shall also be admitted into the beit ha-kneset and beit ha-midrash of the world to come, as it is written, 'Happy are they who dwell in Your house; they shall [in the future as well] sing Your praise (Psalm 84:5).'" This statement is attributed to Joshua ben Levi in Devarim Rabbah 7:1, cf. also Midrash Tehillim 84:3 to Psalm 84:5.

[32] Midrashic wordplay highlights these thematically related terms; note, for example, the assonance between the Aramaic terms for plow (*karvi*) and bread (*krakhi*).

[33] Rubenstein, *Talmudic Stories*, pp. 112–113.

[34] Abraham Joshua Heschel, *The Sabbath* (New York: Farrar, Straus, and Young, 1951), pp. 38–39 and 45.

[35] Initially the cave is a shelter from political persecution, just as David's cave in Ein Gedi was his safe haven from King Saul who sought to kill him (1 Samuel 23–24). Caves in the Land of Israel were often used during revolts, as places of refuge in the Roman period. The Dead Sea Scrolls and many other documents from this era have been found in caves, where the refugees from the Romans found temporary relief. In the Yerushalmi's version of our story (at Y. Sheviit 9:1, [38d]), the cave is only a place to hide; emergence from the cave is seen as analogous to the liberation of a bird from imprisonment. Nothing therefore of the life in the cave is retold.

[36] B. Berakhot 28b.

[37] B. Niddah 30b.

[38] To Martin S. Cohen, the senior editor of this volume, I owe the observation that *kever*, grave, is also a metaphor for womb (M. Ohalot 7:4).

[39] In the version of the tale as preserved in the Babylonian Talmud; cf. note 34 above for how the Yerushalmi treats the element of the cave differently.

[40] The voice of heaven in the Babylonian version may be contrasted with the "voice in the world," the rumors about Roman persecution that Bar Yoḥai sought to consult before daring to leave the refuge, in the Yerushalmi's version of the tale.

[41] While God is willing to forgo divine honor in order to bring peace in the world, Rashbi is not. Consider the following text (B. Nedarim 66b): Once a husband told his wife [who had burned his food]: "I swear that you may not benefit from me [sexually or materially, through my legal obligation to support my wife] until you make Rabbi Judah and Rabbi Shimon taste this dish [that you burned]." Rabbi Judah tasted it [to release her from her husband's vow]. He explained: "My behavior can be learned logically by *kal va-ḥomer* [from

God], for the Torah commands that in order to bring peace between a husband and wife [in the case of the woman suspected by her husband of committing adultery, they may be united if she drinks] the accursed water into which My name that has been written in sanctity has been dissolved. So too for me, even more so [I who am far lower than God must agree to forfeit my honor and to eat this burned dish]!" But Rabbi Shimon refused to eat it. He said: "May all the sons of widows die, and yet Rabbi Shimon bar Yoḥai will not budge from this position, so that people will not treat vows lightly."

42 This contrast is highlighted by the use of similar-sounding Aramaic verbs: *maḥei/masei* = destroy/heal.

43 Hellner-Eshed made this point this in a lecture at the annual rabbinic seminar at the Hartman Institute in Jerusalem.

44 B. Bava Metzia 83b-84b.

45 Jacob Joseph Hakohen, *Toldot Yaakov Yosef* (ed. Koretz, 1780), *Va-yeitzei*, p. 27a. *Toldot Yaakov Yosef* is the earliest published version of the teachings of the Baal Shem Tov. Translations of Hebrew originals in this essay are taken from Menachem Lorberbaum's unpublished work, *Rethinking Halakhah in Modern Eastern Europe: Mysticism, Antinomianism, Positivism*.

46 Lorberbaum, *Rethinking Halakhah*.

47 *Toldot Yaakov Yosef, Va-yeitzei*, p. 27b.

48 Lorberbaum, *Rethinking Halakhah*. The Scholem quotation comes from his *Major Trends in Jewish Mysticism* (1941; rpt. New York: Schocken, 1978), p. 268.

49 Y. Sheviit 9:1 (38d).

50 See B. Sotah 49a: "Pinḥas ben Yair said: 'Since the destruction of the Temple, scholars of Torah (*ḥaveirim*) and people of pedigree are shamed and cover their heads; men of good deeds have diminished, while men of violence and the informers (*baalei lashon*) have increased…So on whom may we rely? On our Parent in Heaven."

51 In the Yerushalmi's version (Sheviit 9:1 [38d]), Bar Yoḥai realizes how easy it is to catch a fugitive hiding in a cave and how God must have decreed his untouchability: "At the end of thirteen years, he [Rashbi] said: 'Perhaps I shall go out and see what is happening in the world.' He went out and sat at the mouth of the cave, where he saw a hunter tracking birds and spreading his net. He heard a heavenly voice saying, 'You are dismissed'— and it [the bird] escaped. He said, 'Without [the decree of] heaven, [even] a bird does not perish; so much more so a human being!' When he saw that things had quieted down, he said: 'Let us go down and bathe (literally, 'warm ourselves) at the baths of Tiberias.' He said: 'We ought to fix something (*takkana*), as our ancestors of old have done."

52 See Genesis 32:10–13: "Then Jacob said: 'O God of my father Abraham and God of my father Isaac…Deliver me, I pray, from the hand of my brother, from the hand of Esau; else, I fear, he may come and strike me down, mothers and children alike."

53 Martin S. Cohen notes that the same word, spelled the same way, can also

mean "to respond with grace or mercy to one who placates" (cf., e.g., 2 Kings 13:23).

[54] In the rabbis' day, the city of Shechem—Neapolis, today called by the Arabs Nablus—was a thriving Greek town.

[55] See note 42 above.

[56] Recall that Judah related to his non-Jewish parents the conversation among the three rabbis about the Romans, passing along not only the participants' positions but also their names—and that information made its way to the Roman authorities, either intentionally or unintentionally. It was in the era of Rabbi Shimon bar Yoḥai that the rabbis added to the daily Amidah prayer a request that God curse informers (*la-malshinim al t'hi tikvah*).

[57] Robert Payton and Michael Moody, *Understanding Philanthropy: Its Meaning and Mission* (Bloomington, IN: Indiana Univerity Press, 2008), p. 154.

[58] Ibid.

[59] Joseph B. Soloveitchik, "Confrontation," in *Tradition* 6:2 (1964), part II, no. 2, p.20.

[60] Joseph Soloveitchik, "The Lonely Man of Faith," in *Tradition* 7:2 (1965), p.16.

[61] Joseph Soloveitchik, *Halakhic Man* (Philadelphia: Jewish Publication Society, 1984), p. 101.

[62] *Guide for the Perplexed* III 27.

Noachide Laws, Universal Justice, and *Tikkun Olam*

Michael J. Broyde and Ira Bedzow

There is a principle in Jewish law that *kol yisrael areivim zeh ba-zeh*, "All members of the people Israel are responsible for one another."[1] This principle underscores people's responsibility to work together to fulfill the Torah's ideals of justice. Because this dictum speaks only to the Jewish people and not to the world at large, many have wrongly assumed that Judaism does not also ask its adherents to work toward justice on a broader, more universal scale—seeking to establish and maintain justice for humanity as a whole. But this narrow view is antithetical to the notion of *tikkun olam*, which calls on us to repair the world as a whole, focusing on the needs of all of humanity. While it is true that Jewish law has a particularistic orientation, the Jewish tradition nevertheless recognizes that there is also a greater obligation for Jews to see themselves as part of a larger humanity—who also have certain basic responsibilities of working toward justice, as set out in the Noachide commandments (which the rabbis understood to be incumbent on all non-Jews).[2] The origin and scope of these commandments will be explained more fully below.

In this essay, we will examine various halakhic attitudes toward the nature of Noachide law as it pertains to establishing a just community, as well as the specific nature of Jews' obligations and responsibilities vis-à-vis these commandments. The scope of our inquiry is threefold, exploring the issues of compliance, enforcement, and petition. The fundamental question to be explored is: as Jews, are we obligated simply to ensure the administration of justice in our own communities, or are we in fact commanded to work toward the establishment of justice in the world as a whole—for both Jews and gentiles? And this, of course, relates directly to the issue of *tikkun olam*: what are the parameters of the world that we are asked to work toward repairing?

We will examine the two major views regarding the relationship that Jews have to the Noachide laws, insofar as they are concerned with increasing justice among gentiles. The dominant view is that Jews do not have an obligation to impose Noachide law on gentiles, nor are they obligated to teach them about it—except, perhaps, by example. The second view maintains that Jews do have an obligation to teach gentiles about the Noachide laws; doing so (in this view) could be considered tantamount to working toward *tikkun olam*. In this essay, we do not advocate for either opinion; rather, we present them as two different understandings of the rabbinic tradition's treatment of the nexus between the particularistic Jewish imperative for pursuing justice, on the one hand, and the broader universalistic concerns for seeking justice for humanity at large, on the other.

Noachide Law: What Is It?

According to the Talmud, God's covenant with Noah after the flood included seven specific commandments, which were deemed binding on him and his descendants—that is, all humanity. Noachide law (*sheva mitzvot b'nei no·ah*, literally "the seven commandments of the descendants of Noah") is composed of six prohibitions and one positive injunction: (1) the prohibition against idolatry, (2) the prohibition against taking God's name in vain, (3) the prohibition against murder, (4) the prohibition against prohibited sexual activity, (5) the prohibition against theft, (6) the prohibition against eating flesh from a living animal, and (7) the obligation to ensure the promulgation and enforcement of just laws (*dinim*).[3]

The talmudic discussion regarding the precise nature of what the Noachide laws include, as well as the origin of these laws, gives rise to divergent opinions regarding both the source of authority of Noachide law and also the substance of its details. For example, there is a debate among the rabbis as to whether Noachide law was revealed along with Jewish law at Sinai, or if its authority stems from natural law. If (according to the first view) Noachide law is taken to have been revealed alongside Jewish law at Sinai, then there is an intimate, two-way relationship between the two systems: Noachide law must recognize the theological and political authority of the Jewish tradition, and Jews have a responsibility to enforce Noachide law among the gentiles. This position is held by Maimonides.[4] Alternatively, if the establishment of Noachide law is separate and distinct from Jewish law, then the relationship between the two systems is pragmatic—that is, a relationship only develops as the two actually interact in real-life situations.

Today, when Jews and gentiles live among each other, there is no practical difference between these two views. In both cases, Jews must be cognizant of Noachide law and the obligations it may place on them. In fact, many latter-day rabbinical scholars—including Rabbi Yosef Engel,[5] Rabbi Meir Simḥah of Dvinsk,[6] Rabbi Yeḥiel Yaakov Weinberg,[7] Rabbi Shlomo Zalman Auerbach,[8] and Rabbi Moshe Feinstein[9]—seem to indicate that there is a halakhic imperative for Jews to follow Noachide law when living in a gentile country, even though Jews are considered to be under the jurisdiction of Jewish law and not Noachide law—since, when Jews live in a gentile country, they are not completely under the jurisdiction of Torah law. Moreover, Jews are further obligated to respect the Noachide laws because of the commonality they share with the rest of humanity. With respect to the issue of how Jews should act vis-à-vis their gentile neighbors regarding the latter's observance of Noachide law, however, the matter is not nearly as clear-cut.

There is disagreement among the rabbis over whether the particular, practical details of the Noachide laws must be the same as in Jewish law, or if the details may be grounded in an independent legal tradition within the Noachide legal system. This disagreement, as it pertains to issues of *tikkun olam*, directly affects one's understanding of the Noachide mandate to establish a just legal system and create courts of justice. With respect to the prescription to create just laws, there are two vastly different interpretations found among the early Jewish juridicial authorities. Maimonides rules that the obligation to create just laws and provide for their enforcement requires only that gentiles ensure that the specific prohibitions delineated in the Noachide laws be enforced in practice. No demands regarding the determination of the particular, practical details concerning the specifics of commercial law (or any other subcategory of law) are made; therefore, they may be different than the details that Jewish law provides. He states:

> How are [Noachides][10] obligated to create just laws (*dinim*)? They must create courts and appoint judges in every province to enforce (*la-dun*) these six commandments...for this reason the inhabitants of [the city of] Shechem were liable to be killed, since Shechem [the person] stole [Dinah], and the inhabitants saw and knew this and did nothing.[11]

According to Maimonides, other types of regulations that gentile society might make are not formally part of *dinim*, as prescribed by the Noachide laws. Yet, even though they are not part of *dinim*, Jews living in gentile countries must nevertheless observe them, under the rubric either of "laws of the land (*dina d'malkhuta*)" or of "laws of the king (*din melekh*)." Moreover, the authority of laws created by gentiles themselves stems from quite a different source than the authority of Noachide law—and this fact may have practical ramifications regarding whether Jews must observe them, if they are in conflict with Jewish law.[12]

Naḥmanides (1194–1270), on the other hand, argues that the obligation for gentiles to create just laws and establish courts of justice goes beyond just enforcing the other six Noachide laws. Rather, it encompasses the obligation to create detailed rules to govern many particular cases of wrongdoing—such as fraud, overcharging, repayment of debts, and the like.[13] Among those who agree with Naḥmanides, seeing a broader mandate for gentiles to establish just laws, there is a disagreement as to scope of what such laws should cover. Rabbi Moses Isserles (1520–1572) interprets Naḥmanides to mean that in those areas where gentiles are supposed to create laws (since, after all, gentiles must follow Noachide law), they are obligated to incorporate Jewish law into Noachide law—unless it is clear that it is inappropriate to do so.[14] For example, Jewish legal norms concerning civil law, such as those that deal with property disputes, would be adopted by Noachide law, but ritual laws or laws prohibiting demanding interest among Jews would not apply to gentiles and thus would not become a part of Noachide law. Other authorities who accept Naḥmanides' opinion construe it more narrowly: rules created under the rubric of *dinim* need to be, like Jewish law, fair and just—yet they need not be identical to Jewish law in their particular details.[15] This debate is significant because all of the subcategories and ramifications of the seven broad Noachide laws encompass nearly sixty of the 613 biblical commandments incumbent on Jews; omitting those commandments having to do with the Temple service, this encompasses a significant part of Jewish law.

Noachide Law: Must Jews Comply With It?

Following this second interpretation of Naḥmanides, the obligation for gentiles to create *dinim* allows them to create rules that differ from Jewish law. Thus, it would seem that there is no Jewish obligation to participate in the enforcement of gentile *dinim*—because it would not be appropriate for Jews to be obliged to enforce two different legal systems. This is not to say that Jews need not obey the laws created by the Noachide government; indeed, they **are** obligated to obey secular law! Rather, the obligation to follow such laws does not stem from the authority of Noachide law over the Jewish community, but rather it is based on the principle of *dina d'malkhuta dina*.[16] As minority members of a broader community, Jews voluntarily accept to live under the terms of the ruling government, the majority culture, by virtue of participating in society. While Jews are obligated by *halakhah* to **obey** Noachide law, and thus its implementation as the law of a gentile government, that does not necessarily include an obligation to **assist in its enforcement**.

To illustrate this last point, the Ḥazon Ish (Rabbi Abraham Isaiah Karelitz, 1878–1953) writes that Jewish law requires that a Jew respect Noachide legal pronouncements, even in a situation where the Noachide judges do not themselves fully observe Noachide law. To the question of whether one must follow a ruling of a court that does not generally observe (or enforce) all of the seven commandments, but that does "observe the law concerning sanctity of life and theft of property," the Ḥazon Ish responds that if the court enforces even just a section of the Noachide laws properly, it is necessary—as a matter of Jewish law—to respect those pronouncements.[17] However, personal respect for the law does not necessarily mean that one must ensure that others respect it as well—and hence, he does not think that Jews have an obligation to assist in the enforcement of gentile law, whether it be the seven provisions of Noachide law or any subsequent *dina d'malkhuta* promulgated by the governing authorities.

In sum: gentiles are obligated to create a legal system designed to enforce the provisions of Noachide law (and Maimonides even includes Jews in this obligation). Jews have an obligation to recognize and respect this system, even when the system is not perfect. This obligation stems from a residual impact of Noachide law on Jews and is recognized in Jewish law—by which we mean that Noachide law is still applicable at times, even though Jews have Jewish law as well.

Must Jews Enforce Noachide Law or Petition for Its Implementation?

Let us begin by examining the following three statements of Maimonides:

Moses, our teacher, only willed Torah and *mitzvot* to the Jewish people, since it states, "An inheritance to the community of Jacob" (Deuteronomy 33:4)…As for one [who is not Jewish] and does not wish to, we do not compel [such a person] to accept Jewish law. So too, *Moses our teacher was commanded by God to compel the commandments obligatory to the Noachides. All who do not accept are killed.* One who accepts them [voluntarily] is called a *ger toshav* [literally: resident alien]…[18]

A Jewish court (*beit din*) is obligated to appoint judges for *gerim toshavim* [plural of *ger toshav*; i.e., resident aliens], to judge them in order that the world not be destroyed. If the Jewish court wishes to appoint judges from within their midst [i.e., from among the *ger toshav* population], it may; if it wishes to appoint judges from the Jews, it may.[19]

One who takes an adult slave from an idol worshipper, and the slave does not wish to be circumcised—[in such a case,] one may delay up to twelve months….If one agreed concerning this slave with his previous owner not to circumcise him, it is permitted to keep the slave uncircumcised; however, the slave must keep the seven commandments obligatory on Noachides and if not, he is killed immediately.[20]

Two fundamental questions that arise from Maimonides' statements:

(1) Does the obligation to compel Noachides to comply with

Noachide law fall on each individual Jew, or on the *beit din*—
and if on the *beit din*, which one? or does Jewish law not follow
Maimonides in this respect?[21]

(2) Is there an obligation to induce or persuade a Noachide to comply
with Noachide law? or, at the very least, is there an obligation to
teach gentiles about Noachide law?

The answer to each of these questions is subject to debate, and how
one approaches these issues will have an impact on one's perception
of the relationship between Jews and gentiles vis-à-vis Noachide law.

Maimonides' Approach

A simple reading of Maimonides' rulings would indicate that either
Jews or a Jewish court are obligated (at the minimum) to compel
Noachides to observe their laws, though one might understand
Maimonides in a more limited sense to mean that this obligation is
only in effect in circumstances when Jews have the political authority
to do so. Yet this is not the only interpretation of Maimonides found
in the rabbinic literature. Rabbi Zvi Hirsch Chajes (1805–1855)
interprets Maimonides' rulings simply as a historical recounting of
facts rather than as normative law. He states:[22]

> B. Sanhedrin 56b recounts that the Jews were commanded
> the ten commandments at Marah. These ten commandments
> included the seven laws of Noah, and the Sabbath laws,
> just civil laws (*dinim*), and the command to respect one's
> parents. Why did the Jews need to be commanded [to follow
> the seven Noachide laws] again, since Jews were already
> commanded from the time of Adam and Noah?...This is
> because we conclude that if the commandments had been
> given prior to Sinai to Noachides but not repeated at Sinai,

they would then be obligatory only for Jews; therefore, the seven commandments had to be repeated at Sinai in order *to obligate Noachides* as well.[23] Considering this comment of Rashbash, the assertion of Maimonides that "Moses, our teacher, only willed Torah and *mitzvot* to the Jewish people, since it states 'An inheritance to the community of Jacob'"... and his assertion that 'Moses our teacher was commanded by God to compel the commandments obligatory to the children of Noah' appears logical. Why was Moses also the messenger to the rest of the world, to compel observance of the seven commandments—perhaps they are obligated by Adam or Noah? [We do not say this, but] rather we see that Moses was commanded at Marah regarding the seven Noachide commandments, even though gentiles were already commanded, in order to make them obligated in the *mitzvot* even now.[24]

Rabbi Chajes continues, arguing that there is no obligation for any Jew in any circumstance to compel a gentile to observe Noachide law. Rather, he explains, Maimonides is merely setting forth the jurisprudential basis for the obligation of Noachides to their seven commandments. Without their repetition at Sinai, only Jews would have been obligated to follow Noachide law. Based on this argument, one could claim at most that Moses was obligated to compel gentiles to observe the Noachide laws, but that latter-day Jews certainly are not obligated to do so—neither through a *beit din* nor as individuals. Rabbi Chajes also understands Maimonides' rule about establishing courts and appointing judges relative to Noachide matters to be limited: Jews are only obligated to do so in situations where Noachides formally accept the obligations of a *ger toshav* (resident alien), and are thus subject to the authority of the Jewish community where they live. The obligation to enforce Noachide law then becomes necessary so as to maintain order, "lest the world be destroyed"—but that obligation does not extend to any other circumstances. Others who also do not think that Maimonides' rulings create a practical legal obligation for Jews to enforce compliance with Noachide law are: Rabbi Yeḥiel Michel Epstein (1829–1908),[25] Rabbi Yehudah Gershuni (1908–2000),[26] Rabbi Shaul Yisraeli (1909–1995),[27] and Rabbi Menaḥem Mendel Kasher (1895–1983).[28]

This explanation of Maimonides' rulings, however, is difficult to reconcile with the simple meaning of his words. In fact, Rabbi Joseph Karo, author of the Shulḥan Arukh, clearly understands Maimonides' ruling to require compulsion whenever possible, even by an individual; yet, even he does appear to limit the application of Maimonides somewhat by not demanding that Jews try to compel gentiles to observe Noachide law whenever they can do so.[29] The medieval *Sefer Ha-ḥinnukh* also follows Maimonides literally, in stating: "The rule is as follows: In all that the nations are commanded, any time they are under our jurisdiction, it is incumbent upon us to judge them [and impose penalties in the event of noncompliance] when they violate the commandments."[30]

The Approach of Ravad, Naḥmanides, Tosafot, and Others

A substantial number of medieval Jewish legalists (*rishonim*) disagree with the opinion of Maimonides, and rule that there is **no** obligation upon an individual Jew to enforce Noachide law among gentiles. Included in this group are Rabbi Abraham ben David of Posquières (Ravad), Naḥmanides, Tosafot,[31] and perhaps even Rabbi Shlomo Yitzḥaki (Rashi) and Rabbi Shlomo ben Aderet (Rashba) as well. Ravad, commenting on Maimonides' ruling that a slave who refuses to accept one of the seven commandments is to be killed, states: "The slave should be sold. We cannot, now, kill a person."[32] While one could understand this assertion as stemming from practical considerations (and Rabbi Karo, writing in his *Kesef Mishnah*, does see it as such), it is more likely that Ravad is limiting the judicial power of the Jewish community to punish Noachides for violations of Noachide law. Ravad would thus be requiring that such a case (of gentile violation of Noachide law) be adjudicated by an authorized court (*beit din*) of twenty-three judges (which could only function when the Sanhedrin was legally empowered to impose capital punishment), and would not give such authority to a court that consists of three people, such as the courts we have today.

Naḥmanides, commenting on Deuteronomy 20 concerning Israel's conquest of the promised land, writes that Jews are not required to impose Noachide law on gentiles if their cohabitation is the result of a negotiated peace between Israel and its Noachide neighbors,[33] and he thus agrees with Ravad's position. According to Naḥmanides, military goals alone should determine the terms of any negotiated peace treaties between Israel and her neighbors— and imposing Noachide law on the other nations living in Canaan is not an appropriate military stratagem. (Note that Maimonides would reject this position, and would permit war purely for the sake of imposing Noachide law on a gentile society.) We may infer that Naḥmanides would likewise not want to see any Jewish body politic ever impose Noachide law on any gentiles—except, of course, in the case of a *ger toshav*.

The Tosafot have a similar position as the rulings of Ravad and Naḥmanides and deny that there is an obligation, even for a Jewish government, to impose Noachide law on nations under its control.[34] Rashi as well seems to side with Ravad on this issue.[35] Rashba in his responsum also appears to agree.[36] Rabbi Asher ben Yeḥiel also has a similar approach; he writes: "[Concerning] a Noachide—even though he violates the seven Noachide commandments [and would be liable for the death penalty]…nonetheless every moment prior to his conviction in court (*beit din*), he is not liable for the death penalty and it is prohibited to kill him."[37] It would seem logical that the *beit din* necessary to impose this type of punishment is the same type of *beit din* necessary to execute Jews—which would mean that this opinion is the same as that of Ravad. Yet, even if this understanding of Rabbeinu Asher is not correct and he intended that any regular *beit din* could fill this role, it is nevertheless clear that he believes there is no obligation for individual Jews to punish Noachides for violations of Noachide law.

A similar situation is discussed with respect to a gentile living in the home of a Jew, either as a "conditional slave"[38] or as an employee; presumably, the homeowner would have considerable influence over these non-Jews. Neither Rabbi Jacob ben Asher (1270–1349) nor Rabbi Moshe Isserles,[39] nor any of the classical commentaries on Shulḥan Arukh, say that there is any obligation to impose Noachide law on such individuals. Note that Maimonides' explicit ruling that one must compel his Noachide slaves to observe Noachide law is ignored by the later authorities—which indicates that his opinion was not considered to be binding in this matter.

Moreover, Rabbi Karo states in his *Beit Yosef* that there is no obligation to kill gentiles who do not obey the Noachide laws;[40] similar sentiments are also found in the writings of Rabbi Jacob ben Asher,[41] Rabbi Joel Sirkes,[42] and Rabbi Joshua Falk.[43] Rabbi Moses Isserles, in his *Darkhei Moshe He-Arukh*, adopts this position as well.[44] Rabbi Karo explicitly incorporates this rule into the Shulḥan Arukh.[45] Rabbi Shabbetai Hakohen states: "There is no obligation [*mitzvah*] to kill gentiles, even if they violate the Noachide laws,"[46] and Rabbi David Halevi agrees with this assertion.

This ruling not to mandate the punishment of gentiles for violating Noachide law stands in clear contrast to the assertion in the Shulḥan Arukh that encourages a person to punish (and even kill) a Jew who intentionally defies Jewish law. This distinction between punishing a Jew and not punishing a gentile for transgressing their respective legal obligations makes it abundantly clear that the Shulḥan Arukh and the other rabbinic authorities rule that, according to Jewish law, gentiles need not be punished by Jews for violating Noachide law;

this is contrary to Maimonides' assertion (cited above). Likewise, these authorities see no obligation or duty to compel observance of Noachide law by gentiles.

Even though it is not obligatory to do so, *Sefer Ha-ḥasidim* nonetheless states that it is a meritorious thing to do, since by doing so one imitates God's conduct towards the Noachides at Nineveh.[49] Maimonides is clear that, when possible, Jews must enforce Noachide law; however, the overwhelming majority of legal decisors, both medieval and modern, disagree with his conclusion and asserts that today there is no obligation for any individual Jew to compel a gentile to stop violating Noachide law.

The Approach of Rabbi Menachem Mendel Schneerson

Despite the preponderance of the opinion that Jews are **not** obligated to compel Noachides to stop violating Noachide law, Rabbi Menachem Mendel Schneerson of Lubavitch—the last Lubavitch Rebbe (1902–1994)—argues, in one of his classical responsa, that Jews **do** have the obligation to teach and persuade, though not necessarily to compel, a gentiles to keep the seven Noachide commandments. His interpretation of Maimonides' rulings is as follows:

It is obvious that this obligation[50] is not limited only to a Jewish court, since this commandment is unrelated to the presence of a *ger toshav* [resident alien], and thus what is the need of a *beit din*....Thus, this obligation is in place in all eras, even in the present when no *ger toshav* can be accepted, and it is obligatory on all individuals who can work toward this goal. So too, this commandment is not limited to the case when we can force [others to obey]—meaning that in a situation where we cannot use force, we could be excused from our obligation—since the essence of the obligation is to do all that is in our power to ensure that the seven Noachide commandments are kept, whether such can be done through force or through other means of pleasantness and peace, which means that one should explain [to Noachides] that they should accept the wishes of God, who commanded them in these rules. This is obviously what is intended by Maimonides.[51]

Rabbi Schneerson concludes his responsum as follows:

From all of the above, it is clear that anyone who has in one's ability to influence, in any way, a Noachide to keep the seven commandments, that person has an obligation to do so, since that was commanded to Moses our teacher. Certainly, for anyone who has connections with Noachides in areas of commerce and the like, it is proper to sustain the connection in order to convince and explain to that person—in a way that will reach that person's heart—that God commanded Noachides to keep the seven commandments...[52]

Rabbi Schneerson's view is unique in that he not only assumes that Maimonides is correct in ruling that there is a general obligation to compel gentiles to observe Noachide law, but he also assumes that the obligation to compel observance includes within it the obligation to persuade. Rabbi Schneerson thus extends to the obligation to cover a much greater area than any other rabbinic authority, both in terms of the responsibility to do so and in the means by which to do so.

Conclusion

We began this essay with a general analysis of Noachide law and the obligation for Jews to abide by it. We then showed that even though Maimonides appears to rule that Jews are obligated to use force to get gentiles to obey the Noachide law, many authorities (both medieval and modern) reject Maimonides' opinion and deny that there is any halakhic obligation for individual Jews to compel gentiles to observe Noachide law. We concluded with the fascinating position of Rabbi Menachem Mendel Schneerson of Lubavitch, who argues that Jews do have an obligation to force gentiles to observe Noachide law when it is possible to do so, and to encourage them when it is not possible to use force.

The difference between these two opinions regarding Jews' relationship to the Noachide law informs one's views on the moral imperative of *tikkun olam*. Is repairing the world a matter of participating in justice by coercing people to act justly, or does it lie in persuading people to live more humanely? The answer to that question lies in how one perceives the relationship between Jews and Noachide law.

NOTES

[1] B. Shevuot 39a.

[2] The Noachide commandments are deemed to be normative for non-Jews, and

were considered by the rabbis to be prescriptive for Jews before the giving of the Torah (B. Ḥullin 100b). The Noachide legal system consists of seven general instructions concerning adjudication, idolatry, blasphemy, sexual immorality, bloodshed, robbery, and eating a limb torn from a living animal (T. Avodah Zarah 8:4–6; B. Sanhedrin 56a–b), and they are identified as being within the first commandment given to the first human being: "And the Eternal, God, commanded regarding the human saying, 'Of every tree of the garden you may certainly eat'" (Genesis 2:16). Even though the laws were given to the first human being, they are still called the "Noachide laws," since humanity is considered to be descended from Noah after the flood. The general nature of the Noachide laws allows for the existence of differences in moral temperament among different societies, even if the broader ethical outlines are the same. Given a certain location, customs can develop that may differ from those in other places due to the constraints of geography, demography, and economy. With varying customs will come varying social perspectives and, hence, different nuances in moral temperament. The relationship between law and ethics is therefore easier to see through a more comprehensive legal system, such as Jewish law, than through a more general one.

[3] B. Sanhedrin 56a.

[4] In his commentary on M. Ḥullin 7:6. In M.T. Hilkhot Melakhim U-milḥemoteihem (subsequently referenced as Hilkhot Melakhim), Maimonides writes specifically, with respect to gentiles, that a wise person is one who accepts the Noachide laws not out of intellectual conviction alone, but from a belief that God commanded their observance (8:11). This seems to be the most plausible interpretation of this halakhah, as supported by textual and contextual analysis. See, however, Steven S. Schwarzschild's "Do Noachides Have to Believe in Revelation? (A Passage in Dispute between Maimonides, Spinoza, Mendelssohn, and H. Cohen): A Contribution to a Jewish View of Natural Law," originally published in 1962 in the *Jewish Quarterly Review* but now available in *The Pursuit of the Ideal: Jewish Writings of Steven Schwarzschild*, ed. Menachem Kellner (Albany: State University of New York Press, 1990), pp. 29–60.

[5] See Rabbi Yosef Engel, *Beit Otzar Marekhet* (Petrokov, 5663), vol.1, §1:7, 9: "The seven Noachide commandments are still obligatory on Jews, and their authority derives from their pre-Sinai obligation. The Torah…merely added to Noachide laws…"

[6] Rabbi Meir Simḥah of Dvinsk, *Or Samei'aḥ, Issurei Biah* 3:2.

[7] Rabbi Yeḥiel Yaakov Weinberg, *S'ridei Eish* 3:22; Rabbi Menashe Klein, *Mishnah Halakhot* 9:278 also agrees with this.

[8] See Auerbach's appendix, included in Rabbi Pinḥas Ḥayyim Sheinman, "T'shuvah B'inyan Y'ladim M'fagrim L'gabbei Ḥinnukh U-mitzvot," in Moriah 11:9–10 (1982), pp 51–65.

[9] See *Ig'rot Moshe, Yoreh Dei·ah* 1:6, where Rabbi Feinstein discusses whether one who is legally excused from observance of positive commandments generally

because of blindness (according to one opinion) is nonetheless obligated to follow the Noachide laws.

[10] Note that the terms "gentile" and "Noachide" are not synonymous, but in fact refer to different populations. The term "gentile" refers to all of humanity, excluding the Jewish people. The term "Noachide" refers specifically to the gentile population living in the Land of Israel who obey Noachide law at a time when the Sanhedrin is the legal authority of an autonomous Jewish state.

[11] M.T. Hilkhot Melakhim 9:14. The story of Dinah and Shechem is told in Genesis 34.

[12] See generally Abraham Sofer, *T'shuvot Hakhmei Provence* (Jerusalem, 5227), §48, at p. 143, which clearly distinguishes between regulations based on the Noachide laws and regulations based on the law of the land or the law of the king. For more on this distinction, see Arnold Enker, "Aspects of Interaction Between the Torah Law, the King's Law, and the Noachide Law in Jewish Criminal Law," in *Cardozo Law Review* 12 (1991), pp. 1137–1156.

[13] Commentary of Naḥmanides to Genesis 34:14.

[14] Responsa of Rema, responsum no. 10 (ed. Asher Siev; Yeshiva University Press, 1970). His ruling is also accepted by Ḥatam Sofer, *Hoshen Mishpat* 91 and Rabbi Yaakov Lorberbaum (of Lissa, also called Leszno), Responsa *Naḥalat Yaakov* 2:3 (Breslau, 1849).

[15] See Rabbi Y. Elḥanan Spector, *Naḥal Yitzḥak, Ḥoshen Mishpat* (Vilna, 5644), §91, p. 280; Rabbi Abraham Isaiah Karelitz, *Ḥazon Ish*, on M.T. Hilkhot Melakhim 10:10 and M. Bava Kamma 10:3 (Jerusalem, 1972); Rabbi Isser Zalman Meltzar, *Even Ha-azel, Ḥovel U-mazzik* 8:5 (Jerusalem, 1955); Rabbi Yeḥiel Michel Epstein, *Arukh Ha-shulḥan He-atid, Hilkhot M'lakhim* 79:15 (Mosad Harav Kook, 2003); Rabbi Naftali Tzvi Yehudah Berlin, *Ha·ameik She·eilah* 2:3 (Mosad Harav Kook, 1960); Rabbi Abraham Kook, *Eitz Hadar* 38, 184 (Bar Ilan Responsa Project, version 22, 2014); Rabbi Tzvi Pesaḥ Frank, *Har Tzvi, Oraḥ Ḥayyim* II (Kuntres Mili D'berakhot 2:1) (Bar Ilan Responsa Project, version 22, 2014); Rabbi Ovadia Yosef, *Y'ḥavveh Da·at* 4:65 (Bar Ilan Responsa Project, version 22, 2014); Rabbi Yitzḥak Yaakov Weiss, *Minḥat Yitzḥak* 4:52:3 (Bar Ilan Responsa Project, version 22, 2014). For a more complete analysis of this issue see Nahum Rakover, "Jewish Law and the Noachide Obligation to Preserve Social Order," in *Cardozo Law Review* 12 (1991), pp. 1073–1136.

[16] *Dina d'malkhuta dina* ("the law of the land is the law") is a halakhic principle that means that *halakhah* incorporates the law of the land in which Jews live into the Jewish legal framework; therefore, where *dina d'malkhuta dina* applies, observance of secular law becomes a halakhic obligation as well. For further discussion of this principle, see B. Bava Kamma 113a, Nedarim 28a, Bava Batra 54b–55a, and Gittin 10b, with their relevant commentaries.

[17] Ḥazon Ish, commenting on Bava Kamma chap. 10, n. 15.

[18] Maimonides, M.T. Hilkhot Melakhim 8:10. In explaining the source for this ruling of Maimonides, Rabbi Karo states in *Kesef Mishnah* to M.T. Hilkhot Milah 1:6 that "Rabbeinu [Moshe ben Maimon = Maimonides] learned this

rule from what is stated in Sanhedrin 57a"; see also B. Yevamot 48a. The dispute between Maimonides and others revolve around the talmudic statement that "on account of seven commandments Noachides are killed" (B. Sanhedrin 57a). Maimonides believes that this not limited to judicial punishment in a court of twenty-three when the Sanhedrin is functioning (as is required to execute a Jew for a violation), but includes "extra-judicial" activity. Maimonides believes that this is not limited to judicial punishment in a court of twenty-three when the Sanhedrin is functioning (as is required to execute a Jew for a violation), but includes "extra-judicial" activity; others limit this statement to judicially sanctioned executions by Jewish courts.

[19] Maimonides, M.T. Hilkhot Melakhim 10:11. As noted by Radbaz (Rabbi David ben Solomon ibn Abi Zimra [c. 1479–1573]), commenting on Hilkhot Melakhim 10:14, *ab initio* it is preferable that Noachides serve as judges on their own tribunals; it is only *ex post facto* that Jews should seek such roles. We would suggest that the rationale for this assertion is that it is generally better that a *mitzvah* be performed directly by the one commanded to do it and not through an agent. In this case, the *mitzvah* is *dinim*; the Noachide is the principal (because he is obligated to establish laws) and the Jew would be the agent. It is worth noting that Maimonides explicitly adopts a universalistic formulation of the obligation to love our Maker in his *Sefer Ha-mitzvot*, positive commandment # 3.

[20] Maimonides, M.T. Hilkhot Milah 1:6. Ravad notes, "Nowadays we cannot kill a person." See below for a discussion of this assertion.

[21] The question, as it relates to a *ger toshav*, is more theoretical than practical since the status of *ger toshav* does not apply today. For a discussion of who is a *ger toshav*, see Rabbi Berel Wein, *Ḥekrai Halakhot* 5:45 (Jerusalem: Mosad Harav Kook, 1988) and Rabbi Yeḥiel Michel Epstein, *Arukh Ha-shulḥan He-atid, Hilkhot Yovel* §49 (Jerusalem: Mosad Harav Kook, 2003).

[22] Quoting Rabbi Shlomo ben Shimon Duran (Rashbash).

[23] See Encyclopedia *Talmudit* 3:359–360. The presumption is that universal commandments (i.e., those given as part of Noachide law prior to the revelation at Sinai) are binding only on Jews, unless they were repeated at Sinai.

[24] Rabbi Zvi Chajes, *Responsa Maharatz Ḥayyot* §2, as reproduced in *Kol Kitvei Maharatz Ḥayyot* 2 (Jerusalem, 1958), p. 614.

[25] *Arukh Ha-shulḥan, Yoreh Dei·ah* 267:12–13 (Jerusalem: Mosad HaRav Kook, 2003).

[26] *Mishp'tei M'lukhah*, 2d ed. (New York, 1950), pp. 232–234.

[27] *Amud Y'mini*, 3rd ed. (Jerusalem, 2000), 12:1:12.

[28] *Torah Sh'leimah* (Jerusalem, 1982), 17:220.

[29] See Karo's *Kesef Mishnah* commentary to M.T. Hilkhot Milah 1:6. Similar sentiments regarding the opinion of Maimonides can be found in *Leḥem Mishneh*, commenting to M.T. Hilkhot Avodah Zarah 10:1.

[30] *Mitzvah* 192 (*parshat Aḥarei Mot*).

[31] Tosafot are medieval commentators on the Talmud who lived in northern

France and the German Rhineland, the centers of Ashkenazic Jewry in the medieval period.

[32] Comment to M.T. Hilkhot Milah 1:6.

[33] Commentary of Naḥmanides on Deuteronomy 20:1 and 20:11.

[34] Tosafot to B. Avodah Zarah 26b, s.v. *v'lo mor'dim*.

[35] Cf. Rashi's comment to Deuteronomy 20:1, 11, which cites only the obligation of taxation, and omits the obligation of observance of the Noachide commandments. This is also in harmony with Rashi's opinion that Noachide slaves of Jews are not required to observe Noachide law (B. Yevamot 48a, s.v. *eved ish v'lo eved ishah*), and it is consistent with his broad conception of *dina d'malkhuta* (noted in his comment at B. Gittin 9b, s.v. *k'sheirin*). Merely because there is an obligation to obey does not necessarily imply an obligation for Jews to assist in enforcement. It may be inferred that that concept is present in Noachide law, also according to those who accept Nahmanides' general framework; see Nahmanides on Genesis 34:11.

[36] Responsa of Rashba 1:59 (Jerusalem: Machon Yerushalayim, 1999).

[37] *Hagahot Ashrei, Avodah Zarah* 64b (printed in the standard Vilna Shas, on the fifth chapter of Avodah Zarah).

[38] A conditional slave is one that is acquired with the explicit condition that conversion not be done; Maimonides nonetheless explicitly required such an individual to observe the Noachide law (see M.T. Hilkhot Milah 1:6).

[39] The opinion of Rabbi Karo in the Shulḥan Arukh itself is unclear. In Yoreh Dei·ah 276:4, Karo appears to simply disallow any temporary slavery absent circumcision, and thus he does not even discuss the imposition of Noachide law. However, in his commentary on the Tur, *Beit Yosef* commenting on Yoreh Dei·ah 267 (s.v. *v'ha-Rambam*), Karo appears to accept the approach of Maimonides. On commenting on that passages in his *Bedek Ha-bayit* (on his final notes in the book), he appears to retract this ruling and make this whole issue conditional on the presence of a *ger toshav* (resident alien)—something that is currently impossible, in his opinion. Thus, it appears that he rules that these rules are applicable currently, in *Kesef Mishnah* and in *Beit Yosef* (in accordance with Maimonides); but in *Bedek Ha-bayit* he rules that (at the least) Maimonides' opinion is inapplicable currently, or the *halakhah* is not in accordance with Maimonides. The Shulḥan Arukh itself is unclear on this matter. See generally Ḥayim Hiskai Medini, *S'deih Ḥemed* (New York, 1964), 9:16, for a discussion of these types of situations in the writings of Rabbi Karo. One is inclined to understand the Shulḥan Arukh as being in agreement with the Rema in this instance.

[40] Yoreh Dei·ah 158, s.v. *rebbeinu u-mikol makom*. For more on this, see the uncensored version of *Beit Yosef Ḥoshen Mishpat* 425 that has recently been incorporated into various new and uncensored editions of the Tur.

[41] Tur, Yoreh Dei·ah 158:1.

[42] See his *Bayit Ḥadash* commentary on the *Arba·ah Turim* of Rabbi Jacob ben Asher, Yoreh Dei·ah 158, s.v. *u-mikol makom*.

43 See his *Drisha* commentary on Tur, Yoreh Dei·ah 158:1. Similar sentiments can be found in his commentary on the Shulḥan Arukh, the *Sefer Me'irat Einayim* (also called the *Sema*) oshen Mishpat 425:15–19, in his attempts to distinguish gentiles from heretics.

44 Rabbi Moshe Isserles, commenting on Tur, Yoreh Dei·ah 158, s.v. *ein mor'dim*. For a long discussion of this topic that reinforces this understanding of the *halakhah*, see the commentary of Rabbi Yoḥanan Kramnetzor, *Arukh Meishar* on *Darkhei Moshe, Yoreh Dei·h* 158.

45 Yoreh Dei·ah 158:1.

46 Rabbi Shabbetai ben Meir Ha-kohen (called the Shakh) in his *Siftei Kohein* commentary to Yoreh Dei·ah 158:2. It is worth noting that he cites Rabbi Shlomo Luria, in his *Yam Shel Shlomo* commentary on *Sefer Mitzvot Ha-gadol* (*Semag*), *mitzvah* 48, as being in agreement with that. The Shakh in his *N'kudat Ha-kesef*, commenting on the same passage, is equally clear on this issue. (All of these commentaries are found in the standard edition of the Shulḥan Arukh or *Sefer Mitzvot Ha-gadol* [popularly called the *S'mag*].)

47 See his *Turei Zahav* commentary (commonly called the *Taz*) to S.A. Yoreh Dei·ah 158:1.

48 Yoreh Dei·ah 158:2.

49 Rabbi Judah the Pious, *Sefer Ḥasidim*, ed. Reuben Margoliot (Jerusalem: Mosad Harav Kook, 2004), §1124. And in this regard, cf. also Jonah 3:1–10.

50 Found in Maimonides, M.T. Hilkhot Melakhim 8:10.

51 Rabbi Menachem Mendel Schneerson, "*Sheva Mitzvot B'nei No·aḥ*," in *HaPardes* 59:9 (5745 [1985]), pp. 7–11. This responsum has been reprinted in a number of places; see, e.g., Rabbi Shmuel Tuvia Stern, *T'shuvot Ha-shavit, Oraḥ Ḥayyim* 7:1 (2nd ed., 2005). For Rabbi Stern's reply, see idem, *Ḥoshen Mishpat* 8:3 (2nd ed., 2005), asserting that Maimonides' ruling is limited to enforcing acceptance, rather than observance.

52 However, even Rabbi Schneerson concedes that the obligation to induce compliance is limited to situations where "no financial loss is caused, even the loss of future profits." This limitation is itself a little difficult, as *halakhah* does not generally recognize "loss of profit" as a mitigating claim.

Mi-p'nei Tikkun Ha-olam (In Order to Preserve the Social Good): Chinks in the System, Humility, and Mimesis

Melanie Landau

If my life was hooked up to a GPS, you'd constantly hear "recalculating."

Every wisdom tradition I know urges us to cultivate active awareness of our mortality—because keeping that simple reality before our eyes enhances our appreciation of life, even when things get tough. It also increases the odds that we will come to some new resolve about how we want to live.

—*Parker Palmer*[1]

Humans are so fallible, so far from perfected beings. And yet, for many reasons—including our own fears and insecurities—we are often scared to notice ourselves and show each other exactly how imperfect we are. As mortal beings our impending physical death is a stark reminder of our very real limits. This essay explores how the concept of *mi-p'nei tikkun ha-olam* (which I propose to translate as "in order to preserve the social good") serves as a model of how we as humans can be more forthright about our own vulnerabilities and chinks. It functions as an open acknowledgment of chinks in the traditional Jewish legal system and it articulates efforts to repair those chinks. By experiencing the process of acknowledgment and repair in relation to the halakhic system, we can also internalize the possibility of what such acknowledgment and repair may mean for us as individuals. However, perhaps more importantly than that, we may find an opportunity to claim the sense of vulnerability, humility, and not knowing that being human and being fallible implies. This means dropping the pressure of having to be something we are not.

It is important to emphasize that the idea of having imperfections is not simply a fall from an ideal version of the human being; rather, it is an important part of what is actually means to be human, enabling us to unfold ourselves in a process of growth and transformation. It is only through this process that one can truly embody that aspect of infinity that being created in the image of the Divine connotes. It is because humans are in relationship with the infinite Divine that we can continue to grow and change and learn. The Ishbitzer *rebbe*, Rabbi Mordechai Yosef Leiner (1801–1854), frames human experience and understanding as an ongoing process. In the section on the Torah portion *Yitro* in the *Mei Ha-shilo·ah*, his book of hasidic teachings arranged according to the weekly Torah portions, he says that there is great importance in the fact that the text of the Ten Commandments presents God using an unusual first-person pronoun, anokhi, instead of the more common form *ani*. This, the author suggests, is not accidental: the word *anokhi*, he teaches, is comprised of the word *ani* ("I") and a *kaf ha-dimayon* (the letter of the Hebrew alphabet that means "like," thereby creating a simile) added to it:

> And if God's name were only written as "I" [as *ani*] it would be as if God had, so to speak, revealed all divine light in its entirety without the opportunity for further deepening…the *kaf* [the letter present in *anokhi* that is lacking in *ani*] shows that it is not whole but only a likeness, an estimation of the great light that the Divine will reveal in the future…As a person more deeply comprehends Torah wisdom, one sees how until this moment one had been in darkness.[2]

The nature of the spiritual pursuit is that it keeps unfolding. What we think we know at one point, we come to see in a new light, at a later point. That is what it means to be human, to be in time, and to be in relationship. This is also mirrored in scientific and social knowledge, as well as in our knowledge of Torah. When we learn Torah and understand it, it seems like light to us. In time, we come to see that what was light becomes dark and something else has become light. It is the same with our lives.

Knowing and remembering this limitation and possibility, we cannot but approach our lives with a degree of humility. We are constantly in process, beings unfolding in learning and understanding.

We carry out our lives and relationships with the limited yet great awareness and attention available to us at the moment. Living in time as humans, we do not know the end of things; in a sense we have intention, we carry out actions, and we hope for the best. The ultimate end, our inevitable death, is also not known to us and in a sense that is the mystery that dominates our life, consciously or not.

Those of us defining ourselves as adherents of—or as living our lives in relation to—the halakhic system often look to it to provide us with guidance, to aid us in putting one foot after the other, of having some knowns, some structure and boundaries, in a world of so many unknowns and of potential chaos and falling apart. At least, let us fall apart when there is something holding us! It is the chinks in the halakhic system, drawn out explicitly by the sages, that I want to call attention to in this essay. These chinks in the system are the laws that were modified *mi-p'nei tikkun ha-olam* ("in order to preserve the social good"), so that exercising a certain halakhic stipulation or practice would not result in undesirable consequences for society.

In the cases we are examining, we shall see that there is one halakhic position expressed by the *halakhah* itself, and then a counter-position expressed in the rabbinic enactment to the *halakhah*. The rabbis are modeling, through the use of *mi-p'nei tikkun ha-olam*, how we can become that walking Torah, human beings who embody the bringing together of different opinions. This is the true meaning of the rabbinic remark that Torah scholars by their very existence increase peace in the world[3]—which includes creating space inside the self for holding conflicting opinions and multiple possibilities, and for staying away from either/or paradigms that increase polarization and may even lead to enmity.

We will now examine more closely how the rabbis used this instrument of enactments made *mi-p'nei tikkun ha-olam*—which may be considered as a model of being able to rework something when it doesn't have the consequences that we intend. Interestingly, the phrase appears ten times in the Mishnah and many of those times in relationship to laws of divorce. Only a man can give a Jewish divorce to his wife, not the other way around. If the husband refuses to grant a divorce, then the wife is ostensibly bound to him until he releases her. She is called an *agunah* (literally, "a chained woman") or a *m'surevet get*, someone to whom a Jewish divorce has been refused. In a sense, the rabbis of the Mishnah may have been pre-empting the problems and heartache that these laws have caused women throughout history, of which awareness and activism around the issue has strengthened in the last few decades.

As mentioned above, the power to grant a divorce is solely in the hands of the husband. There were many ways in which men could exercise their right concerning the get that could be problematic for women. For example, the Mishnah relates:

> At first, a man [who had already sent his wife a *get* by means of a messenger] would set up a *beit din* (court) in a different place [from where the wife lived] and cancel the *get*. Rabban Gamliel the Elder established (*hitkin*) that this should not be done, for the sake of *tikkun ha-olam*.[4]

In this case, a man sent his wife a *get* through a messenger but then changed his mind about the divorce; he could annul the *get* after it had already been dispatched, with no guarantee that the woman would know that it had been annulled. The woman who received the *get* could later *get* remarried, relying on its strength—without realizing that the original *get* had been cancelled. This remarriage would then in fact be forbidden (since the woman is still technically married to her first husband), resulting in problematic ramifications for any children born out of the new union: they would be considered *mamzeirim*, who can only marry other *mamzeirim*. Therefore, a decree was established by Rabban Gamliel that a husband may not cancel a *get* by means of a *beit din*—specifically to avoid confusion over the status of the divorce, and in order to avoid unintentional adultery and to assuage fears of illicit remarriage.

In this case, the practice that was banned *mi-p'nei tikkun ha-olam*—namely, annulling a *get* through a court—was, technically, permitted. However, since it could lead to problems for the system as a whole, it was changed. This process, whereby an original law is altered by enacting a decree, evinces a rabbinic self-awareness of humility and fallibility, as well as the need for human rabbinic agency to act in order to change things, when they are not working out the way they should.

Finding the internal place where we can bring together aspects of ourselves that are in tension, resonates with what the rabbis sought to do through enactments made *mi-p'nei tikkun ha-olam*. These can be seen as "self-correcting," offering imminent critique to the halakhic system, in a transparent way. By observing their method, we may come to learn to take joy in the transformative process of our own personal growth.

Maintaining that relationship between things in tension with each other—between the original version and the new improved one—is not always an easy dance. Rabbi Abraham Isaac Kook (1865–1935) was a great teacher in the area of embracing paradox.[5] In fact, he maintains that in order to reach our potential of service to the Divine, we *must* somehow touch that place of paradox. He writes, in *Eight Notebooks*:

> Sometimes from an excess of fear/awe more than one's soul can sustain, a person comes to hate Torah. And each person needs to measure his or her soul, and whenever the flow

of moralistic thoughts are overpowering, and all the good inside feels as if it has disappeared, one will find in oneself all the dross and all the lack in the world; one shouldn't hold up one's hands and be shocked, and one should know that within all of this is hidden much goodness. And one should also know that within all the many reprimands in the texts—even though through them one can despair greatly—inside them is hidden the light of life and of salvation, a great kindness and bravery of heart. And it is precisely from the depth of the falling that one comes to the depth of rising...and from the emptiness of Torah that is inside one will come to love of Torah, and one will be empowered by its greatness and its beauty. And the disconnection of desire can bring everything to goodness. And one will be wise and will understand that the situation of the broken world is also for good and for blessing, and to give life the Divine made it, and the end of everything will be a complete fixing.[6]

In this teaching, Rav Kook is warning against polarization to any particular side. Yet, at the same time he acknowledges that the extreme movement in one direction will give rise to its opposite movement— that is, from an extreme falling down, the opposite uplifting will emerge. At once, he is acknowledging both that we can have a "depth of falling" where a person "comes to hate Torah," and yet also that from this very place, from "the emptiness of Torah," one can come to a love of Torah and be "empowered by its greatness and beauty." This offers us a transformative paradigm: instead of judging the fall, the mistake, the darkness in negativity and disdain, we may come to regard the fall, the mistake, the darkness as a most vital process in the coming to fruition of human goodness and revelation, where the hidden becomes revealed through the process of growth.

The fact that a mechanism such as *mi-p'nei tikkun ha-olam*

exists, which allows for self-correction, actually enables much light and goodness beyond itself. The more models we have of "chinks" in the system—and "chinks" in the self—the more we can create a space of safety, where people can feel okay about showing their vulnerability. Ultimately, we will all be transformed and enriched in this process. When faced with another person showing his or her vulnerability, we cannot help but relate to them with compassion and deep understanding, acknowledging the "other" and evincing an awareness of the power of what it means to be a human being.

It is not only through rabbinic enactments *mi-p'nei tikkun ha-olam* that the sages demonstrate their capacity to be upfront about problems in the system and to work toward their solutions. We can see another example of this in the following excerpt from the Babylonian Talmud, where the wealthy Rav Ashi (an amoraic sage and himself an editor of the Talmud) realizes that he has made a mistake and corrects himself:

> Ravina asked Rav Ashi: "What does one do about the knives on Passover?" He replied, "I provide [make] new ones for myself."
> "That is well for you, who can [afford] this," said [Ravina] to him, "[but] what about one who cannot [afford] this?" [Ravina] replied, "I mean like new ones: [I thrust] their handles in loam, and their blades in fire, and then I place their handles in boiling water. But the law is: both the one and the other [need only be put] into boiling water, and in a 'first' vessel."[7]

In this case, Ravina asked Rav Ashi what he does with knives during Passover, when one cannot use the same dishes and utensils as the rest of the year. At first, Rav Ashi answers that he has new knives for Passover. Ravina responds that this is fine for Rav Ashi, because he can afford to do so; but what about the people who cannot afford new knives? Rav Ashi's response to this challenge is remarkable: he goes back on what he has just said and, rephrasing his answer, totally changes its meaning. It's not that he *actually* gets new knives, he now explains, but it is as *if* his knives are new. And this feat he accomplishes by sticking the blades in the earth and immersing the handles in boiling water. (The Talmud rules that both the handle and the blade can be made new—and hence fit for Passover—through placing them in a "first" vessel, which is the technical term for a vessel that is directly on the fire and assumed to have a certain degree of heat and capability to purify.) The point here has less to do with the halakhic status of knives, and more with Rav Ashi's willingness to adjust his practice, in order to place the law within the grasp of ordinary people who do not share his wealth—thus providing some ancient analogue to Kant's categorical imperative. I understand this to mean that Rav Ashi is depicted not just as someone who thinks about what he himself is doing, but as a leader, who is obliged to consider whether he is setting a reasonable example for others, which can be easily emulated.

Rav Ashi demonstrates his own capacity to learn in the moment. Up until Ravina challenged his response, he had one answer. After Ravina challenged his response, he adjusted it so that his teaching was more resonant with his values, and so that his teaching could be more universally applicable to his community, and to future communities. This anecdote, relating an interchange between Rav Ashi and Ravina, takes place within the context of discussions about how ritual requirements may, at times, be at odds with social values— and how the ritual requirements can be adjusted so that they don't breach social values. At the same time, due care is given to respect, and not to shame, other rabbis—even if one may not agree with their judgment in a certain case.

The rabbinic category of *mi-p'nei tikkun ha-olam* applies to enactments that were made by the rabbis as they tinkered with the halakhic system in order to preserve the social good; it is an important reminder of the importance of transparency and openness. In the case of their legal enactments, the rabbis expose the flaws of the system and correct them. And outside of the halakhic system, we can use this model in our lives as human beings, as well—if we see that being alive means that we humans are in a constant process of learning and growing. This is a good thing. We were, and are, meant to be this way. When faced with the necessity to change, we can also adopt the flexibility to know that we are not going to be getting it right all the time, and for good reason. Without shame or denial, we must always feel called upon continually to recalibrate, concomitantly attending to the chinks in our own spiritual lives as well as to those in the legal system.

NOTES

1 Parker Palmer, "How Then Shall I Live?" (May 21, 2014), at www.onbeing. org/blog/how-then-shall-i-live/632.

[2] Mordechai Yosef Leiner, *Sefer Mei Ha-shilo·aḥ* (ed. Brooklyn, 1984), p. 25a, s.v. *anokhi*.

[3] B. Berakhot 64a.

[4] M. Gittin 4:2.

[5] Rav Kook was the first Ashkenazic chief rabbi of the British mandatory Palestine and one of the foremost Jewish thinkers of the twentieth century.

[6] Abraham Isaac Kook, *Sh'monah K'vatzim* (ed. Jerusalem, 5759 [=1998–1999]), 6:88, p. 216.

[7] B. Pesaḥim 30b.

Darkhei Shalom: Communities Built on Peace and Harmony Repair the World

Raḥel Berkovits

In rabbinic thought, harmonious interactions among people and the pursuit of peace, *darkhei shalom*, are presented as crucial values that will lead to ultimate repair of the world. Respecting and acknowledging the feelings and emotions of all of human beings created by God leads to building communities that reflect God's image in the world as a whole. The larger rabbinic concept of *tikkun ha-olam*,[1] of which *darkhei shalom* is an integral part, first appears in the Mishnah, in the fourth and fifth chapters of Gittin, the tractate that deals with Jewish divorce law. The first *mishnah* in the series about *tikkun ha-olam* (4:2) discusses the laws of divorce and so, from a technical perspective, one can understand the unit's placement specifically in this tractate. However, it seems that the editor of the Mishnah is presenting a deeper, more meaningful idea with this placement. The unit on *tikkun ha-olam* appears in the middle of a tractate that focuses on the ultimate breakdown of human relationships; it seems that this literary placement is intended to express the rabbis' view that in working to repair the world at large, people need to expend effort first and foremost in the realm of their interpersonal interactions. The importance of harmonious interpersonal relations also figures prominently in the last two *mishnayot* of the unit (5:8–9[2]), which specifically deal with rules governing human behavior and interaction undertaken in the interest of peace. Interestingly, these latter *mishnayot* use a different phrase to explain the rationale behind the laws: *mi-p'nei darkhei shalom* ("in the interest of peace"), rather than the phrase *mi-p'nei tikkun ha-olam* ("for the sake of repairing the world") that is found throughout the earlier part of the unit.[3]

However, the effect of the literary construction is striking: anchoring these *mishnayot* that invoke *tikkun ha-olam* and *darkhei shalom* together in this two-chapter unit, in the midst of legal material concerning divorce, indicates that harmonious interpersonal interactions lies at the heart of creating a more just world at large.

The thematic link between *tikkun olam* and *darkhei shalom* is strengthened by repeated ideas and language, as many of the words in the first half of chapter 5 are repeated in the final *mishnayot* (5:8–9), which list actions undertaken "in the interests of peace."[4] Moreover, similar general themes also appear in both sections of the chapter.[5] Also creating a link and parallel structure between the two chapters, both chapter 4 and chapter 5 end with a *mishnah* (4:9 and 5:9) about interactions between Jews and non-Jews, land, and agricultural commandments (which will be discussed further below).

Legally, the laws that are grounded in a concern for *tikkun olam* and those that are grounded in a concern for *darkhei shalom* function in a similar manner. Common to both sets of laws is a proposed deviation from the basic application of the *halakhah*. Although certain behaviors might technically be licit, they could lead to an undesirable outcome; therefore, in order to right a moral ambiguity, have society function in an optimal manner, or foster peace between people, the rabbis "repair" the law and require people to adhere to a different standard. For example, in the case of *tikkun olam* (5:3), to ensure that people will try to return lost objects to their rightful owners, the finders will not be required to swear that they honestly have returned the entire package and did not keep anything for themselves, despite the fact that legally the owners could require them to do so. Similarly, in a case of *darkhei shalom* (5:8), to ensure that a deaf-mute, the mentally disabled, or a minor does not feel angered, hurt, aggrieved, and robbed, one is forbidden to take from them an object that they found (for which the owners cannot be identified), even though legally it would be permitted to do so (since people of their status—lacking adult cognizance—cannot legally acquire objects for themselves).

With the examples done in the interests of peace, explained below, the deviation in law is sometimes done despite the legal reality (as in the case just cited), and at other times the law prescribes a particular behavior that otherwise is legally not required.

Ten situations and the appropriate behavior for each one, to avoid strife between people, appear in Mishnah Gittin 5:8–9. The list is introduced with the statement: "These are the things they [the rabbis] said in the interests of peace"; and the theme is reinforced by the repetition of the phrase "in the interests of peace" (*mi-p'nei darkhei shalom*) to explain each example. Some of the examples create order and give rules and guidelines where none are legally prescribed, so as to avoid situations that could lead to discord, argument, and in-fighting. Other cases ensure that individuals go beyond the legal norms to prevent other people from feeling hurt and mistreated. The choice of specifically ten examples, and the knowledge that these cases cannot possibly be the only ones in which human beings need guidance on how to avoid enmity and strife, suggest that these examples were chosen not just because of the specific laws that are contained within them, but also because they convey some broader message and represent paradigmatic ideas on the topic of fostering peaceful and harmonious interactions between people.

A closer examination and reading of the text is required to understand the rabbinic message embedded within it[6]:

Mishnah Tractate Gittin 5:8

These are the things they said in the interests [literally "ways"] of peace (*mi-p'nei darkhei shalom*):

[1]   A priest reads [from the Torah] first, and after him a Levite, and after him an Israelite—in the interests of peace [i.e., to prevent fighting about who should receive which *aliyah*].

[2]   An *eiruv* [consisting of food, to enable carrying objects in a joint courtyard on Shabbat] is placed in the old [i.e., previously

used for this purpose] house [in the courtyard]—in the interests of peace.[7]

[3]   The cistern [used to water fields] that is nearest to the [head of the] canal is filled [from it] first, in the interests of peace [to prevent fighting between the field owners, each of whom has to take a turn to stop up the canal to fill their cistern].

[4]   [The taking of] animals, birds, and fish from traps [set by others] is counted as a kind of robbery [even though legally the animals have not yet been acquired by the trap-setter, for he has not yet taken possession of them]—in the interests of peace.
        Rabbi Yossi says it is actual robbery.

[5]   [To take away] anything found by a deaf-mute, a mentally incompetent person, or a minor is counted as a kind of robbery [even though legally they do not have the full cognizance required to acquire objects]—in the interests of peace.
        Rabbi Yossi says it is actual robbery.

[6]   A poor person who gleans [by hitting] on the top of an olive tree, [if another takes the fruit] that is beneath him it is counted as a kind of robbery [even though the poor person did not yet legally acquire them by physically taking possession].
        Rabbi Yossi says it is actual robbery.

[7]   We do not prevent the poor non-Jews from gathering gleanings (*leket*), forgotten sheaves (*shikh·ḥah*), and the corner of the field (*pei·ah*) [which were left for the Jewish poor]—in the interests of peace.

Mishnah Tractate Gittin 5:9

[8]   A woman may lend to her friend, who issuspected [of transgressing the laws] of the Sabbatical year, a fine sieve, or a coarse sieve, or a hand mill, or an oven [even though the friend may be using them with ingredients which are prohibited] but she [the lender, who does keep the laws of the Sabbatical year]

must not sift nor grind with her [friend].

[9]   The wife of a *haveir* [a member of the elite rabbinic faction who is scrupulous in the observance of ritual purity and tithes] may lend to the wife of an *am ha-aretz* [one who is suspected of transgressing the laws of ritual purity and tithes] a fine sieve, or a coarse sieve, and she may winnow or grind or sift with her; but when she [i.e., the wife of the *am ha-aretz*] pours the water, she [i.e., the wife of the *haveir*] must not touch it [i.e., the formed dough] with her,[9] because one does not strengthen the hand of those that transgress.[10]—And all these have only been said for the interest of peace.

[10] And they strengthen the hands of non-Jews in the Sabbatical year [by blessing their labor for success] but not the hands of Jews, and one greets (*sho·alim bi-sh'loman*) them [i.e., non-Jews]—in the interests of peace.[11]

Interestingly, each *mishnah* ends with laws concerning interactions with non-Jews, thus structurally breaking the two *mishnayot* into two parallel units. The theme of peace is doubly reinforced in the last case, as the Hebrew idiom for greeting people is to inquire about the *shalom* of another: How are you? Are you at peace?[12] Concern for the well-being of the ultimate other is the pinnacle example of the collection.

Much can be said about each case brought in these *mishnayot*, and the *g'mara* and the traditional commentaries unpack each law individually. It is instructive to consider, in each case, what creates peace and what is required to bring about harmony. Is the Mishnah simply trying to avoid fighting between people (for example, in legislating the order in which people are to receive *aliyot*, [1] above; or the order in which cisterns are to be filled, [3] above)? Or are the rabbis advocating that one must "do the right thing" even when not legally required to do so (for example, in the cases that may not technically constitute theft, but in which case people will most certainly feel that they have been robbed; [4], [5], and [6] above)? These important issues are beyond the scope of this essay, which will only analyze the literary structure and the ideas presented therein.

The beauty and power of these *mishnayot* lies in the thematic messages imbedded within the halakhic text. Besides delineating technically what is required in order to maintain peace, the Mishnah paints a clear picture of a community and presents a strong argument for harmonious interaction among community members. The Mishnah stresses that interactions with others should be grounded in, and reflect, the value of *shalom*/peace, and it explains that this value must even be extended to people whom one might not necessarily at first glance define as being part of the community (as will be explained below).

Why are these specific cases discussed, and why are they presented in this specific order? If one considers the physical locale in which the first four laws mentioned in M. Gittin 5:8 are operative, the settings mirror the geographic layout of a small rural town (see Diagram A):

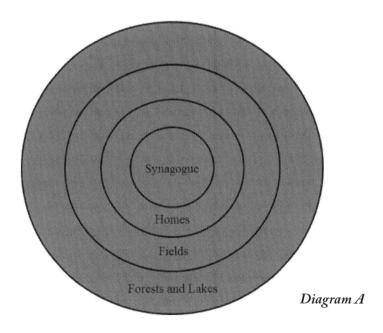

Diagram A

The synagogue lies at the center, and here the Torah is read [1]. Houses and courtyards are built around this most important edifice, and it is there that the *eiruv* is placed [2]. Surrounding the houses are the fields, water for which is supplied by the cisterns [3]. And the forests and lakes are found on the outskirts of town, and it is there that animals are trapped [4].

On closer examination, however, it becomes clear that the *mishnah* does not just describe the physical structure of a town; it also makes a statement about the people one might encounter within that community. Unrest and discord can arise in every segment of community, and the synagogue is listed at the outset as a prime example of a place in which communal in-fighting may arise. The cases listed in this mishnah begin by addressing an individual's core community and proceed outward, widening to include those on the periphery (see Diagram B):

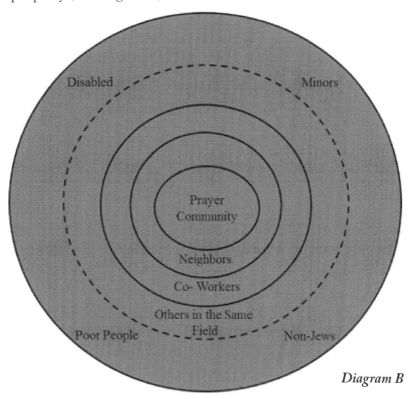

Diagram B

The nucleus of a Jew's community consists of people with similar belief systems and ritual practices. The *mishnah* includes all segments of the Jewish people—priests, Levites, and Israelites—in the description of one's prayer community, at [1]. The text then goes on to address interactions outside of the synagogue, discussing those who live nearby—one's neighbors, at [2]—and those who work nearby and with whom one must share nature's resources—one's co-workers (those in the "same field," so to speak), at [3]. The *mishnah* suggests that other people, even those with whom one does not interact daily, are still part of a Jew's community. The case involving animal traps, at [4], addresses individuals that one does not see but who work in the same profession. While such people are portrayed as peripheral, perhaps due to the solitary nature of their work, they are still within the community and need to be treated appropriately, even if one does not routinely encounter them face-to-face.

The *mishnah* then emphasizes that there are other groups who are also less visible, due to their marginalized social status: the disabled, minors, and poor people, at [5] and [6]. Yet, they are included here in the description of community specifically for that reason: they deserve the same regard and consideration allotted to others in the core community. Although, according to the majority view as expressed in the *mishnah*, the disabled and minors do not legally have a claim, due to their diminished mental capacity, and moreover they may have a lesser legal status within society as a whole, they definitely do have human feelings and emotions that are equal in importance to those of the core or full-functioning community members, and so they would be troubled if they could not keep that which they had found. Similarly, a poor person who has worked hard to glean from the top of the tree may not understand the legality of the situation, and may feel that others are stealing from him and treating him with contempt and disrespect. A community that strives to live harmoniously must not take advantage of those on the margins, but must actively acknowledge and respect their feelings as individuals worthy of respect, for they too are created in the image of God. Interestingly, the *mishnah* chooses to include in its picture of community non-Jews as well, at [7]. The *mishnah* began its description of the Jewish community by listing those included in the covenant of Torah, and it ends by acknowledging that the same high standard of human interaction must be afforded to those who may seem to be the diametrical opposite of the original group: those with different religious beliefs and practices. Not only that, but the particular laws that were set in place by the Torah itself to care for those in need within the Jewish community—such as gleaning, forgotten sheaves, and the corner of the field[13]—must be extended to those on the periphery, the poor of the non-Jewish community, as well.

Within Jewish law and community, women too are often considered to be on the sidelines of society; but in this text, which gives them their own parallel treatment (in 5:9), women become a reflection of the community as a whole. Even though (or possibly because) the sphere of women is in the home, attending to domestic chores, they have strong neighborly and communal relationships that can be a model for all. Another way of categorizing members of the Jewish community may be according to their level of religious practice and adherence to Jewish law. Inevitably, those who are punctilious in the performance of *mitzvot* are well aware of those whom they deem to have a lesser commitment to law than they themselves do. In modern times, this often leads to creating distance and separation; the different groups do not socialize and may not live in the same neighborhoods. Yet here, in the second *mishnah* (5:9), one finds two examples of interactions with Jews who do not follow *halakhah* as the rabbis would desire. At [8] the text describes a woman suspected of not following the rules of the Sabbatical year, and at [9] the case is presented of a woman who belongs to a group other than the *ḥaveirim*, the elite rabbinic faction that is scrupulous regarding observance of ritual purity and tithes. The woman is married to an ignoramus, an *am ha-aretz*—a group that the rabbis generally did not trust to keep the laws of purity and tithes correctly. In both cases, it seems that the women of the rabbinic community live close to—either next door to or in the same courtyard as—these other, less observant Jews. In fact, the woman in [8] who is suspected of transgressing the Sabbatical year is referred to as "her friend," *ḥavertah*—a word from same Hebrew root as the *ḥaveirim*, the very elite rabbinic faction mentioned in the following law, at [9]. The text instructs observant women to maintain neighborly ties and lend cooking utensils to these other women, just as long as they themselves do not transgress the law and aid in any prohibited actions. Not only is there is no requirement to reprimand the other for transgressing, but the mishnah's desire to prevent embarrassment or upset (which might occur if one were to refuse to share or help a neighbor) far outweighs the worry that it may look as if one is sanctioning a transgression.

The *mishnah* ends by once again discussing interactions with non-Jews, focusing on the fact of religious differences between people. Non-Jews are not bound by Torah law and are therefore permitted to work the land during the Sabbatical year, unlike Jews. The whole unit concludes with the idea that one should inquire after the well-being (*shalom*) of the ultimate other[14]—clearly completing the overall structure of the entire *darkhei shalom* unit.

Interestingly, the theme of greeting (*she'eilat shalom*) is also mentioned elsewhere in the Mishnah, and an examination of these other texts may shed some light on the importance the rabbis placed on the act of greeting other human beings. Mishnah Berakhot 2:1 discusses the rules about interrupting one's recitation of the Shema, the ultimate statement of faith in the Divine and the acceptance of God's reign, in order to greet or respond to others. Whether or not the interruption may be made depends on one's relationship to the other person, whether one is initiating or responding to the greeting, and whether one is in the middle of one of the three paragraphs or its surrounding blessing that comprise the *mitzvah* of reading the

Shema or at a break between the paragraphs or at a break between the paragraphs. This *mishnah* concludes with Rabbi Judah's view that "at the paragraph breaks…one responds shalom to all human beings," thus underscoring the supreme value of acknowledging others by greeting them. This link between one's belief in God and one's interactions with others is also seen at the end of the entire tractate, at Berakhot 9:5. After discussing various blessings in which one is permitted to recite God's name, the text states that one may greet another by evoking the power of God's name, just as is done with blessings and prayer: "They [the rabbis] decreed that a person should greet one's friend with the name of God [*sho·eil sh'lom haveiro b'sheim*]." This mishnah seems to be the flip side of the earlier text about the Shema—for it considers greeting another person to be a religious act, worthy of revealing God's presence in this world. Indeed, the word shalom itself is considered by the rabbis to be one of God's names (B. Shabbat 10b). To inquire about someone's well-being, to really see another person, is in fact to acknowledge the divine image imbedded within each individual. And to ignore another person while reciting the Shema, proclaiming that God is One, would ultimately be a farce. All human beings—Jews and non-Jews, men and women, young and old, rich and poor, able-bodied and not—are created in the image of God (Genesis 1:27) and so should be treated with the respect and dignity that the divine image demands. Concern for the *shalom* of all others is an acknowledgment of the divine presence in this world.

Returning to Mishnah Gittin 5:8 and the discussion about achieving harmonious interactions among people: it is important to note that the text includes the dissenting view of Rabbi Yossi ("it is actual robbery") three times (at [4], [5], and [6]). It is not unusual to find opposing voices throughout the Mishnah. However, it may seem, at first glance, somewhat ironic to include a rabbinic dispute precisely in this context of discussing peaceful community-building and the desire to avoid discord and fighting. However, including a dissenting voice on particularly this issue, of striving for peaceful interactions, forces one to notice the impressive way in which the community of *tanna·im* (the sages living in the time of the Mishnah) were able to respectfully differ and disagree with each other. One may disagree even with people from one's own core community— let alone with others, who have different commitments to law and ritual, or even different faiths and religions altogether. In the realm of ideas and the search for truth, one may—and even possibly *should*— voice disagreement. Different views should be acknowledged and respected, as one sees throughout the Mishnah. However, different opinions and ideas should not in any way impact upon how one interacts with others on a daily basis; such interactions should always be conducted respectfully and socially. An understanding of others' feelings, a respect for their well-being, and an acknowledgment that they too were created in the image of the Divine should always be at the forefront of all human interaction—despite any differences of opinion. This point alone is a lesson that any Jewish community today should strive to inculcate and emulate, and in doing so would no doubt bring a small measure of peace as part of repairing this world.

An examination of the earliest *mishnah* to present the concept of *tikkun olam*, with a verse explaining the origin of the phrase, will further solidify the link between this central concept and action undertaken in the pursuit of peace. Mishnah Gittin 4:5 presents a dispute between the schools of Hillel and Shammai concerning a person who is half free and half a slave:

> One who is half slave and half free works for his master one day and for himself one day; these are the words of the School of Hillel.
> The School of Shammai said to them: "You have repaired [benefited][15] his master, but he himself you have not repaired! To marry a[nother] slave is [legally] impossible for him, as

he is already half free. [To marry] a free woman is [legally] impossible for him, as he is still half slave. Should he be annulled [by never marrying and producing descendants]? Was not the world created only for reproduction, as it is said: 'Not as a void [did God] create it [i.e., the world; rather,] to be inhabited [did God] create it' (Isaiah 45:18)? Rather: in order to repair the world (*mi-p'nei tikkun ha-olam*), we force the master and make him a free man, and he [the slave] writes a bond [to the master] for half his worth.

The School of Hillel retracted and taught like the School of Shammai.[16]

The School of Shammai is from the earliest generation of *tanna·im*[17] to use the phrase *tikkun ha-olam,* and this *mishnah* is the only one in the entire unit concerning *tikkun olam* to bring a verse to support its enactment. In this case, the meaning of the decree is very specific. The individual in question, due to his status within human society, cannot legally marry and have children. The desire to reproduce is assumed not only to be a natural human need and right, but actually the sole purpose for which God created the world. God desires that human beings fill the world by reproducing and thus avoiding personal extinction. Repairing the world means setting it back on the course to which God had planned from the beginning—that is, with the goal of human reproduction—but which human constructs such as slavery at times seem to thwart. Although this case describes an uncommon occurrence, it is presented as the paradigmatic example of rabbinic legislation enacted to bring about the betterment of human society, for it requires both a breaking down of human social divisions and also the capability of seeing the other as an individual human being with needs and feelings. The Mishnah seems to be teaching that God wants all of God's creations to enjoy this world and inhabit it, without the distinctions between people that exist in the constructs of human society and hierarchy.

The rabbis saw it as their job to bring the world back to the state that God intended for it: one in which *all* human creation would flourish and inhabit the world. They took the example of empathy and understanding for the needs and situation of the half free man (as taught by the School of Shammai) and they expanded on it, applying the same measure of empathy toward people in other situations, beyond the narrow issue of reproduction. And so they legislated about various issues concerning divorce laws with particular sensitivity toward women (4:2, 3), and about the Sabbatical year with an eye toward the plight of poor people in need of loans (4:3). Apparently the rabbis felt that this concern and respect for the other, also created in God's image, was itself a value, worthy of its own category and legal construct. Creating and living in a peaceful community (and, ultimately, a peaceful and whole world) is not just a good thing that happens randomly to some lucky individuals; rather, one of the great goals of Jewish behavior is the pursuit of justice and peace in the world for all. The Mishnah's laws enacted *mi-p'nei darkhei shalom* are delineated specifically so that they are not lost in the larger context of the laws enacted *mi-p'nei tikkun ha-olam*— because they are important in their own right. Strict but mindless adherence to the law will not bring peace, nor will it constitute a real *tikkun ha-olam*, as God originally intended. The ideal is punctilious observance focused through a moral prism, so that one never ends up doing wrong to others by following the law, and so that concern for all people and their well-being is always at the forefront of one's thoughts and actions.

NOTES

[1] The Mishnah uses the formulation *tikkun ha-olam*, but the definite article (*ha-*) is not usually employed in modern colloquial English use of the term. In this essay, I use both locutions, *tikkun olam* and *tikkun ha-olam*, interchangeably.

[2] In the Kaufman manuscript, they appears as *mishnayot* 9 and 10.

[3] The phrase *mi-p'nei tikkun ha-olam* appears in chapter 4:2–7 and 5:3. The phrase *mi-p'nei darkhei shalom* appears only in chapter 5:8–9. Not every *mishnah* or case mentioned in these two chapters states explicitly *mi-p'nei tikkun ha-olam*. Some, however, remark that the law is a *tikkun* for a more specific reason than to generally repair the world—for example, to prevent kidnapping (4:6) or to encourage repentance (5:5), both of which in the end do repair the world. In other cases, *m'pnei tikkun ha-olam* is understood by the *g'mara* to be the unstated reason for the law taught in the *mishnah*; see, e.g., B. Gittin 48b.

[4] Both the first and last *mishnayot* of the chapter (5:1 and 5:9) mention a woman, thus creating an "envelope structure" for the entire chapter, which is reinforced in the middle of the chapter in 5:3 and 5:6. Found objects are discussed in both 5:3 and in the fifth case of 5:8; priests are mentioned in 5:4, 5:5, and first case of 5:8; the deaf-mute appears in 5:5, 5:7, and the fifth case of 5:8; Israelites (and their relationships to priests) are discussed in 5:5 and first case of 5:8; stolen objects are discussed in 5:5 and in the fourth, fifth, and sixth cases of 5:8.

[5] Issues of impurity with respect to tithes are treated in both 5:4 and 5:9; issues related to the question of whether minors and deaf-mutes have cognizance so that they can acquire objects are treated in 5:7 and 5:8; and the general theme of concern for those who are disadvantaged is seen throughout the chapter as a whole, with cases of feeding a widow and her daughters, a guardian caring for orphans, marrying off a minor girl whose father is deceased, taking into account the feelings of a the mentally and physically disabled, and finally concern and protection for the poor.

[6] I thank my *ḥevruta*, Dr. Meesh Hammer-Kossoy, with whom I first seriously examined these *mishnayot*.

[7] It is difficult to understand why this action would create peace between people. Rambam, in his commentary on this *mishnah*, explains that one in which whose house the eiruv was placed did not have to contribute to the food that made up the *eiruv*—and so there was a benefit to having the eiruv placed in one's home. However, this fact would lead to fighting about where it should be placed, and so the rabbis imposed a rule about its placement—thus preventing any such fights. Alternatively, the *g'mara* (at B. Gittin 60b) explains this as a rule to prevent suspicion, but even this explanation is difficult to understand. Rashi's commentary ad locum (s.v. *mi-shum ḥashada*) explains that if the *eiruv* was normally kept in one house and then it is suddenly moved, if people enter the old house and do not see an *eiruv*, they will suspect that the people of that courtyard are breaking Shabbat and carrying objects without an *eiruv*. The Tosafot (s.v. *ella mi-shum ḥashada*) suggest that when people see the *eiruv* is

missing from the old house they will suspect that the people of the household stole the bread.

[8] In the interests of peace, the observant woman is permitted to share her utensils—even though she knows that most likely they will be used to aid her friend in transgressing the laws of the Sabbatical year when the friend bakes bread with grain that is forbidden. However, the observant woman may not actively assist her friend in the act of baking by sifting or grinding with her, since a transgression is thereby being committed.

[9] In this case, as there is no explicit transgression, the more observant woman only has to stop assisting her friend at the moment when the dough could become ritually impure at the hands of the wife of the *am ha-aretz*—that is, at the moment when the water is added to the dough. For the interests of peace, the observant woman can rely on the fact that, at least most of the time, the wife of the *am ha-aretz* does in fact tithe, and so she can winnow or grind or sift with her friend; however, when the dough surely becomes impure and then the portion of *ḥallah* that must be given to the priest from the bread baked also becomes defiled, the wife of the *ḥaveir* must not participate in aiding that transgression.

[10] This line applies to both cases: those who transgress the Sabbatical year and those who transgress the laws of purity.

[11] It is not the case that it was forbidden to greet non-Jews; just there was no mandated practice requiring that it be done until the rabbis instituted that it should—for the interests of peace. Based on *mishnayot* that appear earlier in the unit—such as 4:6 (which discusses captives and religious objects taken and ransomed by non-Jews), 4:9 (which discusses Jews who either sell themselves [as slaves] or alternatively their fields to non-Jews), and 5:6 (which deals with land confiscated by non-Jewish rulers)—one can imagine that in many cases, relationships with non-Jews during this time period could well have been very strained and filled with strife.

[12] Similar to the modern Hebrew greeting *mah sh'lomkha*—literally, "What is your *shalom*/peace?"

[13] These laws, known in Hebrew as *leket, shikh·ḥah*, and *pei·ah*, are set forth in Leviticus 23:22.

[14] This rule also appears in two other places in the Mishnah: Sheviit 4:3 and 5:9 (and the latter is in fact a word-for-word repetition of M. Gittin 5:9, in its entirety).

[15] Hebrew *tikkantem*, from the same verbal root (*tav-kof-nun*) as *tikkun*.

[16] Compare to the discussion above, concerning rabbinic disagreement. The School of Hillel also knew when to admit they were wrong and to change their minds, when presented with a challenge to their view and a differing opinion that they found compelling.

[17] M. Gittin 4:3 states that Hillel instituted the *prozbol* because of *tikkun ha-olam*; however, cf. M. Sheviit 10:3–4, where the law originates and the phrase *mi-p'nei tikkun ha-olam* is not found.

The Pilgrimage as *Tikkun Olam*

Rivon Krygier

Translated from the French by Martin S. Cohen

The pilgrimage to God's sanctuary is an unambiguous commandment of the Torah that requires every male Israelite to present himself three time a year—at the festivals of Passover, Shavuot, and Sukkot—"before" God and to commune with that God in that place in some sort of sensory context, to which Scripture alludes but does not precisely explain.[1] What might it mean for contemporary Jews to speak about such a thrice-annual pilgrimage, called in later sources *aliyah la-regel*, to Jerusalem? To answer that question, I do not plan to review all the details found in ancient sources about how the pilgrimage was performed historically or imagined ideally. Instead, I wish to write here about the spiritual meaning—and thus the ultimate goal—of the pilgrimage from a comparative perspective, inspired both by biblical and rabbinic sources.

The Book of Deuteronomy underscores the importance of Israel's covenantal loyalty to God, and insists that cultic worship can only occur at one designated place.[2] Maimonides was certainly right to argue that the point of this requirement was the regular gathering of the Jewish people around the Temple—here understood as the earthly pole of the axis *mundi*[3] around which all creation rotates—in order both to maintain ties of allegiance to the Creator and to ensure the social and religious cohesiveness of the Jewish people.[4] But my examination of the biblical and rabbinic texts regarding this *mitzvah* leads me to consider the concept of pilgrimage in the broader context of itinerancy itself: it may be seen not solely as a goal to be attained in physical space, but as a type of spiritual journey in time as well. The concept is not simply about the desire to ensure the ongoing divine presence in the Holy City (nor, later, to restore it, once the Temple itself no long stood in Jerusalem). Rather, I believe that *aliyah la-regel* in antiquity was intended to speak to the need to strengthen the relationship between God and the Jewish people in the long term. In this context, it is the journey itself that is the point: the pilgrim makes an *aliyah*, an ascent, to the Land of Israel, to Jerusalem, to the Temple Mount—thus undertaking a journey, through sacred and transcendental topography, toward a peak. And indeed, different sources suggest that this *aliyah* brings in its wake an elevation of the soul, a modification of the consciousness that can give access and exposure to the Divine in the kind of face-to-face meeting to which Scripture alludes.[5]

Psalm 24, for instance, frames the concept of pilgrimage in terms of the moral behavior required of those deemed worthy of visiting the Temple. I would render verses 3–6 of the psalm as follows, with the translation reflecting my sense that this poem is about the pilgrim's moral progress:

> Who may participate in an *aliyah* to the Temple Mount?
> Indeed, who may enter the site of God's holy sanctuary?
> One who has clean hands and a pure heart, who has never
>   taken a false oath invoking My name or sworn deceitfully.
> Such a one shall carry away the blessing from the Eternal,
>   a just reward from the God of such a pilgrim's ultimate
>   deliverance.
> Such would be the generation of Jacob's people who truly
>   seek Your face.

The very concept of making oneself visible to God—a meaningless thought with respect to an all-seeing Deity, if taken solely literally—suggests its own deeper interpretation: to be "seen" by God is to seek divine approval for attaining a high level of moral rectitude. And this notion is precisely what is suggested by the positioning of the golden cherubs atop the ark in the holy of holies, as stated clearly in an ancient midrash:

> How exactly were the cherubs positioned? Rabbi Yoḥanan and Rabbi Eliezer differed in this matter, one imagining them facing each other and the other imagining them facing the front of the Temple…but these positions are not really mutually exclusive and can be reconciled easily: when Israel's actions reflect the will of God the cherubs faced each other, but when Israel's actions did not do so, they [turned away from each other and instead] faced the front of the Temple.[6]

This idea of pilgrimage, of course, is not a purely individual matter; it is also about a collective odyssey—undertaken not only by individuals once or thrice a year, but indeed by the Jewish people throughout our history, even going as far back as Abraham, the earliest of our patriarchs. Indeed, the psalm can be taken as a kind of call to arms challenging the Jewish people, dispersed and exiled, to rededicate itself to the virtues that will lead to the construction of a true "city of God," one reflective of the ideals of Judaism and its utopian universalism. Jerusalem here is to be understood in its prophetic sense as the place where all the nations will one day converge to worship a God who has become no less universal than unique: "Then, I shall endow the nations with a common language so that I may call to them all in the name of the Eternal, inviting them as one people to the worship of God" (Zephaniah 3:9). Or, resonating even more strongly with the idea of the pilgrimage, consider the following verse from Zechariah: "And it shall come to pass that all those who survive of those nations who array themselves against Jerusalem shall come year after year to prostrate themselves before sovereign God, the Eternal One of Hosts, and [there] to celebrate Sukkot" (Zechariah 14:16).

How could a people be so possessed by a deep respect for its past, yet also fully engaged by the future-oriented desire to bring the nations of the world to Jerusalem, in the specific way the prophet foresaw? And in many ways, this is still a live question for Jews today. Jerusalem is the Gordian knot of the Arab–Israeli conflict, the key to establishing peace for the entire region. Jews in our time are fully aware that, for the first time in modern history, the Temple Mount is under the control of an independent Jewish state; yet, the voltage generated by the issue of Jerusalem somehow also feels at least slightly unnerving. Nor is it at all surprising that the political future of the Temple Mount lies at the crux of any possible peaceful resolution of the conflict in the Middle East. And in addition to the political issues, there is also another set of issues to consider, rooted in the ethnic and religious conscious (or subconscious) of the peoples involved, as they negotiate in terms bordering on the eschatological. It is in this sense that we find ourselves at the heart of *tikkun olam*, the reparation of the world and the edification of a redemptive age to come. It should be noted that the idea of *tikkun olam* also appears in the second paragraph of the Aleinu,[7] in the context of a prayer for the establishment of divine sovereignty over the world—which would presumably begin with the locus of the divine presence on earth, Jerusalem…and from there to spread over the entire world. Aleinu as such is a prayer for universal, not only national, ultimate redemption.

And it is in this sense that moderns should sing the verse from Psalms, known to most Jewish worshippers from the Hallel liturgy, that predicts that the stone once scorned shall yet become a cornerstone (Psalm 118:22): the *tikkun* will install the cornerstone in its place by establishing peace in the Holy City and the Holy Land. Such a reading, as we shall see, effectively calls upon Jews to undergo a kind of interior moral growth process, which will be outwardly expressed through both the renunciation of the thirst for exclusive political power and also of the mindset that defines security as total hegemony over others.

"What Happened to Abraham
Shall Yet Happen to His Descendants"[8]

To understand and to appreciate the ultimate meaning of, and the challenge inherent in, the commandment to "see" God in a specific place, we must begin with the journey of Abraham, whose own journey may be considered the archetypical precursor of the pilgrimage to Jerusalem. Indeed, the nature of the underlying enterprise reveals itself in a particularly striking way in the story of the very first—but surely, when the traditions of other monotheistic religions are taken into account, not the only—pilgrim who, prompted only the desire to serve God, sets out for a distant place he himself could never find on his own:

> The Eternal said to Abram, "*Go forth on your own* from your country, from your homeland, and from your father's house to the land that *I shall show you*. I make you into a great nation: I will bless you and make great your name and you shall be a blessing. I will bless those who bless you and curse those who wish you ill, for all the families of the earth shall know blessing through you." At age seventy-five Abram went forth from Haran just as the Eternal had said he was to do, and Lot went with him. Of course, he didn't only take his nephew Lot along! He also took his wife Sarai and all the property they had acquired in Ḥaran, including a vast entourage of living souls, and thus did they leave Ḥaran for the land of Canaan and eventually they arrived there. After crossing into the land, Abram continued their journey to the region of Shechem and stopped only when they reached the place called Alon Moreh. (The Canaanite was in the country at that time.) And it was at that spot that the Eternal appeared to Abram and said, "I shall give this land to your progeny." Hearing those words, Abram promptly constructed an altar that he dedicated to the *Eternal who appeared to him there*.[9]

Everything is already condensed in the initial two words of the call: *lekh l'kha*. Not necessarily just "go forth," as in our translation, but possibly these words may be translated as "go forth for yourself" or "go forward to yourself," or even "go forth for your own benefit and advancement," as Rashi suggests. The Hebrew phrase denotes movement both centripetal (*lekh* is about travelling forward, toward a distant destination) and centrifugal (*l'kha* is about travelling into oneself, toward the core of one's being). And such a command must surely mean: in order to become oneself (that is, to realize one's own identity and destiny), one must undertake a journey that is at first one's own—consisting primarily of the effort to "infuse," bringing oneself to personal maturity on one's way, and secondarily to "diffuse," making oneself a blessing for others.

Far from being the story of a simple migration, the trajectory that Abraham followed from Mesopotamia to Canaan is, at its heart, a story of interior growth and development.[10] And it is significant that God specifically does *not* reveal to Abraham his final destination, preferring to vaguely reference the end of the journey as "the land that I shall show you." This suggests that completing the journey will require attaining the transcendent, the unforeseeable, perhaps even the unimaginable—something that clearly will never happen without a concomitant experience of profound inner metamorphosis. This notion is suggested almost explicitly when the narrative relates how the names of both of our ancestral pilgrims actually grew along the great journey (as promised literally by God: "I will make great/ enlarge your name"), each acquiring the Hebrew letter *hei*—as Abram becomes Abraham and Sarai becomes Sarah.[11]

The duty to pilgrimate—if my readers will permit me my own neologism—was understood by the Jewish tradition to suggest a kind of initiatory journey capable of leading to growth of the identity, to an enlargement of the self. Rabbinic tradition speaks of the "ten tests of Abraham"[12] to which God subjected him on his journey. It is striking to note that the very roadmap of his journey is mentioned in the above-cited biblical passage (Genesis 12) as consisting of three steps, located in each of the three first verses: (1) first, get out of the place in which you are stuck; (2) then, become a great and blessed nation, both in terms of descendants and territory; (3) and finally, bring blessing to all the families of the earth. Indeed, these three stages are reflected in the three pilgrimage festivals that are rooted formally in the agricultural cycle of ancient Israel, but which more profoundly suggest a nation's growth toward God: (1) first Pesaḥ, celebrating the departure from Egypt as the archetype for any departure from exile and alienation, agriculturally tied to the beginning of the harvest; (2) then Shavuot, celebrating the arrival of the nation at its most sacred Temple bearing the *bikkurim*, the first fruits of the earth, which symbolize national maturity and prosperity; (3) and finally Sukkot, celebrating the end of the harvest and associated with the nation's collective blessing to the peoples of the earth—as symbolized by the sacrifice of seventy bulls, taken from earliest times to represent the seventy nations of the world—and not just to themselves.[13]

Let us go back to the foundational biblical story itself, and note the uncomfortable situation in which God has, from the outset, placed its hero. God promises the land to Abraham's descendants, but he has barely set his feet on its soil when the reader learns with amazement that "the Canaanite was in the country at that time" (Genesis 12:6). Thus, from the very beginning of the saga the reader is alerted to the complexity of the situation into which Abraham has (in this case, literally) wandered: the land to which he has been led is already inhabited, and so this "gift" to Abraham and his descendants comes intrinsically wrapped up in the challenge of *coexistence* with the locals—a challenge that remains even in our day unmet. Surely it would have been simpler and easier for the biblical narrator to take a hand-in-glove approach and describe the gift of a land-without-people to a people-without-a-land! Will Abraham's descendants, the nation-to-be, be able to accept God's gift, without ending up either as an unwelcome guest in someone else's home or as the unfeeling usurper of another people's property? That is the existential question which haunts all the journeys of Israel, and which presents the real challenge of the pilgrimage throughout subsequent Jewish history.

Abraham's precarious situation was bequeathed to the later generations of Israel, who too became obliged to negotiate the complicated situation of being indigenous neither in a land of their own (toward which they must endlessly migrate after prolonged periods of unwanted exile elsewhere) nor in the lands of their exile (where they must live, if they are to retain their identity). And, indeed, this existentially challenging condition serves as the background to the "apocalyptic"[14] moment when God reveals the reason for Abraham's election: "Because if I have known (y'datvi)[15] him [Abraham], that was merely in order that he command to his sons and his house after him to keep to the path of the Eternal, to practice fairness and justice in order that the Eternal might bring to fruition what God has said with respect to Abraham's future" (Genesis 18:19). Such are the ramifications and, indeed, such is the core of the injunction spoken earlier in the text: "Walk before Me and thus become whole" (Genesis 17:1). To become "whole" (tamim), Abraham must voluntarily withdraw something of his own power (and it is precisely such willingness that circumcision represents). Circumcision introduces the notion that completeness comes through the exercise of restraint itself, which notion will eventually be applicable to the way we relate to the "other" in our midst as well. This is why Abraham agrees to share the occupation of land with his nephew Lot (Genesis 13:8–11) and why he is welcomed by God in "negotiating" with him about Sodom and Gomorrah, invoking the sense of justice and compassion that he feels (Genesis 18:22–32). In this instance, Abraham is concerned not only with his own people (he could just as easily negotiated to save Lot and his family alone) but also with the fate of two entire pagan cities. And this is surely the ideal narrative against which to read the commandment addressed later on to Israel concerning strangers in general: "The stranger that sojourns among you shall be for you as the Israelite by birth, and you shall love such a one as yourself, for you yourselves were strangers in the land of Egypt" (Leviticus 19:34).

Reading Abraham's story in this way suggests at least obliquely that the ultimate goal of the pilgrimage is to effectuate a transfiguration in the relationship of the pious individual to the "other," allowing one to find the courage to befriend one's enemies and to treat them with dignity and respect. Surely, the biblical lesson is not to love those who may currently hate us! Rather, treating strangers—even churlish, difficult ones—with a certain respect can become a first step toward co-existing with them. Such a metamorphosis along the journey is the lesson of the beautiful rabbinic adage derived from *Avot D'rabbi Natan*, which teaches that a real hero is "anyone who manages to make an enemy into a friend."[16] It certainly sounds utopian even to contemplate behaving in this way in our own time, but it would be even worse *not* to feel called upon to undertake the great migration, the great pilgrimage, from where we are now to the unimaginable place that Scripture imagines we might yet reach.

The Metaphor of the Graft

Indeed, we cannot minimize the importance of this third and final part of the journey laid out in the roadmap revealed to Abraham: the process by means of which his descendants are to become a source of blessing for the nations of the world. The rabbis of the Talmud drew attention to the verb *nivr'khu* in Genesis 12:3—and their reading highlights a second, far less expected meaning:

> Rabbi Eleazar taught: What is the [deeper, more subtle] meaning of the verse: "…and all the families of that place shall know blessing by you (*v'nivr'khu v'kha*)"? The blessed Holy One was [in effect] saying to Abraham: "I have two

good blessings to graft onto you (*l'havrikh v'kha*): Ruth the Moabitess and Naamah of Ammon.[17]

This interpretation is based on the dual meaning of the root *bet-resh-kaf* as it was used in mishnaic Hebrew, a usage that permits "shall know blessing" to be read as "shall be grafted."[18]

This interpretation—which is also found in the commentary of Rashbam—inverts the expected meaning of the verb: it is not that the nations of the world will be *blessed by* Abraham's progeny, but rather that Abraham's descendants will profit by *having grafted onto them* individuals from outside the Israelite nation, who are distinguished by their fine moral traits.[19] It is true that the two nations mentioned, Moab and Ammon, are depicted in Scripture as themselves being offshoots cut off from the Abraham's family—and so this restoration of their earlier status as part of the Abrahamic family is, effectively, a type of *tikkun*.[20] But the more important detail here is that Ruth and Naamah, the paradigmatic characters in this text, provide a meaningful precedent for the notion that this process of "grafting" other nations onto the Israelite root will ultimately be a source of blessing for all involved: both for Israel, who will only become stronger and better as a result of the graft, and also for the other nations, for whom the process of becoming "related" to the Jewish people will be ultimately beneficial and a source of blessing. Moreover, Rashbam also notes that although the *v'nivr'khu* passage appears in a narrative "about" Abraham, the first patriarch of Israel (Genesis 12:3), it is also "about" Jacob/Israel, whose descendants became the Israelites, insofar as the promise is repeated with respect to him personally later in Scripture (at Genesis 28:14).[21]

To emancipate oneself from illusory self-sufficiency, to work up to the level of being capable of piercing the outer bark in order to accept the graft (and this too is what circumcision is ultimately about)—this is the true purpose of the odyssey of Abraham's descendants. Of course, one cannot attain this level of bi-directionality—encompassing both an acceptance of an other and a willingness to share with that other (as in the relationship between the tree and its graft)—without successfully facing one's own anxieties and fears, especially the multifaceted fear of death. Indeed, we realize later in the story that Abraham does not fear that the divine promise of land may be compromised nearly as intently as he fears the potential negation of the divine promise of progeny. And thus it could not possibly be more significant when we hear God's original, simple *lekh l'kha* call of Genesis 12:1 echoing almost painfully in its subsequent iteration, in the narrative of the *akeidah*, the greatest of all tests: "Take now your son, your only son, the one whom you love, Isaac, and *lekh l'kha* to land of Moriah, and offer him there as a wholly-burnt offering on the mountain that I will show you."

It is key to note here that God's first *lekh l'kha* makes a point specifically of omitting mention of a destination; it simply invites Abraham to a place that God will, presumably, designate once it is reached. I propose therefore that we should see the material between the first *lekh l'kha* and the second as a sort of aside; doing so suggests that the end of the journey, the original journey to which Abraham was called, is the land of Moriah—and even more specifically, the unnamed mountain henceforth to be named "God will be seen (*yeira·eh*)" and "God will see (*yireh*)."[22]

This ultimate test imposed on Abraham presumes a kind of almost superhuman selflessness on Abraham's part—or, at the very least, a willingness to quash his doubts even to the point of risking his own future as the patriarch of a nation. But in the end, what does this test actually prove? Isaac, of course, is not sacrificed. His father passes the test by remaining confident and willing to persevere down a very steep path toward an unknown, potentially disastrous destination. But what does this story imply about Abraham's relationship to his unsacrificed son, to Isaac? Why was it as necessary for him to bring his son up to the top of the mountain at all? It is critical to understand that the test of Abraham rests on a paradox. On the one hand, the story is about the confirmation of Isaac as the "only" and beloved son (Genesis 22:2), and thus the legitimate heir to his father's estate—as opposed to Ishmael, now the disenfranchised child (see Genesis 21). But on the other hand, the story is also about Abraham's readiness to sacrifice this uniqueness (which the loss of Isaac would inevitably entail), in order successfully to go through his ordeal![23] Everything seems to point to the goal of guaranteeing that the line Abraham now stands to father through the elected Isaac will be born, so to speak, aware of and awake to this readiness to sacrifice its "unique" status. Indeed, the story of Ishmael's brutal expulsion from his father's household may be seen as testifying to how things were at the beginning, when fraternity between Isaac and Ishmael had been impossible. The question that the story will prompt the thoughtful reader to ask, therefore, is whether reconciliation between the brothers will be possible in the future. Will Israel be able to renounce exclusivity in the future,[24] as their progenitor was once able to do in the past? In that case, Israel-to-come might be willing to graft the descendants of Ishmael (and they might be willing to be grafted) on to the spiritual tree of Abraham and Israel.

This idea was expressed by Yehudah Halevi (1075–1140) as follows:

> These religions [Christianity and Islam] exist for naught else than to pave the way and prepare the ground for the Messiah, the object of our yearning [no less than theirs]. And, indeed, when they [finally] recognize this truth, then shall the tree again become one. At that time, they shall hold in great esteem the root that they themselves formerly vilified.[25]

And, indeed, a talmudic midrash, in discussing this vision of the future, specifically connects its vision of the future inclusion of the nations to the concept of *aliyah la-regel*:

Rabbah taught a lesson based on the verse from the Song of Songs, "How beautifully shod are your feet, O daughter of nobility" (Song of Songs 7:2). The text can be taken as follows. "How beautifully shod are your feet" can be understood as, "How lovely are your feet, O Israel, when you ascend [to Jerusalem] in pilgrimage." And the phrase "O daughter of nobility" can be taken as a reference to Israel as the descendant of Father Abraham who is indeed called a noble, as is written in the Psalms: "Therefore do the nobles of the nations gather to ally themselves with the people of the God of Abraham, for the weapons of the world are naught but tools of God Most High" (Psalm 47:9). And why does the verse reference the Eternal as the God of Abraham, rather than as the God of Isaac or of Jacob? Because it was he [i.e., Abraham] who first brought [outsiders to faith in God, through the process of accepting converts to monotheism].[26]

Let us remember, however, that this famous peak will, at least spiritually and certainly literarily, resonate with similar visions in the so-called "daughter religions" of Judaism, even though there will obviously also be sharp differences. Within the context of Islamic tradition, for example, the event at Moriah is celebrated with the well-known Islamic festival called *Eid al-Adha* ("the festival of sacrifice"), also known as *Eid al-Kabir* ("the great festival"), the narrative behind which emphasizes that it was Ishmael, not Isaac, whose life Abraham put in peril. And Christians will see in this episode a kind of foreshadowing of Jesus, here taken as the lamb sacrificed but subsequently resurrected, thus—just like Isaac in earlier times—saved. Other details of the larger passion story—for example, including references to Passover and to Moriah in the narrative, are also suggestive and arresting.[27] In the same vein, we must remember that Palm Sunday certainly has its roots in the Festival of Sukkot, the liturgical context for the rabbis' most profound eschatological theorizing. Even the apostle Paul, who claimed to have studied Torah at the feet of Rabban Gamliel, expresses the hope that at the end of time Israel, currently cut off from its own roots, will self-graft back onto the "trunk" of Abraham.[28] The *hadj*,[29] the annual pilgrimage to Mecca, features circumambulatory processions that derive directly from the *hakkafot* undertaken with such fervor in the Temple of Jerusalem on the occasion of the Festival of Sukkot.[30] The Kaaba in Mecca is the Islamic equivalent of the altar of the Temple in Jerusalem.

Despite the emergence of new religious centers, none of the three monotheistic religions has ever forgotten its primary ties with Jerusalem. As is widely known, every synagogue in the world must in principle be oriented toward Jerusalem. Maimonides, relying on a passage in the Targum Onkelos, recalls the rabbinic tradition that it was Abraham who first determined the orientation of the prayer toward Jerusalem:

> Abraham served God and prayed in this place, then declared to the Eternal: "Here shall future generations worship God and say, 'In this day, on this mountain, Abraham served the Eternal.'"[31]

The Western Church kept this orientation of the prayer service toward Jerusalem until the fifteenth century (and it continues to this day to be the tradition maintained in at least some Eastern Churches). Likewise, Jerusalem was the first *kibla* (i.e., direction toward which one should orient oneself in prayer) introduced by Mohammed, before switching to Mecca in 624 C.E.[32] I should also stress that the identification of Mount Moriah and the Temple Mount in Jerusalem find its roots within the biblical tradition itself, since the (only) other biblical reference to that place is at 2 Chronicles 3:1, where we read: "Then Solomon began to build the house of the Eternal *at Jerusalem in Mount Moriah*, where the Eternal had appeared to David his father, in the place that David had prepared in the threshing floor."

I am not trying to assert there is any real historicity to the identification of Moriah with the Temple Mount. What I am interested in here is the symbolic importance of the identification of Jerusalem with the place where Abraham achieved the peak of faith in God's saving power, through his readiness to sacrifice that which was to him most dear and important. And the fact that this specific place also features prominently in the ritual and mythology of other monotheistic religions only makes the identification that much more interesting to consider, and that much more significant for the future.

The symbolic identification of Moriah with the Temple Mount is powerfully underscored in 1 Chronicles 21, in the famous episode of the counting of "sword-bearing men" undertaken by King David that so irritated God. As a result of God's pique, a severe sentence is pronounced against the people as a scourge begins to ravage the citizenry. But then, at the very last moment and no doubt in recollection of the *akeidah*, the binding of Isaac, God relents and calls back the destroyer, an angel, with the famous words: "Enough! Withdraw your hand!" (verse 15). At that very moment, the angel has just reached the threshing floor of Ornan the Jebusite. And then, lifting up his eyes, David sees this angel standing between heaven and earth, "the sword unsheathed and pointed toward Jerusalem."[33] It is this blade that symbolizes the self-aggrandizement that then leads the king to place his trust in the power of his army rather than in obedience to God to ensure the salvation of Israel. Such is the Jewish version of the "sword of Damocles" hanging over the Holy City! And yet David learns his lesson as he realizes that military power is not the solution, and he then asks God to forgive him his hubris. By virtue of this act of repentance the scourge is ended, and the prophet Gad then says clearly to David that it is in *this specific place* that he shall establish the altar—that is to say, the future Temple in Jerusalem, whose construction will be completed by Solomon. The lesson is stated explicitly in the text itself, when God says that

David, has "shed much blood and conducted many wars," and that is for that reason that it will not fall to David to build "a house in [God's] honor."[34] Indeed, God states specifically that this task will fall to Solomon, whose name (*Shelomo*) derives from the same root as shalom, the word in Hebrew for "peace."[35] Solomon's very name thus points to the fact that he will be a man of peace—*the* king of peace who establishes peaceful relations with former enemies in all directions.[36] We have here a *topos* in the technical sense of the term, that is: a motif that serves to link disparate ideas within a single narrative setting. In this case, the *topos* includes three concepts: (1) the need to face head-on a menace that threatens to harm the entire people, (2) a salvific act rooted in bravery, in self-abnegation, and in renunciation of strength as the source of ultimate power, and (3) a context symbolically created and justified in advance for peaceful coexistence.[37]

The Mountain of God

Jerusalem is therefore the place in the world that, more than any other, is redolent of memory and suffused with hope. That the Temple Mount subsequently comes to represent fratricidal rivalry and existential worry is thus a huge and challenging paradox. There is a path toward resolution, however, but one that by its nature requires adopting the same kind of courage and selflessness that the place itself also symbolizes. To rise to such a challenge we must be ready, like Abraham, to wander toward the unimaginable—by renouncing feelings of untoward hegemony toward the place, by renouncing the need to anchor respect for other people's faiths in the unspoken supposition that one's own faith is the superior one, and by retaining in this place allegiance only to the one and universal God.

In the story of the binding of Isaac, the *akeidah*, we read that the place at which the drama unfolds is henceforth to be called *Har*

Adonai (Yeira·eh), the Mountain of (the Ever-Visible) God (Genesis 22:14). I propose that this detail in the biblical text not be considered an afterthought, but should instead be taken as a visionary element in the larger importance of the story, as the Torah urges us to consider the site as a place that belongs to God and *solely* to God.

We read in the Psalms that Jerusalem is "built up, as a city knit together" (Psalm 122:3). The poet probably had in mind the fact that ancient Jerusalem was really two towns: the lower town, which contained the city's homes and shops, and the upper town, in which were located the Temple and the city's higher institutions. But the concept of pilgrimage is also central to the psalm, as is clear from the poet's description of the city as a place "to which tribes ascend, the tribes of the Lord—as enjoined upon Israel—to praise the name of the Eternal" (verse 4). The Temple and its mountain epitomize the nerve-center of the just society that the poet hopes to see established, for it was "there that the thrones of justice were set up, the thrones of the house of David" (verse 5). We read then the poet's injunction to "seek out the peace of Jerusalem" and his prayer that those who love the city themselves be no less at peace (verse 6), and this is followed by three verses that constitute a prayer for serenity that eventually gained a place of importance in Jewish liturgy:

> May there be peace on your ramparts, tranquility in your palaces.
> For the sake of my brethren and my friends, I can only say,
>   "May there be peace in you."
> For the sake of the Temple of the Eternal, our God, I shall
>   ask only for good for you, O Jerusalem (verses 7–9).

In short, this psalm can be taken as a prayer that Yerushalem (the original name of the city) become Yerushalayim (the later name, which also appears in the Bible—although only in three passages—and which can be interpreted as a dual form of the first name). It is almost as though the poet imagines the lower part of the city making some sort of *aliyah* to join the upper city in one united municipality at peace. How odd it is to consider that all these centuries later Jerusalem is still, if not *de jure* then certainly *de facto*, a divided city.

And so it remains relevant to wonder how the poet's vision might yet come to pass. And this brings us to a mystical passage of rabbinic literature that suggests that this conjoining of the city's quarters is also a matter of peace in the heavens:

> Rabbi Yoḥanan taught as follows: The blessed Holy One said, "I shall not enter celestial Jerusalem for as long as I cannot enter terrestrial Jerusalem." Is there a Jerusalem on high? Yes, as it is written: "Jerusalem built up, as a city knit together."[38]

What a strange resolution, that places God in a position of dependence! And yet the lesson seems clear: God is somehow unable to complete the divine analogue of the human pilgrimage, with all its eschatological implications, as long as humankind does not make peaceful and perfect the Holy City below. Peace, *shalom*, which is mentioned extensively in the psalm, is therefore not to be understood as a gift from God or even as something that God on high can manufacture and then bestow on humankind below. Rather, it is the essential commandment *from* God *to* humankind. In other words, the peace that God will establish on high will follow, not precede, the peace built below, which will ensue only as a result of humankind's striving to bring it about.

Another rabbinic midrash expresses this idea with special eloquence, focusing on the pilgrims' feet:

> Great is the peace that the blessed Holy One grants to Zion, as it is said: "Present your wishes for peace to Jerusalem" (Psalm 122:6)....Great is peace, because God will not announce the final redemption to Jerusalem other than after the establishment of peace in that place, as it is written:

"How beautiful upon the mountains are the feet of the one who brings good news, who announces peace, who brings news of happiness, who announces salvation, who says to Zion: Your God reigns!" (Isaiah 52:7).[39]

Anticipating this situation, when King Solomon dedicated the Jerusalem Temple, he invited foreigners to address God in prayer, and requested of God that such prayers by non-Israelites be granted special attention.[40] In the same vein, the prophet Isaiah expressed his hope for the ultimate mission of the Temple and the role its destiny would play in the ultimate mission of all Israel, declaring: "For My house shall be called a house of prayer for all nations" (Isaiah 56:7). And this same prophet also declared:

For the love of Zion, I will not be silent. For the sake of Jerusalem I shall not remain quiet, for as long as *justice* fails to emanate forth from that place as a ray of light, her salvation like a lighted torch. For then shall the nations see your righteousness, and all sovereigns your glory. And then shall you be called by a new name, one that the mouth of the Eternal will designate. (Isaiah 62:1–2)

What is meant here by *tzedek*, "justice"? I believe that the prophet was thinking about the same idea expressed in the Book of Deuteronomy: "And you must do that which is right and good in the eyes of the Eternal, in order that you may be prosperous and thrive in the good land that the Eternal swore to your ancestors that you would possess" (6:18). Commenting on this verse, Rashi notes: "This verse speaks of the willingness to compromise, even beyond the strict letter of the law." And what of the prophet's prediction that someday Jerusalem will have a new name? Perhaps this is the idea mirrored in a passage in which a different prophet, Jeremiah, declared that "in those times shall Jerusalem be called 'throne of the Eternal,' and so shall all nations throng to it" (3:17).

"When We Return to Zion, We Shall Be like Dreamers"[41]

The violent, wrenching conflict in the Middle East between Israelis and Palestinians has at its epicenter the territorial dispute regarding the site in Jerusalem that Muslims know as the Noble Sanctuary (*Haram al-Sharif*) and that Jews call the Temple Mount (*Har Ha-bayit*). (At the same time, we should remember that the Church of the Holy Sepulchre itself is divided into discrete areas under the control of diverse, contentious groups.) But neither Muslims nor Jews appear to be interested in a political agreement, with each side wishing for the whole pie and not even the larger of two slices. An ancient midrash suggests a rather startling starting-point for compromise regarding this ongoing dialogue of the deaf, one that derives from a peculiar ellipsis in the Hebrew text of Scripture. The text in of Genesis 4:8, depicting the prelude to Cain's murder of Abel reads: "Cain said to Abel his brother...[and] then, when they were in the field, Cain rose up against his brother Abel his and slew him" (Genesis 4:8). The midrash attempt to fill in the apparent textual lacuna as follows:

> Rabbi Joshua of Sakhnin said in the name of Rabbi Levi: What was the object of their discussion? One said, "The Temple will be built on my territory!" And the other said, "No, the Temple will be on my territory!" This is hinted at by the use of the word "field" in the verse, which is used elsewhere in Scripture to designate the Temple, as in the verse from the prophet Micah, "Zion [i.e., the Temple] will be plowed as a field" (Micah 3:12). And it was then that "Cain rose up against his brother Abel and slew him."[42]

In recent years, a number of solutions to the problem of the Israeli-Palestinian conflict have been proposed—some going to the heart of the matter, and others primarily addressed at ancillary issues. One proposal that, in my humble opinion, deserves our full attention was penned by Sari Nusseibeh and Ami Ayalon in the fall of 2002.[43] The relevant part reads as follows:

> *No party will exercise sovereignty over the holy places.* The State of Palestine will be appointed as a guardian of the Haram al-Sharif...on behalf of the Muslims. Israel will be the custodian of the Western Wall on behalf of the Jewish people. The status quo concerning the Christian holy places will be maintained. No excavation will be performed in or under the holy places without a mutual agreement.

Proposing that the communities involved renounce any national, exclusive claim on the "Mountain of God" would be a very powerful statement, but human beings *need* powerful symbols if they are to find the strength to step away from old paradigms that have locked them in vicious, ongoing cycles of violence and mistrust. The suggestions of some ancient traditions may be taken as the basis for such an agreement. Jerusalem very early on was called the "Mountain of the Eternal," in which phrase the "Eternal One" is the God common to all involved groups, all of whom self-define as the Abrahamic religions. Moreover, since Jerusalem is considered by our tradition as the great and ultimate goal of pilgrimage, it naturally suggests itself as the one place that should be immune to chauvinism or egotistical claims of superiority. Finally, common sense and common interest endorse the notion that the holy mountain should not (now or ever) be deemed the property of one specific nation or religion, but rather be the exclusive "property" of the one God, the God of all the earth.[44]

A vision for the future along these lines, or at least close to them, was expressed by one of the great rabbinic figures of modern times, Rabbi Ḥayyim Hirschensohn (1857–1935). Considering it impossible to consider the restoration of sacrificial worship in a future Temple without the explicit permission of a *bona fide* national prophet, Hirschensohn envisioned the future of the place along the following lines:

> The Temple site should be a sanctuary devoted to the singing both of [King] David's songs of prayer and praise and also new songs by modern poets capable of composing analogous sacred songs. From this sacred place, our sages should teach righteousness and justice to the people. And in that place should be situated the seat of the High Court of Justice, the specific place from which should go forth Law and Light to the whole world. Such a house should be a house of prayer for all nations (Isaiah 56:7). In that place, therefore, would be no religious symbols that would not be acceptable to all peoples, just as there was nothing in the [ancient] ark [housed in the holy of holies in the ancient Temple] other than the two tablets of stone on which were engraved the Ten Commandments, the foundation of the life of all civilized peoples, so that all nations, together and united, could stream to such a place and there stand before the God of Jacob to learn of the law of God, saying: "Come, let us go up to the mountain of the Eternal, to the House of the God of Jacob, so that God may instruct us in the ways of the divine that we may walk along God's paths. For surely from Zion shall come forth the law, and from Jerusalem the word of the Eternal" (Isaiah 2:2). This is the character we wish to grant to the House of the Eternal in our new State in the Land of Israel: what we wish for is precisely for Law to go forth from Zion and the word of the Eternal from Jerusalem…This is a vision in which the *Mountain of the Eternal serves as a temple of peace*, and, at that, one with far greater potential than the analogous court in the Hague, a court of all nations in which peoples shall be judged justly, in which national avarice shall be roundly condemned, and in which the reprehensible

notion that noble ends can be achieved on the national level through oppression and wickedness will, once and for all, be set aside...[45]

"If we wish it, it need not be a mere fairytale." But it will take time and a lot of persuasion. Still, our classical Jewish sources indicate that peace comes to nations from the bottom up and that peoples can influence their governments. Interreligious dialogue can play a major role here. Indeed, all that it will *really* take for this to happen will be for the men and women of the Abrahamic religions to mobilize around a manifesto that enables them to announce in unison—and *because of*, not *despite*, the virtue of interreligious dialogue on the matter—that they formally waive any claim of political or religious sovereignty over the "Mountain of God"...and that no army of theirs shall ever penetrate those sacred precincts...and that the place is instead permanently and effectively to be guarded by a neutral police force whose make-up and character would be acceptable to all sides. By doing so, the religions in question would gain, not lose, stature, and would become more than ongoing contexts for endless fractiousness and querulous, ongoing strife between peoples.

The world seems fixed on the idea that the dispute regarding the ultimate disposition of the holy places in Jerusalem must be left for the very last stage of negotiation, because it is by its very nature the most resistant to compromise. How remarkable, therefore, it would be for religious souls of every suasion to undertake a common pilgrimage to Jerusalem and, in so doing, to set aside vain pretensions and prejudices—in order that Jerusalem be not merely the eventual locale of eschatological peace, but rather the actual setting for peace today between peoples. To proclaim such an event would not even require new language; the call has already been set forth by two of our ancient prophets, both of whom proclaimed the true destination and goal of the pilgrimage:

In the final days it shall come to pass that the mountain of the house of the Eternal shall be established atop the mountains and exalted above the hills, and people shall flow to it. And, indeed, many nations shall come and say, "Come, and let us go up to the mountain of the Eternal and to the house of the God of Jacob, so that God may teach us of God's ways and that we may walk in God's paths, for Torah shall go forth from Zion and the word of the Eternal One from Jerusalem. And God shall judge between many peoples and shall rebuke remote nations, even distant ones, so that, [knowing peace,] they come to beat their swords into plowshares and their spears into pruning hooks. [As a result,] nation shall not lift up sword against nation, nor shall [their citizenry] any longer learn [the practice of] war. Instead, they shall sit, all citizens, beneath their vines and fig trees, and none shall make them afraid, for the mouth of the Eternal One of Hosts has spoken. For each people shall walk forward in the name of its own god, and we shall walk forever forward in the name of the Eternal our God. (Micah 4:1–5)

Then I shall endow the nations with a common language so that I may call to them all in the name of the Eternal, inviting them as one people to the worship of God. (Zephaniah 3:9)

NOTES

[1] Cf. Exodus 23:17 and 34:23, and Deuteronomy 16:16. The precise linguistic formulation differs slightly from verse to verse, but the point seems to be specifically that the pilgrim experiences some sort of visual communion with God.

[2] See, for instance, Deuteronomy 12:14.

[3] Mircea Eliade has convincingly argued that sacred space in many religions (including Judaism) is often conceptualized in terms of a central axis, which is believed to connect heaven and earth; spirituality—and thus the structural organization of a society—rotate around it. See Mircea Eliade, *The Sacred and the Profane: The Nature of Religion*, trans. Willard R. Trask (1959; rpt. Orlando, Austin, New York et al.: Harcourt, Inc., 1987), pp. 20–68.

[4] Cf. Maimonides' comment in the *Guide for the Perplexed* III 43 that the festivals of the Jewish year are "all for rejoicings and pleasurable gatherings, which in most cases are indispensable for man; they are also useful in the establishment of friendship, which must exist among people living in political societies" (trans. Shlomo Pines [Chicago: University of Chicago Press, 1963], p. 570). And cf. also the comment just two chapters later (*Guide* III 45, idem., pp. 575–581, where he discusses the universal human need to create unique spiritual centers on earth by building temples (or a sole Temple) to the gods (or to God).

[5] See the biblical sources mentioned above in note 1. The pilgrimage may also serve to inspire prayer or prophecy. Concerning prayer, see 1 Samuel 2 (where Hannah prays while on a pilgrimage). Regarding prophetic inspiration, see Y. Sukkah 5:1 (55a), which suggests that Jonah was prophetically inspired while en route to Jerusalem; and cf. also Bereshit Rabbah 70:8, associating a prophetic vision of Jacob with a pilgrimage experience.

[6] B. Bava Batra 99b.

[7] In Aleinu, the idea is expression with the verbal phrase *l'takkein olam*.

[8] See the famous formula of Rabbi Joshua of Sikhnin: "God gave a sign to Abraham to the effect that everything that was to happen to him would also befall his descendants" (*Midrash Tanḥuma, Lekh L'kha* §9:9, s.v. *va-y'hi bimei*).

[9] Genesis 12:1–7, my emphasis.

[10] The story of Abraham's call in Genesis 12 is set in Haran, a city in northern Mesopotamia. But Scripture itself later understands the journey to have begun in Ur, the city of Abraham's birth; cf. Genesis 15:7 and also Nehemiah 9:7, both of which should be read in light of the brief note presented in Genesis 11:29–32.

[11] What does the *hei* actually symbolize? Is it meaningful that Abraham's *hei* is a simple addition to his name, whereas Sarah's is a substitution for a different letter? In rabbinic literature, the letter *hei* has the symbolic function of signaling a breakthrough or an opening where things and beings might otherwise be enclosed (cf. B. Menaḥot 29b). The *hei*, according to an ancient midrash preserved at Bereshit Rabbah 12:10, is a letter "that is not gripped by language" when it is pronounced. It is "breath," thus no less fluid than the very spirit of

God once breathed into Adam and that hovered over the waters on the first day of creation.

[12] Cf., e.g., Pirkei Avot 5:3.

[13] See the eschatological vision of the prophet Zechariah (14:16) quoted above. Regarding the sacrifice of the seventy bulls offered on behalf of the seventy nations, see Bemidbar Rabbah 9:24 and Shir Hashirim Rabbah 4:2.

[14] In the etymological sense of the term, meaning "revelatory of divine secrets."

[15] The Hebrew *y'dativ* may also have the sense of "elected."

[16] *Avot D'rabbi Natan*, text A, ch. 23, ed. Solomon Schechter (3rd ed.; New York: Feldheim, 1967), p. 38a, and cf. the parallel sources listed by Schechter there in note 7.

[17] B. Yevamot 63a.

[18] The root *bet-resh-kof* has a primary meaning of "to bless," with a connotation of addition and juncture. The same root in a different grammatical construction (the Hiphil) was also used in the Mishnah to mean "to graft" (i.e., in the sense of adding something on).

[19] Rabbi Shimon ben Meir (1080–1160), called Rashbam, was the grandson of Rashi.

[20] Recall the incestuous origin of both Moab and Ammon (cf. Genesis 19), as well as the prohibition regarding their subsequent admission to the "assembly of God" because of their hostile behavior to Israel in the wilderness (cf. Deuteronomy 23:4–5). Note that the "excision" mentioned here (*kareit*) is the usual talmudic term derived from Scripture to designate the sanction of exclusion from the community. The concept of being grafted onto the trunk is precisely the opposite idea of this excision.

[21] Cf. Rashbam's commentary to Genesis 12:3 and 28:14.

[22] Cf. Genesis 22:14. Scripture itself finds the name of the mountain, *Adonai Yireh*, sufficiently obscure to warrant an on-the-spot gloss, fleshing out its meaning in more detail. Exodus 23:17 and 34:23, and Deuteronomy 16:16 (the verses that command the thrice-annual pilgrimage) all connect the journey with idea of God seeing and being seen by the pilgrim.

[23] Note how the underlying theme of the future blessing for the multitude of nations, which first surfaces in the original *lekh l'kha* of Genesis 12, reaches its natural culmination at the end of the story of Isaac's ordeal, in God's blessing to Abraham: "Through your progeny shall the nations of the world be blessed (*v'hitbar'khu*), because you have obeyed Me" (Genesis 22:18).

[24] Abraham separates from Ishmael unwillingly in a kind of first test regarding filial sacrifice: Ishmael is sent into the wilderness where he and his mother would surely have died, had an angel not come to their rescue—much as a different angel materialized to save Isaac's life later on. The two sons can and must live separately. But the ties with Ishmael are not totally severed. Abraham receives a divine promise that Ishmael's descendants too shall be considered Abraham's blessed progeny (Genesis 21:13). Taking the pericope of Genesis 21:9–19 seriously is key to grasping the ultimate meaning of the story of Abraham's near-sacrifice of Isaac, as told in Genesis 22.

[25] *Kuzari* IV 23, trans. Hartwig Hirschfeld (New York: Schocken, 1964), pp. 226–228.

[26] B. Sukkah 49b.

[27] New Testament passages that see a parallel between the binding of Isaac and the passion of Jesus include Hebrews 11:17–19 and Romans 8:32. According to the Essene calendar that underlies the Book of Jubilees, Abraham's great test at Moriah took place on the date that would later be Passover (cf. Jubilees 17:1), which passage may be compared to the rabbinic midrash preserved at Shemot Rabbah 15:11 where it is specified that Abraham's test took place in the same month as Passover (although the midrash does not give an exact date).

[28] This claim to have studied at the feet of Rabban Gamliel is found at Acts 22:3. The metaphor of the graft back onto the trunk of Abraham is found at Romans 11:16–24.

[29] Note that this word is cognate to Hebrew *ḥag*.

[30] See 2 Chronicles 5:3 and Nehemiah 8:14, where the Festival of Sukkot is already called *ḥag*—that is, **the** feast *par excellence*. Later, this became the standard way of referring to the festival in the Mishnah and Tosefta (cf., e.g., M. Megillah 3:5). According to the apocryphal Book of Jubilees, it was Abraham who introduced the Festival of Sukkot, as well as the seven circumambulations around the altar; see Jubilees 16:20–31.

[31] *Guide* III 45, p. 571, citing the Targum Onkelos to Genesis 22:14. Maimonides refers also to a source in the talmudic tractate Yoma, but it has not been clearly identified. (Some think that he was referencing the comment that "the prayer of Abraham is to be recited when the walls begin to grow dark" found at B. Yoma 28b.) See Michael Schwarz's comment in his translation of the *Guide* (Tel Aviv: Tel Aviv University Press, 2002), vol. 2, p. 601, n. 6, citing the remarks of Solomon Munk in the latter's French translation of the *Guide*.

[32] Cf. Koran, Sura 2, 136/142–147/152. According to the Koran (Sura 22, 26/27–27/28), Allah indicated to Abraham the location of the Temple (*al Bayti*) that was to become the goal of an annual pilgrimage and the attendant circumambulations. The place is, however, identified in Muslim tradition as the Kaaba of Mecca (although that is not stated explicitly in the Koranic text).

[33] This is reminiscent of Abraham's lifting up of his own eyes, to take note of an angel in the sky, at the exact moment he was holding a knife to the throat of his own son; cf. Genesis 22:13.

[34] 1 Chronicles 22:8.

[35] Cf. 1 Chronicles 22:9–10.

[36] The theme surfaces in the midrash found at *Pirkei D'Rabbi Eliezer*, chap. 32.

[37] This is the same theme that surfaces during the tenth plague brought against the firstborn in Egypt, except that there it was necessary to renounce violence directed toward the "other." The Hebrews' sons were also in danger, which is why danger had to be averted by painting the blood of the paschal lamb on their doorways as a sign of allegiance to God. This gesture is presented by the biblical text (as the rabbinic tradition understands it) as a bold break with the

religion of idolatrous Egyptian. Furthermore, it is the consumption of the lamb in Jerusalem each year during the celebration of Passover that will resacralize the sacred alliance between God and Israel. And it was in Jerusalem as well that the first Christians appended a new meaning to the old story by superimposing the image of Jesus as the *agnus dei*—the paragon of the renunciation of violence—to the paschal lamb. And it was also that very place that Muslim tradition later identified as the "distant mosque," *al masjid al-aksa*, at Koran 17:1. Mohammed made a nocturnal pilgrimage in that place as well, which was a kind of mystical ascent during the course of which he received decisive revelations regarding the order of the prayer and the demands of mercy.

[38] B. Taanit 5a, quoting Psalm 122:3. Rashi *ad locum* explains that the point is that the poet wrote that Jerusalem (i.e., the earthly city) is "like" a united city of tightly contiguous precincts, which seems to imply that there is another Jerusalem—"and where would such a city be, if not in heaven?"

[39] Devarim Rabbah 5:15.

[40] Cf. 1 Kings 8:4–43. According to 2 Chronicles 5:3, the dedication of the Temple took place during the Festival of Sukkot.

[41] Psalm 126:1.

[42] Bereishit Rabbah 22:7.

[43] Published in the newspaper *Haaretz* as "The Nusseibeh-Ayalon Agreement: Final Draft Cover Letter" on September 3, 2002.

[44] This, moreover, is the explicit proposal put forward by an American association headed by Rabbi Jerome Segal, the name of which, "Sovereignty Belongs to God," could not possibly be more evocative; see http://www.pa-il.com/2010/07/jerome-m-segal-sovereignty-belongs-to.html. But this group seems to me rooted in complete unreality, insofar as it hopes to realize the principle of non-sovereignty over the whole of the territory of Israel and Palestine (and not just the city of Jerusalem).

[45] *Malki Ba-kodesh*, ed. David Zohar (Ramat Gan, Israel: Bar-Ilan University and Jerusalem: Schechter Institute of Jewish Studies and the Shalom Hartman Institute, 2006), pp. 14–16. I have added a few words from the original Hebrew edition, first published in 1919, that were omitted in the translation.

Fixing *Tikkun Olam*

Reuven P. Bulka

Tikkun olam—a phrase that is so often used, even abused—sounds simple enough. It means, on a superficial level, "the fixing of the world."

But the precise meaning of the phrase is fraught with questions. Is it possible for any single individual to fix the world? Presuming that *tikkun olam* is an obligation, if not an official *mitzvah*, and that it is impossible to do a full fix, how much of a fix are we obliged to carry out?

Is it possible for a person living in any city to fix the world in another city, in another country? Are we obligated to fix the world in places where no Jews are welcome? Which *olam*, which world, is it our obligation to fix? And never mind another city: what about the city in which one lives? Is a "full fix" remotely possible, even in a much more limited area?

And what exactly do we mean by "fix"? Is it using spiritual crazy glue to bring together broken pieces? Is it just improving on the status quo? How is the improvement measured?

As an absurd example: suppose we find out via a survey that, over time, the percentage of the Jewish community that celebrates a given holiday—Shabbat or Ḥanukkah, for example—has gone up. Are there *tikkun olam* implications in this? Does this rise in percentage mean that the world is getting better?

These are just a few of the perplexities surrounding this often employed but seldom understood phrase.

What follows is an attempt to explore some nuances of the phrase *tikkun olam*, and to suggest the kinds of actions that this phrase ought to inspire us to undertake.

Conversion vs. Inspiration

Judaism does not encourage us actively to seek out converts.[1] We are obligated to welcome converts once they have embraced Judaism, but we are not in the business of convincing people to become Jewish.

We firmly believe that all righteous people have a share in the world to come, so we do not need to "save" them by making them Jewish.[2] They are good as they are.

At the same time, we do have responsibilities to the global community. Our major responsibility is not to convert; rather, it is to inspire. We are called on to inspire humanity.

The question is: inspire humanity toward what end? If it is not toward embracing Judaism, then toward what? Certainly not to another religion. That would hardly make sense.

Our responsibility is to inspire the world to acknowledge God, to embrace God, and to behave with the awe of God as the basis of all action.

That is a tall order, but it is an order we dare not ignore. For most of our history we were, to a greater or lesser extent, prevented from carrying out this mandate. So the mandate may have slipped out of our consciousness—but that does not mean that the obligation has disappeared. It simply was suffocated by exile, persecution, and subjugation.

That suffocation has ended. We can now breathe freely, and we therefore need to return to the mandate.

It is not as if we ever totally forgot this responsibility, even in the worst of times. The universal obligation is a recurring theme in our age-old prayers, in our teaching, in our thinking—as we constantly remind ourselves that we must be, as the prophet said, "a light unto the nations" (Isaiah 49:6).

The theme of infusing our lives with Godliness is recurrent throughout our daily prayers. Every day we yearn for the time that God will reign supreme over all the earth. This idea finds powerful expression in the climactic ending of the Aleinu prayer, which concludes the morning, afternoon, and evening services.

How will this reign of God over the world be achieved? We could of course leave it to God, but we know that it is not the Jewish way to do so.

True, our fate is ultimately in God's hands. But it is clear from the mandates in the Torah that we are partners with God, not mere bystanders. This is surely true of personal fate. It is simply wrong to leave our destiny to God, and thus to neglect our own physical and spiritual responsibilities.

It is a sacrilege to consciously adopt bad health habits—such as smoking, excessive drinking, or overeating—and just leave our well-being entirely to God, Who controls our destiny. This is evident from the abundant health directives in the Torah. If how we behave does not matter, why would God ask us to take care of ourselves? Why would God instruct us, for example, to be "exceedingly careful" (Deuteronomy 4:15) concerning ourselves?

What holds true in the personal realm is likewise true in the communal, even global, realm. It is up to us to facilitate the global embrace of God—again: not through coercion, but rather through the inspirational force of our example.

Partnering with God

Any doubts about the centrality of our mission to inspire the world to embrace God are removed once we fully comprehend the second part of the aforementioned Aleinu prayer. It reads as follows:

> Therefore we hope for You, Eternal our God, soon to behold Your majestic glory, to remove idols from the earth, and with the false gods totally eliminated, to perfect the world through the reign of the Almighty. And all humanity will call in Your name, to turn toward You all the earth's wicked. All the

world's inhabitants will recognize and know that to You every knee must bend, every tongue must vow allegiance. Before You, Eternal our God, they will bend and prostrate, and give homage to Your honored name. They will all accept upon themselves the yoke of Your dominion, and You will reign over them speedily forever. For dominion is Yours, and for all eternity You will reign in glory, as it is written in Your Torah, "The Eternal shall reign forever" (Exodus 15:18). And it is said, "The Eternal shall be ruler over all the world; on that day the Eternal shall be One, and God's name One" (Zechariah 14:9).

How can all this happen without us? Remember that prayer is more than just mouthing words without attending to the meaning. Prayer involves understanding the words, and the obligations that derive from the words.

A further word about partnership is in order. If instead of partnership I use the term "covenant," this idea about our mission to inspire the world would resonate more readily.

But a covenant *is* a partnership. Obviously God is the Majority Partner, and overwhelmingly so, but God has brought us into the corporation/covenantal relationship with some significant clout, if you will.

We refer to this partnership daily, by reciting the faith affirmation called the Shema. The second paragraph of the Shema is all about covenant, about partnership. The terms are clear and blunt:

It will be that if you diligently listen to My commandments that I command you today; to love the Eternal your God and to serve God with all your heart and with all your soul—I shall then provide rain for your land in its right time, the early and late rains; then you will gather your grain, your wine, and your oil. I will provide grass in your field for your cattle; you will eat and be satisfied. Be careful with yourselves, lest your heart be seduced; and you stray and serve the gods of others and bow to them. Then the wrath of the Eternal will be kindled against you, God will hold back the heaven and there will be no rain, and the ground will not yield its produce; and you will be quickly expelled from the good land that the Eternal gives to you. (Deuteronomy 11:13–17)

Here, God tells us in graphic terms that if we do our part, then God will take care of the rest.

There are abundant references to this notion of partnership in the Torah. Two well-known examples include: "If you diligently listen to Me and observe My covenant, then you shall be to Me a treasure from all the nations..." (Exodus 19:5) and "If you follow My statutes, then I shall give you rain in the proper season..." (Leviticus 26:3).

The Talmud even speaks about the partnership with God in the creation story itself, declaring: "Whoever prays on Shabbat eve and recites Va-y'khulu [the biblical passage describing the culmination of God's creating the world, Genesis 2:1–3], Scripture considers it as if that person has become a partner with the blessed Holy One in the creation process."[3]

Another better known reference to this partnership is the rabbinic assertion that there are three partners in the creation of a person: God, the father, and the mother.[4] The Talmud actually goes into detail regarding this partnership, spelling out the respective contributions of each partner: God provides the spirit and soul, the countenance, vision, hearing, speech, insight, and understanding; the father provides the bones, sinews, nails, and the brain; and the mother provides the skin, flesh, and hair, among other components.[5] The level of detail in this accounting reinforces how seriously Judaism takes this partnership.

The partnership carries through all the way to the proverbial "end of days." One of Isaiah's prophecies regarding the end of days is read publicly as a *haftarah* during the weeks leading up to the Days of

Awe. The passage concludes with the famous words: "The smallest will become thousands and the youngest into a mighty nation; I am the Eternal, in its time I will hasten it [i.e., the redemption]" (Isaiah 60:22).

The reader will notice an apparent contradiction in the last words of this verse: "I am the Eternal, in its time I will hasten it." If it is truly to occur "in its time," then it is not being hastened. If the messianic redemption is to occur at its pre-ordained time, then what does it mean to say that God will "hasten" that redemption?

The Talmud picks up on this conundrum and offers the following explication by Rabbi Joshua ben Levi: "If the people are deserving, I will hasten it; if they are not deserving, then [it will come] in its time."[6]

Ultimate redemption is part of God's plan, but *when* it happens is up to us. In other words: the redemptive context is one of partnership, not happenstance.

God can surely generate redemption, or anything else, without us. At the same time, God's clear preference is that we be involved in how quickly redemption unfolds…and this can only happen if we are deserving.

The Aleinu Plea

Our deservedness, the way we behave, impacts directly on how God will be acknowledged by the entire world—and it is this acknowledgment that, as reflected in the Aleinu prayer, is so central to ultimate redemption.

The person who truly and profoundly believes in God must then acknowledge God as the Creator of all—meaning that we are all God's creations, created in the image of God, and we are therefore holy.

Deriving from the monotheistic belief in one God, in God as the One and Only, is the imperative of according respect to all of God's creatures. Belief in the One and Only God means that we are all united under the same God, and are all equal—and this belief leads directly to certain kinds of behavior.

Humility, sensitivity, and caring all become sacred and eternal values in a world wherein God is supreme. The message about how life and all humans are sacred extends toward fully affirming the value of each person, since all must be treated respectfully, kindly, and sensitively.

The Aleinu prayer is therefore not a triumphalist rant. Rather, it is a plea for a world of kindness and compassion, a world in which what are clearly identified as Godly values are the governing values of society. This is our ultimate hope, and it is so central to the Jewish hope for the world that we conclude every one of the basic prayer services with not just a passing mention, but rather with a detailed, descriptive statement of how the world should look, as expressed in the words of the Aleinu.

It is indeed a sacred task to be a light unto the nations, to inspire the world. There is no escape from this "mission." It is a mission to infuse the world with Godly goodness. There have been protracted periods throughout our history when we were rendered incapable of engaging in this mission. And at other times, such as the immediate post-biblical era, we were capable of doing so, but failed in this task.

There are no excuses now. The time is right; the world is ripe, for an inspired engagement that will bring out the divine goodness that inheres in every human being.

We have long recognized that it is possible to be good without being Jewish, just as it is possible to be Jewish without being good. It is more crucial to be good. It is an inescapable component of being Jewish that we strive to be good—as defined by the Torah—and that we inspire others, through our example, to likewise be good. And it is through goodness that the world will have enough redeeming qualities to merit God's forbearance.

To be good does not mean to observe Shabbat or to abide by the dietary laws or to fast on Yom Kippur. It is certainly good to do so, but that alone does not define goodness. To be good means to be honest, to be respectful, to be kind, to be appreciative, to be friendly, to be humble.

The Different Realms in Which We Actualize Our Mission

To inspire the world: that is a daunting task, surely beyond the capacity of any single individual or group.

On whose shoulders does the responsibility to inspire the world rest? In this massive mission, there are both individual and communal realms, and therefore both personal and communal responsibilities.

In the individual realm, it is incumbent upon every Jew to inspire the immediate environment, the immediate world in which that person travels.

On the communal level, there is a collective responsibility to put to work the communal resources to attain this goal.

For rabbis, this means alerting their congregations to this goal. For teachers, it means educating their students to this calling. For parents, it means being role models for their children, showing by personal example how to actualize this way of living.

This is a shared responsibility, shared by everyone, in differing degrees. But no one is free from participating in the collective responsibility we all have to God.

The foundational responsibility is to love God. It is a responsibility that flows naturally from the presumed gratitude we have to God for having been born into God's world. And this responsibility is articulated as part of the partnership agreement with God found in the Shema.

It is not surprising that we are commanded to love God (Deuteronomy 6:5). What is surprising, at least initially, is how this was actually understood.

According to the Talmud, it means that "the name of God should become beloved through you,"[7] so that via conducting our business faithfully and through engaging people pleasantly, people will praise those who taught us and will be inspired by our behavior and deeds. That is the foundation of the imperative that we all share, to bring the world under the rubric of God.

The Abraham–Sarah Model

Abraham and Sarah serve as role models of this mandate.

Tradition has it that they were deeply involved in missionizing, that Abraham converted the men and Sarah converted the women.[8] There was no Judaism then; the Torah had not yet been transmitted. To what faith, then, were the converts converted?

From all that we know, the approach of Abraham and Sarah was to move people away from idolatry with its attendant immorality, and closer to the embrace of monotheism, the belief in the One and Only God Who created the world and everyone in it, idolaters included.

Abraham and Sarah were renowned as having an open house and open hearts, a dwelling open on all sides for all travelers to enter and be welcome.

It was in this home that they worked their magic. But the food and drink were not intended as a strategic trick. The welcome that Abraham and Sarah extended to the world flowed directly from their understanding that God was indeed sovereign over everyone. If they were to profess monotheism and live by it, then by definition they would have to embrace all of God's creations.

The eternal legacy of Abraham and Sarah is not merely the promulgation of monotheism. It is also the marriage of monotheism and monanthropism (the one-ness of humankind), the marriage of the Godly and the human, the intimate connection between belief in God and kindness to all—the idea that one necessarily leads to the other, that they are inescapably intertwined.

To this day, we extol Abraham and Sarah as the exemplars of kindness, and we consider them to be present-day role models for the mandate to strive toward *tikkum olam*.

Abraham and Sarah actually had a colossal challenge: to re-orient an entire world. The challenge for us today is somewhat different: it is to address a more subtle idolatry, which presents itself in the guise of worship of the self and its attendant unwelcome consequences.

Admittedly, it is quite harsh to brand narcissism as the modern idolatry, but it is an accurate assessment. Consider that the idols of old were created by the very people who worshiped these idols. These images thus served as the vehicle, the front, for allowing idolaters to do whatever they wanted—in an instance of narcissism truly gone haywire—with the "blessing" of the idols they created. In modern times, we have done away with the idols, but the focus on the self—which too often comes with a negation of any responsibility to others—is still with us. We do not physically bow down to ourselves, but all too often we do surrender to self-infatuation. The end result is a less than caring society, which remains in need of a massive fix, a true *tikkun*.

The *Tikkun Olam* Imperative

The essence of *tikkun olam* may thus be understood as the imperative to continue the Abrahamic agenda of rallying against idolatry—especially in its modern-day guise of self-worship. This unfinished work was started by Abraham, appreciated by God, put on hold through centuries of persecution, and is now finally appearing out of the dark clouds of our history as a beckoning opportunity and obligation that calls out for us to fulfill.

The way we wake up, the thoughts that we contemplate when we wake up, can to a large degree influence our behavior for the day. It is therefore not surprising that the tradition mandates that we begin each waking day with an expression of thanks to God for being alive, by reciting the Modeh Ani prayer. That way, our day is more likely to build on that gratitude, as we go about our routine: at home, at work—literally, everywhere.

There are those who have the wonderful custom, as they begin their daily prayer affirmations, of expressing their intent to fulfill the obligation to "love your fellow as you love yourself" (Leviticus 19:18), an obligation that is as central to Judaism as it is all-encompassing.

If this verse is recited with sincerity and intentionality, it cannot help but impact on how the day will unfold. One who begins the day by saying this (and meaning it) is more likely to avoid insulting or cheating, and is more likely to go out of one's way to be kind and considerate to others.

There is another clarion wake-up call that seems fitting for *tikkun olam*. It is to awaken to the following contemplation: What can I do today to sanctify the name of God (*kiddush ha-Sheim*)? What can I do to inspire others to embrace the universal Godly values that are the foundation of a genuinely caring society?

If we wake up every day to this contemplation, and come up with good ideas that we translate into action, then eventually the whole process will run on automatic pilot, and doing all these inspiring deeds will be natural.

Note that "natural" is not the same as "by rote." Rote refers to doing things like a robot, without thinking or feeling. Natural means that the thought and the feeling are present and real, and do not need to be forced.

We know what Godly values are, because they are clearly articulated by the rabbis: "Just as God is gracious and compassionate, so too should we be gracious and compassionate."[9]

We fulfill God's word by actualizing the commandments—by undertaking what one might call "*mitzvah* obligations." But we become more like God when we are compassionate, kind, and gracious in the way that we fulfill God's commands to us.

If in the end we are accused of trying to bring kindness and compassion to the world, we should unabashedly plead guilty. There is hardly anything better of which to be guilty.

But such a "guilty plea," it must be noted, ought to be suffused with humility. We do not portray ourselves as better than everyone else, simply because we strive to live our lives guided by this mission. Instead, we humbly project God's word as ennobling and redemptive for everyone.

Jumping into *Tikkun*-Oriented Action

Once we make up our minds to do this—to act with kindness and compassion in order to imbue the world around us with a greater measure of Godliness—then the way to go about inspiring others is not that complicated. In fact, it is quite easy. Once we have made it our priority to inspire the world, we can easily draw up a list of things we can do that take little effort and cost nothing.

For example, saying hello to people of all faiths and persuasions and wishing them a good morning (or a good day) goes a long way. And, in fact, this dovetails quite nicely with the famous rabbinic directive to "initiate greetings to all people."[10] Moreover, the Talmud reports that the sage Abaye would continually emphasize that one should increase harmony with others, including people of other faiths, so that the one who proffers greetings will be both beloved above (i.e., in heaven) and desirable below (i.e., on earth), and accepted by everyone.[11]

The Talmud then points to the great sage Rabban Yoḥanan ben Zakkai, about whom it is reported that no one—not even a non-Jew in the market—greeted him first. He was in the meticulous habit of taking the initiative and being the first to greet all people, no matter what their faith was. This is a most effective way to spread good feelings in general society.

A careful reading of this text underscores the critical point that saying hello to everyone is a way to gain the approval of God, and not merely a social nicety. But why would this practice be so important to God? The answer seems obvious: because the way to open up people to a full appreciation of God, and the embrace of Godly values, is for people of God—that is, identifiably religious personages like Rabban Yoḥanan ben Zakkai—to be visible role models of goodness.

There are many opportunities for us to spread such a spirit of warmth and friendliness—for example, when waiting in line at a checkout or ticket counter, waiting for a medical appointment, or riding in an elevator or on an escalator. These waiting times need not be frustrating moments when nothing is happening. Rather, they are opportunities to be friendly and spread goodness. We should eagerly seize them.

Another very easy way to generate good feelings and inspire others is by expressing gratitude to anyone who does nice things— both when they are done directly for us, and even when they are not done directly for us. Thanking a teller at the bank is a thank-you for a direct kindness, as is saying thank-you to a barber or hair dresser, or a bus driver or a taxi driver. Those are no-brainers, as is being gracious to the person operating a highway toll booth or a parking lot attendant, or an operator providing information, or the person at the supermarket checkout. It does not matter that they are only doing their job. That is not an excuse for being oblivious and blasé. Ingratitude has no place in God's world. Less direct, but still very worthy of thank you, is the expression of appreciation to a custodian for keeping a place clean, a bus driver for reaching the intended destination, and the many other ways our lives are made smoother by others that we sometimes only become aware of in their absence.

It behooves us to become sensitive to these niceties performed for us by others and to acknowledge them accordingly. Such acknowledgment should include leaving an appreciative tip, when appropriate. For many people, nothing conveys appreciation more meaningfully than a generous tip, graciously given.

Remember, too, the eloquent observation of the Talmud that the most critical component of any charitable gesture is the warmth and kindness with which it is conveyed.[12]

Gratitude feeds on itself, in that the more gratitude we express, the more grateful we become. The more grateful we become, the more gratitude we express, and the more other people are thereby uplifted, and then become more likely themselves to pass that gratitude on to others. We may consider this to be a "gratitude crescendo."

Bringing Godly goodness to the fore demands that we each get involved in some way to attain this lofty goal. No one can claim exemption, because it is a collective responsibility.

As to how we, the Jewish people—a mere speck on the map, thirteen million people in a world of seven billion—can inspire the world, remember that by refusing to allow our minority status to be a deterrent, and with God on our side and with Godliness as our objective, nothing is impossible.

To Fix or To Perfect?

We began with the presumption that *tikkun olam* means "to fix the world." That is not a bad translation. But it is an incomplete translation.

First, the more lofty goal of *tikkun olam* is not simply to fix; it is to "perfect the world" in line with God's desire that we complete God's work.

Further, the Aleinu, wherein we pray for *tikkun olam* three times a day, contains a fuller articulation of this concept, which we ignore only at our own peril. The passage reads: "to perfect the world through the reign of the Almighty" (*l'takkein olam b'malkhut Shaddai*).

This is obviously God's work, as is clear in the prayer itself. But we are active partners, not mere bystanders, in this work. And, as I have argued at length above, God wants us to be actively engaged in this work.

The perfection can only be achieved under the banner of God— because without God, any repair or fix is illusory and temporary, since it is not rooted in goodness that is linked with the Almighty. It can work for a while but it is transitory, subject to the shifting definitions of goodness that change from generation to generation.

The Talmud[13] records a fascinating insight into the global implications of revelation, based on the following verse: "All the rulers of the world will acknowledge You, O Eternal One, because they have heard the words of Your mouth" (Psalm 138:4).

To what "words" is the verse alluding? The Talmud explains that when God proclaimed the first two of the Ten Statements (Commandments)—namely, the obligation to believe in God and the prohibition against having any other god—the nations of the world said that there was nothing new here, just another self-serving deity interested in self-promotion.

However, when they heard God proclaim the obligation to honor one's parents, they retracted their skepticism and acknowledged the truth of God and of the Ten Statements, including the first two they had previously dismissed. This acceptance of divine governance started with the rulers of the world who controlled their people, and only then filtered down to the masses.

There are many vital messages in this talmudic passage, not the least of which is the revolutionary notion that honoring one's parents does not diminish from honoring God—a prevalent notion then, and even now in some quarters. Instead, honoring parents serves to further enhance the honoring of God.

But for our purposes, the focus is on the nations of the world "listening in" on the great revelation. Although the revelation was meant directly for the people of Israel, the nations of the world were also a target audience (albeit an indirect one).

It was important then that the nations accept the sovereignty of God. We have no evidence that they embraced the faith of the Israelites at the time, but from the Talmud we know that they were inspired; they realized at that time Who the true God was.

The fact that the Talmud stresses this aspect of revelation is further evidence, if indeed any further evidence is needed, that we are called to inspire the world toward the embrace of God as the One and Only God, and thereby to the embrace of the eternal Godly values.

Turning On the Light

The last line of the Aleinu, recited at the conclusion of all regular prayer services, is: "The Eternal shall be ruler over all the world: on that day the Eternal shall be One, and God's name One."

This verse is taken from Zechariah 14:9 and expresses our ultimate hope for this world. But what exactly do these words mean? What precisely is the difference between God being One and God's name being One?

All this becomes more clear if we understand One not as a mathematical concept, but rather as a theological one. A more accurate term for "One" would be "Only." It is more accurate to speak about God's Only-ness, that there is no other god. "The Eternal shall be One" refers to a world that is absent of any polytheism.

"And God's name One" refers, as suggested by many commentaries on the verse, to the time when God will be the only deity mentioned, and that the universal faith expression will be for the Only God, the God of all humankind, the God of creation.[14] The world will then move from passive acknowledgment to active embrace of God.

This is our bottom-line prayer, articulating our great hope for the world. We pray—and work—for a world in which all the false gods, including narcissism, have absolutely no currency. It will be a world permeated with goodness, an Abraham–Sarah world…the world that we are mandated to help bring into existence.

Much has been said about the ultimate Jewish aspiration, to be the light that illumines the nations. This idea finds expression in the verse, "The nations will walk by Your light…" (Isaiah 60:3).

This was understood by Rabbi David ben Aryeh Loeb Altschuler, a Prague rabbi of the eighteenth century, to mean that the nations will learn the ways of God from us and will be illumined (i.e., inspired) thereby.[15]

And this idea is in line with an earlier verse in Isaiah: "I am the Eternal, and have called you with righteousness and will strengthen your hand; and I will protect you and will set you for a covenant to the people, for a light unto the nations" (42:6). In this verse, God clearly calls on the Jewish people to be a light, via righteousness, to the nations. That is our responsibility. Once we have fulfilled that responsibility, the nations will walk by our righteous light. That is the redemptive vision that Isaiah has for us.

The light that we are asked to be is a very precise light: the light that illumines the path to God and Godly goodness.

We must do so individually, and also as a people.

Individually, this mission will unite us via our common purpose, and bring us together as a united people. That is surely a messianic hope. It is simultaneously the messianic vision. And it is mine as well!

NOTES

[1] B. Yevamot 24b and 109b.

[2] Maimonides, M.T. Hilkhot Teshuvah 3:5.

[3] B. Shabbat 119b.

[4] B. Kiddushin 30b and Niddah 31a.

[5] B. Niddah 31a.

[6] B. Sanhedrin 98a.

[7] B. Yoma 86a.

[8] Bereishit Rabbah 39:21, elaborating Genesis 12:5.

[9] B. Shabbat 133b.

[10] Pirkei Avot 4:20.

[11] B. Berakhot 17a.

[12] B. Kiddushin 31a–b.

[13] At B. Kiddushin 31a.

[14] Cf., e.g., the commentaries of Rashi and *M'tzudat David* to Zechariah 14:9.

[15] Cf. the commentary of the *M'tzudat David* to that verse.

Daring Decrees and Radical Responsibility:
Why Rabbinic *Tikkun Olam* Is Not What You Think

Meesh Hammer-Kossoy

In popular conception, the term *tikkun olam* is frequently used as a catchphrase for the Jewish imperative to pursue social justice and service.[1] Ironically, in coining the term *tikkun ḥa-olam*, the rabbis effectively undermined the utopian biblical vision of justice with which many contemporary social activists readily identify. In the mishnaic collection about *tikkun ḥa-olam*[2] found in the fourth and fifth chapters of tractate Gittin, the rabbis trade the Bible's grand program of social equality and economic justice for a set of incremental and realizable social changes. While their approach may seem, on the surface, to be less inspirational than the biblical model that they are reworking, the rabbis are actually deeply radical in their overall approach. By daring use of the rabbinic decree (*takkanah*), the rabbis take responsibility for doing whatever is possible within the constraints of reality to effect change—even at the risk of overruling the Bible. An examination of the Bible's far-reaching, revolutionary approach to regulating society's norms concerning lending money and the Sabbatical and Jubilee years, on the one hand, and the Mishnah's bold methodology but conservative approach to legislation concerning economic norms, on the other, will serve to highlight not only the significant differences between the two approaches, but also to underscore how both are ultimately anchored in a deep optimism about our ability to work toward—and achieve—a better society.

The Biblical Vision of Economic Justice

The most revolutionary expression of the biblical vision of economic justice is found in the legislation concerning the Jubilee and Sabbatical cycles. The Sabbatical year[3] is well known as a once-in-seven-years opportunity for the land to lie fallow. But beyond its restorative environmental merit, the Sabbatical year promotes the value of social and economic equality in at least four distinct ways. First, land is considered ownerless during the Sabbatical year; as Rashi explains, "You may not act as owner; rather, everyone is equal with respect to it."[4] Secondly, since normal gathering and harvesting are prohibited, equal opportunity for consumption apply to all, extending even to the animals: "But you may eat (*lakhem l'okhlah*) whatever the land during the Sabbatical will produce—you, your male and female slaves, the hired and bound laborers who live with you, and your cattle and the beasts in your land may eat all its yield" (Leviticus 25:6–7).[5] The phrase *lakhem l'okhlah* is translated by NJPS as "you may eat," but it may also be translated as "you *shall* eat." Thus, in an ironic and essential turn, the produce is *kodesh*—sanctified.[6] Whereas sanctity regarding foodstuff usually indicates that its use is reserved for a very limited elite (for example, priests), in the case of the Sabbatical year, the sanctity of the produce derives from the fact that it is available to everyone. Thirdly, this egalitarian vision is amplified by the biblical demand that lenders forgive all debts in the Sabbatical year (Deuteronomy 15:1–4). The social hierarchy—of rich and poor, lenders and debtors, slaves and slave-owners—is eliminated, inaugurating a new period of social solidarity, equality, and unity.[7]

Finally, this audacious vision of equality is not merely an economic plan for narrowing social gaps; there is a spiritual aspect at play here, as well. In Deuteronomy, the Sabbatical year is called *sh'mittah*, the year of "release."[8] This notion of release points beyond economic equality toward an overall process of spiritual awareness. By letting go of our focus on material production, *sh'mittah* gives us the opportunity to rest together with our land—thus grounding ourselves, literally and figuratively. As Ibn Ezra explains, we are empowered to direct our thoughts beyond acquiring material wealth.[9] Social solidarity becomes more fundamental than accumulation of wealth and, by consuming less, we become aware of our own excesses. Ibn Ezra finds proof for this communal religious process in the national gathering for Torah reading that marks the end of the *sh'mittah* year, as ordained in the Book of Deuteronomy: "Every seventh year, the year set for remission (*sh'nat ha-sh'mittah*)…you shall read this Teaching (*torah*) aloud in the presence of all Israel" (Deuteronomy 31:10–11). Ibn Ezra understands that the public reading is a kind of closing ceremony, symbolic of what should be done throughout the Sabbatical year— Torah learning and reflection together as a nation. In working less, we enable reflection, which is no less vital to our existence than owning. But again, that release must be available to everyone; Torah learning must be done as a community: "men, women, children, and the strangers in your communities" (Deuteronomy 31:12).

Equality and inclusivity reach redemptive heights in the Jubilee year, which is essentially the Sabbatical year squared: "You shall count off seven weeks of years—seven times seven years—so that the period of seven weeks of years gives you a total of forty-nine years" (Leviticus 25:8). Not coincidentally, both the Jubilee (Leviticus 25:9) and the messianic age (Isaiah 27:13) are inaugurated by the blast of the *shofar*. In fact, the very name of the year, *yoveil*, means "ram" and references the horn that announces the year's onset, thus emphasizing its messianic dimensions.[10] And the *yoveil* trumpets a great egalitarian value: liberty, *d'ror* (Leviticus 25:10). In addition to the regular features of a normal Sabbatical year, the super-sabbatical Jubilee year mandates the release of slaves[11] and the return of all

Israelites to their familial inheritance.[12] It is essentially a return to
a state of Eden: just as the Land of Israel was distributed in equal
portions to all households in the time of Joshua,[13] so too during the
Jubilee year everyone is entitled to return to their ancestral holdings,
rooted as equals.

At the initial level, this is an economic vision of relatively equal
division of wealth, often called distributive justice. As Rashi explains,
"all have an equal part in it."[14] While this aspiration toward equality is
temporary and limited during the Sabbatical year, it is more expansive
and enduring in the Jubilee year. The Torah designates it: "liberty
(*d'ror*) in the land for all (*kol*) of its inhabitants" (Leviticus 25:10).[15]
According to the Talmud, "liberty" and "all" are interdependent—if
everyone is not free, then no one is free.[16] The Talmud notes that the
Jubilee year enshrines economic equality in a way that has the potential
to last beyond the end of the year itself. Not only are debts forgiven;
in addition, slaves are released and given a grant that enables them to
begin a new life.[17] At the same time, it is no less significant that we
are encouraged to work, produce, and purchase for our own personal
benefit in the intervening years: "Six years you *should* sow your field
and six years you *should* prune your vineyard and gather in the yield"
(Leviticus 25:3).[18] Distributive justice is therefore tempered with the
right to be rewarded for hard work by earning and acquiring private
property and wealth (often called retributive justice).

The biblical conception of economic equality is grand in its vision
and scope. However, critics will protest: why bother working hard,
producing, and acquiring property—only to have the results of one's
labors dismantled at the end of fifty years? Surely that undermines
the motivation to be productive! Medieval commentaries have
pointed out that this is exactly where the genius of the biblical vision
kicks in: the accumulation of private property is never an end in itself,
and therefore must be limited. The Akeidat Yitzḥak (Rabbi Isaac

ben Moses Arama, c. 1420–1494) suggests that when we learn to make do with less, we all end up richer.[19] If we wonder, "Is all of our productivity really as fruitful as we thought it was?"—the Torah reassures us: "And should you ask, 'What are we to eat in the seventh year, if we may neither sow nor gather in our crops?' I will ordain My blessing for you in the sixth year, so that it shall yield a crop sufficient for three years" (Leviticus 25:20–21). Rather than a literal promise that the sixth year will produce three times as much, we might understand this as a reassurance that if we plan and reorient ourselves to a reality of less, there will be enough to carry through. By managing in those three years, and even succeeding to experience them as an opportunity, we are triply blessed: with enough to eat, as well as with a willingness to share with those less fortunate and to make time in our lives for things that are of ultimate importance.

To summarize: through the Sabbatical and Jubilee cycles, the Torah balances the ideal of distributive justice with incentives to produce by emphasizing equality, freedom, opportunities to begin afresh, and an inalienable stake in the Land of Israel with the rights of each individual to acquire material wealth. At the same time, the Torah redirects our attention away from individual wealth accumulation toward communal reflection and social solidarity, and reminds us that sometimes enough should be enough. No individual is left behind. A utopian vision indeed! Clearly, this moral grandeur would have been foremost in the minds of the rabbinic legislators who drew on the concept of *tikkun ha-olam* in enacting legislation likewise designed to move toward a more utopian society.

Too Good To Be True?

Sadly, the biblical ideal of economic justice is far removed from our present-day reality. Israel and the United States top the charts when it comes to gaps in wages between the highest and lowest earners.[20] In 2011, more than 450,000 Israelis—roughly six percent of the country's population—hit the streets in a call for "social justice," which was widely understood to be primarily about unfair distribution of wealth.[21] The American "Occupy Wall Street" movement expressed similar concerns.[22] Yet even with all of this recent popular attention being focused on issues of social inequality, the gaps remain enormous.[23]

In truth, the biblical vision of both the Sabbatical and Jubilee years has always been more a dream than a reality. There are no signs in historical sources that the Jubilee year was ever actually observed as prescribed.[24] By emphasizing that full inclusion was considered the *sine qua non* for the Jubilee year, the rabbis assert that the Jubilee had lost even its theoretical legal applicability with the beginning of the Exile.[25] Neither is there any evidence that the Sabbatical year was actually observed in the biblical period. The Torah itself tried to buttress Sabbatical observance with threats as well as promises.[26] But in spite of the rhetoric, it seems that the institution was not observed; indeed, non-observance of the Sabbatical year is cited in biblical texts as a major reason for the Babylonian Exile.[27] In the Second Temple period, there is ample evidence that the Sabbatical year was indeed observed. However, even then its observance came at a great cost and was fraught with tremendous practical difficulty, most notably the challenges of making loans available, eating, and paying taxes.[28]

Thus it is not only the Bible's grand revolutionary vision, but also its impracticalities, that serve as the backdrop against which we must understand the rabbinic use of the expression *tikkun olam*. It is precisely at this juncture of utopian dreams and disappointing reality where the rabbinic institution of *tikkun olam* enters the scene for the first time. The Mishnah states that "for the sake of *tikkun ha-olam*, Hillel ordained *prozbol*."[29] *Prozbol* is a legal loophole that allows an individual lender to transfer a loan to the court and authorize it to collect the loan, on behalf of the lender, at any time. The court is not obliged to release the loan during the Sabbatical year; thus, it becomes permissible for the lender to collect it in the future (through the court), rather than suffering the financial loss that would be entailed by forgiving it. Lenders may even do the collecting themselves, as agents of the court.[30]

Just as the rabbis declare that the Jubilee year was no longer binding because the nation as a whole could not participate,[31] so too, in a bold move, "for the sake of *tikkun ha-olam*," Hillel essentially renders a major part of the Sabbatical year legally inoperative. To understand Hillel's motivation, we must remember that Jews are prohibited from collecting interest from other Jews, so any loan is an act of *tzedakah*.[32] In fact, an interest-free loan, rather than an outright gift, is the primary form of *tzedakah* prescribed by the Torah.[33] Because in an agrarian society these loans were essential for obtaining seed money in years of drought or failed crops, the rabbis considered it a value "not to lock the door in the face of borrowers."[34] Hillel saw that the Sabbatical year was driving a credit crisis: the wealthy were refusing to risk loaning to the poor as the Sabbatical year approached, out of a fear that the loans would be cancelled and they would lose their money—despite explicit Torah disapprobation of such refusal (Deuteronomy 15:9). Therefore, Hillel deemed it essential to encourage loans by enabling the wealthy to collect their loans even after the Sabbatical year, even at the expense of rendering the injunction to forgive loans in the Sabbatical year inoperative. In modern terms, this could be classified as "trickle-down economics"—making conditions better for the rich in hopes that it will benefit the poor people indirectly. Could this really be *tikkun ha-olam*?

Certainly in the short term, we can recognize that Hillel's decree could in fact be beneficial for the poor by ensuring that loans would continue to be available to them, even as the Sabbatical year approached. On the other hand, this rabbinic enactment effectively cancels the loan forgiveness that the Torah grants the poor—and this could hardly be seen as beneficial for them. How can the rabbis deny the poor their Torah-right to periodically start afresh, simply because the rich were unwilling to abide by the Torah's mandate to forgive loans (and the rabbis were powerless to force them to comply)? Eradicating the practice of loan forgiveness does, certainly, result in additional concentration of wealth in the hands of the few and deeper impoverishment of the weak.[35] The utopian vision of distributive justice symbolized by the Torah's provisions for the Jubilee and Sabbatical years is officially abandoned by the rabbis' enactment of the *prozbol*. It is ironic that a measure undertaken for the sake of *tikkun ha-olam* may, in this way, in fact contribute to further economic disparity between rich and poor!

Tikkun Olam of the Mishnah: Incremental Justice and Brutal Realism

Hillel's approach to the Sabbatical year is part of a larger rubric of rabbinic social activism. Designated *tikkun ha-olam*, the rabbis use decrees (*takkanot*) as a methodological and ideological response to the overall biblical economic and social ideal as a whole, and not just the Sabbatical year in particular. While the Mishnah is generally organized topically, Hillel's *prozbol* decree is found in the tractate of the Mishnah that deals with divorce law. The pericope deals with many different topics but is unified by the recurrence of the expression "for the sake of *tikkun olam*,"[36] and it is followed by another collection of material that employs the recurrent formula "for the sake of peace" (*mi-p'nei darkhei shalom*). The average twenty-first century Jew who is familiar with the term *tikkun olam* in its modern usage might be surprised to learn how it is used in this early source.[37] Many of these *mishnayot* do protect the underdog: they make it easier for women to obtain a writ of divorce[38] and for widows to collect what is owed to them,[39] and they make provisions to protect orphans' property[40] and people with disabilities,[41] as well as for improving the conditions of slaves.[42] However, these laws lack the compassionate or mystical tones that are common in modern parlance with respect to *tikkun olam*. On the contrary, many of these *mishnayot* restrict entitlements, and take the approach that sometimes it is necessary "to be cruel in order to be kind."[43] Most importantly: not only does the Mishnah undermine the loan amnesty that the Torah prescribes during the *sh'mittah* years, but these texts even seem to abandon the revolutionary "no Israelite left behind" approach embodied by the Torah's egalitarian vision of the Sabbatical and Jubilee cycles. Instead, the rabbis of the Mishnah enact changes that reflect a concern for the community as a whole. In so doing, they limit and sometimes even undercut the benefit that the most vulnerable members of society would have received, according to a strict application of the Torah's law. While legally innovative, their approach seems to be fiscally conservative.

The changes to the halakah that are justified by the principle of *mi-p'nei tikkun ha-olam* may, in fact, undermine some of the legal protections for the underprivileged that are found in the Bible itself. For example, the Mishnah declares: "A man who sells himself and his children [as slaves] to a non-Jew is not to be redeemed. However, the children should be redeemed after their father's death."[44] The rabbis' laudable goal is to discourage abusive or dysfunctional fathers from selling their children into slavery repeatedly.[45] However, the Torah dictates that even the father "shall be redeemed" (Leviticus 25:48).[46] Clearly, it is even more imperative to redeem an innocent child who has been enslaved to non-Jews against his or her will. Does the Torah not state that "children shall not die for the sins of their parents" (Deuteronomy 24:16)?[47] This *mishnah* seems not only to echo the most conservative positions, arguing for the detrimental effects of welfare, but also to undermine the basic Torah commandment to redeem captives[48] and to give *tzedakah* to those in need.[49] Surely, this would not resonate with liberal activists working under the banner of *tikkun olam*! Nor does it remain faithful to the biblical ideal of the Jubilee cycle, according to which slaves should be freed and the indigent should be given a chance at a fresh start.[50]

Similarly, the rabbis designate redeeming captives as a *mitzvah* of the highest priority. Summarizing the Talmud,[51] Maimonides states:

> The redemption of captives receives priority over sustaining the poor and providing them with clothing. [Indeed,] there is no greater *mitzvah* than the redemption of captives. For a captive is among those who are hungry, thirsty, and unclothed, and he is in mortal peril. Those who pay no attention to their redemption violate the negative commandments: "Do not harden your heart or close your hand" (Deuteronomy 15:7), "Do not stand by when the blood of your neighbor is in danger" (Leviticus 19:16), and "He shall not oppress him with exhausting work in your presence" (Leviticus 25:53). And they have negated the observance of the positive commandments: "You shall certainly open up your hand to him" (Deuteronomy 15:8), "And your brother shall live with you" (Deuteronomy19:18), "Love your neighbor as yourself" (Leviticus 19:18), "Save those who are taken for death" (Proverbs 24:11), and many other decrees of this nature. There is no *mitzvah* as great as the redemption of captives.[52]

The Mishnah, however, states: "One does not redeem captives for more than their value, for the sake of *tikkun ha-olam*."[53] This *mishnah* is shocking, especially because its authors were assuming that captives were being sold on the slave market rather than ransomed by terrorists. How can anyone put a limit on the value of a human being? After all, the Mishnah states elsewhere that "whoever saves a single soul, it is as if they saved an entire world."[54] In fact, over the course of history the restriction on redeeming captives for more than their value was more honored in the breach than observance. So much was this the case that in the sixteenth century Rabbi David ben Solomon Ibn Zimra (1479–1573) resigned himself to accepting the prevalent norms of behavior in light of the noble motivation from which they emerge: "The whole nation of Israel has already become accustomed to redeeming captives for more than their value on the slave market. Leave Israel be—they are doers of kindness, descendants of doers of kindness."[55] Surely it was this same sentiment that led to the national jubilation all across Israel that accompanied the 2011 ransoming of IDF soldier Gilad Shalit for an almost unprecedented exchange of 1,027 prisoners.[56] But the Shalit deal also illustrates precisely the concerns that motivated the rabbis to restrict captive redemption in the first place. The rabbis certainly support redemption of every member of the Jewish community, but not at too high an expense to the community as a whole—either in the short term or in the long term. The laws of the Jubilee cycle embody the utopian concern that genuine freedom must include "all inhabitants" (Leviticus 25:10), and that if that freedom does not include everyone, it does not exist at all (B. Arkhin 32b). However, this biblical idealism is compromised by the rabbis of the Mishnah in the name of rabbinic *tikkun olam*.

One more example will suffice to prove my point. The Mishnah states:

> If a man was half slave and half free,[58] he should labor one day for his master and one day for himself; so ruled the School of Hillel.
>
> The School of Shammai said to them: You have fixed the matter for his master, but for him you have not fixed it. He cannot marry a slave because he is half free. He cannot marry a free-woman since he is half slave. Should he desist? And was not the world only created for fruition and increase, as it is written: "He created it not a waste; he formed it to be inhabited" (Isaiah 45:18)? Rather, for the sake of *tikkun olam*, they should compel his master to set him free; and the slave to write him a promissory note for half of his value.
>
> The School of Hillel retracted and taught according to the opinion of the School of Shammai.

No doubt, this is a *mishnah* about human rights. The slave has the inalienable right to marry and procreate, and that right overrides another's right to private property. However, how can the School of Hillel and the School of Shammai reconcile themselves to slavery and call it *tikkun olam*? Instead of incrementally improving the plight of the slave, why not abolish slavery altogether?[59]

How different is the rabbinic methodology reflected in the idea of *tikkun olam* from that of the biblical Jubilee cycle! So much is learned from the contrast of the two. Unlike the biblical vision, the mishnaic collection that cites the principle of *tikkun olam* works within the existing social order. In the sub-collection about "the ways of peace," the rabbis repeatedly pay homage to the status quo, even when it is not justified legally or morally, "for the sake of peace."[60] Not only do they sanction slavery (even child slavery!), but the rabbis even legally recognize the criminal Roman takeover of Jewish land. Despite the fact that Roman extortionists expelled lawful Jewish landowners by force, the rabbis give *de facto* status to their thievery by allowing Jews to purchase the land from the Roman squatter who is selling land he possesses but does not own, while requiring the Jewish purchaser to make only symbolic payment to the displaced lawful Jewish owner.[61] The rabbis discount the original owner's rights in order to further the overall national interest of encouraging Jewish possession of the land.

In a nutshell: biblical idealism seems to give way to rabbinic pragmatism, as evinced in the legislation of Mishnah Gittin that justifies itself by citing the principle of *tikkun olam*. In every instance, the rabbis are motivated by a well intentioned and deeply felt desire to benefit the Jewish community as a whole. However, this overall betterment comes at the expense of individual entitlements. The rabbis abandon the revolutionary vision of universal entitlement for *every* citizen that is reflected in the Jubilee cycle, in favor of small but attainable improvements in the economic welfare of the community as a whole. Nevertheless, in spite of its conservative appearance, there is actually a bold and radical core of the *tikkun olam* program.

Tikkun Olam as Radical Rabbinic Responsibility

Despite the conservatism that inheres in the incremental steps toward improving the world, the expression *tikkun olam* also reflects the rabbis' bold methodology: the rabbinic decree, or *takkanah*. Generally speaking, the rabbis' authority derives from received tradition. "Moses received the Torah at Sinai and handed it on to Joshua; Joshua to the elders; the elders to the prophets; and the prophets handed it on to the men of the Great Assembly."[62] As the earliest compendium of the Oral Law, the Mishnah could be described as a collection of transmitted traditions or laws derived from the Torah, using a fixed set of hermeneutic principles.

Tikkun olam depends on a different, radical kind of authority in which the rabbis accept upon themselves the responsibility to legislate, independent of Torah tradition. The Hebrew word *tikkun* means "repair," but the same verbal root (*tav-kof-nun*) also generates the word *takkanah*, "decree."[63] Indeed, every law in the *tikkun olam/ darkhei shalom* collection is explicitly or implicitly understood as a rabbinic decree designed either to repair the world or to promote peace.[64] The fact that decrees are utilized relatively frequently by the rabbis does not detract from the radical nature of the institution.[65] After all, the rabbis deem it axiomatic that the world was created for and through the blueprint of Torah.[66] There is no wisdom that is not already contained in the Torah, as Ben Bag Bag taught: "One should turn it over and turn it over, because everything is in it."[67] Thus, the notion that the world is best repaired through rabbinic injunctions that seem to set aside the Torah's vision of justice is poignant. A number of decrees in the collection seem not only to legislate concerning matters about which the Torah is silent; they seem to override Torah commandments![68] The notion that the rabbis would supersede a Torah rule is so radical that later rabbis of the Talmud find themselves incredulous: how could the rabbis of the Mishnah dare to overrule the Torah?[69] "If it were not stated, it would be impossible to say"[70]—it is almost as if the rabbis are suggesting that *they* know better than God how to create a just world. And yet, the very fact that they undertake such a bold approach suggests that the rabbis of the Mishnah believed that their times demanded exceptional measures.

A literary and structural examination of our sources illuminates the overall rabbinic stance regarding *tikkun olam*. The location of our collection in the middle of the section of the Mishnah dealing with divorce law is not coincidental; in fact, the *tikkun olam* corpus is framed with a concern for marriage and family—and thus, ultimately, Jewish continuity (both literally and metaphorically). The destruction of the Temple and the ensuing exile from the Land of Israel was seen by the rabbis as an attempt on God's part to divorce Israel, seen as bride of the Divine.[71] Thus, the collection opens with a series of decrees designed to protect the vulnerable divorced woman[72] and closes with a set of emergency decrees desperately seeking to preserve the Jewish presence in the Land, symbolizing the marriage between God and Israel. Jewish land ownership was threatened by Roman extortion after the military defeats of 70 and 135 C.E., but the rabbis refused to resign themselves to failure. The rabbis confront a world in which God seems to have stepped out of the picture: God has hidden the divine face.[73] The rabbis respond by filling this void through the institution of *takkanah*. By creating a vision of radical responsibility, they demand that God return to the marriage and restore the divine vision of justice in the world.

Furthermore, although speculative, the fact that this collection is found in the middle of tractate Gittin, which occupies a central place in the entire Mishnah, may hint that *tikkun olam* is central to the rabbinic mission.[74] Support for the centrality of the decrees for *tikkun olam* and the sake of peace may also be detected in the "envelope structure" found in the mishnaic corpus, as presented in the printed text.[75] The key words—forms of the root *tav-kof-nun*, and *shalom*—are central in the final *mishnayot* of both the opening and closing tractates of the Mishnah. The final *mishnah* of the Mishnah's opening tractate, Berakhot, reads as follows:

> All blessings made in the Temple were closed with the expression "for eternity" (*min ha-olam*). But after the heretics corrupted [matters] by saying there is only a single world (*olam*), [the rabbis] **decreed** (*hitkinu, from tav-kof-nun*) that that one should say "from eternity and for eternity" (*min ha-olam v'ad ha-olam*). And they also **decreed** (*hitkinu*) that one

should inquire about the **peace** (*shalom*) of one's fellow with the [divine] name, as it says: "And behold, Boaz came from Bethlehem, and said unto the reapers, 'The Eternal be with you'; and they answered him, 'The Eternal bless you'" (Ruth 2:4). And it is written, "The Eternal is with you, valiant warrior" (Judges 6:12); and it says, "Do not disdain your mother when she is old" (Proverbs 23:22). And it says, "It is time to act for the Eternal: they have violated Your law" (Psalm 119:126). Rabbi Natan says: "They have violated Your law because it was time to act for the Eternal."[76]

The root *tav-kof-nun* features doubly in this *mishnah*: not only do the rabbis make *takannot*, but the decrees come to "fix" the corruption wreaked by the heretics. Furthermore, the key words olam (meaning both "world" and "eternity") and *shalom* ("peace") also feature prominently. Since all three of these words do not occur together elsewhere in the Mishnah, the resonance with our collection is strong. Of course, the conceptual connection to our collection is also clear: sometimes it is necessary for the rabbis to make rabbinic decrees that actually uproot Torah law, for God's sake and for the sake of preserving the Israel–God relationship.[77] What looks like rabbinic abandonment of the Jubilee ideal is really a radical attempt by the rabbis to "break it in order to fix it."

The closing of the Mishnah's final tractate also includes the words *olam* and *shalom* and thus seems to resonate with our collection,[78] but with a twist:

Rabbi Joshua ben Levi said: The blessed Holy One will cause every righteous person to inherit three hundred and ten **worlds** (*olamot*), as it says "That I may cause those that love Me to inherit *yesh* (310),[79] and that I may fill their treasuries"

(Proverbs 8:21). Rabbi Shimon ben Ḥalafta said: The blessed Holy One found no vessel that could hold Israel's blessing except **peace**, for it is written, "The Eternal will give strength to His people, the Eternal will bless His people in **peace**" (Psalm 29:11).[80]

In this closing passage of the Mishnah, the rabbis set forth their own utopian vision, in which the key words "world" and "peace"—in that order yet again—continue to feature prominently. But this time, the rabbinic decree (*tav-kof-nun*) is conspicuously absent. That is because in the redeemed world imagined here, the rabbinic decree is no longer necessary. The rabbis' bold decrees—with which they opened the Mishnah, and which they literally placed at the center of their program—have been successful in restoring the intimate relationship between God and Israel. Their demands have been answered, and it is no longer necessary to fill the void created by God's hidden face; as God returns as the primary actor, the rabbis step back. While conjectural, this literary reading is interesting to consider.

So on the one hand, the rabbinic methodology of incremental change justified as *tikkun olam* is diametrically opposed to the utopian, revolutionary biblical approach to justice found in the institutions of the Sabbatical and Jubilee years. The rabbis contend with the world in brutally realistic ways and they work toward equality through incremental steps. However, their understanding of *tikkun olam* should be seen both as deeply radical and also as profoundly utopian—utopian in its visioning of an ideal world, but radical in the formulation of the steps to be undertaken, in order to get there. Their world is in need of *tikkun* because it is broken. But there are two aspects of to this brokenness (and ultimate repair): both the social/economic order on earth, as well as the other-worldly dimension of the relationship between Israel and God—which is, at its source, grounded in Torah (both Written and Oral). In a radical step, the rabbis take full responsibility for restoring that relationship, even if it means temporarily overriding the Torah they treasure so dearly. This is spiritual audacity at its finest.

The Message

I have suggested that the uncompromisingly realistic strategy of mishnaic *tikkun olam* should be seen as a reaction to the impracticality of implementing the utopian biblical model of Sabbatical and Jubilee years. The Torah envisions radical equality and social solidarity in which every individual has an inalienable stake in the national wealth. At the same time, it cultivates a deep connection to the land and eschews the slavery of insatiable acquisition. But this vision remains a dream lacking a handhold in the real world. The rabbis, on the other hand, boldly act in the unredeemed world before them. They take full responsibility for the current state of the world and its repair—so much so that, when necessary, they are even willing to override biblical laws. As courageous as all that may be, their agenda is moderate and realistic in its ambitions, even as it is radical in its tactics. They take incremental (and sometimes painful) steps, which are intended to improve the plight of the weakest members of their society in the long run and to preserve peace in the short term, but to do so, they must relinquish the Torah's ideal of complete equality.

In choosing a spiritual and political path for ourselves, we can draw much inspiration from both the biblical and rabbinic models. The Jubilee cycle, as delineated in the Torah, provides us with the essential vision toward which we must strive, even if we will never quite achieve it: the ideals of equality, freedom, and modest consumption. Rabbi Jonathan Sacks teaches that dreaming is one of the most practical things we can do.[81] Without aspirations we lack direction;

soaring is impossible. And occasionally, even the utopian dream can become a reality. Is there anything more utopian than the Zionist dream? David Ben Gurion, Israel's first prime minister, is reported to have said, "In Israel, in order to be a realist, you must believe in miracles." It was this kind of sheer determination that allowed for Herzl's famous aphorism, "If you will it, it is not a dream"—and that made it possible for the dream of the early Zionists to be realized, in the founding of the State of Israel.

If dreams can become realities, why would the rabbis abandon that utopian dream in favor of smaller, more concrete steps toward attaining a practical, this-worldly justice? To be sure, dreaming carries with it risks—because not every dream will come to fruition, and thus working toward a dream entails a recognition that one may, in the end, fail to achieve the dream…and this is a sobering thought. While Ben Gurion and Herzl's unflagging optimism led to miraculous success, Yossi Klein Halevi has recently documented the unfulfilled utopian dreams of both the left and the right of Israeli society.[82] Both utopianisms had detrimental impact: the utopian vision of the leftist Kibbutz movement led to dangerous flirtation with Stalinism, while the utopianism of the right-wing Gush Emunim movement has led to an unsustainable settlement policy beyond the pre-1967 borders. Similarly, failed messianic delusions in the aftermath of the Great Revolt of 70 C.E. and the Bar Kohkba Revolt in 132 C.E. led not only to the destruction of the Temple but also to huge death tolls and the near-total decimation of the Jewish presence in Judea. The sages of the Mishnah, having witnessed these truly catastrophic consequences of utopianism, caution us to temper our utopian vision with realism.[83] It is better to take two steps forward and one step back, than to misstep and fall off a cliff. However, while no longer utopianists, the rabbis maintained the most important characteristic of the optimist: a belief in the ability to shape their own destiny.

While the Torah teaches a bold agenda of equality and freedom, the rabbis teach us never to give up, but to work slowly and steadily. "The day is short and the tasks are great."[84] With many small steps, we can get far. The road is long, but if we have a clear sense of where we want to wind up, then we can be assured that small, incremental steps will surely lead us in that direction.

NOTES

[1] This is the basic assumption of the entire volume of *Jewish Educational Leadership* 11:1 (Winter 2013); see specifically Zvi Grumet, "Letter from the Editor," p. 2.

[2] The Mishnah uses the formulation *tikkun ha-olam*, but the definite article (*ha-*) is not usually employed in modern colloquial English. I use both locutions, *tikkun olam* and *tikkun ha-olam*, interchangeably.

[3] The laws concerning the Sabbatical year are found in Leviticus 25:1–7, Exodus 23:9–12, and Deuteronomy 15:1–12.

[4] Rashi to Leviticus 25:6, s.v. *v'haytah shabbat ha-aretz*.

[5] The translations of biblical passages throughout this essay are, unless otherwise noted, generally based on the "new JPS" translation of the Tanakh (Philadelphia: Jewish Publication Society, 1985), hereafter referred to as NJPS.

[6] Y. Sheviit 4:7 (35c), based on Leviticus 25:12, reading the verse to reference the *sh'mittah* year.

[7] The social vision addressed in this essay is limited, of course, to relative economic equality for males.

[8] Deuteronomy 15:1; see also Exodus 23:11, where the verbal form of this Hebrew word (*tishm'tennah*) appears.

[9] See comment of Abraham Ibn Ezra (1108–1164) to Deuteronomy 31:12, s.v. *u-l'ma·an yilm'du*.

[10] Rashi to Leviticus 25:8, based on B. Rosh Hashanah 26a. However, Ibn Ezra, Ramban, Ḥizkuni, and others suggest that the word *yoveil* is derived from a root meaning "lead away," thus suggesting a hyper-release or return to roots occasioned by the manumission of slaves. The English word "Jubilee" is an Anglicization of the Hebrew *yoveil*. The contemporary meaning of "jubilee" as a huge celebration relates to the celebratory freedom granted in that year.

[11] Exodus 21:2 dictates the release of slaves after six years of servitude. Some biblical scholars have suggested that this release was intended to correspond to the Sabbatical year, rather than to the beginning of an individual's period of servitude; this understanding is also found in *Targum Yonatan* to Exodus 21:7, 22:2, and in the commentary of Joseph Bekhor Shor (twelfth century, France) to 21:6. This seems to be the way 2 Chronicles 36:12 understands Jeremiah 34:13–14. Others scholars have followed the traditional understanding, found in Y. Kiddushin 1:2 (59a), that the six years are calculated from the beginning of servitude.

[12] The egalitarian vision of the Torah is largely symbolic, and limited, however, since non-Jews are excluded and women do not generally inherit a portion of the Land of Israel. See further Numbers 27:1–8, however, for an example of the willingness of Scripture to enfranchise women even when doing so rejected existent tradition.

[13] The allotment is detailed extensively in Joshua 13–21.

[14] Comment to Leviticus 25:6, s.v. *v'haytah*.

[15] This is my own translation.

[16] B. Arakhin 32b.

[17] Rashi to Leviticus 25:10, s.v. *u–k'ratem d'ror*.

[18] My translation. The imperfect form of the verbs in Hebrew can be understood either descriptively or prescriptively.

[19] *Sefer Akeidat Yitzḥak* to Leviticus, gate 69 (ed. Lvov 5628 [1867–1868]), p. 144b, and see also gate 67, chap. 7.

[20] See, for example, the information provided by the Organisation for Economic Co-operation and Development on their website, at www.oecd.org/els/soc/income-distribution-database.htm.

[21] Bradley Burston, "Some 450,000 Israelis March at Massive March of the Million Rallies Across Country," *Haaretz* English edition (September 3, 2011), available online at www.haaretz.com.

[22] Cf., e.g., Kerry Picket's article, "Occupy Wall Street Protesters Post Manifesto of 'Demands,'" published in the *The Washington Times* on October 3, 2011.

[23] Lev Grinburg, "The Success of Israel Social Protest Failure," in *Haaretz* (January 23, 2013). For a concise list of what was achieved by the protests, see Talia Gorodess, "'The People Demand Social Justice:' How the Israeli Social Protests Ignored the Palestinian Issue, and the Road Ahead," in *Atkins Paper Series* (July 2013), pp. 6–9; John Cassidy, "American Inequality in Six Charts," in *The New Yorker* (November 18, 2013); and Catherine Muldbrandon, "The One Chart You Need to Understand America's Mind-blowing Income Gap," in *Huffington Post* (April 15, 2013).

[24] David L. Lieber, "Sabbatical Year and Jubilee," in *Encyclopedia Judaica* (Jerusalem: Keter, 1971), vol. 14, p. 575.

[25] B. Arakhin 32b. *Sh'mittah* also lost all or some of its biblical force, according to rabbinic interpretation (B. Gittin 36a).

[26] See Deuteronomy 15:9 for a threat, and Leviticus 25:20–21 for a promise.

[27] See 2 Chronicles 36:21 and Jeremiah 34:12–13, and cf. Leviticus 26:34–35 and 43.

[28] 1 Maccabees 6:49, 53 and Josephus *Antiquities* 3:280ff. Cf. also Nehemiah 5:1–13, which some scholars have understood as a sort of Sabbatical year and others as proof that it was not observed. According to rabbinic understanding, once the Jubilee year was defunct, the Sabbatical year had the force of a rabbinic law. As the economic situation in the Land of Israel deteriorated, the rabbis found various leniencies to make the requirements less onerous. For all historical aspects of the Sabbatical year, see the collection of essays in *Sh'mittah: M'korot, Hagut, Meḥkar* (Jerusalem: Amana, 5733 [1972–1973]).

[29] M. Gittin 4:3. I identify this *mishnah* as the earliest occurrence of the term *tikkun olam* even though the term is not used in the parallel, probably original, context (M. Sheviit 10:3–4). Even assuming that the term is a later accretion, the decree represents the ideology embedded in the text perfectly. My goal is a literary–ideological, rather than historical, understanding of *tikkun olam*.

[30] M. Sheviit 10:4.

[31] B. Arkhin 32b.

[32] Leviticus 25:37. This prohibition is still in force today; thus the institution of the Hebrew Free Loan Society in later centuries. However, this prohibition is frequently circumvented with the help of a *heter iska* agreement, a legal loophole designed to allow businesses to circumvent the laws governing lending on interest.

[33] The biblical verses on this topic are understood by Maimonides as requiring not outright gifts, but rather loans to the poor; see his M.T. Matnot Aniyim 7:1.

[34] This expression appears at least nine times in the Babylonian Talmud. See, for example, B. Gittin 50a and B. Bava Kamma 8a.

[35] The approach of the rabbis seems to have won the day: the *prozbol* is still utilized, even in modern times. Furthermore, a similar "halakhic fiction" was employed starting in the late nineteenth century as Jews returned to the Land of Israel with the Zionist movement and engaged in agriculture. Inspired by the leniencies that Rabban Gamaliel and Rabbi Judah the Prince had already implemented to save the Jewish communities in the Land of Israel in antiquity, modern rabbis sought to support the struggling agricultural movement by allowing a fictional sale of the land to non-Jews (called *heter m'khirah*). Rabbi Abraham Isaac Kook (1865–1935) was the most prominent rabbinic proponent of the sale, on a temporary basis, in 1909. The Ḥazon Ish (Rabbi Avraham Yeshaya Karelitz, 1878–1953) opposed the sale even then, and such opposition has increased steadily to the point that in recent *sh'mittah* years, the chief rabbinate of Israel has left it to the discretion of local rabbis whether or not to rely on it.

[36] M. Gittin, chapters 4 and 5. One exception is 4:8, which is appended to 4:7 because of its similar formulation. Similarly, 5:4–7 do not employ the expression explicitly but are closely related to the theme. Hillel's *prozbol* decree is also found in M. Sheviit 10:4.

[37] Modern scholars have critiqued liberals for what they consider to be their manipulative use of the term *tikkun olam* in a way that seems almost to do violence to the non-liberal, non-radical politics of the mishnaic collection. See especially Hillel Halkin, "How Not to Repair the World," in *Commentary* (July 2008), pp. 21–27.

[38] M. Gittin 4:2.

[39] M. Gittin 4:3, 5:1.

[40] M. Gittin 5:2.

[41] M. Gittin 5:5–6.

[42] M. Gittin 4:4–6.

[43] Even before Shakespeare coined this phrase in *Hamlet* (Act 3, scene 4, line 178), it was found in the midrash at Kohelet Rabbah 7:16, where we read: "Whoever is merciful where he should be cruel is destined to be cruel where he should be merciful."

[44] M. Gittin 4:9.

[45] Either the son has been taken captive in payment for an unpaid loan (see 2

Kings 4:1 and B. Gittin 46b), or the sale was a transgression, since the father can sell his daughters but does not have the right to sell his sons into slavery (see Exodus 21:7 and Mekhilta *Nezikin* 3).

[46] My translation is based on Rashi to this verse, who states, "Do not leave him there until the Jubilee year"; so too Rambam, M.T. Hilkhot Matnot Aniyim 8:13. See, however, NJPS translation, "One of his kinsmen shall redeem him," or Harold Fisch, in the Koren 1989 edition of the Tanakh: "After he is sold, he may be redeemed again." Even if redemption is merely a right rather than an imperative, as indicated by Rashi, our *mishnah* seems to undermine it.

[47] My citation of this verse is intended for figurative effect, but as explained in Exodus 21:7 and Mekhilta N *ezikin* 3, the father has literally sinned in selling his son.

[48] Maimonides associates the command to redeem captives with a number of verses: Deuteronomy 15:7, Leviticus 19:16 and 25:57, and negative commandments Deuteronomy 15:8, Leviticus 25:37 and 19:18, and Proverbs 24:11. See M.T. Hilkhot MatnotAniyim 8:10, as well as S.A. Yoreh Dei·ah 352:6.

[49] S.A. Yoreh Dei·ah 352:2.

[50] In fact, the rabbis of the Talmud find the simple reading of this *mishnah* so harsh that they interpret it to only be applicable when the poor sells himself into slavery repeatedly; see B. Gittin 46b.

[51] Primarily B. Bava Batra 8b.

[52] M.T. Matnot Aniyim 8:10, based on the translation of Eliyahu Touger (Jerusalem and New York: Moznayim), 2005, p. 172.

[53] M. Gittin 4:6.

[54] M. Sanhedrin 4:5, cited according to the Parma and Kaufman manuscripts. Some printed editions of the Mishnah contain the text "who saves a single soul from Israel," but the words "from Israel" are a later interpolation.

[55] Responsa of the Radbaz 1:40, ed. Warsaw 5646 [1885–1886], pp. 6a–b.

[56] Gilad Shalit was serving in the IDF when he was abducted by Hamas in 2006. In 2011 Shalit was ransomed by the State of Israel in exchange for 1,027 Palestinian and Israeli–Arab prisoners. Despite the extraordinary price and the attendant security risks incurred by the exchange, polls showed that 79% of Israelis favored the exchange; see "Poll: 79% of Israelis Support Shalit Deal," in *Yediot Aḥronot* (October 17, 2011), available online at www.ynet.co.il. In 1985, Israel agreed to a similar but less extreme exchange (coined the Jibril Agreement), in which three Israeli soldiers were exchanged for 1,150 security prisoners.

[56] M. Gittin 4:5.

[58] The slave was probably freed by one of his or her two owners and is thus technically only half free.

[59] In truth, my critique of the rabbis for falling short of the biblical vision is somewhat overstated in this case. The Torah also could have abolished slavery altogether. Even while the Torah demands "freedom for all inhabitants" and

return to ancestral inheritance, the inheritance only includes (male) Jewish inhabitants. While Hebrew slaves (both male and female) are liberated in the Jubilee year (and after seven years of servitude generally; see Rashi to Leviticus 25:10, s.v. *d'ror*), Canaanite slaves—the subject of discussion in this *mishnah*—are enslaved eternally and can be bequeathed for "all time" (Leviticus 25:46). The limits of the Torah vision of equality, while very real, are a subject for another essay.

[60] M.Gittin 5:8–9. Take, for example, the practice of giving the first *aliyah* of the Torah reading to priests. While the right to this honor may and should be waived in certain circumstances, the rabbis prohibit doing so—for fear of causing quarrels. This pattern holds true in the first three decrees in this mishnaic text.

[61] M. Gittin 5:6.

[62] Pirkei Avot 1:1, trans. Rabbi Jonathan Sacks in the *Koren Siddur* (Jerusalem: Koren 2006), p. 641.

[63] Hebrew words are built on three-letter roots. Thus, apparently disparate words based on those roots should be understood as related, even though the connections may not be apparent in translation.

[64] The verbal infinitive (*l'hatkin*) appears explicitly four times in the collection (M.Gittin 4:2–3), but is implicit in the refrain "because of *tikkun olam*." Take for example M. Gittin 4:4, which contrasts the decree (*takkanah*) with strict law (*halakhah*): "According to the strict law...but for the sake of tikkun olam...." Similarly, in the talmudic treatment of a *mishnah* prescribing a law "for the sake of peace" that seems to match the Torah law, Abaye objects to Rav Joseph: "Is this rule only [a rabbinic one] in the interests of peace? It derives from the Torah?!" (B. Gittin 59b, trans. Maurice Simon [London: Soncino Press, 1960]).

[65] Another important collection appears in the fourth chapter of M. Rosh Hashanah. For more on the institution of *takannah* and its source of authority, see Menachem Elon, *Jewish Law: History, Sources, Principles,* trans. Bernard Auerbach and Melvin Sykes (Philadelphia: Jewish Publication Society 1994), vol. 2, pp. 477–677.

[66] Bereishit Rabbah 1:1.

[67] Pirkei Avot 5:22; the word "Torah" here could be understood in the broadest sense, including even rabbinic decrees.

[68] I have already discussed the case of prozbol, which the Talmud recognizes explicitly as apparently overriding biblical law (see B. Gittin 34b). A number of other laws seem to override biblically prescribed property rights; see, for example, M. Gittin 4:4–5; 5:3, 5–6. Note especially B. Gittin 33a, which states that according to Rabbi Shimon son of Gamaliel (as cited at M. Gittin 4:2), a writ of divorce that is disqualified according to biblical law is accepted by the rabbis.

[69] B. Gittin 36a and B. Yevamot 90b.

[70] See, for example, B. Berakhot 32a.

[71] In traditional Jewish law, the power of divorce lies exclusively in the hands

of the husband. Thus as bride in the rabbinic imagination, any action the Jews take to "save the marriage" is daring and perhaps even brazen. For more explicit sources portraying the Jewish people and God as bride and groom, see for example M. Yadayim 2:5 and Shir Hashirim Rabbah 2:1. Saul Lieberman traces this motif through the eyes of several different sages in his "Mishnat Shir Ha-shirim," in Gershom G. Scholem, *Jewish Gnosticism, Merkabah Mysticism, and Talmudic Tradition* (New York: Jewish Theological Seminary of America, 1965), pp. 118–126.

[72] The decrees are presented as for the benefit of the woman, but they would naturally also protect any future children as well as the second husband. Thanks to my *hevruta*, Raḥel Berkovits, with whom I first began exploring some of these issues.

[73] The image of "hiding God's face" first appears in Deuteronomy 31:18.

[74] For examples of the mishnaic use of chiastic structure, which point to the centrality of the middle point, see the first and third chapters of M. Rosh HaShannah and Avraham Walfish, *Shittat Ha-arikhah Ha-sifrutit Ba-mishnah Al Pi Massekhet Rosh Hashanah* (Ph.D. dissertation, Hebrew University 2001), pp. 262–263; Yosef Tabori, Pesaḥ Dorot (Tel Aviv: Kibbutz HaMeuḥad, 1996), pp. 361–362, Moshe Vilinger, "Mivneh U-mashmaʿut B'ferek Ha-rishon B'bava batra," online at www.etzion.org.il/dk/5767/1098mamar.html. Even though identifying the middle is an inexact science, Gittin is near the middle counting either tractates or orders of the Mishnah.

[75] The "envelope structure" or "inclusion" is a very common literary feature in the Mishnah. See Avraham Walfish, "The Poetics of the Mishnah," in Alan Avery-Peck and Jacob Neusner, eds., *The Mishnah in Contemporary Perspective* (Leiden: Brill, 2002), vol. 2, pp. 165–178. This particular occurrence should be identified as later than the original compilation of the Mishnah, since the final *mishnah* in Uktzin is actually a later addition that does not appear in all manuscripts; see the commentary of Hanokh Albeck and his appendices there.

[76] M. Berakhot 9:5.

[77] See B. Yevamot 89b–90b, where the words "uproot" (from the root *ayin-kof-resh*) and "violate" (from the root ayin-vav-resh) are used by the rabbis themselves; and cf. B. Sanhedrin 46a, where the word "violate" is used in this sense.

[78] I think this is literarily significant, despite the fact that the combination of the words *olam* and *shalom* appears in other places in the Mishnah.

[79] Using a technique called by the name *gematria*, each letter in a word was traditionally assigned a numerical value. This kind of number-play was a feature of rabbinic exegesis and a kind of artistic way of suggesting the validity of truths they wished to assert.

[80] M. Uktzin 3:12.

[81] See his *d'var torah* to *parashat Mikkeitz*, available online at www.rabbisacks.org/mikketz-5774-power-dreams.

[82] Yossi Klein Halevi, *Like Dreamers: The Story of the Israeli Paratroopers Who*

Reunited Jerusalem and Divided a Nation (New York: HarperCollins, 2013), pp. xxiv–xxvi.

[83] The expression *tikkun olam* predates the Roman conquest. But the centrality of the concept in the Mishnah may be understood in no small part as a reaction to it.

[84] Pirkei Avot 2:15.

The Seven-Year Fix

Nina Beth Cardin

The Problem

There is a charming, inspiring hubris in the concept of *tikkun olam*. It says that we, who are but dust and ashes, believe that we—individually and collectively—have the calling and the capacity to change the trajectory of the world. Knowing that your people, your faith, your God, believe deeply in what you do on a daily basis is a good enough reason to get out of bed every morning. But there is a darker side, too, to *tikkun olam*, for though we may be able to resist and deflect the calling part, we cannot deny our capacity part. We humans have now become a geo-physical force. Whereas before we were able to affect parts of this world, for good or ill, today we can affect the entire global universe of creation simply by our mass, our consumption, and our waste. We live; therefore, we affect the welfare of the world. That is a responsibility we must accept and pursue intentionally.

The plotline of the Torah captures that pursuit. It is a relentless dreaming of utopia here on earth. It is a story that teaches that paradise is not a place waiting to be inherited or stumbled upon, but rather a place that must be deliberately and assiduously fashioned and built through the work of our daily lives. The story of the Torah is about seeking and failing, and then trying yet again to make this world as good as it can humanly be. It pursues this quest in and through the shelter of community. Judaism is not primarily concerned with personal salvation, forbearance of suffering, forgiveness of sin, or eternal life. It is, rather, a visioning of what it would take to create a world that is built upon the pillars of justice and peace, prosperity and sharing (*tzedek*, *shalom*, *osher*, and *ḥesed*). Judaism is concerned with how each of us should live in the presence of each other, and the systems that must be in place to bring forth such a society.

The Torah starts with a tough message: life is hard. That is what the Garden of Eden story is all about: things aren't easy. Adam and Eve were gardeners, not lord and lady of the manor. And while food and shelter were abundant, the human appetite is wired to always seek more. This is good when this drive leads to curiosity, discovery, engagement, creativity, and love in healthy amounts—which are all things we need to create utopia. But it is bad when it leads to greed, temptation, jealousy, covetousness, selfishness, and unrelenting dissatisfaction. The biblical story teaches that desire will propel us onward. And the questions then pour out: toward what end? with what intention do we reach for knowledge and beauty? and how much will it take to satisfy us? How do we measure enough?

Other founding stories of the Torah go on to remind us that in our everyday world, we have to work hard with no guarantee of success; sweat equity can still yield thistles and thorns. And even when we succeed (as Cain did with agriculture, and Abel with animals), rewards may not be equitably doled out. Bad things do happen to—and can even be caused by—good people.

And yet. The Torah tells us that the promised land is not a place of mists and myth. It is a land of fields of beauty and abundance, where plenty can exist for all—if we but manage both it and our appetites well. It is up to us to believe it and make it happen. Though suffering is real and only rarely redemptive, still we are not to succumb to quiet resignation, nor to deny the reality of pain. Life is not to be merely endured or conquered, but rather enjoyed and celebrated—on an individual, familial, tribal and global scale. Our task is to make that happen.

The Misplaced Role of Wealth

One critical component to realizing such a world is recognizing the proper role of wealth—more specifically, the equitable and sufficient possession of, access to, and use of those things society assesses as goods and services, both natural and cultural. There is no doubt that money is an essential asset, a source of much that is good. It enables us to eat well; to stay warm in the cold and cool in the heat; to be idle when we are sick and to tend to others when they are in need; to host others and be hosted by them; to offer gifts; to relax and refresh, dream and dare; and to invest in and trust the future. But it is also true that money—inappropriately managed and pursued—is the source of much that is wrong in society. The excess pursuit of (and acquisition of) wealth, accompanied by an insatiable desire to purchase, own, and consume ever more things (both tangible and not), is devastating for the marketplace, society, nature, and the human spirit.

The repercussions are felt in the economic disparity that increasingly characterizes America. For example, in the last thirty years—and particularly in the past five years—only the top 1% of Americans have seen their share of America's total income grow. The other 99% of American earners have *lost* a bit of their share of America's income.[1] As a recent Pew report concluded, "From the end of the recession in 2009 through 2011...the eight million households in the U.S. with a net worth above $836,033 saw their aggregate wealth rise by an estimated $5.6 trillion, while the 111 million households with a net worth at or below that level saw their aggregate wealth decline by an estimated $0.6 trillion."[2] Practically, this means that a fast food worker in New York City (there are 55,000 of them) who made roughly $8.90 an hour in 2013 (about minimum wage) would have to work for almost a century, in order to earn as much as the McDonald's CEO earned in the single year of 2011.[3] Such inequity does not get us closer to our utopian world.

Neither does preferencing profits over people. On November 24, 2012, a fire raced through the Tazreen Fashions factory in Bangladesh, killing 112 people and putting thousands more not only in physical danger, but out of work. Major global companies, most prominently Wal-mart, source some of their products from there. And while the international community[4] has called upon those companies to contribute to the medical needs and financial support of the victims and families of the fire, many companies (including Wal-mart and Sears) have declined to do so.[5] Their answer is usually that Tazreen Fashions was an unauthorized merchant and their suppliers should not have been using them. Yet, the companies in question still sold those products and profited from them. Tazreen workers made as little as $38 a month; Wal-mart makes $34,880 in profit every minute.[6] With $16 billion in annual profit from the products it sells—whether sourced from authorized providers or not—Wal-mart has the means, but not the heart, to help those who make them profitable.

This is not a call for flattening salaries, denying professional rank, or otherwise blunting human drive and expression. Some disparity is not only inevitable but fair. This is a call however, for considering what the renowned former World Bank economist Herman Daly calls the eleventh commandment: "Thou shalt not allow unlimited inequality in the distribution of private property."[7] This is especially true when such economic inequality is built on and reinforces ethical inequities.[8]

Beyond its economic ramifications, the excessive pursuit and accumulation of wealth also takes a heavy toll on nature. Concentrated wealth leads to excess consumption, intentional or not, which in turn leads to the inequitable and unsustainable use of the earth's natural resources. Consider, for instance, the United States. Americans make up only 5% of the earth's population; yet, we consume 20% of the earth's fossil fuels and create 40% of the earth's waste.[9] Globally, as a result of the habits of the developed and fast-developing economies, humans are consuming more of the earth's resources every year than the earth annually replenishes.[10] And we are rapidly depleting some of the resources that are not renewable, like helium and those elements called rare earth metals[11] at a faster rate than ever before. Even more disconcerting, however, is the fact that both the benefits and the negative consequences of this global over-consumption are inequitably distributed, with the haves (i.e., you and me) enjoying our undue share of the benefits and the have-nots enduring their unfair share of the negative consequences.

As anyone who has a wallet or a refrigerator knows, we cannot indefinitely take from a system with finite resources without regularly and appropriately replenishing it. Failing to restock our supply while continuing to draw it down will sooner or later cause it to run dry. If we degrade the earth's soils, drain our aquifers, poison our waters, deplete the world's fishing stock, and strip all the minerals from the mines, we will be left empty. Our appetites, industry, and consumption, therefore, must match the pace in which the earth renews itself. Even the magic of the marketplace cannot make it rain, create exhausted minerals, manufacture more land, or bring extinct species back to life. We can bail out banks and countries that fail but, we cannot bail out Mother Nature. There is nowhere for us to go if she fails. There is no "there" there anymore, only "here."

The spiritual realm also suffers from the excesses of wealth, as an insatiable desire or cultural compulsion to earn ever more money and possess ever more things denies us the deep joy of satisfaction, of enoughness. A marketplace that measures personal worth in dollars and continually moves the goalposts of satisfaction is a marketplace that feeds on the discontent of its members. It fosters the cultivation of consumerist attitudes and behaviors, wherein society becomes subservient to the marketplace rather than the marketplace working to the benefit of its constituents. The French social commentator Jean Baudrillard expressed it as follows: "If a consumer forgets [his role of constant desire and does not continually exercise his consumer capacities], he will be gently and insistently reminded that he has no right not to be happy."

Yet, how can we find happiness if we are always pressed to pursue more? How can we be sated when the marketplace reminds us that we never have enough? Even more, economists tell us that economic growth (which is equated with economic health and society's overall well-being)[13] is dependent on loans—that is, debt. The more we borrow, we are taught, the better off we are as a society. Still, we know the truth: more is not always more. The two greatest economic tragedies of the last one hundred years were caused by the misguided pursuit of economic excess. "The failure of additional wealth and consumption to help people have satisfying lives may be the most eloquent argument for reevaluating our current approach to consumption."[14] For those of us blessed with economic security, the key to happiness lies not in our next purchase, not with keeping up with the Joneses. It is found in knowing when we have enough, *that* we have enough.

The Redemptive Cycles of Seven

How, then, do we build a world that balances wealth and satisfaction, desire and satiety, curiosity and contentment, growth and "enoughness"…mine, yours, and ours?

The Torah speaks of all this: the human desire for consumption and wealth, the market's tendency to concentrate wealth, the attendant growing disparity between the haves and have-nots, the incessant spiritual unsettling that clamorous appetites bring, and the spiritual and economic pursuits that ravage the land. So the Torah offers a corrective, woven into the very fabric of time, and written into the opening chapters of Genesis: Shabbat, the Sabbath.

Fast on the heels of creating the world of production, consumption, and growth, immediately after fashioning man and woman and calling them to learn and master the world about them, God does something remarkable: God creates a pause. On Shabbat, God leaves the world to its own celebration. The wonders of the world are left to unfold as designed.

Once every six days, for as long as time endures, the world of building and tearing down, buying and selling, turning nature into products and time into commodity, ceases. Taking its place is a world that is, in the words of the rabbis, a taste of the world to come.[15] Every six days we put aside the rough and tumble of the work-a-day world. We put aside the measure of each other's worth in terms of dollars and cents. Instead, we live as if a bit of utopia has descended upon us. Like sunrise and sunset, winter and summer, the Sabbath was built into the rhythms of time.

But the Sabbath was not answer enough. It is not a transformation, but just a pause in the rough-and-tumble world; it is not a corrective, but a recurring place of refuge. It gives us a vision but not an on-ramp to that world we seek.

So the Torah stepped it up a bit. Every seven years we are asked to leave the world of the customary economy and live a bit in utopia. This is the world of *sh'mittah*, the Sabbatical or seventh year: "For six years you shall sow your fields and harvest its crops, but during the seventh year you are to release your hold on the land, letting it lie unplowed and fallow. Then the poor among your people may eat from it, and the wild animals may eat what is left over. Do the same with your vineyard and your olive grove." (Exodus 23:10–11)

While still in the throes of slavery—suffering from the worst excesses of wealth, consumption, and power laid against them in the land of Egypt; having no vision of an economy other than the abusive one they were raised in—the Jewish people were being taught to resist repeating the wrongs of Egypt. When you are free, Moses tells them, for six consecutive years you may work as your own masters, tending to the land according to your own desires and capacities Those who benefit from luck and skill will prosper; those whose luck or skill fails them will not. Fates and status will rise and fall. But once every seven years, all that will be suspended. Everyone—landowner and tenant, rich and poor, the high and the low—will live in the equity of shared human dignity. Landowners will tear down their fences, let their fields lie fallow, ignore their boundary stones. Instead, the fields roll on unbroken, and the produce that grows there of its own accord, both from field and from the tree, belong to all.[16] The land with all its goodness returns to the commons.[17] The commons is the cultural and natural resources that are the scaffolding of society. It is our language, our watershed, our libraries, our literature, the internet, Wikipedia, national myths and traditional songs. The very first commons was the Garden of Eden. The commons of the Jewish people is the Bible, the Hebrew language, and the Land of Israel.

Sh'mittah is a celebration of and a return to the commons—particularly seeing the Land of Israel as our great commons. It is not about charity or generosity or magnanimity, wherein the wealthy share a bit of their riches with the needy. Rather, it is about re-envisioning a world in which ownership of critical resources belongs to and is shared by all. It is a taste of Eden, wherein many boundaries are erased and the land and its resources are remembered for what they are: a gift from the Creator to all humanity.

But the Torah does not stop there. *Sh'mittah* is also a year of economic equality. Debts are to be either suspended or, as more standardly and radically understood, forgiven. The economic inequality that invariably builds up in a standard economy is undone here—as are some social barriers, as well. It is harder to maintain the prejudices of social classes when boundaries of exclusion and inclusion disappear and everyone has to gather their food in the same field, in the same way, in the same amounts, with the same frequency. Indeed: during sh'mittah it is not just that food is free for all; food ceases to be a commodity at all. It cannot be measured or sold in bulk, as it is in other years. There can be no hoarding, no classic commerce, and no profits based on scarcity. Land and food and debt are temporarily removed from the economic equation. Social networks cut cross economic lines. Neighbors meet every day gathering food, on more equitable financial and social grounds, gathering what they need in plain sight of each other.

But it would be wrong to see *sh'mittah* as simply a zealous attempt to mandate social and economic equity only once every seven years. Behavior during the other six years is affected by the umbra of sh'mittah as well. Both debtor and lender are more conscious of (and the lender certainly more cautious about) their financial behavior, knowing the consequences looming during the *sh'mittah* year. And they also know that despite their inequitable relationship during the six secular years, both of them will meet on more equitable footing sometime in the not-too-distant *sh'mittah* year.

Even more important is the impact of knowing that for one-seventh of our life, we will not be judged by our money or land holdings, but by what kind of neighbor we are, what kind of friend we are, and what we do beyond our work and wealth. This informs our choices about how to live the other six-sevenths of our life… which leads us to explore the greater purpose of *sh'mittah*.

We know that *sh'mittah* was not an ethic ignored. It was at least occasionally observed in biblical and rabbinic times, even if only in the breach. It was accepted as part of the Jews' regular repertoire of commandments, so that when it chafed in more sophisticated economies, remedies had to be found to protect it. Hillel (first century B.C.E.) is credited with creating the *prozbol*, a legal remedy that skirted the remission of personal debts by allowing lenders to place their claims with a court.[19] As a public institution, the court would be immune from the laws of *sh'mittah*. The lender's financial risk would thus be protected, as the loan was no longer subject to cancellation. This was seen as protecting both borrowers (since potential lenders would not refuse to lend them money as the seventh year approached) and lenders (since they would no longer suffer financial loss due to their largesse).

Seen more deeply, *sh'mittah* falls into the category of "gift"—an antidote to the necessary concept of capital and the reciprocally-bound transactions that capital demands. In his widely-hailed book *The Gift*, Lewis Hyde teaches that societies are stitched together by gifts, something that "moves from one hand to another with no assurance of anything in return."[20] Gifts move freely and engage the emotions, creating ties and evoking drama and value beyond the object itself, for they stir up an inherent imbalance into which all parties are drawn. The giver endures a true diminishing of assets, as opposed to the immediate and balanced exchange in commercial transactions. In a purchase, there are no loose ends and no expectation for ongoing relations between the buyer and seller (unless, of course, the item is faulty or if the contract of the exchange is otherwise violated). No emotion, no ties; all is settled and done at the end of the exchange.

But true gifts go on and on. *Sh'mittah* creates a large circle of gifting by involving and evoking community and nature, neighbors and God. Letting the land lie fallow with its produce accessible to neighbors and animals alike enlarges the gifting circle. The physical removal of field fences and boundaries mirrors the erasure of social, psychological, and existential boundaries of this world, and allows us to enter what Lewis calls "mystery." It is in this world of circulating gifts, a world infinitely bigger than our small transactional lives—a world where there is enough for all—that *sh'mittah* allows us to live, and thrive, ever so briefly.

The idea of *sh'mittah*, then, is more than a way to provide a pause and a corrective to the economic order. It is a rehearsal of sorts for the utopia we seek. We must act as if the land has resorted to common ownership, as if our daily needs come readily to hand, as if our days and worth are not measured only by our commercial labor but by...what? The Torah does not tell us *how* we are to spend our time when we are not working or engaged in commerce. Perhaps in companionship, creativity, experiments and discovery, study and song, comforting and caring for the ill and aged. This is a part of the utopia that *sh'mittah* invites us to explore.[21]

Yet for most Jews, *sh'mittah* is an almost forgotten tradition.[22] Those of us in the Diaspora are challenged today neither by its strictures nor by its freedoms. What would happen if we embraced both?

The question facing us, then, seems to be: given the depth of modernity's economic, environmental, and social challenges, how can we renew our understanding and observance of *sh'mittah*?[23] The *prozbol* was one such effort. It was not designed to do an end-run around *sh'mittah*, but was rather an effort to preserve *sh'mittah* in a way that allowed the community to honor the law while still accommodating it to contemporary times. That seems to be our challenge once again today: how can we take the lessons and values of *sh'mittah*—returning natural resources to the commons, more equitably managing our economy, and creating a society with limited social barriers—and apply them to our lives today?[24] Clearly, the biblical details of the laws of *sh'mittah* are not immediately applicable to a modern, capitalist, diaspora community. But its vision and values are.

What if lenders in the *sh'mittah* year permanently wrote off one-seventh of the interest owed them and deferred the payment of all remaining principal to the eighth year? What if, as consumers in the *sh'mittah* year, we did not purchase anything beyond our monthly capacity to pay it off?[25] What if, as possessors, we emptied our closets and storage units of all those choice items we no longer use, and gave them away to those in need? What "fields" in our businesses do we own and what fences have we erected that should be opened up and pulled down, so that equal access can be given to all? What commons has been walled off for the privileged that should be opened to all? What barriers have we erected between parent and child, brother and sister, friend and friend that should be torn down so that relationships can be restarted and past emotional debts forgiven?

Sh'mittah today calls us to devise ways to challenge the sacred structures of the modern economy and to pierce the fearsome social boundaries that divide us, even for just a brief time, so that we too can re-vision the mystery that we are privileged to be a part of. While we may never actually achieve utopia, it is more than likely that the effort of the pursuit itself will bring us a little closer to it, and enrich us in ways we cannot otherwise imagine.

NOTES

[1] "Trends in the Distribution of Household Income Between 1979 and 2007" (October 25, 2011), online at the website of the Congressional Budget Office at www.cbo.gov.

[2] See "The 2008 Crisis and the Restructuring of Class Relations in America" (June 4, 2013), online at the website of the World Socialist Web Site at www.wsws.org/en/articles/2013/06/04/pers-j04.html.

[3] Paul Krugman, "Better Pay Now," in *New York Times* (December 1, 2013), p. A33.

[4] Including the victims' families, as well as groups such as IndustriALL Global Union, International Labor Rights Forum, UNI Global Union, and United Students Against Sweatshops.

[5] See "Bangladesh: Companies Fail to Compensate Fire Victims" (December 16, 2013), available online at the website of the Human Rights Watch at www.hrw.org.

[6] See "Wal-mart Company Statistics" (as of July 12, 2014), online at www.statisticbrain.com/wal-mart-company-statistics.

[7] Herman E. Daly, "A Biblical Economic Principle" in Beyond Growth: The Ethics of Sustainable Development (Boston: Beacon Press, 1996), p. 206.

[8] For an overview of the contemporary state and impact of income inequality, see the recent documentary film by Jacob Kornbluth, "Inequality for All: A Passionate Argument on Behalf of the Middle Class" (www.inequalityforall.com).

[9] Waste is not a signature of progress but rather a design flaw. America would become even more of a world leader if Americans figured out how to turn waste into goods. See William McDonough and Michael Braungart's *From Cradle to Cradle: Remaking the Way We Make Things* (New York: North Point Press, 2002); and the material gathered at the Biomimicry website (www.biomimicry.net) for ways in which people are seeking to eliminate waste and maximize productivity.

[10] See the information and analysis presented on the website of the Global Footprint Newtwork at www.footprintnetwork.org/en/index.php/gfn/page/world_footprint: "Today humanity uses the equivalent of 1.5 planets to provide the resources we use and absorb our waste. This means it now takes the Earth one year and six months to regenerate what we use in a year."

[11] Rare earth metal are "one of a set of seventeen chemical elements in the periodic table....New demand has recently strained supply, and there is growing concern that the world may soon face a shortage of the rare earths. ...worldwide demand for rare earth elements is expected to exceed supply...unless major new sources are developed." (Information taken from http://en.wikipedia.org/wiki/Rare_earth_element.http://en.wikipedia.org/wiki/Rare_earth_element.)

[12] Jean Baudrillard, *The Consumer Society* (London: Sage, 1998), p. 80. According to Baudrillard, the marketplace tells us that happiness is found only, or at least best, at the end of a sale, and that we must continually buy so that we can

continually be happy. To not buy is to not be happy—or even worse, to seek happiness outside the marketplace and absent new purchases is downright anti-capitalist.

[13] For an alternative to GDP as the measure of economic and social well-being, see, e.g., the Wikipedia article "Genuine Progress Indicator," at http://en.wikipedia.org/wiki/Genuine_progress_indicator. And for a real-life example of GPI in practice, see "Wealth vs. Well-Being: How Do We Measure Progress?" online at the website of the Maryland Department of Natural Resources at www.dnr.maryland.gov/mdgpi.

[14] From "The State of Consumption Today" (December 27, 2013), on the website of the Worldwatch Institute at www.worldwatch.org/node/810.

[15] B. Berakhot 57b.

[16] Sh'mittah literally means "release"; the word suggests a letting go, freeing up that which one had previously held on to. I imagine sh'mittah as the loosing and opening of a fist, both revealing and offering that which it had been holding fast inside.

[17] For a fine definition of the commons, see the Wikipedia article at http://en.wikipedia.org/wiki/Commons. For examples of how groups are reclaiming and implementing this concept in modern times, see www.onthecommons.org.

[18] See Nehemiah 10:32, 2 Chronicles 36:20–21, and 2 Kings 19:20–30.

[19] See M. Gittin 4:3, where we read that "Hillel established the prozbol in order to repair the world"; cf. also M Sheviit 10.3. Prozbol is a Hebrew word of undetermined Greek origins that refers to the document that protected the repayment of loans over the course of the sh'mittah year.

[20] Although there is an air of expectation of return, at some point time and for somebody in the circle—for fundamentally, according to Hyde, the gift (or, at least: gifting) must move and circulate throughout society. A gift that does not translate into other gifts becomes capital, which is the very opposite of a gift. See Lewis Hyde, The Gift (New York: Vintage Books, 1983), p. 9.

[21] For an example of a modern company that went on sabbatical, see the video by Simon Cohen, "Global Tolerance on Sabbatical," at www.globaltolerance.com/simoncohentalksaboutsabbatical.

[22] I write here about diaspora Jewry's modern efforts to observe sh'mittah. Israel has been struggling with this question since the late 1880s, when the Zionist dream slowly began to blossom into a reality. Treating the complicated issues of the economy, debt, and land use in the State of Israel goes beyond the confines of this paper.

[23] Sh'mittah occurs in 5775 (2014–2015) and every seven years subsequent to that.

[24] Looked at this way, sh'mittah can be seen as a biblical forerunner to the triple bottom line of sustainability: people, planet, and profit. For efforts to embrace an ethic that incorporates these three "p's," see http://bteam.org/, http://urbanomnibus.net (and particularly urbanomnibus.net/2013/09/the-five-thousand-pound-life), https://bealocalist.org/ and others.

[25] As with all laws, exceptions would be made for undeferrable expenses: medical bills, college tuition, moving and new home expenses, essential new cars, etc. But what would bar or bat mitzvahs, weddings, and baby showers look like, influenced by *sh'mittah's* call for simpler consumption?

Tikkun Olam: An Over-Used Term and Its Missing "Inner Point"

Admiel Kosman

Translated from the Hebrew by Martin S. Cohen

Speaking as someone who has been involved in the instruction of liberal rabbis for more than ten years now, I feel that the much loved, but far over-used, expression *tikkun olam* is itself in need of some serious *tikkun* (or at least some thoughtful refinement), and I wish to explain in this essay what I mean by that thought.

The expression itself—which, as is well known, derives from ancient halakhic texts—has in our day turned into nothing more than a slogan that people regularly use when arguing for the superiority of a liberal approach to Judaism. I don't imagine this is done consciously, yet it seems obvious to me that we liberal Jews regularly use the expression to underscore the ways in which we suppose our approach to Judaism to be more worthy than its analogue in old-style, fundamentalist/traditionalist Judaism. Indeed, in our effort to free ourselves from untoward subservience to ancient *halakhah*,[1] we (unlike more traditional Jews) like to think that we have adopted a more exalted sense of purpose than mere obedience to the law: our goal is nothing less than the "repair of the world," which is the precise translation of the Hebrew term *tikkun ha-olam*.[2] In this we distinguish ourselves from those whose goal is merely to remain steadfastly observant of the complex collection of laws and rules that have come down to us from the distant, gloomy past and, more recently, from the *shtetlach* of pre-Shoah Europe.

Two points in particular seem worth making explicitly:

1. Even as we self-define in halakhic terms, we reject the notion of observance that is mindless, dryly vague, or pointless. Indeed, for us the *halakhah* as we observe it is part of a larger, more complex program of *tikkun olam*. And when, just a bit exaggeratedly, we invoke the spirit of the late Ashkenazic chief rabbi of British Palestine, Rabbi Abraham Isaac Kook (1865–1935) in this regard, it is specifically to buttress our sense of the reasonableness of connecting the minutiae of observance to greater goals and principles.

2. The expression *tikkun olam* itself has become central in our thinking precisely because it serves to distance us from the isolationist approach of fundamentalist traditionalism. We reject that approach as wrongheaded precisely because, by infusing the concept of Israelite chosenness with unbecoming superiority, it leads not to the great goal of unifying the peoples of the earth under the sovereignty of God, but instead serves to create a sharp, unwarranted distinction between Israel and the gentile nations...and thus also creating an unbridgeable chasm between Judaism and the spiritual bearing of the rest of humanity.

The expression *tikkun olam*, as we have come to use it, thus underscores the degree to which we liberal Jews see ourselves primarily as citizens of the world, whose Jewishness serves us as the specific framework in which we work toward the great and inclusive goal of repairing the world—and in this regard, we are precisely like the spiritually adept of other nations with respect to their own spiritual frameworks.

That, in my opinion, is precisely the problem—and it is a thorny one indeed! As someone both personally involved in and very sympathetic to the liberal beliefs and practices that are subsumed under the general rubric of *tikkun olam*, my problem is not with the expression itself (which is lovely), but specifically with what it has come to mean in the way we use it today.

Anyone who listens closely to the undertones that almost inevitably accompany the term, as people use it today, will recognize easily that it either directly or indirectly serves to trumpet a kind of exalted distinctiveness—not the isolationist distinctiveness mentioned above between Israel and gentile nations (with whom we labor intently to live in peace), but rather between the reasonableness of liberal Judaism and the intransigent obstinacy of pre-modern fundamentalism with which we are so little eager to identify, even accidentally. It is to underscore the exalted distinctiveness of the liberal Jew that we so openly and vigorously wave the flag of *tikkun olam*.

I wish to stress the following points to highlight three interrelated serious problems that I see hiding behind this specific usage of the term *tikkun olam*. First, I believe that it is almost instinctive for people to wave flags vigorously, because they wish to distract onlookers and thus keep them from scrutinizing the underlying ideas that have brought them to act as they do. (People who live mindful lives fully in sync with their own values do not need flags to draw attention away from what they are actually doing in the world.) Second, I believe that it should be possible to learn a lot from tradition, even as we respectfully insist on distancing ourselves from those parts of traditionalist praxis or belief that we find objectionable...and self-confident liberal Jews should not need to demonstrate the validity of their approach to Judaism by using slogans that only serve to draw attention away from their beliefs or activities. And third, I find something objectionable in the mechanical use of a slogan as a pennant to be waved on behalf of a particular religious outlook, and I feel that way even if the slogan and its flag themselves are justifiable and reasonable.

To explain why I feel as I do, I wish now to turn to a brief consideration of a very deep and satisfying hasidic story that, in my opinion, can serve as a useful jumping-off point for considering the relationship of the slogan and the false way it is used today as a banner.

A Hasidic Story about the Gerer Rebbe, Rabbi Isaac Meir Alter

Rabbi Bunim…of Lublin…related how his grandfather once went…to stroll about a bit in the courtyard of the *beis medrash* [study hall] in Gur and he went along with him. It was the month of Elul. Someone asked his grandfather if they had blown the traditional *shofar* blasts that morning in the *beis medrash*, whereupon he responded with these words: "When someone becomes the spiritual leader of an entire generation, he must obviously provide all the necessary accoutrements for that kind of leadership. He needs, for example, a *beis medrash* with rooms and tables and benches. And he needs someone to serve as beadle and someone else to serve as sexton, as well as others to serve in various other positions…But then, shortly after all is finally set in place, the Accuser [i.e., the accusing angel] comes and steals away the inmost point of the whole operation, leaving the rest in place to revolve around a now-empty center…*un dos reidel dreyt zikh veiter* [literally, "and the wheel continues to turn"]! This is what we must fear the most of all: that the day may come when all will be exactly in place as it is right now, but the central point of the whole community will be missing." Afterwards, he called out in a loud voice, "Our blessed God will help us! *Men zoll zikh nisht lozn*—we must not let this thing happen!"[3]

Rabbi Isaac Meir (Rotenberg) Alter (1799–1866), the protagonist of our anecdote, is well known as the founder of the hasidic dynasty of Gur, and this detail alone already suggests the tension between the individual and the community that lies just beneath the surface of the narrative.[4] However, in contradistinction to the brutish iconoclasm we would expect from the standard anti-hero of a modern novel, what we find here instead is the intense tension that derives from the fact that the individual in question, who might well have chosen a different "story" to express his frustration, is also the man who feels called upon to lead his community forward.

Moreover, the individual has fallen into an unexpected trap: when, as leader, he should be acting as administrator (and it is worth mentioning in this regard that Rabbi Isaac Meir was well known in his day as a talented organizer and builder of this hasidic community), he finds himself struggling with a task that goes against his very nature: to build "structures" for the community. And thus we see that the authenticity of the individual is threatened by the monster that is organizational effort—a monster that he is also personally responsible to sustain. Indeed, it is for that very reason that the story begins with a walk around the courtyard outside the *beis medrash*. A walk is generally defined as a stroll with no specific destination, and it usually takes place somewhere within the world of nature. That is what the courtyard represents in the story, I believe, and it is meant to serve as the opposite of the determined march forward of people on their way to some specific goal, the kind of activity that characterizes the effort of an organization to move into the future. The community must exist as a well-oiled machine if it is to survive—yet that is the very effort that its own leader fears will make the larger operation meaningless.

The walk "outside" is far from the "central point" around which all the organizational industry has been orchestrated, which by itself establishes governance over the masses; it is that specific point, inside, from which originally flows the rabbi's authority to lead the community. The "central point" appears to have as its natural locus the *beis medrash*. Our story thus contrasts the "outside"—nature, alive and wild—with culture, with the order found on the inside. The irony in the rabbi's words derives, in fact, directly from the fact that order, once it is established, becomes a threat in its own right. It becomes its own version of the wild "monster" against which the rabbi must struggle.

Only when an individual escapes from the feverish effort to produce and takes the time to go for a walk can that person listen to his or her inner voice. And so, in fact, even though the rabbi is the leader of his community, it becomes clear to him while strolling with his grandson that the monster threatens those who sustain it… because the monster is the embodiment of self-directed unknowing, of self-unawareness that risks swallowing everything in a single, devastating gulp…including the individual who was supposed to be in charge of keeping it in check.

Every couple that goes forth into married life imbued with the freshness of early wedlock and with the positive energy of young love eventually meets this monster. Indeed, this is true for all who start out fresh and pure, vital and alive and filled with potential: all such people eventually risk disappearing into the labyrinthine thicket of details that characterizes human industry at its least appealing. And this surrender eventually renders the industry itself devoid of purpose, as the "heart" within the enterprise that had provided motion and energy and that served as its "central point" is suddenly discovered to be missing.

I have written until now about spatial aspects of this parable, but there is a temporal aspect to consider as well. The story takes place during the month of Elul, the threshold month that serves as the transitional period between the year about to end and the one about to begin, and that is traditionally understood as the ideal time for introspection and renewed inner resolve. The *shofar*, in fact, is the ancient symbol of this out-of-time summons to the kind of inner awakening that leads away from empty industry. (And the hasidic ear hears a link between the word shofar and the Hebrew word for self-improvement, *shippur*...which, in turn, eventually morphs on the common tongue into *tikkun* or *tikkun olam*.) Consider in this regard the words of Maimonides, who wrote as follows in the third chapter of his "Laws of Repentance":

> Even though it is a scriptural law that the *shofar* be sounded on Rosh Hashanah, it also hints at something else [that is, something extra-scriptural]. "Awaken," the *shofar* says, "awaken you who slumber from your sleep...you who have allowed the nonsense of daily life to distract you from the truth, you who have spent an entire year chasing after inanity and silliness.[5]

It is no wonder, then, that the rabbi's walk represents his effort to resolve a deeply stressful interior conflict, one that he allows to surface in a moment of intimacy in the presence of his grandson. And even though it seems as though his words are "about" the organization he must lead (and this is how the story is generally understood), the truth is that he is speaking just as plainly about himself, about his inner fear that **he** is about to become entrenched as "administrator" of an essentially empty, yet nevertheless complicated, hierarchal machine from which he will never escape.

And so he speaks, using code language well known to Gerer hasidim, about the "loss of the central point." The beauty in this description lies in the fact that the "point" is localized in the "center" of the *beis medrash*, the organizational center from which radiates out the great spiritual power of the spoken Torah...but it is specifically from this place, from this inside "point," that the rabbi flees to the outside. And it is exactly there, in the "outside," that he discovers that the "point" is empty and lifeless on the "inside." To harness the vivid energy that once motivated him, he must seek to recover the "inner point" that has been lost. And he seeks it, entirely reasonably, outdoors in the courtyard, rather than in the formal place of Torah.

To describe the paralyzing inertia of the organizational structure, the rabbi uses the symbol of an ever-rotating circle that encircles... nothing at all. (In turn, this notion reminds me of the Tibetan custom of writing a prayer out on a piece of paper and then hanging it on a rotating prayer-wheel on the assumption that the wheel, as it turns, will propel the prayers attached to it toward heaven.)

At any rate, the circle completes whatever there is to say about the point. And it is that point, at least ideally, that can and should serve as the energy source that makes the circle revolve. Even the rabbi understands that he himself is done, his original spiritual energy source drained and depleted...and that he will surely not have it in him further to sustain the circle of hasidim around him, a circle that he now perceives as a noose around his neck. What remains, then, is a kind of lifeless skeleton that is rooted solely in inertia. One could even say that the power of the "inner point" decreases in inverse proportion to the degree to which the "point" becomes swollen and bloated with the kind of authority that derives solely from institutional structure.

The act of choosing the point *and* the circle is fraught with meaning not solely for leaders themselves, but also for the communities they lead and for the ideology that provides those communities with their ideational substructure. The "inner point" of the circle itself houses an energy source that provides power and structure to the entire circle. On the macro level, the prototype of this kind of symbol is the sun, which sends forth its rays to the entire world. On the micro level, the most accessible model would be a piece of fruit, which houses seeds that may grow into similar pieces of fruit. How interesting is it that we consider those seeds to be garbage, and that we only esteem as valuable the part of the fruit that we can eat! Yet from the point of view of natural science, the flesh of the fruit is only of secondary importance and serves solely to house the seeds...and to entice birds to eat them, and thus to carry the seeds throughout the world. It is for this reason, of course, that mystics of every age have tended to such seeds as symbols of the power to sustain the circle: the seed becomes the spirit that sustains the flesh that houses and surrounds it.[6]

In the medieval period, kabbalists—as well as Christian and Buddhist mystics—saw the circle as a symbol of wholeness. Jung in fact cited a medieval alchemist named Maier, who determined that the "circle is the symbol of eternity."[7] Jung himself saw the circle as a symbol of the well-integrated personality; however, that is true only—and we must emphasize *only*—if the core, the "inner point," keeps radiating its spiritual energy to the entire circle.[8] In this regard, it is also worth taking note of the interesting, if hypothetical, concept of "panspermia," a notion that goes back to ancient Greece but that continues to morph forward in different ways even in our own day—for example, in the work of Francis Crick, the co-discoverer (along with James Watson) of DNA. The basic concept, at least in its ancient guise, is that scattered throughout the universe are "seeds" of life, such that every living body contains some sort of "creative point" that is its life-seed. And there are those who think that these "inner points" of life derive directly from God.[9]

Considered from the vantage point of gender, some have identified the force of the "point" that leads to divine order in the universe as male—in light of the way that it sends forth its "seed" into the circle, identified in this context as the essentially female "flesh" of the fruit. If the "female" component responds to the "male" point and accepts its place in the proper hierarchy of things, then this merely constitutes the metaphysical analogue to human conception.[10]

Moshe Idel has even published a section of an old manuscript, which records a vision of Rabbi Isaac of Acre (fl. 13th–14th centuries). In the vision, Moses is seen receiving the Torah from God in the form of a circle (perhaps the image is meant to suggest a ball of fire), and it is by means of this circle that the visionary understood that Moses had become able to see everything in the world. In that medieval text, we read: "Seek to find the beginning of the circle or its end or its middle and you will not succeed…for it has no such place of entry, but is rather completely whole."[11] In later Kabbalah, it became commonplace to observe that the beginning of the circle is its "inmost point," as Moses ben Shem Tov de Léon (c. 1250–1305) wrote: "The beginning of existence lies in the secret of the hidden point [that is, *s'firah* of Ḥokhmah]…and that point is the basis of all hidden things, and it was from thence that they spread out in all their variegated diversity."[12]

The Missing Point of *Tikkun Olam*

But, of course, all this is relevant solely to the social circle in which the "inner point" actually dwells. But to my regret, even for us liberal Jews, the normal situation is that the organizing principle— the "point" from which power flows out to the world and which is supposed to constitute the life-giving point embedded in the flesh of the fruit—has turned, just as Rabbi Isaac Meir feared, into a monster that consumes the seeds of spiritual vitality, leaving us burdened with an endlessly revolving wheel of empty ideologies. The truth is that, in the end, any great idea will begin to exist as a bureaucratic behemoth when it eventually morphs into an unwieldy, bloated organizational structure—even truly exalted and worthy ideas, capable of serving as "inner points" that can generate sufficient vitality and spiritual power to effect good in the world. This is because such ideas cannot avoid distorting their original nature—ironically, the very "inner point" that originally served as the conduit to the divine realm. And this is no less true of the idea of *tikkun olam*: the idea presents itself as a "slogan" that sounds praiseworthy and desirable, but upon closer examination we find that beneath the slogan resides merely emptiness, as the idea has been deprived of its inmost meaning and spiritual worth.

This inner situation so in need of *tikkun* finds expression mostly in the spreading about of shop-worn, tired slogans like *tikkun olam*;

and the matter seems especially tragic as we hear the phrase again and again in the mouths of so many who have no actual intention to embody its inmost principle in their own lives, by seeking to adapt in their own selves and actions the great call to true *tikkun olam*, the repair of a broken world.

A Path Forward

How might it be possible to revivify the original spirit that animates the "point" that was lost…and, in so doing, to rouse us to undertake anew an honest, forthright discussion—and a truly heartfelt one at that—about *tikkun olam*?

It seems that a solution to that question lies hinted at within the folds of the hasidic story we have been parsing in this essay as well. In order to awaken from its slumber, the Jewish community is going to have to pass two hurdles: the first is the hurdle of attaining self-awareness, and the second is what we could reasonably call the hurdle of becoming ready to open the door to the unknown.

Let me explain what I mean. A community that yearns to awaken from its slumber must first come to terms *both* with the fact that it has up until now been asleep and *also* with the fact that, since the situation cannot be fixed with speeches (even passionate ones) or with flowery slogans, the solution is going to require going "outside," to a kind of exile from the comfortableness of home (whether one's spiritual home is in the *beis medrash*, or any other place one is accustomed to and in which one feels at ease)…so as to be able, *by looking from the outside in*, to identify the specific parts of the cultural and institutional structures that, having become frozen with the passage of time, have wreaked such havoc with our lives. In past centuries, the hasidic masters developed—for this very reason—the habit of leaving their own communities now and then dressed as regular people and, so deprived of their rabbinic outfits, going out into exile and wandering from place to place in the manner of simple people, sometimes even masquerading as paupers or beggars wandering from door to door in search of alms.[14]

It was not for no reason at all that the hasidic master in our story goes out for a walk in nature, at a distance from his regular home in the study hall—because only at a great enough distance to be able to fully ignore his status as rabbi and communal leader (who occupies a central position in the communal hierarchy) would it become possible for him to awaken to the inner point of divine worship. Indeed, only once our status as standard-bearers of importance and worth is completely eradicated—that is, once we finally come to see ourselves as simple and wholly *un*important people—only then can our inner awakening occur.[15]

Nevertheless, it is crucial to stress that this first stage of self-awareness lacks the power to bring us to real inner awakening…but it *can*, perhaps, bring us to the brink of that kind of awakening. A well-known hasidic lesson explains that although no one can force the sun's rays to enter one's home, one can indeed prepare one's home for that light by keeping the windows spotlessly clean.

This effort to achieve the first stage, then, is simply the basic cleaning that makes it possible for the light of the sun to shine into our personal windows. But we ourselves cannot control the shining forth of the divine light any more than we can dictate to the sun where to direct its rays; *that* is a function of God's grace, and in the normal course of events that kind of divine beneficence rarely comes to us from the expected corner, and neither does it arrive dressed in same garb it wore when it last crossed our path. For his part, Buber wrote succinctly: "The Thou meets me through grace—it is not found by seeking."[16]

It is for this specific reason that I prefer to describe the second stage as the opening of a door to the unknown and the unfamiliar. And, indeed, when we do not stifle with our own hands the possibility of God's light coming into our lives—and when we freely offer all we have of God's presence to all whom we encounter, and when we do so generously and openly—then we can reasonably say that Elijah has been sent to us from heaven to guide us forward. In this way, the prophet will be garbed in an unexpected and unfamiliar outfit, and it will be in his company that the "awakening" we seek shall also come to us—that awakening for which we yearn and which we have anticipated for longer than any of us can remember.

NOTES

[1] As, for example, at M. Gittin 4:3, where mention is made of an innovation by Hillel, the *prozbul*, that basically undoes the obligation to remain faithful to the clear intent of Scripture.

[2] The term as it appears in classical sources includes the definite article, *tikkun ha-olam*. In modern parlance, the article is elided and the concept is referred to simply as *tikkun olam*. (It might well be that the modern phrase is some kind of back-formation from the liturgical phrase well known from Aleinu, where it appears without the definite article: *l'takkein olam b'malkhut Shaddai*.)

[3] Avraham Issachar Binyamin Eliyahu Alter, *Sefer Mei·ir Einei Ha-golah* (ed. Warsaw, 1932), vol. 1, §547, p. 48. The Accuser, called the *satan* in Job, is the angel in heaven who exists to mock human piety and to accuse people of wrongdoing.

[4] Gur, also called Ger, is the Yiddish name of Góra Kalwaria, a town on the Vistula about sixteen miles southeast of Warsaw.

[5] Maimonides, M.T. Hilkhot Teshuvah 3:4.

[6] See Omraam Mikhaël Aïvanhov, *The Symbolic Language of Geometrical Figures* (Fréjus [France]: Prosveta, 1985), pp. 23–44; and see also Jill Purce, *The Mystic Spiral: Journal of the Soul* (New York: Avon, 1974).

[7] C. J. Jung, *Psychology and Religion* (1938; rpt. New Haven: Yale University Press, 1966), p. 128.

[8] Ibid., p. 96.

[9] Ibid., p. 124.

[10] See Aïvanhov, *Symbolic Language*, pp. 26–27.

[11] Moshe Idel, *The Mystical Experience in Abraham Abulafia*, trans. Jonathan Chipman (Albany: State University of New York Press, 1988), p. 115.

[12] As cited in Isaiah Tishby and P. Lachover, *Mishnat Ha-zohar* (Jerusalem: Mosad Bialik, 1949), vol. 1, p. 142, and cf. the discussion there about the importance of the "point" as a symbol in Kabbalah.

[13] See in this respect the theory of Max Weber as set forth in *From Max Weber: Essays in Sociology*, ed. Hans Gerth (London: Routledge & Kegan, 1967), pp. 245–264. As an example one could mention the famous case of the sociological research on the *kibbutzim* in Israel that clearly showed the same phenomenon: while the first generation was motivated by the "inner point" that radiated naturally out to influence the entire arrangement of life of the *kibbutz* (which, at that time, was motivated almost solely by the concept of *tikkun olam*), the later generations were interested more in establishing their own solid financial status. See Yonina Talmon-Gerber, *Yahid V'hevrah Ba-kibbutz: Mehkarim Sotsiologi·im* (Jeruslem: Magnes Press, 1970), pp. 222–230 and p. 232, n. 4.

[14] In this regard, see the list of hasidic rabbis mentioned by Netanel Lederberg in his *Sod Ha-da·at: D'muto Ha-ruhanit V'hanhagato Ha-hevratit shel Rabbi Yisrael Ba·al Sheim Tov* (Jerusalem: Reuben Mass, 2007), p. 260, n. 149. Cf. also the relevant material gathered together by Elliot R. Wolfson in "Walking as Sacred Duty: Theological Transformation of Social Reality in Early Hasidism," in his

Along the Path: Studies in Kabbalistic Myth, Symbolism, and Hermeneutics (Albany: State University of New York Press, 1995), pp. 89–109. Similarly, see in this regard the essay by Haviva Pedayta, "*Halikhah V'tiksei Galut: Ritualim shel Geirush V'havnayat Ha-atzmi B'merhavei Eiropa V'eretz Yisrael*," in *Yahadut: Sugyot, K'ta·im, Panim, Z'huyyot: Sefer Rivkah*, ed. Haviva Pedaya and Ephraim Meir (Beer Sheva: Ben Gurion University Press, 2007), pp. 7–147, esp. pp. 137–139, where the author focuses particularly on the questions of exile and wandering in hasidism.

[15] In the book *Shivḥei Ha-ran* by Nathan Sternharz (as published in Sefer *Shivḥei Ha-ran Im Siḥot Ha-ran* [s.a.; rpt. Jerusalem, 1992), §154, p. 122, we find the following tradition regarding Rabbi Naḥman of Bratzlav: "I heard it was said in his name that he once remarked that he only attained his level [i.e., of spiritual awareness] by assuming the demeanor of a *prostik* [i.e. by behaving like a simple layperson]."

[16] Martin Buber, *I and Thou*, trans. Ronald Gregor Smith (New York: Scribner's, 1958), p. 11. And cf. also what I wrote regarding those words of Buber's in my essay "*Mavo L'mishnat Buber*," in *Mordekhai Martin Buber: Ani V'attah*, trans. Aaron Fleischmann (Jerusalem: Mosad Bialik, 2013), pp. 160–231, esp. pp. 206–207.

Human Artistry and *Tikkun Olam*[1]

Roberta Rosenthal Kwall

The idea of of *tikkun olam*—repairing the world—has evolved greatly through the centuries. In the earliest rabbinic sources, the focus of *tikkun olam* was exclusively on preserving *halakhah* and caring for the most vulnerable in Jewish society. Gradually, however, *tikkun olam* came to be regarded as having a more universal application.[2] According to both of these perspectives, the notion of repairing a broken external world is of critical concern. Yet, the history of *tikkun olam* also reflects a concern for the spiritual journeys of the individual—that is, seeking to attain the perfection of one's soul.[3] And this more personal approach to *tikkun olam* is focused on repair that is inner-directed, rather than an outer-directed repair of an external environment (be it the Jewish community or beyond).

This essay examines the realm of artistic expression, defined broadly to include many types of human creativity, as a vehicle for engaging in *tikkun olam*. Although I assume that creating works of beauty has the potential to help repair a broken external world, my primary focus here is the internal dimension of human creativity as an exercise of *tikkun olam*. I argue that human creativity can embody *tikkun olam* insofar as it represents a path to observing God's will and perfecting one's soul. In making this case, this essay mines the depths of the Jewish tradition, particularly the creation narratives in Genesis and selected commentaries, both ancient and modern, on those texts.

A profound understanding of the nature of the artistic soul can be achieved by examining narratives that recount, or seek to explain, the creative process as inspirationally or spiritually motivated.[4]

Human beings have an innate urge to create. This is suggested by the urge to create demonstrated by children,[5] as well as by the works of artists lacking any expectation or hope of remuneration—such as the cave drawings of prehistoric humans,[6] the artistic creations of death row inmates,[7] and Nazi death camp prisoners.[8] Elisabeth Kübler-Ross, the psychiatrist who outlined the five stages of grief in her groundbreaking work on the emotional components of dying, often spoke of her experience in volunteering in an internment camp after World War II as the catalyst that influenced the course of her research. Specifically, she was struck by the beautiful butterflies carved all over the walls of the barracks housing the prisoners about to be put to death; she contemplated those butterflies for the rest of her life, as they helped her realize that even in the midst of tragedy, human beings still can strive for beauty.[9] This point is also underscored in the book *Art Against the Odds*, which features works by inmates and other artists who were isolated, self-taught, and totally disinterested in showing or profiting from their works.[10] Art made the worlds of these artists more comforting and tolerable; it was their way of repairing not only a very broken external world, but also a fractured internal spirit.

The creation narratives in the Book of Genesis reflect Western society's understanding of the human creative enterprise. Although the unique creation stories of other religions and cultures can help illuminate the spiritual and artistic creations of those cultures,[11] the Genesis narratives probably are the most celebrated stories about creativity in Western society. These narratives, and their interpretation through the rabbinic tradition, are the basis of my exploration of human creativity and *tikkun olam* through the Judaic perspective. These sources attest to the strong spiritual underpinnings that animate human innovation[12] and furnish the basis for the view that human creativity exemplifies *tikkun olam*.

A nuanced examination of the creation texts in Genesis discloses two distinct creation stories, each depicting a different image of

Adam. Although these two images of Adam can be interpreted as "two representatives of humanity,"[13] for purposes of this discussion it is important to underscore that both creation narratives contain significant insights about inspirational motivations for human creativity. These insights can be derived from a careful exegesis of the biblical text and its interpretive theology.

First Creation Narrative

The first creation narrative recounts God's creation of the world in six days, culminating with the creation of humankind on the sixth day (Genesis 1:26). The text states: "God created man in His image, in the image of God He created him" (Genesis 1:27), and then tells us that God commanded the newly created human being to "fill the earth and master it" (Genesis 1:28).[14]

Through this language, the first creation narrative provides important support for a fundamental insight regarding inspirational motivations for artistic creation. It depicts the first human as a spiritual being whose affirmative creative acts are undertaken in response to divine command. According to the late Rabbi Joseph Soloveitchik, an influential twentieth-century theologian, the Torah tells us the story of creation so that humans could derive the law that God obligates us to create; Soloveitchik believed that "the peak of religious ethical perfection to which Judaism aspires is man as creator."[15] Thus, the Jewish religion introduced to the world the idea that "the most fundamental principle of all is that man must create himself."[16]

The rabbis of antiquity taught: "All that was created during the six days of creation requires improvement."[17] The role of humans was to partner with God in creating an improved world, thus renewing the cosmos with creative enterprise.[18] Another early rabbinic narrative involving a dialogue between the great talmudic sage Akiva and the evil Roman governor, Turnusrufus, also expresses this fundamental concept.[19] Turnusrufus challenges Akiva by asking which is more beautiful: the work of God or of humans. Akiva replies that the latter is better, with respect to those things where human art is effective (in contrast to things where humans and God are operating in completely different spheres—such as the creation of heaven and earth). Pressing further, Turnusrufus asks why male babies are not already born circumcised; Akiva replies that this is because God gave the commandments in order to refine the people of Israel.

The Hebrew verb used in the first creation narrative is *bara* ("created"), which derives from the root *bet-resh-alef*. This root appears in the Torah only in conjunction with divine creativity; however, the first creation narrative in Genesis is understood by Rabbi Soloveitchik as "challeng[ing] man to create, to transform wilderness into productive life."[20] The text of the first creation narrative reinforces this perspective. The human being of this story dominated the "elemental natural forces" and invoked a "will to learn the secrets of nature."[21] In so doing, however, the human being obeyed God's command to "rule the fish of the sea, the birds of the sky, the cattle, the whole earth, and all the creeping things that creep on earth" (Genesis 1:26). After God created man and woman, he blessed them and said: "Be fertile and increase (*p'ru u-r'vu*); fill the land and master it" (Genesis 1:28). Significantly, the earliest appearance of the phrase *tikkun olam* in rabbinic literature is in the Mishnah's tractate Gittin, where it is linked to the divine commandment about procreation.[22]

Human creativity exercised in response to divine command figures prominently in the story of the construction of the Tabernacle, beginning in Exodus 31. God instructs Moses to single out, as the supervisory master craftsman for this project, Bezalel—who has been endowed "with a divine spirit of skill, ability, and knowledge (*b'hokhmah u-vit'vunah u-v'da·at*) in every kind of craft; to make designs for work in gold, silver, and copper, to cut stones for setting and to carve wood, to work in every kind of craft" (Exodus 31:3–5).

And then Bezalel (and his associate Oholiab) are assigned the task of supervising the construction of the Tabernacle and all of the accoutrements necessary for the service of God. (Exodus 31:7–11) This text thus presents a confluence between obedience to God, worship of the Divine, and human artistic creativity.

Although the construction of the Tabernacle exemplifies a specific link between human artistry and obeying God, Jewish tradition sees human artistry, on an even broader level, as acting in accord with God's commandment to humans to create. In carrying out God's instructions, the human beings in the first creation narrative are viewed as the prototypes for "collective human technological genius."[23] This idea embodies the concept of "practical spirituality," which recognizes that a spiritual connection to God can be achieved even through the performance of ordinary tasks.[24] Thus, an important lesson from this creation narrative is that an author who labors toward even a physical or material end can be empowered through a sense of practical spirituality, in much the same way as the humans depicted in the biblical text.

Practical spirituality is prevalent in Judaism. For example, the twelfth-century philosopher and legalist Maimonides seems to recognize this concept when he affirms that people should perform even ordinary tasks for the service of heaven; he writes: "A person should direct one's heart and the totality of one's behavior to one goal: becoming aware of God, the Blessed One."[25] The concept of practical spirituality also is steeped in the hasidic teaching that every object reflects and expresses the Divine; according to this view, "not only study and prayer are religious acts but also commerce, *artisanship...* [and] all human behavior has the potential to reveal God to His people, and each person can aspire to that revelation."[26] According to this view, the body is the source of concern for the physical, whereas the soul is the source for the spiritual. Judaism strives to maintain an appropriate balance between body and soul, or the physical and the spiritual. Thus, "when the physical is engaged for spiritual purposes, the conflict is transformed into peace and harmony."[27] This harmony can be achieved even through the creation of mundane physical objects or other artistic creations that, in fact, can allow the author to, in the words of Marc Chagall, "take flight to another world."[28]

The first creation narrative provides a second important insight regarding inspirational motivations for artistic creation. This insight can be called the mirroring argument: humanity's capacity for artistic creation mirrors or imitates God's creative capacity.[29] Rabbi Joseph Soloveitchik notes that phrase *tzelem elohim*, "the image of God" (found in the first account of creation), underscores "man's striving and ability to become a creator."[30] This language clearly lays out a path for humans to see themselves as potential creators, underscoring an unprecedented parallel between God and humanity—and this has been recognized even by those who approach the Bible from a non-theological perspective.[31] This view sees creativity as rooted in inspirational elements, because the motive for human creativity is to mirror the Divine.

An additional example of the mirroring argument in connection with human creativity is found regarding the laws of Shabbat, embedded in the Tabernacle narrative in the Book of Exodus. Israel is commanded to mirror God not only with respect to creating, but also with respect to ceasing to create on Shabbat. An injunction for the Israelites to observe Shabbat appears following the delineation of all the instructions for constructing the Tabernacle and its accoutrements, which are necessary for the service of God (Exodus 31:16). The textual juxtaposition is telling: the injunction to observe Shabbat immediately follows the instructions for the construction of the Tabernacle, directed to the skilled craftsmen, and thus furnishes a reminder to humans to mirror the Divine in this regard as well—that is, in cessation from labor, no less than in the creative enterprise. Indeed, the last verse of this section concerning Shabbat reads: "For in six days the Eternal made heaven and earth, and on the seventh day God ceased from work and was refreshed (*va-yinnafash*)" (Exodus 31:17).

Further, the "Godlike notion of creation" in the opening chapters of Genesis provides the basis for the parental metaphor of authorship.[32] Both God and humans "give birth" to their creations, and therefore manifest a particular type of connection to their handiworks. In fact, the word "creativity" derives from the Latin verb *creo*, which means "to give birth to."[33] Indeed, the opening verses of Genesis may be seen as providing a description of a womb: "The deep, unformed darkness is the womb, ripe with potential. The water is the amniotic waters that protect the fragility of life."[34] The first creation narrative thus serves as a highly significant source that reflects the inclination of humankind to view themselves as creators, with the potential for possessing a parental connection to the created works.[35] This is yet another way in which humanity mirrors the Divine.

There are many textual examples of God's parental connection to humanity. This concept appears very concretely in the Book of Jonah, for example, which concludes with the idea that God has pity on the Ninevites because they are God's creation, and refrains from destroying the city out of a parental concern for its inhabitants (4:11). Similarly, the Torah relates that God had "heartfelt sadness (*va-yinnaḥem*)" concerning the evil generation in the time of Noah (Genesis 6:6).[36] Rashi explains this phrase as meaning that God "mourned over the loss of the divine handiwork (*ma·aseih yadav*)."[37] Yet another example of God's parental concern with humanity appears in the weekday Amidah, recited by observant Jews three times a day: "Hear our voice, our God, take pity and be compassionate to us…" The specific Hebrew word for "take pity" used in this prayer is *ḥus*, which refers to an artisan's special regard for the product of his hands. The underlying concept here is that God should pity us because we are God's handiwork.[38]

Thus, we see from the first creation narrative that the traditional Jewish approach to human creativity emphasizes the underlying spiritual motivations for physical creative action. These motivations are rooted in the spiritual elements of obeying God and mirroring

God's capacity for creativity, ceasing creativity on a periodic basis, and connecting to one's works of authorship in a particular type of way. I now turn to the second creation narrative in the Book of Genesis, which reveals additional spiritual motivations for human creative enterprise.

Second Creation Narrative

The second creation narrative, beginning in Genesis 2:4,[39] also is significant for its understanding of humanity's inspirational creative spirit. The biblical text reads: "Eternal God formed [the first] man from the dust of the earth. God blew into his nostrils the breath of life (*nishmat ḥayyim*), and man became a living being (*nefesh ḥayyah*)" (Genesis 2:7). Classical interpretations of this narrative suggest that human creativity derives from an intrinsic drive that, although endowed by an external source, enables people to suppress their egos and focus on the emergence of their work. These themes reinforce the notion, seen above in the first creation story, that creativity is spiritually motivated.

Initially, this passage illuminates the idea that human ability to engage in expression, including through artistic skill, is endowed by an external source. The thirteenth-century Jewish commentator Naḥmanides (Ramban) interprets this passage to mean that God's own breath was blown into Adam's nostrils.[40] God's breath is understood to mean "the soul of life,"[41] thus establishing the way in which the creation of human beings differs from all other creations.[42] Rashi explains that the human soul is more alive than the souls of animals because only the former contains the powers of speech and reasoning.[43] Further, according to Rabbi Soloveitchik, "the Biblical metaphor referring to God breathing life into Adam alludes to the actual preoccupation of the latter with God, to his genuine living experience of God."[44] In other words, Adam enjoyed a closeness with God that facilitated God's direct endowment in humanity of expressive, creative capacities. Moreover, this perspective understands human artistry as a reflection of knowledge of the divine will. This point is illustrated further in the passages about the Tabernacle that refer to the artistic contributions of the "wise-hearted" men and women.[45] This text illustrates the Jewish tradition's inclination to equate creativity with wisdom and knowledge.[46]

The second creation narrative also emphasizes the connection between creative endowment and self-abnegation, which can be understood as "the denial or abasement of oneself."[47] From a theological perspective, self-abnegation facilitates spiritual transcendence, to the extent that an individual focuses on God as the Center of the Universe rather than on oneself.[48] Thus, the concept of self-abnegation also relates to the idea that creativity is endowed by an external source.

According to Jewish authorities, speech is singularly reflective of the quality of self-abnegation. For both God and humans, speech is an indication of the ability to transcend the self and relate to someone or something else. In describing the divine act of creation, the Torah does not say that God *made* a world, but rather that the world was *spoken* into existence. Every creative act was preceded by a speech-act, declaring in advance what God was about to do; for example, "God said, 'Let there be light,' and there was light" (Genesis 1:3). These "speakings" are referred to as the "Ten Utterances" (*asarah ma·amarot*) with which, according to the text, God created the world.[49] According to this view, the Adam of the second creation narrative, whom God infused with a special soul, possessed the ability to speak and express himself in a way that mirrored the divine capacity for self-abnegation.[50]

In sum: the two creation narratives in Genesis depict humans as inspired, creative beings. Classical Judaism's interpretation of these narratives facilitates the development of a theory of spiritual motivation that focuses on an intrinsic dimension of human innovation. The way in which humans partner with and relate to God has important implications for human creative enterprise and its role in *tikkun olam*. These motivations for human creativity are consistent with the view of *tikkun olam*, especially prominent in kabbalistic thought, which emphasizes the restoration of "harmony, balance, and oneness among the forces that constitute the manifested aspects of God."[51] The idea of *tikkun olam* as a means of perfecting one's soul through engaging in physical activities that can also positively impact the world was skillfully articulated by law professor and former prosecutor Samuel Levine: "As a prosecutor, I feel that I… further the purpose of creation, by helping the criminal justice system return order to the world.…As a result of my work, society is better able to function in accordance with God's plans, in an orderly and productive manner.…I am a partner with God in creating a better world."[52] Although Levine was not speaking about artistic creativity, the same reasoning clearly applies to the process of human creative enterprise. Indeed, as this discussion has demonstrated, human creativity entails the very type of contemplation and concentration that is a fundamental component of this vision of *tikkun olam*.

Judaism's Lessons on Human Creativity as a "Light Unto the Nations"

From a profound biblical standpoint suggestive of the concept of *tikkun olam* as it would later evolve, Israel is imagined as "a light unto the nations."[53] This essay has explored how the Jewish tradition understands human creativity to facilitate spiritual self-development. The lessons derived from our tradition regarding the potential for spiritual self-development in connection with artistic creativity can be such a "light unto the nations." Indeed, studies have documented how Christian theology and culture, as well as the narratives of secular authors and creativity theorists, comport with the Jewish tradition, by attesting to the strong spiritual underpinnings that Jewish tradition believes animate human creativity and innovation.[54] For example, the renowned Christian author Madeleine L'Engle explicitly invoked several of the themes discussed in this essay, without specifically attributing her insights to the Jewish tradition. She embraced the parental metaphor in combination with the "gifted" aspects of creativity when she spoke of the work coming to the author, saying "Here I am. Enflesh me. Give birth to me."[55] Moreover, Director Elliot Silverstein, representing the Directors Guild of America, also relied on the parental metaphor of authorship explicitly when he referred to the film colorization process as a means of torturing and butchering "our children" (i.e., the films), in his testimony before Congress opposing this technological process.[56]

The classical Jewish tradition views God as the external source of expressive and creative ability. However, there is also a more generalized idea that creative expression, though driven by an intrinsic mechanism, is "gifted"—that is, it comes from a source beyond the author's control. Some degree of self-abnegation is critical to the development of an artistic soul. Creativity derives from a higher power, and therefore, if true artistic creation is to occur, an artist must transcend the self in order to focus on the source of one's gift. Contemporary psychologists and creativity scholars John Dacey and Kathleen Lennon have extensively explored the connection between creativity, faith, and self-abnegation, and they emphasize the importance of spirituality and faith in the creation process: "Being spiritual…means striving to enlarge one's connection to that force lying within, a force that can make it possible to transcend the ordinary self and reach one's fullest potential."[57]

Another universal lesson derived from the creation text in Genesis concerns the cyclical nature of creativity. After Adam and Eve partake of the forbidden fruit, God admonishes them, "For dust you are, and to dust you shall return" (Genesis 3:19). The text thus ensures that the starting-point of humanity is the same as its end-point: dust. According to Rashi, the human being is a combination of the earthly and the Divine.[58] After death, the soul returns to its source, God, while the body returns to its source, the earth.[59]

While alive, however, every person—as God's creation—serves as a testament to God's message for humanity.[60] The universal message concerning human creativity embedded in this text is powerful: just as God's creations are cyclical and return to their source, the author's creations are cyclical and return to their source.[61] According to this view of creativity, the author's creation is an embodiment of the work's spiritually motivated message. Moreover, an author has the responsibility for preserving the message of the work and its meaning during his or her lifetime, after which the work returns to its source. Jewish tradition thus provides the basis for a well developed set of secular laws, applied throughout the world, that are designed to preserve the message and meaning of an author's works. These laws are known as moral rights, and they serve as a practical application of the spiritually focused basis for human creativity that is emblematic of the internal potential for *tikkun olam*. Unfortunately, the moral rights laws in the United States are substantially under-developed as compared to the rest of the world. A primary reason for this discrepancy is that in the United States, human creativity is seen largely as a means to an economic end rather than as a spiritually motivated enterprise.[62] Perhaps, then, lawmakers in the United States need a bit more education on the potential for tikkun olam as it applies to human spirituality and improvement of the soul.

NOTES

[1] This essay is an adaptation of sections of chapter 2 of my book *The Soul of Creativity: Forging a Moral Rights Law for the United States* (Stanford: Stanford University Press, 2010).

[2] Byron L. Sherwin, "*Tikkun Olam*: A Case of Semantic Displacement," in Jewish Political Studies Review 25:3–4 (Fall 2013), pp. 11 and 14; and see also the essay by Vernon Kurtz elsewhere in this volume. Note that Sherwin is critical of contemporary understandings of *tikkun olam* on the ground that they "have little or nothing in common with the various understanding of the term in classical Jewish literature" (p. 14).

[3] See Sherwin, "*Tikkun Olam*: A Case of Semantic Displacement," p. 10.

[4] I use the terms "inspirational" and "spiritual" synonymously throughout this essay. See *Soul of Creativity* (cited in note 1 above).

[5] Frank Barron et al., eds., *Creators on Creating: Awakening and Cultivating the Imaginative Mind* (New York: Penguin Group, 1997); see especially Barron's "Introduction," pp. 1 and 18.

[6] See Daniel J. Boorstin, *The Creators: A History of Heroes of the Imagination* (New York: Random House, 1992), pp. 151–152, for a discussion of depictions of animals of prey as early as 15,000 B.C.E.

[7] See Roberta Harding, *Gallery of the Doomed: An Exploration of Creative Endeavors by the Condemned*, in 28 NEW ENGLAND JOURNAL ON CRIMINAL & CIVIL CONFINEMENT 195, 196 (2002). Please note that throughout this essay, all citations to legal sources (such as law review articles) appear in accordance with conventional legal citation format, rather than in the style used elsewhere in this volume. In these citations, the title of the article is italicized, and the name of the journal (printed in small caps) is preceded by the volume number and immediately followed by the page number on which the article begins, and if applicable, by the page number(s) for the specific proposition or quotation being referenced in the body of this essay.

[8] See, for example, *The Diary of Anne Frank*, which is one of the greatest classics of Holocaust literature (*Anne Frank: The Diary of a Young Girl*, trans. B.M. Mooyaart-Doubleday [Garden City, NY: Doubleday, 1952]).

[9] See Judith Graham, "Pioneer Who Taught World to Live with Death, Dying," in *Chicago Tribune* (August 26, 2004), section 1, p. 1.

[10] Susan Goldman Rubin, *Art Against the Odds: From Slave Quilts to Prison Paintings* (New York: Crown Publishers, 2004).

[11] See generally in this regard, Boorstin, *The Creators*. In this comprehensive work on heroes of the imagination, historian Daniel Boorstin explores the creation stories of other cultures, and their impact on the specific works of art produced.

[12] Consider Thomas Wolfe's account of sculptor Frederick Hart's "Ex Nihilo," which adorns the tympanum over the Washington National Cathedral. See Wolfe, "The Artist the Art World Couldn't See," in *The New York Times*

(January 2, 2000), 6 (Magazine), at pp. 16 and 18, available online at www.jeanstephengalleries.com/hart-wolfe.html.

[13] Joseph B. Soloveitchik, *The Lonely Man of Faith* (New York: Doubleday, 1965), p. 10. The character Adam (Eve's partner) actually is mentioned by name only in the second creation narrative.

[14] Unless otherwise indicated, the translations of biblical passages throughout this essay are based on the new JPS translation of the Tanakh (Philadelphia: Jewish Publication Society, 1985), hereafter referred to as NJPS.

[15] Joseph B. Soloveitchik, *Halakhic Man*, trans. Lawrence Kaplan (Philadelphia: Jewish Publication Society, 1983), p. 101.

[16] Ibid., at p. 109.

[17] Bereishit Rabbah 11:6.

[18] According to Jewish tradition, humans were not intended to be passive recipients of the Torah; rather, in Soloveitchik's words, the human being is to become "a partner with the Almighty in the act of creation" (*Halakhic Man*, p. 81).

[19] *Midrash Tanḥuma, Tazria* 5, and cf. the extended discussion of this midrash in the essay by Benjamin Blech elsewhere in this volume.

[20] Abraham R. Besdin, *Reflections of the Rav* (1979; rpt. New York: KTAV, 1993), pp. 27–28.

[21] Soloveitchik, *Lonely Man of Faith*, p. 14.

[22] See M. Gittin 4:1–5:3, together with the discussion in Sherwin, "*Tikkun Olam*: A Case of Semantic Displacement," p. 4 (citing Sagit Mor, "*Tikkun Ha-olam* in the Thought of the Sages"; Ph.D. dissertation, Hebrew University, 2003). The Mishnah's discussion of procreation (*p'riyah u-r'viyah*) is found in Gittin 4:5.

[23] Soloveitchik, *Lonely Man of Faith*, p. 17 n.†. Soloveitchik also notes that man also acquires dignity by exercising control over his environment (p. 15).

[24] Ibid., pp. 18–19.

[25] See M.T. Hilkhot Dei·ot 3:2.

[26] Moshe Rosman, "Innovative Tradition: Jewish Culture in the Polish–Lithuanian Commonwealth," in David Biale, ed., *Cultures of the Jews* (New York: Schocken Books, 2002), pp. 519 and 563 (emphasis added).

[27] "Chanukah in a New Light," in *Farbrengen* (Winter 2001), pp. 9 and 11.

[28] Barry Oretsky, "Making the Mystical Transition," in *Farbrengen* (Winter 2001), p. 7. Oretsky, a painter, also notes that he finds "a wonderful spirituality occurs when the creative process is expressed in paint" (ibid.).

[29] Cf. Mark Rose, Copyright and Its Metaphors, in 50 UCLA LAW REVIEW 1, 11 (2002). Rose notes that "some creative spark…if unpacked could be shown to carry a numinous aura evocative ultimately of the original divine act of creation itself."

[30] Soloveitchik, *Lonely Man of Faith*, p. 12.

[31] See Boorstin, *The Creators*, p. 41.

[32] See Rose, *Copyright*, p. 9.

[33] Russ VerSteeg, *Rethinking Originality*, in 34 WILLIAM & MARY LAW REVIEW 801, 826 (1993).

[34] Karyn D. Kedar, "The Many Names of God," in Elyse Goldstein, ed., *The Women's Torah Commentary* (Woodstock, VT: Jewish Lights Publishing, 2000), p. 129.

[35] Parents often view their children as reflections of themselves, just as authors do their works. See generally Nancy Friday, *My Mother/My Self: The Daughter's Search for Identity* (New York: Delta Trade Paperbacks, 1997).

[36] The translation "heartfelt sadness" comes from *The Chumash: The Stone Edition*, eds. Nosson Scherman et al. (New York and Jerusalem: Moznaim Publishing Corp., 1993), p. 29.

[37] Rashi to Genesis 6:6, s.v. *va-yitatzeiv el libbo*.

[38] *The Complete Artscroll Siddur*, eds. Nosson Scherman and Meir Zlotowitz (Brooklyn, NY: Mesorah Publications 1984), p. 109, referencing an observation of the Vilna Gaon.

[39] The first half of verse four finishes the first story of creation; the second half begins the second story. The NJPS translation, for example, reads: "Such is the story of heaven and earth when they were created. When the Lord God made earth and heaven..." The *Etz Hayim* commentary to that verse observes that the inversion of "heaven and earth" and "earth and heaven" "signals a shift in the focus between the two creation stories" (*Etz Hayim: Torah and Commentary* [New York: Rabbinical Assembly and the United Synagogue of Conservative Judaism, 2001], p. 12).

[40] Naḥmanides to Genesis 2:7, s.v. *va-yippaḥ b'appav nefesh ḥayyim*.

[41] Cf. Rashi to Genesis 7:22, s.v. *nishmat ruaḥ ḥayyim*.

[42] According to many traditional commentators, although humans were created alive, their true form was not attained until God took this further step of infusing them with a soul, cf. the comments of Rabbi Yaakov Culi in his *Mei-am Lo'eiz* Torah commentary, trans. Aryeh Kaplan (Brooklyn, NY: Moznayim, 1977), vol. 1, p. 245.

[43] Rashi to Genesis 2:7. Cf. also Maurice Merleau-Ponoty, *Phenomenology of Perception* (London: Routledge & Kegan Paul Ltd., 1976), pp. 178–179 (likening authentic speech—that which is the creative, original descriptions of feelings—to the expression of artists); and Russ VerSteeg, *Defining "Author" for Purposes of Copyright*, in 45 AMERICAN UNIVERSITY LAW REVIEW 1323, 1339, 1365 (1996) (affirming communication as the essential component of authorship).

[44] Soloveitchik, *Lonely Man of Faith*, p. 23.

[45] See, e.g., Exodus 35:25, where this phrase appears in conjunction with the women's contributions specifically; and 36:1–2, where it appears in conjunction with the men's work.

[46] Interestingly, in her speech accepting the 2013 Tony Award for directing *Pippin*, Diane Paulus quoted Harvard President Drew Faust as saying that "creativity is a form of knowledge." See Sarah Rodman, "ART's Diane Paulus,

'Pippin' Win Big at Tony Awards" (June 9, 2013), online at www.boston.com.

[47] *Oxford American College Dictionary* (New York: Spark Publishing, 2002), p. 1239.

[48] Sue Fishkoff, *The Rebbe's Army: Inside the World of Chabad-Lubavitc*h (New York: Schocken, 2003), p. 77.

[49] See Berel Wein, *Pirkei Avos—Teaching for Our Times* (Brooklyn, NY: Birnbaum Edition/Shaar Press, 2003), pp. 184–185.

[50] See Soloveitchik, *Lonely Man of Faith*, p. 2.

[51] Sherwin, "*Tikkun Olam*: A Case of Semantic Displacement," p. 12.

[52] Samuel J. Levine, *The Broad Life of the Jewish Lawyer: Integrating Spirituality, Scholarship, and Profession*, in 27 TEXAS TECH LAW REVIEW 1199, 1206 (1996).

[53] Isaiah 49:1–6; 51:4. And cf. in this regard Elliot N. Dorff, *For the Love of God and People* (Philadelphia: Jewish Publication Society, 2007), p. 109, as well as the essay by Dorff elsewhere in this volume.

[54] See generally Roberta Rosenthal Kwall, *The Soul of Creativity; and idem, Inspiration and Innovation: The Intrinsic Dimension of the Artistic Soul*, in 81 NOTRE DAME LAW REVIEW 1945 (2006).

[55] Madeleine L'Engle, *Walking on Water: Reflections on Faith and Art* (New York: Macmillan, 1980), p. 18; see also p. 195, which present a Christian perspective on the "gifted" aspect of creation.

[56] United States Senate, Committee on the Judiciary, Subcommittee on Technology and the Law, *Legal Issues that Arise when Color Is Added to Films Originally Produced, Sold, and Distributed in Black and White* (Washington, D.C.: Government Printing Office, 1987); statement of Elliot Silverstein.

[57] John S. Dacey and Kathleen H. Lennon, *Understanding Creativity* (San Francisco: Jossey-Boss, 1998), p. 130.

[58] Cf. Rashi's comment to Genesis 2:7, s.v. *va-yippaḥ b'appav*, where he notes that "[God] made the human being from the terrestrial realms and the celestial realms: the body from below and the soul from above."

[59] Cf. Kohelet 12:7.

[60] See Boorstin, *The Creators*, p. 42.

[61] Over time, the notion of stewardship, which assumed a prominent theological focus particularly in Christianity, embraced this cyclical view of creativity.

[62] These themes are explored in depth in Kwall, The Soul of Creativity.

A Theology of Jewish Social Justice[1]

Sid Schwarz

Among the most defining characteristics of American Jewry is its deep commitment to progressive social change. In the American Jewish community this activity is often labeled as *tikkun olam*, literally "the work of repairing a world [that is broken]." There are numerous examples of this brokenness: the growing gap between the rich and the poor, intolerance between members of different groups fueled by growing religious extremism and ethnic tribalism, oppressive political systems that do not respect basic human rights of persons within their borders, the subjugation and abuse of women in societies that continue to view women as chattel, environmental degradation exacerbated by human inattention to sustainable patterns of living, human trafficking that has become a multi-billion dollar international "industry." Unfortunately, the list can go on and on. Indeed, any cursory study of the labor movement, the civil rights movement, the women's movement, the field of human rights, and more recently the gay rights movement and environmentalism, will reveal that Jews have played leadership roles as thought leaders, as funders, and as the activists who have done important work in advancing the goals of these movements. Many opinion surveys conducted among Jews reveal that some version of "making the world a better place" usually ranks first, second, or third as the most defining feature of Jewish behavior.[2]

In this essay, I will explore the historical and theological roots of this phenomenon. In the American Jewish setting, the social justice phenomenon that I will be discussing has become synonymous with the Hebrew expression *tikkun olam*. It is an evocative term that means "the repair of the world," suggesting that the world we have inherited is broken. The mere fact that this Hebrew expression has become one of a handful of Hebrew terms widely familiar to American Jews already suggests the appeal of the concept. But whether we call it *tikkun olam* or social justice, the questions remain: Why is it that, even as Jews have moved up the socio-economic ladder in America and gained entry to the top corridors of power in American society, there has been a close correlation in Jewish voting patterns, attitudes, and activism with those of marginalized minority groups? What is it about the history, culture, and values of the Jewish people that have made so many of them champions of social justice for the most vulnerable in society?

From Slavery to Freedom

The national consciousness of the Jewish people was forged in the context of slavery. The story of the Jewish enslavement in Egypt, recounted in the biblical book of Exodus, is seared into the memory of Jews via the annual observance of Passover. A Jew need not be learned nor frequent a synagogue to know the story of his or her enslaved ancestors building the pyramids of Pharaoh, until they escaped under the leadership of Moses—an experience that the Israelites saw as a redeeming act of God.

Part of the genius of the rabbinic sages was to take the central parts of the Jewish historical narrative and concretize them in annual festivals replete with memorable rituals, symbols, liturgy, and pageantry. The holiday of Passover is one of the most beloved and observed festivals in the Jewish annual cycle. The rituals and melodies of the Passover *seder* are especially designed to captivate the attention of children, forming memories that last a lifetime. There are several ways that Jews are affected by the Passover story:

First, it sets the stage for the motif "from slavery to freedom" (*mei-avdut l'heirut*), which runs throughout Jewish history. Whenever the Jewish people experienced persecution, oppression, or expulsion, they re-lived the experience of their ancestors in Egypt. Precisely because the Exodus story concludes with the redemption of the Jewish people from Egyptian bondage, Jews throughout history—especially those who found themselves in the most dire of circumstances—believed that they too would ultimately be redeemed from their suffering.

Second, because the motif "from slavery to freedom" played itself out in Jewish history over and over again, Jews came to see the trajectory of their history as essentially redemptive or messianic: there would always be a better tomorrow. For religious Jews, this was an article of faith. God's hand was active in history, and so the redemption of Jews from a specific circumstance was a sign of divine love for God's chosen people. When Jewish suffering persisted, that suffering was understood by the rabbis as a divinely ordained punishment. Since all of history was understood to be under God's dominion, then it must be the case that God was punishing the people for a reason: presumably, because they had not been faithful to the covenant at Sinai. And yet, that very theology fortified the belief that, in the end, evil would be vanquished and the world would come to enjoy a state of peace and harmony.[3] This sense of hope, deeply embedded in the soul of the Jew, is reflected in the national anthem of the State of Israel, called Hatikvah, "the hope."

Third, the Jewish people have internalized the message of Exodus 23:9: "You shall not oppress the stranger, for you were strangers in the land of Egypt." This commandment is reinforced again and again in the Jewish tradition, leading Jews to have a particular concern for the "stranger in their midst." This sense of being outsiders is deeply rooted in the collective consciousness of the Jewish people and has served as a powerful force impelling Jewish activism toward social justice.

The Jew as Outsider

The status of Jews as outsiders is based on more than just the biblical origins of the Jewish people. In the year 70 C.E., the Romans destroyed the Second Temple in Jerusalem and Jews effectively lost their political sovereignty. Banished from the Land of Israel, Jews needed a survival strategy. In a remarkable historical transformation, credited in the Talmud to Yoḥanan ben Zakkai, the Jews set up an academy outside of Jerusalem, in Yavneh, and began the process of making their national identity portable. In the centuries following the fall of Jerusalem, the rabbinic sages—through their interpretations of the laws of the Torah—provided Jews with a carefully defined way of life. This body of Jewish law, called *halakhah*, provided specific guideposts for daily life. In addition, a corpus of non-legal material (popularly called *aggadah*) came to undergird and inform the ritual practices that became the defining hallmarks of Jewish existence. Both of these bodies of literature were used as a prism through which Jews of every generation understood their individual and collective existence. It tied them not only to generations of Jews that had preceded them, but also to Jews across the globe, in their own generation. This expanded body of Torah provided Jews with the tools to survive an exile that lasted almost 2000 years.

Jews were able to survive the loss of their ancestral land because, wherever they lived, they clustered in communities that accepted the authority of the rabbinic sages. The sages used halakhic decisions and aggadic teachings to connect the Jews of their generation with the master narrative of Jewish history. In addition, Jews developed communities that had well-developed social structures, addressing a wide range of individual and communal needs. In many ways, Jews were living out the biblical observation that they were "a nation that dwells apart" (Numbers 23:9). Jews throughout the Middle Ages enjoyed an advantage that many non-Jews did not enjoy: within their semi-autonomous communities, and with their own political, judicial, and social welfare systems, they were able to create both the intellectual and social structures that gave them a sense of purpose and a way to survive.

Jewry in Freedom

As much as these semi-autonomous communities helped Jews negotiate less-than-hospitable host cultures during the Middle Ages, it was a system that would not survive the transition to modernity. Just as feudalism and the system of guilds gave way to the emergence of the modern nation–state in Christian Europe, so too did the communal governance system of Jewish communities need to adapt to new circumstances.

A seminal moment in Jewish history took place in 1807 when Napoleon Bonaparte convened an assembly of rabbis from across Europe and dubbed it, in the grandiose way that only an emperor might, "the Sanhedrin." Napoleon wanted to use the Sanhedrin and the authority it might exert on European Jewry to advance his own imperialistic agenda. Though the ancient Sanhedrin had not actually met since the fifth century C.E. (when its last head, Gamliel VI, died), there was a method to Napoleon's madness. Desperately wanting to unite Europe under his political authority, he needed to break down the medieval feudal system under which clergy, nobility, artisans, and peasants each had their own separate arrangements with local authorities. Laying the foundations for the modern nation–state, Napoleon understood that effective governance over a vast territory would require laws that applied equally across the spectrum of the subject population. He was willing to grant the subject population certain rights, in exchange for their political loyalty and their fulfillment of certain financial obligations to his empire. The Jews represented a political entity that functioned semi-autonomously throughout the empire, and thus stood in the way of

Napoleon's ultimate design. Napoleon did not love the Jews; rather, the Sanhedrin was Napoleon's clever ploy to break down Jewish separateness and to make the Jews like everyone else.

Nevertheless, his offer was not an ungenerous one. In return for defining Jewish identity as a faith (rather than as a separate national or ethnic community, with loyalties different from those of other people in the empire), Jews would acquire full citizenship and the rights attending that status. It was the Jews' ticket out of the ghetto, an entry-pass into the emerging, modern European nation–state. It was also a break with almost 2000 years of diaspora Jewish history. If Judaism represented a creative tension between holy apartness and an expectation that Jews would be fully engaged in the world that they inhabited, medieval Europe had effectively denied Jews the opportunity to achieve the second part of that mandate. But the new arrangement offered by Napoleon to the Jews held out the possibility that they might engage more fully with gentile society—in a way that had happened only rarely in their history.

The rabbis of Napoleon's Sanhedrin were given a series of questions that clearly had right and wrong answers from Napoleon's perspective. The Sanhedrin gave the emperor the answers he wanted, and they did so in a way that carefully respected existing halakhic norms. The following are included among the rulings issued by the Sanhedrin: polygamy was prohibited; a religious bill of divorce (get) was required, and had to be accompanied by a prior civil divorce; a mixed marriage would be binding on Jews from a civil/legal perspective, even if not recognized by Jewish law; Jews were required to regard their country of residence as their fatherland, living by its laws as full citizens and pledging loyalty to its political authority; Jews were called on to treat their fellow (non-Jewish) citizens according to universal laws of moral conduct, treating them as they would fellow Jews in all business matters—including the exacting of interest on monetary loans. Effectively, these rulings set the groundwork for full Jewish participation in the modern nation–state.

Ever since Napoleon's historic Sanhedrin, Jews have wrestled with the trade-off represented by these rulings. Was Judaism simply a profession of faith, or were there national and historical elements to Judaism that ensured that the Jews would always be "a people apart"? If Jews were being offered an opportunity to join the international brotherhood of humanity, free from all of the limitations and disabilities that had characterized their diaspora existence for centuries, should the offer be spurned—for the sake of exclusivist Jewish historical consciousness and group identity? Could Jews engage with gentile society without losing their distinctiveness? Might this new status be the messianic "end of days" foretold by the Bible, or was it a modern "golden calf"—that is, a false idol that appeared to offer redemption but was, in fact, a betrayal of the biblical mandate that Jews remain a people apart?[4]

It was not until the twentieth century that theories of democratic and cultural pluralism emerged in the United States, which changed the model for social and political integration that had been introduced by Napoleon. These new ideas suggested that a democracy did not require all cultural, religious, and ethnic identities to be relinquished. America, it was argued, was a cultural mosaic and not a melting pot. But even before these theories gained prominence in America, laws guaranteeing the separation of church and state and the free exercise of religion had allowed the United States to forge a society far more hospitable to Jews than had ever been the case in Europe. This new "social contract" allowed Jews to attain levels of prominence and prosperity in America that had been unprecedented in any other country of their historical experience. But it also opened the door to the highest level of assimilation in Jewish history.

The period between the emancipation of Napoleon until the end of World War II was a time of great ferment in the world, bringing many new forms of Jewish identity to the Jewish community. Reform Judaism was born in Europe, as an attempt to provide the kind of faith that would preserve essential parts of the Jewish religion but without the national and historical dimensions that would stand in the way of full integration of Jews into their European host countries. Conservative Judaism would emerge as a reaction to Reform, trying to balance some of the stringencies of Orthodox Judaism with the demands of living as members of multi-religious societies. Even large segments of the Orthodox community underwent a change of worldview under the banner of Neo-Orthodoxy, the watchword became *torah im derekh eretz*, "being faithful to observance but consistent with the ways of modern society." The revolutionary political movements of Eastern Europe included many Jews, who were seeking to find secular ways to advance a messianic vision of society. And within those revolutionary movements existed the kernel of the idea for Jews to create a society of their own, an idea that would give birth to the Zionist movement.[5]

History, however, does not run in straight lines. The opportunity provided by modernity for Jews to integrate themselves into European society was intoxicating, and many Jews seized it. Some went so far as to convert to Christianity. But the Holocaust turned back the historical clock, tapping into the Church's demonization of the Jews that dated to the first centuries of the Common Era.[6] Cutting the cancerous Jews out of the European body politic was an idea that found ready acceptance among many in Christian Europe.

In the years after the Holocaust, the debate over Jewish identity re-emerged. If Zionism was an alternative for Jews seeking to escape persecution, could there be another form of Jewish identity for those Jews living in relative freedom? The Zionists were convinced that Jews would disappear, either through physical annihilation in countries where anti-Semitism raged (such as the Soviet Union) or through assimilation in societies that offered Jews full embrace (such as much of Western Europe and the United States). Indeed, there is much in the history of the Jewish communities of the world since World War II that bears out this analysis. At the same time, it is hard to ignore the thriving Jewish communities around the world today that provide a wide array of Jewish identity options. It is here that probing the meaning of the twin impulses of Jewish identity—Exodus and Sinai—will prove illuminating. These impulses have a direct bearing on the Jewish affinity for tikkun olam.

Exodus: Political/Ethnic Consciousness

Nations search their past for symbolic starting-points to define the master narrative of a people. America may be said to have several such starting-points: as part of Western civilization, America's origin can be traced to Columbus' discovery of the New World; as a nation free of European control, it can be dated to the victory of the colonies against Britain in the Revolutionary War; as democracy, America traces its origin to the framing of the United States Constitution.

The Jewish people's narrative also has several possible starting-points. While Abraham is the first Jew, insofar as bringing the idea of monotheism into the world is concerned, it is the Exodus story that represents the beginning of Jewish national consciousness. A group of slaves shared a common predicament (slavery) and a common oppressor (the Egyptians). What shaped the national consciousness of the people that the Bible will call "the Children of Israel" (*b'nei yisrael*) is the pairing of that enslavement experience with the people's subsequent escape to freedom. Their consciousness was forged not only by an experience of common suffering but, more importantly, by a shared experience of redemption. Immediately after the Israelites' redemption at the Sea of Reeds, Moses impressed upon the people the significance of what they had just experienced: "Remember this day that you went out from the house of bondage; by virtue of the strong hand of the Eternal were you redeemed" (Exodus 13:3).

This verse will be used again and again in the Bible, in rabbinic writings, and in the liturgy that Jews recite in worship. Its power to shape the consciousness of the Jewish people cannot be overestimated. The experience of the Exodus is passed down through the generations, not only in the celebration of Passover. The sacred literature of Judaism uses that experience as the foundation for Jewish peoplehood. It is impossible to know what elements of the Exodus story, as passed down in the biblical account, were known to those who were enslaved. The biblical account is a theological interpretation of those events, recorded centuries after their occurrence. And even if it were a contemporaneous account, it is unlikely that the average slave would have been aware of the high drama being played out between Pharaoh and his upstart nemesis, Moses. But what could not have escaped the notice of the common slave was this truth: the political regime that had overseen their enslavement was being challenged by some combination of a spokesperson for the enslaved (Moses), environmental calamities (the plagues), and perhaps even by a God who was more than a match for the deities of Egypt. By the time the slaves followed Moses out of Egypt and escaped the pursuing Egyptians, they were well on the road to nationhood. The Bible records the moment as follows: "When Israel saw the wondrous power that the Eternal employed against the Egyptians, the people were in awe of the Eternal, expressing their loyalty to God and to God's servant, Moses" (Exodus 14:31).

All the elements of political consciousness were now in place: a common history (Egyptian slavery), a founding myth (being redeemed from the Egyptians by a God more powerful than any other), and a leader (Moses). The Exodus dimension of Jewish existence would remain at the very core of Jewish consciousness throughout the Jews' long history. For a time, it would play itself out in the form of political sovereignty, as it did with the ancient kingdoms of Israel and Judah. In the twentieth century, the Exodus impulse would manifest again with the creation of the modern State of Israel.

But the Exodus consciousness described here transcended conventional political arrangements. The Jewish people manifested this consciousness during their wandering in the desert, in their early settlement in the Land of Israel arranged by tribal affiliation, and during the two millennia that Jews lived in the Diaspora. Exodus consciousness caused Jews to identify with each other regardless of the fact that they might be living thousands of miles apart, under different political regimes, speaking different languages, and developing different regional variations on the practice of Judaism, which often synthesized elements of traditional Jewish practice with the specific gentile culture in which they lived. This consciousness also meant that Jews took care of one another—not only when they lived in close proximity to each other, but even when they became aware of Jews in distress in other locales. During the time that Jews lacked political sovereignty, they became a community of shared historical memory and shared destiny. They believed that the fate of the Jewish people, regardless of temporal domicile, was linked. This is what explains the success of the Zionist movement, the historically unprecedented resurrection of national identity and political sovereignty after 2000 years of dispersion. The Exodus consciousness of the Jewish people was the glue that held the Jewish people together; it was the secret to Jewish survival.

For the Israelites, however, there was a dimension of national identity that transcended political consciousness. It would be an encounter with sacred purpose that would create a direct connection between the slaves who experienced the Exodus from Egypt and the vision that drove the patriarch, Abraham.

Sinai: Spiritual/Religious Consciousness

Scholars, clergy, and lay readers alike can debate the veracity of the Bible's account of the revelation of the Torah at Mount Sinai, but none doubts its mythic power. If the Exodus gave the slaves who left Egypt a sense of a common past and a shared destiny, it was the experience at Sinai that made it abundantly clear that the people

Israel were expected to live out a higher calling. If the Jewish people thought that their redemption from bondage was "a free ride," the covenant entered into at Sinai was a rude awakening. It made many demands on the Jewish people, and they would often be judged to fall short of those demands. The Book of Exodus relates God's words to the fledgling nation: "You have seen what I did to the Egyptians, how I bore you on eagle's wings and brought you to Me. Now then, if you will obey Me faithfully and keep My covenant, you shall be My treasured possession among all the peoples....You shall be to Me a kingdom of priests and a holy nation" (Exodus 19:4–6). God thus reminded the people that they were redeemed from slavery in order to be God's treasured people—on the condition that they obey God's laws and live faithfully in accordance with the covenant.

Throughout the centuries, part of the Jewish people's loyalty to the covenant manifested itself in their observance of ritual laws. Over time, the level of ritual observance would wax and wane. But the ethic of Sinai had greater resonance and staying power than the observance of any particular ritual law. It conveyed to Jews throughout the generations that their task was to replicate, in the temporal world, the kingdom of heaven. While in some religious traditions this phrase would take on otherworldly meanings, Jews have generally understood it to bespeak a rich body of core values that guided their behavior in this world. Jews thus became a people of compassion: they were guided—both by their history of persecution and by their understanding of the revelation at Sinai—to lend their hands and their hearts to the most vulnerable members of society, both Jewish and non-Jewish. The Talmud states: "If anyone has compassion on all created beings, then it is certain evidence that he or she is from the seed of Abraham, our ancestor."[7] Compassion for others defines the Jew.

Classical rabbinic commentators focus on the Israelites' response to the giving of the Ten Commandments and the laws that follow in the Book of Exodus. Repeatedly the Israelites proclaimed that they will obey all that God has asked of them, culminating with the famous phrase *na·aseh v'nishma*, "we will do and obey" (Exodus 24:7)—which the commentators take as a sign of ultimate obedience. The commitment to follow the laws, even before they were fully revealed, represents the highest form of religious obedience. It is the standard that God and Moses demand and expect.

There are other significant aspects of the Sinai moment that make it so central to the essence of Judaism and to the consciousness of the Jewish people. First, the revelation is given in the desert, in a place lost to history. The sanctity of the revelation will not inhere in any physical place, but rather in the message. Second, the revelation is given to the entire nation, and not merely to a subset of its priests; it is thus the possession of the entire people of Israel. Third, the covenant is entered into by a free people in an act of volition. The Hebrew word *avodah* carries two meanings. It is can mean "slavery," experienced by the Israelites in Egypt, but it can also mean "serving God," behavior that will be demanded of the Israelites at Sinai. The difference between the two is that "slavery" (or servitude) is coerced, whereas "service" is an offering of the hearts of the faithful.

The German–Jewish philosopher Leo Baeck beautifully articulated the concept of a people with a sacred purpose when he wrote:

A difficult task was assigned this people [Israel] in history. It is so easy to listen to the voices of idols, and it is so hard to receive the word of the One God into oneself. It is so easy to remain a slave, and it so difficult to become a free man. But this people can only exist in the full seriousness of its task....Man lives within the universe and within history. This people [Israel] understood that history and the universe testify to a Oneness, and reveal a totality and order. One word has dared to be the one expression for that which keeps everything together: "covenant."[8]

Baeck's characterization typifies Jewish self-perception from the earliest stages of Jewish history. He is describing what we are calling here "Sinai consciousness." Even if we cannot establish the historicity of God's revelation to the Jewish people at Sinai and the divine "choosing" of the people Israel, the fact that the people lived with a belief that they were the chosen people led them to conduct themselves in such a way that they more than earned the label. In other words, the Jewish people lived at a higher moral level, in order to live up to the expectation of the covenant.

It must nonetheless be noted that whatever combination of gratitude, fear, and/or religious ecstasy evoked the full-hearted response of obedience from the Israelites at Sinai, they would soon stray far from that commitment. The further they got from their enslavement in Egypt and from the revelation at Sinai, the more they complained about the conditions of the wilderness and the more they fell short of meeting their covenantal responsibilities. One of the themes of this early history of the Israelites is unworthiness, and it provides the traditional theological justification for all subsequent travail of the people: the forty years in the desert, the problems that beset the early Israelite monarchies, the chastisements of the prophets, the military defeats at the hands of Israel's neighbors, and ultimately the loss of Jewish sovereignty and the exile of the Jewish people from the Land of Israel.[9]

The contemporary political philosopher Michael Walzer, in his seminal work *Exodus and Revolution*,[10] points to the gap that almost always exists between the vanguard of a revolution, on the one hand, and the masses who are supposed to benefit from the change in political circumstance, on the other. While the vanguard is filled with high theory about the ultimate meaning of the revolution and the ultimate destiny of those who are to be liberated, the masses are driven by more basic concerns: Will we eat better? Will we enjoy better living conditions? Will we be able to raise our families in relative peace and security? Perhaps this explains why the promise of bringing the Israelites to "a land flowing with milk and honey" (Exodus 3:8) is mentioned even before the struggle with Pharaoh commences. The willingness to engage in revolution is based on the people's belief that it will lead them to a better life.[11]

On the heels of the Exodus, the Israelites are filled with gratitude and they have good reason to expect that all of their self-interested needs will be met. They promise Moses and God anything and everything ("we will do and we will obey"). But the covenant at Sinai requires a people that is deeply committed both to justice and to holiness. Sinai consciousness can only be fulfilled over the course of many generations, for the proof of fulfillment is revealed only to the extent that the people who accept the challenge "teach the words diligently to their children" (Deuteronomy 6:7). From a theological perspective, the history of the Jewish people is about bridging the gap between the materialist and self-interested longings of the people and the sense of sacred purpose commanded by God and conveyed through Moses.

Exodus/Sinai in Historical Perspective

Central to the understanding of Judaism and the Jewish people is the tension that exists between being the people of the Exodus and being the people of Sinai. The two aspects of Jewish self-conception are by no means mutually exclusive; in fact, they are meant to be complementary. Yet time and again, history has shown that one impulse conflicts with the other. Specifically, every nation is challenged to find a way to survive. To do so, nations find ways to organize themselves socially, economically, and politically. They acquire a piece of territory that they defend against others who covet it. They develop a particular culture unique to themselves. All of these are the elements of nationhood. And just as with other nations in history, the elements of the Jewish people's unique culture—which includes their Sinai consciousness—comes to be subservient to the demands on the nation to ensure its physical survival.

To be the "holy nation" of Exodus 19:6, the Jewish people will adopt practices that will set them apart from the rest of the world. But to fulfill God's charge to Abraham, *la-asot tzedakah u-mishpat* (Genesis 18:19)—literally meaning "to do righteousness and justice," but more liberally understood as meaning "to extend the boundaries of righteousness and justice in the world"—will require that the Jewish people become fully engaged with the world around them, with Jews and non-Jews alike.

Through the course of Jewish history, Exodus impulses and Sinai impulses are often at odds with each other. Yet, examples can be found in the Jewish tradition where this tension is engaged creatively and productively. Despite the fact that Abraham brings into the world a theology that forces him to leave his father's house and forge an uncharted religious path, the rabbinic commentators admire Abraham for the fact that he does not wall himself off with his own clan. The nineteenth-century commentator Rabbi Samson Raphael Hirsch reflects the standard rabbinic perspective on Abraham. Admiring Abraham's behavior in his appeal for the sinners of Sodom and Gomorrah, Hirsch writes: "A righteous person who lives in an atmosphere like Sodom is not permitted to abandon the nation and to close himself off in his own world, thinking that he will fulfill his obligation just in order to save himself and his family."[12]

The tension between Exodus consciousness and Sinai consciousness and can also be found in the early history of Zionism. The early Zionists saw two threats to the future of the Jewish people. One was the allure of assimilation in those Western countries that granted the Jews a certain level of political emancipation. What would keep the Jews committed to any group consciousness without the hostility and rejection of the host culture? The second challenge was the deep-seated anti-Semitism of Europe, a culture that would never fully tolerate Jews in their midst, the Zionists were certain. The response of the political Zionists, led by the likes of Theodore Herzl, was to solve the problem by founding a Jewish homeland.

A small but influential group of thinkers who were contemporaries of Herzl had another answer. These "spiritual Zionists" were as concerned about the future of Judaism and the soul of the Jewish people as they were about saving Jewish lives. They, too, sought to establish a Jewish homeland for the Jewish people, but their priority was focused on the establishment of a society that fulfilled the highest ethical and moral principles of Judaism. Some, but not all, of these spiritual Zionists were Orthodox. The most prominent of this group was Aḥad Ha-am (Asher Ginzberg), who was steeped in traditional Jewish learning but was effectively a secular Jew who considered himself part of the Jewish enlightenment movement that came to be known as the *haskalah*.[13]

As the Zionist movement evolved, and even after the establishment of the State of Israel in 1948, it is easy to see these two strands of thought—political and spiritual Zionism—competing with one another. Though it is easy to admire the idealism of the proponents of spiritual Zionism, the horrors of World War II and the Holocaust made the strategies and approaches of the political Zionists seem far more appropriate. Jews were being slaughtered; they needed to be saved. Instinctively the Jewish people went into Exodus mode, engaging themselves in the task of bringing a beleaguered remnant from slavery to freedom. There was no time to debate the extent to which one or another element of the *yishuv* (pre-state Israel) was consistent with the highest ideals of Sinai consciousness.

Many in Israel continue to argue, even today, that the principles of spiritual Zionism need to be more fully heeded. In fact, there are numerous examples of how Israeli society has tried to live by core Jewish values and principles. Yet most would admit that such concerns are virtually always relegated to secondary status, taking a back seat to concerns about Israel's safety and security. It would be admirable if the Jewish people could live in the world solely as the people of Sinai, but for as long as the world presents threats to Jewish survival, history seems to demand that Jews continue to be a people of the Exodus as well.

The philosopher Rabbi David Hartman points to this tension in the Jewish condition when he writes:

> Sinai permanently exposes the Jewish people to prophetic aspirations and judgments….Sinai requires of the Jew that he believe in the possibility of integrating the moral seriousness of the prophet with the realism and political judgment of the statesman. Politics and morality were united when Israel was born as a nation at Sinai….The prophets taught us that the state has only instrumental value for the purpose of embodying the covenantal demands of Judaism. When nationalism becomes an absolute value for Jews, and political and military judgments are not related to the larger spiritual and moral purpose of our national renaissance, we can no longer claim to continue the Judaic tradition.[14]

While the tension that Hartman highlights has existed throughout Jewish history, it became more acute when the Jewish people established the State of Israel. Situated in a region surrounded by nations sworn to her destruction, the Jewish state has been willing to use every means at its disposal to defend itself, even in the face of world condemnation. Still, rarely does a day go by in modern Israel when Jewish voices don't call out for the government to find a way to uphold the moral vision of Sinai and act with compassion, even toward those who might intend harm to the state. Indeed, this Sinai consciousness is embedded in Israel's Declaration of Independence: "The State of Israel…will be based on freedom, justice, and peace as envisaged by the prophets of Israel."

The Psychology of Jewish Survival

The Exodus/Sinai continuum provides a theoretical framework that helps to explain not only how the sages of the Jewish tradition interpreted sacred texts, but also Jewish collective behavior through the course of history. To some extent, the Exodus/Sinai continuum we suggest here parallels more familiar frameworks that have been used to interpret Judaism and the history of the Jewish community, such as particularism/universalism or conservatism/liberalism. Yet those continua are often characterized by polarized thinking. A particular interpretation or communal action is seen as either particular or universal, either conservative or liberal. By applying the Exodus/Sinai analysis to Judaism and to the Jewish community, one can see how both elements are often at play at the same time. The thesis proposed here leads to a more accurate understanding of the factors that influence both Judaism and the actions of the Jewish community.

The Exodus/Sinai continuum is organic; each pole on the continuum contains elements of the other. Although the term "Exodus consciousness" suggests how Jews might act defensively, in a fashion that is protective of group self-interest (because the Exodus experience is at the core of Jewish political consciousness), the Exodus biblical narrative also contains one of the phrases that is the cornerstone for Jewish universalism: "You shall not oppress the stranger, for you were strangers in the land of Egypt" (Exodus 23:9). Even in the present day, the tendency of Jews to identify with those who are most weak and vulnerable can be understood as the historical conditioning of a people born in slavery.

Sinai consciousness is no less complex. Although the term "Sinai consciousness" describes the way that Jews aspire to be altruistic, engaging in other-directed behavior in accordance with a pursuit of justice and a sense of sacred purpose, the holiness inherent in Sinai contains a strong impulse for the Jews to remain a people apart. The life of holiness entails many customs that reinforce Jewish distinctiveness, which is a prerequisite for the Jewish people to be bearers of a prophetic heritage to the world. While social justice initiatives are usually aligned with the Sinai-consciousness impulse of Jewish tradition, the Jewish people would have disappeared long ago without a healthy dose of the Exodus impulse as well. It is instructive that a prayer for the welfare of the State of Israel issued by the office of the Israeli Chief Rabbinate in 1948, just after the declaration of Israel as a state (and now widely used in synagogues across the world), blesses Israel as "the first promise of our redemption." This wording recognizes that although the current Jewish state may aspire to manifest the highest ideals of Sinai, it has yet to attain goal. Each impulse—both Exodus and Sinai—is meant to be a corrective to the other.

Sinai represents the Jewish people's encounter with a moral calling and with God. The outcome from that encounter—essentially, the teachings of Judaism—are written all over the face of Jewish history. Exodus represents the Jewish people's experience with their history, moving again and again from a situation of persecution, oppression, and annihilation to a place of liberation and freedom. The Jewish people are shaped by Sinai consciousness, just as Judaism is shaped by Exodus consciousness. Both are part of a larger oneness. Judaism and the Jewish people are best served when the twin impulses are integrated and are in balance.

Tribal Versus Covenantal Identity

This understanding of the origins of the Jewish people, and the emergence of two equally compelling visions of the central mandate of Jewish life, go to the heart of the contemporary Jewish condition. The Exodus impulse informs the strong sense of tribal loyalty that exists among many Jews. The Sinai impulse informs the many Jews whose identity I would call "covenantal."

Modernity has brought into bold relief the growing gap between covenantal and tribal approaches to Jewish identity. Tribal Jewish identity is relatively easy to recognize. The State of Israel is the single largest tribal Jewish polity; one either is a citizen of the state or is not. A Jew living in the Diaspora has several ways of being considered part of the tribe. One option is to join an organization that works to raise money or political support for the Jewish state. Jews can also make a financial contribution to their local Federation, which supports a wide range of local and international Jewish needs; payment of this voluntary "tax" essentially makes one a member of the tribe. The same is true for memberships in synagogues and other Jewish cultural, philanthropic, public affairs and/or educational organizations. While the population of the State of Israel continues to grow, the affiliation numbers in the rest of the Jewish world show a steady decline—a phenomenon that leads those most invested in a strong Jewish community to have a heightened sense that the future of the Jewish people is at risk. One of the rallying cries of the American Jewish community over the past few decades has been "continuity." Those committed to the perpetuation of the Jewish people will continually be challenged to find ways to capture a larger percentage of those Jews who do not choose to belong to the tribe in any tangible way.[15]

It is here that it is so critical to understand covenantal Jewish identity. Throughout the generations, the rabbis recognized that the **spirit** of Abraham's legacy was as important as were the specific behavioral commandments that later made up the substance of Jewish life and observance. Rabbi Joseph Soloveitchick, one of the most widely read and highly esteemed sages in the history of American Jewry, asserts that *b'rit avot*, God's covenant with Abraham and the other patriarchs, was more important than the specific rules given in the Torah and later rabbinic codes. He was here referring to God's charge to Abraham in Genesis 18 quoted earlier: la-asot *tzedakah u-mishpat*, "to extend the boundaries of righteousness and justice in the world." That charge is the meta-goal of Judaism—which is why Soloveitchick ascribes to it a higher priority than the 613 *mitzvot*, which provide the means to the ends. The legacy of Abraham's response to God's call to righteousness and justice has shaped the values and subconsciousness of Jews for all time.[16]

In a similar vein, Rabbi Abraham Isaac Kook, who served as the first Chief Rabbi of Palestine from 1921–1935, believed that the early Zionists—who observed few, if any, of the ritual commandments of Judaism and who wore their secularism proudly—were agents for a divine plan for the Jewish people in the world. Unlike Herzl, Kook did not see a Jewish homeland primarily as a place to provide safe refuge for persecuted Jews. Rather, he believed that the settling and building of Israel was part of a divine plan to bring healing to the entire world. This more universal understanding of Jewish faith and destiny is at the core of covenantal Jewish identity. Rabbi Kook challenged the normative rabbinic reading of the verse "You shall love your neighbor as yourself" (Leviticus 19:18) as referring only to other Jews; he believed that Jews must read the verse to refer to all humanity.[17]

It is not easy for the organized Jewish community to assess how Jews might be living out covenantal Jewish identity, when this notion is stripped of all elements of tribal association. It is easier to identify a Jew who takes on the particular details of Jewish observance and faith, than it is to identify a Jew who has no such practice but yet lives in accordance with Jewish ethical and moral principles. There is data that can tell us how many Jews belong to synagogues, how many contribute money to Federations, and how many travel to Israel—or even how many Jews keep kosher and or how many light Ḥanukkah candles. What cannot be as accurately determined however, is how many Jews *feel* Jewish.

It is here that we enter the realm of what we have called Sinai consciousness, or what the sociologist Herbert Gans calls "symbolic ethnicity."[18] Many Jews define large parts of what drives their actions in the world in the context of the Judaic heritage, even when they have no Jewish affiliations and engage in no Jewish religious practices. These Jews typically have a hard time finding a place in the organized Jewish community, since the leaders of these institutions often view with some suspicion those who cannot "check the boxes" on conventional modalities of Jewish group affiliation. Of course, such attitudes toward marginally affiliated Jews become a self-fulfilling prophecy. Jews who might otherwise be open to initiatives or programs of the Jewish community when such endeavors align with their values and ethics are effectively driven away, by an implicit attitude coming from communal institutions that they have "not paid their dues" to the tribe—not only financially, but also by dint of their failure to associate regularly with communal institutions.

The organized Jewish community is not very good at understanding and validating this kind of covenantal Jewish identity. The leadership of the American Jewish community often feels that the community is under siege or at risk. Any manifestation of anti-Semitism at home or abroad, and any threat to the security of the State of Israel, sends the community to its battle-stations. When in this mode, the Jewish community has a tendency to circle the wagons and ostracize those Jews whose opinions stray too far from the party line. This behavior is most noticeable around the issue of support for the State of Israel.

Jonathan Woocher has argued that as American Jews became increasingly secular, loyalty to Israel replaced religious observance as a yardstick for ethnic loyalty.[19] As a result, the attempts by American Jews to form organizations that challenged the organized Jewish community's uncritical support of policies of successive Israeli governments were not only met with determined resistance by Jewish leaders, but in fact with attempts to delegitimize those very organizations. This is what happened to Breira (founded in 1973), to New Jewish Agenda (founded in 1980) and to J-Street (founded in 2008). All these organizations attracted Jews who believed that the values of Judaism required them to speak out about policies of the

State of Israel that they felt were misguided, if not immoral. All three organizations could be seen as manifesting the Sinai consciousness that derives from the core teachings of Judaism. Yet all three found themselves on the defensive, facing challenges to whether they were in fact loyal to Israel and to the Jewish people. Breira closed after five years; New Jewish Agenda closed its doors after twelve years. J-Street has been far more successful than either Breira or New Jewish Agenda when measured by the size of budget, staff, and public profile. At the same time, in many Jewish communities J-Street is marginalized because, unlike the mainstream Jewish community, they are not uncritically supportive of all Israeli policies. Many rabbis who might be sympathetic to J-Street policies will not lend their names to the organization because of concerns for their careers. In 2014, J-Street was denied admission into the Conference of Presidents of Major American Jewish Organizations.

During rare moments when Israel seemed to be on the road to peace and the Jewish community did not feel besieged by outside enemies—such as during the mid-1990s—the demons became internal. Predicting "death by demography," communal leaders sounded alarm bells over the results of Jewish population studies that showed soaring rates of intermarriage and assimilation and declining patterns of affiliation. In either mode—under siege or at risk—the Jewish community tends to draw hard-and-fast lines on who belongs and who does not. And the harder the lines, the less likely it is that covenantal/Sinai Jews, whose Jewish identity is soft and ambivalent, will identify themselves with the Jewish community.

It is here that the organized Jewish community has created for itself a catch-22 situation. In a social milieu where fewer and fewer Jews deem ethnic affiliation a necessity, the Jewish community is nevertheless desperate to get marginally affiliated Jews to overtly commit themselves to communal institutions, either by joining Jewish organizations or by contributing money to Jewish causes. The target audience is large and growing. The 2013 Pew study of

American Jewry revealed that while 75% of American Jews had "a strong sense of belonging to the Jewish people," that percentage was only 42% among Jews who identified themselves as "Jews with no religion"—a category heavily skewed towards Jews in their 20s and 30's.[20] These Jews may be open to deeper involvement in the Jewish community, but only on their own terms. They don't feel that they need it. But if inspired and convinced that it will add meaning and purpose to their lives, they are "available" for such an affiliation. The form that their commitment will take is very tentative. They are more likely to dabble in a Jewish event here or make a modest gift to a Jewish cause there, rather than becoming flag-waving, highly affiliated Jews overnight. For a Jewish organization that invests money in an outreach strategy, this is an unsatisfactory short-term return. At the same time, the language used by Jewish organizations to rally the highly committed—constantly sounding the warning bell of imminent extinction—is the least likely language to attract marginally affiliated Jews to the fold. Why would anyone join a sinking ship if they did not have to?

The divide between Exodus/tribal Jews and Sinai/covenantal Jews is wide and getting wider. The Holocaust and the birth of the State of Israel were singular events for Exodus/tribal Jews. It would be hard to invent a more compelling narrative for why Jews need to band together—whether in a nation-state or through diaspora Jewish organizations—in order to protect themselves and watch out for each other in a hostile world. Yet those two experiences are becoming more remote with every passing year. They are not the life-experience of Jews born after World War II. And while Exodus Jews still see the State of Israel as a kind of biblical David—doing battle against an array of Goliath enemies in the world, and thus worthy of unqualified support—to many Jews, the narrative is much more morally complex. Israel is no longer the primary engine, driving Jewish identity or Jewish philanthropy, as it once was.

All of this brings us back to the millennial tension in Judaism between the Exodus and Sinai impulses. Every faith community is committed to the survival and perpetuation of its own, and Judaism is no exception to these tendencies. Judaism has often fallen prey to the proclivity, endemic to all groups, to see itself in parochial terms and to believe that the interests of the group supersede all else. This is especially true in times of crisis. In the modern era, this defensiveness extends to times when Israel is at risk—either from war, terrorism, or worldwide campaigns to discredit Zionism and the right of Jews to collective existence in their ancestral homeland.

Still, the Jewish tradition's universal teachings about responsibility toward all human beings and to the entire world continue to bring us back to the needed equilibrium between self-interest, as embodied in the Exodus impulse, and the interests of humanity, as expressed in the Sinai impulse. Even when—or, perhaps, especially when—the Jewish world tends toward the parochial, there are voices in our midst that call us back to our prophetic legacy: to be agents for *tikkun*, the repair of the entire world.

NOTES

[1] This chapter is adapted from my *Judaism and Justice: The Jewish Passion to Repair the World* (Woodstock, VT: Jewish Lights Publishing, 2006) and appears here with that publisher's consent.

[2] The Pew Research Center's "A Portrait of Jewish Americans" (October 2013; online at http://www.pewforum.org/2013/10/01/jewish-american-beliefs-attitudes-culture-survey) found that 56% of Jews polled listed "working for justice and equality" among the most important elements of their Jewish identity. The Public Religion Research Institute's survey, "Chosen for What: Jewish Values in 2012," found that 84% of Jews surveyed rated "pursuing justice" or "caring for the widow and the orphan" as very, or somewhat, important. It should be noted that Orthodox Jews do not rate social justice issues as highly as non-Orthodox Jews do. Religious observance and commitment to social justice tend to be inversely correlated among American Jews. See Steven M. Cohen and Leonard Fein, "American Jews and their Social Justice Involvement: Evidence from a National Survey," Amos—The National Jewish Partnership for Social Justice (November 21, 2001), available online at the website of the Berman Jewish Policy Archives (www.bjpa.org).

[3] See, for example, Isaiah 2:4 for an eloquent statement of this sentiment: "[God] will judge among the nations and arbitrate for the many peoples; and they shall beat their swords into plowshares and their spears into pruning hooks. Nation shall not take up sword against nation; they shall never again know war."

[4] These themes are addressed well in Jacob Katz, *Out of the Ghetto: The Social Background of Jewish Emancipation*, 1770–1870 (Cambridge, MA: Harvard University Press, 1973).

[5] For a good treatment of the many variations of Jewish expression that emerged in the encounter with modernity, see David Rudavsky, *Modern Jewish Religious Movements: A History of Emancipation and Adjustment* (New York: Behrman House, 1967).

[6] See Daniel Jonah Goldhagen, *A Moral Reckoning: The Role of the Church in the Holocaust and Its Unfulfilled Duty of Repair* (New York: Knopf Doubleday, 2007).

[7] B. Beitzah 32b.

[8] Leo Baeck, *This People Israel: The Meaning of Jewish Existence* (Philadelphia: Jewish Publication Society, 1965), p. 402.

[9] See Ephraim Urbach, *The Sages: Their Concepts and Beliefs* (Cambridge, MA: Harvard University Press, 1987), chap. 11.

[10] Michael Walzer, *Exodus and Revolution* (New York: Basic Books, 1986).

[11] See Walzer, *Exodus and Revolution*, especially pp. 102–104.

[12] Samson Raphael Hirsch, *Commentary on the Torah, Vol. 1, Genesis*, trans. Isaac Levy (London: Judaica Press, 1966), pp. 324–325.

[13] The *haskalah* was the intellectual and cultural counterpart to the political emancipation that Jews were experiencing in Europe in the eighteenth and

nineteenth centuries. It promoted the use of the Hebrew language and intensive study of Jewish history. As its objective was to help Jews integrate themselves in European society, it also advocated secular education among Jews.

[14] David Hartman, *A Heart of Many Rooms: Celebrating the Many Voices within Judaism* (Woodstock, VT: Jewish Lights Publishing, 1999); see chap. 15, "Auschwitz or Sinai? In the Aftermath of the Israeli-Lebanese War," pp. 259–266.

[15] Both the "National Jewish Population Survey, 2000-01" (available online at http://www.jewishfederations.org/local_includes/downloads/4606.pdf)   and the "Portrait of Jewish Americans" (cited at n. 2, above) found that membership in Jewish organizations and philanthropy given to Jewish causes declined with each successive generational cohort, with younger Jews being far less "connected" to such Jewish associations than were previous generations.

[16] Comment of Rabbi Joseph Soloveitchik in Abraham Besdin, *Man of Faith in the Modern World* (New York: KTAV, 1989), pp. 67–69.

[17] Rav Avraham Kook, *Orot Yisrael*, ed. David Weitzner (Israel: Machon Har Bracha, 2008), vol. 1, pps. 288–290. For a more extensive discussion of Rav Kook's vision of *tikkun olam*, see the essay by Aubrey L. Glazer elsewhere in this volume.

[18] Herbert Gans, "Symbolic Ethnicity: The Future of Ethnic Groups and Cultures in America", in *Ethnic and Racial Studies* 2:1 (January 1979), pp. 1–20. For a fuller discussion of the notion of "secular" Jewish identity, see Seymour Martin Lipset and Earl Raab, *Jews and the New American Scene* (Cambridge, MA: Harvard University Press, 1995), pp.66 and 175.

[19] Jonathan Woocher, *Sacred Survival: The Civil Religion of American Jews* (Bloomington, IN: Indiana University Press, 1986).

[20] The study is cited in note 2 above.

You Must Not Remain Indifferent:
Personal Decency and Social Justice

Bradley Shavit Artson

Judaism has a message that the world very much needs to hear: a vital insistence on the intersection between personal ethics and social justice. And that integration is made possible precisely because of our commitment to social justice and our commitment to *derekh eretz*— that is, personal decency expressed in an embracing commitment to Torah and to its commanding authority. For me personally, this is the definition of *tikkun olam*—the Jewish mandate to repair the world and make it into a place suffused with divine values—that inspires and energizes; it is the path I have personally chosen to travel in my own effort to repair a broken world and effect its redemption.

Our concern for social justice is legitimately Jewish—and psychologically adequate—only when it is the result of our loyalty to the Torah and to *mitzvot*. Unfortunately, we live in a world of shattered fragments. We live in a world in which it is impossible to hold on to the kind of politeness that demonstrates a shared humanity, a recognition of another's dignity—and this challenge threatens to destroy our society from within. Consider the following two telling examples.

I was once at the John Fitzgerald Kennedy Library outside of Boston and saw a film clip whose sole purpose was to glorify the deceased President. The film documented the period of the Cuban Missile Crisis, and it began with President Kennedy calling the Senate Majority Leader, Hubert Humphrey, and the Vice President, Lyndon Johnson. These two important and powerful men were summoned by their President in the midst of a national emergency, so they got into the chauffeur-driven limo and were rushed to the White House. There were guards at the door to ensure their security. The film showed the men emerging from the car. First came the Vice President. Summoned by the nation's leader at this time of crisis, he acted like any important man at such a moment would: he got out of the car and strode purposefully into the White House. The Vice President was followed by the Senate Majority Leader, Hubert Humphrey, who did the same thing. But as Humphrey got out of the car, he caught himself, turned to the guard who had opened the door, and thanked him. Only then did he stride into the White House. That little gesture is so telling precisely because it was not the point the film wanted to make—because Humphrey never made it into the White House as President, and because it is so rare to find someone who combines a passion for social justice (particularly in the public sphere) with an unwavering commitment to personal ethics (especially in one's private conduct).

Or consider the now nearly-forgotten "Nannygate" incident of the 1990s, in which President Clinton decided, in the first few days of his administration, not to appoint Zoë Baird as the first female Attorney General of the United States. She was removed from consideration after it was revealed that she had hired an undocumented worker as her child's nanny. Whether Baird had done so simply in order to save money, or whether she had consciously turned a blind eye to the legal issues, the question remains: how is it possible that Zoë Baird, who earned half a million dollars a year, chose not to secure childcare that was in full compliance with the legal requirements? The Clinton administration sought to whitewash the incident by underscoring that except in this regard, her record was unblemished. She was fully and strictly within the law—other than her crime, which she knowingly committed. (She later paid $2900 in fines.) Leaving aside for the moment the fact that male political leaders are rarely (if ever) scrutinized regarding their childcare arrangements, one still has to wonder: how is it possible that a woman passionate about social justice could have oppressed someone, by paying them too little to be able to have some retirement money later on?

It appears that in our secularized culture, we have bifurcated between following the dictates of the letter of the law, on the one hand, and doing the right and decent thing, on the other. Thus a high-ranking official who deals with the big picture—the equality of human beings, the liberation of the world, freedom from hunger and want, and poverty—does not have time to say "thank you" and an affluent political figure does not pay her own employees a living wage. On the other hand, too many of those concerned with individual acts of kindness and beauty think that politics is pointless, that all politicians are necessarily corrupt, and that mendacity is the way of the world. To that bifurcation, Judaism says: "No, it cannot be." So long as we sever the letter of the law from its spirit—perhaps upholding the former in practice, but giving the latter little more than lip-service—then we are trapped. Only when we see these two as complementary approaches, and dedicate ourselves to both of them equally, can we hope to transform the world.

I have often asked the children in a bar mitzvah class to share with me who their heroes are. Sadly, I have to report that they don't have any heroes; indeed, from the puzzled looks on their faces when I pose the question, it seems that the very idea of heroes strikes them as hopelessly old-fashioned. How is it possible to be a teenager and not have a hero? Granted, the heroes that I had as a teenager were not as heroic in reality as I had imagined. But most important was not the particular identity of the heroes themselves, but rather the very fact that I *did* a particular image of them in my mind. How is it possible for a person grow up without ideals? How can someone grow up thinking that, deep down, everyone is only looking out for number one and that nobody cares about decency any more? What kind of children are we raising in this increasingly callous and self-centered world?

That cynical assessment has nearly paralyzed Judaism as well. We are so used to accepting the paltry standards of our secularized culture that we take those standards as norms—and then diminish and constrain our Judaism to fit inside that prison. We have abandoned what is truly breathtaking about our sacred heritage. Severing justice from ethics silences Judaism's distinctive voice and robs its real message of a hearing. Think of the image (suggested by Rabbi Milton Steinberg, of blessed memory[1]) of the ends of a string, each pulled in opposite directions. In our case, we have the perception of a tension between a commitment to social justice, on the one hand, and personal decency, on the other—pulling in opposite directions. Rabbi Steinberg said that the beauty of Judaism is to recognize that when opposing forces pull in two different directions, the only way to harmonize them is to introduce a third force, lifting up at the middle of the string. The upward lift removes the opposition: suddenly the two ends are united again, now pulling in the same direction. That lift-up force is God. Judaism insists that ethical righteousness and social justice both come from the same source, because the living God commands both. God cares how we treat each other—both at the one-on-one level of personal decency, and also at the more universal level of social justice. Both virtues, righteousness and justice, gain coherence when they are understood to derive from the same source. The sovereignty of God is the basis for the dignity of all human beings: every single one of us is a child of God, and every single one of us represents some unique facet of the Divine that nothing and no one else can replicate. We need to train ourselves to see each person as nothing less than a brand-new source of knowledge of God.

God's Sovereignty and Human Dignity

There are several implications to the notion of the sovereignty of God, as explained above, that remain pertinent today. The first is the affirmation of the U.S. Declaration of Independence that all people—or, at least, all free men (in Jefferson's conception)—are created equal and that they are endowed by their Creator with certain unalienable rights. Thomas Jefferson knew that people are not equal, if only the here-and-now is used as the standard of measurement. Some people are better looking than others, some are brighter, and some are smarter, stronger, or more eloquent. We are clearly not equal, when it comes to qualities such as these; human equality is a lie, if judged on the scale of secular materialism. What does make us equal is our relationship to the Holy One, who created us and who is utterly and transcendently beyond any of us. Relative to that God, our differences become insignificant. We are equalized in God's parenthood. And so the Declaration of Independence is based on the recognition that it is God, as Creator, that gives us our equal worth.

We need to return to that recognition. All of us are equal because God is equally concerned for all. If God is the Creator of All, then we need to recognize that the world that we inhabit is not ours. The world is not ours to do with exclusively as we please. We are not the only living creatures that matter; in fact, the Creator clearly intended for this to be a rich and variegated world with all kinds of living things teeming over it. *All* of those creatures are part of the symphony of praise that God receives with each new dawn. We need to recall that when we endanger other living things, when we treat the world with scorn, we are slapping God in the face, as it were. We are scorning God's gift of creation, a beautiful planet. Moreover, the sovereignty of God is the linchpin for that preciousness—otherwise, the world and other people would be merely tools to be used for our own pleasure and short-term gain.

Finally, the sovereignty of God implies that all people have an intrinsic dignity. Whenever we belittle the dignity of any other human being, we are doing nothing less than belittling God.

The Torah makes those implications clear in several places. God says, at the creation of humanity, "Let us make people in our own image" (Genesis 1:26). What does it mean to be made in God's image? Surely not that God shares my appearance, or yours. It means that our ability to distinguish good from evil, our ability to be compassionate and kind and loving, our ability to hurt when other people hurt, and our ability to cry at other people's pain and rejoice at other people's triumphs is a way that we can most Godlike.

The Torah instructs us, "You shall love your neighbor as yourself" (Leviticus 19:18). What a remarkable teaching that is! The Torah is not asking us to give precedence to another person at the expense of our own human dignity. Instead, this passage from Leviticus expresses the remarkable idea that if all of us are God's children, and if all of us are made in God's image, then we need to see that in divine image each other. Ultimately, one who cannot love one's neighbor cannot love oneself.

Rabbi Akiva comments in the Jerusalem Talmud that this teaching from Leviticus is the guiding principle of the Torah, a *k'lal gadol*.[2] In our bifurcated world, we have split into two camps: we have one group of Jews who worry only about the big picture and let the details slip through their fingers, and we also have another camp of Jews who worry exclusively about the little deeds of kindness, ignoring the big picture.

Social Justice and Personal Decency: The *Talmid*, the *Tzaddik*, and the *Ḥasid*

What we need is Jews who will stand up for both sides of the equation: for a Judaism of both social justice and personal decency. What we need, in our day, is a return to a full-bodied Judaism. Surely in that richer, holistic Judaism there is a symbol that can unite these dual, competing aspirations into one synergistic fusion! According to the great scholar Gershon Scholem,[3] there are three ideal models for precisely this union in the Jewish tradition: the talmid ḥakham, the tzaddik, and the ḥasid.

The first model is that of the *talmid ḥakham*, the scholar or sage. This image teaches that we can use our minds in the service of God. A Judaism that prohibits asking certain questions or thoughts is a perversion of what Judaism ought to be. God demands the service of our mind no less than that of our heart. In fact, there is in Judaism such openness to the life of the mind that it even extends beyond the borders of our own people and of our own tradition. For example, Midrash Rabbah affirms that if someone insists that there is wisdom among the nations of the world, we are to believe it.[4] And Maimonides instructs us to accept truth from any source.[5]

What a remarkable heritage: a Judaism unafraid to face the truth no matter who articulates that truth, and no matter what the context. A faithful Jew need not fear truth. To the contrary: we have elevated truth to a sign of God, *ḥotamo shel ha-kadosh barukh hu*, the sign of God is truth.[6] And yet, says the midrash, if a person says that there is Torah among the nations they should not be believed, because wisdom and Torah are not one in the same thing.[7] There is a hallowed place for knowledge in the service of goodness. But a truncated wisdom, removed from a context of personal decency, nurtures the perversions that so rankle contemporary life: people who can be passionate about justice but do not care about goodness, or a neighbor who loves goodness yet doesn't bother voting.

The second Jewish role model is the *tzaddik*, a righteous person. The Talmud offers various degrees of righteousness. There is the run-of-the-mill *tzaddik*, which can be any of us, and then there is the *tzaddik gamur*, the completely righteous person.[8] The *tzaddik* is the role model for all of us, a person who takes God's will as his or her own personal agenda. A *tzaddik* makes his or her own pathway through life, seeking to become a walking *sefer torah*, so that the black words on the white page live through their actions and their deeds.

Doesn't the Torah itself say that people should see the way we behave and, based on the way we act, they should say "what a wise people, what a loving God"?[9] How many people can look at the way we conduct our daily lives and make that inference? And yet, the *tzaddik* is the very core of who we are to be. But even with the example of the *tzaddik*, our tradition refuses to be overly particularistic. According to one midrash, the prophet Elijah is reported to have said, "I call heaven and earth to witness that whether one be Jew or gentile, man or woman, manservant or maidservant, the Holy Spirit will come to rest on each in direct proportion to [the worthiness of] the deeds that he or she has performed."[10] Goodness is what defines a *tzaddik*. One who claims to be pious without being good is a fraud.

The third role model is the *hasid*, a religious enthusiast. A *hasid* is someone for whom God is the reason to wake up in the morning and do one more sacred act, one more good deed. One who seeks to make every moment holy time, and who sees each new action as a chance to unite with God—such a person is able to cultivate the passion and energy needed to repair the world.

While the *tzaddik*, the *hakham*, and the *hasid* all have unique qualities , the truth is that they are not separate categories. Instead, they overlap in important ways—so much so, in fact, that Rabbi Hanina ben Idi could ask: "Why are the words of Torah likened to water? To teach you that just as water flows from a higher level to a lower level, so too do the words of Torah abide only with one who is meek in spirit."[11] In short, one cannot be a sage without also being a *tzaddik*—although one can be a *tzaddik* and still be an ignoramus. Judaism values learning highly, yet values goodness even above learning.

The Messiah as Fusion of Personal and Social Ideal

These three types of holiness merge and enrich each other, leading us to Judaism's pre-eminent symbol for that fusion of the personal and the global, that blend of personal ethics, individual kindness, and social justice: the Messiah. One need not believe literally that an anointed person is coming to redeem the world, in order to yet find value in a metaphor that is inextricably linked to the personal. Why does the Talmud often prefer to speak of a Messiah rather than of a "messianic age"? I believe it does so precisely to prevent the bifurcation of what is politically right from what is personally compassionate. The Messiah is social justice personified. There can be no justice in theory only, that is indifferent to particular people.

The Talmud tells us that the Messiah will be found engaging in selfless acts of *ḥesed* such as binding the wounds of the leper by the gates of the city.[12] This is the same Messiah who will bring to an end depression and injustice, and who will gather us to our homeland in peace. This Messiah of world peace and healing spends time binding the wounds of sick individuals, thus embodying the goal for all Jewish piety: the fusion of the general and the particular, of kindness with justice. Maimonides was absolutely right when he said that it is a waste of time to speculate on when the Messiah is coming or who the Messiah will be.[13] The Messiah is best understood as a hope, as an aspiration, as a dream. As such, the image of the Messiah *must* be irreducibly personal. Advancing social justice and caring about the individual needs of human beings is the epitome of the personal dimension, a messianic mission that summons us now.

Our role in that age of the Messiah is curiously similar to what our role is our own time. To answer the question of "When will the Messiah come?" the Talmud quotes from the book of Psalms: "Today, if you will only listen."[14] In other words, we have to open our hearts now, acting as though the messianic age is already here. When our hearts are attuned to the point that we love all human beings, that we see in every individual person someone sacred, precious, irreducible, and beautiful—that is when the Messiah will come.

That same talmudic passage relates: "Rabbi Zeiri said in the name of Rabbi Ḥanina that the Messiah will not come until the arrogant in Israel cease to be."[15] This seems paradoxical: when there are no longer any arrogant people and the Messiah will be able to come, then we will no longer need the Messiah, because the messianic age will have already arrived! If we live in such a way that we take the wounds of other people to be our own, to heal; if we live in such a way that one hungry person is an affront to our conscience, and then act to provide food; if we can't sleep so long as there is one homeless person, and we can't sleep because we were rude or cruel to someone—then the day of the Messiah's arrival will be too late, because we will have already brought the messianic age ourselves.

That is what rabbinic tradition conveys. When the King Messiah appears, he will proclaim to Israel: "Humble one, the time of your redemption is near!"[16] In other words, the reality that will characterize the age of the Messiah is precisely the morality that must precede the coming of the Messiah. The Messiah waits for us to act messianically, and won't come until we do.[17]

What, then, can we do? I believe that the pertinent mitzvah is *lo tukhal l'hitalleim*, (Deuteronomy 22:3), that we must not remain indifferent. A Jew who is indifferent to the plight of others is effectively blaspheming against the memory of our people. A Jew who is indifferent to human suffering is denying God. Recognizing the sovereignty of God as Creator of the world implies a simultaneous acceptance of the supreme value of human dignity, together with the obligation to work to uphold that dignity in all people. Rabbi Joshua ben Levi said, "When a human being walks on the road, a troop of angels walks in front of that person shouting 'make way for the image of the blessed Holy One.'"[18] Imagine what a world it would be if we could train ourselves to hear those angels, if we could see the heavenly host standing in front of everyone here, pointing to each one of us and saying "This is the image of God"—imagine how people would treat each other! "Great is human dignity," the Talmud says, "since for its sake we may violate a prohibition of the Torah."[19] Imagine the kind of world it would be if all of us took the negative commandments of the Torah seriously, and then took human dignity even more seriously than that! Imagine if we were able to say that upholding the dignity of the most repulsive human being is more important than refraining from violating a negative commandment in the Torah—and we could make our assertion mean something, precisely *because* we revere the negative commandments of the Torah.

Communities as Centers of Social Justice

Many different organizations actively pursue agendas of social justice, and Jews are often among the leaders of those activist groups. Why, with such a plethora of other opportunities for involvement, should Jews, as part of the Jewish community, become involved in the broader arena of social justice? Why should religious organizations get involved in political controversies? And what should our agenda be, if we *do* feel impelled to become involved?

As Jews, we frequently turn to our religious traditions for life-cycle events, for history lessons, or for deepened spirituality. But our political convictions generally emerge from contemporary political theories, as though our ancient heritage has no wisdom to contribute to the question of how people ought to live together to create a just, fair world—that is, what our traditional liturgy calls "working to establish God's sovereignty on earth." In deriving our politics from Adam Smith or from Karl Marx (or even from John Maynard Keynes), we deprive ourselves of historical depth and Jewish authenticity—even as we accede to the reduction of the human animal to an economic pawn.

Most modern theories of political organization begin with the assumption that human happiness is to be found in economic justice, that people are motivated primarily by economic questions, and that oppression is primarily an issue of economic relations. Such a mono-dimensional view of humanity and of human society ignores the tremendous complexity of each of us and of our societies. Our motivations—whether emerging from patriotism, jealousy, idealism, or bitterness—often have little to do with economic theory, and a great deal to do with the difficulties of being truly human.

It is precisely here—in wrestling with our own impulses, in learning how to cultivate our own better natures—that economic and political theories have the least to offer. And it is precisely here that Torah has been working to transform and to elevate the Jewish people for millennia.

To reiterate: our concern for social justice is legitimately Jewish—and psychologically adequate—only when it is the result of our loyalty to the Torah and to *mitzvot*. Social justice is a mitzvah, neither more nor less obligatory than the *mitzvot* of Shabbat or *kashrut*. The same God who commands that we fast and pray on Yom Kippur also insists that we show deference to the aged. Recorded in the same Torah are the *mitzvot* of circumcising firstborn males and of prohibiting wanton destruction of the earth's natural resources. Both ritual profundity and acts of social justice are expressions of our obedience to the *M'tzavveh*, the Commander—whose authority, presence, and passion permeate the Torah (and later rabbinic teachings as well). One cannot claim to be a servant of God without a commitment to make this world more just, more compassionate, and more Godly. We often quote the verse *tzedek tzedek tirdof*, "justice shall you pursue" (Deuteronomy 16:20). As stirring as those words are, they have become muted through overfamiliarity.

As previously mentioned, I prefer to derive the impetus for Jewish social justice from another commandment found in the same biblical book: the verse that commands *lo tukhal l'hitalleim*, "you must not remain indifferent" (Deuteronomy 22:3). The essential insight here is that the opposite of good is not evil, but rather indifference. And indifference—to human suffering, to human isolation, or to human hatred—contradicts everything that the Torah represents, and everything that Judaism holds sacred.

As Jews, we look to our ancestral traditions not merely for some ethnic color or occasional comfort, but as a pathway of response to God, as a tool for infusing sanctity and holiness into our own lives and into the world around us. Thus, our involvement in social issues must emerge from those traditions themselves. In other words, our context is the heritage of Torah.

It is no coincidence that the commandment most often repeated in the Torah is to be solicitous of the *ger*, the resident alien. It is surely deliberate that the most frequently repeated refrain is: "for you were slaves in the land of Egypt."[20] Serious, committed Jews must be involved in questions of social justice because the Torah itself is passionately concerned with social justice. The very core of our tradition—the story of our liberation from Egyptian slavery—is a story about freedom and liberation, the story of a God who fights for the oppressed and for justice. To accurately reflect the priorities of the Torah, then, means that we must also become zealous on behalf of those who are excluded, downtrodden, or despised. A midrash in the Babylonian Talmud remarks that the first and last deeds recorded in the Torah were both deeds of kindness: God made clothes for Adam and Eve when they had no clothes, and God saw to the burial of Moses when there was no one around to bury him.[21] To perform deeds of lovingkindness is to make the world more compassionate and more just. To walk in God's ways is to act on political concern.

Rabbi Ben-Zion Gold of the Harvard-Radcliffe Hillel once offered a yardstick for evaluating the Jewish content of any practice. Noting the observation in the book of Genesis that humanity is made in God's image, Rabbi Gold insisted that any practice that enhances or illumines God's image in other human beings is properly Jewish, and any standard that obscures or diminishes the reflection of God's image is anti-Jewish—regardless of its source or its antiquity. We act as good Jews when we cultivate the image of the Divine in our fellow human beings.

Rabbi Simon Greenberg, founding President of American Jewish University and for almost thirty years Vice Chancellor of the Jewish Theological Seminary of America, taught that the central task facing all of God's servants is to validate God's judgment at the end of Creation that the world is "very good." When we bolster that claim, we sign on as God's partners in the ongoing task of perfecting creation.

We must not remain indifferent.

Given that a vital part of a religious Jewish commitment is a passion for social justice, we still must ask about the details of that commitment. A religious Jewish agenda of social justice would include the following:

- Given that all human beings are made in God's image, we must actively support the equality of women. Women also reflect the divine image, and any diminution of women is a derogation of God. The dignity of women in the workplace and in the home, the right of women to control their own reproductive capacity, the right to childcare and equal pay for equivalent work—all these flow out of our Torah's conviction that there should be one law for all.[22]
- Given that all human beings are created in God's image, asserting the dignity of people of all abilities (including those struggling with special needs) is a mandate for any social agenda. The right to access public spaces and buildings, the right to communicate, and the right to housing and meaningful work and social relations are all

fundamental to being human—for those with special needs as well as for the neurologically typical.

- That same conviction mandates that racial and ethnic prejudice cannot co-exist with God's rule on earth. The practice of discrimination based on race—in housing, employment, social opportunity, or education—strikes at the heart of the Torah's message of social justice. As religious Jews, we must speak out clearly and consistently for the dignity of all human beings and all human groupings. That insistence also means that the age of the jokes about a *goyishche kop*, or remarks about *shikses* and *shkotzim*, are no less offensive and improper than jokes about "jewing someone down" or comments about "Jewish-American princesses." Characterizing and slandering ethnic, religious, or racial groups must be seen as no less than a rebellion against God and Torah, a violation of our covenant of peace.

- Hillel taught, "Do not to others what you would not have them do to you."[23] It is time that our diverse communities welcome gay, lesbian, and transgender Jews. For too long, such people (and their parents, siblings, friends, and relatives) have been isolated by the all-encompassing silence or hostility of our communities. Gays, lesbians, and transgendered people have a right to acceptance and understanding within the synagogues and communities of their childhood and their future. There are too many eager Jews among them who want to live Jewishly and who desire to contribute to Jewish life for us to continue a *de facto* policy of silent neglect.

- *Lo am ha-aretz ḥasid*, the Mishnah records: one cannot be pious if one remains ignorant.[24] Our Jewish traditions depend on the centrality of learning. In fact, Judaism may be unique among the world's religions in insisting that study is itself a form of worship. Consequently, the level of education available to the public is a matter of Jewish religious concern, as is the level of scholarship and intellectual prowess that the Jewish community requires of its leaders. Judaism cannot survive, let alone flourish, in a culture that does not cultivate learning. The mediocre quality of the nation's schools and colleges are a religious matter for us: the Jewish principle *talmud torah k'neged kullam* ("the *mitzvah* of Torah study equals all the rest") can and should be applied to education in general, and most definitely be broadly enough interpreted to include secular studies that bring increased learning to the world at large.[25]

- A *midrash* teaches that God instructed the first humans to care well for this world, since there would be no creations to replace it.[26] We demonstrate gratitude for the gift of life and the marvel of creation by living responsibly with the rest of nature, by assuring that our children's children will also have clean air, water, food, and access to pristine, unspoiled wilderness in their own time.
- Finally, and arching above all the rest, we must involve ourselves in the *mitzvah of bakkeish shalom v'rodfeihu*, "seeking peace and pursuing it."[27]

Humankind now has the power to reject all of creation, to undo the very foundations of biological existence on earth. It is our duty as Jews and as human beings to pressure our government to seek solutions to the constant possibility of nuclear annihilation. We may not have the answers ourselves, but we must convey our concern and our rejection of nuclear terror as a continuing way of life.

This list could go on and on: activism on behalf of the security of the State of Israel and peace with the Palestinians, the fate of the homeless in our urban centers, oppressed Jewry in Ethiopia, Arab lands, and elsewhere. So long as our agenda reflects the clarion call of Torah and *mitzvot*, so long as we are responding not to the news media but rather to the injunction to love our neighbors, some may fault our religion, but they cannot fault our responsiveness.

Judaism is not content merely with decorous and vibrant synagogues. Judaism aims to mend the world and to transform the streets. To undertake a life devoted to *tikkun olam* means to be servants of God, and to be a servant of God means to care. That being the case, we cannot remain indifferent: "This is what the Holy One said to Israel: My children, what do I seek from you? I seek no more than that you love one another and that you honor one another."[28]

Imagine a world in which we all loved and honored each other. Such a world would surely hasten the coming of the Messiah, the symbol of social justice with human decency. In such a world, the children in today's bar mitzvah classes—and all children—would have no shortage of heroes. They would know that they themselves are called to be heroes, and that they themselves must testify by their own actions that the hosts of angels are not liars. We would know that, just as the angels shout out that we reflect God's image, our deeds announce the same beautiful truth. In such a world, the coming of the Messiah would be redundant…and that is precisely the purpose of Judaism.

NOTES

[1] Milton Steinberg, "To Hold With Open Arms," in Jack Riemer, *Wrestling with the Angel: Jewish Insights on Death and Mourning* (New York: Schocken Books, 2006), pp. 134–140.

[2] Y. Nedarim 9:4.

[3] Gershom Scholem, originally published in *Eranos-Jahrbuch* 38 (1969), pp. 346–364, and reprinted as "Three Types of Jewish Piety," in *On the Possibility of Jewish Mysticism in Our Time*, ed. Avraham Shapira, trans. Jonathan Chipman (Philadelphia: Jewish Publication Society, 1997), pp. 5–23.

[4] Eikhah Rabbah 2:13.

[5] Maimonides, *Sh'monah P'rakim*, foreword.

[6] B. Sanhedrin 64a.

[7] Eikhah Rabbah 2:13.

[8] B. Berakhot 7a.

[9] Deuteronomy 3:7.

[10] *Seder Eliyahu Rabbah* 10:1, ed. Meir Friedmann/Ish-Shalom (1904; rpt. Jerusalem: Wahrman, 5729 [1968–1969], p. 48.

[11] B. Taanit 7a.

[12] B. Sanhedrin 98a.

[13] M.T. Hilkhot Melakhim 12:2.

[14] B. Sanhedrin 98a, citing Psalm 95:7.

[15] Ibid.

[16] *Pesikta Rabbati* §§35–37.

[17] These rich legends about the Messiah make it clear that a true "Messianic Jew" is a traditional Jew who continues to wait for a Messiah—an individual who cherishes Jewish tradition and hopes and works toward a future of salvation for all.

[18] Midrash Tehillim 17:8.

[19] B. Berakhot 19b, Shabbat 81b and 94b, Eruvin 41b, and Menaḥot 37b.

[20] Deuteronomy 6:21 and elsewhere.

[21] B. Sotah 14a.

[22] This principle appears several times in the Torah, sometimes in the context of ritual law (e.g., at Exodus 12:49 and Numbers 9:14, 15:15–16 and 29) but also in a more general context (e.g., at Leviticus 19:33–34, 24:16, or 24:22), implying the broader legal principle that a just society cannot maintain separate sets of laws for citizens and sojourners.

[23] B. Shabbat 31a.

[24] Pirkei Avot 2:5.

[25] M. Peah 1:1.

[26] Kohelet Rabbah 7:20.

[27] Psalm 34:17.

[28] *Seder Eliyahu Rabbah* 26:6, ed. Friedmann, p. 143.

Tikkun Olam, Tikkun Atzmi: Healing the Self, Healing the World

James Jacobson-Maisels

Beginning with the Self

Rooted in its mishnaic meaning denoting "enactments undertaken for societal benefit" but also incorporating its broader kabbalistic meaning of "repairing the brokenness of both God and the world," the phrase *tikkun olam* has taken on the contemporary meaning of "pursuing justice and repairing the broken world in which we live, through social and political activism." This worthy modern reimagining of *tikkun* can yet benefit from the richness and expansiveness of earlier kabbalistic sources, which see the repair of this world in a broader context: one that includes the repair and transformation of the self. I wish to briefly explore the place of self-transformation in that broader task, and in particular how self-transformation is crucial to a genuine and sustainable healing. I will argue for a kabbalistic–hasidic political and social activism that is based on love and not hate, which does not make opponents into enemies and which does not undermine its work for compassion and justice by pursuing it from a place of anger and animosity.

We can see the beginnings of this approach to *tikkun* in the Zohar, in *Parshat Va-yak·heil*, where it is taught:

> In prayer, the body and soul of a person are healed (*mitatkan*) and one becomes whole. Prayer is reparative reparations that repair (*tikkunim mitaknan d'mittaknan*) as one, and they are four. The first *tikkun* is the *tikkun* of the self for its perfection.

The second *tikkun* is the *tikkun* of this world. The third *tikkun* is the *tikkun* of the upper world....The fourth tikkun is the tikkun of the holy name....[1]

Each of these four *tikkunim* (self, world, upper world, holy name) is then associated with a particular part of the prayer service: the *tikkun* of the self, with the introductory parts of the service (Birkot Ha-shaḥar, the recitation of the sacrifices, and the introductory blessings); the tikkun of this world, with P'sukei D'zimra; the *tikkun* of the upper world, with the Shema and its blessings; and the *tikkun* of the holy name, thus the *tikkun* of God, with the Amidah.[2] Prayer here serves as a technique to heal the self, the world, the divine worlds, and God.

The Interdependence of *Tikkun Atzmi* and *Tikkun Olam*

This image of *tikkun* has some profound lessons to teach us.[3] First, it sees these various levels of *tikkun* as interconnected. One is not possible without the other. *They are one, which is four.* On the one hand, this means that one cannot repair the self without repairing the world. To do so is to be lost in a kind of false narcissistic understanding of self-transformation. This illusory self-work is mistaken not only in its abandonment of the world, but in its very focus on the self. This self-centeredness is contrary to the very nature of genuine self-transformation, which is a loosening, softening, and letting go of the self in compassionate service of the world. Self-transformation, to be genuine, must always be directed outward as well as inward.

On the other hand, one cannot repair the world without repairing the self. To do so is to care about the suffering out there while neglecting the suffering in here: the suffering of one's partner, co-worker, children, and self. It is to work for a social justice organization that is doing tremendously beneficial work while creating a toxic work environment. It is to become, as my grandfather noted of one prominent Jewish activist and colleague, someone who "would sell his mother for the cause." It is to pursue change from a place of aggression, hatred, and anger—and so to sow the seeds of the very cruelty and injustice one is fighting against. Perhaps even more frighteningly, it is to become what one is fighting against—a legacy of too many revolutions, where the victorious oppressed merely become another brutal oppressor.[4]

We can see this inseparable connection between acts of compassion and self-transformation in a teaching by the sixteenth-century kabbalist Rabbi Benjamin ben Matatyah on *tzedakah*, the giving of charity. He teaches:

> The essence of the giving of *tzedakah*, which God commanded us in order that a person might aid one's brother, is to show that we are all the descendants of one person and that we are all one spark and one limb and a divine portion from above. And if one has pain in a single limb, then all of one's limbs are pained concerning it....Thus all Israel is one limb from a portion above, and if one [person] is impoverished and oppressed with the sufferings of poverty, then the other must support and strengthen that one through *tzedakah*.[5]

Here, giving *tzedakah* to another person is not only an act of compassion toward that other, but it is also a practice of self-transformation whereby both giver and receiver are meant to understand, enact, and embody the truth of their fundamental connectedness. That is: in giving charity, one is meant to simultaneously challenge one's sense of self, to see oneself not as an independent entity but as an interconnected aspect of a greater whole. Giving charity is a practice directed at both the recipient and the giver, and it is meant to provide both material sustenance and self-transforming insight. This insight of non-separation applies across the board and governs every manner of relationship—whether a familial, political, communal, or workplace relationship, or a relationship to oneself.

In addition, repairing the self is crucial to repairing the world, for the transformation of the self is essential to sustaining the work of transforming the world. Transforming the world without transforming the self too often leaves the self burnt out, despairing, and overwhelmed. Unable to sustain the commitment to transformation, because one is acting from a place of anger, attachment, and demand, the activist eventually drops out—an unhealthy relationship to justice work that leads some, at least, to abandon the field and temper their passion.

Beginning with *Tikkun* of the Self

Tikkun olam, the repair of the world, must then involve *tikkun atzmi*, the repair of the self, as the Zohar teaches. Yet the second insight we can glean from the Zohar comes from the order in which the series of *tikkunim* takes place. The repair of the self is first. We begin with ourselves, with what is closest, so that we do not mistakenly pursue the broader work of *tikkun* from a place of hatred and enmity, a place that would ultimately damage that which we aim to heal. Indeed, the insight of non-separation that we are meant to learn in the giving of *tzedakah*, according to Rabbi Benjamin, has important implications for the work of *tikkun olam*—for this insight of non-separation makes it impossible to make anyone an "enemy," since they too are ultimately part of that "one spark and one limb." They too are "a divine portion from above." We must recognize that no person is ever completely separate from us. We must rather see every person—ally or opponent; victim or victimizer; colleague, employee, or boss; partner, parent, or child—as in fact intertwined with ourselves. Moreover, we start first with the *tikkun* of ourselves so that we are able to pursue this work of healing with wisdom and compassion, without feeling overwhelmed, and without becoming burnt out from the magnitude of the task we face.

But beginning with the self does not mean that we wait until we have perfected ourselves before we start doing the work of transforming the world. Rather, the Zohar has us move through all of the various stages of *tikkun* every day. Beginning always with the self, grounding our work in self-reflection and self-transformation, we must always move outward to the world around us, always doing the best we can, given who we are at any particular moment. Yet, that beginning with the self colors the whole process. It incorporates a kind of self-reflectiveness, a questioning as to whether any given action is not only in service of the broader cause but whether it is also in service of, and consistent with, who we most want to be, on every level. It means pursuing *tikkun olam* from a place of love, rather than from a place of anger, hatred, and enmity. It means making no one into our enemy, but always recognizing that even the worst perpetrator and our most strident opponent is just another human being—perhaps mistaken and twisted, perhaps lost in anger, hatred, fear, and cruelty, but never separate from us and always, though perhaps hidden, a portion of divinity from above.

How Anger Hurts Us: The Suffering of Anger

Yet why not? Why shouldn't we fight for justice from a place of anger? Why shouldn't we see our opponents, especially when they are supporting and perpetrating profound injustices, as our enemies? Perhaps the answer to this question may be found in the following inquiry: Who is suffering from our anger? To whom is the anger causing pain? Who is the anger hurting? If we objectively investigate this question, we will discover that it is in fact we ourselves who suffer most from our anger, as well as those people around us—mostly our loved ones, who must encounter our angry self. It is not the perpetrator, opponent, or enemy who primarily suffers from our anger but ourselves and those around us. We have all said and done things in anger that in a calmer frame of mind we wish we had not. Rabbi Ḥayyim Vital (1543–1620), transmitting the wisdom of his teacher, Rabbi Isaac Luria (1534–1572, popularly called the Ari) tells us:

> The quality of anger, aside from serving as an obstacle to mystical inspiration altogether, [has other injurious consequences]....My teacher (the Ari), of blessed memory, used to be more exacting when it came to anger than with all other transgressions, even in a situation where one loses one's temper for the sake of some religious obligation....This is because all other transgressions injure only a single limb of the body, whereas the quality of anger injures the soul in its entirety, altering its character completely. This is the issue: when one loses one's temper, one's holy soul absconds altogether; in its place a spirit of an evil nature enters. And this is the esoteric meaning behind the verse: "You who tear yourself in your anger" (Job 18:4). For such a person actually tears one's soul, rendering it unfit, and kills it at the moment of this wrath and anger....[6]

Perhaps this description of anger feels familiar: does it not sometimes feel that we are possessed? that a "spirit of an evil nature" has taken control of our body, and some part of us wonders, "Who is this crazy person, yelling at his beloved!?" A friend has related that she sometimes sees her children looking at her that way when she loses herself in anger, as if they are saying, "Who is this monster, and what have you done with our mother?!" Does it not sometimes feel as if our soul—our wisdom, compassion, clarity, and love—has been torn from us, that we have betrayed and in some way damaged who we truly are? We kill ourselves in such moments, teaches the Ari. We injure ourselves and those around us. When we reflect on our own experience, we start to see that we and those we most love are ultimately the ones who suffer from our anger. If we are the primary target, then our friends, families, and children bear the brunt of the collateral damage inflicted by our anger.

Yet no matter how angry we become, the anger itself does not change anything. We can rage at the world all we want, as many of us have, without anger itself accomplishing a thing. This is not to say that anger cannot motivate us to act; indeed, it can. Yet what our tradition suggests is that we can act more effectively from a place of love and compassion than from a place of anger. It is love and compassion, healing and repair, that can be not just the final goal of our actions but the very means and process whereby we attain that final goal, as well.

Anger and Unwise Action

We aim to act with love and compassion not only because doing so cultivates and manifests those very qualities of healing, but also because when anger is present wisdom is lost. When we act from anger, we act in inexpedient and unskillful ways. As Rav Huna teaches in the ancient midrash on Leviticus, Vayikra Rabbah: "In three places Moses became angry, and his teachings (*halakhah*) disappeared."[7] When we become angry, we lose our wisdom. Our mind narrows and is only able to see the current situation through the constricted lens of anger and the distortions it effects. In our anger we lose our stability and openness; we lose that quality of a settled mind so crucial to making wise choices. As Rabbi Shimon bar Yohai reminds us in Bereishit Rabbah, "hatred ruins judgment."[8] Caught up in hatred, anger, or enmity, we cannot see clearly. We falsely ascribe pernicious motives where there are none, make situations black and white and all-or-nothing, see our opponents as demonic and incapable of dialogue and fall into a host of other cognitive distortions that prevent us from seeing things as they truly are. We therefore make foolish and harmful choices, damaging ourselves and others.

Binding Ourselves to the Object of Hatred

Perhaps even worse, we bind ourselves to the object of our hatred. We make that which we oppose central to who we are, obsessing over our anger and enmity. As Vaclav Havel taught, "The fixation on others, the dependence on them, and in fact the delegation of a piece of one's own identity to them" is part of the nature of hatred; this is so much so that "the hater longs for the object of his hatred."[9] We are imprisoned by our hatred and anger. We ironically give ourselves over into the power of that which we oppose. We become trapped by our anger and by whatever the anger is directed against, causing our mind and self to unhealthily wallow in thoughts of resentment, revenge, and destruction.

This trap of anger can hurt us and others even when arising from the most profound of injustices, and even in situations where anger, hatred, and a desire for revenge seem not only understandable but even appropriate. For their book *How We Choose to be Happy*, authors Rick Foster and Greg Hicks interviewed many happy people, including Hannah, a Jewish Dutch Holocaust survivor. They asked Hannah how it was possible for her to lead a life that is happy; given all that she had experienced, how was it possible for her to live her life without constantly aching for revenge? She responded:

> These events were so horrible, so traumatic, that it took me a number of years to reconcile my feelings about them. But I never considered myself a victim of what happened during the war. Certainly, I have been terribly hurt. I felt extreme sadness, pain, and loss. But carrying around a feeling of victimhood? No, that would do nothing more than keep such horrors alive. I will not allow myself to be enslaved by the past. From the start, my interest is in positive ways to ensure that this will not happen again. Being a victim, blaming the Nazis, is not one of them....

> Feeling that I'm a victim of the Nazis gives them a perverse power over me. It would keep me in their hands and allow them to continue damaging me and my family fifty years later. Letting go leads to happiness.[10]

I cannot begin to imagine Hannah's experience, nor her strength and clarity in her refusal to be a victim; but I have profound and stunned admiration for her refusal to be trapped by the past, to be trapped by hatred that would only hurt herself and those she loved, to be trapped in relationship to those who perpetrated horrors against herself, her family, and her people. Her abandonment of an attitude of hatred and victimization is not a refusal to see that she has "been terribly hurt," nor a refusal to feel "extreme sadness, pain, and loss." Nor is it an abandonment of the pursuit of attaining a just society and preventing such unimaginable cruelty. Rather, she is committed to "working in positive ways to ensure that this will not happen again." But in her staunch refusal to be chained to the Nazis and thus trapped by the perpetrators of unimaginable evil, Hannah poignantly shows us how letting go of anger can be transformative, allowing the self to grow into places from which it can accomplish good in the world. In this way Hannah demonstrates how, even in the face of the most unimaginable horrors, we can choose to free ourselves from the prison of hatred.

Anger, Control, and False Protection

Our anger is also misguided because it is ultimately only another strategy to preserve and protect our sense of self. Rabbi Jacob of Radzin, a nineteenth-century hasidic rebbe, teaches that our anger is "like a person who thinks that he is the master of the house, and becomes angry when things are not according to his intent...but does not become angry when he is in a friend's house."[11] That is: our anger is connected to our sense of self. Only when we mistakenly think of ourselves as having mastery and ownership of the world, only when we think that we ought to be in control, does anger arise. We see ourselves as an independent self who should rightly be able to control what is ours. The constant violation of that control, when things regularly do not turn out the way we would like, gives rise to anger. Yet if we gave up the illusion of control, the misconception of some self who could be in control (as we might do when visiting a friend's home), then anger need not arise.

This connection to mastery is crucial. It is not having a preference, or even a strong desire, that gives rise to anger. One may, in this analogy, have a strong desire that things could be otherwise at a friend's house—but, recognizing that one is not in control, anger does not arise. According to Rabbi Jacob, it is the illusion of control, and the tension and neurotic striving that it produces, that give rise to anger. Rather, as this hasidic school teaches, "the earth is the Eternal's and all that is in it" (Psalm 24:1).[12] We are called upon to recognize that we are not the owners or masters of this world, only God is— and in that recognition, anger dissipates.

No longer struggling under the illusion of control, a kind of acceptance becomes possible when things do not go as we would like them to. When this acceptance is present anger does not arise, because we become angry only because we are not willing to accept the reality of some situation. Anger is our attempt and desire to control that which we find unacceptable, to change it or make it go away—or to at least let ourselves *feel* that we have some control, some ability to manage the situation. It gives us a sense of power and efficacy in some way, even if it is just armchair anger, even if we actually do nothing. The anger makes us feel justified and strong. We feel less vulnerable to the sense of loss, hurt, fear, failure, or sadness that underlies our anger. Anger in this sense is a form of protection, a way to protect our fragile self from what feel like unacceptable and overwhelming emotions.[13] It is an attempt to shield ourselves from full truth of the situation, just as it is. It is easier to blame and become angry, in small and large ways, than to really feel what is so painful, vulnerable, and threatening in the injustice and hurt.

Anger is, then, just another avoidance strategy, but we do not have to succumb to it. We can instead turn to the current situation with a deep acceptance, acknowledging that we are not in control but that rather "the earth is the Eternal's and all that is in it." This acceptance is not an affirmation that what has happened is good. It is not a Pollyanna-ish acceptance which says that "all is for the best in the best of all possible worlds."[14] We may still work hard to make the world a different place, but we can do so in a non-neurotic way because we recognize that though we are not impotent we are also never in control. We cannot determine how things will be. We are not the masters. We can only do our best and then accept, in the sense of acknowledging the truth of, the world as it is in this moment—though we may work to change it the next.

Anger Making and Becoming Enemies

Finally, anger is hurtful because it turns the object of anger into an enemy, into a demon. In our family, our beloved or our child is suddenly an object of rage and scorn. In our community, our anger creates tension, "sides," distance, and suspicion, rather than enabling us to work together to solve whatever difficulty is arising. In our political lives, our lives of social activism, hatred ultimately demonizes and dehumanizes the opponent, making such people no longer worthy of our respect and care. At its extreme, this results in the victorious oppressed merely becoming the next brutal oppressors, the conquered having no claim on our compassion; but in less radical ways, we can see the roots of this pattern in our own life. Consider your worst political enemy, whoever that may be: the head of the party you despise, the human rights perpetrator, etc. How do you feel towards that person? Do you see them as a human being created in the image of God? Do you have feelings of anger, hatred, and violence towards that person? Does this kind of reflection help you become more aware of your anger? Making others into demons creates the conditions that fuel the cycle of hatred, violence, and anger. It traps us in a distorted and unhealthy relationship with the other and leads us to indifference and even cruelty, dispositions unbecoming to our divine nature.

How to Be with Anger

Yet being aware of the danger of anger and hatred does not mean that we repress it, nor that we berate ourselves when anger arises. Doing so merely adds a kind of self-violence to the violence of anger, reinforcing the very energy we mistakenly seek to reject. The question, rather, is how we can be wisely present with anger as it arises, so that we are not trapped in it and the suffering that it produces.

The first step to wise presence with anger is to actually *be with* the anger, to allow oneself to feel it fully. There is no need to control and banish the anger. Indeed, as Rabbi Israel Baal Shem Tov (the seventeenth-century founder of Hasidism, popularly called the Besht) explains, attempting to do so is only a kind of violence toward the self and merely makes the anger stronger. The Besht instructs that when these psychic "enemies" assault the self they must rather be embraced. "And if not," he teaches, "if [one] rejects them, more haters are made through thickness and corporeality."[15] It is therefore necessary to not reject the anger but to only hold it in compassion. When we do so, we start to experience those emotions, discussed above, that are hovering underneath—such as a sense of injustice, threat, vulnerability, loss, discrimination, fear, and hurt. When we genuinely allow ourselves to feel these emotions, we are no longer trapped by them but can instead respond to them wisely with compassion. Following the divine command to "circumcise the foreskin of your hearts" (Deuteronomy 10:16), we courageously open our hearts to all that arises, exposing its soft flesh, cutting it open, and making it vulnerable.

In particular, we become open to the felt sensation of anger, rather than to the story-line that accompanies the anger. We notice what we feel in the body and heart, the tension in the throat or the burning in the chest, while dropping the story in the mind. By dropping the story, we step out of that which is fueling the anger and making it overwhelming. We stop reinforcing the illusion of control or the thoughts that "things shouldn't be this way." We give up the sense of mastery. We step out of the projections and distortions of the mind that are supporting and maintaining the anger, and so the anger no longer controls us. As Rabbi Kalonymus Kalmish Shapira, an early twentieth-century hasidic rebbe, teaches,

> Gaze inward, listening and attentive person, and see that it is a human law, if you engage in any of the sensations that rustle in your soul whether a sensation of imagination, will or feeling, love, fear or the other qualities, including if one is engaging with one's consciousness, if one's consciousness is engaging in the sensation, then through this engagement the sensation becomes more active, stronger, and agitated. And if consciousness does not engage in the sensation but rather about the sensation, about the imagination, about the will, or about love and fear, etc., then on the contrary— through engagement of consciousness about it, the sensation will fade and even cease completely.[16]

Rabbi Shapira's use of the term "about" (in Hebrew: *odot*) can be confusing, but here it has the technical meaning of being mindfully present with a sensation (an emotion, thought, or feeling), rather than thinking, being trapped in, or falling into the "sensation." That is: when we are simply trapped in the story of the anger, engaging in the sensation of anger, then the anger is fueled, becoming "more active, stronger, and agitated." But if we engage "about the sensation" of anger—that is, we mindfully observe the sensation itself, dropping the story-line and staying with the felt experience of the anger—"then on the contrary…the sensation will fade and even cease completely." Rabbi Shapira continues:

> And if a vice is aroused in you, whether jealousy or hatred of some person, or some other vice…or any bad thought that strikes you, God forbid, and it is difficult for you to repel it and annul it, use this means…Be careful that you do not think the bad thought, but only about (*odot*) the bad thought.[17]

Rather than getting lost in the story of the anger, rather than engaging *in* the sensation, we open ourselves to the pain of the anger itself and we engage *about* the sensation. Not rejecting it, but not supporting it either, we stay with the anger itself. And precisely in that pain and discomfort, we find a new way to be with our anger: a path of compassion that allows us to honor the anger without being trapped by it. It is as the Jewish teacher-sage-musician Leonard Cohen tells us: "There is a crack in everything, That's how the light gets in."[18] Only by paying attention to the crack, the place that feels broken and scary, are we able to experience the light that enters in precisely that place.

Such work is of course quite challenging and it requires both creating a container of safety to allow that work to take place and also significant courage. Training in meditation, mindfulness, and presence; communicating with the scared parts of ourselves, and letting them know we will go no faster than they are able; and cultivating the supportive power of love and compassion—all of these can help make this work possible. In addition, just as we acknowledge and embrace the anger, we must acknowledge and embrace the fear of working with it. We let ourselves know that it is fine to feel whatever is arising and that we will give ourselves all the necessary support to be with it, whether it is fear, anger, or something else. We accept our feelings with compassion and love, and are even prepared to forgive ourselves when we are not able to fully be with what is arising.

Present in the body and heart and no longer trapped in the story, we can now turn to the mind itself, lovingly challenging the thought patterns that give rise to the anger. One of the main thought patterns is being trapped in the illusion of requirements or needs, rather than the truth of desires. We can see this in a mundane way in Rabbi Shapira's imaginative modeling of this technique, where he envisions the practitioner reflecting on the desire and saying: "My whole self is handed over to my desire, so much so that it is difficult for me to separate myself from this food. For I will not die if I don't eat of it, and yet in any case how bound I am to it!" Here, in the case of food, one can recognize the desire itself and the illusion of needs that accompany the desire. One will not, after all, die if one does not have this food, though our mind sometimes acts as though we will. Similarly, we all want the world to be a certain way, often with great justification. Anger arises when that desire is expressed as a demand or requirement rather than as a desire, the thought that the world *must* be a certain way. The difference between demands and desires is not the depth of caring, but rather the recognition of not being in control: that no matter how much we may want things to be a certain way, there is no guarantee that they will be that way. One can deeply desire justice and struggle for it with all of one's might, but when it becomes an internal demand or requirement, then anger and other forms of suffering may arise if that desire is not fully realized. Yet when the desire stays and is recognized for what it truly is—a deep desire and aspiration for change, accompanied by the wisdom to see that the desire for change may not be fully fulfilled—there is an open passion and energy in the aspiration, which can fuel the work of transforming society.

In that sense, an important part of this work of *tikkun* is simply to deeply admit what it is that we really want, to *be* with the longing itself. Often anger is a way to escape from the discomfort of that longing, of really noticing our desires. This is one of the key roles of prayer: to help us touch and express, on a daily basis, that which we most deeply aspire toward. When we are really *with* the wanting itself, it does not have to turn into anger. The wanting can become a force of connection rather than of separation.

Love, Not Anger

No longer being trapped by our anger does not mean that we fall into apathy and indifference. Rather, it means that another path of *tikkun olam* opens up for us: a path of love. Having done, and constantly doing, the work of *tikkun atzmi*, stopping ourselves from becoming trapped in anger and hatred, we can turn to the work of *tikkun olam* with no less passion but with more wisdom, compassion, and sustainability, caring about every person and every step in the process. When we shift to the perspective of love, something extraordinary happens: there is a lightness, hope, and clarity in our work that was not present before.

This attitude is described in the talmudic passage that teaches, concerning the righteous: "They suffer insults but do not respond by insulting [others], they hear shameful things being said of them but do not reply, they act out of love and take pleasure in their own misery. And regarding them Scripture notes, 'May His lovers be as the sun rising in its might (Judges 5:31)."[19] Those who are genuinely filled with love, those who are God's lovers, feel no need to protect themselves from insult and offense. They have let go of their strategies of defense and so "act from love." This does not mean they are passive. They act, but they act from love rather than self-protection. The Talmud recognizes the awesomeness, majesty, and courage of such a transformation. Such people are, following the verse, like "the sun rising in its might." The response of love, of seeking healing and connection, is not a sign of weakness but rather of extraordinary strength. Such people can experience joy even in the midst of their suffering, maintaining a wider perspective in the midst of life's difficulties.[20]

What would it feel like to choose to respond from a place of love instead of from anger? What would it feel like to stop trying to protect ourselves, to stop trying to answer insult or injury with the same, but instead to act only from love? The Talmud here calls on us to be warriors of love, to be profoundly vulnerable and compassionate even in the midst of threat and uncertainty. In doing so, we respond and act from a place of compassion rather than anger, bringing healing rather than destruction in our wake.

Acting from love means leaving no room for blame. We may see what went wrong, we may assign responsibility and work to correct whatever was wrong, but we do not blame (in the sense of condemning) the individual personally. We respond to the wrong someone has done from a wider perspective, which sees their divine goodness. Rabbi Menaḥem Naḥum Twersky of Chernobyl (1730–1787), called the Chernobyler, interprets the injunction to "love your fellow as yourself" (Leviticus 19:18) as follows: "Even when you see something bad in your fellow, you must despise only that bad thing, so that you can love the holy portion in that person as yourself."[21] The Chernobyler asks us to never allow the recognition of wrongdoing to turn into a view of the individual person as essentially bad. Rather, we must always keep in mind that they too are a holy portion of divinity and divine limb from above. They may have acted in a harmful way, even an extremely harmful way, but that fact does not make them personally evil; it merely makes them trapped in their own confusion, hatred, and anger. This charge to abandon blame is quite challenging. It can be scary to let go of the thought patterns of blame, which so often seem to protect us and define our world.

It invites us continually to be open to the pain of every person in a given situation, rather than conveniently labeling some participants in a situation as evil—which would then allow us to able to ignore their suffering and confusion.

My teacher Amita Schmidt encouraged me to inquire, whenever I am caught in anger: "What would love do?" This simple but profound question can completely re-orient our approach to a specific situation. Though we may begin with hatred and anger, asking this question can shock us into responding instead from a place of love and wisdom. We do not stop seeking to pursue justice, but we do so from a place of love rather than revenge. This allows us to remain acutely aware of the suffering and injustice of the world and be deeply committed to alleviating it, but to do so without turning the perpetrators into demons. Instead, we confront the perpetrators as an act of love, rather than as an act of blame and vengeance.

This is the meaning of the biblical injunction that "You shall not hate your kinsman in your heart; reprove your neighbor, and incur no guilt because of him" (Leviticus 19:17). We are commanded to reprove, but not from a place of hate. Indeed, proper rebuke happens precisely because we do not hate the other, but rather see our essential connection with the other person: that that individual is our kinsman. Indeed, this verse seems to imply that hate would often lead us to do nothing, allowing our kinsman to continue to act in damaging ways. That indifference is itself the product of our hatred, our unwillingness to be near or in conversation with such a person due to our antipathy, or simply our inability to communicate effectively with such a person due to our conflict—and it would mean that we are impotent to stop harmful behavior. It seems, according to the continuation of the verse, that we are then in some way held guilty for the behavior of others. It is our responsibility to not be trapped in our own hatred, so that we can effectively encourage others to reform their ways. When we see our own kin—and we are all each other's kin, a portion of a limb of the divine body—acting harmfully, we can ask, "What would love do?" We can rebuke from love, a rebuke that perhaps has the ability to be heard and to make an actual difference in the other person's life.

When we act from love rather than hate, we give up the illusion of control. We recognize that love is calling on us to act in a particular way and to pursue a particular goal, but there is no guarantee as to the outcome. In a certain sense, acting through love is actually surrendering to love. It is about allowing the Divine to act through us, which constitutes more of a listening than a demanding. Indeed, Rabbi Dov Baer, the Maggid of Mezritch, tells us: "The better way to say Torah is when one does not feel oneself at all, but rather one's ear listens to how the World of Speech speaks through one's own self. In such a situation, the speaker himself only appears to be speaking: as soon as the speaker begins to listen, that person's own words cease."[22] In a sense it is less about us acting, and more about us praying for the right action to be given to us. It is less about figuring it all out, and more about listening to the divine wisdom already within us, asking what our body already knows in a way broader than does our mind.

All this is not to say that anger has nothing to teach us. It does. It can teach us when and how to say "no," how to cut through surface appearances, and how to see when something is wrong. It can be a kind of clear penetrating wisdom that helps us see the problem in situations. This will not happen if we allow ourselves to become lost in our anger, consumed by it. But if we are prepared to be *with* it, as described above, and then respond to the wisdom it gives us with love, then our anger can be the goad that propels us to act wisely with action that will be healing both to ourselves and to others.

Making Enemies into Lovers

One of the tendencies of anger that we have explored is that it makes our opponents into our enemies. Those who act in ways we oppose become demons who lack the divine nature granted to every aspect of reality, according to the hasidic masters. We have seen how damaging such demonization can be, from the mental suffering it produces in us to the persecution and revenge it can lead to. How do we move beyond this demonization, to a broader view that is able to see the damage people are doing without turning them into enemies or demons? How do we explore the possibility of turning an enemy into a beloved?

No Enemies, No Demons

We begin by again recognizing that there are no enemies, no demons, no forces of pure evil who are fundamentally separate from us. Rather, we must recognize two truths: that every human is created in God's image (with no exceptions), and that we are not fundamentally separate from perpetrators of evil, for the roots of their acts are present in us as well. Of course, we often deeply wish that there are people who are forces of pure evil, for that would make things easier for us. As Aleksandr Solzhnitsyn expresses it:

> If only it were all so simple! If only there were evil people somewhere insidiously committing evil deeds, and it were necessary only to separate them from the rest of us and destroy them. But the line dividing good and evil cuts through the heart of every human being. And who among us is willing to destroy a piece of their own heart?[23]

Despite his own history as a victim of persecution, Solzhnitsyn denies that there are evil people out there somewhere, whom we need only destroy in order to make everything alright. Rather, it is the case that evil, expressed in the actions of some particular people, is actually a part of every one of us.

On a mundane level, we can fight this illusion of the "enemy" by "not judging another until you are in that person's place," as the sage Hillel suggests. Rabbi Elijah de Vidas (1518–1592) expands on this aphorism in his work *Reishit Ḥokhmah* by bringing in the comments of Rabbi Joseph Yavitz, who teaches:

> Most quarrels between people are caused by the fact that we do not apply the same standard in judging ourselves as we do in judging others...therefore we are instructed to withhold judgment of others until we can emotionally and intellectually empathize with them....For example, if someone has shamed you for something you have done, do not respond until you first judge yourself in the following manner: Were that person to have done to you that which you did, would you have not shamed that individual even more than that person shamed you? This is an important and comprehensive principle by which to increase peace in the world.[25]

When we consider how we might think, feel, and act if we were in others' situations, we start to realize that those others are merely faulty human beings like us, not demonic perpetrators of evil. It is not that, upon considering their situation, we would always have acted the in the same way, but rather that we are able to understand, without necessarily condoning, how it was that they came to act in the way they did. We start to reflect on the times that we have acted in ways that we are not proud of, and what it was that caused us to do so. We see that they are also responding, even if in a more systematic way, from their own fear, anger, suffering, and confusion.

Seeing Our Connectedness

Through such reflections and our own work of mindful observation, we see that we are not fundamentally different from those whom we oppose. We see the violence in ourselves, the craving for power and control, the resentment and anger, the jealousy and fear, that are all part of every human being's experience. We see how, but for the grace of God, we could have been that perpetrator. I was recently watching a documentary called "The Interrupters," about former gang members who work with kids in violence-ridden areas in order to teach them how to interrupt the cycle of violence. It included a discussion among middle schoolers about how to respond to threats and provocations. In a moment of insight, I realized: had I been a middle schooler in a place where weapons were available and violence was a socially acceptable option, I too might have responded to my own pain in middle school with violence and even deadly force. Only by luck was I raised in the context of a community and family that made such a response extremely unlikely, if not impossible. There are no "evil people" out there. Rather, as Solzhnitsyn reminds us, "the line dividing good and evil cuts through the heart of every human being."

Recognizing ourselves in others, even in the most painful acts of others, is a deep part of the work of transformation, the *tikkun atzmi* that leads to a wise and compassionate *tikkun olam*. This is the practice that Rabbi Jacob Joseph of Polnoye (1710–1784), the primary disciple and amanuensis of the Baal Shem Tov, teaches. He explains that when we cannot find a way in which to share the sin of another person, when we cannot "find him 'close' to you, as your 'brother,'" then we, in a sense, bring that sin home with us. We cannot heal the sin and we cannot relate to our fellow properly. We must then "study Torah, and in that manner find the sin." That is, we must find the place by which we are connected to the person and their damaging act, the way in which we truly are that person's sibling, their compatriot in this human experience. We must find the way in which that sin, perhaps in only a nascent form, is present in us.[26] Through Torah we learn that we are not separate and alien from those who sin, but rather that the same sin has a place in us as well.

It is in this way that we can turn our enemies into our friends. It is painful and courageous work. It is challenging to be able to admit all of the ways that violence, hatred, and injustice are present in us as well. Indeed, in *Avot D'Rabbi Natan* we are are told: "Who is a warrior of warriors? One who conquers their inclination (*yitzro*)... And anyone who conquers their inclination is considered as if they had conquered a city full of warriors..."[27] This work is not for the faint of heart. It is like confronting a whole host of warriors, an army of demons, waiting to destroy us. It requires us to see, confront, and not become lost in our own hatred, anger, pain, and fear. It requires us to sit in the shakiness, pain, and discomfort of those feelings, the burning that can be sometimes feel unbearable, and refuse to escape the discomfort by lashing out or retreating into self-induced numbness.

Doing so is challenging, but the rewards are extraordinary. As the text in *Avot D'Rabbi Natan* continues, "And there are those who say: [Who is a warrior or warriors?] One who makes one's enemy into a beloved."[28] When we are truly courageous, when we are really able and willing to see the humanity of the other, the way we are fundamentally connected to the other—even an other who is acting in terrible ways—it is then that we can make them a beloved instead. Sometimes, this may be only internal, a shift in how we see and relate to that person. But sometimes, if we are lucky, there may also be an external manifestation, and the relationship itself changes—and someone with whom we had previously been embroiled in conflict can actually become a beloved friend.

From Victory to Transformation, From Destruction to Healing

This orientation shifts our broader work of *tikkun olam*, which now becomes less about defeating the enemy and more about creating healing. Though in any particular situation we may still be fighting for a political victory, and we may correctly see those pitted against us as opponents to be overcome, in a deeper sense our goal is not to defeat our opponents but rather to help everyone (including them) transform, so that we can all act with more love, compassion, and wisdom. Indeed, this is the lesson that Beruriah famously taught to her husband Rabbi Meir when he, wrapped up in his own pain, anger, and confusion, sought vengeance on those who were "causing him pain," praying for them to die. Beruriah rebukes her husband, reminding him that the verse asks that "sin cease from the earth," not "sinners" (Psalm 104:35) and that the meaning of "there being no more evildoers" in the continuation of the verse is that those evildoers should return in repentance and hence cease being evildoers rather than that they should be destroyed. Rather than seeking his bulliers' death, Beruriah instructs Rabbi Meir to "request compassion upon them so that they return in repentance."[29] Indeed, the classic talmudic language for prayer, "to request compassion upon," is particularly appropriate here—as Rabbi Meir's act of compassion toward both himself and his tormentors is his prayer for them to return to who they truly are: to return to God, to abandon their acts of malice, and to act from their genuine nature of love.

Beruriah make clear that the real hope is for the transformation of those who are acting harmfully, not for their destruction. Indeed, I believe that this is the meaning of the "blessing on heretics" in the Amidah. The *b'rakhah* reads, "may all evil perish in an instant" and "may the willfully sinful (*zeidim*) be quickly uprooted, crushed, overthrown, and humbled speedily in our day." Immersing myself in the meaning of these words day after day, I suddenly realized one day that this blessing was not talking about some others out there, but about me. I was praying for the parts of myself that were willfully sinful—that sought to cause harm and that lashed out from their own fear and pain—to be uprooted, crushed, overthrown, and humbled. I was not praying to wipe out the evil *out there*, but rather the evil *in here*. That includes the evil "in here" in each one of us. My prayer is not just for myself, but is for the confusion and hatred in all of us to be uprooted and overthrown.

We see that others, just like us, act harmfully—not because they (or we) are essentially evil, but because they (like us) have turned away from who they truly are, they have gotten lost, confused, and fearful, and they have forgotten their genuine divine nature. Rabbi Nathan Sternharz (1790–1844, popularly called Reb Noson), the primary disciple of Rabbi Naḥman of Bratzlav (1772–1810), calls upon us to follow the example of King David in the psalms, who

> prayed for very much to God to be saved from oppression and theft and violence of the Husks, which are the Evil Inclination and its armies who oppress—God forbid—the souls in their sins and who remove their holy garb, until their faces change [with shame] and they no longer recognize their preciousness and [as a result] they confuse good and evil.[30]

David, according to Reb Noson, recognizes sinful people because "they no longer recognize their preciousness and [as a result] they confuse good and evil." We know this is the case because we see it in ourselves, and from seeing it in ourselves we can understand the parallel process in others. When, due to the "oppression" of the evil inclination, we forget our genuine nature, our inner nobility, clarity, and goodness, then our selfishness, jealousy, anger, hatred, and unhealthy desires manifest themselves, and we lose our wise discernment and act in ways that we know, in a deeper place, to be wrong. Seeing this in ourselves and others, we see that those acting destructively are not enemies but simply other humans, fumbling along just as we are. They are not evil but just mistaken, confused, and suffering, tragically taking out their own suffering on others.

Stopping the War

What this perspective makes clear is that repairing the world, *tikkun olam*, and repairing the self, *tikkun atzmi*, cannot be separated. The personal is political and the political is personal.[31] At a certain level, all conflict and hatred is one and so, as our opening passage from the Zohar taught us, healing must be done each day at every level. Reb Noson beautifully conveys just this insight when he teaches:

> The whole world is filled with strife. There are wars between the great world powers. There are conflicts within different locales. There are disputes within families. There is strife between neighbors. There is conflict within a household, between husband and wife, parents and children. Life is finite; people die each day. Every day death comes closer. But people continue to fight and forget their true goal in life. All strife is identical. The friction within a family parallels the strife between nations. Each person in a household is the counterpart of a world power, and their fights are the wars between those powers....You may wish to live in peace, but you are forced into conflict. It is the same for nations, which might wish to avoid war yet still become caught up in war. Two other powers might demand its allegiance until it is forced to choose a side and join the war....A person living alone can become insane. Within such a person are the warring nations and that person's personality is that of the victorious nation. Each time a new nation is victorious, such an individual must change completely, and this can lead to insanity. Such a person is alone and so cannot express the war within. But when such a person lives with people, these inner battles are expressed toward family or friends....When the Messiah comes, all wars will end. The world will then have eternal peace.[32]

Whether the war is between nations, family members, or aspects of the self, the basic nature of the war is the same, Reb Noson tells us. True healing, the messianic time, is when all of these wars will end. And indeed, if they are all the same, then it must be all or nothing. We cannot have political peace and social justice without familial peace and compassionate relationships. So too, we cannot have healed families and selves without healed societies and nations. Each level of *tikkun*—the self, the family, the community, the society, the state, the world, and the Divine—are inextricably connected with each other. We cannot hope to heal oppression and injustice by creating war. We cannot heal the world through hatred and anger, for the acts of healing themselves—our social activism—are undermined by the hatred and violence that accompany them. Rather, true healing must be multi-layered, pursuing *tikkun* at multiple levels at once. Our work of *tikkun olam*, our compassion toward the world more broadly, must be imbued with the qualities of *tikkun atzmi*, our compassion toward ourselves and those with whom we are in relationship. Only then can true healing take place. Only then can the war—both inner and outer, both private and public, both personal and political—truly stop.

This is the message of Reb Noson's beautiful prayer for peace. He prays:

> May it be Your will, the One who bestows peace, Sovereign to whom peace belongs, that You may place peace among Your people Israel. And may the peace grow until it spreads out over all the inhabitants of the world. And let there not be any hatred, jealousy, competition, or triumphalism between human beings. Instead, let there be love and great peace among all, and let everyone know the love of the other, that the other seeks that person's good, seeks that person's love, and desires that person's success eternally—until they will be able to come together and gather together, all as though with friends, and they will speak to one another and explain the truth to one another. Master of peace, bless us with peace![33]

True *tikkun* comes in this way: from a peace that grows from the inside out, spreading until it encompasses the whole world. This is how injustice finally stops, when "everyone knows the love of the other, that the other seeks that person's good, seeks that person's love and desires that person's success eternally." Of course, in the meantime, we must struggle for justice and *tikkun olam* even when that awareness is not present, but we must do it with the aspiration to make that awareness present, to perfect ourselves as well as the world. We do not wait to achieve complete self-perfection before pursuing a perfected world but, as the Zohar teaches us, we start with it each day, committing ourselves to the inner healing that is necessary for the true outer healing to take place.

NOTES

[1] Zohar II 215b. All translations are mine, unless otherwise noted. Thanks to Martin S. Cohen for the alliterative English translation.

[2] Zohar II 216b–217a.

[3] Putting aside our relationship to Zoharic metaphysics for the moment, the invitation here is to see how the Zohar might speak to us on a non-metaphysical level.

[4] The Reign of Terror during the French Revolution is perhaps the modern model for such an unfortunate outcome.

[5] *Sefer Tohorot Kodesh* (ed. Amsterdam, 1732), p. 44c.

[6] Ḥayyim Vital, *Sha·ar Ru·aḥ Ha-kodesh* (Tel Aviv: Eshel, 1961), pp. 33–34. The translation presented here is substantially based on the one published by Lawrence Fine in his *Physician of the Soul, Healer of the Cosmos: Isaac Luria and His Kabbalistic Fellowship* (Stanford, CA: Stanford University Press, 2003), p. 90.

[7] Vayikra Rabbah 13:1, ed. Mordechai Margoliot (Jerusalem: Wahrman, 1972), vol. 1, p. 269.

[8] Bereishit Rabbah 55:8, ed. Theodor-Albeck (Jerusalem: Wahrman, 1965), vol. 2, p. 593. In the same aphorism, Bar Yoḥai also claims that love ruins judgment, in the sense of untoward favoritism. I would maintain that love only ruins judgment in precisely that sense of favoritism, though genuine impartial love supports fair-mindedness and balanced clear judgment. Hatred, on the other hand, spoils our judgment in general, and not only toward those we hate.

[9] Cited in Sharon Salzberg, *Loving Kindness* (Boston: Shambala, 2011), p. 69.

[10] Rich Foster and Greg Hicks, *How We Choose to Be Happy* (New York: Perigee, 2004), p. 63.

[11] Jacob of Radzin, *Sefer Beit Yaakov* (Warsaw, 1909), *Parshat No·aḥ* §19, p. 34a, as cited and translated in Don Seeman's essay, "Martyrdom, Emotion, and The Work of Ritual in Rabbi Mordecai Joseph Leiner's *Mei Ha-Shiloaḥ*," in *AJS Review* 27:2 (2003), p. 254.

[12] See Seeman's discussion in ibid., pp. 254–255.

[13] I am deeply influenced in this analysis by my teacher, Amita Schmidt.

[14] It may be that such a statement is not far from the view of the Izbica-Radzin, but I believe that even this most radical school does not hold such a view (though there is not space to substantiate such a claim here).

[15] *Keter Shem Tov Ha-shaleim*, ed. Yaakov Emanual Shoḥet (Brooklyn: Kehot, 2004), §75, p 40.

[16] *Hakhsharat Ha-avreikhim* (Jerusalem: Va·ad asidei Piaseczno [Committee of Piasczno Hasidim], 2001), ch. 9, part 4, pp. 119–120. The slightly confusing shift from second to third person to third is a feature of the original text.

[17] Ibid., pp. 123–124.

[18] Lyrics from the song "Anthem," as reproduced online at www.leonardcohen.com.

[19] B. Shabbat 88b, based on Isadore Epstein's translation (London: Soncino Press, 1960).

[20] That is, I read the term *s'meiḥin b'yissurin* (translated here as "joy in suffering") to reference their ability to experience joy in the midst of their suffering, not to suggest that they are happy that they are suffering.

[21] Menaḥem Naḥum of Chernobyl, *Sefer Me'or Einayim* to *Parashat Ḥukkat, s.v. zot ha-torah adam ki yamut ba-ohel*, as translated by Jonathan P. Slater in his "A Better Way of Being in the World, a Way of Compassion" in *Jewish Mysticism and the Spiritual Life: Classical Texts, Contemporary Reflections*, eds. Lawrence Fine, Eitan Fishbane, and Or Rose (Woodstock, VT: Jewish Lights Publishing, 2013), p. 99.

[22] Dov Baer, the Maggid of Mezritch, as cited by Zev Wolf of Zhitomir in his *Sefer Or Ha-mei·ir*, in the section labelled *Rimzei Tzav* (ed. New York, 1954), p. 95c–d. "To say Torah" is a typical hasidic turn of phrase.

[23] As cited by Jack Kornfield in his *The Wise Heart* (New York: Bantam, 2008), p. 155.

[24] Pirkei Avot 2:5.

[25] Elijah da Vidas, *Sefer Reishit Ḥokhmah*, ed. Jósefów 5628 (1867–1868), pp. 182a–b. This translation is substantially based on the translation offered in Solomon Schimmel's essay, "Education of the Emotions in Jewish Devotional Literature: Anger and Its Control," in *Journal of Religious Ethics* 8 (1980), p. 271.

[26] Rabbi Jacob Joseph of Polnoye, *Sefer Toldot Yaakov Yosef* to *Parashat Ki Teitzei*, §3, as translated and discussed by Rabbi Jonathan P. Slater in "A Better Way of Being," pp. 100–101.

[27] *Avot D'Rabbi Natan*, text A, 23:1, ed. Schechter (Vienna, 5647 [1886–1887]), p. 38a.

[28] Ibid.

[29] B. Berakhot 10a.

[30] Nathan Sternharz, *Likkutei Halakhot, Birkot Ha-shaḥar* 3:3, as cited and translated by Ariel Burger in *Hasidic Nonviolence: Rabbi Noson of Bratzlav's Hermeneutics of Conflict Transformation* (Boston University: Ph.D. dissertation, 2008), p. 181.

[31] There is an interesting connection between these kabbalistic–hasidic views of *tikkun* and this feminist insight: they both see how the modern tendency to separate the private and public, the personal and political, is fundamentally flawed.

[32] *Siḥot Ha-ran* §77, based on the translation by Ariel Burger in his *Hasidic Nonviolence*, p. 123 (and slightly altered here, for clarity).

[33] Nathan Sternhartz, *Liklutei T'fillot* §27, based on the translation offered in Burger, *Hasidic Nonviolence*, p. 243.

Tikkun Olam: Particular or Universal?

Vernon H. Kurtz

The phrase *tikkun olam* is a very popular one today, which has become part and parcel of Jewish vocabulary. A story is told, for example, about an American Jew traveling to Israel for the first time. Greeted at the airport by his Israeli cousin, his first question is: "How do you say *tikkun olam* in Hebrew?[1] Remarkably, the phrase has moved beyond Jewish parlance and has become accepted as appropriate terminology in our society at large. Even the President of the United States has mentioned it many times: in his speeches to the Union of Reform Judaism, the American–Israel Public Affairs Committee, and in a Passover message to the Jewish community at large, President Barack Obama has either used the term *tikkun olam* in its original Hebrew form or has referred to the concept of "repairing the world," which is seen by most as the normative translation of the term. In fact, President Obama has been termed by some as the "*tikkun olam* President."[2]

Why does this phrase enjoy such popular and widespread use? It is understood by most people, including the President of the United States, in its present parlance, as a synonym for social action—that is, it is a call for taking personal action to make the world a better place, to improve the lot of all humanity. Even in the Jewish world it is often seen as such. However, if one examines the term as it is found in Jewish sources, one will see that this is not necessarily the meaning it has always had. The phrase has been used differently in different contexts and at different points in time. More specifically: we will see that the concept of *tikkun olam* has reflected different underlying definitions and conceptions in rabbinic literature, in kabbalistic literature, and in the liturgy.

At the same time that we examine the concept of *tikkun*, "repair," we must also examine what the word *olam*, "world," suggests. This latter word raises a question: are we referring to a better world for Jews in particular, or for all humanity? I believe that the latter understanding is assumed by most people, whether they are Jewish or not. But is this the true meaning of the concept? Where does the idea originate, and how did it become a synonym for social action, making the world a better place for all?

The phrase is first used in the Mishnah in tractate Gittin, edited in the early third century C.E. In the fourth chapter and in the beginning of the fifth, there appear a number of laws that are justified with the phrase *mi-p'nei tikkun ha-olam*, "because of *tikkun ha-olam*." Many of these laws refer to social policy legislation providing extra protection to those potentially at a disadvantage—for example, legislating conditions for the writing of divorce decrees and for the freeing of slaves. In these cases, it seems that the rabbinic legislation is meant to articulate rules and regulations that might not have risen to a state of obligation, but were made obligatory because of the concept of mi-p'nei tikkun ha-olam. Herbert Danby, a classic translator of the Mishnah, renders the phrase as "a precaution for the general good."[3] As these laws specifically deal with Jewish society, he sees this legislation as bettering the Jewish world.

One example of such legislation concerns protocols surrounding divorce. In Jewish law a husband may divorce his wife by granting her a *get*, a divorce document, either delivered in person or by means of a messenger. As soon as the woman accepts the *get*, she is divorced and free to marry another man. The Mishnah suggests that men may change their minds about whether to divorce their wives and therefore, after sending a messenger, they could annul the *get* (albeit in the presence of a court) without the woman knowing that it has already been cancelled. The woman might then assume that she is divorced and she may thereupon marry another man, even though she was still officially married to her first husband (since the divorce had been nullified). This would be unfair to her and any children produced from this new union. M. Gittin 4:2 relates that Rabban Gamliel the Elder established that annulling the *get* in this fashion should not be done, *mi-p'nei tikkun ha-olam*.

Perhaps the most famous mishnaic example of justifying rabbinic innovation by invoking the concept *mi-p'nei tikkun ha-olam* is Hillel's institution of the *prozbul* (M. Gittin 4:3). According to the Torah, every seven years all debts owed by Jews to other Jews are forgiven. Hillel was concerned that people would refrain from lending money to each other, because they would fear that they would not be repaid as the Sabbatical Year approached. He therefore established the *prozbul*,[4] a legal maneuver whereby lenders authorize the court to collect all debts owed to them. This effectively circumvented the legislation of the Torah and allowed for the collection of loans even after the *sh'mittah*, the Sabbatical Year, when all loans are to be forgiven. In this way no debts are cancelled by the sabbatical year, and the economic well-being of the community could thus be maintained.

It seems from these two examples (as well as the others mentioned in the Mishnah) that the phrase *mi-p'nei tikkun ha-olam* is used to solidify the social order and to take care of those—whether it be women, the poor, or (in other examples) slaves—who are less able to take care of themselves. According to Jill Jacobs, "preserving this current social order might sound like a politically conservative move. It is worth noting, however, that the majority of these rabbinic cases involve the protection of a person or set of people who typically found themselves toward the bottom of the social order."[5] The concept thus seems to protect the most vulnerable members of society.

The phrase *tikkun ha-olam* is found some fifteen times in the Mishnah, thirty-odd times in the Babylonian Talmud, eight times in the Yerushalmi, and a handful of times in the the halakhic *midrashim* and the Tosefta. Gilbert Rosenthal suggests that we should translate *tikkun ha-olam* as "the improvement of society."[6] Byron Sherwin quotes a Ph.D. thesis written by Sagit Mor: "After its initial application to divorce law, the use of the term *tikkun ha-olam* was expanded to include various other types of halakhic legislation which establish conditions aimed at supporting and sustaining various types of Jewish communal and individual needs."[7] David Widzer suggests that *mi-p'nei tikkun ha-olam* is used to justify the rabbinic enactment to promote social welfare; he writes: "maintaining the community's well-being may require an amendment to an existing law, often (but not exclusively) in financial affairs and interpersonal relationships."[8] Elliot Dorff writes: "In these first usages, the term probably means, as the Reuben Alcalay and the Even-Shoshan dictionaries suggest as their first definitions, 'guarding the established order in the physical or social world.'"[9] Jane Kanarek suggests that it be understood as "a recalibration of the world, a recognition that the world is out of balance and that legal remedies are needed in order to readjust the world to a better balance."[10]

If , in today's world, the concept of *tikkun olam* is understood to mean "repairing the world" in a more universal sense, it is clear that in its rabbinic understanding, the world that the Mishnah, Talmuds, and Midrash are referring to is solely a Jewish one. Eugene Lipman writes that *olam* literally means "world," meaning the whole world: "That certainly is the way the phrase is used in our time as a major *mitzvah* for contemporary Jews and for the Jewish community: to move the entire world toward our messianic goals. It is universalistic." However, he continues, "It was not so in the Talmud. None of the material which has been adduced here could serve to bring me to the conclusion that the talmudic sages were speaking of all humanity in their enactments."[11] As an example, he brings a comment of Rashi in which he clearly understands the concept of the world (*olam*) as denoting solely "all of Israel."[12]

Sherwin agrees with this understanding as he, too, believes that the concept of *olam* refers to maintaining the social order in the Jewish world rather than seeing it in universal terms. Quoting Mor, he writes: "The earliest appearance of the term *olam* refers to 'Jewish culture and civilization' rather than to universal humankind."[13] In fact, if one examines the mishnaic passages and the terminology as it appears there, it is quite clear that both Rabban Gamliel and Hillel are referring to the ordered society of a Jewish community—whether in regard to the laws of divorce or to the laws of lending money. In both cases, they are concerned with Jewish law only as it pertains to the Jewish community, and not as some universal approach that might be more in line with "repairing the world"—as understood in the common parlance of either President Barack Obama or most of the modern Jewish community at large.

Most people who are familiar with the concept know it from the liturgy, as it appears in the Aleinu. This prayer may have been written as early as the second century and was originally part of the liturgy for Rosh Hashanah. Probably around the thirteenth century, it was moved to the daily liturgy and it is now recited three times daily, toward the conclusion of the morning, afternoon, and evening services. The prayer itself consists of two paragraphs. The first speaks of the greatness of God and of the particular relationship between God and the Jewish people, while the second is much more universalistic in tone, suggesting that divine sovereignty will encompass the entire world. The second paragraph of Aleinu includes the phrase *l'takkein olam b'malkhut Shaddai*, which has been variously translated as "perfecting the earth by Your kingship" (Siddur Sim Shalom),[14] "to perfect the universe through the Almighty's sovereignty" (ArtScroll),[15] "when the world will be perfected under the sovereignty of the Almighty" (Koren Sacks Siddur),[16] and "when the world will be perfected under the kingdom of the Almighty" (Hertz Siddur).[17] But in order to understand the phrase, it is important to look beyond the words themselves to the larger context in which they appear.

Clearly, the focus of the first paragraph of the Aleinu is on the Jewish people. They are the ones, in contrast to all other peoples, who bow down to the Sovereign of sovereigns, the blessed Holy One. However, the second paragraph (in which the line about *tikkun olam* appears) is not only about the Jewish people. According to Levi Cooper, the universalistic theme of the second paragraph of the Aleinu "has its eyes set on repairing society in general, both Jewish and non-Jewish."[18] Jacobs suggests that this section focuses on the promise of God's ultimate sovereignty, as the text speaks of a time "when all the people of the world will call out God's name."[19] The triumph of divine sovereignty, according to the text, requires the elimination of any pockets of resistance to God's exclusive rule. Alyssa Gray writes that "the Aleinu thus takes a concept that denoted only certain, but not all, rabbinic enactments and expands it to mean God's ultimate repair of the world."[20] While we commonly think of *tikkun olam* as a human project, here it is presented as God's responsibility: it is God who is to repair the world in this case, not humans. And it is clear that the concept of *olam*, in this context, is not merely the Jewish world, but the entire world—as God is understood here to be the sovereign of all humanity.

In the Middle Ages, at least in kabbalistic circles, the term *tikkun olam* was understood differently. Daniel Matt suggests the Zohar, the mystical text ascribed by most scholars to Moses de Leon of Spain near the end of the thirteenth century, understands the idea of *tikkun* in many different ways. For example, Daniel Matt's dictionary of the Zohar includes the following in its definition of *tikkun*: "social order; welfare; rearranged the world for them; working the earth; preparing the soil."[21] In the kabbalistic understanding of the term, we thus move to an entirely new concept, quite different from the valence it held in earlier rabbinic sources.

Isaac Luria (1534–1572) takes the kabbalistic concept of *tikkun* to yet another level. He describes creation as a process by which God contracted the Divine Self in order to make room for the world. In this creation story, God then emanated into the world through ten *s'firot*, aspects of the Divine Presence. Luria conceptualized the divine *s'firot* as vessels of divine essence, then went on to imaging some of the vessels becoming too weak to actually contain the stuff of Divinity assigned to them. The vessels shattered, resulting in the mixture of divine light with the *k'lipot*, or shells, of the vessels themselves. This process resulted in the introduction of evil into the world.[22] Luria understood the concept of tikkun as the idea that human actions can have an effect far beyond the action itself. He maintained that as Jews fulfill their obligations under God's commandments, they literally help to fix the shattered world.[23] For Luria, Jews observing the commandments would, quite audaciously, fix God. According to Sherwin, for the kabbalists, the goal of *tikkun ha-olam* was to restore harmony, balance, and oneness among the forces that constitute the manifested aspects of God—that is, the *s'firot*.[24]

This understanding takes the concept of *tikkun* to a level not envisioned by the rabbinic sages. Rosenthal suggests: "The great novelty of the Lurianic approach to *tikkun* is that it elevates the role of human beings far beyond that envisioned by the Talmudic sages who devised the concept. It is now in the hands of every man and woman to lift the sparks and redeem the supernal and lower worlds by our own actions."[25] The ancient rabbis had been interested in "repairing" their own contemporary Jewish society. The kabbalistic notion of *tikkun*, however, went far beyond that concept, suggesting that human behavior can have an effect—positive or negative—on the world; and that *mitzvot*, Jewish ethical and ritual commandments, have an impact even beyond the immediate effect of a particular action.

To what *olam* was Luria referring? Did he believe that our actions would have an impact on the entire cosmos, or was the *tikkun* that he envisioned more limited in scope? Lawrence Fine suggests that "while it is true that by its nature Lurianic myth spoke in cosmic, and thus in some sense, 'universal' terms, the Lurianists were not curtailed by any sense of 'shared fate' with humanity at large."[26] According to Fine, sixteenth-century Jews were not concerned with the entire human condition. In a similar vein, Byron Sherwin writes that "the focus of the kabbalistic view is not primarily the social sphere, the terrestrial realm, but the divine realm. The kabbalistic approach is blatantly and unabashedly theocentric."[27] And Gilbert Rosenthal, in assessing the use of the term by other medieval kabbalists, suggests that "*Tikkun* is directed toward three goals: the repair of the flaws in the world from creation, the perfection of humans, and the repair of the primordial sin of Adam and purging of the pollution injected by the serpent into Eve in Eden." Thus, the kabbalistic understanding of the phrase *tikkun olam* is clearly quite different from how it was used in rabbinic literature and in the liturgy. For the kabbalists, it has become a term referring to individual self-improvement, by which process an individual can also have an effect on the world—and "the world" in this usage refers both to the inner world of the person doing the *mitzvot* and also to the expanded world of the Jewish people.

With this background, it is now possible to explore how we understand *tikkun olam* in our own day. Lawrence Fine writes that the originators of the new meaning of this term in the United States— Shlomo Bardin, Leonard Fine, and Michael Lerner, for example— surely consciously based themselves on the way the term was used in ancient times, as they created its modern meaning.[29] I would like to suggest that the term today is an amalgam of all these understandings. From the rabbinic sphere, we have taken the concept of helping the most vulnerable in society, repairing the world, readjusting its balance, and consolidating the social order. From the Aleinu prayer, we have embraced the concept of repairing the world—moving from a particularistic formulation about Jewish society to a universalistic one, making us responsible for humanity at large. And from the mystical Lurianic approach, we have added the concept of human activity improving the self, and thus perhaps even the world above.

There are some who believe that we have gone beyond the limits of what the historical understanding of the term should allow for. Byron Sherwin, for example, writes: "The contemporary use of tikkun olam is an example of the semantic displacement of American Jewry, an expression of verbal abuse. It is a metamorphosed version of 'Prophetic Judaism,' which like 'Prophetic Judaism' has come to be understood as being synonymous with Judaism."[30] And Arnold J. Wolf believes that popular modern usage has distorted the concept of *tikkun olam*: "A teaching about compromise, sharpening, trimming, and humanizing rabbinic law, a mystical doctrine of putting God's world back together again, this strange and half-understood notion becomes a huge umbrella under which our petty moral concerns and political panaceas can come in out of the rain."[31]

But others, like Jonathan Sacks,[32] are more sanguine with the current usage of the term, and seize the opportunity to appreciate the possibility of human beings creating a better world order. And this is especially true of the many modern writers for whom *tikkun olam* has become a synonym for social action and repairing the world, and who lack an understanding of the term's historical background. Levi Cooper suggests that for these people, "it is most commonly heard as a catch cry for activism, political involvement, and social justice. As a banner, *tikkun olam* helps people rally around a value that sounds like it is drawing on traditional Jewish sources, while at the same time championing contemporary liberal values."[33]

No matter what the particular historical usage of the term may be, it has now become part of our modern lexicon. But when we moderns use the phrase, whose *olam* are we referring to? Are we talking about the world of rabbinic society, the universe under God's dominion as portrayed in the Aleinu, or about the inner self as defined by the mystical tradition? It seems to me that the real understanding of the definition of our modern-day term is best captured by a confluence of these three understandings.

Tikkun olam, in its modern parlance, is seen as a human activity. Whether the term is used by youth groups, synagogues, communal organizations, or even non-Jewish organizations, the imperative of *tikkun olam* is invoked in order to motivate human beings to repair society, to create a better social order, and to support the vulnerable— much as it was understood in rabbinic times. At the same time, it has also been universalized to refer to the entire world order. While most people are not familiar with Lurianic Kabbalah and might not feel comfortable with some of its tenets, many of those for whom tikkun olam is a live concept do appreciate some deeper theological or spiritual meaning, perhaps emanating from the mystical approach of the Lurianic kabbalists.[34] Doing social action in this world bears with it the theological imprint of the person doing the action, whether or not it has an effect upon the unification of God's self. And finally, the universal approach found in the second paragraph of Aleinu seems to have moved the concept of *tikkun olam* from a Jewish-centric societal and communal formula to one that is much more universal. In this day and age, it seems to be much more fashionable to think in terms of universal values rather than in particularistic Jewish ones. If we find a Jewish value that allows universal thinking and action, how much better would that be? *Tikkun olam* is just such a value.

In Jewish life there are sometimes conflicts between responsibilities to the Jewish community and to the non-Jewish world, and these conflicts exist in many different realms. Where, for example, should we donate our limited philanthropic dollars: to Jewish or non-Jewish causes? In working toward creating a better community and society, should we prioritize our efforts on behalf of Jewish or non-Jewish institutions? The question has been aptly put by Elliot J. Cosgrove: "Embedded deep within the foundation of Judaism exists a tension— an anxiety wrought by an unresolved question that has been with us since our very beginning. Is our faith, our Judaism, universal or particular in its orientation? To put it another way, is our greatest concern as Jews the condition of our collective and shared humanity, or are we meant to focus on the particulars of our own peoplehood?"

For some, this is a real conflict. It is the responsibility of Jews, they feel, to care for their own and not to be involved in society at large. For such people, isolation is not necessarily a negation of responsibilities toward humanity; rather, one's first responsibility is simply to one's own family. On the other hand, there are those who believe that since we are part of humanity at large, global issues should come even before our own particular ones—for as members of humanity we have a responsibility toward all. And there are still others who believe that there really is no conflict between the two concerns. For example, Yosef Green writes: "I am an incurable universalist precisely because of my Jewish particularity, which emphasizes the fatherhood of God and the brotherhood of man."[36] His views are also those of Jonathan Sacks and a number of others, who see no real conflict between being a member of the Jewish people and a member of the family of humanity.[37]

We live today as members of both families: both our Jewish family and our greater human family. As it is currently understood, tikkun olam allows us to take a Jewish concept as it has evolved through the ages and use it to anchor our actions in ancient values as we strive to contribute in a Jewish fashion not merely to our immediate family, but to our larger family: the family of all humanity. "Repairing the world," doing *tikkun olam*, is simply assumed to be a part of what it means to be a responsible Jew today. Organizations such as The American Jewish World Service, Project TEN of the Jewish Agency for Israel, and others encourage Jews to focus on this value of their heritage, as they partake of social action activities in the world at large.[38]

If President Barack Obama can use the term *tikkun olam* in Hebrew and know that it is compatible with his own philosophy of attempting to create a better world order, then surely the term has now become totally universalized. On the one hand, this is good: as Jewish tradition teaches, it is our responsibility to create a better world order. On the other hand, to universalize so totally the concept detracts from its specifically Jewish meaning, as understood by Jewish sources and sages throughout history. This is a representation of one of the major challenges of the modern Jewish world.

Gerald J. Blidstein suggests that "*tikkun olam* assumes that the acting party—whether it be an individual or a community—is one with the *olam*, or the society, whose benefit he seeks. At times, this society is the Jewish community itself; in other instances, it is the general community."[39] He continues: "Perhaps the point is that the Jew must answer to the human imperative both as an individual and as a community, that both aspects of this imperative are to be heard and answered."[40]

Today, as the American tourist understood it, *tikkun olam* has simply become part of the American Jewish vocabulary; and repairing the world is not confined to the Jewish community alone, but it has become a universal concept. The danger, though, is that if Jews let it remain that way, without being concerned with their own immediate family, then the term itself will have morphed into a concept far beyond its original rabbinic meaning. It seems to me that this is one of the challenges of both being a Jew and being a citizen of the world today—that is, being both particular and universal at the same time, being supportive of the Jewish community while still being an active citizen of the world.

The challenge today in understanding the concept of *tikkun olam* is to frame it within its Jewish context and at, the very same time, to use it appropriately to convey responsibility both to the Jewish world and the world at large—motivating us to act to create a better world order for the Jewish world and the non-Jewish world alike.

NOTES

[1] Byron L. Sherwin, "*Tikkun Olam*: A Case of Semantic Displacement," in *Jewish Political Studies Review* 25:3–4 (Fall 2013), available online at http://jcpa.org/jewish-political-studies-review-home.

[2] See: Jodi Rudoren, "Shalom, Mr. President: Obama Tries to Charm Israelis With Hebrew," *New York Times* (March 23, 2013), at www.nytimes.com/2013/03/23/world/middleeast/obama-tries-to-charm-israelis-with-hebrew.html?_r=0; Avraham Infeld, "Obama's 'Tikkun Olam': Lost in Translation?" in *The Times of Israel* (March 10, 2012) at http://blogs.timesofisrael.com/obamas-tikkun-olam-lost-in-translation; Steven M. Bob, "The 'Tikkun Olam' President," in *The Jerusalem Post* (August, 11, 2013).

[3] Herbert Danby, *The Mishnah* (London: Oxford University Press, 1933).

[4] Explained more fully in M. Sheviit 10:3.

[5] Jill Jacobs, "The History of 'Tikkun Olam,'" in *Zeek* (June 2007), at www.zeek.net/706tohu.

[6] Gilbert S. Rosenthal, "*Tikkun Ha-Olam*: The Metamorphosis of a Concept," in The Journal of Religion 85:2 (April 2005), p. 217.

[7] In Sherwin, "*Tikkun Olam*: A Case of Semantic Displacement."

[8] David S. Widzer, "The Use of *Mipnei Tikkun Ha'Olam* in the Babylonian Talmud," *CCAR Journal* 56 (Spring 2008), p. 38.

[9] Elliot N. Dorff, *The Way Into Tikkun Olam: Repairing the World* (Woodstock, VT: Jewish Lights Publishing, 2005), p. 7.

[10] Jane Kanarek, "What Does *Tikkun Olam* Actually Mean?" in *Righteous Indignation*, eds. Or. N. Rose, Jo Ellen Green Kaiser, and Margie Klein (Woodstock, VT: Jewish Lights Publishing, 2008), p. 19.

[11] Eugene J. Lipman, "*Mipnei Tikkun Ha'Olam* in the Talmud: A Preliminary Exploration," in *The Life of Covenant: The Challenge of Contemporary Judaism— Essays in Honor of Herman E. Schaalman*, ed. Joseph Edelheit (Chicago: Spertus College of Judaica Press, 1986), p.108.

[12] Rashi on B. Shabbat 54b, s.v. *b'khol ha-olam kullo*.

[13] Sherwin, "*Tikkun Olam*: A Case of Semantic Displacement."

[14] Siddur Sim Shalom, ed. Rabbi Jules Harlow (New York: The Rabbinical Assembly and United Synagogue of Conservative Judaism, 1985), p. 161.

[15] *The Complete ArtScroll Siddur*, trans. Rabbi Nosson Scherman (Brooklyn: Mesorah Publications Ltd., 1984), p. 161.

[16] *The Koren Siddur*, ed. Rabbi Sir Jonathan Sacks (Jerusalem: Koren Publishing, 2009), p. 180.

[17] *The Authorized Daily Prayer Book*, ed. Rabbi Dr. Joseph H. Hertz (New York: Bloch Publishing Company, 1961), p. 211.

[18] Levi Cooper, "*The Tikkun Olam* Catch-All," in *Jewish Educational Leadership* 11:1 (Winter 2013), p. 47.

[19] Jacobs, "The History of *Tikkun Olam*."

[20]   Alyssa Gray, in *My People's Prayer Book: Traditional Prayers, Modern Commentaries*, vol. 6, *Tachanun and Concluding Prayers*, ed. Lawrence A. Hoffman (Woodstock, VT: Jewish Lights Publishing, 2002), p. 142.

[21]   Matt's dictionary of Zoharic vocabulary is not yet published; the definition cited here reflects his understanding of *tikkun olam* at Zohar I 38a.

[22]   Jacobs, "The History of *Tikkun Olam*."

[23]   Dorff, *The Way Into Tikkun Olam*, p. 10.

[24]   Sherwin, "*Tikkun Olam*: A Case of Semantic Displacement."

[25]   Rosenthal, "*Tikkun Ha-Olam*: The Metamorphosis of a Concept," p. 226.

[26]   Lawrence Fine, "*Tikkun*: A Lurianic Motif in Contemporary Jewish Thought," in *From Ancient Israel to Modern Judaism, Intellect in Quest of Understanding: Essays in Honor of Marvin Fox*, eds. Jacob Neusner, Ernest S. Frerichs, and Nahum M. Sarna (Atlanta: Scholars Press, 1986) ,vol. 4, p. 43.

[27]   Sherwin, "*Tikkun Olam*: A Case of Semantic Displacement."

[28]   Rosenthal, "*Tikkun Ha-Olam*: The Metamorphosis of a Concept," p.228.

[29]   Fine, "*Tikkun*: A Lurianic Motif," pp. 50–51.

[30]   Sherwin, "*Tikkun Olam*: A Case of Semantic Displacement."

[31]   Arnold Jacob Wolf, "Repairing *Tikkun Olam*," in *Judaism: A Quarterly of Jewish Life* 50:4 (2001), p. 482.

[32]   Jonathan Sacks, *To Heal a Fractured World: The Ethics of Responsibility* (New York: Schocken Books, 2005), p. 265.

[33]   Cooper, "The *Tikkun Olam* Catch-All," p. 49.

[34]   Ibid., p. 50.

[35]   See Cosgrove's sermon "Judaism—Universal or Particular?" (October 3, 2009), online at http://pasyn.org/resources/sermons/%5Bfield_dateline-date%5D-6.

[36]   Yosef Green, "Universalism and/or Particularism," in *Jewish Bible Quarterly* 30:1 (2002), pp. 3–10.

[37]   Sacks expresses himself in this regard particularly eloquently in his book *To Heal a Fractured World* (see note 32 above).

[38]   For more about the American Jewish World Service, see www.ajws.org; for more about Project Ten, see www.tenprogram.org.

[39]   Gerald J. Blidstein, "*Tikkun Olam*," in *Tikkun Olam : Social Responsibility in Jewish Thought and Law*, eds. David Schatz, Chaim I. Waxman, and Nathan J. Diament (The Orthodox Forum Series; Northvale, NJ: Jason Aronson, 1997), p. 18.

[40]   Ibid., p. 20.

Community and the Individual

Yehonatan Chipman

I first conceived of this essay in wake of a competition, some eight years ago, calling upon people to suggest ideas for an "important Jewish book." Having written, for a number of years, a paper on the weekly Torah portion—with a different theme each year—I found myself asking the question: Were I given the opportunity, including time and money, to write a book, what would I write about? What is the central message that I feel Judaism has to give to the world at this historical junction? This essay constitutes my answer.

The Problem

Throughout the twentieth century, much of Western Jewry enthusiastically embraced modernity and all it has to offer, attempting to harmonize Jewish identity with modernity and accepting many of its central values and ways of thinking. Yet historically, Jews have always been, and have thought of themselves as, "nay-sayers." A well-known midrash derives Abraham's name, *Avraham Ha-ivri* ("Abraham the Hebrew"), from the idea that "the whole world was on one side (*mei-eiver ehad*) and he was on the other."[1] Thus, the very first Jew is portrayed as the archetypal non-conformist, as one who did not fear to criticize and call to account things that were done improperly in the world. Jews said no to Canaanite paganism; to the Hellenistic culture of late antiquity; to medieval European Christianity; and, as

Maurice Samuels persuasively argues in *The Gentleman and the Jew*,[2] to the culture of warfare, colonialism, militarism, and the celebration of combat sports and the hunt that "trained" for these pursuits, which have characterized much of European and English history.

The question that arises is: What phenomena in today's world call for "nay-saying"? Of course, there are many things that call for refutation on every level in economic, cultural, and political life, in the United States, in Israel, and elsewhere. These include, most strikingly, the very real threats to the environment, which in recent years have been dramatically manifested in frightening signs of world climate change; and the ongoing threat of nuclear warfare, with which we have "learned to live" for a half-century or more, but which constitutes no less a potential mortal threat to our civilization.

But there is another phenomenon that stands out in my mind, one that I have observed over my adult lifetime (roughly speaking, since the mid-1960s) that, while less immediately cataclysmic than the two mentioned above, nevertheless represents a very serious threat to the ongoing life of society; and is one so obvious that it is often overlooked. I refer to the decline of the sense of society, of community, and the rise of individualism, at times in extreme form.

I believe that in recent years a kind of extreme individualism has emerged as the covert ideology of much of Western society, with a corresponding decline in community values and in what has been called "social capital." This is a problem that urgently needs to be addressed; I see this struggle as a central focus of the Jewish call for *tikkun olam*, for attempting to rectify the faults of the world in which we live. In the second half of this essay, I will discuss the manner in which Judaism provides certain answers or alternative models to this problem, in the form of a proper balance between individual and society.

Decline in Communal Values: Examples from Current Life

During the past half-century, I have observed a series of changes in the social world in which we live, all of them pointing in the direction of greater emphasis on the individual and a concomitant decline in community values.[3] If at times I shall engage below in overly sweeping generalizations, I offer my apologies. Notwithstanding certain exceptions, I believe that my description of the overall trends is nevertheless a correct one. A few examples:

Marriage and Sexuality: The past half-century has been marked by a series of dramatic changes related to family and sexuality: (a) an unprecedented rise in the incidence of divorce in Western society; (b) the so-called "sexual revolution"—that is, the widespread acceptance of premarital intercourse as a behavioral norm among the educated middle class in Western countries among all but the most traditional religious circles (including Protestants, Catholics, and Jews alike); (c) the widespread acceptance and legitimation of homosexual behavior; and (d) the emergence of a powerful feminist movement (the so-called "Second Wave"), many of whose norms have been widely accepted among the educated classes in the West. All of these phenomena, taken in aggregate, indicate a radical change in attitudes toward sexuality and the family, whose common denominator might be described as thinking about sexuality in individualistic terms: that is, as a basic human need and source of pleasure for the individual, rather than as a basis for marriage and for the family (which serves as the smallest and most basic unit of society, and as a normative framework for procreation and raising the next generation). Some have described these changes in terms of the privatization of sex or, in religious terms, as the desanctification of relations between men and women.

There are, admittedly, many positive aspects to these changes. First and foremost, perhaps, are the positive changes in the role of women in society generally, and greater opportunities for women in the professions. The de facto legitimation of homosexual behavior has served as a liberating change for gay people, who have hitherto lived dual lives, in shame and secrecy. More generally, the frankness and honesty regarding sexuality and the open discussion of sexual issues in today's society may be seen in positive terms. But there is also a downside to many of these developments: by severing the connection between sexuality and morality, by declaring any consensual relation between two people as legitimate, the sense of awe has been removed from the sexual act. Moreover, the very possibility of raising ethical issues concerning sexuality in public discourse has been nullified. In addition, certain schools of feminism have fostered the idea of relations between sexes as largely combative rather than cooperative, leading to a new "war of the sexes." The emphasis on women as individuals has tended to undermine the family unit—the very smallest social unit, which as such functions as the basis of society. Divorce has become so widespread as to have become almost normative, causing the breakup of large numbers of families—often unnecessarily—and with dire results to these families' children during their most impressionable years. In my understanding, taken together these changes in the nature of the family constitute a threat to the cohesion and viability of society as a whole.

Economic: On the economic level, there has been a resurgence of capitalism, in the form of globalization or "neo-liberalism." Capitalism, as a philosophy, sees the human being first and foremost as homo economicus: its core belief is the notion that the profit motive, the desire for wealth, is the basic motivation of all human activity. Margaret Thatcher expressed this idea succinctly in her oft-repeated statement that "There is no such thing as society, only individuals." Hence the culture of capitalism emphasizes competition rather than cooperation. Over recent decades we have seen the decline of the welfare state, a process of privatization, and an increasingly harsh economic environment. This change has been pronounced in the State of Israel, which over the past forty years has been transformed from one of the more economically egalitarian countries in the world to one of the least so. Moreover, in recent decades there has emerged a pattern, in high-power, high-paying professions such as law and technology, in which people are expected to work twelve- and fourteen-hour days. There is an expectation of total devotion to one's career, fueled by a covert acceptance of the notion that career and high income are the highest values in society. This ethos is one of the factors that contribute directly to delayed marriage, as well as to a decline in family life and in the ability of parents to spend substantial time with their children. (Sabbath observance among traditional Jews serves to counter these forces somewhat, but is not in itself sufficient to stem the socio-economic forces confronting families in the twenty-first century.)

Legal Theory: The emphasis on individuality has affected legal discourse as well. The discourse of individual rights, praiseworthy in itself, tends to emphasize the rights of special groups or of individuals, with a corresponding rejection or reduction in the notion of social responsibility. For example: some years ago Israel considered adopting a "Good Samaritan Law," under which, among other things, bystanders would be required to attend to a person who had been injured in an accident. Surprisingly, several secular left-wing Knesset members, whom one would have expected to back such a proposal, were troubled by the idea of society imposing a legal responsibility of this sort on individuals, even in such a drastic case; it was perceived by them to constitute a violation of individual liberty.[4]

Spirituality: In recent decades there has been a renewal of interest in spirituality, often referred to by the phrase "New Age"—something which, as a religious person, I cannot but see as praiseworthy. However, the emphasis of this movement tends to be on the individual and his or her own personal, subjective experience. Thus, for example: Pesaḥ is reinterpreted as the individual being freed from one's own personal Egypt, Shavuot as focused on accepting one's own personal Torah, and so forth. (Admittedly, this approach does have roots in Judaism— particularly in Hasidism, where such ideas originally flourished, albeit in a very different context.) In the current context, these trends seem to express a kind of post-modernist relativism, downplaying both *halakhah* and Jewish covenantal, collective existence.

Historical Consciousness: My own admittedly subjective impression is that an increasing number of people no longer feel themselves part of any historical continuum. The idea of historical continuity is, as we shall see below, a central idea in Judaism; indeed, it is a necessary component of any meaningful notion of cultural identity. This implicit rejection of history was strongly articulated by Existentialist thinkers, one of whose core ideas was that the only meaning of life is that which the individual—whose own purview is limited by his or her own birth and death—gives to it. I first encountered these ideas in my youth, and at the time was much impressed by them—largely because such central figures of the movement as Jean-Paul Sartre and Albert Camus behaved quite heroically during World War II in the anti-Nazi underground in France. But, upon closer examination, I came to believe that these ideas are highly problematic; moreover, they can be equally used in support of fascism and other questionable moral position.

New Technology: On the concrete, practical level, much of the new technology separates people from one another. This trend already began with television, but it has been greatly exacerbated by personal computers, smart phones, the internet, and various forms of social media, whose ubiquity seems to have created a society in which people are increasingly isolated from one another, with less and less face-to-face contact and more and more contact by electronic means. I submit that such modern technological innovations, useful as they may be (and at times even necessary, for example in facilitating communication between people separated by great distances), cannot substitute for the depth and intimacy possible through face-to-face contact between people.

Causes of this Decline

What has led to this change? And is it really such a bad thing? To a great extent, the swing of the pendulum toward individualism is an understandable reaction to the exaggerated emphasis on community and the collectivity that characterized the period preceding the present one. The first half of the twentieth century was characterized, inter alia, by such totalitarian movements as communism, fascism, and Nazism, all of which regimented society, disregarded the value of the individual, and engaged in mass murder when it allegedly served collective aims. (Such tendencies can still be found today in societies such as North Korea, in which the individual is seen as existing to serve the state or its ideology; and it appears to me that there may be a similar mood in Islamic radicalism.) Indeed, a great deal of the attractiveness of such radical movements is that they provide individuals with a powerful sense of purpose, of *esprit de corps*, and of a meaning in life found by sharing in a cause greater than themselves.

Even Zionism (which as such could hardly be called a totalitarian movement) made great demands upon the individual during the early years of the State, when the newly-created State of Israel was engaged in collective tasks such as absorbing hundreds of thousands of immigrants, creating state institutions, and building an economy— all this while fighting for its very survival. Indeed, even the literature and popular music of that period reflected those concerns. But at a certain point, perhaps in the 1960s or early 1970s, many Israelis began to ask themselves: when can I live for *myself*? Such prominent leaders as the late Shulamit Aloni began to raise human rights as a political issue, while fiction authors such as Amos Oz and A. B. Yehoshua began to write in a more personal vein. Today, in marked contrast to earlier societal tendencies, there is a growing trend in Israeli culture toward privatism and individualism.

But radical individualism runs the very real risk of ignoring certain central human values. Such values as kindness, generosity, and helping others—known in Hebrew as *hesed*—are predicated on human beings living within community, and can as such only be actualized within the context of society. At least in its extreme form, individualism leaves little or no room for *hesed*: when one lives for oneself alone, acts of charity are conceived of as private, purely voluntary acts, rather than as moral obligations incumbent upon each individual by virtue of being a human. Indeed, the moral concept of responsibility toward others is premised on the concept of society as the natural state of humanity. It is this concept that lies at the root of the controversy within American society surrounding such issues as governmental involvement in social welfare, even concerning such basic areas as education or health.

Individualism

What is the basic idea of individualism? In a word, it is the idea that the proper focus of life—the central criterion of determining value—is the welfare and happiness of the individual human being.

Some scholars find the roots of individualism in Christianity, which was founded as a religion based upon a redemptive message of salvation of the individual soul, and which converted individuals in line with this theology. (In this respect it differed from Judaism which, as I shall discuss in detail below, is based upon community, and upon a covenant between a specific family-become-nation and its God; conversion to Judaism involves symbolic adoption or even rebirth as a Jew.) But by the Middle Ages, the Christian Church had grown to function as an all-embracing community, so that the emergence of Protestantism in the sixteenth century revived the focus of religious life upon the individual.

From the Renaissance on we find increasing expressions of the individual in Western culture and literature: Cervantes, in *Don Quixote*, writes of an eccentric individual who pursues his own vision, "tilting at windmills"; Daniel Defoe's *Robinson Crusoe* may be seen as a paradigm of the lone individual who survives entirely on his own; the philosopher René Descartes coined the phrase *Cogito ergo sum* ("I think, therefore I am"), pinpointing the essence of humanness in the process of thought, which is by definition an individual process; John Stuart Mill's essay *On Liberty* celebrates the autonomy and freedom of the individual. In America, the "conquest of the West" during the nineteenth century was largely a movement of individuals or small family units moving West in covered wagons, each one establishing itself on its own homestead, expressing what came to be called "rugged Yankee individualism."

Closer to our own period, the emergence of modern capitalism coincided with the ideas of individual initiative, the myth of the "self-made man," and the notion that the capitalist system allowed each individual to realize his or her full potential, if one but worked hard enough. These ideas found extreme expression, for example, in such novels as Ayn Rand's *The Fountainhead* and *Atlas Shrugged*.[5]

The problem is a difficult one on several levels. On a practical level, the growth of individualism is the result of deeply-rooted factors in modern society, beginning with urbanization and persisting in light of such economic changes as the domination of the economy by huge, anonymous corporations, creating a sense of alienation on the part of the individual worker or consumer. All these macro-societal factors make a return to the old-fashioned type of intimate community, such as that of the pre-modern village, all but impossible.

On the level of values: just as an excessive emphasis on individualism creates the problems mentioned above, an excessive emphasis on the collective, with its concomitant suppression of individual rights and identity, presents its own dangers, as mentioned above. Hence, the solution cannot be a return to all-embracing societies of the type that existed in the past—and certainly not to the totalitarian models of the mid-twentieth century, which governed and dictated, often in oppressive ways, the lifestyle, values, and life patterns of the individual. Rather, the goal toward which we ought to strive is a happy medium between individualism and vital community life. There is need for a new approach that, while allowing wide latitude for individual differences, will mitigate the alienation and anomie resulting from the dissolution of society and social cohesion that is so pervasive within contemporary Western culture.

One may find examples of tightly-knit, highly supportive communities within the Jewish religious world. Examples of this are to be found, in very different ways, in many West Bank settlements, and in the Haredi (ultra-Orthodox) world—but in both cases demanding conformity to a very specific set of norms. While I do not agree with the political ideology of the West Bank settlers' movement, I admire their passion—which is related to the fact that they have in many places created a rich community life in a new type of communal settlement, the *yishuv k'hillati*, which has perhaps overcome some of the failings of the kibbutz movement. Thus, part of the sadness felt as a result of the 2005 evacuation of Jewish settlements in the Gaza Strip was the breakup of such communities and the relocation of the families to new places—without the communal fabric, institutions, and friendships that had given them great support.

Community

One of the buzzwords of contemporary social criticism is "alienation," which is seen as one of the diseases of modern mass, anonymous society. Already in the early twentieth century many people began writing about the anomie felt by the individual in mass society, in urban settings in which neighbors do not know one another. The revival of a sense of community, which is of course no simple matter, would help to solve or ameliorate this problem.

In the late nineteenth century, the German sociologist Ferdinand Tönnies wrote a book entitled *Gemeinschaft* und *Gesellschaft* ("Community and Society"),[6] in which he drew a contrast between two differing kinds of societal organization: the intimate community, marked by living human interaction, and the anonymous, mechanized big city, in which relations among people are instrumental, based upon formal rules.

In recent decades, a communitarian movement has grown in the United States, which has developed a critique of the above-mentioned exaggerated individualism.[7] This movement is neither "Right" nor "Left" in the classic sense. Rather, it focuses upon what it calls the "loss of social capital"—that is, the disintegration of social structures, including such voluntary organizations as the PTA, church groups, or even bowling leagues (hence the title of one popular book on the subject, *Bowling Alone*)—which brought people together, in earlier times.[8] The movement notes the disconnection of people from one another, resulting in harm both to society and to the individual's emotional (and even physical) health by the breaking of these bonds—and issues a call for the renewal of such groups.

Michael Lerner, editor of *Tikkun* magazine, has made an interesting observation related to this point.[9] He notes that liberals in the U.S. are often critical of those who speak of "family values," who generally advocate a conservative approach toward such issues as abortion and homosexuality. However, Lerner asserts that such people are largely motivated by their longing for a sense of lost community. He argues that the competitive values of the marketplace promote selfishness and materialism, undermining our capacities to sustain loving relationships; therefore, families need to be embedded in communities that unabashedly affirm the value of love and solidarity.

I find it significant, and more than a little disappointing, that the communitarian literature points specifically to various places in southeast Asia (such as Singapore, the Philippines, and Taiwan) as models for strongly community-oriented societies, whereas Jewish communities are not mentioned in this context—certainly not those of Jews living in Western countries, nor those in contemporary Israel. There is a certain anomaly here, as in principle Judaism is strongly rooted in the idea of community. However, today this is no longer the case—at least not in practice—for the Jews in U.S. and other Western diasporas. Jews have been extremely successful in the United States in business, in the professions, in media, and in the academic world; many Jews like to cite the disproportionate number of Nobel Prize winners among Jews. But all these accomplishments have been of an individual nature. Why is this so? Because Jews, for numerous reasons, have largely assimilated into Western society (in some cases even trying to conceal their Jewishness) and, in the process, have thrown off much of traditional Judaism, including its strong communal structure, adopting instead a Western individualistic approach to life.

Judaism and Community

Notwithstanding, I submit that Judaism has important things to say about our problem. Traditional Judaism recognizes the importance of both the individual and the community, fostering insights that may prove fruitful to our own age.

Judaism—as a religion, as a literature, as a system of thought—greatly values community; indeed, it is based upon it.[10] One needn't search far to prove this point. The central idea in Judaism, the covenant between God and the people Israel, which lies at the heart of the Sinai revelation, is based upon a collective covenant between God and the people. In similar fashion, the major festivals revolve around community and peoplehood. Shavuot celebrates the covenant with the community; see the verse regarding the Sinai revelation, "you shall be a kingdom of priests and a holy nation" (Exodus 19:6); Passover signifies the birth of the nation, celebrated by the consumption in extended family groups of the paschal lamb, the sacrificial ritual upon which the modern *seder* meal is modeled; and so on.

Even a key individual ritual such as *b'rit milah*, circumcision, by which each male individual is initiated into Judaism shortly after birth, is conceived in communal terms. In recent public disputes about circumcision—in San Francisco, in Germany, in other places in Europe—the argument has been made that an infant child "has no religion." But this argument is predicated on the assumption that religion is a function of personal belief, which by definition can only apply to a person with an ability to think, choose, and formulate a worldview—which an infant clearly cannot do. But from a traditional Jewish perspective, the Jewishness of the individual begins as part of a collective identity, in a communal covenant—and only later, and in a supplementary way that does not displace this earlier aspect, does it become a personal commitment. Similarly marriage, which as such is a union between two individuals, is celebrated in Judaism in a communal fashion.

The famous rabbinic dictum concerning the "three things upon which the world stands"—Torah, religious devotion or worship, and acts of lovingkindness[11]—may similarly be interpreted with both individual and communal emphases. One can pray alone, one can study by oneself, one can perform individual deeds of kindness by oneself, even anonymously. But all three can, and often are, performed in community—and are arguably enhanced thereby.

The study of Torah is often conducted through fixed public study sessions, while the *beit midrash*, the study house, is a central public institution. *Yeshivot*, autonomous study institutions devoted wholly to study, are likewise collective bodies.

Regarding prayer: the *minyan*, symbolically representative of an entire community, is seen as essential for public worship. The Talmud contains an interesting dispute between Rabbi Yossi ben Ḥanina and Rabbi Yehoshua ben Levi concerning the nature and origin of the three daily prayers: are they rooted in the personal prayer of the three patriarchs, or in the daily sacrifices? I believe that at the heart of this dispute is a debate as to whether prayer is essentially an individual act or a communal one. Is its essence the subjective, individual experience, the "service of the heart" rooted in the emotional life of the individual, which is by definition located within each person's psyche? Or is it quintessentially a public act of the community standing before God, serving the Almighty as a collective?

Regarding the practice of *ḥesed* (lovingkindness) in community: traditionally, Jewish communities have established *ḥevrot*, societies for the organized practice of *ḥesed*, of providing for the needy—be it marrying off indigent brides, providing interest-free loans to the needy, visiting the sick, burying the dead, or providing food and clothing for the needy. I have had the good fortune to have been personally involved in two communities in which the practice of *ḥesed* was of central importance. In one, that of the late Bostoner Rebbe (Rabbi Levi I. Horowitz) in Brookline, Massachusetts, the practice of hospitality (*hakhnasat or'ḥim*), of inviting Shabbat guests to one's home week in and week out, encouraged and often organized by the community, was a fact of everyday life. Another community, a Shabbat *minyan* in Jerusalem, exemplified dedication to the ongoing care of seriously ill members of the congregation. Whenever a person took sick, a group of people would gathered in his or her home every Shabbat afternoon, to visit, to talk with him or her, to study Torah, and to pray.

Even such inner psychological and spiritual processes as *t'shuvah* (repentance) and *kapparah* (atonement), which lie at the heart of the High Holy Days, have strong collective or communal elements. Yom Kippur is celebrated in community, in mass confession and prayer for forgiveness, all of which are phrased in the plural. We also recall the ancient ceremony of the *se'ir ha-mishtalei·aḥ*, the "scape goat" sent into the wilderness, which served as an instrument of collective atonement, without any specific individual acts of *t'shuvah*.

On the other hand, there is great importance attached to the individual in Jewish tradition. An important passage in the Mishnah describes the warning delivered to witnesses in a criminal case, stressing the value of the individual life:

> How does one chasten the witnesses in capital cases [so as not to impose the death penalty too lightly]? One says: ... Therefore the first human being was created alone, to teach you that whoever destroys a single individual [from Israel] is considered by Scripture as if they had destroyed the entire world; and whoever sustains one soul [from Israel] is considered by Scripture as if they had sustained the entire world.
>
> An additional reason [that humanity was created with a single person] is for the sake of peace among people, so that a person will not say to another: "My father was greater than your father." And so that the heretics not say: "There are many dominions in heaven." And to teach the greatness of the blessed Holy One: for a human being makes several coins with one seal, and all of them are similar to one another; but the King of Kings, the blessed Holy One, makes every person in the seal of the first Adam, and yet not one of them is similar to any other one. Therefore each person must say: "For me the world was created."[13]

Aviva Zornberg, in her book, *Genesis: The Beginning of Desire*,[14] notes that the human being is the only creature who lives in the tension of a dual nature—both horizontal and vertical. She sees humankind's standing erect as symbolizing its domination, related to its individuation, in contrast to "the swarm"—the "horizontal spread" of the other creatures who lack this consciousness, and who are driven solely by the instinct to proliferate, to "swarm"—that is, the automatic, instinctual drive for biological life.

Underlying the importance of the individual is the concept that the consciousness, the intellect, is located in the individual mind, which is the seat of the religious awareness of the individual. Hence, such philosophical views as that of Maimonides, who sees the ultimate goal of the religious life as knowledge of God,[15] perceive the individual as central. The same holds true, in a different way, for mystical schools; while they have very different cognitive contents, they are also ultimately concerned with the function of soul/spiritual consciousness.

Conclusion

The above is a very brief presentation of what can and should be said about this vital subject. My purpose here has been to describe the phenomenon of gradual decline of community. Unfortunately, I do not have any concrete program for dealing with this problem, but simply wished to issue a call for awareness of the problem.[16]

I wish to conclude with two brief comments. First, it is important to cultivate the growth of local communities—in synagogues, in small neighborhoods and settlements, and in various types of voluntary organizations, including political and social activist groups. (It should be noted that my emphasis on religious community should not be taken as implying that the "solution" lies specifically in that direction; there is a great deal of room for non-religious people to organize rich community life around shared values of their own, whether political, social, cultural, or otherwise; I have simply written about what I know best.)

Secondly, community exists on the level of the macro as well as the micro. That is, beyond cultivating local, face-to-face communities, it is important for people to be aware that society is not some impersonal, cold, alienated entity, but rather that society as a whole may—and should—be transformed into something based upon rich human interaction among its members, and that it is important for the individual to identify in a positive way with society as a whole.

NOTES

[1] Cf. Bereishit Rabbah 42:8.

[2] Maurice Samuel, *The Gentleman and the Jew* (New York: Alfred A. Knopf, 1950).

[3] On the growth of individualism in American life, see Christopher Lasch, *The Culture of Narcissism: American Life in an Age of Diminishing Expectations* (New York: W. W. Norton & Co., 1978).

[4] Note the controversy in Israel's Knesset concerning the Good Samaritan Law (5758/1998), discussed by Yair Eldan in his paper, "'You Shall Not Stand Over the Blood of Your Neighbor' as a Basis for Understanding and Dialogue between Religionists and Secularists in the State of Israel" (Hebrew), in *Akdamot* 17 (2001), pp. 7–37.

[5] On individualism, see, inter alia: Christian Eugene Ehrhardt, "Individualism" and Rudolph Christoph Eucken, "Individuality," in *Encyclopaedia of Religion and Ethics*, ed. James Hastings (Edinburgh: T & T Clark; New York: Charles Scribner's Sons, 1914), vol. 7, pp. 218–225.

[6] Ferdinand Tönnies, *Gemeinschaft und Gesellschaft* (Leipzig: Fues's Verlag, 1887); published in English as *Community and Civil Society*, ed. Jose Harris; trans., Jose Harris and Margaret Hollis (Cambridge [U.K.] and New York: Cambridge University Press, 2001).

[7] On the communitarian movement, see: *The Essential Communitarian Reader*, ed. Amitai Etzioni (Lanham, Boulder, New York, and Oxford: Rowman & Littlefield, 1998) and *Habits of the Heart: Individualism and Commitment in American Life*, eds. Robert n. Bellah et al. (1985; rpt. Berkeley, Los Angeles, and London: University of California Press, 2008), and cf. also Robert Putnam's book mentioned in the following note.

[8] Robert D. Putnam, *Bowling Alone: The Collapse and Revival of American Community* (New York: Simon and Schuster, 2000).

[9] See Michael Lerner, *The Politics of Meaning* (Boston: Addison Wesley, 1996); and idem, *The Left Hand of God* (San Francisco: Harper, 2006).

[10] On community in Judaism, see Jacob Neusner, *Fellowship in Judaism: The First Century and Today* (London: Valentine, Mitchell, 1963) and Mark Zborowski and Elizabeth Herzog, *Life Is with People: The Culture of the Shtetl* (1952; rpt. New York: Schocken, 1995).

[11] The Hebrew is *torah, avodah,* and *g'milut ḥasadim*; see Pirkei Avot 1:2.

[12] B. Berakhot 26b.

[13] M. Sanhedrin 4:5.

[14] Philadelphia: Jewish Publication Society, 1995, pp. 10–13.

[15] See, e.g., M. T. Hilkhot Melakhim 12:4, Hilkhot Talmud Torah 1:12, Hilkhot Teshuvah 8:10, etc.

[16] But see, e.g., Ron Wolfson, *Relational Judaism: Using the Power of Relationships to Transform the Jewish Community* (New York: Jewish Lights, 2013).

Tikkun Olam: What's a Rabbi To Do?

Daniel Greyber

I know the world must be mended. I know I have a role to play. But when someone tells me, "The problem is clear! I know what I must do!" or, worse, "I know what you must do!"—I want to check my pockets to see if they've taken my wallet. I distrust those who claim that the world's problems are clear to all and easily fixed. It's a big world we live in. As a rabbi, the phrase *tikkun olam* seems to be all around me—on websites and blogs, in newspaper articles and mission statements—but it's found much more rarely in the Jewish texts that are the basis of whatever authority I might have as a rabbi. I feel like a curmudgeon, old before my time. I am forty-two years old and suspicious of *tikkun olam*.

Every discussion about *tikkun olam*, repairing the world, begins in the middle. One only repairs a world that is both broken and also capable of being redeemed. One only repairs a world with both a history one did not choose and also a future that one can choose. **People** are called to repair the world, but the second paragraph of the Aleinu prayer hopes that **God** will repair the world to make it worthy of divine sovereignty. *Tikkun olam* forces us to see the world as it is, and demands that we dream of a world that is yet to be. *Tikkun olam* is both impatient and irritable, hopeful and hardworking. Rabbi Bunim of Przysucha famously taught that we are told to carry two notes in our pocket: one that says, "The world was created for me" (M. Sanhedrin 4:5), and another that says, "I am but dust and ashes" (Genesis 18:27). *Tikkun olam* begins when my hands are already full, because I'm holding both notes, saying, "I know you're busy, but you have more work to do!" That is how I feel: already too busy and a bit frustrated because I know that there's more work to do.

Rabbis and Politics and Repairing the World

I got asked, again, just this week, to say something publicly about North Carolina politics. For me to speak out on the record would make most people in my congregation happy, and a minority of them unhappy. I could do it. Some of my colleagues in the rabbinate blog about gun control, sermonize about health care, and inspire synagogue communities that thrive on the fusing of social action and Judaism. Some in my own congregation yearn for me and our community to move in this direction, for me to involve myself in politics, because Judaism calls on us to repair the world. "You're our rabbi," someone said to me. "We're looking to you for guidance, inspiration." But I'm plagued by a nagging question: what qualifies *me* to preach about this? I read the same newspapers as everyone else. I do consider myself well read and I try to keep up with current events. But there are many people in my congregation who are considerably better versed in North Carolina (and other) politics than I am. Even if I possessed some sort of expertise in an area of public policy, I remain suspicious: the whole mixing of religion and politics is fraught with danger, for both politics and religion.

Religion can stifle political debate. I don't want a society in which politicians make decisions about issues affecting society by quoting Scripture. I love the Bible, but too often it is a conversation stopper. Someone quotes a verse—and then, what else is there to say? Too often the use of religious language stops, rather than engenders, the debate that I believe helps us to arrive at wisdom. My teacher, Rabbi Elliot Dorff, has written:

I believe in the Aristotelian model for attaining social wisdom—namely, that all views should be aired in the marketplace of ideas, with none given a priori authority…I would seek to determine America's commonalities in thought and values inductively, testing for agreement amid the diversity of traditions and attitudes brought to the table. This approach also parallels both the method and "the sound and fury" of each page of the Talmud, where multiple opinions must be heard and evaluated before a decision is made…[1]

In debating critical societal matters, religion *should* play a role—but I don't think it should be the trump card that it too often is.

I also worry about too much religion in politics because the understanding of morality found in the majority religion often tramples upon the religious freedom of minorities. In the spring of 2013, the North Carolina Senate passed a draft of a law (HB 695) which, in its own words, aims "to protect its citizens from the application of foreign law that would result in the violation of a fundamental constitutional right of a natural person"—but that very law contains within it provisions that threaten the Jewish community's constitutional right to practice Judaism with regard to abortion. Jewish legal sources oppose abortion in many cases, but the Jewish tradition does not believe that the life of the fetus is equal to the life of an already-born baby. Consequently, if the fetus threatens the life or health of the mother, according to Jewish tradition, the fetus *must* be aborted.[2] Reasonable people can and do disagree with Judaism's approach to abortion and its understanding of when life begins. Neither I nor the Jewish community seek to impose Judaism's beliefs upon the body politic, but Jews—and people in general—must be able to continue to practice our own understanding of what is right. Thomas Jefferson once wrote that the practice of morality is "necessary for the well-being of society."[3] He also wrote, "The interests of society require observation of those moral principles *only in which all religions agree.*"[4] Our society must be moral. There is widespread agreement on the immorality of murder and incest; secular law can rightfully forbid them. Not all religions agree about what is moral when it comes, for example, to abortion, as discussed above. Similar arguments might be made for issues such as gay marriage. Whereas for hundreds of years most religions in America considered gay marriage immoral, no such consensus exists today, as many religious leaders argue that gay marriage is a moral right provided for not only by the Constitution but by the Bible itself. In the absence of broad agreement, the understanding of any particular religion on issues such as abortion or gay marriage should not be a determining factor in how and when citizens can obtain a safe and legal abortion or be married in the eyes of American law.

I worry not only about what religion can do to politics, but also about what politics can do to religion. Politics is high-stakes, nasty warfare with strategies and tactics. Language is used to put people on one side or another of an issue. If I am pro-life, you must be anti-life. If I am pro-choice, you are anti-choice. The polarizing language and tactics of politics tears at the fabric of our society and makes more difficult the healing that religion, in its best form, seeks to bring into the world. By participating in the public arena, religion risks losing itself and embodying the very destructiveness of political discourse for which it can be a healing balm.

So I worry about what religion does to politics, and I worry about what politics can do to religion. And yet, I worry as well about what happens to both when they are kept too far apart. Our public discourse is impoverished without the values and insights of religion. Let me again quote from Rabbi Dorff, who writes:

> Jews have been badly burned when governments have enforced religious norms. In America, though, we do ourselves, religion, and the nation a disservice if we think that religion should have no role in shaping national policy. No religion should have

the power or right to determine national policy, because that all too easily leads to intolerance, oppression, and sometimes even bloodshed. On the other hand, if public discussion of important social issues is to reflect the nation as a whole and if it is to attain the richness and wisdom that only multiple parties with differing views can give it, each religion must enter the fray of public debate and contribute its own views.[5]

So while I don't want to live in a world where leaders make public policy decisions by quoting Scripture or by simply declaring themselves to be morally superior by virtue of their religious beliefs, I also don't want to live in a world where our society makes decisions absent religious traditions that contain wisdom refined by generations over thousands of years.

It is not only American discourse that might be impoverished without an articulation of Jewish values; Judaism itself is diminished if it fails to live in the public sphere. I do not believe in a Judaism that tries to build for itself a self-imposed ghetto, simply for the sake of Jewish continuity. Authentic Judaism must live and breathe in relationship with the world, nourished by the wisdom of science and philosophy and medicine, challenged to grow by the advent of the Internet and a world of individual choice and freedom, shining as "a light unto the nations" and speaking a voice of truth to a world in need of a moral beacon. Beyond the physical security offered by the Jewish homeland, perhaps the greatest gift of Zionism has been that it has forced the richness of Jewish thought out of the synagogue and study hall, and thrust it into wrenching debates about diplomacy and public policy. For two thousand years, Judaism had little to say about things such as how to balance a nation's moral imperative to accept refugees fleeing oppression with the need to provide for the economic welfare of that nation's own citizens. We had no country of our own, nor did we live in a place where it mattered what Jews thought, even if we were permitted to speak. Such is not the case today in Israel—or in America either, for that matter. The media and elected leaders pay attention to Jews and Jewish values. It is a blessing, not a curse, that rabbis, their congregations, and the Jewish community as a whole seek to formulate a Jewish voice in the public discourse and, at the same time, to navigate and maintain the blurred boundary between religion and politics.

I still feel like a curmudgeon. I still feel suspicious of *fixing the world*, but my own convictions lead me, however begrudgingly, to acknowledge the blessing of living in a time when Jewish values can and should influence the world. I may wonder to myself, "What training did I undergo, what message from on high did I receive, that qualifies me as a rabbi to condemn the state legislature?" Or, more broadly, "Who empowered me to *repair the world*?" But I also must wonder to myself, "Who am I, to ignore a world in need?" I must acknowledge that the world is constantly being remade not just by God, but by people—and, if that is the case, why should I bequeath to my children a world shaped by those in my generation who yell the loudest, rather than by those guided by the wisdom of the Jewish tradition that I so love and respect?

Doing Good, and Dangers to the Religious Self

Once one decides to take the plunge and become a "world repairer," is there any guidance from the Jewish tradition about how to go about doing it? My first instinct is to always remember that doing good is complicated business. "No Good Deed" is a musical number from the Broadway musical *Wicked*. Elphaba, the so-called "Wicked Witch of the West," looks back on all the good that she's tried to do and wonders, "One question haunts and hurts, too much, too much to mention: was I really seeking good, or just seeking attention?" When we set out to fix the world, are we just seeking attention? How can one tell the difference between serving God and serving ourselves?

A danger of *tikkun olam* is that it may run the risk of blurring the distinction between God and me.

Consider this text from the Talmud:

> Rabbi Ḥama son of Rabbi Ḥanina said: What is the meaning of the verse, "Follow the Eternal, your God" (Deuteronomy 13:5)? Is it possible for a human being to walk after God's presence? Has it not been taught: "The Eternal your God is a devouring fire" (Deuteronomy 4:24)? But [the meaning of the verse is that we are] to walk after the attributes of the blessed Holy One. Just as God clothes the naked, for it is written: "And the Eternal God made for Adam and for his wife coats of skin, and clothed them" (Genesis 3:21), so too you must also clothe the naked.[6]

God renews the work of creation, and we too renew the work of creation. God clothes the naked, and we too must clothe the naked. But God is a consuming fire; best be careful where one stands. The high priest entered the holy of holies on Yom Kippur and dared to do God's service, where one false move meant death. Now that the Temple is gone, we have no clear instructions about how to do all this. Who can be certain they are serving God? I am as suspicious of myself as I am of others who proclaim they know with certainty what it is that God wants. Certainty about God's will is arrogance; we make idols of our own knowledge. And yet arrogance, it seems, has a role to play in serving God—which is precisely what makes repairing the world such a dangerous business.

Quite inexplicably, the ashes of the red heifer purify the impure but contaminate the pure. In a commentary explaining the spiritual idea behind this strange *mitzvah* found in Numbers 19, the Baal Shem Tov says that even though the *mitzvah* of the red heifer seems obsolete without the Temple, the laws contain within them a hint of the role of arrogance[7] in the service of God. He teaches:

> When one behaves improperly and is far from God, one's
> repair (*tikkun*) begins through arrogance…for example, [one
> is motivated to do commandments by a desire] for self glory
> or [one acts solely] to obtain the world to come, which is a
> type of hidden arrogance, if one believes that it is fitting for
> God to reward good deeds and [that one he has indeed done]
> something for God. But in truth, what are we in comparison
> to the strength of the Creator? How can we receive a reward?
> But [without this illusion that is based in arrogance,] it is
> impossible to come to this [insight], and [without it] God
> forbid, one would remain "outside." So it is permitted to
> grab hold of arrogance and glory, and to do things not just
> for the Torah's sake, because "by way of not for the Torah's
> sake, one comes to act for the Torah's sake" (B. Pesaḥim
> 50b). But when doing things for the Torah's sake [and not
> for any supposed reward], one must be refined and free of
> any moment of arrogance, because if arrogance mixes in,
> God forbid, the service [of God] will be spoiled. Therefore,
> arrogance purifies the impure who are far from God, and
> makes impure the pure who are close to God, such that, God
> forbid, if a person felt arrogance [as part of one's service of
> God], it would become an abomination before God.[8]

For me to improve as a person, for me to move from being distant
from God to serving God, I must pass through the (illusory?) stage of
believing in my own power, the dangerous, idolatrous, self-centered
moment of saying, "I know God's will! I can serve God and my service
is important!" But for me to actually serve God, I must be free of any
sense of self-importance, of any confidence that I have indeed done
something important. I must make of my life an offering, without
any expectation that it is fitting or acceptable. To return God's light

to God I must become a vessel, empty of ego and arrogance. The moment I think I've achieved something is the moment when the achievement disappears because I think I have it. It slips through my fingers. I must retreat, becoming again distant from my Creator, and I must then ready myself for the whole process to begin anew.

Do Motivations Matter?

Whether we are arrogant in believing too strongly in our own ability to make a difference, or whether we are overly humble in believing too meekly in our ability to create change—when it comes to repairing the world, one can legitimately ask whether motivations should matter at all. The road to hell is, after all, paved with good intentions. In the opening scene of *Fiddler on the Roof*, a villager says to Naḥum the Beggar, "Here, Reb Naḥum, here's one kopeck." Nahum the beggar complains, "One kopeck? Last week you gave me two kopecks!" The villager answers, "I had a bad week," to which the beggar replies, "So? If you had a bad week, why should I suffer?" The scene raises an important question about trying to do good: does it matter to the poor person why one is doing the *mitzvah*?

The lowest level of giving on Maimonides' ladder of *tzedakah* is giving begrudgingly.[9] But just ask the family of a poor person if they'd rather receive a lot of money, given begrudgingly, or a little money, given cheerfully: they'll look at you like you're crazy. First, they need to eat.

Dan Pallota, an American entrepreneur, humanitarian activist, and author, is best known for founding multi-day charitable events such as AIDS Rides and Breast Cancer three-day walks. He is known as a pioneer for rethinking the way that nonprofits operate and raise money. In a March 2013 TED Talk, Pallotta argues that the whole way we approach charity limits the extent to which we can do good in combating large-scale social problems:

We don't like non-profits to use money to incentivize people to produce more in social services. We have a visceral reaction to the idea that anyone would make very much money helping other people. Interesting that we don't have a visceral reaction to the notion that people would make a lot of money not helping other people. You want to make $50 million selling violent video games to kids, go for it; we'll put you on the cover of *Wired* magazine; but you want to make half a million dollars trying to cure kids of malaria and you're considered a parasite yourself. And we think of this as our system of ethics! But what we don't say is that this system has a powerful side effect, which is: it gives a really stark, mutually exclusive choice—between doing very well for yourself and your family, or doing good for the world—to the brightest minds coming out of our best universities, and sends tens of thousands of people who could make a huge difference in the non-profit sector marching every year directly into the for-profit sector, because they are not willing to make that kind of life-long economic sacrifice.[10]

Does the fact that someone makes an annual salary of $500,000 while raising millions of dollars to help millions of people make that person less ethical than someone making $80,000 per year helping a few people? Even if we assume that the well-paid executive is ill-motivated—an unfair assumption—ask all the people being helped by the well-paid executive which they prefer. The answer should be obvious.

Pallotta argues that our puritanical need for people to benefit very little while helping others holds us back from doing a lot more good. Someone can do an awful lot of good while serving their own self-interest, and people with the best motivations may also wreak a lot of havoc. I once made an off-handed remark from the pulpit that if the United States decided to do so, we could grow enough food in the

State of California to put an end to poverty in much of the world. Someone raised their hand and pointed out that in doing so, we would wind up draining the Colorado River and ruining the entire Southwest region of the United States. Without entering into the finer points of water policy, the rebuke was a good reminder that well-intentioned actions are not, by definition, moral. Much havoc has been wreaked by those meaning well. Shouldn't goodness (and wickedness, as well) be measured by what we actually *do*, and not by *why* we do it?

The World Is a Big Place; Leave Room For God

In her book *Epilogue: A Memoir*, Anne Roiphe writes:

> I wake up at 2:45 in the morning...I listen to the sirens wail along the avenue. I pick up my *New Yorker* magazine. I want to read an article about the Sudan. But I am too tired. My head begins to throb. I cannot help those the Janjaweed would kill. I cannot make dictators desist and warlords retreat and land-grabbers grow modest in their needs. I am a widow who can grind her teeth in fury, who can write a letter to her president, e-mail a friend, or just wait for morning at the window, knowing that the blush of dawn will return over the East River when it is ready, good and ready and nothing I can do will rescue a child.[11]

"What good can one person do?" can sound like giving up too easily, or like an excuse to make ourselves feel better for doing nothing at all. It is also the exhaustion of a widow mourning her husband, who does not have the energy to lift herself from grief to fight evils a world away. Roiphe reminds me not to judge or condemn those who cannot rally to a particular cause at any given time. While one shouldn't spend one's life cocooned away from the world's suffering, there are times in life when we need to seek refuge, to help ourselves for a time—so that we can then emerge and be of help to others once again.

But it is also true that we should maintain a healthy humility regarding the role that we play in the unfolding human story. Abraham pleads on behalf of Sodom and Gomorrah, negotiating with God down to ten righteous people: "For the sake of ten, I will not destroy it" (Genesis 18:32). Abraham does what he can, but, in the end, there are not even ten righteous people in the city. Despite all of Abraham's efforts, Sodom and Gomorrah are destroyed.

I want to quote at length from an essay on *tikkun olam* written by Professor Moshe Benovitz, in which he questions the whole idea that God calls upon human beings to involve themselves in repairing the world:

God commands Moses: "Behold, I have given into your hand Sihon, king of Ḥeshbon, the Amorite, and his land; begin to possess it and challenge him to battle" (Deuteronomy 2:24). And what does Moses do? "I sent messengers out of the wilderness of Kedemot unto Sihon king of Ḥeshbon with words of peace, saying: 'Let me pass through your land; I will go along by the highway, turning neither to the right nor to the left" (2:26–27). Moses deliberately violates God's explicit command: he is ordered to provoke battle with Sihon, but instead he sends emissaries on a mission of peace. And God ignores him, arranging things exactly as He had planned originally, without Moses' help: "But Sihon king of Ḥeshbon would not let us pass, for the Eternal your God hardened his spirit, and made his heart obstinate, that he might deliver him into your hand this very day. And the Eternal said unto me: 'Behold, I have begun to deliver up Sihon and his land before you; begin to possess his land.' Then Sihon came out against us, he and all his people, to battle at Yaḥatz. And the Eternal our God delivered him up before us, and we smote him, and his sons, and all his people" (2:30–32).

When Moses smote the rock accidentally instead of speaking to it, God was furious, and decreed that Moses' lifelong dream, to enter the Promised Land, be snatched from him a moment before it was to become a reality. This is the gravest punishment that could possibly be inflicted on a person who devoted his entire life to one goal. Yet here, when Moses deliberately turns his back on God's explicit command, refusing to do his part in establishing international boundaries in accordance with the divine plan, God ignores him, and carries out his plan without Moses' cooperation. God deprives Siḥon of his free will and hardens Siḥon's heart, in order to fix the borders of nations as He pleases.

That is to say: the role that God allots us in *tikkun olam* is not all that significant. Right- and left-wing politics are much ado in the hearts of men and women, but the counsel of the Lord will stand forever, regardless of people's best efforts. To paraphrase Lekha Dodi: "Break out to the right or to the left, but worship Adonai." Note that our prayer in [the second paragraph of the Aleinu] is not "And so we hope to repair the world with the sovereignty of the Almighty," but "And so we hope for you, Adonai our God, to speedily see Your glorious power remove idolatry from the face of the earth and utterly destroy false gods, in order to repair the world with the sovereignty of the Almighty." We don't hope to change God's world. We hope that God will change His world.[12]

What if Benovitz is right? What if Jewish tradition looks to God, not to us, to repair the world? What, then, are human beings called upon to do? Benovitz continues: "There is another world. There is a whole world 'in here,' within each of us, and repairing that world is our responsibility. Moses was not punished when he veered left, in accordance with his conscience, after God told him to turn right, but he was punished severely when he lost his temper with the Israelites and smote the rock."[13] It is not repair of the world that is our task, says Benovitz, but rather repair of the individual soul—and that task is hard enough.

Yet there is a certain irony in Benovitz's essay. A scholar at Machon Schechter in Jerusalem, Benovitz wrote his essay in modern Jerusalem, a city that was reunited in 1967 and that is secure today because Jews stopped leaving their fate up to God. The Zionists who founded the modern Jewish State rejected the idea that changing the course of Jewish history should be left to God; they decided to break with thousands of years of Jewish history and stop waiting for God to redeem the Jewish people, and instead took action to redeem the world for themselves. They stopped praying and waiting for a Messiah. They engaged in politics and international diplomacy; they established newspapers for culture; they raised money, worked the land, raised an army, and built a country. Religious Zionists now claim that it was God who strengthened the hand of the secular Zionists who fought and founded modern Israel. From a spiritual perspective, I find the claim that God continues to act in history compelling, but intellectually I must recognize (1) that I possess no certainty that God mysteriously helped found the State, and (2) that it was largely secular, not religious, Zionists who founded the modern State of Israel. Was God's hand at work? Was it human effort alone that created the (relatively) safe and prosperous city of Jerusalem, from which Benovitz could pen his essay? Where, exactly, divine and human effort overlap is, again, unclear. Again, the boundary is a tricky one—especially in modern Israel, where zealots of different political stripes each cling to their own vision of what a "repaired world" should look like, and who should do the repairing.

Finding One's Place in (Repairing) the World

Before I became a rabbi, I once sat with my father in his living room. He looked at me and said, "Daniel, you should run for office. You could be a senator." As I smiled, he said with greater urgency, "I can tell you're thinking, 'That's what every father believes about his son'"—which was, indeed, exactly what I *was* thinking—"but you really can do it. The country needs people like you to be involved." I listened dutifully and flew home. I have no plans to run for office… but that is not to say I haven't thought about it.

I met the President of the United States a few years ago. I drove from North Carolina to Washington D.C., gathered with a group of Conservative rabbis in the office of a local law firm, made the short walk to the White House, went through security, walked into the West Wing, sat at the end of a table in the Roosevelt Room, and, at approximately 2:20 p.m., shook the President's hand as he made his way around the room greeting each person. What I remember most about the experience was thinking to myself, "Here is the flesh-and-blood person who is making decisions that will affect the fate of the world. He is not so different than I. If I made a decision to move my life in that particular direction—to get the right degrees, to study, to run for office—the American democratic process makes it possible for me to become President. Wow!"

So why don't I try? Is it hubris and arrogance to believe in one's own potential? Shouldn't we all want to be President, so that we can change the world? But even if I committed myself and, in some alternative universe, were to actually become President, it seems that even presidents have a hard time changing the world. What with Congress and politics, natural disasters and those pesky other parts of the world that do not like to listen as much as we'd hope they would, even presidential power is no guarantee that one can change the world for the better. But world leaders *do* seem to have more means at their disposal than the rest of us. Why not, then, run for office? Why not try?

In his commentary on the Torah portion *Va-yak·hel*, Rabbi Mordecai Yosef Leiner of Izbica (1800–1854) writes about the construction of the tabernacle:

> If so much as a nail were missing, the Shekhinah would not rest in the mishkan. Therefore no one could in any way feel superior to another, even the one who made the ark [could not feel superior] to the one [who made] the tent-spikes of the courtyard, for, as it says in the Talmud, "What does it matter, both this and this serve to exalt the Most High?" (B. Sotah 40a)[14]

What is one to do? How does one know one's place in repairing the world? The key is not to try and do everything, or even the biggest thing. Rather, we must each know ourselves and find the part that we want to do—and that God needs us to do—to help God's presence be felt in the world.

It is a weekday morning in December as I finish these thoughts. The sun rises again this morning. Cars stream by. An hour ago, I helped my children get off to school in the early morning darkness. Now I type quietly before the day begins, straining to sew together a few words, to add my voice to a conversation that began long before me and will continue long after. The world is broken; this much I know. It can be redeemed; this too I believe. I am in the middle: between brokenness and redemption, between arrogance and humility, between my family and the world, between hunger to act and resignation. Should I be here, typing away at this screen? Not everyone must run for President. Not everyone must involve themselves in every cause, every issue. No person may feel superior to another because of having done this or that. But each person must do what he or she feels called to do by God; no more and no less. We must listen—to God, to ourselves, to the world—at each and every moment. We must constantly struggle to know ourselves as we really are, without self-deceit. We must constantly judge ourselves and allow ourselves to be judged. Perhaps the question of fixing the world returns to the question the poet Mary Oliver asked so beautifully so many years ago:

> Tell me, what is it you plan to do
> With your one wild and precious life?"[15]

NOTES

[1] Elliot Dorff, *To Do the Right and the Good: A Jewish Approach to Modern Social Ethics* (Philadelphia: Jewish Publication Society, 2004), p. 100.

[2] According to the Mishnah in Ohalot 7:6, "If a woman has [life-threatening] difficulty in childbirth, the embryo within her should be dismembered limb by limb, because her life takes precedence over its life. Once its head or its greater part has emerged, it may not be touched, for we do not set aside one life for another." See also David M. Feldman, "Abortion: The Jewish View" (1983), p. 803, at http://rabbinicalassembly.org/sites/default/files/public/halakhah/teshuvot/19861990/feldman_abortion.pdf.

[3] Cited by E. Raab in an untitled essay published in *American Jews and the Separatist Faith*, ed. David G. Dalin (Washington, DC: Ethics and Public Policy Center, 1993), p. 112.

[4] Ibid., 12:315; emphasis added.

[5] Dorff, *To Do the Right and the Good*, pp. 112–113.

[6] B. Sotah 14a.

[7] The word he uses is *hagbahut*, which might be translated as "accomplishment" or "a lifting up of oneself." It comes from the same root as *hagbah*, the word we use to describe the lifting up of the Torah after it is read.

[8] *Sefer Baal Shem Tov Ha-m'fo·ar* (Jerusalem: Nofet Tzufim, 1987), part. 2, p. 114.

[9] M.T. Hilkhot Matnot Aniyim, ch. 10.

[10] http://www.ted.com/talks/dan_pallotta_the_way_we_think_about_charity_is_dead_wrong.html.

[11] Anne Roiphe, *Epilogue: A Memoir* (New York: Harper, 2008), p. 202.

[12] http://www.schechter.edu/facultyForum.aspx?ID=44. Translations of biblical texts, as well as transliterations of Hebrew words, have been changed from the original in order to accord with the style of this volume.

[13] Ibid.

[14] *Living Waters: A Commentary on the Torah by Rabbi Mordechai Yosef of Isbitza*, trans. and ed. by Betsalel Philip Edwards (Northvale, NJ: Jason Aaronson, 2001), p. 175. "Isbitza" and "Izbica" are alternate spellings of the same village in Poland.

[15] Mary Oliver, "The Summer Day," in *New and Selected Poems, Volume One* (Boston: Beacon Press, 1992), p. 94.

Tikkun Olam as Messianism: Macrocosmic Restoration through Microcosmic Piety in Rav Kook

Aubrey L. Glazer

Throughout the ages, Jewish thinkers have claimed that the Jewish messianic impulse can redeem the world—but what is at stake in such a claim? If we take to heart the insights of Martin S. Cohen's essay in this volume—namely, that *tikkun olam* is about the challenge that confronts *halakhah*, when it at times needs to find a way to ignore its own strictures for the sake of remaining faithful to its own principles—then how far of a stretch is it for mystical Jewish thinking to transform this messianic impulse into a redemptive reality? The present essay will investigate territory only a few centuries removed from that of sixteenth-century Safed, the home of Rabbi Isaac Luria's radically baroque Kabbalah. Nonetheless, the shift into the thinking of Rav Kook,[1] the first Ashkenazic Chief Rabbi of Palestine in twentieth-century Jaffa and Jerusalem, is not as far removed from its Lurianic forerunners as it might at first seem to be. In this essay, I will present a close reading of several of Rav Kook's texts—mostly from his hidden diaries written between 1904 and 1921, known as the *Sh'monah K'vatzim* or *Eight Files*, which were censored and only recently republished.[2] My argument is that by the early twentieth century in Jerusalem, the concept of *tikkun olam* had become even more highly charged with, and inseparable from, its messianic impulse than it had been in earlier generations. Indeed, the concept of *tikkun olam*, as Rav Kook understood it, was a product of the discernible undercurrents of Lurianic messianic impulse which became exacerbated within the context of twentieth-century proto-Zionism, and which came to mark the birth pangs of the State of Israel.

My intention here is to write about *tikkun olam* as the concept finds expression in both the published and the (until-now) unpublished works of Rav Kook. In these texts, it carries a kind of redemptive messianism—a highly utopian and radically new vision of reality in the here and now—that the term almost never has when used by moderns today. I also believe that restoring some of what Rav Kook brought to the idea of *tikkun olam* will enhance the concept for moderns, by infusing it with greater philosophical depth and spiritual grandeur that is often lacking, when the phrase is used merely as a handy Jewish sound-bite about working for social justice outside the larger framework of a philosophy of history. What I find fascinating is how Rav Kook offers a countervailing and unifying approach in his thinking about *tikkun olam*, from a perspective of philosophical mysticism, and how unique this approach is, in its concern with transforming the outer world (or macrocosm) through one's inner world (or microcosm) as a messianic process.

Transforming such a messianic impulse into a reality that strives to work forward toward redemption remains deeply controversial for Judaism, yet Rav Kook's legacy makes it simply impossible to address *tikkun olam* without considering this intricate web of the messianic impulse and its realization, which are always in the offing. While Jewish mysticism may promulgate an esoteric understanding of the importance of the messianic impulse, the exoteric Jewish religion of the masses is, through its "neutralization"—whereby messianic terms were transformed and neutralized, ultimately leading to their allegorization—by and large fearful of (and thus protected from) any overt messianic impulse.[3] Scholem was suggesting that this esoteric messianic impulse courses through the veins of every epoch of Jewish history, and so the stabilizing and conservative elements of exoteric Jewish religion made sure to defang its bite. Even a cursory look at Jewish thinking through history—from the Qumran sect in Second

Temple times to the messianic prophecies of Sabbetai Tzvi,[5] and including both the messianic self-understanding of Rabbi Naḥman of Bratzlav[6] as well as even that of the most recent Lubavitcher *rebbe*, Menaḥem Mendel Schneerson[7]—confirms this tension, in the degree to which such a messianic impulse is allowed to seep into any redemptive reality whatsoever. Consider David Berger's characterization of the late Lubavitcher *rebbe*'s messianic posturing as something suggestive of a separate religion[8]—which is to say exactly what led the head of the Lithuanian Jewish community, the late Rabbi Eliezer Shach, to call Chabad a "cult" and sarcastically define it as the religion closest to Judaism.[9] Or consider Yehudah Amitai's contention that *Gush Emunim* (the settler group whose name means "Block of the Faithful"), its antithesis *Shalom Achshav* (the anti-settler group whose name means "Peace Now"), as well as the militarism of Ariel Sharon all constitute "false messianisms marked by a single-minded evasion of moral and political complexity."[10]

Throughout the course of this essay, I will explore the contours of this fascinating messianic impulse as it relates to the intricate web of ideas known as *tikkun olam* in the writings of Rav Kook—which, until now, have been highly censored. Central to my argument will be a reconsideration of Yehudah Mirsky's remarkable intellectual biography of Rav Kook, in which he claims that while "Rav Kook had no doubt that he was living in messianic times, looking inward, he did not see himself as the Messiah, but did understand his own expansive and healing consciousness as profoundly redemptive."[11] What Mirsky brings to the fore with such a claim is the complex web of messianic impulses that Rav Kook intertwined with the principle of *tikkun olam*. I intend to unpack a complex spectrum within philosophical mysticism that is concerned with the messianic process of transforming the outer macrocosm through the transformation of one's inner microcosm. We shall see how Rav Kook's daring adaptation of *tikkun olam* constitutes both a challenge to embrace spiritual activism and a call to balance a life of outreach in the macrocosm with contemplative spirituality in one's personal microcosm. We shall discover the radical implications of this kind of piety, which results in a rewriting of Judaism's self-understanding on the cusp of its next paradigm.

A brief biographical sketch of Rav Kook is in order. First serving as the rabbi of Zeimel and then of Bausk (in Lithuania and Latvia, respectively), eventually Rav Kook realized his love for Zion by immigrating to the Land of Israel in 1904, where he served as rabbi of Jaffa until 1914 and then accepted the position of Chief Rabbi of Jerusalem in late October of 1919. Then, not three years later, he was voted in as Chief Rabbi of Palestine for the Ashkenazim in February of 1921.[12] In those days, the chief rabbinate remained an office shared between Ashkenazic and Sephardic chief rabbis—an arrangement that was in part a hold-over from Ottoman times, when chief Jewish religious authority had been vested in the *ḥakham bashi* or "head sage."[13] Given that the colonial practice of the British was to rule as indirectly as possible, they were happy to continue the Ottoman system of granting these religious figures authority over personal status.[14]

In the first set of the secret diaries known as *Sh'monah K'vatzim*, composed between 1904 and 1921 and, after being intentionally suppressed by his inner circle of disciples, only eventually published by the family of the late Rabbi Eliyahu Shelomo Raanan, much is revealed about Rav Kook's messianic calling. (Note that his deeper messianic impulses in the other still-hidden files, composed between 1921 and 1935, remain the source of much speculation.[15]) In his love for Zion, Rav Kook was torn between what he saw as the redemptive possibilities of a "New Settlement" and the primarily ultra-Orthodox ways of the so-called "Old Settlement," which community embodied the most regressive elements of his own Eastern European Jewish religious upbringing. Israel provided the context, according to Rav Kook, for cultivating a new spiritual persona whose heart would incline toward transcending boundaries, whose spirit "is beyond all fixed logic…or any practical established *halakhah*, and [whose] heart aspires to ascend on high."[16] By reading journal entries from *Eight Files* like these, and speculating, with Rosenak, about what may be in the yet-to-be-revealed journals, it seems reasonable to posit that Rav Kook's spiritual pendulum swung along a range that encompassed "the normative along with the antinomian, responsibility towards the collective together with a yearning for individuality."[17]

Rav Kook was no ordinary rabbi. Even today, decades after his death, he remains a towering figure in "Israeli politics and Jewish spirituality."[18] As a mystic, halakhic decisor, poet, and activist, Rav Kook transcends boundaries and defies categorization; yet it is his messianic impulse that has likely left its strongest trace, and has led to the greatest reductive misreading of his teachings by his disciples.[19] Redemption, for Rav Kook, was not an externalized person or event from *without*; rather, it was a deeply dialectical process from *within*: "It was about processes originating in God's attempts, through human action, to reconcile His eternity with the world He created."[20] Notwithstanding the deeply personal, inward-turning nature of this process of redemption, Mirsky notes that "central to [Rav Kook's] thought-world was messianism, an apocalyptic energy field that held in place the conflicting elements of his time. He saw in secular Zionists and socialists the unwitting heralds of the Messiah."[21] That messianic impulse was made manifest in more than merely Rav Kook's writings—it also informed his activist piety that embodied *tikkun olam*, as "he spent much of his time visiting the sick, counseling the distressed…and tending to the poor. He regularly gave away his household possessions, and signed as guarantor for pauper's loans until his family convinced the local loan society to stop honoring his signature."[22] For Rav Kook, redeeming reality from its brokenness was the equivalent of redeeming hidden sparks nascent within all realms, including (most controversially) the secular and mundane ones.

To fully appreciate the unique insights in Rav Kook's re-reading of *tikkun olam*, we need to understand why he found the foundations of *tikkun olam* to be so deeply embedded in the mystical notion of "ultimate cosmic and meta cosmic repair and restoration." Developing his own version of Lurianic Kabbalah, Rav Kook accepts the cosmological vision of a cataclysmic divine withdrawal that sets in motion all of cosmic history, right up to the birth-pangs of Zionism. This process of a cosmic *tikkun* that heals the very fissures within the Godhead leads Rav Kook to a radical point of reflection: if the "holy is all that is near the great apotheosis of the *tikkun*" while the profane is "that which has not yet woven itself into the fabric of the final *tikkun*," then "could the seemingly profane be sacred, and the seemingly sacred, profane?" From this, it seems evident that for Rav Kook, only a "slim membrane stands between that radicalism and the coming of the Messiah."[22] The devotional work of the final *tikkun* becomes a perpetual contemplative practice for Rav Kook, as he continuously attempts to unify contradictions in thinking and to heal brokenness in reality that inescapably takes place within messianic time. What takes places in time cannot be extracted from Rav Kook's notion of being, as it necessarily encompasses his very own constitution of self.[26]

To appreciate the volatility and urgency of Rav Kook's messianic impulse, it is important to understand the abiding influence of the rabbinic notion to the effect that "in the time of the footsteps of the Messiah, impudence (*ḥutzpah*) will swell."[27] This rabbinic notion imagined a chaotic pre-messianic eschaton preceding the messianic era, a time in which everything, including morality, becomes topsy-turvy. Such messianic *chutzpah* is crucial in breaking through all the inevitable accretions of exilic existence. In the hasidic thought of Chabad so crucial to Rav Kook's spiritual formation, this is "referred to as *dillug*, skipping, vaulting over seemingly unbridgeable gaps—non-being and being, nothingness and existence, man and God—a skipping that lands on its feet because in the end it is all the same ground." In his inimitably dialectical way of thinking, Rav Kook fuses the rabbinic with the hasidic as a response to "the confusions of modernity."[29] A good part of that confusion, which Rav Kook witnessed first-hand while stranded in exile by the horrors of World War I in St. Gallen, Switzerland, lies with nationalism.[30]

The power of the burgeoning Jewish nationalism that marks Zionism is closely linked to the temptation of heresy for Rav Kook, insofar as most forms of base nationalism tend to be guided by universal ethics, which were in opposition to the specificity of Jewish ethics—and this struck him as morally problematic.[31] And indeed, each of Rav Kook's main disciples managed, tragically, to exacerbate this moral problematic intrinsic to nationalism. Rabbi Yaakov Moshe Charlap "saw around him a time of cosmic rebirth under the sign of Messiah ben Joseph, an era of purest darkness in which the ontologically vapid gentiles, facing spiritual evaporation, had to try to destroy Israel,"[32] with the result that the entire being of the people of Israel is essentialized to the height of holiness. Rabbi Tzvi Yehudah Kook's messianic impudence found expression in May 1967, in his rejection of the 1947 United Nations vote to partition Palestine, as he cried out to throngs of his *Merkaz Harav* students: "Where is our Hebron—are we forgetting it?! And our Jericho... our East Bank?! Where is each and every clod of earth? Every last bit, every four cubits of the Land of Israel? Can we forego even one millimeter of them? God forbid! Shaken in all my body, all wounded and in pieces, I couldn't, then, rejoice"[33]—with the result that the Land of Israel is essentialized to the height of holiness. By raising peoplehood and land to the level of untouchable holy of holies, Rav Kook's legacy was betrayed—losing, in the process, Rav Kook's vision of *tikkun olam* as a macrocosmic, universal vision of his microcosmic, personal piety.

Clearly, a very different tension characterized Rav Kook's own thinking about messianism than the version of that same tension that his students felt. But it was that very tension that led him to distinguish between the pre-Sinaitic Abrahamic/Noahide laws and the Torah of Moses revealed at Sinai. Whereas the former promulgated, in Rav Kook's mind, a kind of natural morality with an ethical goal of creaturely peace and kindness that were intuited and thus predated full revelation at Mount Sinai, the Torah of Moses presents "sacral *mizvot*...[as an] educational means towards the higher morality of the future, [while] they are of as much ethical import as are the simple kindnesses of the present."[34]

Notice how globalized Rav Kook's vision of redemption becomes in the following passage from *Eight Files*, in which Rav Kook interprets a rabbinic dictum regarding redemption; it seems that he imagines Israel–Diaspora relations to hold the very key to *tikkun olam*:

> The sanctity of nature emanates from the sanctity of the Land of Israel, so that [the notion that] the Shekhinah that descended into the Diaspora to accompany the Jews in exile [becomes] the connective tissue that ensures sanctity in opposition to nature. But any holiness that is opposed to nature always remains incomplete. Holiness needs to be swallowed up in its supernal crystallization in holiness—which is the very holiness of nature itself. This is the foundation of *tikkun olam* altogether and [will be] its resolution at the end of time. The holiness in the Diaspora will be connected to the holiness in the Land of Israel, so that in the future all synagogues and academies of Babylonia will become permanently ensconced in the Land of Israel.[35]

Clearly there is a dialectic being set up here within Rav Kook's cosmology between the macrocosm of Israel and the microcosm of the Diaspora. Each institution located therein, whether a place of Torah (such as an academy) or a place of prayer (such as a synagogue) constitutes an entire *olam*, an entire world—and at times, these may be in opposition with one another. Indeed, it is the opposition between these polarities of holiness that Rav Kook seeks to unify through his vision of *tikkun olam*, which is a process of unifying these oppositional energy fields. So it is in this sense that I want to press deeper into Mirsky's claim that "central to [Rav Kook's] thought-world was messianism, an apocalyptic energy field that held in place the conflicting elements of his time," while "he did not see himself as the Messiah, but did understand his own expansive and healing consciousness as profoundly redemptive."[37]

Following Rav Kook's own thought-world of messianism as a process animating and sustaining the collective world soul, rather than merely as potential embodied in a particular person, it becomes somewhat questionable to dismiss his messianic impulse in favor of a seemingly more neutralized redemptive consciousness. After all, redemptive consciousness is part and parcel of the messianic impulse that courses through all beings—from the being of the soul of Rav Kook and other righteous individuals (*tzaddikim*), to the being of the larger world-soul in which his particular soul was nestled. A revision of Mirsky's earlier claims regarding messianic neutralization will be necessary, if we are to take into account the following three facets of messianism in Rav Kook's thought:

1. Rav Kook's scathing, albeit idiosyncratic, critique of the Church for having stripped away the personal messianism of Jesus, thus causing "a crippling absence of spiritual élan vital" as well as leading to the Church's "refusal to believe that the material world could be redeemed on its own terms"[38];

2. The reading of Rav Kook's oeuvre by the self-described "Rav Kook Circle" in the early 1940s, as well as by his later disciples-cum-apostles, according to which it was possible to understand those "teachings as esoteric and entirely sacred, a corpus whose very study was itself part of the redemptive process";[39] and

3. Rav Kook's fear of being punished with afflictions for having revealed too much esoteric knowledge.[40]

With these considerations in mind, there is no escaping the conclusion that it was the primacy of the messianic impulse within Rav Kook's thought-world that influenced his expansive vision of *tikkun olam* as a force that could reach out to the external cosmos only insofar as it delved deeply into the internal piety of the mystic. Put simply, Rav Kook is stretching the term *tikkun olam* to encompass both the macrocosm "out there" *and* the microcosm within himself. Given the desire for the unification of both realms, the distinction between Messiah and world collapses—leaving only the flow of messianic consciousness free to bring redemption to the world.

For such a messianic impulse to be coursing through all of being necessitates quite a different view of the world and the cosmos, starting with the world-soul itself. While the notion of the world-soul really begins with Plotinus, in this regard Rav Kook followed more precisely in the spirit of the modern-style idealism that characterized German Romanticism at its most spiritual, envisioning "the natural course of the world flowing toward its ultimate rectification of *tikkun*…as being interwoven into the fabric of its deepest truth at all times."[41] German Romanticism, especially as expressed in the thinking of Hegel, had posited a developmental model of the *Weltgeist* ("the world spirit") that animates history, in which Judaism represented an early stage that needed to be superseded through the advent of Christianity. Already by 1912, Rav Kook had sought to focus Hegel's biased philosophy of history through the lens of the Jewish thinker Naḥman Krochmal (1785–1840). In so doing, he created a fourfold counter-argument to Hegel, namely:

1. that the "Absolute Spirit" arises precisely in the nation;

2. that the "Absolute Spirit" is realized through the vehicle of commanded morality or *mizvot*;

3. that the "Absolute Spirit" is already embodied within the Jewish people, and

4. that the "Absolute Spirit" is the fusion of body and soul as manifest in the nation, rather than in the state.[43]

The rectification of the world—"from both a particular and universal sense—is the completion of its messianic impulse illuminating it,"[44] from the moment of its being embedded at the incipience of creation. The Hegelian "Absolute Spirit" comes across in Rav Kook as *ru·aḥ*, *n'shamah*, or havayah, and that messianic impulse is not something that "just appears from thin air...but courses through all pathways of the opening heart."[45] And it is in this spirit that Rav Kook explicitly correlates the light of that messianic impulse to *tikkun olam*.[46]

In this next passage, notice how collective human evolution as a revelation of the "Absolute Spirit" in history—a theme that derives directly from Hegel's philosophy of history[47]—is correlated to the specificity of a Jewish approach to the "spirit" (*n'shamah*), through a directing of the heart known as "intentionality" (*kavvanah*):

Humanity desperately needs to evolve to the point where it recognizes the great value of an Intentionality and its Desire, of the hidden idealism within the depths of the soul. [These spiritual aspects] are always adorned in the bounty of new colors, which radiate some of the soul's power and her great splendor. All of the great ethical deeds in the world, both universal and particular, are merely a manifestation of constricted consciousness, miniature sparks from the great flame of an integral Intentionality. Intentionality is everything. The renaissance of Intentionality is the renaissance of the world....Intentionality stands out within the letters, and the names, for every letter and vowel within them are an abyss of both seas and tributaries, great Niles and the expansive hands of life, desire, aspiration and enlightenment, strength and power, unity and splendor. Intentionality is manifest in its grasp of the holy bodies, pure idealistic people, where the upright and good deeds and ethics are the feeling of their vitalization. What illumination becomes manifest in the world, through a vital and invigorated Intentionality!

The supernal secrecy comes and connects the soul, directed in its intentionality, with the eidetic source of life, with the ultimate root; and the limitless light, the light of the living God, progresses and expresses ambitions as manifest in every thought and action. Intentionality is what gives birth to action. *Tikkun olam* is encompassed and integrated within the supernal intentionality invested with divine vitality. *Tikkun olam* is integrated within every thought of peace and encompassed within the battle for what is just and right. *Tikkun olam* is integrated within the endurance of wisdom and the structure of what is good and pleasing, all of which is encompassed within it.

Serving as a communal rabbi of Jaffa early on during his residency in the Land of Israel, Rav Kook was exposed to the ebb and flow of such collective diversity. Regardless of the conflict—whether between the loosely traditional secular Zionist Jews of the "new" *yishuv* and the staunchly traditionalist Jews of the "old" *yishuv*, or between Jews and Arabs—Rav Kook was always extending himself and taking advantage of his position as Chief Rabbi to promote the pathways of peace and friendship. Given his messianic impulse, it is clear that this kind of communal activism was very much integral to his realization of *tikkun olam*.[49] The mystical vision undergirding Rav Kook's vigilance to extend himself beyond the expected halakhic legalism of the old *yishuv* (including matters regarding the status quo of religious devotion) clearly stems from a commitment to do his part as a spiritual agent charged with the task of *tikkun olam*: to restore that primordial harmony to a world now mired in chaos. Such devotion embodies "a kind of *tikkun olam*" just as much as does "a deeply spiritual recitation of the Shema and all the letters of its blessings,"[50] as it is embodied in a spiritual activism that extends the sanctuary walls into a prayer-life of conciliatory outreach within one's own community.[51] The radical implications of this kind of piety result in a rewriting of Judaism's self-understanding, whereby "the seeming sinners, were, in their commitment to the Jewish people, the land, and social justice, closer in themselves to the messianic restoration than were pious Jews."[52] Rav Kook's dedication was to seeing each of these opposing groups, as Mirsky astutely notes, eventually reach and heal each other, as part of the process of incremental messianic development embodied in tikkun olam.[53] This perspective then shines an entirely new light on the role of the messianic impulse within the collective setting of the community, as Rav Kook writes:

When asked about the direction of communal life, the answer cannot be found from within existence itself, unless we merit entering the aspiration of the great and exulted universe, which shimmers slightly through into the world of knowledge, and in all the expansiveness of the world of the spirit. It is here that we already come to the conclusion that it is impossible for all of human aspiration to be immersed only in such communal life alone. Moreover, if communal life stopped being weaned from its supernal nourishment above it, then its purpose would become deficient…And for this to be so, *tikkun ha-olam* [must] demand that we envision a deep redemption from the fonts of supernal redemption. So the eternal hope of Israel—for the illumination of the messianic impulse, for the divine light in the world—is the basis of the world and all its conditions. Even the communal formations with all their fragmentations lead to the necessity that what people are envisioning will be found. All their fountains will be immersed in the same supernal directives, and their visions will ascend and shower upon the communal visions that are holding up such substantial space in our vast universe at present.[54]

While nationalism is the spark that lights the fire of inspiration here for Rav Kook, it is clearly a call to envision the messianic impulse driving Zionism. One must give heed to the messianic impulse, as it is redeemed from exile and opens new pathways to liberation for the "the spiritual renaissance of the integral human being."[55] But one must *also* continually seek a more expansive consciousness that can accommodate the messianic impulse. Rav Kook describes this process in the following ornate passage:

> At this auspicious hour of national revival, each day there comes forth [development] from potentia to actua in different gradations while the entire world is rattling the cries of war, whose direction is concealed, except unto God who knows all outcomes—this is surely the setting up of *tikkun olam* under the sovereignty of Shaddai, through Israel's return to its stronghold, to be a proper and dignified nation whose ways shall be revealed throughout all paths of life, all living things; and all orders of nature from all national police forces to the spiritual seekers are signs of the spiritual renaissance that constitute the integrated human macrocosm (*ha-adam ha-k'lali*). Indeed, even the celestial throngs are moving in this direction of rectifying (*u-m'takknim*, from the same root as *tikkun*) the darkened site of the destroyed Temples, as well as liberating those [dark] forces that are imprisoning the Shekhinah in the depths of her exile—they are all moving forward and evolving. The heavy chains fettering the Messiah's legs are being shattered, falling away like chaff in the fire, like thin threads of flax passing between burning flames. Even though the national renaissance, and the signs of the spiritual renaissance of the integral human being all appear to be occurring from the external and embodied perspective, it is from these very crises that the spiritual [nature] and the light of the supernal soul in all its configurations is being

built. The supernal light of redemption is moving forward and revealing itself in the multiple golden waves. The time has come to embrace all creative thinkers, philosophers, interpreters, and anyone who is inspired by the divine spirit and longs for the presence of the Holy Spirit, to come and [self-]cleanse through the depth of thinking in the secrets of Torah, with free spirit, with discernment and blessing, [with] the great logic and the purifying service so exalted and uplifting. The exultation of this holiness is revealed through singular mystics. So all who envision some kind of a sign from within their spirit, even if it is faint, are actually perceiving a tiding of this holiness, a tiding that will add strength by listening to the secret supernal sounds, uplifting the limited and finite human consciousness to become more expansive within the supernal grove of holiness, where the spiritual light of hidden holiness and the wondrous aroma of the Messiah, herald of the redemptive moment that originates deep within the God of Jacob.[56]

***

By surveying even briefly the voluminous censored writings of a major twentieth-century mystic, we have the opportunity to appreciate the nuances of Rav Kook's innovative philosophical reading and mystical practice of *tikkun olam*. I have attempted to show just how the idea of *tikkun olam* was invested with a kind of redemptive messianism by Rav Kook, who brought a unique philosophical depth and spiritual grandeur to the concept—which it often lacks, when used merely as a handy Jewish sound-bite to working for social justice, outside the larger framework of a philosophy of history. Rav Kook offers a countervailing and unifying approach in his thinking about *tikkun olam*, within a perspective of philosophical mysticism, that is uniquely and simultaneously concerned with the messianic process of transforming the outer macrocosm through the transformation of one's inner microcosm. His unique adaptation of the concept of *tikkun olam* thus becomes a call to spiritual activism—one that extends at once beyond the walls of the synagogue and the house of study, into a contemplative life of conciliatory outreach with the world while also delving deeper into one's own spiritual life. The radical implications of this kind of piety result in a rewriting of Judaism's self-understanding. This kind of *tikkun olam* takes the shape of a form of redemption that is not an externalized person or event from without; rather it is a deeply dialectical process from within, albeit one with deep macrocosmic reverberations.

The spiritual healing that Rav Kook dedicated his life to bring to light could only have been possible as part of a deep, personally pious, and utterly inner *tikkun olam* that has the capacity to precede the restorative *tikkun* of the historical *olam*. The messianic impulse pulsating through this proto-Zionism that gave birth to the State of Israel allowed Rav Kook to paint his thoroughly modern canvas of redemption with a most vibrant and diverse palette of colors. Giving heed to this macrocosmic messianic impulse opens new pathways to liberation for the spiritual renaissance of the microcosmic, integral human being—and that is the ultimate purpose of *tikkun olam*.

NOTES

[1] Rabbi Abraham Isaac ben Shelomo Zalman Hakohen Kook was born in Griva (modern-day Latvia) in 1865 and he died in Jerusalem in 1935. Rav Kook is often referred to as the Rayah (the acronym of his name).

[2] Avraham Isaac Kook, *Sh'monah K'vatzim*, File 1 (Edition for Students of the Academy: Jerusalem, 5764 [2003–2004]). There is much speculation surrounding the censorship that was carried out regularly by Rav Kook's inner circle of disciples and editors, both David Cohen (known as the Nazir) as well as Rabbi Moshe Charlap. The primary reason for editorial censoring of the strong messianic impulse in Rav Kook's writings was his disciples' sense that the world was not yet ripe for such a message. For more on the specifics of editorial censorship, see Avinoam Rosenak, "Hidden Diaries and New Discoveries: The Life and Thought of Rabbi A. I. Kook," in *Shofar: An Interdisciplinary Journal of Jewish Studies* 25:3 (Spring 2007), pp. 111–147.

[3] The thrust of this "neutralization" revolves around how the esoteric impulse is sublimated for the sake of keeping exoteric religion together, in light of previous messianic movements that revealed too much esoteric truth. Cf. Gershom Scholem, *The Messianic Idea in Judaism and Other Essays on Jewish Spirituality* (New York: Schocken, 1971), pp. 176–202, esp. 201. For a revisionist approach to neutralization of messianism in Jewish mysticism, see Moshe Idel, *Messianic Mystics* (New Haven: Yale University Press, 1998).

[4] See Israel Knohl, *The Messiah Before Jesus: The Suffering Servant of the Dead Sea Scrolls* (Berkeley, CA: University of California Press, 2000).

[5] See Gershom Scholem, *Sabbatai Sevi: The Mystical Messiah*, 1626–1676 (Princeton, NJ: Princeton University Press, 1973).

[6] See Zvi Mark and Naftali Moses, *The Scroll of Secrets: The Hidden Messianic Vision of R. Nachman of Breslav* (Brighton, MA: Academic Studies Press, 2010).

[7] See Elliot R. Wolfson, Open Secret: *Postmessianic Messianism and the Mystical Revision of Menaḥem Mendel Schneerson* (New York: Columbia University Press, 2009).

[8] See David Berger's *The Rebbe, the Messiah, and the Scandal of Orthodox Indifference* (London: Littman Library of Jewish Civilization, 2001).

[9] Yeshayahu Ginsburg, "On Chabad," in *The Beacon: An Open Platform for the Orthodox Community* (April 22, 2013), available online at http://thebeaconmag.com/2013/04/opinions/on-chabad.

[10] Yehudah Mirsky, *Rav Kook: Mystic in a Time of Revolution* (New Haven: Yale University Press, 2013), p. 229.

[11] Mirsky, *Rav Kook: Mystic in a Time of Revolution*, p. 237.

[12] Ibid., p. 165.

[13] Ibid., p. 169.

[14] Ibid., p. 169.

[15] Still-hidden files remain suppressed by the inner circle of disciples connected with Mossad Harav Kook and they will eventually be published, presumably,

once the world is ready for the advent of the messianic age.

[16] Rav Kook, *Sh'monah K'vatzim*, File 1, §151, p. 59, quoted and translated in Rosenak, "Hidden Diaries and New Discoveries," p. 115, n. 24.

[17] Rosenak, "Hidden Diaries and New Discoveries," p. 120.

[18] For a wonderful intellectual biography of this fascinating figure, see most recently Yehudah Mirsky, *Rav Kook: Mystic in a Time of Revolution*, p. 1.

[19] Mirsky rightly points out the degree to which the ideological highlighting and editing of Rav Kook's writings by his son, Tzvi Yehudah, continued a process of "blunting the more radical theological leaps and harsher critiques of conventional religiosity, and subtly but unmistakably heightening the nationalist dimensions"; see Mirsky, *Rav Kook: Mystic in a Time of Revolution*, p. 224.

[20] Ibid., pp. 3 and 50.

[21] Ibid., p. 4.

[22] Ibid., p. 51.

[23] Ibid., p. 27.

[24] Ibid., p. 27.

[25] Ibid., pp. 40 and 49.

[26] The French Jewish thinker Emmanuel Levinas will come, by 1948, to a full-fledged critique of this link between being and time in his teacher Martin Heidegger's magnum opus of the same title (*Sein und Zeit*, 1927). However, that same proclivity for considering *exstasis* as a core tenet in mystical thinking, evident in Heidegger's ontology, is already sensed in Rav Kook. Further consideration of the *Zeitgeist* surrounding Kook and Heidegger is beyond the scope of this essay.

[27] M. Sotah 9:15. The original reads: *be'ik'vata di-m'shikha ḥutzpah yasgei.*

[28] Mirsky, *Rav Kook: Mystic in a Time of Revolution*, p. 98. This critical point made by Mirsky deserves much deeper reflection—namely, the correlation between Rav Kook's re-reading of the Chabad concept of *dillug* relative to his idiosyncratic notion of *tikkun olam* within messianic time, and Heidegger's notion of "skipping over." Cf. Martin Heidegger, *Being and Time: A Translation of Sein Und Zeit*, trans. Joan Stambaugh (Albany, NY: State University of New York Press, 1996), I: III: 62, p. 66.

[29] Yehudah Mirsky, *An Intellectual and Spiritual Biography of Rabbi Avraham Yitzhaq Ha-Cohen Kook from* 1865–1904 (Ph.D. dissertation; Harvard University, March 2007), pp. 379–386; compare with Mirsky, *Rav Kook: Mystic in a Time of Revolution*, pp. 59–61.

[30] Mirsky, *Rav Kook: Mystic in a Time of Revolution*, pp. 121–156.

[31] Mirsky, *An Intellectual and Spiritual Biography*, pp. 379–380.

[32] Mirsky, *Rav Kook: Mystic in a Time of Revolution*, p. 223. Rabbi Charlap (1882–1951) was the head of the *Merkaz Harav* yeshiva in Jerusalem, founded by Rav Kook in 1924.

[33] Ibid., p. 226.

[34] Idem., *An Intellectual and Spiritual Biography*, p. 380.

[35] Rav Kook, *Sh'monah K'vatzim*, File 2, §326, p. 342. (All translations in this

essay are my own work unless otherwise indicated.) The word "crystallization" here translates the Aramaic *tamtzita*. In the rabbinic mind, in the messianic era diaspora buildings themselves will be magically be relocated to the Land of Israel; see B. Megillah 29a: "It has been taught: Rabbi Eleazar Hakappar says: 'The synagogues and houses of learning in Babylon will in time to come be planted in the Land of Israel, as it says, *For as Tabor among the mountains and as Carmel by the sea came.* Now can we not draw an inference here *a fortiori*: seeing that Carmel and Tabor, which came only on a single occasion to learn the Torah, are implanted in the Land of Israel—how much more must this be the case with the synagogues and houses of learning, where the Torah is read and expounded!'" In the rabbinic mind, these two mountains (or their angelic guardians) came to Sinai at the time of the giving of the Law. For Rav Kook, however, the teachings and prayers that nourish these institutions will find inspiration in the Land of Israel and will therefore relocate in order to be closer to its source; this is akin to Aḥad Ha-am's model of the land of Israel as the central wheel, emanating and drawing inspiration from its spokes to the circumference back to its center.

[36] Mirsky, *Rav Kook: Mystic in a Time of Revolution*, p. 4.

[37] Ibid., p. 237.

[38] Ibid., pp. 128–129.

[39] Ibid., p. 221.

[40] Ibid., p. 216.

[41] Rav Kook, *Sh'monah K'vatzim*, File 5, §106, pp. 100–101. Plotinus (204–270 C.E.), the famous Neoplatonist philosopher, expounds on this idea in his work, *The Enneads*.

[42] Georg W. F. Hegel, *The Philosophy of History*, trans. J. Sibree (New York: Dover Publications, 1956), pp. 53, 244, and 335.

[43] Mirsky, *Rav Kook: Mystic in a Time of Revolution*, pp. 79–80.

[44] Rav Kook, *Sh'monah K'vatzim*, File 5, §235, p. 163.

[45] Ibid., File #5, §235, p. 164.

[46] Ibid., File # 5, §235, p. 165.

[47] Georg W. F Hegel, *The Philosophy of History*, pp. 53, 244, and 335.

[48] Rav Kook, *Sh'monah K'vatzim*, File #4, §61, p. 21.

[49] Mirsky, *Rav Kook: Mystic in a Time of Revolution*, pp. 83–86.

[50] For more on this call to the particular ritual expression of devotional piety, see Rav Kook, *Sh'monah K'vatzim*, File #6, §275, p. 278.

[51] For more on this universal call to pious living, cf. Rav Kook, *Sh'monah K'vatzim*, File #7, §43, pp. 312–313; and also File #7, §47, pp. 316–317.

[52] Rav Kook, *Sh'monah K'vatzim*, File #2, §21, as quoted and translated by Mirsky, *Rav Kook: Mystic in a Time of Revolution*, p. 98.

[53] Mirsky, *Rav Kook: Mystic in a Time of Revolution*, p. 98.

[54] Rav Kook, *Sh'monah K'vatzim*, File #7, §67, p. 327.

[55] Rav Kook, *Sh'monah K'vatzim*, File #8, §181, p. 454.

[56] Ibid.

Tikkun Olam as Text and Context: Interpreting the Jewish Mandate to Fix the World through Law, Liturgy, and Narrative

Adena K. Berkowitz[1]

The term *tikkun olam* is variously translated as repairing, healing, or improving the world, and it has become, in contemporary times, a shorthand phrase for social justice. Whether referenced by elected officials,[2] Jewish organizations,[3] or children's books and shows,[4] the phrase *tikkun olam* has become a sound-bite that describes the guiding philosophy that Jews (especially younger ones) invoke to find meaning in their Judaism—by reaching out to society as a whole and doing their share to improve communities.[5]

According to Dr. Lawrence Fine, the first use of the phrase *tikkun olam* in modern Jewish history in the United States was by Brandeis–Bardin Camp Institute founder, Dr. Shlomo Bardin, in the 1950s.[6] Bardin looked toward the phrase in the Aleinu prayer, *l'takkein olam b'malkhut Shaddai* ("when the world shall be perfected under the reign of the Almighty"), which in context suggests a utopian vision, and took it instead to refer to the responsibility of Jewish people to work toward a better world.[7] However, the question that arises is: do the biblical, rabbinic, and liturgical sources that discuss the concept of *tikkun olam* support the contemporary usage of the term, as well as the social justice movement associated with it, or is it being taken out of context?[8] And, if that is the case, are there any actual prooftexts within classical Jewish literature for what *tikkun olam* has come to mean: a Jewish imperative to be engaged with the wider world and seek to repair and improve it? If traditional sources that discuss *tikkun olam* cannot be read to imply the greater obligation to achieve social repair, then what sources *do* imply that sacred calling to complete God's creative work by improving, even perhaps trying to perfect, the world?

In rabbinic literature, the phrase *tikkun olam* is used to describe pragmatic legal decrees that promote the appropriate functioning of society.[9] In the Mishnah, the earliest extant compendium of the Oral Law, the phrase *mi-p'nei tikkun ha-olam* ("for the sake of the *tikkun* of the world") is used repeatedly to justify some adjustment to an existing law or practice.[10] Whether it is the rabbis seeking to resolve issues connected with divorce, payments to a widow under her marriage contract, or ransoming captives, the decisions of the rabbis appear grounded in the overall desire to maintain and improve social and legal policy within the Jewish community—specifically by addressing apparent flaws in the system that threaten to overturn the entire system, in order to ensure the ongoing stability of the system as a whole.[11] Yet this is not truly a universal imperative: even when discussing the case of purchasing ritual items from non-Jews, the point of the analysis has to do with the impact of such purchases within the Jewish world; the mishnaic analysis does not point in any way to a larger social good to be achieved outside the boundaries of the Jewish world, but is concerned only with the internal functioning of the Jewish community itself.[12]

Within mystical Jewish thought, in particular Lurianic Kabbalah,[13] the concept of *tikkun* refers to "repairs" that are performed on an individual level. When God contracted part of the Divine Self into vessels of light in order to create the world, these vessels could not contain God's essence and they shattered, scattering God's light. In order for the world to be restored to its holy perfect state, humanity must be engaged in cosmic repair. In the popular reconstruction of classic Lurianic mysticism, the idea then becomes for humankind to reunite the scattered shards of God's light, and thus to bring about the perfection of the world, by reparation—specifically, by engaging in prayer and fulfilling religious commandments. And it is this great effort that is labeled *tikkun*, the repair.[14]

But we can find traces of the idea that *tikkun* is a Jewish imperative to repair the world and seek the welfare of society in a far earlier text. The source for this is the Aleinu prayer:

It is our duty to praise the Ruler over all, to acclaim the greatness of the One who forms all creation. For God did not make us like the nations of other lands, and did not make us the same as other families of the earth. And neither did God place us in the same situations as others, nor make our destiny the same as anyone else's [for they prostrate themselves before nothingness and emptiness and pray to a god who cannot effect salvation, whereas[15]] we bend our knees, and bow down, and give thanks, before the Ruler, the Ruler of rulers, the Holy One, blessed be God—the One who spread out the heavens and made the foundations of the earth, and whose precious dwelling is in the heavens above and whose powerful Presence is in the highest heights. The Eternal is our God, there is none else. Our God is truth, and nothing else compares. As it is written in Your Torah: "And you shall know today, and take to heart, that the Eternal is the only God, in the heavens above and on earth below; there is no other" (Deuteronomy 4:39).

Therefore we put our hope in You, O Eternal One, our God, to soon see the glory of Your strength, to remove all idols from the earth, and to completely cut off all false gods; to repair the world, Your holy empire; and for all living flesh to call Your name, and for all the wicked of the earth to turn to You. May all the world's inhabitants recognize and know that to You every knee must bend and every tongue must swear loyalty. Before You, O Eternal One, our God, may all bow down, and give honor to Your precious name, and may all take upon themselves the yoke of Your rule. And may You reign over them soon and forever and always. Because all rule is Yours alone, and You will rule in honor forever and ever. As it is written in Your Torah: "The Eternal shall reign forever and ever" (Exodus 15:18). And it is said: "The Eternal will be Ruler over the whole earth; and on that day, God will be One and God's name will be One" (Zechariah 14:9).

If Manny Rivera was known as the "Great Closer" for the New York Yankees, then the Aleinu prayer can be considered the "great closer" in the framework of daily Jewish prayer. Aleinu originated as an introduction to the section of the High Holy Day Rosh Hashanah liturgy called Malkhuyot ("the Kingship Prayers"), where Jews declare God to be the Sovereign, but sometime in the Middle Ages it migrated to the daily prayer service and is now universally recited at the end of morning, afternoon, and evening services, as well as at the conclusion of certain other prayer services.[16] Where does it come from originally? Some traditional sources claim that it was authored by Joshua as he captured the city of Jericho.[17] Others, including such luminaries as Manasseh ben Israel (1604–1657), attribute the prayer to the men of the so-called Great Assembly of the Second Temple period;[18] still others posit Rav, the third-century rabbinic sage, as the author.[19] Some claim that there is a version of Aleinu going back even earlier to the time of Rabbi Akiva, who died decades before Rav was even born. This would then imply that Rav did not compose the prayer but merely included an already-extant Aleinu prayer in the Rosh Hashanah liturgy.[20]

Aleinu speaks of God in the third person and comes across more as a declaration of faith than as a prayer.[21] It speaks of a Jew's duty to worship and prostrate him or herself before God, acknowledging God as the Creator and Sovereign of the universe, praising God for allowing the Jewish people to serve God, and then expresses the hope that one day the whole world will recognize God and abandon idolatry.[22]

But Aleinu is a composite prayer and lays out a distinctly particularistic model in its first paragraph—which stands in sharp contrast to the universalistic theme of the second paragraph, where the words *l'takkein olam b'malkhut Shaddai* are found. While we do not find words that depict Jews as the chosen people picked to serve God as a role model to others, the first paragraph of Aleinu does describe the Jewish nation as distinct from other nations. In the words of the Aleinu prayer, it is the Jews alone who—unlike the other nations of the world—worship and prostrate themselves before God.

Because of the singular emphasis on Jewish particularism in the first paragraph of Aleinu, the placement of the *tikkun olam* reference in the second paragraph becomes that much more significant—especially when contrasted with the original text of the first paragraph, where a textual reference that was excised from European prayerbooks by Christian censors originally described non-Jews as those who "bow down to vanity and emptiness, and who pray to a god that cannot save."[23]

Despite the original connection of this phrase to condemnation of pagan idolatry, no different from countless analogous texts found in the prophetic writings[24] (or even in other liturgical texts composed prior to the rise of Christianity), it was nonetheless censored by church and governmental officials working under the impression that it had been written *specifically* to speak to the Christian claim that there was no possibility of salvation outside the church. Jewish apostates pointed out that the word for "emptiness" (*va-rik*) is numerologically equivalent to 312, which happens to also be the numerological equivalent of *yeshu*, the most well-known Hebrew version of Jesus' name.[25] While the phrase remained in Sephardic and Mizrachi prayerbooks published in the Muslim world (for example, in Yemen), it was removed from Ashkenazic prayerbooks published in the lands of Christendom, due to pressure from Christian censors in Europe. In some prayerbooks, however, a space was left to indicate that something was missing from the text.[26] In recent times, however, these words have reappeared in several contemporary prayerbooks, including the very popular Artscroll and Koren/Sacks *siddurim*.[27] Its return is justified as a simple effort to restore the text to the original version, and specifically not as a contemporary attack on Christianity.[28] Whether or not worshippers take it that way, of course, is a different question entirely.

Although the placement of this phrase was apparently not originally directed against Christians per se, the phrase clearly was read as an anti-Christian phrase during the Middle Ages.[29] But regardless of why it was placed in Aleinu in the first place, it provides a stark contrast when juxtaposed with the expansive theology expressed in the second paragraph. The first paragraph provides a very clear denunciation of the beliefs of the nations of the world, in contrast to Jewish views of one God—who is here referred to in the third person. However, the tone of the second paragraph is completely different: it takes on the form of a prayer in which one turns directly to God and prays that the entire world will reject idolatry and instead recognize and worship God as Jews do—that is, that all human beings will follow the example set by the people Israel and accept upon themselves the sovereignty of God.[30]

The popular interpretation of *l'akkein olam b'malkhut Shaddai* is "so that the world will be perfected under the sovereignty of God," and this implies that by accepting God's sovereignty and seeing ourselves as created in God's image, the *tikkun* that is to take place requires humanity to work to overcome social misery. This understanding of *tikkun olam* then provides an encompassing call to practice social justice as a religious imperative.

There are two problems with this interpretation, one from a linguistic perspective and the other more theological in nature. The first concerns recent scholarship, which has focused on whether translating the word *tikkun* as "repair" is itself reasonable. Versions of the prayerbook exist in which the Hebrew world *l'takkein* is spelled with the letter *kaf* instead of the more common *kof*, with the meaning "to establish" rather than "to fix" or "to repair."[31] (The word spelled in that way, for example, can be found in the prayerbooks of Rav Saadiah Gaon [c. 882–942], Maimonides [in the version of the liturgy included as an appendix to the Sefer Ha-ahavah section of his Mishneh Torah[32]], and in many prayer texts found in the Cairo Genizah.[33] In current Yemenite prayerbooks, it is spelled that way as well.[34]) As this second section of Aleinu is fundamentally a prayer for the establishment of God's kingdom, Mitchell First (who has documented these variant spellings) points out that the reading of *l'takkein* spelled with a *kaf* is a more appropriate fit: in this context, it makes sense to speak of "establishing" the world under God's sovereignty, rather than "repairing" it.[35] However, as First also points out, there are many other sources within the early European prayerbook tradition—such as *Maḥzor Vitry* and *Siddur Ḥasidei Ashkenaz*—where the word is indeed spelled the more familiar way, with the *kof*.[36]

But regardless of the spelling, there may be a second barrier in understanding Aleinu to be the source for the contemporary understanding of *tikkun olam*. The plain reading of the entire second paragraph doesn't outwardly seem to appeal to humanity to accomplish that goal, but rather implies that it is God alone who will bring this about…and presumably without any human input.[37]

If Aleinu then fails as the source of *tikkun olam* (in its contemporary usage), either for linguistic or theological reasons, can we find an alternate source for this idea, within the large corpus of rabbinic literature?

One approach has been to analyze the roots of *tikkun olam* through the prism of Jewish–gentile relations, in particular through the seven so-called Noachide laws, rules that have traditionally been understood to lay out moral and ethical standards for humanity as a whole.[38] (Noah is identified in the Torah at Genesis 6:9 as a righteous person, at least in his own generation, and so it follows logically that God would give these laws as a binding set of laws to the descendants of Noah—that is, humankind—as guidelines for living as righteous a life as their progenitor.) In the view of the rabbis, righteous people of all nations have a share in the world to come if they follow these precepts.[39] As enumerated in the Talmud, these seven laws are: the prohibitions of idolatry, blasphemy, murder, sexually immoral behavior, theft, and the ingestion of an animal's flesh while the animal remains alive, and also the requirement to set up courts designed to enforce laws. In the traditional Jewish conception, Jews are required to observe 613 commandments while gentiles are bound solely by these seven Noachide laws.[40]

In contemporary times, Rabbis J. David Bleich and Michael Broyde have examined whether the Noachide laws can serve as a basis for Jewish involvement in social justice and the welfare of general society.[41] They explain that the significance of the seven Noachide laws is that these laws provide the outline for a just and stable culture. As such, the desire to create a more just and stable world would be based on a form of *tikkun olam* arising out of these laws, as they provide the foundational examples for the correct functioning of secular society. According to Bleich, the Noachide code exists not just for the benefit of humanity (namely, by regulating human conduct and preventing anarchy), but also to fulfill a divine mission. Jewish thought is "bound by divinely imposed imperatives that oblige him [i.e., the Jew] to be concerned with the needs—and morals—of his fellow."[42] As a result, the Jewish people—themselves elected to serve God—are obligated to assure that God is served by all of God's creatures. If these rules provide the outline for joint interest in being engaged in the welfare and betterment of general society, what then are the requirements for Jews vis-à-vis their implementation? Is the mandate that Jews only provide non-Jews with detailed instructions as to the specific ways to obey the Noachide commandments? Or do Jews have a general obligation formally to compel, as best they can, gentile observance of Noachide law?[43] Both Bleich and Broyde conclude that while the seven Noachide laws are binding for non-Jews, there is no requirement for Jews to demand their acceptance by gentiles, but rather only a voluntary approach to encouraging them to fulfill these commandments.[44] This stands in contradistinction to the view of Maimonides, who argued that Moses commanded Jews by the word of God specifically to compel all people on earth to accept these commandments bequeathed to the descendants of Noah; Maimonides thus believed that Jews *are* required to compel gentiles to follow these laws.[45] In contemporary times, as Broyde points out, the Lubavitcher Rebbe, Rabbi Menachem Mendel Schneerson (1902–1994), taught that Jews *are* obligated to teach and persuade Noachides to observe these commandments.[46] Broyde cites many authorities, including Rabbi Moses Isserles (1520–1572, called the Rema), who disagree with Maimonides and who thus do *not* see any obligation to attempt to compel non-Jews to follow these rules. Rather, according to them, Jews can see themselves as being able to set an example as a form of providing *or la-goyim* ("light unto the nations") and to impart specific knowledge to non-Jews when requested.[47] Both Broyde and Bleich agree that while there is no actual legal requirement to enforce compliance, there are grounds for a meta-halakhic practice of encouraging non-Jews to observe these commandments.[48]

What we have to consider, however, is that the moral order described in the Noachide laws are not neutral principles connected only to social justice. While setting up courts or not stealing or murdering are moral values that all can embrace, the prohibition against blasphemy and not engaging in idolatry require a particular theological orientation of those non-Jews who accept these laws—and, thus, of society as a whole. As Gerald Blidstein explains, the realm of *tikkun olam* that may flow from the Noachide laws asks us to share with others what we see as a religious vision of the world that all of humanity can accept. It means, then, that universal concepts regarding social justice and ethics are wrapped up in acceptance of a monotheistic faith and worldview.[49]

How do we make the leap that calls upon Jews to embrace a mandate to be concerned with the welfare of general society, which does not necessarily endorse a religious position? Are we merely concerned with what was bequeathed to us at Sinai as the bearers of a unique covenant, or do we also see ourselves as part of the general picture of all humanity created in the image of God?[50] As Blidstein writes, there exists a "paradoxical possibility that Israel best fulfills whatever responsibility it has for the welfare of mankind by acting in devotion and probity before the Lord, rather than by busying itself in attempting to directly affect the spiritual or material state of the world...."[51] And he writes further that, in his opinion, "We can safely say that 'responsibility for the welfare of general society' is not the highest priority in our scheme of things, at least on the day-to-day level. The people Israel seems called upon primarily to keep its house in order and to care for its own, to serve God and to witness to Him. At the same time this exemplary life ought to have an overall incremental impact on mankind as a whole."[52]

One aspect of this "paradoxical possibility" is explored in a seminal essay of Rabbi Joseph B. Soloveitchik, "Confrontation."[53] Soloveitchik, the pre-eminent authority for the Modern Orthodox movement in the twentieth century, identifies a double confrontation that characterizes the Jewish role in the world. The Jewish people are called upon to maintain their own unique relationship with God but also, and at the same time, to take part in the universal confrontation of humanity with the cosmos. He makes the point that up until the modern era, the Jew's engagement with the modern world was not ideological, but rather born out of historical reality. Ironically, in this essay Soloveitchik calls upon Jews to be engaged in relationships with non-Jews regarding general civic issues, standing "shoulder to shoulder with mankind...for the welfare of all."[54] But when it comes to theological dialogue, Soloveitchik feels that *that* is part of the intimate relationship that each faith community has with God, which should neither be trespassed upon nor engaged with.[55] Yet the question we are left with is whether the theological realm can really be divorced from the political or civic realm.

Thus, on the one hand, Jews must see themselves as human beings sharing the destiny of Adam in his general encounter with nature—which means Jewish involvement in "every civic, scientific, and political enterprise" and as "human beings committed to the general welfare and progress of mankind," which leads to Jews being seen as useful, engaged citizens.[56] On the other hand, Jews are part of a unique covenantal community that cannot be shared with the world, and thus they need not set up for public scrutiny matters of personal issues of faith. Ironically, this appears to imply that it would be better if any Jewish involvement in the betterment of society *not* invoke any broad theological basis that could possibly lead to the kind of interfaith dialogue to which Soloveitchik was personally opposed.[57]

It would seem then that a more neutral way to invoke—and ground—the concept of *tikkun olam* would be as part of general moral impulses, by refashioning the parallel concept of laws undertaken "for the sake of preserving peace" (*mi-p'nei darkhei shalom*). Blidstein notes that Jews who live in a democratic society are obligated by mutuality of civic responsibility: "It is unfair, ugly, and eventually impossible," he writes, "to make claims on society without feeling part of it and making one's own contribution."[58] Nor, in his view, should we limit the application of this idea when we invoke laws enacted *mi-p'nei darkhei shalom*. While the spirit of *mi-p'nei darkhei shalom* has obvious pragmatic value,[59] it also expresses a "value of the spirit"[60] and could therefore be translated as "for the sake of harmonious relations." He takes it a step further and says that while there is a Jewish value to social justice,[61] we can rely on something beyond general notions of mutuality, respect, and moral impulse to develop a general notion of *ḥesed*, of righteous behavior, emphasized by the prophets and infused with the religious conviction that we are all God's children.[62] In other words, we should follow the admonition of the rabbis that we must visit non-Jews who are sick as seriously as we take the injunction to visit Jews who are ill. Similarly, we must provide for all who are poor and not just the Jewish poor. This view is reflected in a relevant passage in Maimonides: "The sages commanded us to visit the sick of the gentiles and to [provide the means for them to] bury their dead [just as we provide for the burial of] the dead of Israel, and to provide for their poor together with the poor of Israel, because of 'the ways of peace.' Behold, it is written, 'God is good to all, and His mercy is upon all of His creations,' and it is also written, "Its [the Torah's] ways are pleasant ways and all of its paths are peace.'"[63] Rabbi Jonathan Sacks further elaborates the connection of *darkhei shalom* to *ḥesed* by defining the former as "*ḥesed* universalized"—that is, applied to those who are not members of the Jewish faith.[64] He points to the phrase found in Genesis 2:18, "It is not good for man to be alone" (speaking literally about the need for Adam to have a soulmate), as the birth of the concept of *ḥesed*, which he then identifies as the redemption of solitude, the bridge we build across the ontological abyss between I and Thou.[65]

There may be another theme that can be connected to *darkhei shalom*, one in which Jewish engagement with the wider community is defined not only as *ḥesed* but in fact as a form of *kiddush ha-sheim*, the sanctification of God's name.[66] To illustrate this point, I would like to draw on an account from outside the Jewish world, one written by African–American Yale Law School Professor Stephen Carter, describing his experience of moving, as a pre-teen, together with his family, into an all-white neighborhood in Washington, D.C., in 1966:

> In the summer of 1966, my parents moved with their five children to a large house near the corner of 35th and Macomb Streets in Cleveland Park, a neighborhood in the middle of Northwest Washington, D.C., and, in those days, a lily-white enclave…My first impression was of block upon block of grim, forbidding old homes, each of which seemed to feature a massive dog and spoiled children in the uniforms

of various private schools. My two brothers and two sisters and I sat on the front steps, missing our playmates, as the movers carried in our furniture. Cars passed what was now our house, slowing for a look, as did people on foot. We waited for somebody to say hello, to welcome us. Nobody did.…I watched the strange new people passing us and wordlessly watching back, and I knew we were not welcome here. I knew we would not be liked here. I knew we would have no friends here. I knew we should not have moved here. I knew.…And all at once, a white woman arriving home from work at the house across the street from ours turned and smiled with obvious delight and waved and called out, "Welcome!" in a booming, confident voice I would come to love. She bustled into her house, only to emerge, minutes later, with a huge tray of cream cheese and jelly sandwiches, which she carried to our porch and offered around with her ready smile, simultaneously feeding and greeting the children of a family she had never met—and a black family at that—with nothing to gain for herself except perhaps the knowledge that she had done the right thing. We were strangers, black strangers, and she went out of her way to make us feel welcome. This woman's name was Sara Kestenbaum. Sara died much too soon, but she remains, in my experience, one of the great exemplars of all that is best about civility.[67]

Professor Carter recalls that Kestenbaum and her family were deeply religious Jews, and he saw her behavior arising not just from a loving and generous nature, but as a result of deeply held religious beliefs:

Civility creates not merely a negative duty not to do harm, but an affirmative duty to do good. In the Jewish tradition, this duty is captured in the requirement of *g'milut ḥasadim*—

the doing of acts of kindness—which is in turn derived from the understanding that human beings are made in the image of God. This understanding imposes a duty to do as God would do...civility itself may be seen as a part of *ḥesed*; it does indeed require kindness toward our fellow citizens, including the ones who are strangers, and even when it is hard.[68]

Whatever proofs we may or may not find for current social justice efforts having their roots in rabbinic and liturgical understandings of tikkun olam, in the final analysis it would seem that the related concepts of *ḥesed* and *g'milut ḥasadim* provide wider catchment for understanding *tikkun olam*.[69] In turn, the need to resort to a legally mandated model becomes less compelling once we realize we have a model of *ḥesed* in which our definition of *tikkun olam* is grounded. Holocaust survivor and Nobel laureate Elie Wiesel expressed this idea well, when he said that "Judaism integrates particularist aspirations with universal values, fervor with rigor, legend with law....A Jew must be sensitive to the pain of all human beings. A Jew cannot remain indifferent to human suffering, whether in other countries or in our own cities and towns. The mission of the Jewish people has never been to make the world more Jewish, but to make it more human."[70] Whether an ethical or legal mandate, *tikkun olam* is a Jewish necessity, and a vital part of our community and our DNA.

NOTES

[1] I would like to thank my son Menachem Leib Brenner (Yeshiva University, 2017) for his incisive comments and suggestions on earlier drafts of this essay. `
[2] See, for example, President Obama's speech to the AIPAC Policy Conference on March 4, 2012, available online at www.whitehouse.gov/the-press-office/2012/03/04/remarks-president-aipac-policy-conference: "The concept of *tikkun olam* that has enriched and guided my life…" Cf. also the remarks made by the President and by (then) House Majority Leader Eric Cantor at the Conference of Presidents of Major American Jewish Organizations gala on October 13 2013, in which Obama remarked, "together we have upheld the principle that each of us has the obligation to repair the world" and Cantor declared that "we as Jewish leaders must continue the sacred religious tradition of communal leadership and *tikkun olam.*" Both the President's remarks and Eric Cantor's are available online, at www.youtube/chGu-WiBjGE and www.youtube/6zO8vXBO714 respectively.
[3] See, for example, how the term is used by the following organizations on their websites: American Jewish World Service (www.ajws.org/what_we_do/advocacy), BBYO (formerly the B'nai B'rith Youth Organization, www.bbyo.org/about/mission, under "Core Values: Active Leadership"), and the United Synagogue Youth (www.usy.org/yourusy/sato/tikun_olam). Cf. also the remarks of Rabbi Rick Jacobs, president of the Union of Reform Judaism, "Opening Plenary Speech" (November 15, 2012), available online at www.urj.org; as well as the comments of Rabbi Shmuel Yanklowitz, founder of the social justice organization Uri L'Tzedek, in his "A Jewish Call for Social Justice," in *The Jewish Press* (July 29, 2009); and "The Role of the Divine in Social Change: Where is God in *Tikkun Olam?*" in *The Jewish Week* (December 14, 2011; available online at www.thejewishweek.com).
[4] See, for example, Vivian Newman, *Tikkun Olam Ted* (Minneapolis: Kar-Ben Publishing, 2012). And cf. also how the concept of *tikkun olam* was featured on the children's television show "Shalom Sesame" (see the "*tikkun olam* songs" at www.shalomsesame.org).
[5] A possible unintended definition of *tikkun olam* can be found in a 2012 interview with American music artist Bruce Springsteen: "We're repairmen, repairmen with a toolbox, if I repair a little of myself I'll repair a little of you, that's the job." See David Remnick's essay, "We Are Alive: Bruce Springsteen at Sixty-Two," in *The New Yorker* (July 30, 2012), pp. 38–57, available online atwww.newyorker.com/magazine/2012/07/30.
[6] Lawrence Fine, "Tikkun: A Lurianic Motif in Contemporary Jewish Thought," in *From Ancient Israel to Modern Judaism: Essays in Honor of Marvin Fox*, ed. Jacob Neusner, et al. (Atlanta: Scholars Press, 1989), vol. 4, p. 51.
[7] Fine, "Tikkun: A Lurianic Motif," p. 51.
[8] See, for example, the critique of Joel Alperson, "Abusing Tikkun Olam: Repairing the World Isn't Any One Political Stripe," in *The Jewish Daily*

Forward (March 23, 2012), available online at www.forward.com.

⁹ See Barry Freundel, *Why We Pray What We Pray: The Remarkable History of Jewish Prayer* (Jerusalem and New York: Urim Publications, 2010), p. 204.

¹⁰ M. Gittin 4:1–5:3, and cf. also 5:4–7.

¹¹ See Jill Jacobs, "A History of Tikkun Olam," in *Zeek* (June 2007), available online at www.zeek.net/706tohu.

¹² The *mishnah* that prohibits the purchase of scrolls, *t'fillin*, and *mezuzot* from gentiles for more than their fair market price is M. Gittin 4:6. As Gerald Blidstein points out, legislation relating to gentiles, which is discussed in M. Gittin 4:8–9, is justified differently: in these cases, the rationale is given as *mi-p'nei darkhei shalom*, "because of the ways of peace" (i.e., harmonious relations). See Gerald Blidstein, "*Tikkun Olam*," in *Tikkun Olam: Social Responsibility in Jewish Thought and Law*, eds. David Shatz, Chaim I. Waxman, and Nathan J. Diament (Northvale, NJ: Jason Aronson (1997), p. 27, n. 12, and also p. 56. (This usage suggests a pragmatic approach, as opposed to an idealistic one.) Blidstein does reference one source in aggadic literature, in *Midrash Ha-gadol* to Exodus 21:1 (ed. Mordechai Margulies [Jerusalem: Mossad Harav Kook, 1956]), p. 452, where the phrase conveys a universalistic meaning of repairing the world, describing human (political) activity after the great flood.

¹³ The adjective "Lurianic" references the kabbalistic system developed by Rabbi Isaac Luria (1543–1572) in sixteenth-century Safed.

¹⁴ See, for example, Fine, "Tikkun: A Lurianic Motif," pp. 38–39.

¹⁵ The passage in brackets is usually omitted from the ancient hymn, but has lately been re-introduced in some prayerbooks, as explained in the course of the essay.

¹⁶ Ismar Elbogen, *Jewish Liturgy: A Comprehensive History*, trans. Raymond P. Scheindlin (Philadelphia: Jewish Publication Society, 1993), p. 63. And cf. also the detailed commentary on Aleinu in the medieval *Maḥzor Vitry* §330, ed. Shimon Hurwitz (1923; rpt. Jerusalem: Yitzḥak Malkah, 5748 [1987–1988], pp. 369–370, or the comment of Rabbi Eliezer ben Yehudah of Worms in his *Sefer Rokei·aḥ Ha-gadol* §324 (Jerusalem, 5720 [1959–1960]), p. 221. Some surmise that Aleinu was to be said at the conclusion of services due to its emphasis on God's sovereignty and uniqueness and its stress on God's unity. See also Freundel, *Why We Pray What We Pray*, p. 227, n. 94, referencing Israel Ta-Shma, *Ha-t'fillah Ha-ashk'nazit Ha-k'dumah* (Jerusalem: Magnes Press, 2003), chap. 10. Ta-Shma sees the origin of Aleinu as a concluding prayer arising from the custom to recite special prayers called *ma·amadot* at the conclusion of services. Based on Joseph Heinemann's work (*Prayer in the Talmud: Forms and Patterns* [Berlin and New York: Walter De Gruyter, 1977], pp. 273–275), Ta-Shma viewed the ma·amadot service, which began during the time of the Second Temple and continued on even after its destruction, as including an early version of Aleinu. Freundel also points to Rabbi Eliezer of Worms as an influence for its placement at the end of services: noting Rabbi Eliezer's association with esoteric mystical teachings and the mystical understanding of Aleinu as a prayer offering angelic protection for

one's "journey" as one travels from the spiritual experience of prayer back into the physical universe, it would make sense to place it at the end of the service as a point of transition back into the real world (see Freundel, p. 227).

[17] In *Peirush Siddur Ha-t'fillah La-rokei·ah* §132, ed. Moshe Herschler (Jerusalem: Mekhon Harav Herschler, 5752 [1991–1992], p. 656–657), Rabbi Eliezer writes that when Joshua entered the Land of Israel and witnessed the religion of the Canaanites, "he began to lift his hands up toward heaven, fell on his knees in fear, and said aloud in a melody that gladdens the hearts, *aleinu l'shabbei·ah*." He also points out that the words *bin nun*, which comprise the patronymic of Joshua's name (*Yehoshua Bin Nun*, meaning "Joshua the son of Nun") is equal in the kind of Hebrew numerology called *g'matriya* to the number of words in one part of the Aleinu prayer. See also *Siddur Hasidei Ashkenaz*, ed. Moshe Herschler (Jerusalem, 5732 [1971–1972]), p. 126, and Rabbi Avraham Ben Azriel, *Sefer Arugat Ha-bosem* (thirteenth century), ed. Ephraim Urbach (1939; rpt. Jerusalem: Mekitzei Nirdamim, 1962), p. 98, and also *T'shuvot Ha-ge'onim Sha·arei T'shuvah* (ed. Livorno, 1869), §43.

[18] Manasseh ben Israel, *Vindiciae Judaeorum* (London, 1743), p. 2. See also Joseph Heinemann, *Prayer in the Talmud, Forms and Patterns*, trans. Richard S. Sarason (Berlin and New York: Walter DeGruyter, 1977), pp. 270–273. The Men of the Great Assembly lived in Israel from the time of the rebuilding of the Second Temple in the sixth century B.C.E. until the time of Alexander the Great. Since the Aleinu specifically mentions bowing and kneeling, which were practices connected to the Temple, but contains no mention of rebuilding the Temple, some connect it to this period when the Temple was still in existence. See Joseph H. Hertz, *The Authorized Daily Prayer Book with Commentary, Introductions, and Notes* (rev. American ed.; New York: Bloch Publishing, 1948), p. 208.

[19] Rav is the universally used sobriquet for Rabbi Abba bar Aybo (175–247 C.E.), one of the most important talmudic sages of his day. And cf. further Y. Avodah Zarah 1:2, as referenced by Abraham E. Millgram, Jewish Worship (Philadelphia: Jewish Publication Society, 1971), p. 455. Ruth Langer points out that although Rav lived in Babylonia, he had been a student of Rabbi Judah the Patriarch in the Land of Israel. And cf. also Langer's essay, "The Censorship of Aleinu in Ashkenaz and Its Aftermath," in *The Experience of Jewish Liturgy: Studies Dedicated to Menahem Schmelzer*, ed. Debra Reed Blank (Leiden and Boston: Brill, 2011), pp. 148–149. (Langer believes that the first and second paragraphs of Aleinu were written at the same time, unlike other scholars who think they were written at separate times.) And cf. too Mitchell First, "Aleinu: Obligation to Fix the World or the Text?" in *Hakirah* 11 (Spring 2011), pp.187–197.

[20] Freundel, *Why We Pray What We Pray*, p. 212.

[21] Reuven Hammer, *Entering the High Holidays* (Philadelphia: Jewish Publication Society, 1998), p. 53.

[22] Reuven Hammer, *Entering the High Holidays*, pp. 79–80.

[23] See, for example, the Artscroll prayer book *Siddur Kol Yaakov*/The Complete Artscroll Siddur (Brooklyn: Mesorah Publications, 1984), pp. 158–161, and the newer Koren prayer book, *The Koren Siddur*, ed. and trans. Jonathan Sacks (Jerusalem: Koren Publishers, 2009), pp. 180–183.

[24] In Isaiah 30:7 and Jeremiah 10:15 we see a similar theme where God, who made the heavens and the earth, is contrasted with the false gods who did not— and this is meant to contrast pagans, who worship nothingness, with Jews, who worship the true God, the only Creator. See also Isaiah 45:20, which describes the pagan nations living at that time who pray to a god that cannot save. This phrase is present in the Aleinu prayer, dating to the period of the Second Temple, but the "they" that is referenced is understood to be Hellenistic and pagan cults. See Heinemann, *Prayer in The Talmud*, pp. 270–273.

[25] Pesach Peter, as cited in Elbogen, *Jewish Liturgy*, p. 72, and cf. Millgram, *Jewish Worship*, pp. 455–456. Another coincidence is that the word *rik* is similar to the regular word for "sputum" in Hebrew (*rok*), and a custom developed among some to spit when saying this phrase. In 1703, the Prussian government issued a decree that not only required that this line be removed, but that also forbade spitting—with an added requirement that a government official be present at Jewish services to ensure compliance (Elbogen, p. 72). The act of spitting is believed to be the origin of the Yiddish expression *er kummt tzum oysspeien* ("he comes at the spitting"), which refers to someone who comes so late into the service that he has arrived at the conclusion of prayers, at the point when Aleinu is said (see Freundel, *Why We Pray What We Pray*, pp. 234–235). Freundel also references the thirteenth-century Rabbi Abraham Ben Azriel, who writes that the Hebrew words *la-hevel va-rik* has the numerical equivalence of the words "Jesus" and "Muhammed" (whom he calls Mahmat); cf. the *Sefer Arugat Ha-bosem*, ed. Ephraim Urbach (Jerusalem: Mekitzei Nirdamim, 5723 [1962–1963]), p. 468. Cf. also Freundel's citation of Yaakov Elbaum's essay "*Al Sh'nei Tikkunim Bi-t'fillat Aleinu*" in Tarbiz 42 (1973), p. 206, where Elbaum notes that many medieval Ashkenazic sources call Muhammed by the name "Mahmat," but cf. in this regard Freundel, p. 233, where this is disputed.

[26] See, for example prayerbooks from Venice 1545, Amsterdam 1699, and Dessau 1700, as cited in: Kenneth Berger's doctoral dissertation, *Issues and Developments in the Liturgy of Ashkenaz during the Sixteenth and Seventeenth Centuries* (New York: Jewish Theological Seminary, 2006), p. 225, n. 136.

[27] See *The Complete Artscroll Siddur*, pp. 158–160 and the Koren Prayer Book, pp.180–183.

[28] Ibid.

[29] In *The Vale of Tears*, a sixteenth-century martyrology, Rabbi Joseph Hakohen reports that the Jews of Blois, who were martyred by Crusaders in 1171, chanted the Aleinu on their way to their deaths. Some have suggested that introducing Aleinu into the daily service was an act of defiance against Christianity and its persecution and murder of Jews. Others view the recitation of Aleinu as the

Jews were led to their deaths as a legend. See, for example, Jacob Rader and Marcus Berger, *The Jew in the Medieval World* (New York: Atheneum, 1969), pp. 127–131.

[30] Heinemann, *Prayer in the Talmud*, pp. 270–273.

[31] Mitchell First, "Aleinu: Obligation to Fix the World or the Text?" in *Ḥakirah* 11 (Spring 2011), pp. 187–197. First credits Meir Bar Ilan for first pointing out the possibility of this spelling, referencing the latter's essay, "*M'korah shel T'fillat Aleinu L'shabbeiʿaḥ*," in *Daat* 43 (1999), p. 20, n. 72.

[32] The passage is glossed over in many printings of the Mishneh Torah, but I am citing the Yemenite text published online by the Mechon Mamre at www.mechon-mamre.org.

[33] First, "Aleinu," p. 189, n. 6, referencing *Siddur Rav Saadiah Gaon*, ed. Israel Davidson, Simchah Assaf, and Issachar Joel (Jerusalem: Mekitzei Nirdamim, 5723 [1962–1963]), p. 221; and p. 190, nn. 7 and 8, referencing sources in Maimonides and many texts found in the Cairo Genizah.

[34] Cf., e.g., the text in the *Ha-tikhlal Ha-m'voʿar, Nusaḥ Baladi* (B'nei Barak: Ḥayyim ben Naḥum Shalom, 5766 [2005–2006], part 1, p. 99. The expression *nusaḥ baladi* references the followers of Rabbi Yiḥye Tzaliḥ (1713–1805), called the Maharitz.

[35] First, "Aleinu," p. 187.

[36] Ibid., p. 191, nn. 15 and 16. *Maḥzor Vitry* was compiled in the twelfth century by Simḥah ben Shemuel of Vitry, a student of Rashi, the pre-eminent Bible commentator. This work contains many liturgical poems, responsa by Rashi, and laws connected with prayer and religious practices. It is the closest source to the Ashkenazic prayer practice of today. *Siddur Ḥasidei Ashkenaz* was written in the twelfth and thirteenth centuries by German pietists (called *Ḥasidei Ashkenaz*, literally "the pious ones of Germany").

[37] We see this from the opening words: "We therefore hope in *You*...to rid the world of idolatry..." The phrase *l'takkein olam* seems to flow naturally from the idea that God—and not humans—will be effecting the "repair."

[38] According to Genesis, Noah and his family were the only humans to survive the flood. God made a covenant with Noah and his descendants to never destroy the world and also laid out a blueprint of basic moral rules required of all humanity. For more on the idea of the Noachide laws and their relationship to the idea of *tikkun olam*, see the essay by Michael Broyde and Ira Bedzow elsewhere in this volume.

[39] B. Sanhedrin 105a.

[40] B. Sanhedrin 56a.

[41] J. David Bleich, "*Tikkun Olam*: Jewish Obligations to Non-Jewish Society," in *Tikkun Olam: Social Responsibility in Jewish Thought and Law*, pp. 61–102; and cf. Michael J. Broyde, "The Obligation of Jews to Seek Observance of Noahide Laws by Gentiles: A Theoretical Review," published in that same volume, pp. 103–143.

[42] Bleich, "*Tikkun Olam,*" p. 101.

[43] See the introduction to the volume, "Tikkun Olam," quoting Bleich, p. 7; and also Bleich, "*Tikkun Olam,*" p.77.

[44] Bleich, "*Tikkun Olam,*" p. 73, and Broyde, "The Obligation of Jews," p. 139. Bleich takes a middle-ground approach that Jews have to set an example and are obligated to respond to a request for specific information by non-Jews. Reference is made to the thirteenth-century compendium of Ashkenazic lore and practice called the *Sefer Ḥasidim,* in which it is noted that when one sees a Noachide sinning, one should correct that person if one feels able to do so. The text "proves" this with reference to God's readiness to send Jonah to Nineveh to bring non-Jews back to God's path.

[45] M.T. Hilkhot Melakhim U-milḥ'moteihem 8:10. Maimonides codified the requirement to compel gentile compliance with these laws as follows: "Our master Moses did not bequeath the Torah and [its] commandments except to Israel...And similarly, Moses commanded [us] by word of God to compel all people on earth to accept the commandments that were commanded to the descendants of Noah."

[46] Broyde, "The Obligation of Jews," p.136.

[47] Bleich, "*Tikkun Olam,*" p. 73.

[48] Bleich, "*Tikkun Olam,*" p. 73. Broyde, "The Obligation of Jews," p. 139.

[49] Blidstein, "*Tikkun Olam,*" p. 19.

[50] Ibid. Michael Broyde notes that what is permissible according to *halakhah,* Jewish law, is not necessarily the same as that which is morally laudable. In the world of contemporary politics, *tikkun olam* is often invoked by Jews for a number of different issues, such as gay marriage or pro-choice legislation. How should an observant Jew seek to influence public policy, if one's view of *tikkun olam* in the public sphere would mandate being against the prevailing political ethos? If there is no technical obligation to do so, may Jews decide not to enforce Noachide law—especially if doing so would hurt Jewish self-interest and create a backlash against Judaism? (See Broyde, "The Obligation of Jews," p. 143.) How that notion should be applied practically, of course, is a different matter entirely.

[51] Blidstein, "*Tikkun Olam,*" p. 25. For a contemporary view that reflects the perspective that all Jews, including the Orthodox-affiliated, need to engage in universal social justice, see Shmuly Yanklowitz, *Jewish Ethics & Social Justice: A Guide for the 21ˢᵗ Century* (Pompano Beach, FL: Derusha Publishing, 2012).

[52] Blidstein, "*Tikkun Olam,*" p. 55.

[53] Joseph B Soloveitchik, "Confrontation," in *Tradition* 6:2 (Spring–Summer 1964), pp. 5–29.

[54] Blidstein "*Tikkun Olam,*" p.19; Soloveitchik, "Confrontation", pp. 20–21.

[55] Soloveitchik, "Confrontation." pp.19–20.

[56] Blidstein, "*Tikkun Olam,*" quoting Soloveitchik in "Confrontation," p. 20.

[57] Soloveitchik, "Confrontation," pp. 23–24.

[58] Blidstein, "*Tikkun Olam,*" p.56.

[59] Often this term was understood as being based on broad self-interest, that of placating the gentiles with whom we live not to harm us or see us negatively, as opposed to doing it from a clear moral stance.

[60] Blidstein, "*Tikkun Olam*," p. 56.

[61] See, for example, Jacob J. Schacter, "Tikkun Olam: Defining the Jewish Obligation," in *Rav Hesed: Essays in Honor of Rabbi Dr. Haskel Lookstein*, ed. Rafael Medoff (Jersey City, NJ: Ktav, 2009), vol. 2, pp. 183–204.

[62] We can see it within religious terms as *k'vod ha-b'riyyot*, respect for the inherent dignity of every person.

[63] M.T. Hilkhot Melakhim U-milḥ'moteihem 10:12, based on B. Gittin 61a and referencing Psalm 145:9 and Proverbs 3:17.

[64] Jonathan Sacks, *To Heal a Fractured World: The Ethics of Responsibility* (New York: Schocken Books, 2009), p. 98.

[65] Ibid., p. 47.

[66] Blidstein, "*Tikkun Olam*," pp. 20–22.

[67] Stephen L. Carter, *Civility: Manners, Morals, and the Etiquette of Democracy* (New York: Harper Perennial, 1999), pp. 70–71.

[68] Ibid., p.71.

[69] For a different attempt to locate the concepts of social justice underlying the phrase *tikkun olam* in ancient Jewish sources, see the essay elsewhere in this volume by Elliot Dorff.

[70] Elie Wiesel, "What Being Jewish Means to Me," advertisement sponsored by the American Jewish Committee and published in the *New York Times* on September 29, 2000.

Pinḥas, the Quest for Purity, and the Dangers of *Tikkun Olam*

Geoffrey Claussen

The popular Jewish idea that human beings are obligated to "repair the world" (to engage in *tikkun olam*) is a valuable idea and, also, a dangerous idea. It can inspire much good but also, potentially, much evil. While visions of *tikkun olam* may reflect humility, thoughtfulness, and justice, they are often marked by arrogance, overzealousness, and injustice.

All of us who hope to improve the world need to guard against these sorts of vices. As we advance our visions for the repair of the world, we also need to tend to what the Jewish tradition has often called "repairing the soul" (*tikkun ha-nefesh*). It is good to be inspired by calls to repair the world—but only if we are careful to scrutinize our inclinations, realize the limits of our own visions, and listen to the criticism of others.

It is, unfortunately, generally easier to see the brokenness in the external world than the brokenness within one's own soul. Focusing oneself on the brokenness of one's own character and worldview requires that one admit one's weaknesses—a task that most of us human beings do our best to avoid. Addressing the brokenness of the world, on the other hand, offers attractive opportunities to serve others—and opportunities to feel the sense of one's righteousness that may accompany such service. When one is taking action in public, one may also be enticed by the promise of power and recognition. There is nothing inherently wrong with making use of power and being recognized for what one is doing. But efforts motivated by the desire for power and recognition—and so, too, efforts motivated by the desire to bring great benefits to others—need to be subjected to continual scrutiny.

Moreover, the metaphor of "repair" can be enticing in potentially problematic ways, insofar as *tikkun* may suggest perfection, transcendence, and purity. The word is often translated as "perfection," and the process of "repair" can be envisioned as a process that attempts to eliminate any flaw whatsoever. Indeed, many Jews throughout history have pinned their hopes on a world that would be perfectly repaired, unlike the world that we know—a world that would truly be perfect, harmonious, and unified in its devotion to God. At times, we have been guilty of imagining that we can articulate what that perfect world would look like—and, like most people imagining a perfect world, we have had trouble imagining that anyone other than us should have power within that world.

The alluring idea that human beings can envision perfection, be perfected, and perfect our societies or the cosmos can be catastrophic on many levels. Notions of "repairing the world" can be particularly dangerous when they are not tempered by a deep understanding of human limitations. Our efforts to "repair the self" require a similar sort of humility, as we should not think that that our souls have been—or can ever be—"perfected." Some of the most troubling programs for *tikkun olam* in Jewish literature and history have arisen from those who have been confident that they have perfected their own souls, that they can access perfect truth, and that they can therefore envision the perfection of the world—a perfection in which they stand at the center. One of the tasks incumbent upon the Jewish people is to oppose such programs, helping their authors to reflect more deeply on their ideas and their limitations.

Pinḥas: Zealotry as a Form of Repair

One figure in Jewish literature who plays a key role in many dangerous visions of repairing the world is Pinḥas, the priest praised in the Book of Numbers for his zeal in executing the Israelite tribal leader Zimri and Zimri's Midianite consort, Kozbi. According to the biblical account, while encamped at Shittim, Israelite men engage in sex and idolatry with local Moabite and Midianite women. God is incensed and, when Zimri appears with Kozbi before the whole Israelite community, Pinḥas takes matters into his own hands: "He left the assembly and, taking a spear in his hand, he followed the Israelite into the chamber and stabbed both of them, the Israelite and the woman, through the belly" (Numbers 25:7–8).[1] A plague brought by God against the people of Israel is ended, and God commends Pinḥas for his zealotry, rewarding him with a "covenant of peace" and the "covenant of priesthood for all time." Pinḥas then leads Israel as the "priest on the campaign" (Numbers 31:6) that seeks "to wreak the Eternal One's vengeance on Midian" (Numbers 31:3).[2] As one classical *midrash* explains, Pinḥas's presence in the war against Midian is crucial: it was he who had initiated the violence against the Midianites, and so he is now entitled to "complete the sacred task (*mitzvah*)."[3] The task is finally completed when the Israelites wreak God's vengeance by killing all Midianite men, boys, and non-virginal women (Numbers 31:17).

While some classical rabbinic texts caution against emulating Pinḥas's violent zealotry,[4] there are many sources that praise it. The Mishnah even codifies the opinion that Jews are authorized to emulate Pinḥas's model and attack Jewish men who engage in intercourse with non-Jewish women.[5] Kabbalistic sources go further in describing Pinḥas's soul as "perfect" and his violence as an act of "repair." In the Zohar, for example, Pinḥas is described as having a "perfect (*shalim*) existence before God."[6] He has, as the commentator Rabbi Yehudah Ashlag puts it, "repaired himself (*tikkein et atzmo*)."[7] Moreover, by killing Zimri and Kozbi, Pinḥas "repaired what had initially been distorted" within the Israelite community.[8] In the previous generation, Pinḥas's uncles Nadav and Avihu had sought to purify the camp, but inadvertently brought an "alien fire" (*eish zarah*) into it (Leviticus 10:1).[9] Pinḥas, on the other hand, with his perfected soul, successfully exterminates the "alien woman" (*ishah zarah*) who is now threatening Israel. He "repairs" his uncles' souls, and he repairs the cosmos.[10] There is, from this perspective, nothing positive to be learned from foreign nations like Midian or Moab, and there is certainly no interest in hearing how Midianites or Moabites might envision a repaired world. Instead, the narrative indicates that these foreign nations are entirely evil, and that the repair of the world depends on those who can see truth most clearly, and who use violence to keep all sources of evil at bay.[11]

Meir Kahane and the Purity of Jewish Ideas

Among the modern figures who drew on Pinḥas's example in constructing their own visions of "repairing the world" was the militant demagogue Rabbi Meir Kahane (1932–1990).[12] For Kahane, Pinḥas was a Jewish hero distinguished by his confidence, his willingness to use violence and to take revenge against enemies, and his zealous commitment to the Jews' uniqueness, purity, and superiority.

Kahane was fond of arguing that contemporary Jewish leaders should seek to be like Pinḥas at Shittim. They should act with force, he contended, rather than engaging in endless deliberations. According to one midrashic tradition,[13] Pinḥas rose up to act at precisely the moment when the elders of the Sanhedrin were discussing what to do in response to Zimri and Kozbi. From Kahane's perspective, the Sanhedrin failed when they chose to deliberate rather than taking action to immediately kill Zimri and Kozbi. Pinḥas, by standing up and choosing to act, rightfully "overthrew the Sanhedrin. They forfeited their authority, and he received it."[14]

Kahane urges his fellow Jews to learn from this example that "zealotry and vengeance are necessary against the wicked."[15] Especially when God's honor is threatened, one must rush in to punish those who are causing the threat—like Pinḥas did, by "burn[ing] with zealousness over the desecration of God's name."[16]   At times, an entire nation will threaten God's honor, as the Midianites did, and that whole nation should be targeted. The same is true of any nation, for Kahane, that "cries its hatred of the Jewish state"—like, in the contemporary world, "the Arabs" with their "refusal to bow to Jewish sovereignty." The zealotry of Pinḥas against the Midianites, for Kahane, should be a model for contemporary Jewish leaders in the state of Israel, who must act in "removing, burning out, the evil that is the Arab nation in our midst."[17]

Kahane acknowledges that zealotry is not always a positive trait— but, he argues, it certainly is a positive trait when one knows that one is acting correctly, as Pinḥas did:

> Zealotry and vengefulness are crucial attributes, but only if exercised for the sake of Heaven, as done by Pinḥas, Elijah, and others like them. If vengeful acts are motivated by sinful anger, however, that anger must be condemned. There is greatness in the very urge to zealotry and revenge, yet this must be tempered so as always to be for the Sake of Heaven. We must know when not to apply these traits.[18]

What gives Pinḥas his authority to kill rather than to listen to the Sanhedrin's deliberation, then, is his purity of motivation. As Kahane puts it elsewhere, there is a "repair" at work here: Pinḥas is able to kill others for the sake of heaven, "repairing" the error of his ancestor Levi who had been overly motivated by pride in his violence against the city of Shechem.[19]

Since Pinḥas has achieved a level of perfection where his motives cannot be doubted, there is then no room to criticize him. There is no need to imagine that he might have benefitted from listening to the discussions of the Sanhedrin. Indeed, from Kahane's perspective, the Book of Numbers makes it clear that Pinḥas is deserving of the highest praise. And Kahane is certain that the text "is perfect, for it emerged from the mouth of the Perfect G-d."[20] Kahane thus sees those who would question the justice of Pinḥas's actions as unbearably arrogant. Proper "zealotry," such as that of Pinḥas, is only questioned by people who are taking their cues from foreign cultures. Zealotry, Kahane writes, "has turned into a negative trait in the eyes of the nations and assimilationist devotees of the alien culture. Once more the contradiction arises between G-d's perfect Torah and the alien culture that has pervaded the sanctuary."[21] Questioning the Torah with ideas from foreign cultures, here, is a sin comparable to Zimri's sin—an act of compromising the purity of Torah with alien ideas. What is most appalling to Kahane is that those who learn from other nations, and often criticize the Torah's ideas as "immoral," sometimes claim that their ideas are in fact "Torah":

> There is no greater abomination than the brazen distortion of Judaism perpetrated by those who have cast off G-d's yoke. They try to weave a forbidden amalgam of Torah and alien culture and present it as holy garb, the mantle of Elijah, i.e., Pinḥas, when their deeds are really those of Zimri.[22]

Students of history might well respond to Kahane by pointing out that much of the written and oral Torah that Kahane views as perfect has, in fact, been shaped by a diverse array of foreign cultures. But Kahane is insistent that his Torah is perfect, that Jewish ideas as he understands them are distinct and superior to the ideas of other nations, and that the ideas of other nations are contaminating Israel's purity:

> Israel has been contaminated by the nations with loathsome falsehoods, such as the equality of the heathen non-Jew and the holy Jew, and the non-Jewish concept of "Democracy," which transforms evil and good, bitter and sweet, darkness

and light, to equals. These people have introduced leprosy into the holy camp! Their clothing must have a tear in it, they must go without a haircut and must cover their heads down to their lips. "Unclean! Unclean!" they must call out.[23]

And, for Kahane, Jews must respond to these threats with zeal: "Who shall rise up like Pinḥas and, spear in hand, execute zealous judgment against the alien culture and abominable concepts which have destroyed the uniqueness, holiness, and separateness of the chosen, supreme people?"[24]

As Kahane makes clear, he and his students are like Pinḥas: they are part of a pure remnant of Jews, uncorrupted by foreign wisdom, possessing an "authentic" Torah. Upon founding his yeshiva—"The Yeshiva of the Jewish Idea"—he thus spoke of his hopes that it would produce "the people of the true and authentic idea" who would bring authentic Torah "to the world." And this, he proclaimed, "is the great and awesome task of repairing the world (*l'takkein olam*) under God's reign."[25]

Tikkun olam, from Kahane's perspective, is thus only accomplished to the degree that Israel maintains its uniqueness, ensuring that there is "no nation like it" and thus that it is fit to partner with God ("Who has no one like Him"). Precisely to the degree that Israel joins God in maintaining its perfect and unique morality—in particular, its ideas about zealotry, vengeance, and chosenness that are often mocked by more liberally minded nations—it is able to "demonstrate the partnership between God and Israel in which these two unique entities are linked together to perfect the world (*l'takkein et ha-olam*) under G-d's reign."[26]

This "repair" also requires Jews to seek out political power and to create a state in which threatening, non-Jewish ideas cannot be heard. The State of Israel, for Kahane, has the potential to become such a state, but only if it builds up the "walls of separation" that the "foreign women" at Shittim had sought to breach.[27] In Kahane's view,

Only separation, only isolation, can protect the Chosen People from the poisonous influence of that [foreign] culture....G-d therefore established for His holy nation a holy land. It would be a vessel to house the Jewish people and their society, the Torah state G-d obligated them to create, and to separate them from the straying nations and their culture, which both errs and leads others astray. After all, whatever separates between Israel and the nations necessarily separates between holiness and the non-holy.[28]

Non-Jews, for Kahane, are poisonous, impure, and less than fully human: "Unlike Israel, who are called 'Adam' [the Hebrew word for "human"], the other nations are not called 'Adam' [and so they are therefore less than human]. In contrast to the holiness and purity of Israel, there is only impurity and unholiness among the nations; and how can holiness exist with impurity?"[29] Indeed, non-Jews are only permitted to live in the Land of Israel if they accept the superiority of Jews and accept their own "slave status."[30] They are, clearly, not permitted to influence the "perfect Torah state and society" that Jews are commanded to establish there.[31]

For Jews who imagine *tikkun olam* as leading to perfect clarity, homogeneity, and purity, one can imagine how this vision might be enticing. This is a path of *tikkun* that can transcend the ordinary messiness of political compromise, ambiguous texts, or dissenting opinions. Kahane can promise a sort of "repair" that might seem more complete and authentic than what more liberal modern Jewish thinkers have endorsed.

Kahane's rhetoric offers an extreme but illustrative example of how a vision of *tikkun olam* may be animated by a certainty about one's ability to understand perfection and an unwillingness to accept criticism from others. Kahane—like Pinḥas—is deeply convinced of his own righteousness. He writes off as impure (like Kozbi) those non-Jews who criticize him, and he writes off serious challenges from his fellow Jews as reflecting the "assimilationist" mindset of Zimri. Kahane sees himself as largely beyond criticism, as he sees himself as having internalized the virtues of humility, justice, and zealousness commended by God in Numbers 25. He sees himself like Pinḥas: humble (having submitted to God's will), just (ensuring that both Israel and the impure nations are given what they deserve), and appropriately zealous (knowing that it is appropriate to kill others "for the sake of heaven").

From the perspective of most other Jews, of course, Kahane appears in desperate need of *tikkun ha-nefesh*—the repair of his own soul. He lacks humility, as demonstrated by his self-righteousness and his inability to listen to perspectives other than his own; he lacks the qualities of justice that would recognize the fundamental equality of all human beings; and he lacks the qualities of moderation that would restrain his zealotry. Kahane's followers, however, have continued to praise Kahane for his faith in himself, his justice, and his zealotry. Their efforts to follow their teacher's vision have not always been successful, but have led to at least one successful mass murder: the killing of twenty-nine Muslim worshippers in Hebron in 1994 by Kahane's student Baruch Goldstein, directly answering his teacher's call to "repair the world" by "removing, burning out, the evil that is the Arab nation in our midst."[32]

Yitzchak Ginsburgh:
Repairing the Spirit, the State, and the World

Among the rabbis who publicly praised Goldstein's violence in Hebron, Rabbi Yitzchak Ginsburgh, a rabbi from the Chabad Lubavitch sect of hasidism, was perhaps the most prominent. A fellow traveler of Meir Kahane in many respects, Ginsburgh is a contemporary Israeli *rosh yeshiva* who shares Kahane's stress on Jewish superiority and the importance of vengeance. Like Kahane,

Ginsburgh also stresses the need to cultivate inner virtues such as humility, justice, and zealousness, and to act so as to effect change in the world. He stresses the importance of inner spiritual development somewhat more than Kahane, though, and his writing is more suffused with the language of "repair" (or, in his preferred translation, "rectification"), both when speaking about the inner life and about the external world. Ginsburgh's rhetoric regarding internal and external "rectification" can help us to see, further, how morally pernicious these concepts can be.

Like Kahane, Ginsburgh sees *tikkun olam* as a concept that should inspire human activism: "More than just accepting the world as it is, we are commanded in the Torah and implored by the sages and prophets to become partners with God in rectifying and elevating the world."[33] At the root of the task is the "the sincere probing of the heart and mind" and the repairing of the inner brokenness that one finds[34]—for "all physical rectification must be predicated by spiritual rectification."[35] The spiritual *tikkun* that is essential for *tikkun olam* includes rectifying "our emotional makeup"—specifically, emotions that correspond to the seven lower divine *s'firot*, which Ginsburgh understands as "love, fear, mercy, confidence, sincerity, devotion, and humility."[36] One must also develop intellectual clarity about the three ideas that Ginsburgh sees as essential truths for all human beings to understand (and which correspond to the three upper *s'firot*): that the Torah is completely authoritative; that all Jews must live in Israel, settling all of the land and building a kingdom guided by all of the Torah; and that Jews are superior to non-Jews.[37]

There is, here, a critique of those who would view *tikkun olam* in purely material terms, focusing on physically building the State of Israel while neglecting the spirit;[38] at the same time, there is a critique of a traditional hasidic posture that would focus on the inner life but neglect political activism.[39]

Pinḥas is one of the numerous figures who serves as an inspiration for Ginsburgh's vision. Like Kahane, Ginsburgh sees Pinḥas as a perfected individual, whose act of killing Zimri and Kozbi was solely for the sake of heaven. According to Ginsburgh, Pinḥas had no self-interest; as he tells the story, Pinḥas proved his moral excellence when he refused to take pride in his deed, despite the fame that he achieved among the people of Israel.[40] Pinḥas was a *tzaddik*—as Ginsburgh defines it, "someone who has fully overcome the evil inclination of his animal soul (and converted its potential into good)."[41]

Jonathan Garb has argued that, in Ginsburgh's thought, the *tzaddik* (in traditional hasidic parlance, "the rebbe") is a sort of embodiment of God—that is, someone who can intuit the truth directly and who does not generally need to seek the advice of others or seek out "halakhic backing or precedents to justify his actions."[42] In Ginsburgh's own words, the rebbe "is sure of himself, and has no need for precedents....More than anyone else, the 'rebbe' is able to recognize the exceptional needs of the generation."[43] As Garb points out, Ginsburgh's vision is grounded in traditional hasidic teachings regarding the centrality of the *tzaddik*, the perfected spiritual leader; but Ginsburgh is in fact advancing a "modern, anti-traditionalist" conception of authority, in which the accumulated tradition, with all of its ambiguities, can be replaced by the clear vision of a single charismatic leader.[44]

Pinḥas, for Ginsburgh, is an ideal Jewish leader of this sort. As Ginsburgh notes, one interpretive tradition teaches that Pinḥas "did not even ask Moses what the *halakhah* in such a case is." Rather, his "youthful vigor...burned within him," and he knew that in a place where God is dishonored, he could not "wait for someone else to do what is needed."[45] This was precisely what Ginsburgh admired about Baruch Goldstein's massacre of Muslim worshippers in Hebron: Goldstein understood that "the honor of heaven takes precedence over the honor to one's teacher"—such that, as Don Seeman has explained, Goldstein could ignore those rabbis who would criticize him, "the community of scholars who would tend to prohibit acts of zealotry."[46] He did not, needless to say, seek out the counsel of anyone who might have criticized him, just as Pinḥas did not seek to listen to the caution that members of the Sanhedrin might have offered him.

For Ginsburgh, developing the confidence to act in unconventional ways and developing the courage to risk condemnation, punishment, or death is a part of the "rectification" work that is essential for repairing the State of Israel and, ultimately, the world. Speaking of the centrality of Israel in the scheme of redemption in his book *Rectifying the State of Israel* (in Hebrew, *Tikkun Ha-Medinah*), Ginsburgh argues that "national rectification (*ha-tikkun ha-le'umi*) demands deviation from the 'rules of the game.' It demands a new, definitive source of authority, different from that recognized today, which must be honored and obeyed in building a rectified society."[47] Such authority lies in the clear words of the Torah and its authentic interpreters and, when one commits oneself to that truth, one should develop the courage to boldly implement the Torah's vision. "Boldness comes with a sense of direct, clear vision of the truth," and "clear recognition of truth empowers one to act without fear of unwarranted criticism."[48]

Ginsburgh is careful to note that he is not opposed to all criticism—one should have the humility to listen to "constructive criticism"—but that one must be "bold enough to stand up against those that mock him in his service of God. To be bold in the face of mockery is in fact the very first instruction of the Code of Jewish Law."[49] And a wise leader must allow for courageous individuals to fulfill this instruction, as did Moses in response to Pinḥas's outbreak against Zimri and Kozbi. Thus, according to one commentary on the story of Pinḥas published by Ginsburgh's students,

> True leadership is one that knows how to give a place of honor to the outbreaks of individuals. A leader who is terrified by any outbreak that is not "according to the rules" and immediately and categorically rejects it is not a true

leader. Such a leader believes that it is only the dry legal system that maintains the people, and does not realize that without the inner burning, the engine that drives the people forward will be lacking. A true leader can appreciate the positive impulse that drives people to action.[50]

Ginsburgh positions himself as a "true leader" of this sort—one who understands that Jews may sometimes need to act boldly, in unconventional ways, in order to bring about the repair of the world.

Ginsburgh's outline for what must be done to repair the world closely resembles that of Kahane. "Our first act of rectification must be to declare Jewish sovereignty over the entire Land of Israel."[51] At first, this means ruling over the whole West Bank of the Jordan and replacing the current secular State of Israel (and, of course, the Palestinian Authority) with a new Jewish "theocracy." "Within these borders," all Jews must do the work to "rectify, on the communal level, the seven emotions."[52] And "the Israeli government must undergo a process of spiritual metamorphosis" and "rectification" "in order to open its ears to the truth of the words of the Torah."[53] Establishing control of the West Bank and undergoing a spiritual transformation there is just the beginning of the process, though. Soon after, Jewish sovereignty should be expanded to encompass the land promised to Abraham, "from the Nile to the Euphrates" (Genesis 15:18). Eventually, when the world is truly rectified, "the borders of Israel will expand to encompass the whole earth," and the laws of the Torah will govern the entire world.[54]

For now, while the Land of Israel is confined to a more narrow space, Ginsburgh joins Kahane in recommending the expulsion of non-Jews from that land—with the exception of those who recognize the chosenness of the Jewish people and the truth of the Torah. Non-Jews must realize that "in the Divine plan for the rectification of reality the Jew has been chosen to be the spiritual giver to humanity";[55] but they reject this truth and, instead, threaten

Jews, both spiritually and physically. When in the land alongside Jews, non-Jews have a negative spiritual influence, "arousing in the hearts of the Jewish people—whether consciously or unconsciously—a desire to mingle and assimilate with them."[56] When they purchase land in Israel, they are "blemishing the integral wholeness of the land."[57] And Ginsburgh is certain that most non-Jews seek Israel's physical destruction as well; whenever they do so, "the threat must be eliminated."[58] Even those among Israel's enemies who seem to be innocent civilians may be targeted, in Ginsburgh's view. As Ginsburgh's close disciples Yitzhak Shapira and Yosef Elitzur noted in their 2009 book *The King's Torah* (*Torat Ha-Melekh*), a book strongly endorsed by Ginsburgh, it is permitted to kill "even those who are innocent, according to the needs of the moment and for the sake of repairing the world [*l'tikkun ha-olam*]."[59] As Shapira and Elitzur argue, even innocent children must sometimes be killed—as one can learn from examples such as the war against the Midianites.[60]

The use of violence to purify the land, for Ginsburgh, must go hand in hand with extreme measures to purify the soul. At the heart of repairing the world is "rid[ding] the land of foreign, hostile elements," and "this external act reflects an internal process that takes place within our souls, a process of purification (that is, ridding ourselves of undesirable character traits)."[61] Ridding oneself of ego is at the heart of the internal process—just Israel needed to destroy Midian because Midian was characterized by self-centeredness, so one must nullify one's own ego and humbly submit to God's will.[62] Humility before God, of course, does not mean passivity. As Pinḥas understood, it sometimes means engaging in the acts of vengeance that God requires.[63] Purifying the soul also depends upon the character trait of "sincerity" (*t'mimut*), the trait that seeks inner purity. In Ginsburgh's view, the work of social purification will help Jews to purify their souls; the increasingly "sincere" and purified Jews will, in turn, feel the need to further purify the world around them.[64]

The spiritual task of holding the goal of perfection in mind is crucial to this process. For Ginsburgh, such a goal should inspire Jews to be unsatisfied with a State of Israel that has compromised its Jewish identity, given up its utopian aspirations, and accepted non-Jews and non-Jewish ideas. On the spiritual level, Jews must rectify these errors by constantly holding in mind the ideal world, which contains no such compromises: "Throughout the entire rectification process…the Messiah and the rectified Jewish state, the Kingdom of Israel, must remain in the forefront of our consciousness."[65] "The full power of the will" can only be activated if we have an "inspired focus on the end of the process."[66] If we recognize "how the complete rectification of the Jewish state and the area of redemption it will usher in is truly 'good for the Jews (and the entire world),' how it is an enticing, attractive, delightful, and achievable reality—the will to create that reality here and now is aroused."[67]

Facing the Dangers of *Tikkun Olam*

For most contemporary Jews, these profoundly racist, ethnocentric, utopian visions are easy to reject. But the ideas of Kahane and Ginsburgh continue to have influence, especially in contemporary West Bank settlements.[68] Their promises of a "repaired" world, with total purity and no compromises, continue to strike some Jews as "enticing, attractive, delightful, and achievable." Their visions of purity are well-grounded in certain narratives of the Torah—such as the story of Pinḥas, among others—and in certain streams of the Jewish tradition. And a good deal of their appeal lies in their distinctly modern emphasis on values like authenticity, inner purity, and individual self-expression.

As Adam Seligman has argued, such values are best described as values of "sincerity," and they are values often privileged in modernity, both among religious and secular thinkers. At the heart of the commitment to sincerity is "the belief that truth resides within the authentic self, that it is coherent, and that incoherence and fragmentation are therefore themselves signs of inauthenticity."[69] Rejecting traditional attitudes that acknowledge and accept the imperfections of the world, "the sincere orientation rejects the fundamental brokenness of the world in a search for wholeness and totality."[70] Seligman contrasts this orientation with an orientation that privileges ritual behavior and accepts the "imperfect" practices, motivations, meanings, and outcomes that may accompany the performance of ritual. Traditional Jewish practice, in Seligman's analysis, has often permitted such ambiguities, rather than claiming to bring about perfection.[71]

Kahane and Ginsburgh, however, pick up on the strains of the Jewish tradition that are less tolerant of ambiguities and that lead to the very "sincere" idea of *tikkun olam*. The sorts of extremist movements that they have helped to lead—what are often called "fundamentalist" movements—are, as Seligman points out, characteristically modern movements in that they privilege values of sincerity, "striving for an integrative wholeness, an overcoming of dissonances" both within the self and within society.[72] In fundamentalist movements, conventional rules and practices are devalued; aligning oneself with a transcendent reality requires a "deviation from the 'rules of the game,'" to use Ginsburgh's phrase.

With their programs for repairing the world, Kahane and Ginsburgh can appeal to Jews who seek experiences of transcendence, who want to join others in bringing their visions of perfection into the world, and who delight in their non-conformity. Perfect transcendence, after all, requires rejecting the ordinary world and refusing to compromise with it. This is typical of fundamentalist efforts; the goal of fundamentalist movements, as Seligman puts it, is to "overcome the chasm between the religious terms of meaning, transcendence, and unity on the one hand, and the simple fact that the taxonomic orders of the world do not, on the whole, recognize these orders of meaning."[73] From the fundamentalist perspective that Ginsburgh and Kahane exemplify, spiritually awakened Jews have bridged that chasm, and are able to see the transcendent clearly. They must be permitted to express the pure truths that burn within them, even when (or perhaps especially when) that expression requires killing those who reject these truths.[74]

Most visions of *tikkun olam*, of course, do not lead to fundamentalist violence of this sort. But considering how they may sometimes do so is important for all of us who seek to develop visions of repair. Considering visions like those of Kahane and Ginsburgh can help us to develop better visions of improving the world that guard against the dangers of ideas like theirs.

This is important work precisely because most of us deny that our visions have anything in common with these sorts of "extremist" vision. But part of our work of "repairing the self" should involve considering whether that is the case. We should examine ourselves, for instance, to see if there are ways in which we also share some of the impulses to wipe out "foreign" threats that Pinḥas acted upon. A good deal of evidence suggests that these impulses are found within all human beings, in various ways. Human nature is such that we tend to demonize those who are viewed as total outsiders; we view them as less than human, think that the world would be better off without them, and often call for their extermination.[75] When human beings imagine what it would be like to live in a perfect world, we tend to imagine that the world would be governed by people like us, and that all people would accept the ideas of nations or communities like ours. And when we are inspired by our visions of a perfect world, we are often indifferent or cruel to those who disagree with us. These are by no means uniquely Jewish tendencies, but they are tendencies that Jews should seek to avoid in interpreting the Jewish tradition and in responding to other traditions.

And so, as Jews dream of a repaired world, we should be careful not to place ourselves at the center of that world. Tempting though it may be to imagine, with Meir Kahane, that there is "no nation" comparable to Israel, it is important to heed the prophecy of Amos that Israel is, in crucial ways, very much comparable to other nations, who were also liberated by God for their own purposes: "To Me, O Israelites, you are just like the Ethiopians—declares the Eternal One. True, I brought Israel up From the land of Egypt; but also the Philistines from Caphtor and the Arameans from Kir" (Amos 9:7).[76] And tempting though it may be for Jews to imagine a future in which Jews reign over others—as, indeed, many biblical prophets imagined—it is important to heed the caution from Maimonides that "the Sages and Prophets did not long for the days of the Messiah so that Israel might exercise dominion over the world, or rule over the heathens, or be exalted by the nations."[77] Hermann Cohen, building on Maimonides, argued that the prophets instead hoped for "the eventual restoration also of [even] those states and nations which had fought against their own people."[78] In this vision, true prophets, characterized by true humility, would hope for the persistence of a world of diverse nations from whom Israel might learn. As Pirkei Avot famously teaches, after all, the wise person is one "who learns from all human beings."[79] There might even be something to learn from Midianite visions of repairing the world.

Many biblical scholars suspect that Israel did in fact learn from Midian in profound ways. There are reasons to think that much of what came to be called Israelite religion drew on Midianite models; for example, the story of Moses discovering God at a burning bush in Midianite territory may preserve a memory of how Midianite culture inspired Israel's ideas about God.[80] The historical research that has led to such a hypothesis suggests that Israel was not a nation with "pure" ideas that were in radical disagreement with the "impure" ideas of its neighbors. Quite the contrary, Israel adapted ideas and practices of its neighbors in all sorts of ways. Maimonides had famously theorized that this would have to be the case, arguing that Israel could only access transcendent truths through ideas and practices that made sense to them—ideas and practices that would have to resemble those of Israel's neighbors. Israelite ideas and practices, from this perspective, were not "pure" or "perfect"; they were imperfect concessions that closely resembled the ideas and practices of groups such as the Canaanites and Midianites.[81]

Even the Bible itself describes Israel learning from Midianite visions in profound ways. In tension with the biblical narratives that glory in Israel's destruction of Midianites are other biblical narratives that describe Midian as instructing Israel. In the Book of Exodus, for example, the Midianite priest Jethro is not only Moses's father-in-law but is also one of Moses's central teachers. When Moses is struggling with how to hear all the cases that his people bring to him, Jethro comes, criticizes Moses, and teaches him how to better organize a system of justice, suggesting the appointment of many more judges and a new system of social organization for Israel. Moses could have responded to Jethro's ideas by invoking the language of Meir Kahane, complaining that Jethro's "alien culture" that was threatening to pervade and contaminate Israel's holy precincts; he could have protested that he alone possessed ultimate insight.[82] Instead, "Moses heeded his father-in-law and did just as he had said" (Exodus 18:24).[83] Jethro makes his mark in helping to repair the fabric of the Israelite community, and then he "returns to his own land" (Exodus 18:27).

Jews who have preferred to see Israel at the center of the world have, of course, retold this story of Moses and Jethro as a story in which Jethro acknowledges the superiority of the people of Israel, converts, leaves the impure Midianites behind, and ends up teaching Israel to be suspicious of Midian.[84] According to one tradition, Jethro is himself "zealous" in his devotion to his new God and new people; and he seems to pass this trait on to Pinḥas—because, in fact, according to another tradition, he is Pinḥas's maternal grandfather.[85] Meir Kahane, accepting this storyline, adds that Jethro was willing to risk his life by rejecting his community and therefore merited to have a grandson who would also risk his own life in rejecting that same community (and the Israelites that it enticed).[86] With these narratives, the purity of Israel can be affirmed; outsiders will not become teachers to Israel unless they are the sorts of converts who zealously reject the impure nations from which they came.

But those who are tempted to develop narratives like these should, again, inspect their souls. Why, indeed, is it tempting to tell the story in this way? Why reject the biblical story in which Jethro "returns to his own land"? Here, too, we should critically examine our impulses to eliminate the possibility of wisdom coming from outsiders. If we are to speak the language of *tikkun olam*, we should be particularly careful not to understand *tikkun olam* as a state of perfection that fails to respect the challenges that other communities may offer.

We can, in fact, only come closer to the transcendent if we hear those challenges, acknowledging our own individual limitations and the limitations of our communities. Grasping revelations of profound truth requires listening to as many voices as we can, critically considering the wisdom that those voices might offer, and seeking to repair our own imperfect visions of *tikkun olam* in light of the challenges that other voices offer. As the Jewish philosopher Emmanuel Levinas has put it, "The totality of the true is constituted from the contribution of multiple people: the uniqueness of each act of listening carrying the secret of the text; the voice of the Revelation, as inflected, precisely, by each person's ear, would be necessary to the 'Whole' of the truth." The acceptance of such a conception of revelation, of course, means accepting ambiguity, uncertainty, and contradiction. Such a conception is familiar to most Jews, who are used to understanding their tradition as possessing precisely these characteristics. But it is, of course, a deeply problematic notion for sincere zealots who believe that their souls have been repaired and that they clearly see perfect truths that need to be brought to the rest of the world.

Rejecting such notions, and accepting human limitation and the very real ambiguities that inevitably accompany the human search for truth should, then, be at the heart of the work of repairing our own notions of *tikkun olam*. We should seek to repair ourselves and, in doing so, we should see our own limits; and, to the degree that we can, we should help others to do the repair-work that brings them to see their own limits as well.

Keeping in mind the notion of the transcendent should help us to realize this. Such was the counsel of Rabbi Simḥah Zissel Ziv, one of the founding figures of the nineteenth-century *musar* movement, which emphasized the work of "repairing the soul" like no other movement in Jewish history. We learn from the Psalms, Simḥah Zissel taught, to "seek out the Eternal One and [God's] might! *Continually* seek [God's] face!" (Psalms 105:3-4)[88] Why must the work be continuous? "Because," Simḥah Zissel says, "in all the days of your life, you will not have arrived at the end." If you think that you have reached the end, he cautions, "you should have doubts: perhaps you have not arrived at the truth, and you must seek further."[89]

As we seek to improve the world, we can always seek further. Whenever we think that we have achieved clarity of vision, we must have doubts, inspect our souls, and make sure that we are walking humbly on a path toward a better world.[90]

NOTES

[1] NJPS translation.

[2] Based on NJPS translation, substituting "Eternal One" for "Lord."

[3] Bemidbar Rabbah 22:4. The translation of *mitzvah* as "sacred task" follows *Midrash Rabbah: Numbers II*, trans. Judah J. Slotki (London: Soncino Press, 1951), p. 856.

[4] See Eliezer Segal, "Disarming Phineas: Rabbinic Confrontations with Biblical Militancy," in *The Twenty-First Century Confronts Its Gods: Globalization, Technology, and War*, ed. David J. Hawkin (Albany: State University of New York Press, 2004), pp. 141–156; Alan Mittleman, "The Problem of Religious Violence," in *Political Theology* 12:5 (2011), pp. 722–726.

[5] M. Sanhedrin 9:6. See Robert Eisen, *The Peace and Violence of Judaism: From the Bible to Modern Zionism* (New York: Oxford University Press, 2011), p. 33.

[6] Zohar III 215b. (*Shalim* is the Aramaic equivalent of the Hebrew *shaleim*, meaning "perfect.")

[7] Yehudah Ashlag, "*Ha-Sullam*," on Zohar III 213b, in Sefer Ha-Zohar (New York: Yeshivat Kol Yehudah, 2004), vol. 15, p. 4 (sect. 11).

[8] Zohar III 57b; and see *Ha-Sullam*, vol. 12, p. 9 (sect. 26).

[9] See Isaiah Tishby, *The Wisdom of the Zohar*, trans. David Goldstein (Oxford: Oxford University Press, 1989), pp. 884 and 1199. Nadav and Avihu's own sexual abstinence made them unable to unite God's masculine and feminine aspects.

[10] Zohar III 57b, III 213b–217a. The reference to the "alien woman" uses the language of Proverbs 2:16 and 7:5. Nadav and Avihu, according to the Zohar, become reincarnated within Pinḥas.

[11] On the demonization of foreign nations in kabbalistic anthropology, see Elliot R. Wolfson, *Venturing Beyond: Law and Morality in Kabbalistic Mysticism* (New York: Oxford University Press, 2006).

[12] S. Daniel Breslauer, *Meir Kahane: Ideologue, Hero, Thinker* (Lewiston, NY: Edwin Mellen, 1986), p. 156, argues that "*tikkun olam* plays no role in [Kahane's] theology," as Kahane fails to recognize that "the Jew has responsibilities here and now, obligations that demand action with both Jew and non-Jew for the sake of improving the world" (pp. 155-156). Kahane's theology does not give a role to the sort of tolerant and cooperative vision of *tikkun olam* that Breslauer refers to. As I argue in this essay, however, a deeply intolerant and xenophobic concept of *tikkun olam* does play an important role in Kahane's theology.

[13] See Bemidbar Rabbah 20:25.

[14] Meir Kahane, *Tzofeh U-Manhig*, ed. Netanel Ozri (Jerusalem: Institute for Publication of the Writings of Rabbi Meir Kahane, 2005), Part One; available online at http://www.rabbikahane.org/ArticleView.aspx?id=296.

[15] Ibid.

[16] Meir Kahane, *Beyond Words: Selected Writings of Rabbi Meir Kahane*, 1960-1990, ed. David Fein (Brooklyn: Institute for Publication of the Writings of Rabbi Meir Kahane, 2010), vol. 3, p. 436; cf. vol. 3, p. 441.

[17] Ibid., vol. 3, pp. 441–442. Cf. Meir Kahane, *Commentary on Exodus: Perush HaMaccabee*, trans. Daniel Pinner (Jerusalem: Institute for Publication of the Writings of Rabbi Meir Kahane, 2014), p. 598, on Exodus 3:5, where Kahane draws the parallel between the immediate need for vengeance against Midian in the Numbers 31 narrative and the immediate need for "driving out the Arabs" in the present day.

[18] Meir Kahane, *The Jewish Idea*, trans. Raphael Blumberg (Jerusalem: Institute for Publication of the Writings of Rabbi Meir Kahane, 1996), vol. 1, p. 288. To bring this citation into line with the general transliteration standards of this volume, I have substituted "Pinḥas" for the original "Pinchas."

[19] Meir Kahane, *Peirush Ha-Makabi: Al Sefer D'varim* (Jerusalem: Institute for Publication of the Writings of Rabbi Meir Kahane, 1995), on Deuteronomy 33:18; available online at http://www.rabbikahane.org/ArticleView.aspx?id=456.

[20] Kahane, *The Jewish Idea*, vol. 1, p. 138. Kahane here avoids writing out the word "God" out of concern that the word might be desecrated, a common practice within certain Jewish circles.

[21] Ibid., vol. 1, p. 281. Cf. Meir Kahane, *Uncomfortable Questions for Comfortable Jews* (Seacaucus, NJ: Lyle Stuart, 1987), p. 177.

[22] Ibid., vol. 1, pp. 107–108. I have substituted "Pinḥas" for the original "Pinchas."

[23] Ibid., vol. 2, p. 996, with reference to Leviticus 13:14.

[24] Ibid. I have substituted "Pinḥas" for the original "Pinchas."

[25] Kahane, *Tzofeh U-Manhig*, Part One; online at http://www.rabbikahane.org/ArticleView.aspx?id=222.

[26] Kahane, *The Jewish Idea*, vol. 2, p. 699. Kahane brings the language regarding the uniqueness of God and Israel from Sifrei Devarim, §355.

[27] Ibid., vol. 2, pp. 740–741.

[28] Ibid., vol. 2, p. 543.

[29] Ibid., vol. 2, p. 747.

[30] Ibid., vol. 1, p. 320.

[31] Ibid., vol. 2, p. 587.

[32] Kahane, *Beyond Words*, vol. 3, pp. 441–442.

[33] Yitzchak Ginsburgh, *Awakening the Spark Within: Five Dynamics of Leadership That Can Change the World* (Jerusalem: Linda Pinsky Publications, 2001), p. 60.

[34] Ibid., p. 61.

[35] Yitzchak Ginsburgh, *Rectifying the State of Israel: A Political Platform Based on Kabbalah*, 2nd ed. (Jerusalem: Linda Pinsky Publications, 2003), p. 173.

[36] Ibid., p. 16.

[37] See ibid., p. 71.

[38] See Julia Schwartzmann, "Rabbi Yitzchak Ginsburgh and His Feminine Vision of the Messianic Age," in *Journal of Modern Jewish Studies* 12:1 (2013), p. 55.

[39] Jonathan Garb, *The Chosen Will Become Herds: Studies in Twentieth-Century Kabbalah*, trans. Yaffah Berkovits-Murciano (New Haven: Yale University Press, 2009), p. 67.

40 Yitzchak Ginsburgh,"Pinchas, Eliyahu, the Or Hachayim, and Rebbe Shlomo of Karlin" (July 18, 2006), available online at the website of the Gal Einai Institute, at www.inner.org.

41 Ginsburgh, *Rectifying the State of Israel*, p. 216.

42 Garb, *The Chosen Will Become Herds*, p. 81.

43 Ibid.

44 Ibid. I have substituted "*tzaddik*" for the original "*tzaddiq*," to conform to the general transliteration standards of this volume.

45 Ginsburgh, "Pinchas, Eliyahu, the Or Hachayim, and Rebbe Shlomo of Karlin," with transliteration of Hebrew modified to fit the general transliteration standards of this volume. The interpretive tradition cited stems from B. Sanhedrin 82a.

46 Don Seeman, "Violence, Ethics, and Divine Honor in Modern Jewish Thought," in *Journal of the American Academy of Religion* 73:4 (December 2005), pp. 1026–1027. Cf. Kahane, *Beyond Words*, vol. 3, p. 437.

47 Ginsburgh, *Rectifying the State of Israel*, p. 54.

48 Ibid., pp. 54, 159.

49 Ibid., p. 159, referring to *Shulḥan Arukh Admor Ha-zakein, Oraḥ Ḥayim* 1:1.

50 Motti Inbari, *Jewish Fundamentalism and the Temple Mount: Who Will Build the Third Temple?* (Albany: State University of New York Press, 2009), pp. 143–144.

51 Ginsburgh, *Rectifying the State of Israel*, p. 77.

52 Ibid., p. 176.

53 Ibid., p. 95.

54 Ibid., p. 177.

55 Ibid., p. 67. Cf. Ibid., p. 66: "Although our ultimate goal is the rectification of the entire world so that all nations serve God together, the rectification of all humanity depends first upon our and the world's recognition of the essential difference between Jew and non-Jew."

56 Ibid., pp. 59–60.

57 Ibid., p. 59.

58 Ibid., p. 89.

59 Yitzhak Shapira and Yosef Elitzur, *Torat Ha-Melekh* (Yitzhar: Yeshivat Od Yosef Chai, 2009), p. 209. As Shipira and Elitzur indicate, this phrase draws on the language of Maimonides (M.T. Hilkhot Melakhim U-milḥ'moteihem 3:10) and legal precedents from a variety of authorities. Ginsburgh's words of introduction may be found in the volume on pp. 1–5. The authors are characterized as Ginsburgh's close disciples on p. 1; see also Ginsburgh's reference there to "the repair of reality" (*tikkun ha-m'tzi·ut*).

60 Shapira and Elitzur, *Torat Ha-Melekh*, p. 220.

61 Ginsburgh, *Rectifying the State of Israel*, p. 106.

62 Yitzhak Ginsburgh, "*Parshat Matot* 5771: The Five Kings of Midian," available on youtube.com (July 20, 2011). As Ginsburgh explains in his discussion, Midian represents "evil" and "the source of self." He notes (9:14) that "there is a hasidic source that says that the general name of evil, all the evil that exists in the world, is self, [and] it is all from Midian" which represents the ego.

[63] Ibid.; *Rectifying the State of Israel*, p. 167 n. 24, and p. 183, n. 12; and see also Yitzchak Ginsburgh, "*Barukh Ha-Gever*," in *Barukh Ha-Gever: Sefer Zikkaron La-Kadosh Barukh Goldstein* (Jerusalem and Golan: Shalom al Yisrael 1995), p. 20.

[64] Ginsburgh, *Rectifying the State of Israel*, chap. 12; as Ginsburgh notes in the glossary, p. 214 (and in various charts throughout the book), *t'mimut* is "the inner experience" linked with that chapter's theme, "expelling hostile elements."

[65] Ibid., p. 44.

[66] Ibid., p. 43.

[67] Ibid., p. 42–43.

[68] For some documentation of this influence, see Max Blumenthal, *Goliath: Life and Loathing in Greater Israel* (New York: Nation Books, 2013), esp. pp. 308–310 and 325–329. For some important cautions regarding Blumenthal's book, see Shaul Magid, "Goliath the Israel Slayer: Why Max Blumenthal's New Book is a Painful Read," available online at http://religiondispatches.org/igoliathi-the-israel-slayer-why-max-blumenthals-new-book-is-a-painful-read. Magid has offered further reflections on Kahane's influence in an important recent paper, "Was Meir Kahane a Zionist?" presented at the 2014 Association for Jewish Studies Conference, Baltimore, Maryland.

[69] Adam B. Seligman, "Modernity and Sincerity: Problem and Paradox," in *Hedgehog Review* 12:1 (Spring 2010), p. 54. I am grateful to colleagues at the Institute for the Advanced Studies in Culture at the University of Virginia, especially James Davison Hunter, for first introducing me to Seligman's work on this theme.

[70] Ibid., p. 60.

[71] See, e.g., Adam B. Seligman et al., *Ritual and Its Consequences: An Essay on the Limits of Sincerity* (Oxford: Oxford University Press, 2008), pp. 24, 36–38, 66, 115–118, and 136.

[72] Adam B. Seligman, "Ritual, the Self, and Sincerity," in *Social Research: An International Quarterly* 76:4 (2009), p. 32; Seligman et al., Ritual and Its Consequences, p. 123.

[73] Adam B. Seligman, "Ritual and Sincerity: Certitude and the Other," in *Philosophy & Social Criticism* 36:1 (2010), p. 32; Seligman, *Ritual and Its Consequences*, p. 125.

[74] See Seligman, "Ritual and Sincerity: Certitude and the Other," p. 32; Schwartzmann, "Rabbi Yitzchak Ginsburgh and His Feminine Vision of the Messianic Age," p. 56.

[75] See David Livingstone Smith, *Less Than Human: Why We Demean, Enslave, and Exterminate Others* (New York: St. Martin's Press, 2011).

[76] NJPS translation, substituting "Eternal One" for "Lord." Meir Kahane cites Sifrei Bemidbar §99 in showing how this verse can, however, instead point to Israel's distinctiveness: "The Cushite is distinguished by [the colour of] his skin, and similarly Israel is distinguished by having more mitzvot than all the other nations of the world" (Kahane, *Commentary on Exodus*, p. 472, on Exodus 2:21).

[77] Maimonides, M.T. Hilkhot Melakhim U-milḥ'moteihem 12:4; following the translation of Abraham M. Hershman in *The Code of Maimonides, Book 14: The Book of Judges* (New Haven: Yale University Press, 1949), p. 242.

[78] Hermann Cohen, *Reason and Hope: Selections from the Jewish Writings of Hermann Cohen*, trans. Eva Jospe (New York: Norton, 1971), p. 120.

[79] Pirkei Avot 4:1.

[80] See Joseph Blenkinsopp, "The Midianite-Kenite Hypothesis Revisited and the Origins of Judah," in *Journal for the Study of the Old Testament* 33:2 (2008), pp. 131–153. A briefer discussion may be found in James L. Kugel, *How to Read the Bible: A Guide to Scripture, Then and Now* (New York: Free Press, 2007), pp. 424–428.

[81] Moses Maimonides, *The Guide of the Perplexed*, trans. Shlomo Pines, vol. 2 (Chicago: University of Chicago Press, 1963), III 32. See Menachem Marc Kellner, *Maimonides' Confrontation with Mysticism* (Oxford: Littman Library of Jewish Civilization, 2006).

[82] Kahane sees Moses as having indeed sinned in Exodus 2 by taking refuge with Jethro when Jethro still lived among the Midianites and had not yet joined the Jewish people, as discussed in Kahane, *Commentary on Exodus*, p. 481 (on Exodus 2:22). Kahane concludes his discussion of Moses's encounter with Jethro in Exodus 2 (on p. 485 of the translation) with the message that "all intimacy with foreign influences can only undermine the authentic Jewish Idea." Cf. also Kahane, *Commentary on Exodus*, p, 592, on Exodus 3:5 Kahane's commentary on Exodus did not reach Exodus 18 and he has relatively little to say about Jethro's encounter with Moses there, but he gives no indication that Jethro should still be identified as a Midianite at that point or as drawing on non-Jewish wisdom at all.

[83] NJPS translation.

[84] See Zohar II 68a–69a, III 122a. Kahane accepts these sorts of traditions; see, e.g., Kahane, Commentary on Exodus, pp. 400 and 403, on Exodus 2:16; and p. 478, on Exodus 2:22. I imagine that Ginsburgh endorses these traditional narratives as well, though I have found little discussion of the character of Jethro in Ginsburgh's published writings to date.

[85] On the connection between Pinḥas and Jethro, see B. Sanhedrin 82b. Mekhilta, *Yitro* 1, and Mekhilta D'Rabbi Yishmael, *Amalek* 3 tell of Jethro's zeal as the source of his name, "*Keini*." In its context, *Keini* would seem to indicate Jethro's foreign, "Kenite" identity, whereas the midrash understands the term as pointing to his rejection of that identity. Kahane refers to this midrash in his *Commentary on Exodus*, p. 430, on Exodus 2:18.

[86] Kahane, *Commentary on Exodus*, p. 401, on Exodus 2:16.

[87] Emmanuel Levinas, "Revelation in the Jewish Tradition," in *Beyond the Verse: Talmudic Readings and Lectures*, trans. Gary D. Mole (Bloomington, IN: Indiana University Press, 1994), pp. 133–134.

[88] Based on the NJPS translation, modified for gender neutrality and with emphasis added.

[89] Simḥah Zissel (Broida) Ziv, *Sefer Ḥokhmah U-Musar* (Jerusalem: Me'orei Oros Hamusar Publications, 2003), vol. 2, p. 15.

[90] I began formulating this essay while debating with my uncle, Yoel (Joel) Lerner (1941–2014), a disciple of Meir Kahane and an admirer of Yitzchak Ginsburgh, who aspired to "repair the world" in line with many of the disturbing and dangerous ideas presented here. I dedicate this essay to my uncle's memory, and I am sorry that I never had the opportunity to share it with him in its completed form.

Authentic *Tikkun* in the Writings of Emil Fackenheim[1]

Jeremy Gordon

Testimony of an Auschwitz Camp Guard

Witness: Women carrying children were always sent with them to the crematorium. The children were then torn from their parents outside the crematorium and sent to the gas chambers separately. When the extermination of the Jews in the gas chambers was at its height, orders were issued that the children were to be thrown into the crematorium furnaces or into the pit near the crematorium without being gassed first.

Smirnov (Russian Prosecutor): How am I to understand this? Did they throw them into the fire alive, or did they kill them first?

Witness: They threw them in alive.[2]

This infinitesimal moment, among so many million moments, is enough to break my heart. As a human, as a Jew, and certainly as a rabbi, my heart breaks all the time—but never more so than when I dare confront the Holocaust. And yet I persist. I persist in wanting to know more about the horrors visited on my people. I persist in a congregational rabbinate where there is not only good news, but heartbreaking loss also. And perhaps most outrageously of all, I persist in celebrating—laughing and falling in love—even though I know of a million heartbreaking moments. The only way I can justify this outrage, to explain this persistence, is by paying homage to an unfashionable Jewish philosopher and Holocaust survivor, Emil Fackenheim—who pioneered a new use of the term *tikkun*, quite different from the valence it had carried in earlier periods of Jewish history, and thus set the stage for other innovative uses of the term in modern Jewish discourse.

Fackenheim was born in Saxony in 1916.[3] Arrested by the Nazis on Kristallnacht in November of 1938, he survived a three-month internment in the Sachsenhausen concentration camp before fleeing, first to Scotland and then to Canada, where he was imprisoned as an enemy alien. Eventually he received his Ph.D. and he joined the philosophy faculty at the University of Toronto in 1960. At the age of 68 he made *aliyah* to Jerusalem.

Fackenheim freed the word *tikkun* from its original rabbinic and Lurianic connotations, applying it instead to matters of contemporary importance. Sadly, the word has become so used and overused in recent years that its mooring to Fackenheim's novel and profoundly brave treatment has disappeared. That, as I hope to show, is a loss in ways more important than the mere academic desire to understand a key moment in the evolution of contemporary Jewish thought.[4]

Emil Fackenheim's First and Second Questions

Fackenheim was an ordained rabbi,[5] but he was not concerned with the technical fixes—for example, to Jewish divorce law—that the rabbis of ancient times enacted in the name of *tikkun olam*.[6]

Fackenheim is often referred to as a theologian, but this is not a helpful term to hold in mind when considering his contribution to Jewish thought. Certainly he offers no justification of God's ultimate omnipotence or beneficence. (Confronted by burning babies, what goodness could one possibly find in the world?) Nor does he have much to say about a human etiology of evil; he takes as a given that the great hope of the Enlightenment—the ever-improving lot of humanity—is, after the Holocaust, something best discarded. Nor, certainly, was Fackenheim a theosophist in the kabbalistic sense of the term. He seems uninterested in the inner workings of the Godhead, and the esoteric cosmogony of Isaac Luria seems to interest him only cursorily.[7] Rather, Fackenheim was a man who encountered the Holocaust, and he continued throughout a long academic career to be nagged by the sense that the experience of this singular horror rendered all other achievement, all other possibility, somehow empty.

As a young academic, Fackenheim attempted to avoid dealing with the Holocaust; his early work focused on Kant and Hegel. But he found that he was unable to escape confronting this ultimate human horror.

Fackenheim's first foray into post-Holocaust thought began with this question: *In the face of the Holocaust, what should the authentic Jew do, and why?* This is the driving question of his God's Presence in History, published in 1970.[8] And over the twenty years that followed, his interests shifted to the more inchoate and more universal problem: *Can there ever be an authentic response, in the face of the Holocaust?*—the driving question of *To Mend the World*, published in 1982.[9] Fackenheim's famous (or, perhaps, infamous) answer to his first question—that refusing to grant Hitler a posthumous victory is, as of now, the 614th commandment—can hardly be considered under-discussed;[10] but the answer to the second question needs rescuing from an even deeper spiral into cliché than history has afforded the notion of a 614th commandment.

In Search of an "Authentic" Response to the Holocaust

The Holocaust pricks our conscience; it is the ultimate test of the authenticity of any response to a world that appears, too often, nasty, brutish, and short. If we fail the test of the Holocaust, we are left with nothing but foolish words. But if we can find a response to the question of life that passes the test of Auschwitz then, surely, we have discovered something important.

That Fackenheim sees history and the Holocaust as a test of the authenticity of thought and action can be seen from an extended attack on Heidegger that takes up thirty pages of his *To Mend the World*.[11] Fackenheim doesn't critique Heidegger's logic or reasoning; rather, he simply claims that Heidegger must be wrong (or "inauthentic," to use Fackenheim's term), since he failed to speak against the horrors of Auschwitz. The Nazi, so Fackenheim claimed, may not be judged on the technical merits of his own philosophizing, but must be held accountable for everything that happened because of his silence. Auschwitz, as a historical event, becomes the standard against which all theorizing about "good" and "evil" must be judged. But this high bar serves only to raise a more profound dilemma: does not *all* thought become unauthentic? Toward the end of the work, Fackenheim—still struggling with whether anything he has to offer can have meaning in a post-Auschwitz world—puts the problem of thinking about the Holocaust this way: "Perhaps *no* thought can be where the Holocaust is…perhaps all thought is 'paralyzed' vis-à-vis that event and…perhaps paralysis at this catastrophic point calls into question [all] thoughts everywhere."[12] His reticence about the possibility of post-Auschwitz thought can, perhaps, be sensed most clearly in an extraordinary passage where Fackenheim considers Adolf Eichmann, one of the foremost drivers of the "Final Solution," a "good" Kantian. Eichmann, deems Fackenheim, acted as a dutiful idealistic mass murderer, thus obeying the first of Kant's categorical imperatives: that one should act from a principled position. The Nazi also obeyed the second imperative of acting with the intention that his own actions could become a universal law. And, finally, Fackenheim feels forced to acknowledge that if one considers Jews as sub-human (as Eichmann did), then sending them to their extermination could be excused—from Kant's requirement that all "full" human beings are treated as ends in themselves. Fackenheim admits his own "horror" at the findings he feels compelled to admit. One can feel his despairing of the value of the philosophic heroes whose work drove Fackenheim's own early professional endeavor.

The point is not that philosophy is rendered unauthentic after the Holocaust. It is that everything becomes vacuous, at best, when tested against the horrors of Auschwitz. Fackenheim cites Kierkegaard's assertion that a "single event of inexplicable horror 'has the power to make *everything* inexplicable, including the most [otherwise] explicable events.'"[13] The challenge of the Holocaust was physical, but is now existential; we—even those of us who have physically survived—remain in danger of losing everything.

Learning from History: The "Q" and the "A"

The testimony of the Auschwitz camp guard found at the beginning of this essay is, in many ways, typical of *To Mend the World*. The work is full of historical excurses, but Fackenheim finds something truly precious in the rubble of European Jewry: the very building-blocks of a response. Auschwitz brings us all to a halt. But it is not the end of our tale; rather, it is its beginning. As Fackenheim says, "It is at this point that our going-to-school-with-life…begins in earnest… and only in [the] context of [engaging with the destruction of the Holocaust] can the 'central question' of our whole inquiry be *both asked and answered*."[14] History thus provides not only the "Q" (i.e., "Can anything be authentic after the Holocaust?"), but also the "A."

Central to Fackenheim's thought is his commitment to look to the dark places of history, until the darkness becomes its own source of meaningful engagement with something, somehow redemptive. It brings, if not a downright epiphany, then at least its own reward. We have a record of the moment Fackenheim himself came to this understanding:

[While studying the story of Pelagia Lewinska] I made what

to me was, and still is, a momentous discovery: that while religious thinkers were vainly struggling for a response to Auschwitz, Jews throughout the world had been responding all along…with an unexpected will to live—with, under the circumstances, an incredible commitment to Jewish group survival.[15]

Lewinska was a Holocaust survivor who in her memoir, *Twenty Months at Auschwitz*, depicts the horrors of "the ditches, the mud, the piles of excrement," and comes to understand that the Nazis have committed themselves not only to the physical annihilation of Jews, but also to their systematic abasement: "They wished to destroy our human dignity, to efface every vestige of [our] humanity…to fill us with horror and contempt."[16] However, Lewinska's experience of being so utterly overpowered, instead of stripping her of her decency and humanity, becomes its own extraordinary motivation:

> From the instant when I grasped [this Nazi] motivating principle…it was as if I had been awakened from a dream…. I *felt under orders to live*…And if I did die in Auschwitz, it would be as a human being, I would hold onto my dignity. I was not going to be the contemptible, disgusting brute my enemy wished me to be.[17]

The answer, claims Fackenheim, had been there all along; it was simply waiting for someone to come and find it.

> The world itself is philosophically intelligible after Auschwitz in the exact sense in which it was already understood—in Auschwitz and Buchenwald, in Lublin and the Warsaw Ghetto—by the resisting victims themselves. No deeper or more ultimate grasp is possible for philosophical thought that comes…after the event. This grasp—their grasp—is epistemologically ultimate.[18]

Lewinska, who discovered in the face of Nazi dehumanization that she felt commanded never to surrender her humanity, becomes the model for the possibility of choosing a path of "faithfulness unto death."[19] The Buchenwald hasidim, who swapped four rations of bread for a pair of *t'fillin*, become the paradigm for the possibility of retaining categories of commandedness even in a post-Auschwitz world.[20] And even thought—philosophy—finds the possibility of an authentic post-Holocaust existence, because of a moment of authenticity forged in the crucible of Nazi Germany.

Kurt Huber (1893–1943) was a professor of philosophy in Munich when he came into contact with a collective of philosophy students known as The White Rose. The group's members were arrested, and after a sham trial, killed—for distributing anti-Nazi pamphlets. Huber became their most eloquent spokesperson. In a "Final Statement of the Accused" placed before the court that found him guilty, Huber sought to justify the legality of the group's acts of philosophical resistance, using philosophical discourse. Of course, the court had no truck with his claims. Huber was stripped of his position, his doctorate, and his life—but even in the face of this bastardized injustice, Huber retained his engagement with philosophy. Extraordinarily, while in prison awaiting his inevitable fate, Huber completed work on a biography of Gottfried Leibniz.

One has the impression that Fackenheim was not particularly impressed with the quality of Huber's work; but just as Fackenheim accuses Heidegger of failing as a philosopher despite his intellectual brilliance, Huber succeeds regardless of his lack of academic genius: "What the greatest German philosopher of the age failed to achieve was accomplished, at least in principle, by an obscure German professor of philosophy in the midst of the *Ereignis* [Event] itself."[21] Huber and the White Rose's engagement in philosophical thought in the midst of "the Event" justifies the possibility of philosophical thought after "the Event."

These acts of resistance, philosophical and otherwise, are not the actions of those who looked away from the horrors of Auschwitz. Fackenheim claims that these resisting actors all engaged honestly with their surroundings. Lewinska understood Auschwitz. The prayers of the Buchenwald hasidim were a "rejection of all pious explanations of the purpose of prayer."[22] Huber and the members of the White Rose knew the futility of their actions and were aware of their all-but-certain-death; "they knew it, but they did it."[23] This awareness, claims Fackenheim, made their actions holy, authentic, and meaningful. And whereas before this epiphany we may have feared that there could be no authentic response in the face of the rupture of such horror, once an archetypal reaction is discovered to be authentic, the path is then open for other possible responses. Or, as Fackenheim put it: "We do not mean that [these cases of heroic response are] the only one[s]; we do mean that even a *single* case, provided it was genuine, is a *novum* that alters everything."[24] Notwithstanding the futility of life *and* the failure of piety *and* the certainty of death in our contemporary existence, we too are capable of achieving holiness and authenticity…and even meaning.

Authenticity and *Tikkun*

We have jumped too quickly, accepting without comment Fackenheim's claim as to the holiness of the actions of these resisting heroes. For Fackenheim, the source of this possibility of holiness is the very term—*tikkun*—that is the focus of this volume's efforts.

Tikkun is a term much used (and, arguably, even overused) in contemporary Jewish discourse. Nevertheless, at time of *To Mend the World's* publication in 1982, its use must have been quite shocking. Not only was a very particularistic Hebrew term making an appearance in the work of a thinker known in the secular academy, but the term, prior to the publication of *To Mend The World*, had been the preserve of talmudic sages and theosophistic kabbalists. Fackenheim professes no special fidelity to the term *tikkun* as understood in Lurianic writings. Many of the areas in which he uses the term—such as in discussing the possibility of rebuilding a broken church, or to vouchsafe the possibility of authentic philosophical discourse—are wholly foreign concerns to the Lurianic corpus. Moreover, the notion that the Godhead itself is broken—a central Lurianic axiom—figures only peripherally in *To Mend the World*. But in one vital sense, Fackenheim does base himself on a foundation of Lurianic cosmogony—and that is a foundation in danger of becoming forgotten in the contemporary focus given to the term. In Lurianic Kabbalah, *tikkun* is the third element of a cosmology that begins with a divine withdrawal from a previously unbordered infinite omnipresence of divine energy— *tzimtzum*. *Tzimtzum* prepares the way for the manifestation of a finite creation, but the limited divine energy that trickled into this emptiness was still too powerful to be contained—resulting in a destruction, known in Lurianic thought as *sh'virah*. It is only at this point—after and directly connected to cosmic destruction—that Lurianic discourse about *tikkun* has meaning.

Fackenheim's *tikkun*, as a contemporary philosophical construct, entails a direct encounter with a shattered existence. Time and time again, To Mend the World binds the notion of *tikkun* with a willingness to encounter rupture, the Lurianic *sh'virah*. To take one example:

> A *tikkun* here and now is mandatory, for a *tikkun* then and there was actual. It is true that because a *tikkun* of that rupture is impossible we cannot live, after the Holocaust, as men and women have lived before. However, if the impossible *tikkun* were not also necessary and hence possible, we could not live at all.[25]

The notion that this *tikkun* must be bound to *sh'virah* ought not to be such a radical claim; but in the thirty years since the publication of *To Mend the World*, the word *tikkun*—especially in the phrase *tikkun olam*—has become so overused that it is in danger of becoming trite. Richard Hirsh, in a special edition of *The Reconstructionist* magazine entitled "*Tikkun Olam*: Theory and Practice," acknowledges and seemingly accepts that "*tikkun olam* has gone the way of other traditional Jewish categories, notably *mitzvah* and *tzedakah*, and has become a generic term for social action policies."[26]

Of course social action is important, and indeed there is much work that needs to be done to better the lot of those dispossessed by contemporary society, but to use *tikkun* only in the context of "thou shalt not wrong a stranger"[27] seems to traduce the term. To strip *tikkun* of its relationship to rupture renders the term *pareve*. Perhaps a better analogy can be drawn from the world of antibiotic resistance. We are over-medicating, and in so doing we weaken our ability to fight that most terrifying of spiritual diseases: not the loss of our physical life (which remains inevitable), but the loss of the possibility of authentic living even while alive (a thought that is truly terrifying).

For Fackenheim, the special quality of *tikkun* is its reality. Traditional rabbinic categories that speak about suffering do not "presume to penetrate the divine nature but...rather [offer] a human metaphorical way of speaking...God only 'as it were' weeps or roars like a lion...[However] no such restraint is shown by kabbalistic Judaism."[28]

The Lurianic system makes an ontological claim: in the minds of the kabbalists, the *sh'virah* really happened;[29] therefore *tikkun*, as a type of authentic action, really was (and is) possible. Again, we see the importance of history in Fackenheim's thought. What for Luria was religious and theological reality becomes, in Fackenheim's hands, an eminently this-worldly focused existential foundation, on which a quest for holiness can be constructed. The authenticity of a category of the past has been established, and therefore the category may be carried into the future. It may continue to engender holiness, even after Auschwitz.

Fackenheim and Me

Fackenheim's conception of *tikkun* as authentic action, lived in the face of the rupture, is one I hold dear—even as I find the general use of the term often hackneyed. As a philosophical response to radical evil, it seems indestructible (if only because its foundation is already one of wreckage and destruction). As an existential approach, it echoes other articulations I hold dear. James Fowler, in his 1981 work *Stages of Faith*,[30] attempts to articulate the parallels between child development and theological sophistication. Fowler suggests that children, and childish theologians, are drawn to certainties and absolutes. Adolescents, and adolescent theologians, Fowler suggests, know such childish notions to be unutterably deceitful and reject them all. But eventually (for some), the thrill of destructive iconoclasm passes…and then what? The adult stage of faith (by Fowler's reckoning, the "Fifth Stage") entails re-appraising the value of conceptions known in youth and returning to them not for their scientific accuracy but in search of insight, inspiration, and the sort of truth that cannot be subject to laboratory protocols. I locate myself, and my relationship with God and revelation, in Fowler's "fifth stage of faith"—the place where, after the iconoclasm of adolescence fades, one is ready to resubmit to the power of religious tradition. Fackenheim's use of *tikkun* echoes, for me, this relationship with past modalities. I'm not looking for certainties. I am not looking to re-create worlds that have gone and are never to return. But I do look to the past in search of value and values. I do look to the past in search of authentic possibilities for living well today.

I also find Fackenheim's sense of *tikkun* enormously helpful in my work as a congregational rabbi. The weddings and such are fine, and even many of the sadder occasions provoke no existential threat. But there are also occasions, without wishing to suggest anything comparable to Auschwitz, that can empty out a person. There are occasions when, as a rabbi, I am called to stand with those who face *sh'virah*—the loss of existential possibility—in their own lives, and it is a contagious threat. I believe empathy is the strongest gift I have to share with those suffering; but attempting to share pains that cause existential rupture is a dangerous business—even a rabbi (this rabbi) can be emptied out. It is when I stand with those suffering rupture (even if—and perhaps especially when—there is nothing "to do"), and also when I retreat home to lick my own existential wounds, that I cherish Fackenheim's notion of *tikkun*: authentic possibility in the face of rupture, both in a generalized, humanist sense, and also in offering for those bereft and bereaved the specific religious ritualized responses of the Jewish tradition.

I find, in Fackenheim's articulations, guidance in the search for ways to live authentically in the face of the nasty, the brutish and the short. For me—in my, life and especially as a rabbi confronted by the often heartbreaking experiences of both my congregants and my people—Fackenheim's notion of *tikkun* after *sh'virah* works.

NOTES

[1] An earlier version of this essay was published in *Conservative Judaism* 66:1 (Winter 2014), pp. 59–69.

[2] Cited in Emil Fackenheim, *To Mend the World: Foundations of Future Jewish Thought* (New York: Schocken, 1982), p. 212. The author offers a fuller bibliographic citation for this testimony on p. 340, n. 15.

[3] The following biographical information owes a debt to Lawrence Joffe's obituary published in *The Guardian* (October 10, 2003), available online at www.theguardian.com/news/2003/oct/10/guardianobituaries.

[4] Leonard Fein, in his study of the development of the use of the motif, is, I think, the first to acknowledge Fackenheim's pre-eminent role in using the term as a response to the ills of society. See Leonard Fine, "*Tikkun*: A Lurianic Motif in Contemporary Jewish Thought," in *From Ancient Israel to Modern Judaism: Essays in Honor of Marvin Fox*, eds. Jacob Neusner, Ernest S. Frerichs, and Nahum M. Sarna (Atlanta: Scholars Press, 1989), vol. 4, pp. 35–53.

[5] His ordination was granted by the bastion of Berlin Reform Jewry, the Hochschule für die Wissenschaft des Judentums. Staggeringly, he seems to have been awarded ordination in 1939—after Kristallnacht.

[6] Other essays in this collection address the use of the term in historical perspective; see especially the essay by Gail Labovitz.

[7] Other papers in this collection address the Lurianic sense of *tikkun*.

[8] Emil Fackenheim, *God's Presence in History* (New York: Harper & Row, 1970).

[9] Emil Fackenheim, *To Mend the World* (New York: Schocken, 1982). This analysis is based on Michael L. Morgan's "The Central Problem of Fackenheim's *To Mend The World*," in *Journal of Jewish Thought* 5(1996), pp. 297–312, particularly p. 299.

[10] Fackenheim was already citing his own "canonical" rendition of the Commanding Voice of Auschwitz—not to hand Hitler a posthumous victory—in 1968; see *God's Presence in History*, p. 84, and also p. 103 n. 44 and p. 100, nn. 10 and 11. Rabbinic discourse has long presumed a total of 613 commandments in the Torah; see B. Makkot 23b in the name of Rabbi Simlai.

[11] *To Mend the World*, pp. 151–181.

[12] *To Mend the World*, p. 249.

[13] Cited in Kierkegaard's name, but with no citation, in *To Mend the World*, p. 191. Emphases here and throughout are my own.

[14] *To Mend the World*, pp. 23–24.

[15] Emil Fackenheim, *The Quest for Past and Future* (Bloomington, IN: Beacon, 1968), pp. 19–20.

[16] *Twenty Months at Auschwitz* (London: Lyle Stuart Inc., 1968), p.41, cited in *To Mend the World*, p. 25.

[17] Ibid., p. 50, and cited in *To Mend the World*, p.25; italics per Fackenheim's citation of the passage. Fackenheim is clearly drawn to the notion of the "commanding voice" that Lewinska "hears." There is in Lewinska's heroic refusal

to surrender her own humanity something of Victor Frankl's insistence that even the horror of Auschwitz cannot strip everything from a human; see *Man's Search for Meaning* (1959, under the title *From Death Camp to Existentialism*; rpt. New York: Simon & Schuster, 1985).

[18] *To Mend the World*, p. 248.

[19] *God's Presence in History*, p. 74, cf. the discussion of Lewinska in *To Mend the World*, pp. 25, 217, 219, 223, 229, 248, and 302.

[20] Though the notion of commandedness is clearly central for Fackenheim, he does not advocate the wholesale importation of pre-modern halakhic norms into a post-Holocaust world. It is a central tenet of Fackenheim's self-claimed canonical statement of the Commanding Voice of Auschwitz that the "religious Jew who has stayed with his God may be forced into new, possibly revolutionary relationships with Him" (*God's Presence in History*, p. 84). See his discussion of the Buchenwald hasidim in *To Mend the World*, pp. 218, 223, 229, 254, and 303.

[21] *To Mend the World*, p. 266.

[22] Ibid., p. 230.

[23] Ibid., pp. 266–267.

[24] Ibid., p. 266.

[25] *To Mend the World*, p. 254.

[26] "From the Editor," in *The Reconstructionist* 68:1 (2003), p. 2. This is certainly the general approach to *tikkun* in the essays published in that volume. There is nothing, even in the supposedly more theoretical papers, that seeks to understand *tikkun* in the context of *sh'virah*.

[27] As Laurence Kushner suggests in *The Book of Words* (Woodstock, VT: Jewish Lights Publishing, 2003), p. 83.

[28] *To Mend the World*, p. 253. Fackenheim likewise rejects earlier biblical models of protest as not sufficiently concrete; see *God's Presence in History*, p. 76.

[29] I do not think that Fackenheim is making a scientific "God and the Big Bang" type of claim; rather, I believe he is acknowledging the claimed religious truth of the Lurianic cosmology as a faith construct.

[30] James Fowler, *Stages of Faith* (San Francisco: Harper & Row, 1981).

Tikkun Olam as an Antidote to *Hash·ḥatat Yishuvo shel Olam* (The Destruction of Society)

Jill Jacobs

Today, the term *tikkun olam* conjures up images of activists, lawmakers, and rabbis trying to create a more just and perfect world. But contemporary usage results from a long and rich tradition in which the term works its way through the worlds of prayer, law, and mysticism.

As I have laid out more fully elsewhere,[1] the term *tikkun olam* goes through at least four distinct major periods. The earliest known usage, in the Aleinu prayer, equates a repaired world with the elimination of idol worship and the full expression of God's sovereignty. The Mishnah employs the idea of *tikkun olam* as a means of closing loopholes, changing laws, or establishing policies in the face of a threat to the social order. Lurianic Kabbalah sees *tikkun olam* as the reunification of the divine being and a restoration of the world to its original state. In the United States in the 1950s and 1960s, the term began to refer to social justice or social service. While some authors have pointed to the differences between the earlier uses of the term *tikkun olam* and its contemporary meaning as an argument against applying it to contemporary justice work, I see these four categories as building on and enriching one another. In speaking of *tikkun olam* today, we might ask what changes we need to make in law and policy in order to help society to flourish, while also drawing inspiration from the possibility of summoning the divine presence and moving closer to the messianic era.

One use of the term *tikkun olam*, however, seems to defy these four categories and presents a far less positive image of the phrase that is most often associated with justice and perfection. In his Mishneh Torah, Rambam[2] references—and justifies—the right of the king to carry out capital punishment without due legal process, or after the legal process has resulted in acquittal, as an act of *tikkun olam*:

> If someone kills another person and there is no clear evidence, or no warning was given [to the perpetrator before the crime], even in the case in which there is only one witness; or if one person accidentally kills someone he or she hates—in these cases, the king has permission to execute that person and [thus] *l'takkein ha-olam* ("to fix the world," or "to engage in *tikkun olam*"), according to what the hour requires. He may execute many on one day, and may hang and leave the bodies hanging for many days, in order to instill fear and to break the hand of the evildoers of the world.[3]

> In all of these cases of murderers and the like who are not liable for capital punishment at the hands of the court, a king of Israel who wishes to execute them in accordance with *din ha-malkhut* ("the law of the land") and *takkanat ha-olam* (a variation of the phrase *tikkun ha-olam*) has permission to do so. Similarly, if the court saw it necessary to execute them because of the exigencies of the moment (*hora·at sha·ah*)—if the hour required this, they have permission to do as they see fit.[4]

> As for those whom the king did not execute, and in the case in which the hour did not require strictness, the court is obligated in any case to flog them severely, to the point of near death, and to imprison them in harsh conditions for many years, and to afflict them with all types of afflictions, in

order to sow fear and terror among the rest of the evildoers, so that this event will not become an obstacle and a stumbling block for them, that they should say, "I will arrange to have my enemies killed just as so-and-so did, and I will go free."[5]

The laws of criminal justice, as laid out in the Talmud, strive to prevent any possibility of executing an innocent person or someone unaware of the consequences of his or her actions. Thus, the rabbis established strict laws of evidence that require, among other stipulations, that the two witnesses be cross-examined on points not directly relevant to the crime, that the two must have viewed the crime from the same vantage point (and not, for example, from two different windows), and that the perpetrator must have been warned of the punishment for his or her action and must have indicated formally that he or she understands the consequences before actually committing the crime. Unlike the king in the Mishneh Torah text above, the court may not hear two capital cases in a single day—lest the judges fail to devote their full attention to either.

These strictures should certainly prevent the conviction of an innocent person—and should serve as a sharp rebuke to the American courts, which too often have convicted, and even executed, people based on unreliable or coerced testimony. On the other hand, these conditions make it almost impossible to convict anyone. Even a person known beyond all reasonable doubt to have committed murder may be acquitted based on a technicality.

One famous passage reflects both the rabbinic ambivalence about the death penalty and the concern that the absence of such punishment in a system that does not normally allow for imprisonment will lead to murderers roaming free:

A Sanhedrin that puts a person to death once in seven years is called a murderous one. Rabbi Eleazar ben Azariah said: Or even once in seventy years. Rabbi Tarfon and Rabbi Akiva said: If we had been in the Sanhedrin, no one would ever have been given a death sentence. Rabban Shimon ben Gamliel said: If so, they would have multiplied murderers in Israel.[6]

The very existence of capital punishment in classical Judaism begins with a paradox. The Torah teaches us: "Whoever sheds human blood, by the human hand shall that person's blood be shed" (Genesis 9:6). Since human beings are created in the image of God (*tzelem Elohim*), the murder of a human being represents the ultimate sin: the simultaneous desecration of humanity and the desecration of God. Capital punishment seems only to compound this crime.[7] Thus, each of the first three statements of this *mishnah* advocates for a rarer and rarer use of the death penalty. And yet, Rabban Shimon ben Gamliel worries that a Sanhedrin that acquits everyone will let murderers roam free, and perhaps even encourage potential murderers who might otherwise be deterred by the prospect of death by execution.

The rabbis themselves understood that they had effectively legislated capital punishment out of existence. For this reason, they invented the penal institution of the *kippah*—a sort of solitary confinement cell leading to certain death, which was to be employed in certain cases in which a person escapes capital punishment on a technicality. While we have no evidence that any Jewish court ever actually implemented the *kippah*, we may view this institution as evidence of the rabbis trying to create an alternative to the capital punishment system they had rejected.

The Power of the King

Rambam proposes an entirely different solution to the question of how to punish murderers whom the Sanhedrin cannot convict. As we saw in the passages above, he allows the king—and, in some cases, the court—to carry out capital punishment, even without the necessary evidence. The court gains permission to do so in the case of *hora·at sha·ah*, an emergency situation. The king's power falls under a different rubric, *takkanat ha-olam*, which we might understand according to the mishnaic definition of the term as "maintaining the social order."[9] While the court acts according to the needs of the moment, the king must keep in mind the broader picture of the long-term needs of society.[10] This distinction becomes even clearer in the words of the Ran, who defines the king's role as "repair of the societal order" (*tikkun ha-siddur ha-m'dini*) and "repair of general matters" (*tikkun inyanim*). In contrast, the role of the Sanhedrin is to "judge the people according to *mishpat tzedek* (righteous judgment)."[11]

The king, then, has far broader powers than the court has. But where does the king get such powers?

Commentators on Rambam generally understand him to base the broad permissions for the king to carry out his own justice on an incident reported in the Talmud Yerushalmi, in which two men engaging in sex with a female dog worry that a righteous (and solo) passerby will report their crime, and that King David will kill them. This story seems to suggest that a king—or at least one as powerful as David—has the authority to enact capital punishment based on the testimony of a single witness.[13]

This incident alone hardly seems to justify granting the king broad powers to carry out capital punishment. Our historical knowledge of the behavior of kings and dictators tells us that such leniency will almost definitely lead to abuse. No wonder Radbaz emphasizes that "the king must concentrate [on using this power] for establishing faith and repairing injustice, and not for his own glory."[14]

Menachem Lorberbaum notes that the Rambam's permission for the king to carry out capital punishment applies only to the crime of murder, and not to any other capital crimes such as idolatry or certain sexual transgressions.[15] He ascribes this distinction to the nature of *din ha-malkhut*, which he defines as an extra-legal system of law that operates in conjunction with the normative legal system, and whose purpose is *tikkun ha-olam*:

The expression *hash·ḥatat yishuvo shel olam* appears to be the opposite of the expression *tikkun ha-olam*. The first describes the result of the actions of the murderer, and in the second, one should see the result of the actions of the king—and, by extension, the result of his actions in regard to the social order.[16]

Therefore, Lorberbaum writes: "The severity of the crime of murder—the destruction of civilized society—calls for the king to take action in order to mend the world."[17] Unlike the Sanhedrin, which is charged only with addressing individual criminal cases, the king carries the burden of maintaining a functional social order. For this reason, the king has license to take action to prevent any threat to this social order—specifically, the possibility of widespread murder.

Limits on the Power of the King

How can a king know whether the acquittal of a murderer will lead to more murders? One modern response comes from Rabbi Isaac Herzog, who served as the Ashkenazic chief rabbi of British Palestine and Israel from 1937–1959, who counts on the king to assess the general ethical state of society:

Capital punishment falls under the authority and the role of the Sanhedrin, but even after the Sanhedrin has acquitted the accused, the king has the power—for the sake of *tikkun ha-olam*, and in accordance with the needs of the hour—to execute. But, this does not mean that the Israelite kings had a special law that was not in accordance with the Torah— for they judged in accordance with it, and appointed judges and confirmed witnesses in accordance with it. But, in the case of the laws of murder, the matter is turned over to the

conscience of the king, and depends on the moral state of
the people. If there are very few murderers, and there is no
danger that acquitting the accused will multiply murderers
among Israel, the king need not do this at all.[18]

Herzog provides a significant check on the broad powers that
Rambam confers on the king. As discussed earlier, the king must
maintain a focus on *tikkun olam*, the protection of the societal order
for the long term. Per Herzog, though, the king needs to develop
a keen sense of the current state of society and of the likely effects
of his policies. Thus, in a society rife with murderers, in which he
believes that the release of a murderer will lead to *hash·hatat yishuvo
shel olam* (i.e., the destruction of society), then the king may—or
perhaps must—carry out capital punishment himself. If, however,
the execution will have little or no discernible effect on murder rates,
the king should not take this liberty.

One potential resolution for our contemporary unease with the
image of a Jewish king singlehandedly convicting and executing
probable murderers would be to note that capital punishment, in
modern times, has little or no deterrence effect.[19] Regardless of how
we define the moral state of our own society, the knowledge that
widespread executions will not reduce murder should be enough to
declare that the category of *tikkun olam* as understood by Herzog
simply does not apply.

We could also argue that Rambam's philosopher-king has never
existed and will likely never exist. While a perfect king might be able to
make determinations of guilt on his own, none of the leaders we know
from history or contemporary life approach this ideal. Instead, we are
familiar with dictators who abuse their power to carry out widespread
and unjustified murders of their citizens. We might also note that
modern judicial systems do not require the level of proof that the
rabbis demanded. In the United States, evidence "beyond reasonable
doubt" suffices to convict. Rambam's case specifically addresses the

situation in which there is evidence beyond reasonable doubt—but not beyond *any* doubt, per the criteria set out by *halakhah*.

For these three reasons, we can safely say that Rambam's permission for a king to carry out unilateral executions may not be taken literally or used in any way to justify capital punishment.

At the same time, those of us committed to understanding and integrating halakhic texts into our justice work must ask what, if anything, we can profitably adopt from Rambam's innovation in the use of the term *tikkun olam*. To address this question, I now turn to another problematic, if more benign, use of the term *tikkun olam*, this time from the Mishnah.

Prozbul and the Economic Order

As mentioned earlier, the Mishnah uses *tikkun olam* to refer to instances of closing a loophole or changing a policy that threatens to destroy the social order. For example: several *mishnayot* eliminate practices that might lead to confusion about the validity of a get, thereby throwing a woman's marital status into question. This situation would have massive societal repercussions. A woman who erroneously believes herself to be divorced might remarry and produce children, who would then be *mamzeirim*, and neither they nor their descendants would be permitted to marry non-*mamzeirim*.[20] Or, a woman who does not believe herself to have received a valid *get* might refrain from marriage and subsequent child-bearing. Since "the world was only created to be populated,"[21] her unnecessary abstention from having children would also constitute *hash·hatat yishuvo shel olam*, the destruction of society.

It is beyond the scope of this article to go into depth about the reasons for each of the uses of *tikkun olam* in the Mishnah.[22] Rather, I will look closely at the most radical applications of this concept: as a justification for uprooting a stipulation of the biblical law of *sh'mittah*, the Sabbatical Year.

As laid out in the Torah, *sh'mittah* includes the forgiveness of debts. This provision allows those who have accumulated significant debts over the course of six years to start again from zero. This is not a wholescale redistribution of wealth, but rather a chance for those deep in debt to work their way out of poverty.

Even the Torah, though, notes a potential problem with this law. Few creditors will likely agree to lend money in the sixth year, knowing that the debt will likely not be repaid. For this reason, the Torah warns:

> Beware lest you harbor the base thought, "The seventh year, the year of remission, is approaching," so that you are mean to your needy kinsman and give him nothing. He will cry out to the Eternal against you, and you will incur guilt. Give to him readily and have no regrets when you do so, for in return the Eternal your God will bless you in all your efforts and in all your undertakings. (Deuteronomy 15:9–10)

It seems that neither the biblical threat of punishment nor the promise of divine reward was sufficient to persuade lenders to part with their money as the *sh'mittah* year approached. Thus, regardless of this biblical warning, it seems that potential lenders—quite understandably—resisted parting with their money in advance of *sh'mittah*. According to the Mishnah, the great rabbi Hillel "saw that people were avoiding lending to one another, and were transgressing what is written in the Torah."[23] In response, "Hillel established prozbul for the sake of *tikkun ha-olam*." This institution of prozbul allows the court to take control of debts and to collect these after *sh'mittah*, since the provision for forgiving debts applies only to those from a private lender.

In creating the institution of *prozbul*, Hillel simultaneously protected the system of lending and borrowing that allowed the economic system to function, and eliminated debt forgiveness altogether. While the consequences of this decision may not be as immediately dramatic as Rambam's king executing murderers, both situations prioritize positive long-term outcomes over more difficult short-term ones. In the case of *prozbul*, individuals lose the chance to erase their debts, and they may therefore end up stuck in poverty, or even forced to become indentured servants. Hillel apparently determined that this possibility paled in comparison to the more dire prospect of an entire year, once in every seven-year cycle, in which no one would ever lend or borrow money. Similarly, Rambam assumed that a few executions were a small price to pay if it would lead to a world less plagued by murder. In both cases, the focus on tikkun olam leads to the abrogation of Torah law, rather than simply an elimination of loopholes, as in other cases of *tikkun olam*.

The concept of *tikkun olam* forces us to consider the long-term consequences of any action or legal stipulation. At the same time, *tikkun olam* does not permit for gross disregard of individual laws. For Rambam, the king does not have full power to enact laws, try cases, and carry out sentences. Instead, he has some specific—if problematic—leeway to act in cases in which the system of justice proves inadequate. As we have seen, later commentators see the danger in this permission, and restrict the power of the king even further. As for Hillel, he seems to have recognized *prozbul* as a necessary correction at a time when people were disregarding Torah law. This case parallels Herzog's permission to act differently according to the moral state of society.

In contemporary Jewish life, it has become popular to use the term *tikkun olam* to refer to everything from serving lunch in a soup kitchen to giving *tzedakah* to advocating for legislation. The difficult example of Rambam's king instead asks us to view *tikkun olam* as a challenge to keep our vision on long-term change, without going too far in ignoring short-term needs.

At first glance, Rambam's use of *tikkun olam* may offend those of us who oppose capital punishment and are distrustful of kings (or other powerful rulers) to do what is best for society as a whole. Without letting go of these anxieties, we can acknowledge that Rambam's understanding of *tikkun olam* parallels that of the Mishnah: both cases force us to think about the effect of law on large social and economic structures, rather than simply consider the correct ruling in a given situation. The Sanhedrin and a *beit din*, as judicial bodies, can address only the presenting case. The king, who has the broad view, can and should consider long-term implications and act accordingly.

Today, we have no such figure as Rambam's king—a perfect ruler concerned only with the betterment of society. Perhaps no such leader has ever existed. We should not, therefore, engage with the text in question literally, as permission for our own rulers to carry out capital punishment. Instead, we might ask: What are the laws, policies, loopholes, or absences that lead to *hash·ḥatat yishuvo shel olam* today? How can we, like the ideal king, take the long view toward addressing these? What laws, policies, or structures must we put into place in order to achieve the state of *tikkun olam* to which both the Mishnah and Rambam aspire?

NOTES

[1] For a more detailed overview of the history of the term *tikkun olam*, see Jill Jacobs, *There Shall Be No Needy: Pursuing Social Justice Through Jewish Law and Tradition* (Woodstock, VT: Jewish Lights Publishing, 2009), pp. 24–40.

[2] Rambam is Rabbi Moses ben Maimon, also known as Maimonides (1138–1204).

[3] M.T. Hilkhot Melakhim U-milḥ'moteihem 3:10.

[4] M.T. Hilkhot Rotzei·aḥ U-shemirat Nefesh 2:4.

[5] M.T. Hilkhot Rotzei·aḥ U-shemirat Nefesh 2:5.

[6] M. Makkot 1:11.

[7] For more on the concept of *tzelem Elohim*, see Yair Lorberbaum, *Tzelem Elohim: Halakhah Va-aggadah* (Jerusalem: Schocken, 2004). Much has been written on capital punishment in Judaism. See, for example, Beth A. Berkowitz, Execution and Invention: *Death Penalty Discourse in Early Rabbinic and Christian Cultures* (New York: Oxford University Press, 2006).

[8] For more on the institution of the *kippah*, see Jacobs, *There Shall Be No Needy*, pp. 204–208.

[9] Ibid., pp. 28–34.

[10] For more on this, see Menaḥem Lorberbaum, "*Tikkun Olam Al-Pi Ha-rambam: Iyyun B'takhliyyot Ha-halakhah*," Tarbiz 64:1 (1998), pp. 65–82.

[11] The Ran is Rabbeinu Nissim of Gerona (1320–1376). His comments may be found in his sermon no. 11 in *Sh'neim Asar D'rushim L'ha-rav Rabbeinu Nissim* (ed. Warsaw, 1875), p. 38a.

[12] Y. Sanhedrin 6:6, 23b–c.

[13] See, for example, *Migdal Oz* on M.T. Hilkhot Melakhim U-milḥ'moteihem 3:10.

[14] Radbaz is Rabbi David ben Solomon ibn Abi Zimra (c. 1479-1573); see his comment on M.T. Hilkhot Melakhim U-milḥ'moteihem 3:10.

[15] Lorberbaum, "*Tikkun Olam Al-Pi Ha-rambam*," passim.

[16] Ibid, p. 69, my translation. There is a difference of opinion between Lorberbaum and Gerald Blidstein regarding the relationship between *din ha-malkhut* and the ordinary system of law. Blidstein argues that the existence of the king's law is a pragmatic approach to balancing the ideal law with the needs of society, whereas Lorberbaum sees *din ha-malkhut* as a built-in system that works alongside the regular legal system. See Yaakov (Gerald) Blidstein, *Ekronot M'diniyim B'mishnat Ha-rambam: Iyyunim B'mishnato Ha-iyyunit* (Ramat Gan: Bar-Ilan University, 1983), pp. 118–130; Lorberbaum, "*Tikkun Olam Al-Pi Ha-rambam*," and idem, *Politics and the Limits of Law: Secularizing the Political in Medieval Jewish Thought* (Stanford, CA: Stanford University, 2001), pp. 51–61.

[17] Lorberbaum, *Politics and the Limits of Law*, p. 59.

[18] *T'ḥukkah L'yisrael al Pi Ha-torah* (Jerusalem: Mossad HaRav Kook, 1989), pp. 76–77.

[19] See, for example, Daniel S. Nagin and John V. Pepper, "Deterrence and the Death Penalty" (Committee on Law and Justice at the National Research Council, April 2012), available on the website of the National Academies Press (www.nap.edu); Jeffrey Fagan, "Death and Deterrence Redux: Science, Law, and Causal Reasoning on Capital Punishment," in *Ohio State Journal of Criminal Law* 255 (2006), pp. 6–105.

[20] *Mamzeir* is the technical term for the offspring of two parents who could not licitly be married, generally the product of an incestuous union or of one between a married woman and a man other than her husband; it does not refer to someone simply born out of wedlock.

[21] M. Gittin 4:5.

[22] For such a discussion, see particularly the essay of Gail Labovitz elsewhere in this volume.

[23] M. Sheviit 10:3.

[24] M. Gittin 4:3.

The Relationship Between Spirituality and Morality in Deepening the Commitment to *Tikkun Olam*

Jonathan Wittenberg

"Great is learning," runs the conclusion of the famous debate between Rabbi Tarfon and Rabbi Akiva as to whether study or good deeds is greater, "because learning leads to action."[1] My argument in this essay is that attentiveness to the sacred leads us to action, while action in turn brings us back to the sacred, to seek replenishment and renewed inspiration. There thus exists a profound and compelling relationship between the spiritual and the moral. Sensitivity to God's voice makes us aware of what we must do here on earth, while the commitment and courage required for action is most deeply sustained by a rich and disciplined life of the spirit.

I shall begin by considering how God's presence touches us and motivates us to care for and love the world around us. I will then suggest how this can lead to a response of *tikkun*, of commitment to both the inner task of spiritual renewal and restoration, and also the outer work of practical engagement and reparation. I will consider the importance of prayer and Torah study as part of this process and briefly outline some of the principles that should, I believe, guide our actions.

If God is present in all things, then all things speak God's commandments. Traditionally, Judaism understands these commands to have been communicated by God to Moses, delivered by him to Israel, and interpreted by subsequent generations to create the structure of Jewish laws and observances that are intended to govern our lives.

But there is a parallel mystical tradition that God's voice can also be heard throughout all of nature, through the *asarah ma·amarot* ("ten utterances") by which God formed the world and which still reverberate through all created matter.[2] Sometimes, seeing even a bird, a dragonfly, or a fox pausing in the road before disappearing behind the hedge, I feel I am hearing that voice. Often it fills me with a sense of wonder, occasionally with shame; but it always possesses great power. With a compulsion deeper than any language, it calls us to be mindful of the presence and oneness that connect us all. Perhaps it is to this kind of awareness that Isaiah refers in his vision of universal redemption: "They shall not hurt nor destroy in all of My holy mountain, for the earth shall be full of the knowledge of the Eternal as the waters cover the sea" (Isaiah 11:9). I never think of that mountain solely as a specific geographical location, the Temple Mount in Jerusalem, but rather as an image of the entire world and all of life in its diversity. Isaiah thus gives expression to what is, to me, the root and the essence of all the commandments: the demand that we respect and cherish all life, and strive to never wantonly or carelessly harm it.

At the moments when we apprehend this reality, this claim on our attentiveness and respect transcends any theoretical underpinnings for belief in revelation. Here is God's presence directly before us—in these trees, this bird, this human being—and it speaks immediately to our feeling of kinship with it, because we too belong to the one spirit

> ...that impels
> All thinking things, all objects of all thought,
> And rolls through all things.[3]

"Don't hurt" and "don't destroy": these commandments—whether expressed as words of admonition, as a silence tense with outrage or desolate with mourning, or as quiet reverence—can be intuited from

all being. We may hear them in the voice of an anxious child or in
the cry of a tormented animal; we may infer them from the semi-
desert of dead stumps where a forest formerly grew and birds fed in
the branches.[4] This call is at one and the same time the most potent
and the most powerless in the world. It is consistently unheeded, yet
it is there for all to hear.

That paradox is captured in the psalmist's assertion, in
contemplating the wonders of God's creation, that "day talks with
day and night whispers knowledge to night" (Psalm 19:3). Yet, the
psalm continues: "There is no speech and there are no words; their
voice is not heard at all" (*ein omer v'ein d'varim b'li nishma kolam*,
19:4), as if the communication were no more than an illusion—or,
at best, so secret as to be hidden entirely from human apprehension.
However, the Hebrew also suggests the very opposite interpretation:
ein omer v'ein d'varim, "there is no speech and there are no words";
b'li nishma kolam, "without their voice being heard"—that is, there
is no living being in all of creation that does not participate in the
sacred, and there is no form of expression in which the voice of God
is not articulated. It is precisely this tension between the two possible
meanings of the verse that Yehudah Halevi (c. 1075-1141) captures
in his great poem, *Yah, Anna Emtza·akha* ("God, where shall I find
You?"):

> God, where shall I find You; for Your place is exalted and hidden!
> And where shall I find You not, for Your glory fills the world!
> Who can claim that they have not seen You? Behold, the heavens
> and their hosts
> Proclaim the awe of You, *b'li nishma kolam*, without their voice
> being heard.[5]

Throughout the ages, mystics of all faiths have addressed our yearning
to hear—and our deep conviction that we can and do apprehend—
God's voice within creation. Thus the Maggid of Mezeritch (c. 1700-

1772), successor to the Baal Shem Tov in the leadership of the early Hasidic movement, understands the sentence from the daily morning prayers, *malah ha-aretz kinyanekha*, not according to the conventional meaning that "the world is full of what is Yours, God," but rather as teaching us that "the world is full of ways of acquiring You"—that there is nothing that does not speak of God's presence and there is no place in which God's presence cannot be found.[6]

The nineteenth-century British poet Gerald Manley Hopkins (1844–1889), who took his vows as a Jesuit in 1870, used the simile of a shaft of light dazzlingly reflected off bright metal to evoke the brilliance of God's presence:

> The world is charged with the grandeur of God.
> It will flame out, like shining from shook foil.[7]

I cannot be alone in experiencing that sacred radiance as "shining out" only rarely, in privileged but infrequent moments of great wonder or joy. This is not because the light is absent, but because my attention is not present. I have to re-attune myself, to remind myself to observe it.

The presence of the sacred within creation does more than simply arouse our feeling of wonder. It calls out to our sense of responsibility; its demands on us are urgent and immediate. In his final address, delivered just three days before he died, the moral philosopher Hans Jonas (1903–1993), best known for his essay "The Concept of God after Auschwitz," spoke of "the outcry of mute things." Reflecting on the Holocaust, during which his mother had been murdered, Jonas observed that humanity was now confronted by a danger of even greater import, the all-embracing challenge of which had rendered questions of race "anachronistic, irrelevant, almost farcical." He was speaking of the fate of the earth itself. He concluded, in what was to be the final sentence in a lifetime of engagement with questions of the origins, nature, and compass of our moral responsibility: "The latest revelation—from no Mount Sinai, from no Mount of the

Sermon, from no Bo (tree of Buddha)—is the outcry of mute things themselves that we must heed by curbing our powers over creation, lest we perish together on a wasteland of what was [that] creation."[8]

It is from within this silent cry—which in moments of exaltation the prophets and psalmists understood as the song of the forests and the dancing of the hills, and in moments of pain the rabbis described as the call of the dying tree whose voice "reverberates from one end of the world to the other, yet no one hears"—it is from within this silent cry that God speaks to us.[9] Jonas apprehends in it not the spontaneous outburst of natural joy, but rather the powerless plea of a voiceless world that demands our urgent attention. This appeal addresses us in the totality of our being—heart, soul, and conscience—and it pulls at the core of our moral and spiritual being.

It is of course possible to live a life of moral commitment without any engagement with or interest in the spiritual quest. The greatness of the need provides sufficient motivation in and of itself: the need of the hungry for food, of the homeless for shelter, of the refugee for a safe haven, of the ravaged hillside for replanting. Many people experience the desire to do what is right and good as deriving from a moral imperative unconnected to either religion or spiritual intuition. Indeed, the appeal to God may seem like a pious distraction, when suffering demands our immediate and practical involvement. Thus Elliot Dorff writes that "Jewish sources provide a series of rationales for caring for others, and some of them…invoke God much less than others do. As a result, atheistic or agnostic Jews can find ample grounds in the Jewish tradition for the duty to help others, and even those who affirm a belief in God will at times be motivated more by Judaism's nontheistic reasons than by its theistic ones."[10] He is surely correct, and this is no doubt a significant benefit; after all, the greater the range of reasons that draw us into doing what is right and good, the better.

Yet to the person to whom God is important, the realms of the spiritual and the moral cannot be separated. They converge to form a compelling sense of inescapable commitment. They require each other. Furthermore, unless spirituality expresses itself in moral action, it is liable to degenerate into a sophisticated form of narcissism. At the same time, moral engagement is most profoundly sustained by a spiritual communion that restores our vision and replenishes our energy.

The desire for *tikkun*—for reparation, restoration to how things should be according to the demands of justice and compassion—has different but interrelated dimensions. Combined with *nefesh* ("soul"), it becomes *tikkun ha-nefesh*, which can be understood as the personal journey of inner spiritual and moral development through which we refine both who we are and how we perceive the world.[11] Connected to *olam* ("world"), it becomes *tikkun olam*, "putting the world right." Loosely translated as "social action," the root meaning of this phrase is "the reparation or perfection of the world." It refers to activity that is essentially restorative, requiring us to care for and protect the earth so that it can be healed and re-established according to a vision of how it might and ought to be. The broad concept of *tikkun* thus connects the redemption of the self with the ultimate goal of the redemption of all life. While these objectives can be understood quite independently from each other, the two aspects of *tikkun* can also be seen as intimately connected.

Tikkun ha-nefesh may be described as the desire to attune one's own spirit to God's spirit, to align one's own consciousness with the sacred oneness that fills all being. The value of prayer can be understood in this way, as a regular and disciplined endeavor to realign and refocus our awareness. Haunted by thousands of nagging demands on our attention, the consciousness is unrelentingly assailed by distractions of every color. Many of them may indeed be important, but they may distract us from the call that is much less voluble yet far more urgent: the sound of God's voice in all being, what Hans Jonas called "the mutely insistent appeal of [God's] unfulfilled goal."[12]

Thus *tikkun ha-nefesh* may begin with listening. In this way it is profoundly connected with *yirat shamayim*, awe before heaven, before the sacred in all being. *Yirat shamayim* is misunderstood if it is taken to imply little more than fear of God's power or punishment. Rather, at its highest it is an expression of respect and reverence—not just for God, as if God were solely a separate and distant being, but before the sanctity of life itself, before the integrity and uniqueness of all created being. True awe, implies Rabbi Kalonymus Kalman Shapiro (later known simply as the *rebbe* of the Warsaw Ghetto), is not simply *yirah* but *yirah she-b'ahavah*, that reverence which is an essential part of love, which may be understood as the desire not to hurt or harm in any way the object of our concern because of the respect, appreciation, and ultimately love that we feel toward it.[13] Thus *yirah* coupled with *ahavah*, awe and love together, express the heartfelt concern that we should not in any way damage what we care about most deeply and thereby bring upon ourselves sorrow and shame because of our failure to protect and cherish something so precious. Such feelings might be stirred by a lonely child, a destitute refugee, the raw heart of a friend, a calf on the way to the slaughterhouse, or a needlessly uprooted tree.

Crucial to *tikkun ha-nefesh* is the combination of such sensitivity—which I, like many of us, fail to attain the great majority of the time—with an awareness of our accountability. This is expressed in classical rabbinic literature as the recognition that we are judged for all our deeds, both in the present and the hereafter: "Know what is above you: an eye that sees, an ear that hears, and all your actions written in a book," teaches Rabbi Judah the Patriarch.[14] The image of God in heaven recording our every deed, and especially misdeed, in a Book of Memories (*sefer ha-zikhronot*, as it is called in the liturgy)—which the verdict is read out yearly on the High Holy Days—provokes in many people a sense of disbelief, which only our residual feelings of guilt and anxiety prevent us from dismissing entirely. Yet those very fears (or intuitions) indicate that whatever we may feel about so literal a picture of the deity passing sentence, the feeling that we both are and want to be known and judged, is anything but irrelevant to our conscience and to our moral life. Accountability before God may therefore be more vividly understood within the immediacy of our historical context and relationships, as our answerability to each other and to all life for our actions, words, and even thoughts in every situation and interaction in which we are engaged. We exist in constant kinship with all other living beings and the quality of our responses— whether to other creatures or to our shared environment—is always felt, always registered somewhere, and somehow and always makes a difference—even if the effect is imperceptible to us at the time. Because God is present in all life, the way in which life around us is aware of and takes note of us is also, in effect, a measure of God's judgment of us. Stephen Duncan poignantly captures this sense of ethical and spiritual interconnectedness in his remarkable voice poem "Grandma's Philosophy":

> She even said
> Be nice to the trees
> Because even the breeze is your companion
> And the sun sees every hand that moves wrongly
> And scorches the serenity of its present calm…
> So be careful when you shout
> Because the universe can hear you.[15]

Such apprehension leads to a profound and disturbing understanding of the implications of being commanded. It never lets go of us. Awareness of it is never, and never can be, simply an end in itself. Rather, it is a ceaseless call to service, an appeal that knows of no escape and no time off. The failure to act, the refusal to care, is always a multiple betrayal; I at once let down the spirit within me, the life before me, and that aspect of the sacred or divine that is present and embodied within in it. Thus *tikkun ha-nefesh* leads compellingly and ineluctably to *tikkun olam*.

The specific commandments and duties described by the Torah and defined and refined over millennia by rabbinic analysis can be understood as the means of directing this consciousness of the depth and value of the life of all things into appropriate attitudes and actions. Precisely what these must be at any given time requires a constantly renewed consideration of context, of both the intellectual and moral continuity of the rabbinic tradition and the exigencies of the hour in which we are called upon to respond. Thus the culture of ceaseless debate as to what is right and just, as to what constitutes God's will in any and all of the circumstances of human life—which is the hallmark of Jewish, and specifically of talmudic, culture—is and must be ongoing, impassioned, and relentless.

There is no single formula for the relationship between action and intention: does the motivation precede the deed, or does action itself engender deeper motivation? The answer must be both: sometimes, our inner conviction leads us to act; at other times, involvement in a task subsequently leads us to deeper awareness.

Returning to the discussion of *yirat shamayim*, awe before heaven, the Talmud offers two challenging analogies. In the first, Rabbah son of Rav Huna asks rhetorically what a person is like who has knowledge of Torah but no awe before heaven. Such a person, he explains, is like a treasurer whose money is kept in a safe within a safe, and who has the keys to the inner chest but not those to the outer container. How, Rabbah asks bluntly, is one to get in? Here, knowledge of Torah represents the inner chamber, God's secret treasure house; but without the first key of *yirat shamayim*, awe before heaven, a person lacks the essential means to access it.[16] The inference is as clear as it is radical: knowledge of Torah undirected by reverence and wonder is of limited spiritual value. Indeed, we cannot even understand what such knowledge truly entails. Yet, at the same time that very sense of reverence now leads us to Torah; it requires knowledge of Torah in order to bring it into full focus. Torah and *halakhah* guide the vital experience of the sacred into channels of appropriate action and response.

Equally, though, right actions have the power to lead us back to a deeper awareness of the sacred. In our daily lives, actions often precede feelings. There are many situations when we are called upon to take action, and when dwelling on our thoughts and motivations would be an indulgence. One doesn't ask oneself what one feels when a child is on the pavement bleeding. Often one just has to get on with doing what is necessary and right. Even then, though, as Abraham Joshua Heschel so beautifully wrote, the commandments do not function solely as ends in themselves but rather "lead us to wells of emergent meaning, to experiences which are full of hidden brilliance of the holy."[17] Doing what we have to do in the moment guides us back to a reconsideration of our values.

Thus, in the same discussion of *yirat shamayim*, awe before heaven, the Talmud offers a second, different analogy: "Alas for the person who has no courtyard," declares Rabbi Yannai, "but makes a gateway into it."[18] In other words, what's the point of having a gate if you have no land to which it leads? Here, the gate represents the "doorway" of Torah: it comes first because in passing through it we are subsequently made aware of the need to create the kind of home, the sort of world, that its precepts demand. Through our deeds, our motivation is deepened and refined, leading us to a deep sense of reverence. Indeed, Judaism has always maintained the view that *mi-tokh she-lo li-sh'mah ba li-sh'mah*, that "out of doing things for the wrong motive we can arrive at doing them for the right reasons"— that good actions have the power to purify those who do them.[19]

For these reasons, Torah study is an essential part of *tikkun olam*. This is not simply because Torah and Talmud are our heritage and we should study them out of respect for the past and for the sake of Jewish continuity. Nor, as it has been put somewhat cynically, is it so that we should appreciate that what we are doing anyway is actually something Jewish. Rather, the study of Torah—both the specific texts of Torah, and also Torah in its widest sense as embracing the whole discourse of Judaism through the ages—is essential, because it immerses us in an enduring and incisive conversation defined and refined by the search for what is just and right before humanity, creation, and God.

Furthermore, as in every generation, we are responsible for creating a full and deep engagement between Torah and those specific issues that beset us in our day. This is important both so that we can examine them through the moral and spiritual disciplines that Judaism has given us, and also so that whatever may be learned from our own age can become part of the legacy of the vital and contemporary Judaism that we bequeath to our children.

Some of the key concepts that must inform this ongoing discourse include:

- moral responsibility and its inescapability, based on the core beliefs that we have the capacity for both moral discernment and freedom of action, and on the understanding that the other person is always our brother, sister or neighbor, be he or she rich or poor, in health or in need of care;
- the equally shared dignity of all human life, based on the creation narrative, wherein all people are made in God's image; on the commandment that no innocent blood must ever be shed; and on the belief that God hears the cry of the oppressed;
- the centrality and impartiality of justice, rooted in the commandment that we must not attend to the status of the plaintiff but rather to the merit of the case, and especially in the core or meta-narrative of Judaism to which we refer every day— namely, that we were slaves in the land of Egypt, that our very identity was formed out of the experience of being the victims of injustice, and that we are therefore eternally committed to the implementation of justice at every level and in every sphere of life;
- compassion, based on the understanding that we are the instruments of God's desire that there should be compassion on earth, and on the insistence that we are not allowed "to hide

ourselves away from our own flesh" (Isaiah 58:7)—that is, from the basic necessities of food, drink, clothing, healing, shelter, protection, and companionship, which we all experience and which every human being requires;

- respect for the natural world, founded on the awareness that it belongs not to us but to God, that it is entrusted to our care, and that we are thus bound not to destroy it, not to waste its gifts, not to treat it as our rubbish bin, and not to bring suffering or destruction to any species with which we share the privilege of life;

- the primacy of deeds, the realization that it is not our beliefs alone that matter, or our adherence to the forms of culture or religion, but our actions, the way we live and implement our values every day.

All these principles, and the many texts that underlie them, require attentive debate; only our generation can determine how they should be interpreted and fulfilled in our world today. One of our most important tasks is therefore to develop a contemporary dialogue with these core concepts of the Torah. A key aim must be to articulate for our own time, within the language of Judaism, the principles of a universal ethic within open and democratic societies, in which Jews participate fully and equally alongside people of other faiths and philosophies, and carry a proportion of the shared responsibility for the moral conduct of the country in which they live, as well as of the world as a whole. Jewish law has never been a hermetically sealed system bound solely by its own rules; it has always existed in dialectic tension with new ideas and realities—because "it is not in heaven" but on the earth, and it does not lack the creative capacity to respond to the needs of that earth and the people and life that it sustains.[20]

An especially urgent part of this task is the need to extend and apply the laws of *bal tash·ḥit* (the prohibition of wanton destruction) and tza·ar ba·alei ḥayyim (the prohibition of causing suffering to animals) so as to formulate an adequate approach to action concerning the environment.[21] Not long ago I saw the film *A Sacred Duty: Applying*

Jewish Values to Help Heal the World, produced by the American Jewish Vegetarian Society. One of the closing scenes shows a pen in which a calf is trapped among scores of terrified animals, pressed against the wire fence of the enclosure into which they have been herded prior to their transportation to the slaughterhouse, and from which there is no escape. The calf weeps in utter desolation. In its tears I glimpsed a fraction of the unbounded measure of the helpless suffering of innocent life in the face of the calf's tormentors and oppressors, and I felt that I was witnessing the indictment of our entire civilization for its immeasurable cruelty and brutality toward the rest of creation. Can such behavior possibly be considered as God's will?

One evening when I was in my early twenties and unsure what path to follow and what I wanted to do with my life, my father and I happened to watch a television program about the work of the charity organization "Doctors Without Borders." After a few minutes, during which we saw a group of young people struggling to treat sick and destitute people in what looked like the middle of nowhere, my father said to me, "And what about you?" My father was never prolix in his criticisms, with the result that I remember very clearly those moments when he did chide or challenge me. Although I have tried to better the world, I often still feel as if I'm still watching that program with him and struggling to respond to his question. There are many thousands of people who show remarkable compassion, courage, and selflessness in what they do for others and the world. They serve by their actions as a goad and an example—whatever their faith, nationality, or motivation. It is what they do, and what each of us does, that matters most.

Yet alongside the necessity of responding to the suffering around us, there is an existential and spiritual need to answer with our lives the question that Elijah heard in the voice of fine silence, in the mute articulacy of life itself, and which the prophet intuited as God's question not only to him but to every human being: "What are you doing here, Elijah?" (1 Kings 19:12,13). What am *I* doing here?

What are *you* doing here? Then, once we have found our particular response to the commandment implied within the question, and made the inner resolution to try to live by it, we need the sustenance and restoration offered by grace and beauty, by reverence and awe, by God's presence within all life that so wondrously surrounds us.

NOTES

[1] B. Kiddushin 40b, where the intention of the majority of rabbis is to side neither with Rabbi Tarfon (who advocates the primacy of learning over action—that is, the performance of the *mitzvot*) nor with Rabbi Akiva (who espouses the opposite view), but rather to emphasise the interdependence of the study of Torah and carrying out its precepts. Neither enterprise on its own makes sense without the other.

[2] The *asarah ma·amarot* (M. Avot 5:1), the ten divine utterances, are the ten times that God spoke in the creation of the world. The Talmud (at B. Rosh Hashanah 32b and Megillah 21b) notes that there are in fact only nine such references, and therefore counts *b'reishit*, "in the beginning" (Genesis 1:1), as the first such utterance. These *ma·amarot* are understood in many places in Jewish mystical literature to constitute a channel of divine revelation that is parallel to the Ten Commandments (thus, see Zohar III 11b).

[3] William Wordsworth, "Lines Composed A Few Miles Above Tintern Abbey," cited from *The Poems of William Wordsworth* (London: Edward Moxon, 1845), pp. 160–161.

[4] The commandment of *lo tash·ḥit* or *bal tash·ḥit*, "do not destroy," originates in the injunction in Deuteronomy 20:19 that a besieging army may not cut down fruit-bearing trees to use the wood to make instruments of war. From here, the scope of the prohibition expanded to include such acts of wanton destruction as tearing clothing, smashing dishes, pulling down buildings, or ruining food for no reason (M.T. Hilkhot Melakhim 6:10).

[5] *Yah, Anna Emtza·akha*, a a liturgical poem (*piyyut*) by Yehudah Halevi, opening couplet and end of third verse. This is my translation of the text published by Samuel Philipp in his edition of Halevi's poetry, with notes by Samuel David Luzzatto (Lemberg: Wolf, 1888), pp. 81–82.

[6] Referred to in the name of the Maggid of Mezeritch by Rabbi Shalom Noah Berezovsky of Slonim, "On Rosh Hashanah," in *Sefer N'tivot Shalom: On the Festivals*, vol. 2 (Jerusalem: Yeshivat Beit Avraham Slonim, s.a.), p. 134b.

[7] Gerald Manley Hopkins, "God's Grandeur," in his *Poems and Prose*, selected and edited by W. H. Gardner (London, New York, et al.: Penguin Books, 1976), p. 27.

[8] Hans Jonas, "The Outcry of Mute Things," in his *Mortality and Morality: A Search for the Good after Auschwitz*, ed. Lawrence Vogel (Evanston, IL: Northwestern University Press, 1996), pp. 201–202.

[9] *Pirkei D'Rabbi Eliezer*, ch. 34, quoted in *The Book of Legend, Sefer Ha-aggadah: Legends from the Talmud and Midrash*, ed. Ḥayyim Naḥman Bialik and Yehoshua Hana Ravnitsky, trans W. G. Braude (New York: Schocken Books, 1992), §773, p. 138.

[10] Elliot Dorff, *The Way Into Tikkun Olam* (Woodstock, VT: Jewish Lights Publishing, 2005), pp. 12 and 23.

[11] *Tikkun ha-nefesh* is not a well-established expression in Jewish spiritual literature, although there does exist the eleventh-century moralist work *Tikkun Middot Ha-nefesh* by the Spanish Jewish poet and Neoplatonist philosopher Solomon ibn Gabirol. I am using the phrase to refer to the inner process of *tikkun*—that is, spiritual development and purification in contrast to and in partnership with the outer work in the wider world that is generally meant when speaking of *tikkun olam*.

[12] Hans Jonas, "The Concept of God after Auschwitz: A Jewish Voice" in *Mortality and Morality*, p. 141.

[13] Rabbi Kalonymus Kalmish Shapiro, *Sefer Derekh Ha-melekh* (Tel Aviv: Va·ad Ḥasidei Piaseczno, 1976), *passim*.

[14] Pirkei Avot 2:1.

[15] Stephen Duncan, "Grandma's Philosophy," online at www.youtube.com/watch?v=_fBQUnHsZPc.

[16] B. Shabbat 31a–b.

[17] Abraham Joshua Heschel, *Man's Quest for God: Studies in Prayer and Symbolism* (1954; rpt. New York: Crossroad, 1987), p. 105.

[18] B. Shabbat 31b.

[19] For this idea, see, e.g., B. Pesaḥim 50b, Sotah 22b and 47a, Sanhedrin 105b, Horayot 10b, and Arakhin 16b. This view seems to me axiomatic in understanding Jewish views about motivation. A person is not to be rejected for doing things for the wrong reason, but appreciated for doing them at all—in the confidence that the process of engagement can be trusted to purify the motive.

[20] The words "it is not in heaven" are from Deuteronomy 30:12 and were later used by Rabbi Joshua in his fierce argument with Rabbi Eliezer in order to "prove" that the interpretation of the Torah is a matter not of divine revelation (i.e., "in heaven") but rather belongs to the realm of human debate and reasoning (B. Bava Metzia 59b).

[21] See note 4 above. We think of *tikkun* as action, yet it is also understood in the world of hasidic thought as perception, how we see the world, as the capacity for *yiḥudim*. See *Derekh Ha-melekh*, pp. 288–289.

Tikkun of the Self

Kim Treiger-Bar-Am

Tikkun olam can be understood to point to what one is to do for the *tikkun* of oneself. Even working with the conceptions of *tikkun olam* as regarding social justice and global change (in its current versions), or repairing the world by joining together the pieces shattered at the time of creation (in the kabbalistic view), it is the individual who undertakes the efforts of repair. I would like to propose that the term can be used to reference the self-repair of that individual. Where the goal of *tikkun* becomes the fixing of the self, the focus is narrowed from a wide scale to the individual; it denotes a move from the macro to the micro. What can be done with that change of perspective, looking to the *tikkun* of the individual self? I invite exploration of the effect that repair of the individual can have on correcting social ills and repairing the world.

Judaism shows great concern for the individual. Humanity is partnered with God in creation and tasked with repair of the world. Also, the individual's well-being is a predominant focus: the individual is called upon to aspire toward self-perfection. This notion of consciously bettering oneself has strong roots in Jewish heritage. A predominant aspect of *tikkun* of the self is learning. This facet of *tikkun* of the self is also a *tikkun* of the world both because the one is part of the many, but because one's learning facilitates the fixer's fixing of the world. I would like to put forward that the Jewish approach to repairing the self be seen as within *tikkun olam* strictures.

We can do *tikkun*, and we must. In Judaism, freedom and

obligation converge.[1] People are to aim to become the best that they can be. We have both the capacity and the responsibility for it. Our capacity to create is to be exercised and our potentiality fulfilled. Our capacity and also our responsibility reflect the moral dimension of our freedom.

The first use of the term *tikkun olam* in the Mishnah, the early codification of rabbinic law, was when adjustments to the *halakhah* were made "*mi-p'nei tikkun ha-olam*"—for the sake of repairing the world. So too, for the sake of the *tikkun* of the self through learning, adjustments to the practice of *halakhah* may be made. One example regards women's learning. Women's learning—including Torah study and prayer—should be promoted as part of Jewish women's self-*tikkun*. Supporting women's study and prayer *mi-p'nei tikkun ha-olam* will allow women to perfect themselves, and also will strengthen society.

The discussion in this essay begins with the centrality of the human in Judaism. Consideration of the *tikkun* of oneself, in particular through learning, follows. The Jewish approach to women's learning and prayer is then explored. *Tikkun olam*—or rather the mishnaic doctrine of *mi-p'nei tikkun ha-olam* ("for the sake of the world's repair")—is then offered as a means of amending the system and easing tensions in the Jewish community worldwide.

Centrality of the Human in Judaism

Judaism affords to the human a pivotal place. According to Jewish tradition, humankind is a partner with God in creation of the world.[2] In the Garden of Eden, God instructs the first person, Adam, to safeguard the world (Genesis 2:15). We are to complete creation[3] and keep it from dissolving.[4] The partnership between God and humankind is symbolized for example in the blessings at the time-honored Sabbath evening meal over wine and bread, which people make from the grapes and wheat that God allows to grow. The prominence of the human is seen in the process of *tikkun olam* and self-repair.

Tikkun olam sets for the individual an important task. The human being must play a part in the pursuit of social action: "[e]ach and every act upgrading the universe is of cosmic significance."[5] According to one school of Kabbalah, God placed tremendous energy into vessels of light that were shattered at the time of the creation of the world; human beings are tasked with reuniting the pieces into a whole. The bringing on of redemption depends on human beings.[6]

The repairer is to engage in self-repair. The kabbalistic understanding of *tikkun* begins with the perfection of the self.[7] Jewish tradition pays a great deal of attention to helping us reach towards perfection. The *mitzvot*—God's commands—are said to instruct us in bettering ourselves. The esteemed twelfth-century biblical commentator Maimonides (known as the Rambam) teaches that *mitzvot* are for education, i.e., to assist us in our effort to reach for perfection.[8] According to the thirteenth-century biblical commentator Nahmanides (known as the Ramban), all of the commandments are to refine and purify God's creatures.[9]

We are not required actually to *realize* perfection; we need not *be* perfect. Striving for self-betterment is a continuous process of *becoming*. Because of our creation in the image of God (*b'tzelem elohim*), we are able to become holy. The Bible affirms that the Jewish people are capable of becoming holy.[10] Just as becoming holy is a process, so too perfecting oneself can be considered a process.

How does one repair oneself? *Tikkun* of the self begins with learning.

Tikkun of the Self in Learning

Learning relies on our intellect, our engaging in Torah study, our passion for discovery, and our willingness to learn from others. Learning is both a freedom and an obligation. It is a freedom: upon their creation *b'tzelem elohim*, human beings possess the capacity to understand and discern.[11] Learning is also an obligation for humans,[12] and a duty to ensure education for all in the community.[13]

The intellect is a focal point in Jewish heritage. Biblical narrative is suffused with accounts of free intellectual debate in arguments with God, for instance in the negotiations with God undertaken by Abraham (Genesis 18) and by Moses (Exodus 32–33 and Numbers 14).[14] Intellectual rigor is further lauded in the Talmud. Even prophetic visions are said to come through the intellect.[15] The advancement of the intellect is the aim of humankind.[16]

The intellect is the touchstone of the human being. Maimonides points to rationality as the bond between humans and God, and teaches that with an active intellect human beings can approach seeing God.[17] The individual's perfection both intellectually and morally thus enables the individual to realize inner affinity with God, the transcendent Active Intellect.[18] In addition to intellectual perfection, Maimonides holds that perfection is to be sought on a moral plane.[19]

Jews are instructed to study Torah. Bible study, in Maimonides' view, is to continue beyond childhood.[20] But the prescription for education is much wider. Maimonides' substantial work on Jewish philosophy, *The Guide for the Perplexed*, begins with an Epistle Dedicatory in praise of the comprehension of mathematics and science. Also, for instance, the great Vilna Gaon (1720-1797) formally acknowledges the importance of education in science and mathematics alongside the study of *halakhah*.[21]

Humans are set the task of discovery. We are to uncover multiple approaches from different points and perspectives of earthly truth.[22] This prescription comes along with acknowledging and valuing the pluralism that the world offers. Haim Cohn, a former Justice of Israel's Supreme Court, writes of the obligation to have all matters on earth investigated in the most variegated and multifarious manner possible.... Anyone whom God has blessed with intellect and with the drive and curiosity to investigate on his own, by rational methods ... is in duty bound to make use of the capabilities and talents that God has bestowed [on us] by embarking on such investigations.[23]

The Jewish ethic teaches the need to learn from others. Wisdom, *ḥokhmah*, is what one learns from other people and from experience in the world.[24] The significance of wisdom is indicated in conjunction with understanding and knowledge.[25] All three are associated with Bezalel, the chief artisan of the Sanctuary that the Jews carried in their wanderings in the desert after their exodus from Egypt, as recounted particularly at Exodus 31:2-3 and 35:30-31. Bezalel's wisdom allowed him to learn from others. The chief artisan of King Solomon's Temple is also described as having the same three gifts.[26]

Women's Learning and Prayer

When I was a bat mitzvah at a Conservative synagogue back in the 1970s, girls were only allowed to recite the *haftarah* reading at Friday evening services. You may ask with surprise: *haftarah* on a Friday evening? What was that all about? At the time, it was deemed a progressive step to allow girls on the synagogue's *bimah*, its central platform, at all. This was as far as the synagogue would go to respect women and girls approaching the age of commitment to the *mitzvot*. Since that time various Jewish denominations have moved ahead in that sphere, but many challenges for women remain

The active roles in religious life that women have been taking include women's gatherings for prayer and study. Houses of study (*yeshivot*) for women and girls have been founded, and in some *yeshivot* women learn alongside men. Recently women have been ordained and become rabbis, and appointed *halakhic* advisers for rabbinic courts, congregational advisers and spiritual leaders. Efforts are underway to create "new possibilities of meaning in the existing corpus of Jewish tradition."[27] The synthesis of Jewish law with modern values of equality is said to move toward the covenantal goal of humankind being in the image of God,[28] from which Judaism will emerge stronger.[29] At the time of these efforts for increased active participation in prayer, the Women of the Wall are facing a challenge in Jerusalem.

In 2019—2019!—women are not allowed to pray in groups with their voices raised in prayer and read from a Torah scroll at the Western Wall (popularly called by its Hebrew name, the Kotel) in Jerusalem. A group of women known as Women of the Wall have been meeting for thirty years on the first each month (i.e., on Rosh Ḥodesh) to hold prayer services. Each month they face opposition; despite myriad appeals to the Israeli courts, their practice is still not protected.

In March 2019, the women planned a festive prayer service on Rosh Ḥodesh to mark the thirty-year anniversary of the Women of the Wall. I was planning to go. But the opponents of Women of the Wall arranged for thousands to appear and interrupt the prayers. I stayed away; fear kept me from attending the celebratory prayer service. Indeed some of the participants of Women of the Wall and others were hurt. The police said that the Women of the Wall were provocative. What was their provocation of the violence? That they were present for prayers.

There have been interpretations of *halakhah* according to which the style of Women of the Wall's prayer has been accepted. Former Deputy Chief Justice Menachem Elon, a practicing Orthodox Jew well-versed in Jewish law, reviewed *halakhah* in the first ruling before the Supreme Court on the issue of Women of the Wall's prayer. He referred to numerous rabbinic opinions that do not prohibit women's prayer in a group with articles of religious dress worn during prayer services, including *tallit* and *t'fillin*.[30] Moreover, an argument has been made that social changes affect the *halakhah* regulations regarding the donning of these items. Pursuant to *halakhah*, wearing the *tallit* and *t'fillin* in prayer are commandments involving a commitment of time, to which women are not obligated.[31] Yet some rabbis today take the position that this ruling is no longer applicable, as it was made during a period when women were fully dependent and had no control over their time.[32] Even when *halakhah* is taken to prohibit Women of the Wall, the way the rabbis developed the concept of *tikkun olam* suggests a manner of resolving the conflict.

How does *tikkun olam* enter the picture to help us here? Where the interpretation of *halakhah* bars Women of the Wall's prayer services, *tikkun olam* may call for halakhic adjustments *mi-p'nei tikkun ha-olam*, i.e., for the sake of *tikkun olam*. For the sake of the *tikkun* of the self, women's learning is to be encouraged, and mercy shown to them. *Tikkun* of the self is a part of *tikkun olam*.

The Mishnah prescribes modifying the *halakhah* and directing behavior considered good practice for the smooth functioning of society, in tractate Gittin, on the laws of divorce. For example, a woman needs a divorce decree, a *get*, from her husband in order to be able to remarry, but the *halakhah* allowed a *get* to be invalidated by a husband even while in transit to the wife and without the woman's knowledge. This loophole was annulled by the rabbis for the sake of *tikkun olam*.[33]

Another well-known example set forth in that tractate is the *prozbul* recommended by Hillel. Because all debts are canceled in the Sabbatical year pursuant to a Torah commandment, fewer loans ended up being made because potential lenders knew that debts would be canceled. To mitigate this result of the Torah commandment, Hillel devised a method whereby debts could be transferred to the ownership of the court and so were not canceled in the seventh year. The *prozbul* enabled loans to continue to be made for the poor, *mi-p'nei tikkun ha-olam*.[34]

Supporting Women of the Wall would be a means of *tikkun olam* in a variety of ways:

- Allowing Women of the Wall's worship practice will enable *tikkun* on the personal level by furthering the learning and prayer of the individual women participants and observers of Women of the Wall's Rosh Ḥodesh prayers. Women and girls will be encouraged to learn more, in terms of Torah study and prayer, and to participate in them both.

- *Tikkun* on the individual level also may be present for those who oppose the prayer services of Women of the Wall, as they will be brought to bestow mercy (*ḥesed*) upon women with whom they disagree. Showing *ḥesed* to others is a part of becoming holy.[35] Humans are created in the image of God, *b'tzelem elohim*, and as *ḥesed* is included among the attributes of God, human beings are to embody and display *ḥesed* as well.[36] Acting with *ḥesed* is in imitation of God. Indeed, God's spirit is to be brought down to earth.[37] The *ḥesed* we show to others is part of one's perfecting both oneself and the world around us.

- Endorsing the participants of Women of the Wall in their efforts to learn and worship will uphold the Jewish and democratic values of the State of Israel, and will be a *tikkun* for the entire nation. Jewish values will be promoted when Women of the Wall are permitted to pray, pursuant to the Talmudic principle known as *eilu v'eilu* ("these and those") according to which varying interpretations of Jewish practice and *halakhah* made in good faith are to be respected.[38] Democratic values of the state will also be advanced when Women of the Wall's worship is protected, as the principles of free speech and equality will be upheld. Permitting Women of the Wall's prayer practices will foster the coherence of the terms that constitutionally define Israeli society, and encourage the knitting together of the social fabric.[39]

- Permitting Women of the Wall's prayer services and bolstering its participants will improve relations between Israel and Jewish communities around the world, fostering an inner-Jewish *tikkun* on the international level. For instance, in the United States support for Women of the Wall is widespread. Endorsing Women of the Wall's efforts will further the accord between the parts of the whole Jewish people. The unity of the Jewish nation will thus be strengthened.

Hence *tikkun* of the self, of Israeli society, and of relations between Jews around the world will be cultivated by the encouragement of women's learning and prayer, including by Women of the Wall. The Israeli government, Israeli courts, Israeli society, and Jews throughout the world should take that stand proudly and unambiguously. *Tikkun ha-olam* will be enhanced.

Conclusion

The role and well-being of the individual have prominent places in Judaism. The tradition calls for *tikkun* of the self through learning. The *tikkun* of the individual affects the world, just as the micro always affects the macro. Torah study and prayer for women and girls bring this lesson forward. Women's prayer at the Kotel in Jerusalem is to be fostered. This is so for the sake of the *tikkun* of the individual women in prayer, of Israeli society, and indeed of the world, all *mi-p'nei tikkun ha-olam*. We have the freedom to do *tikkun* of our individual selves and *tikkun olam*, and we must: in Judaism, freedom and obligation go hand in hand. *Tikkun* of the self is a process of becoming, as also is *tikkun olam*. A saying of the Sages proclaims: "It is not your responsibility to finish the work [of perfecting the world], but you are not free to desist from it either."[40]

NOTES

[1] I address the continuum of freedom and obligation in Jewish tradition in my book *Positive Freedom and the Law* (Abingdon, England: Routledge, 2020), and my essay "Choice and Obligation," published in *Jewish Thought and Spirituality: U-Vacharta Ba-Chayim*, eds. David Birnbaum and Martin S. Cohen (New York: New Paradigm Publishing, 2018), pp. 11–30.

[2] Joseph B Soloveitchik, *The Lonely Man of Faith* (New York: Doubleday, 1965), p. 12 ("The peak of religious ethical perfection to which Judaism aspires is man as creator."); idem, *Halakhic Man* (Philadelphia: Jewish Publication Society, 1983), p. 101.

[3] B. Shabbat 119b in the name of Rabbi Hamnuna; *Etz Hayim: Torah and Commentary*, eds. David L. Lieber et al. (1985; rpt. New York: Rabbinical Assembly-Jewish Publication Society, 2001), p. 12 on Genesis 2:1.

[4] Avivah Gottlieb Zornberg, *Genesis: The Beginning of Desire* (Philadelphia: Schocken, 1995), pp. 27-28, citing the comments of Resh Lakish in B. Shabbat 88a and Rashi's comment on Psalms 75:4.

[5] Irving Greenberg, *The Jewish Way: Living the Holidays* (New York: Simon and Schuster, 2011), pp. 121 and 161.

[6] Gershom Scholem, *Kabbalah* (Jerusalem: Keter Publishing House, 1988), p. 142.

[7] Ibid., p. 178, citing Zohar II 215b-216a; David Patterson, *Emil L. Fackenheim: A Jewish Philosopher's Response to the Holocaust* (Syracuse: Syracuse Univ. Press, 2008), p. 165; David S. Ariel, *Kabbalah: The Mystic Quest in Judaism* (Lanham: Rowman & Littlefield, 2008), p. 180 (*tikkun* is a remedy designed to "heal the individual soul and repair the tear in the cosmos").

[8] In Maimonides, *Guide for the Perplexed* III 28 and 31, *mitzvot* are seen to inculcate truth, remove erroneous opinion, improve social relations, clear away injustice, and teach good morals.

[9] Naḥmanides on Deuteronomy 22:6. See also Ze'ev W Falk, "Can Judaism Incorporate Human Rights, Democracy, and Personal Autonomy?" in *On Liberty: Jewish Philosophical Perspectives*, ed. Daniel H Frank (New York: St. Martin's, 1999), p. 119.

[10] In Exodus 19:5, God prescribes: "If you abide My commandments, you *shall become* a special people," and in Leviticus 19:2, God instructs that the people of Israel *shall be* holy, for God is holy. The people are instructed to fulfill their potentiality and become holy—in the future tense. (But see Deuteronomy 14:2.)

[11] Maimonides, *Guide for the Perplexed* I 1, and Sforno on Genesis 1:27, where the authors discuss the human power of intellectual perception and discernment.

[12] Haim Cohn, *Human Rights in Jewish Law* (New York: KTAV, 1984), p. 18.

[13] Robert M. Cover, "Obligation: A Jewish Jurisprudence of the Social Order" in *Law, Politics, and Morality in Judaism*, ed. Michael Walzer (Princeton: Princeton University Press, 2006).

[14] See also Lenn E. Goodman, "*On Liberty* Reconsidered" in *On Liberty*, ed.

Frank, p, 19; Yoram Hazony, *The Philosophy of Hebrew Scripture* (Cambridge: Cambridge University Press, 2012), pp. 104 and 138–139.

[15] In Maimonides, *Guide for the Perplexed* II 36, II 41, and II 42, prophetic visions or dreams are deemed not antithetical to the intellect but as working in conjunction with it, the imagination is said to be the expression of the intellect and thus free from the senses, and people are called to aim towards (and the prophets begin to master) the rational faculty, the imaginative faculty, and moral habits.

[16] Maimonides, *Guide for the Perplexed* III 27.

[17] Ibid. III 52.

[18] Herbert Davidson, "Maimonides on Metaphysical Knowledge" in *Maimonidean Studies*, ed. Arthur Hyman (New York: Yeshiva University Press, 1992–1993), vol. 3, pp. 89–98; Kenneth Seeskin, *Autonomy in Jewish Philosophy* (Cambridge: Cambridge University Press, 2001), pp. 104–106.

[19] Maimonides, *Guide for the Perplexed* III 54.

[20] M.T. Hilkhot Talmud Torah 1:8.

[21] See his comment on Proverbs 6:4. On the relation of science and religion, see also Jonathan Sacks, *The Great Partnership: Science, Religion, and the Search for Meaning* (London: Hodder & Stoughton, 2011). Rabbi Elijah ben Shlomo Zalman, one of the foremost Jewish scholars of his day, was popularly called the Vilna Gaon ("the Genius of Vilna").

[22] Tanya White, "The Process of Truth and impact of Time," available at: https://contemplatingtorah.wordpress.com/2014/05/30/the-process-of-truth-and-impact-of-time-shavuot-5774/.

[23] Cohn, *Human Rights in Jewish Law*, p. 127.

[24] *Etz Hayim: Torah and Commentary*, citing Rashi's commentary to Exodus 35:31.

[25] The Habad hasidic movement is named for the acronym of *ḥokhmah*, *binah*, and *da·at* ("wisdom, understanding and knowledge").

[26] 1 Kings 7:14, part of the *haftarah* portion of the Prophets read in synagogue following the reading of the Torah account of Bezalel's work.

[27] Tamar Ross, *Expanding the Palace of Torah: Orthodoxy and Feminism* (Waltham, MA: Brandeis University Press, 2004), p. 176.

[28] Irving Greenberg, *The Voluntary Covenant* (New York: National Jewish Resource Center, 1982).

[29] Blu Greenberg, *On Women and Judaism: A View from Tradition* (Philadelphia: Jewish Publication Society, 1998), p. 37.

[30] HCJ 257/89, 2410/90 *Hoffman v Western Wall Commissioner*, IsrSC 48(2) PD 265 (1994) (Justice Elon) (para 26: on women's donning of *tallit* and *t'fillin* being permitted by Maimonides, Rabbenu Tam, and Ravad; paras 28D, 29, 38: on women's prayer groups; para 27: on reading the Torah). Former Justice Itzhak England refers to the ruling under Jewish law according to the rabbinic authority of the Wall, in the Additional Hearing HCJ 4128/00, *Director of Prime Minister's Office v Hoffman*, IsrSC (April 6, 2003) (Justice England, para

13).

[31] M. Kiddushin 1:7.

[32] *Gender Equality and Prayer in Jewish Law*, eds. Ethan Tucker and Micha'el Rosenberg (Jerusalem: Urim Publication, 2017); Ross, E*xpanding the Palace of Torah*, pp. 304 and 326, notes 12 and 13.

[33] M. Gittin 4:2–3 and 6.

[34] Ibid. 4:3.

[35] Kindness and mercy to others is behavior commanded for becoming holy in Leviticus 19. On the command to become holy, see above, n. 10. Acts of loving kindness – *gemilut ḥasadim* (a term related to *ḥesed*) – are said to be one of the three things upon which the world stands (instead of) M. Avot 1:2 (in the name of Shimon Ha-tzadik).

[36] B. Sotah 14a (in the name of Rabbi Ḥama son of R. Ḥanina) and B. Shabbat 133b (in the name of Abba Shaul). In the Guide for the Perplexed (at III 54), Maimonides writes that perfecting the human intellect allows an individual to approach the knowledge of God, which in turn leads to imitating God's attribute of *ḥesed*. Maimonides, M.T. Hilkhot De·iot 1:6.

[37] Soloveitchik, *Halakhic Man*, pp. 41 and 108.

[38] B. Eruvin 13b (in the name of Rabbi Abba, citing Shmuel). On varying practices based on varying interpretations, see B. Yevamot 14a.

[39] See my *Positive Freedom and the Law* (2019).

[40] M. Avot 2:16 (in the name of Rabbi Tarfon).

special acknowledgement to

Nora Frydman

Translation
Grant peace everywhere goodness and blessing,
Grace, lovingkindness and mercy to us and unto all Israel

.

Transliteration
Sim shalom tovah u-v'rakhah
ḥein va-ḥesed v'raḥamim aleinu ve-al kol Yisrael amekha

שִׂים שָׁלוֹם*

שִׂים שָׁלוֹם טוֹבָה וּבְרָכָה
חֵן וָחֶסֶד וְרַחֲמִים עָלֵינוּ וְעַל כָּל יִשְׂרָאֵל עַמֶּךָ

---

* **Sim Shalom** (Hebrew: שִׂים שָׁלוֹם; "Grant Peace") is a blessing that is recited near the end of formal Jewish prayer services. The precise form of the blessing varies depending on the service and the precise denomination along the Jewish spectrum.

www.BlechTapes.com

a focused YouTube channel

Benjamin Blech Exegesis

on 10-theme Mesorah Matrix

sequence of 12 twenty-minute tapes:

intro + 10 themes + outro

www.UnifyingScienceSpirituality.com

About the Contributors

Bradley Shavit Artson, Ph.D., (www.bradartson.com) holds the Abner and Roslyn Goldstine Dean's Chair of the Ziegler School of Rabbinic Studies and is Vice President of American Jewish University in Los Angeles, where he is a member of the Philosophy Department. Rabbi Artson is particularly interested in theology, ethics, and the integration of science and religion. He supervises the Miller Introduction to Judaism Program and mentors Camp Ramah in California. He is also Dean of the Zacharias Frankel College in Potsdam, Germany, ordaining rabbis for Europe. A regular columnist for the Huffington Post and for the Times of Israel, he is the author of 10 books and over 250 articles, most recently *God of Becoming & Relationship: The Dynamic Nature of Process Theology* (Jewish Lights).

Ira Bedzow is the director of the Biomedical Ethics and Humanities Program and assistant professor of medicine at New York Medical College. He is also senior scholar of the Aspen Center for Social Values.

Raḥel Berkovits teaches Mishnah, Talmud and *halakhah* at the Pardes Institute of Jewish Studies in Jerusalem. She writes articles and lectures widely in both Israel and abroad on topics concerning women and Jewish law, and recently published the book *A Daughter's Recitation of Mourner's Kaddish*.

Adena K. Berkowitz, M.A., D.H.L., J.D., is Scholar in Residence and co-founder of Kol HaNeshamah NYC, dedicated to re-energizing the spiritual life of both affiliated and not-yet-affiliated Jews. She is the co-author of *Shaarei Simcha: Gates of Joy*, a mini prayerbook—the first liturgical work in the modern era written by Orthodox women, and is also a visiting lecturer at Yeshivat Chovevei Torah Rabbinical School.

Benjamin Blech has served as a Professor of Talmud at Yeshiva University since 1966 and is the author of fifteen books and hundreds of articles. He has been recognized as an American Educator of the Year and is Rabbi Emeritus of the Young Israel of Oceanside.

Michael J. Broyde is a professor of law at Emory University as well as project director and senior scholar in the Emory University Center for the Study of Law and Religion.

Reuven P. Bulka, C.M., Ph.D., is the Rabbi of Congregation Machzikei Hadas in Ottawa, Ontario, Canada, chairs Trillium Gift of Life Network, the government agency responsible for Organ & Tissue Donation and Transplantation in Ontario, and is the author of over 35 books.

Nina Beth Cardin founded the Baltimore Jewish Environmental Network and was the founding co-chair of the Associated Jewish Community Federation of Baltimore's Sustainability Initiative. Rabbi Cardin currently serves as the Sustainability Advisor to the Central Maryland Ecumenical Council.

Yehonatan Chipman lives in Jerusalem. He is a professional translator of academic Judaica and an independent thinker who has written extensively about Jewish thought and theology. For the past fifteen years he has published a weekly commentary on the Torah portion entitled *Hitzei Yehonatan*.

Geoffrey Claussen is the Lori and Eric Sklut Emerging Scholar in Jewish Studies, director of the Jewish Studies Program, and Assistant Professor of Religious Studies at Elon University. He is current president of the Society of Jewish Ethics and is the author of *Sharing the Burden: Rabbi Simhah Zissel Ziv and the Path of Musar* (SUNY Press).

Martin S. Cohen, Ph.D., is the rabbi of the Shelter Rock Jewish Center in Roslyn, New York, and the senior editor of the Mesorah Matrix series. He also served as the senior editor of *The Observant Life*, a compendium of Jewish law and custom published by the Rabbinical Assembly in 2012. Rabbi Cohen's weekly blog can be viewed at www. theruminativerabbi.blogspot.com. His published works include *The Boy on the Door on the Ox* (2008) and *Our Haven and Our Strength: A Translation and Commentary on the Book of Psalms* (2004). He is currently writing a translation and commentary on the Torah and the Five Megillot.

Elliot N. Dorff, Rabbi, Ph.D., is Rector and Distinguished Service Professor of Philosophy at American Jewish University in Los Angeles. His service as a past President of Jewish Family Service of Los Angeles and Co-Chair of the Los Angeles Jewish Federation's task force on Serving the Vulnerable is directly relevant to this topic, as are two of his books: *To Do the Right and the Good: A Jewish Approach to Modern Social Ethics, and The Way Into Tikkun Olam (Repairing the World)*.

Aubrey L. Glazer, Ph.D. serves as senior rabbi at Congregation Beth Sholom, San Francisco. Aubrey is the author of *Mystical Vertigo: Kabbalistic Hebrew Poetry Dancing Cross the Divide (Academic Studies Press, 2013), A New Physiognomy of Jewish Thinking: Critical Theory After Adorno as Applied to Jewish Thought* (New York: Continuum, 2011), and *Contemporary Hebrew Mystical Poetry: How It Redeems Jewish Thinking* (Edwin Mellen Press: New York, 2009).

Jeremy Gordon was ordained at the Jewish Theological Seminary and serves the New London Synagogue in London, England. He has worked as a chaplain with the Red Cross in the aftermath of the 2001 9/11 attacks in New York and in a number of hospital and hospice environments. He is the author of the *Spiritual Vagabondry and the Making of a Rabbi* and blogs at www.rabbionanarrowbridge.blogspot.co.uk.

Daniel Greyber is the rabbi of the Beth El Synagogue in Durham, NC, and author of *Faith Unravels: A Rabbi's Struggle With Grief and God*. Formerly a nationally ranked swimmer, he served as USA Team Rabbi at the 2013 World Maccabiah Games. His articles have been featured in a wide range of Jewish publications.

Meesh Hammer-Kossoy teaches Talmud and Social Justice at the Pardes Institute of Jewish Studies in Jerusalem. She holds a Ph.D. in Talmud and Rabbinics from New York University.

Jill Jacobs is the Executive Director of T'ruah: The Rabbinic Call for Human Rights, which brings the moral voice of 1800 rabbis, cantors, and their communities to protecting human rights in North America, Israel, and the occupied Palestinian territories. She received rabbinical ordination and an MA in Talmud from the Jewish Theological Seminary. Her most recent book is *Where Justice Dwells* (Jewish Lights).

James Jacobson-Maisels, Ph.D., is the founder of Or HaLev: A Center for Jewish Spirituality and Meditation (http://orhalev.org/). Rabbi Jacobson-Maisels teaches at Haifa University, the Pardes Institute of Jewish Studies, and in a variety of settings in Israel and around the world.

Admiel Kosman, a renowned poet, is Professor for Jewish Studies at Potsdam University as well as the academic director of Geiger College, a training school for liberal rabbis, in Berlin. The author of several books and many articles in the field of talmudic research, and of collections of Hebrew verse, he also writes a regular column for Haaretz in which he interprets traditional stories in a postmodern light. His latest academic book is *Gender and Dialogue in the Rabbinic Prism* (Berlin, Walter de Gruyter), and his most recent collection of poetry is *Approaching You in English: Selected Poems* (Boston, Zephyr Press).

Rivon Krygier is the rabbi of the Adath Shalom, the first Masorti congregation in Paris. He holds a Ph.D. from the Sorbonne in the Science of Religions.

Vernon H. Kurtz is the rabbi of North Suburban Synagogue Beth El in Highland Park, Illinois. He is Adjunct Professor of Rabbinics at Spertus Institute for Jewish Learning and Leadership, a senior Rabbinic Fellow at the Shalom Hartman Institute in Jerusalem, and the author of Encountering Torah: Reflections on the Weekly Portion. He is currently president of the American Zionist Movement and a past president of the international Rabbinical Assembly.

Roberta Rosenthal Kwall is the Raymond P. Niro Professor of Law at DePaul University College of Law. She is the author of *The Myth of the Cultural Jew: Culture and Law in Jewish Tradition* (Oxford University Press, 2015).

Gail Labovitz is Associate Professor of Rabbinics at the American Jewish University, where she teaches primarily for the Ziegler School of Rabbinic Studies, and is an ordained rabbi. She is the author of *Marriage and Metaphor: Constructions of Gender in Rabbinic Literature* (Lexington Books, 2009) and numerous articles on topics including rabbinic literature and culture, Jewish law, and gender and sexuality.

Melanie Landau served for eight years as Lecturer and Community Educator at the Australian Center for Jewish Civilization at Monash University in Melbourne A past Mandel Jerusalem Fellow, she is currently on the Advanced Kollel track at Yeshivat Maharat (Class of '15) and she is the Director of Facilitation for Encounter in Jerusalem.

Sid Schwarz is a senior fellow at Clal: The National Jewish Center for Learning and Leadership. He was the founding president of PANIM: The Institute for Jewish Leadership and Values for 21 years and is the founding rabbi of Adat Shalom Reconstructionist Congregation in Bethesda, MD where he continues to lead services and teach. He is the author of *Finding a Spiritual Home: How a New Generation of Jews can Transform the American Synagogue* (Jewish Lights, 2000) and *Jewish Megatrends: Charting the Course of the American Jewish Community* (Jewish Lights, 2014).

Kim Treiger-Bar-Am has taught law at various institutions in Israel and England. She made aliyah to Israel after her studies of philosophy and law at Yale, and later wrote her doctorate in law at Oxford. Her main research and teaching interests extend to the intersection between speech rights and the rights of authors and artists under copyright doctrine. She is currently writing a book on positive freedom in Jewish and Kantian thought in which she shows how the Jewish and democratic values of the state of Israel accord with each other.

Jonathan Wittenberg has been rabbi of The New North London Synagogue since 1987 and Senior Rabbi of Masorti Judaism UK since 2008. He combines his deep attachment to Judaism with a love of nature and a love of literature.

Noam Zion, on the faculty of the Hartman Institut   =e in Jerusalem since 1978, specializes in in-service learning for rabbis, educators, and theologians. His popular publications include books about the Jewish holidays: *A Different Night: Haggadah; A Different Light: Hanukkah; A Day Apart: Shabbat at Home; and A Night to Remember: A Haggadah of Contemporary Voices. His academic books are a trilogy on Jewish Giving in Comparative Perspectives* (Biblical, Greek, Rabbinic, Christian, and Muslim narratives of generosity) and forthcoming, six volumes on Talmudic Marital Dramas (available from noam.zion@gmail.com).

MESORAH MATRIX

10-BOOK SERIES
150+ Essayists

dimensions of

Spirituality & Kedushah

THE SPARK OF THE INFINITE DIVINE

Mesorah Matrix Series

David Birnbaum

Editor-in-Chief

MESORAH
MATRIX

Sanctification
2015

TIKKUN OLAM
2015

BIRKAT KOHANIM
2016

KADDISH
2016

Modeh Ani
2017

HAVDALAH
2017

SEARCH FOR MEANING
2018

U-VACHARTA BA-CHAYIM
2018

Ehyeh asher Ehyeh
2019

U'shamru
2019

200+ original essays

jewish thought & spirituality

150+ global thought leaders

a decade-long unified endeavor

David Birnbaum

LIGHTS OF CREATION & TRANSCENDENCE / Mesorah Matrix Series

MESORAH MATRIX

10-BOOK SERIES
150+ Essayists

Sanctification

Tikkun Olam

Birkat Kohanim

The Kaddish

Modeh Ani

Havdalah

Search for Meaning

U-VACHARTA BA-CHAYIM

Ehyeh asher Ehyeh

V'Shamru

THE SPARK OF THE INFINITE DIVINE

Mesorah Matrix Series

Sanctification ("Kedushah")

Tikkun Olam ("Repair the World")

Birkat Kohanim (The Priestly Blessings: a contemporary take)

The Kaddish (specifically, The Mourner's Praise of God)

Modeh Ani (The solo daily morning prayer of Gratitude)

Havdalah (separating Holy from Secular: Sabbath > secular)

Search for Meaning (pegging-off of Viktor Frankl's classic)

U-VACHARTA BA-CHAYIM (The 613th precept-Choose Life)

Ehyeh asher Ehyeh ("I Will Be That Which I Will Be" – at the Burning Bush)

V'Shamru (The Sabbath)

21st CENTURY PUBLISHING

David.Birnbaum.NY@gmail.com

www.NewParadigmMatrix.com

MESORAH MATRIX
VOLUME 1

David Birnbaum / Mesorah Matrix Series
LIGHTS OF CREATION & TRANSCENDENCE

Sanctification

Editors

David
Birnbaum & **Blech**
Benjamin

LEAD ESSAY: **Jonathan Sacks**

New Paradigm Matrix™

EXPLORING HIGHER DIMENSIONS

TIKKUN OLAM

JUDAISM, HUMANISM & TRANSCENDENCE

David Birnbaum / Mesorah Matrix Series
LIGHTS OF CREATION & TRANSCENDENCE

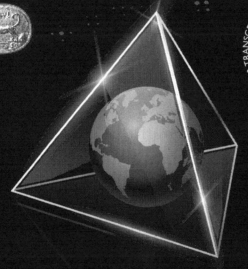

Editors

David
Birnbaum & Martin S.
Cohen

Associate Editor: **Saul J. Berman**

EXPLORING HIGHER DIMENSIONS

New Paradigm Matrix™

VOLUME 3

BIRKAT
KOHANIM

David Birnbaum / Mesorah Matrix Series

LIGHTS OF CREATION & TRANSCENDENCE

Editors

David
Birnbaum & Cohen
Martin S.

Associate Editor: **Saul J. Berman**

New Paradigm Matrix™

EXPLORING HIGHER DIMENSIONS

VOLUME 4

KADDISH

Editors

David
Birnbaum &

Martin S.
Cohen

Associate Editor: **Saul J. Berman**

New Paradigm Matrix™

EXPLORING HIGHER DIMENSIONS

VOLUME 5

David Birnbaum / Mesorah Matrix Series
LIGHTS OF CREATION & TRANSCENDENCE

Modeh Ani

THE TRANSCENDENT PRAYER OF GRATITUDE

Editors

David
Birnbaum & Martin S. **Cohen**

Associate Editor: **Saul J. Berman**

New Paradigm Matrix™

EXPLORING HIGHER DIMENSIONS

MESORAH MATRIX
VOLUME 6

LIGHTS OF CREATION & TRANSCENDENCE
David Birnbaum
Mesorah Matrix Series

EXPLORING HIGHER DIMENSIONS

HAVDALAH

Editors

David
Birnbaum & Cohen
Martin S.

Associate Editor: **Saul J. Berman**

New Paradigm Matrix™

MESORAH MATRIX

VOLUME 7

David Birnbaum / Mesorah Matrix Series

LIGHTS OF CREATION & TRANSCENDENCE

SEARCH FOR MEANING

Editors

David
Birnbaum &
Martin S.
Cohen

Associate Editor: **Saul J. Berman**

New Paradigm Matrix

EXPLORING HIGHER DIMENSIONS

MESORAH
MATRIX
VOLUME 8

David Birnbaum / Mesorah Matrix Series
LIGHTS OF CREATION & TRANSCENDENCE

U-VACHARTA
BA-CHAYIM

Editors

David
Birnbaum & Cohen

Martin S.

New Paradigm Matrix™

EXPLORING HIGHER DIMENSIONS

David Birnbaum / Mesorah Matrix Series
LIGHTS OF CREATION & TRANSCENDENCE

Ehyeh asher Ehyeh

Editors

David
Birnbaum & Martin S. **Cohen**

New Paradigm Matrix

EXPLORING HIGHER DIMENSIONS

MESORAH MATRIX

VOLUME 10

U'shamru

Editors

David
Birnbaum & Martin S. **Cohen**

New Paradigm Matrix

EXPLORING HIGHER DIMENSIONS

ESSAYISTS

Avivah Zornberg
Author

London, UK

David Ellenson
HUC-JIR

New York, NY

Saul Berman
Y.U. / Stern

New York, NY

Jonathan Sacks
United Hebrew
Congregations
London, UK

James Kugel
Bar Ilan University

Ramat Gan, Israel

Shalom Carmy
Yeshiva University,
Tradition Magazine
New York, NY

Rachel Barenblat
Bayit

Williamstown, MA

Rachel Friedman
Lamdeinu

New York, NY

W. Zeev Harvey
The Hebrew University of Jerusalem
Jerusalem

Rachel Adelman
Hebrew College
Newton Centre, MA

Shlomo Riskin
Ohr Torah Stone Colleges
Efrat, Israel

Mark Goldfeder
Emory University
Atlanta, GA

Hillel Goldberg
Intermountain Jewish News
Denver, CO

Lawrence Schiffman
NYU
New York, NY

Alan Cooper
Jewish Theological Seminary
New York, NY

Yonatan Feintuch
Bar Ilan University
Tel Aviv, Israel

Jacob Schacter
Yeshiva University

New York, NY

Aryeh Cohen
American Jewish
University
Los Angeles, CA

Avram Reisner
Chevrei Tzedek
Congregation
Baltimore, MD

Elliot Dorff
American Jewish
University
Los Angeles, CA

Michael Graetz
Congregation Eshel
Avraham
Omer, Israel

Steven Kepnes
Colgate University

Hamilton, NY

Reuven Bulka
Congregation
Machzikei Hadas
Ottawa, Canada

Adena Berkowitz
Kol Ha-neshamah

New York, NY

Alan Mittleman
Jewish Theological
Seminary
New York, NY

Tzvi Sinensky
Rosh Beit Midrash

Lower Merion, PA

Bradley Artson
American Jewish
University
Los Angeles, CA

Jill Jacobs
T'ruah: The Rabbinic
Call for Human Rights
New York, NY

Michael Broyde
Emory University

Atlanta, GA

Noam Zion
Hartman Institute

Jerusalem

Sid Schwarz
CLAL

New York, NY

Rahel Berkovits
Pardes Institute

Jerusalem

Howard Addison
Temple University

Philadelphia, PA

Robert Harris
Jewish Theological
Seminary
New York, NY

Samuel Lebens
Rutgers University

New Brunswick, NJ

Richard Hidary
Congregation
Shearith Israel
New York, NY

Jonathan Schorsch
Universität Potsdam
Potsdam
Germany

Eliezer Shore
Hebrew University
of Jerusalem
Jerusalem

Roberta Kwall
DePaul University
Law School
Chicago, IL

Alon Ferency
Heska Amuna
Synagogue
Knoxville, TN

Aubrey Glazer
Congregation Beth
Shalom
San Francisco, CA

Rebecca W. Sirbu
Rabbis Without
Borders, CLAL
New York, NY

Geoffrey Claussen
Elon University

Elon, NC

Jeremy Gordon
New London
Synagogue
London, U.K.

Shoshana Klein
Poupko
Ahavath Torah
Englewood, NJ

Michael
Wasserman
The New Shul
Scottsdale, AZ

Daniel Greyber
Beth El Synagogue

Durham, NC

Gail Labovitz
American Jewish
University
Los Angeles, CA

James Jacobson-Maisels
Or HaLev, Center for Jew-
ish Spirituality & Meditation
New York, NY

Yeshaya Dalsace
Dor Vador Com-
munaute Massorti
Paris, France

Kari Tuling
Congregation
Kol Haverim
Glastonbury, CT

Karyn Kedar
B'nai Jehoshua
Beth Elohim
Deerfield, IL

Nina Cardin
Rabbinical
Assembly
New York, NY

Aryeh Klapper
Center for Modern
Torah Leadership
Sharon, MA

Jonathan Wittenberg
New North London
Synagogue
London, UK

Michael Knopf
Temple Beth-El
Richmond, VA

Rivon Krygier
Congregation
Adath Shalom
Paris

Elie Spitz
Congregation
B'nai Israel
Tustin, CA

Ira Bedzow
Aspen Center for
Social Values
Aspen, CO

Yitzchak Blau
RCA

Jerusalem

Alfred Cohen
YU High School

New York, NY

Elliot Cosgrove
Park Avenue
Synagogue
New York, NY

Yehonatan
Chipman
Hitzei Yehonatan
Israel

David Flatto
Penn State Law

University Park, PA

Shohama H. Wiener
Temple Beth-El

City Island, NY

David Evan Markus
Temple Beth-El

City Island, NY

Nathaniel Helfgot
Yeshivat Chovevei
Torah
New York, NY

Cass Fisher
University of South
Florida
Tampa, FL

Admiel Kosman
Postdam University

Germany

Simcha Krauss
Eretz Hatzvi

Jerusalem

Melanie Landau
Monash University

Australia

Vernon Kurtz
North Suburban
Synagogue Beth-El
Highland Park, IL

Rolando Matalon
B'nai Jeshurun

New York, NY

Shmuly Yanklowitz
Valley Beit Midrash
President & Dean
Scottsdale, AZ

Peter Knobel
Beth Emet

Evanston, IL

Harvey Meirovich
Zacharias Frankel
College
Berlin, Germany

Aryeh Frimer
Bar-Ilan University

Ramat Gan

Martin Lockshin
York University

Ontario, Canada

Shai Cherry
Shaar Hamayim

Del Mar, CA

David Shatz
Yeshiva University

New York, NY

Jeremy Rosen
Persian Jewish
Center
New York, NY

David Greenstein
Congregation
Shomrei Emunah
Montclair, NJ

Avraham Walfish
Herzog College and
Michala Jerusalem
Tekoa, Israel

David Mescheloff
RCA

Israel

Barbara Thiede
UNC Charlotte

Concord, NC

Lawrence Troster
GreenFaith

Highland Park, NJ

Ruth Walfish
Herzog College and
Michala Jerusalem
Tekoa, Israel

Lenn Goodman
Vanderbilt
University
Nashville, TN

Dan Ornstein
Ohav Shalom

Albany, NY

Dena Freundlich
Ma'ayanot AMIT

Jerusalem

Elaine Goodfriend
California State
University
Northridge, CA

Berel Dov Lerner
Western Galilee
College, Herzl Inst
Northern Israel

Orna Triguboff
Neshama Life
Organisation
Sydney, Australia

Nehemia Polen
Hebrew College

Newton Centre, MA

Mark Greenspan
Oceanside Jewish
Center
Oceanside, NY

Richard Claman
Zeramim Journal

New York, NY

Avi Olitzky
Beth El Synagogue
St. Louis Park, MN

Michelle J. Levine
Stern College for Women
Yeshiva University
New York, NY

Yehuda Gellman
Ben-Gurion
University
Negev, Israel

Herbert Bronstein
Lake Forest
College,
Lake Forest, IL

Avraham Feder
Beit Knesset
Moreshet Yisrael
Jerusalem

Elyse Goldstein
City Shul

Ontario, Canada

Kerry M. Olitzky
Big Tent Judaism

New York, NY

Dalia Marx
Hebrew Union
College
Jerusalem

Jason Rubenstein
Mechon Hadar

New York, NY

Herbert Yoskowitz
Adat Shalom
Synagogue
Farmington Hills, MI

Mark Sameth
Pleasantville Com-
munity Synagogue
Westchester, NY

Catharine Clark
Congregation
Or Shalom
London, Ontario

Jacob Adler
Temple Shalom of
Northwest Arkansas
Fayetteville, AR

Jonathan Jacobs
John Jay College,
CUNY
New York, NY

David Kunin
Beth Shalom
Synagogue
Edmonton, AB

Michael Marmur
Hebrew Union
College
Jerusalem

Mordechai Luria
Institute for Jewish
Ideas & Ideals
New York, NY

Noah Farkas
Valley Beth Shalom

Encino, CA

Alex Maged
Yeshiva University

New York, NY

Hayyim Angel
Yeshiva University

New York, NY

Elie Kaunfer
Mechon Hadar

New York, NY

Alex Sztuden
The Herzl Institute

Jerusalem

David Golinkin
Schechter Institute
of Jewish Studies
Jerusalem

Mark Washofsky
Hebrew Union
College
Cincinnati, OH

Edwin C. Goldberg
Temple Sholom of
Chicago
Chicago, IL

Baruch Frydman-Kohl
Beth Tzedec
Congregation
Toronto, Canada

Ora Horn Prouser
Academy for
Jewish Religion
Yonkers, NY

Howard Wettstein
University of
California
Riverside, CA

Zvi Grumet
Yeshivat Eretz
Hatzvi
Jerusalem

Erica Brown
The Jewish
Federation
Rockville, MD

Meesh Hammer-Kossoy
Pardes Institute
of Jewish Studies
Jerusalem

Michael J. Cook
Hebrew Union
College
Cincinnati, OH

James Diamond
University of
Waterloo
Ontario, Canada

Shira Weiss
Ben Gurion
University
Beer Sheba, Israel

Gidon Rothstein

Bronx, NY

Ariel Mayse
Stanford University
Stanford,
California

Dr. Elyssa Wortzman
Mindful art-based
spiritual education
San Francisco

Ellen LeVee
Spertus Institute

Chicago, IL

Kim Treiger-Bar-Am
Tel Aviv

Israel

David Maayan
Boston College

Newton, MA

Senior Editors

Benjamin Blech
Yeshiva University

New York, NY

Martin S. Cohen
Shelter Rock,
Jewish Center
Roslyn, NY

21st CENTURY PUBLISHING

David.Birnbaum.NY@gmail.com

www.NewParadigmMatrix.com

Sanctification

'Sanctification'
from Essay by Chief Rabbi Lord Jonathan Sacks

... And there is the priestly task of kedushah, sanctifying
life by honouring the sacred ontology, the deep moral
structure of the universe, through the life of the 613
commands, a life of discipline and self-restraint, honesty
and integrity, respect and love, the code set out in the
chapter of the Torah that opens with the momentous
words, "Be holy for I, the Lord your God, am holy." Other
cultures and faiths drew inspiration from its wisdom and
prophetic traditions, but kedushah remained a specific
Jewish imperative that made us different. Even so, it
contains a message for the world, which Jews bear witness
to whenever and wherever they remain faithful to it.
Our vocation remains, to be mamlechet cohanim vegoi
kadosh, "a kingdom of priests and a holy nation."

- The Ethic of Holiness, August 2012

to view series updated authors list,

see www.MesorahMatrix.com

Mesorah Matrix
Series

Editors

David Birnbaum

Martin S. Cohen

Benjamin Blech
Editor

- born in Zurich in 1933, is an Orthodox rabbi who now lives in New York City.

Rabbi Blech has been a Professor of Talmud at Yeshiva University since 1966, and was the Rabbi of Young Israel of Oceanside for 37 years. In addition to his work in the rabbinate, Rabbi Blech has written many books on Judaism and the Jewish people and speaks on Jewish topics to communities around the world.

Benjamin Blech
Yeshiva University,
"Understanding
Judaism"

Education

Rabbi Blech received a Bachelor of Arts degree from Yeshiva University, a Master of Arts degree in psychology from Columbia University, and rabbinic ordination from the Rabbi Isaac Elchanan Theological Seminary.

Milestones

Rabbi Blech is the author of twelve highly acclaimed and best selling books, with combined sales of close to half a million copies, including three as part of the highly popular Idiot's Guide series. His book, *Understanding Judaism*: The Basics of Deed and Creed, was chosen by the Union of Orthodox Jewish Congregations as "the single best book on Judaism in our generation".

Martin S. Cohen

Martin S. Cohen

Martin S. Cohen has been a Senior Editor of the inter-denominational Mesorah Matrix series since 2012.

From 2000-2014, he served as Chairman of the Publications Committee of the quarterly journal *Conservative Judaism*, which was under the joint auspices of the JTS (Jewish Theological Seminary) and the RA (Rabbinical Assembly) during that span.

Rabbi Cohen also served as the senior editor of *The Observant Life*, a compendium of Jewish law, custom published by the Rabbinical Assembly in 2012.

Martin's weekly blog can be viewed at www.TheRuminativeRabbi. blogspot.com. He serves as rabbi of the Shelter Rock Jewish Center in Roslyn, New York.

Rabbi Cohen was educated at the City University of New York and at Jewish Theological Seminary of America, where he was ordained a rabbi and received his Ph.D. in Ancient Judaism. He is the recipient of fellowships at the Hebrew University (Jerusalem) in 1983 and Harvard University in 1993.

Martin Cohen has taught at Hunter College, the Jewish Theological Seminary of America, the Institute for Jewish Studies of the University of Heidelberg, as well as at the University of British Columbia and the Vancouver School of Theology.

His published works include *The Boy on the Door on the Ox* (2008) and *Our Haven and Our Strength: A Translation and Commentary on the Book of Psalms* (2004).

Rabbi Cohen is currently writing a translation and commentary on the Torah and the Five Megillot.

Saul Berman
Mesorah Editor

Saul J. Berman is one of the world's leading Jewish intellects.

He is an American Jewish scholar and Modern Orthodox rabbinic.

Saul Berman
Yeshiva University,
Stern College

Rabbi Berman was ordained at Yeshiva University, from which he also received his B.A. and his M.H.L. He completed a degree in law, a J.D., at New York University, and an M.A. in Political Sciesnce at the University of California, Berkeley, where he studied with David Daube. He spent two years studying mishpat ivri in Israel at Hebrew University of Jerusalem and at Tel Aviv University. He did advanced studies in Jewish Law at Hebrew University and Tel Aviv University Law Schools. Since 1971 Rabbi Berman serves as Associate Professor of Jewish Studies at Stern College for Women of Yeshiva University. Rabbi Berman was Rabbi of Congregation Beth Israel of Berkeley CA (1963-1969), Young Israel of Brookline, MA (1969-1971) and of Lincoln Square Synagogue in Manhattan (1984-1990.) Since 1990 he has served as an Adjunct Professor at Columbia University School of Law, where he teaches a seminar in Jewish Law. Aside his academic appointments, from 1997 until 2006.

Rabbi Berman is a contributor to the *Encyclopedia Judaica* and is the author of numerous articles which have been published in journals such as *Tradition, Judaism, Journal of Jewish Studies, Dinei Yisrael,* and others.

Rabbi Berman was the founder and director of the Edah organization for the promotion of Modern Orthodoxy. Edah was ultimately absorbed into Yeshivat Chovevei Torah.

He is married to Shellee Berman; they have four children and seven grandchildren.

Wikipedia online, http://en.wikipedia.org/wiki/Saul_Berman (accessed February 15, 2013) +
The Tikvah Center for Law & Jewish Civilzation online, http://www.nyutikvah.org/fellows/
saul_berman.html (accessed February 15, 2013)

Shalom Carmy
Contributing Editor

Shalom Carmy is an Orthodox rabbi teaching Jewish Studies and philosophy atYeshiva University, where he is Chair of Bible and Jewish Philosophy at Yeshiva College. He is an affiliated scholar at Cardozo Law School of Yeshiva University. He is also Editor of Tradition, an Orthodox theological journal.

Shalom Carmy
Yeshiva University,
Tradition Magazine

A Brooklyn native, he is a prominent Modern Orthodox theologian, historian, and philosopher. He received his B.A. in 1969 and M.S. from Yeshiva University, and received his rabbinic ordination from its affiliated Rabbi Isaac Elchanan Theological Seminary, studying under Rabbis Aharon Lichtenstein and Joseph Soloveitchik. He has edited some of R. Soloveitchik's work for publication. Carmy has written many articles on Biblical theology, Jewish thought, Orthodoxy in the 20th century, and the role of liberal arts in Torah education. He edited "*Modern Scholarship in the Study of Torah*: Contributions and Limitations" (ISBN 1-56821-450-2), "*Jewish Perspectives on the Experience of Suffering*", as well as several other works. He writes a regular personal column in *Tradition*, and contributes regularly on Jewish and general subjects to *First Things* and other journals. In addition to his exegetical and analytic work, Carmy's theological contribution is distinguished by preoccupation with the way religious doctrine and practice express themselves in the life of the individual.

http://en.wikipedia.org/wiki/Shalom_Carmy (accessed May 7, 2014)

Mesorah Matrix
SENIOR EDITORIAL BOARD

LIGHTS OF CREATION & TRANSCENDENCE

David Birnbaum

Mesorah Matrix Series

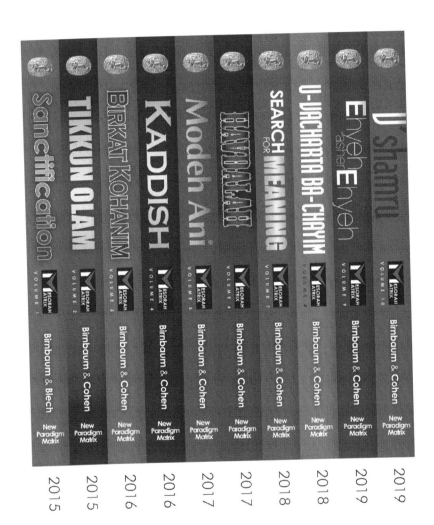

Sanctification — VOLUME 1 — Birnbaum & Blech — New Paradigm Matrix — 2015

TIKKUN OLAM — VOLUME 2 — Birnbaum & Cohen — New Paradigm Matrix — 2015

BIRKAT KOHANIM — VOLUME 3 — Birnbaum & Cohen — New Paradigm Matrix — 2016

KADDISH — VOLUME 4 — Birnbaum & Cohen — New Paradigm Matrix — 2016

Modeh Ani — VOLUME 5 — Birnbaum & Cohen — New Paradigm Matrix — 2017

HAVDALAH — VOLUME 6 — Birnbaum & Cohen — New Paradigm Matrix — 2017

SEARCH FOR MEANING — VOLUME 7 — Birnbaum & Cohen — New Paradigm Matrix — 2018

U-VACHARTA BA-CHAYIM — VOLUME 8 — Birnbaum & Cohen — New Paradigm Matrix — 2018

Enyeh asher Enyeh — VOLUME 9 — Birnbaum & Cohen — New Paradigm Matrix — 2019

U'shamru — VOLUME 10 — Birnbaum & Cohen — New Paradigm Matrix — 2019

March 2018

www.MesorahMatrix.com

www.NewParadigmMatrix.com

Schwarz
Berkovits
Hammer-Kossoy
Claussen
Broyde
Kurtz
Chipman
Cardin
Zion
Bulka
Treiger-Bar-Am
Jacobson-Maisels
Labovitz
Gordon
Greyber
Wittenberg
Cohen
Kwall
Glazer
Krygier
Jacobs
Dorff
Berkowitz
Blech
Kosman
Landau
Artson
Bedzow

For the mountains shall erode

and the hills indeed collapse,

but My grace towards you shall never waver.

- Isaiah 54:10

כִּי הֶהָרִים יָמוּשׁוּ

וְהַגְּבָעוֹת תְּמוּטֶינָה

וְחַסְדִּי מֵאִתֵּךְ לֹא יָמוּשׁ

יְשַׁעְיָהוּ 54:10 –

21st CENTURY PUBLISHING

David Birnbaum
Editor-in-Chief

New Paradigm Matrix
att: David Birnbaum
Tower 49
12 E 49th St.
11th Floor
New York, NY 10017

David.Birnbaum.NY@gmail.com

$16.00 / book

Tikkun Olam

ISBN: 978-0-9961995-0-6

Made in the USA
Monee, IL
30 August 2022

12835205R00386